Poetry for Students

National Advisory Board

Poetry for Students

Presenting Analysis, Context, and Criticism on Commonly Studied Poetry

Volume 16

David Galens, Project Editor

Foreword by David Kelly

GALE®

THOMSON

GALE

Detroit • New York • San Diego • San Francisco • Cleveland • New Haven, Conn. • Waterville, Maine • London • Munich

Poetry for Students

Project Editor
David Galens

Editorial
Anne Marie Hacht, Madeline S. Harris, Michael L. LaBlanc, Ira Mark Milne, Pam Revitzer, Kathy Sauer, Jennifer Smith, Daniel Toronto, Carol Ullman

Research
Sarah Genik

Permissions
Debra Freitas, Lori Hines

Manufacturing
Stacy Melson

Imaging and Multimedia
Lezlie Light, Kelly A. Quin, Luke Rademacher

Product Design
Pamela A. E. Galbreath, Michael Logusz

For permission to use material from this product, submit your request via Web at http://www.gale-edit.com/permissions, or you may download our Permissions Request form and submit your request by fax or mail to:

Permissions Department
The Gale Group, Inc.
27500 Drake Rd.
Farmington Hills, MI 48331-3535
Permissions Hotline:
248-699-8074 or 800-762-4058

Since this page cannot legibly accommodate all copyright notices, the acknowledgments constitute an extension of the copyright notice.

ISBN 0-7876-6035-3
ISSN 1094-7019

Printed in the United States of America
10 9 8 7 6 5 4 3 2 1

Table of Contents

Just a Few Lines on a Page

I have often thought that poets have the easiest job in the world. A poem, after all, is just a few lines on a page, usually not even extending margin to margin—how long would that take to write, about five minutes? Maybe ten at the most, if you wanted it to rhyme or have a repeating meter. Why, I could start in the morning and produce a book of poetry by dinnertime. But we all know that it isn't that easy. Anyone can come up with enough words, but the poet's job is about writing the *right* ones. The right words will change lives, making people see the world somewhat differently than they saw it just a few minutes earlier. The right words can make a reader who relies on the dictionary for meanings take a greater responsibility for his or her own personal understanding. A poem that is put on the page correctly can bear any amount of analysis, probing, defining, explaining, and interrogating, and something about it will still feel new the next time you read it.

It would be fine with me if I could talk about poetry without using the word "magical," because that word is overused these days to imply "a really good time," often with a certain sweetness about it, and a lot of poetry is neither of these. But if you stop and think about magic—whether it brings to mind sorcery, witchcraft, or bunnies pulled from top hats—it always seems to involve stretching reality to produce a result greater than the sum of its parts and pulling unexpected results out of thin air. This book provides ample cases where a few simple words conjure up whole worlds. We do not actually travel to different times and different cultures, but the poems get into our minds, they find what little we know about the places they are talking about, and then they make that little bit blossom into a bouquet of someone else's life. Poets make us think we are following simple, specific events, but then they leave ideas in our heads that cannot be found on the printed page. Abracadabra.

Sometimes when you finish a poem it doesn't feel as if it has left any supernatural effect on you, like it did not have any more to say beyond the actual words that it used. This happens to everybody, but most often to inexperienced readers: regardless of what is often said about young people's infinite capacity to be amazed, you have to understand what usually does happen, and what could have happened instead, if you are going to be moved by what someone has accomplished. In those cases in which you finish a poem with a "So what?" attitude, the information provided in *Poetry for Students* comes in handy. Readers can feel assured that the poems included here actually are potent magic, not just because a few (or a hundred or ten thousand) professors of literature say they are: they're significant because they can withstand close inspection and still amaze the very same people who have just finished taking them apart and seeing how they work. Turn them inside out, and they will still be able to come alive, again and again. *Poetry for Students* gives readers of any age good practice in feeling the ways poems relate to both the reality of the time and place the poet lived in and the reality of our emotions. Practice is just another word for being a student. The information given here helps you understand the way to read poetry; what to look for, what to expect.

With all of this in mind, I really don't think I would actually like to have a poet's job at all. There are too many skills involved, including precision, honesty, taste, courage, linguistics, passion, compassion, and the ability to keep all sorts of people entertained at once. And that is just what they do with one hand, while the other hand pulls some sort of trick that most of us will never fully understand. I can't even pack all that I need for a weekend into one suitcase, so what would be my chances of stuffing so much life into a few lines? With all that *Poetry for Students* tells us about each poem, I am impressed that any poet can finish three or four poems a year. Read the inside stories of these poems, and you won't be able to approach any poem in the same way you did before.

David J. Kelly
College of Lake County

Introduction

Purpose of the Book

The purpose of *Poetry for Students* (*PfS*) is to provide readers with a guide to understanding, enjoying, and studying poems by giving them easy access to information about the work. Part of Gale's "For Students" Literature line, *PfS* is specifically designed to meet the curricular needs of high school and undergraduate college students and their teachers, as well as the interests of general readers and researchers considering specific poems. While each volume contains entries on "classic" poems frequently studied in classrooms, there are also entries containing hard-to-find information on contemporary poems, including works by multicultural, international, and women poets.

The information covered in each entry includes an introduction to the poem and the poem's author; the actual poem text (if possible); a poem summary, to help readers unravel and understand the meaning of the poem; analysis of important themes in the poem; and an explanation of important literary techniques and movements as they are demonstrated in the poem.

In addition to this material, which helps the readers analyze the poem itself, students are also provided with important information on the literary and historical background informing each work. This includes a historical context essay, a box comparing the time or place the poem was written to modern Western culture, a critical overview essay, and excerpts from critical essays on the poem. A unique feature of *PfS* is a specially commissioned critical essay on each poem, targeted toward the student reader.

To further aid the student in studying and enjoying each poem, information on media adaptations is provided (if available), as well as reading suggestions for works of fiction and nonfiction on similar themes and topics. Classroom aids include ideas for research papers and lists of critical sources that provide additional material on the poem.

Selection Criteria

The titles for each volume of *PfS* were selected by surveying numerous sources on teaching literature and analyzing course curricula for various school districts. Some of the sources surveyed included: literature anthologies; *Reading Lists for College-Bound Students: The Books Most Recommended by America's Top Colleges*; textbooks on teaching the poem; a College Board survey of poems commonly studied in high schools; and a National Council of Teachers of English (NCTE) survey of poems commonly studied in high schools.

Input was also solicited from our advisory board, as well as educators from various areas. From these discussions, it was determined that each volume should have a mix of "classic" poems (those works commonly taught in literature classes) and contemporary poems for which information is often hard to find. Because of the interest in expanding the canon of literature, an emphasis was also placed on including works by international, multicultural, and women poets. Our advisory board members—educational professionals—helped pare down the list for each volume. If a work was not selected for the present volume, it was often noted as a possibility for a future volume. As always, the editor welcomes suggestions for titles to be included in future volumes.

How Each Entry Is Organized

Each entry, or chapter, in *PfS* focuses on one poem. Each entry heading lists the full name of the poem, the author's name, and the date of the poem's publication. The following elements are contained in each entry:

- **Introduction:** a brief overview of the poem which provides information about its first appearance, its literary standing, any controversies surrounding the work, and major conflicts or themes within the work.

- **Author Biography:** this section includes basic facts about the poet's life, and focuses on events and times in the author's life that inspired the poem in question.

- **Poem Text:** when permission has been granted, the poem is reprinted, allowing for quick reference when reading the explication of the following section.

- **Poem Summary:** a description of the major events in the poem. Summaries are broken down with subheads that indicate the lines being discussed.

- **Themes:** a thorough overview of how the major topics, themes, and issues are addressed within the poem. Each theme discussed appears in a separate subhead and is easily accessed through the boldface entries in the Subject/Theme Index.

- **Style:** this section addresses important style elements of the poem, such as form, meter, and rhyme scheme; important literary devices used, such as imagery, foreshadowing, and symbolism; and, if applicable, genres to which the work might have belonged, such as Gothicism or Romanticism. Literary terms are explained within the entry, but can also be found in the Glossary.

- **Historical Context:** this section outlines the social, political, and cultural climate *in which the author lived and the poem was created.* This section may include descriptions of related historical events, pertinent aspects of daily life in the culture, and the artistic and literary sensibilities

of the time in which the work was written. If the poem is a historical work, information regarding the time in which the poem is set is also included. Each section is broken down with helpful subheads.

- **Critical Overview:** this section provides background on the critical reputation of the poem, including bannings or any other public controversies surrounding the work. For older works, this section includes a history of how the poem was first received and how perceptions of it may have changed over the years; for more recent poems, direct quotes from early reviews may also be included.

- **Criticism:** an essay commissioned by *PfS* which specifically deals with the poem and is written specifically for the student audience, as well as excerpts from previously published criticism on the work (if available).

- **Sources:** an alphabetical list of critical material used in compiling the entry, with full bibliographical information.

- **Further Reading:** an alphabetical list of other critical sources which may prove useful for the student. It includes full bibliographical information and a brief annotation.

In addition, each entry contains the following highlighted sections, set apart from the main text as sidebars:

- **Media Adaptations:** if available, a list of audio recordings as well as any film or television adaptations of the poem, including source information.

- **Topics for Further Study:** a list of potential study questions or research topics dealing with the poem. This section includes questions related to other disciplines the student may be studying, such as American history, world history, science, math, government, business, geography, economics, psychology, etc.

- **Compare and Contrast:** an "at-a-glance" comparison of the cultural and historical differences between the author's time and culture and late twentieth century or early twenty-first century Western culture. This box includes pertinent parallels between the major scientific, political, and cultural movements of the time or place the poem was written, the time or place the poem was set (if a historical work), and modern Western culture. Works written after 1990 may not have this box.

- **What Do I Read Next?:** a list of works that might complement the featured poem or serve as a contrast to it. This includes works by the same author and others, works of fiction and nonfiction, and works from various genres, cultures, and eras.

Other Features

PfS includes "Just a Few Lines on a Page," a foreword by David J. Kelly, an adjunct professor of English, College of Lake County, Illinois. This essay provides a straightforward, unpretentious explanation of why poetry should be marveled at and how *Poetry for Students* can help teachers show students how to enrich their own reading experiences.

A Cumulative Author/Title Index lists the authors and titles covered in each volume of the *PfS* series.

A Cumulative Nationality/Ethnicity Index breaks down the authors and titles covered in each volume of the *PfS* series by nationality and ethnicity.

A Subject/Theme Index, specific to each volume, provides easy reference for users who may be studying a particular subject or theme rather than a single work. Significant subjects from events to broad themes are included, and the entries pointing to the specific theme discussions in each entry are indicated in **boldface**.

A Cumulative Index of First Lines (beginning in Vol. 10) provides easy reference for users who may be familiar with the first line of a poem but may not remember the actual title.

A Cumulative Index of Last Lines (beginning in Vol. 10) provides easy reference for users who may be familiar with the last line of a poem but may not remember the actual title.

Each entry may include illustrations, including a photo of the author and other graphics related to the poem.

Citing Poetry for Students

When writing papers, students who quote directly from any volume of *Poetry for Students* may use the following general forms. These examples are based on MLA style; teachers may request that students adhere to a different style, so the following examples may be adapted as needed.

When citing text from *PfS* that is not attributed to a particular author (i.e., the Themes, Style, Historical Context sections, etc.), the following format should be used in the bibliography section:

"Angle of Geese." *Poetry for Students*. Eds. Marie Napierkowski and Mary Ruby. Vol. 2. Detroit: Gale, 1998. 5–7.

When quoting the specially commissioned essay from *PfS* (usually the first piece under the "Criticism" subhead), the following format should be used:

Velie, Alan. Critical Essay on "Angle of Geese." *Poetry for Students*. Eds. Marie Napierkowski and Mary Ruby. Vol. 2. Detroit: Gale, 1998. 7–10.

When quoting a journal or newspaper essay that is reprinted in a volume of *PfS,* the following form may be used:

Luscher, Robert M. "An Emersonian Context of Dickinson's 'The Soul Selects Her Own Society.'" *ESQ: A Journal of American Renaissance* Vol. 30, No. 2 (Second Quarter, 1984), 111–16; excerpted and reprinted in *Poetry for Students*, Vol. 1, eds. Marie Napierkowski and Mary Ruby (Detroit: Gale, 1998), pp. 266–69.

When quoting material reprinted from a book that appears in a volume of *PfS,* the following form may be used:

Mootry, Maria K. "'Tell It Slant': Disguise and Discovery as Revisionist Poetic Discourse in 'The Bean Eaters,'" in *A Life Distilled: Gwendolyn Brooks, Her Poetry and Fiction*. Edited by Maria K. Mootry and Gary Smith. University of Illinois Press, 1987. 177–80, 191; excerpted and reprinted in *Poetry for Students*, Vol. 2, eds. Marie Napierkowski and Mary Ruby (Detroit: Gale, 1998), pp. 22–24.

We Welcome Your Suggestions

The editor of *Poetry for Students* welcomes your comments and ideas. Readers who wish to suggest poems to appear in future volumes, or who have other suggestions, are cordially invited to contact the editor. You may contact the editor via E-mail at: *ForStudentsEditors@gale.com.* Or write to the editor at:

Editor, *Poetry for Students*
The Gale Group
27500 Drake Rd.
Farmington Hills, MI 48331–3535

Literary Chronology

1806: Elizabeth Barrett Browning (born Elizabeth Barrett) is born on March 6 in Durham, England, the oldest of her parents' twelve children.

1830: Emily Dickinson is born on December 10 in Amherst, Massachusetts, the second daughter of Edward and Emily (Norcross) Dickinson.

1850: Elizabeth Barrett Browning's "Sonnet XXIX" is published.

1861: Elizabeth Barrett Browning dies on June 29 and is buried in Florence.

1879: Wallace Stevens is born on October 2 in Reading, Pennsylvania, to Garrett (a lawyer) and Margaretha (a schoolteacher) Stevens.

1885: Ezra Pound is born on October 30 in Hailey, Idaho.

1886: Emily Dickinson dies from Bright's disease on May 15 and is buried in Amherst.

1890: Emily Dickinson's "Much Madness Is Divinest Sense" is published.

1911: Czeslaw Milosz is born on June 30 in Szetejnie, Lithuania, the son of Aleksander (a civil engineer) and Weronika (Kunat) Milosz.

1914: William Stafford is born in Hutchinson, Kansas.

1919: May Swenson is born on May 28 in Logan, Utah.

1920: Ezra Pound's "Hugh Selwyn Mauberley" is published.

1921: Richard Wilbur is born on March 1 in New York City into a family of writers and artists.

1923: Wallace Stevens's "Sunday Morning" is published.

1934: Audre Lorde is born on February 18 in Harlem, New York, the daughter of West Indian-born parents, Frederic Byron and Linda Gertrude (Belmar) Lorde, small-scale real estate managers.

1941: Simon J. Ortiz is born at the Pueblo of Acoma, near Albuquerque, New Mexico, the son of Joe L. Ortiz and Mamie Toribio Ortiz.

1943: Tess Gallagher is born on July 21 in Port Angeles, Washington, to Leslie (a logger and longshoreman) and Georgia Bond.

1943: Czeslaw Milosz's "Song of a Citizen" is published.

1947: Ai (born Florence Anthony) is born on October 21 in Albany, Texas. Her father is Japanese, and her mother (who is not married to him) is a mixture of Choctaw Indian, southern Cheyenne, African American, Dutch, and Irish.

1948: Leslie Marmon Silko is born on March 5 in Albuquerque, New Mexico, a child of Laguna Pueblo, Plains Indian, Mexican, and Anglo-American descent.

1949: Victor Hernandez Cruz is born on February 6 in Aguas Buenas, Puerto Rico, to Severo and Rosa Cruz.

1953: Jane Hirshfield is born in New York City. Her father is a clothing manufacturer and her mother is a secretary.

1955: Wallace Stevens receives the Pulitzer Prize for poetry for *Collected Poems*.

1955: Wallace Stevens dies from cancer on August 2 in Hartford, Connecticut.

1956: Richard Wilbur's "Merlin Enthralled" is published.

1957: Martín Espada is born in Brooklyn, New York, to a Puerto Rican father and a Jewish mother.

1957: Richard Wilbur receives the Pulitzer Prize for poetry for *Things of This World*.

1963: May Swenson's "Southbound on the Freeway" is published.

1963: Audre Lorde's "What My Child Learns of the Sea" is published.

1972: Ezra Pound dies in November in Venice.

1973: Victor Hernandez Cruz's "Business" is published.

1976: Simon Ortiz's "My Father's Song" is published.

1980: Czeslaw Milosz is awarded the Nobel Prize in literature, and his books of poetry are published for the first time in Poland.

1981: Leslie Marmon Silko's "Story from Bear Country" is published.

1989: May Swenson dies on December 4.

1989: Richard Wilbur receives the Pulitzer Prize for poetry *New and Collected Poems*.

1990: Martín Espada's "Colibrí" is published.

1991: Ai's "Reunions with a Ghost" is published.

1992: Tess Gallagher's "I Stop Writing the Poem" is published.

1992: Audre Lorde dies from recurrent cancer on November 17 in St. Croix.

1993: William Stafford dies within months of writing "Ways to Live."

1997: Jane Hirshfield's "Three Times My Life Has Opened" is published.

1998: William Stafford's "Ways to Live" is published.

Acknowledgments

The editors wish to thank the copyright holders of the excerpted criticism included in this volume and the permissions managers of many book and magazine publishing companies for assisting us in securing reproduction rights. We are also grateful to the staffs of the Detroit Public Library, the Library of Congress, the University of Detroit Mercy Library, Wayne State University Purdy/Kresge Library Complex, and the University of Michigan Libraries for making their resources available to us. Following is a list of the copyright holders who have granted us permission to reproduce material in this volume of *Poetry for Students* (*PfS*). Every effort has been made to trace copyright, but if omissions have been made, please let us know.

COPYRIGHTED MATERIALS IN *PfS*, VOLUME 16, WERE REPRODUCED FROM THE FOLLOWING PERIODICALS:

ELH, v. 48, Summer, 1981. Reproduced by permission.—*Paideuma: A Journal Devoted to Ezra Pound Scholarship*, v. 27, Spring, 1998. Reproduced by permission.

COPYRIGHTED MATERIALS IN *PfS*, VOLUME 16, WERE REPRODUCED FROM THE FOLLOWING BOOKS:

Cruz, Victor Hernandez. From "Business," in *Mainland (Poems)*. Random House, 1973. Copyright © 1973 by Victor Hernandez Cruz. All rights reserved. Reproduced by permission of Random House, Inc.—Gallagher, Tess. From "I Stop Writing the Poem," in *Moon Crossing Bridge*. Graywolf Press, 1992. Copyright © 1992 by Tess Gallagher. All rights reserved. Reproduced by permission of Graywolf Press, Saint Paul, Minnesota.—Hirshfield, Jane. "Three Times My Life Has Opened," in *Lives of the Heart*. HarperCollins, 1997. Copyright © 1997 by HarperCollins. All rights reserved. Reproduced by permission of HarperCollins Publishers Inc.—Milosz, Czeslaw. From "Song of a Citizen," in *Selected Poems*. Seabury, 1973. Copyright © 1973 by Seabury. All rights reserved. Reproduced by permission.—Ortiz, Simon. "My Father's Song," in *Going for the Rain*. Harper, 1976. Copyright © 1976 by Harper. All rights reserved. Reproduced by permission.—San Juan Jr, E. From "Ezra Pound's Craftmanship: An Interpretation of Hugh Selwyn Mauberley," in *Critics on Ezra Pound*. University of Miami Press, 1972. Copyright © 1972 by University of Miami Press. All rights reserved. Reproduced by permission.—Stafford, William. From "Ways to Live," in *The Way It Is: New and Selected Poems*. Graywolf Press, 1998. Copyright © 1998 by the Estate of William Stafford. All rights reserved. Reproduced by permission of Graywolf Press, Saint Paul, Minnesota.—Stern, Herbert J. From "Adam's Dream," in *Wallace Stevens: Art of Uncertainty*. University of Michigan Press, 1966. Copyright © 1966 by University of Michigan Press. All rights reserved. Reproduced by permission.—Wilbur, Richard. From "Merlin Enthralled," in *Things of This World*. Harcourt, 1956. Copyright 1953 and renewed 1981 by Richard Wilbur. All rights reserved. Reproduced by permission of Harcourt, Inc.—Witemeyer, Hugh. From "Early Poetry: 1908–1920," in *The Cambridge Companion to Ezra Pound*. Cambridge University Press, 1999. Copyright © 1999 by Cambridge University Press. All rights reserved. Reproduced by permission of Cambridge University Press.

PHOTOGRAPHS AND ILLUSTRATIONS APPEARING IN *PfS,* VOLUME 16, WERE RECEIVED FROM THE FOLLOWING SOURCES:

Ai, speaking at Lucite podium, photograph. AP/Wide World Photos. Reproduced by permission.—Browning, Elizabeth Barrett, print. Archive Photos, Inc. Reproduced by permission.—Cruz, Victor Hernandez, photograph. Arte Publico Press Archives, University of Houston. Reproduced by permission.—Dickinson, Emily, c. 1847–1848, photograph. The Granger Collection, New York. Reproduced by permission.—Espada, Martin, photograph. Reproduced by permission.—Four aliens walking toward their spacecraft, photograph. © Darren Winter/Corbis. Reproduced by permission.—Gallagher, Tess, photograph. Jerry Bauer. Reproduced by permission.—Hirshfield, Jane, photograph. © Jerry Bauer. Reproduced by permission.—Lorde, Audre, photograph by Joan E. Biren. Reproduced by permission.—Merlin thumbing through a large book, illustration, photograph. © Bettmann/Corbis. Reproduced by permission.—Milosz, Czeslaw, standing and speaking into microphones, University of Jagellonian, Cracow, Poland, 1981, photograph. Getty Images. Reproduced by permission.—Ortiz, Simon J., photograph by Nancy Crampton. © Nancy Crampton. Reproduced by permission.—People walking around in the back yards of the Warsaw ghetto, photograph. USHMM Photo Archives.—Pound, Ezra (wearing suit jacket, tee-shirt), 1945, photograph. AP/Wide World Photos. Reproduced by permission.—Red maple leaves clinging to a snowy branch in the Mount Naomi Wilderness of Utah's Bear River Range, Wasatch-Cache National Forest, photograph. © Scott T. Smith/Corbis. Reproduced by permission.—Silko, Leslie Marmon, photograph by Robyn McDaniels. © Robyn McDaniels. Reproduced by permission.—Stafford, Dr. William E., photograph by Barbara Stafford-Wilson. Reproduced by permission.—Stevens, Wallace, photograph. Corbis-Bettmann. Reproduced by permission.—Swenson, May, photograph. Rozanne Knudson (Estate of May Swenson) / Corbis-Bettmann. Reproduced by permission.—Wilbur, Richard, photograph by Constance Stuart Larrabee. Reproduced by permission of the author.

Contributors

Bryan Aubrey: Aubrey holds a Ph.D. in English and has published many articles on twentieth-century literature. Entries on *Reunions with a Ghost* and *Song of a Citizen*. Original essays on *Reunions with a Ghost* and *Song of a Citizen*.

Greg Barnhisel: Barnhisel directs the Writing Center at the University of Southern California in Los Angeles. Entry on *Hugh Selwyn Mauberley*. Original essay on *Hugh Selwyn Mauberley*.

Adrian Blevins: Blevins teaches writing courses at Roanoke College. Original essays on *I Stop Writing the Poem* and *Ways to Live*.

Kate Covintree: Covintree is a graduate of Randolph-Macon Women's College with a degree in English. Original essays on *Story from Bear Country* and *Three Times My Life Has Opened*.

Lisa Fabian: Fabian is a former student of poetry. Original essay on *Southbound on the Freeway*.

Erik France: France is a librarian and college counselor, who teaches history at University Liggett School and English at Macomb College near Detroit, Michigan. Entry on *What My Child Learns of the Sea*. Original essay on *What My Child Learns of the Sea*.

Joyce Hart: Hart has degrees in English literature and creative writing and is a published writer of literary themes. Entries on *I Stop Writing the Poem* and *Much Madness Is Divinest Sense*. Original essays on *I Stop Writing the Poem* and *Much Madness Is Divinest Sense*.

Pamela Steed Hill: Hill is the author of a poetry collection, has published widely in literary journals, and is an editor for a university publications department. Entries on *Southbound on the Freeway* and *Three Times My Life Has Opened*. Original essays on *Colibrí, Reunions with a Ghost, Southbound on the Freeway, Three Times My Life Has Opened*, and *What My Child Learns of the Sea*.

Beth Kattelman: Kattelman holds a Ph.D. in theatre from Ohio State University. Original essay *Much Madness Is Divinest Sense*.

David Kelly: Kelly is an instructor of creative writing and literature at Oakton Community College. Entries on *Merlin Enthralled* and *Ways to Live*. Original essays on *Merlin Enthralled, My Father's Song*, and *Ways to Live*.

Laura Kryhoski: Kryhoski is currently working as a freelance writer. She has also taught English literature in addition to English as a Second Language overseas. Original essays on *Story from Bear Country* and *Sunday Morning*.

Deneka Candace MacDonald: MacDonald is an instructor of English literature and media studies. Original essays on *Much Madness Is Divinest Sense* and *What My Child Learns of the Sea*.

Daniel Moran: Moran is an instructor of English and American literature. Entry on *Sonnet XXIX*. Original essay on *Sonnet XXIX*.

Josh Ozersky: Ozersky is a critic and essayist. Original essay on *Song of a Citizen*.

Wendy Perkins: Perkins teaches American literature and film and has published several essays on American and British authors. Entry on *Sunday Morning*. Original essay on *Sunday Morning*.

Frank Pool: Pool is a published poet and a teacher of high school English. Original essay on *Ways to Live*.

Michelle Prebilic: Prebilic is an independent author who writes and analyzes children's literature. She holds degrees in psychology and business. Original essays on *Business* and *Three Times My Life Has Opened*.

Chris Semansky: Semansky is an instructor of English literature and composition. Entries on *Business*, *Colibrí*, and *My Father's Song*. Original essays on *Business*, *Colibrí*, and *My Father's Song*.

Kathy Smith: Smith is an independent scholar and freelance writer. Entry on *Story from Bear Country*. Original essay on *Story from Bear Country*.

Paul Witcover: Witcover is an editor and writer whose fiction, book reviews, and critical essays appear regularly in magazines and online. Original essay on *Sunday Morning*.

Business

Victor Hernandez Cruz

1973

"Business," first published in the collection *Main-land* in 1973, is a portrait of a street performer who gets arrested for doing what he does best—selling whistles and puppets and playing guitar for eager crowds. Written by one of the leading contemporary Hispanic-American poets, this work, like many others from the same collection, chronicles the lives of everyday people in New York City, where Victor Hernandez Cruz lived for many years after moving from Puerto Rico. The poem, in its simple tone and straight-forward narrative, humorously satirizes a judicial system that would arrest a man for entertaining people with what the author calls "monkey business." On a larger scale, perhaps this poem raises other questions of authority, such as why a person is not allowed to make an honest living doing what he or she does best, in this case, entertaining people or selling puppets and whistles on the street.

Author Biography

Cruz was born in Aguas Buenas, Puerto Rico, February 6, 1949, to Severo and Rosa Cruz. Because of the difficult economic conditions in Puerto Rico, Cruz's family migrated to New York City in 1955 and settled on the Lower East Side of Manhattan, in one of the areas designated as *el barrio*. Following the divorce of his parents soon after the move, Cruz's mother begain working to support the family. When he was about fourteen years old, Cruz

Victor Hernandez Cruz

began to write verse, and, at seventeen, he composed his first collection of poetry, titled *Papo Got His Gun! and Other Poems.* Cruz's career got an early boost when an avant-garde New York magazine, the *Evergreen Review*, featured several poems from the collection. Six months before he was to have graduated from high school in 1967, Cruz quit school. Cruz joined *Umbra* magazine in 1967 as an editor. In 1968, Cruz cofounded the East Harlem Gut Theater, a Puerto Rican collective of actors, musicians, and writers. The theater closed after a year.

Cruz moved to California in 1968, where he soon made contact with other authors. He accepted a job teaching a group of junior high school boys in a Berkeley experimental public school that same year and began his first major work, *Snaps*. Cruz taught a poetry workshop at the University of California at Berkeley in 1972 and served as an instructor of ethnic studies at San Francisco State College. He received a Creative Artists Program Service (CAPS) grant in 1974, which supported him while he composed his third volume of poetry. In 1975, Cruz married Elisa Ivette, and the couple had a son, Vitin Ajani, later that year. He became a contributing editor for *Revista Chicano Riqueña* in 1976. That same year, he began an association with the San Francisco Neighborhood Arts Program, working with schools, senior citizen centers, prisons, and city festivals. The job supported him

while he completed his third book, *Tropicalization*. Cruz won another CAPS grant in 1978 to write fiction. Although some of his short fiction was published in avant-garde reviews, an early novel he had written had still not been published. In 1979, Cruz took part in the One World Poetry Festival in Amsterdam. Cruz's second child, Rosa, was born in 1980, and, in 1982, he published a collection of prose and poetry entitled *By Lingual Wholes.* That same year, Cruz's first novel was published. Cruz has concentrated on fiction more than poetry since the early 1980s but has remained a leader among the "Neorican" writers, a group of authors who share Puerto Rican heritage.

Poem Text

Don Arturo says:
There was a man
who sold puppets and whistles
for a living
He also played guitar   5
He used to go
to the shopping areas
and draw huge crowds
They bought his whistles
and puppets   10
They threw money into
his guitar
This was against the law
So he was arrested at
least three times a week   15
When his turn came up
in the courtroom
He took a puppet out
and put a show on
All the detectives   20
and court clerks
rolled on the floor
When he finished
they all bought puppets
and whistles from him   25
The judge got angry
and yelled:
What kind of business
is this
And the man said   30
I am the monkey man
and the
Monkey man sells
Monkey business.

Poem Summary

Line 1

This opening line establishes that the following story was first told to the speaker by Don Arturo. This person might be a friend of the poet's, or an authority figure in the neighborhood ("Don" is a title of respect); in either case, by mentioning the source of the anecdote, Cruz emphasizes the influence of story and urban myth on his childhood.

Lines 2–4

The story begins the way most stories do, introducing the central character, who seems like a simple man, perhaps a street vendor selling toys to kids in order to make a living. The very easy level of vocabulary is reminiscent of stories one is told as a child.

Line 5

Not only does he sell puppets and whistles, he is also a musician, entertaining the crowds.

Lines 6–8

These lines give a sense of how popular the man was. According to the story, he would draw "huge crowds," an observation which helps establish how satisfied and appreciative the people were.

Lines 9–12

Here the reader learns more specifically how successful the man was, both in his sales of puppets and whistles, and in his performances. Many street performers leave their guitar or saxophone cases open while they play so people can toss in money, usually small change, for tips. Again, this was probably the man's only source of income, and the poet does not give any indication that the man was disturbing or bothering anyone in any way.

Line 13

Contrasting the man's popularity and success at making a living, the speaker bluntly announces that what he was doing was against the local law, which probably required that he possess a vendor's license of some kind.

Lines 14–15

Perhaps an exaggeration, which stories are prone to, these lines seem to show the humorous side to the situation; they also show the stubborn persistence of the police in arresting him and the man's stubborn persistence to keep doing what he does best, regardless of laws.

Line 16–17

The man's court date arrived.

Media Adaptations

- *Lannan Literary Videos: 12* features a poetry reading and interview with Cruz recorded April 17, 1989, at the Los Angeles Theatre Center. Cruz reads from *Rhythm, Content and Flavor* and *Red Beans*. Their address is Lannan Foundation, 313 Read Street, Santa Fe, New Mexico 87501–2628.

- Cruz is a featured speaker in the Lannan Foundation's *Where Poems Come From*, released in 1991.

- The Poetry Center at San Francisco State University has a number of audiotapes of Cruz reading his poetry from the 1970s and 1980s. Tapes can be ordered from The Poetry Center and American Poetry Archives, San Francisco State University, 1600 Holloway Avenue, San Francisco, CA 94132.

Lines 18–19

In these humorous lines, the man shows no regard for court room protocol, instead putting on his performance (a puppet show) and making a circus out of the proceedings.

Lines 20–22

The surprising and extreme behavior of the detectives and court clerks indicates that they are as impressed with the man's show as the other crowds have been.

Lines 23–25

As if rolling with laughter were not enough, the detectives and court clerks want to buy the man's goods after he's finished. Again, the reader is left wondering how much of the story is exaggerated, but in any case the poet sets up a very unexpected courtroom scene, perhaps satirizing or mocking the stiff and highly organized proceedings most courtrooms observe.

Lines 26–29

In juxtaposition to the out of control proceedings in the court—everyone having fun—the judge is not happy, perhaps pounding his gavel over the laughter, demanding order, asking the man "what kind of business is this?"

Line 30

This is the first time in the poem that the reader hears the man speak and learns his side of the story.

Lines 31–34

"Monkey man" was perhaps slang for any street performer, referring to the technique some entertainers would use of training a spider monkey to take tips and small change from the crowd after each show. Or perhaps the man was known around the neighborhood as the "monkey man." In this courtroom farce, though, he gets the last word, turning his wit back on the angry judge. Of course, "monkey business" is also a phrase that refers to any kind of playful misbehavior and is perhaps the man's way of pointing out to the judge how harmless the performances really are, and, further, how unreasonable it is to be arrested for making people happy and trying to earn a living.

Themes

Reality and Appearance

Human beings often behave in ways that their job or circumstances require, and this behavior frequently conflicts with who they believe themselves to "really" be. Such conflicts are not uncommon in a society that has put the needs of big business and government ahead of those of individuals. Cruz uses a confrontation between a street performer and the government to point out the hypocrisy at the root of these conflicts. He suggests that behind all of the masquerading and posing that goes on during the course of one's work are human beings that can laugh, love, and recognize the difference between what is legal and what is right. Cruz spells this out most vividly in the responses of the court clerks and the detectives to the monkey man's courtroom puppet show. Their ability to enjoy themselves stands in stark contrast to the judge's inability to enjoy himself and his steadfast insistence on following the law, even if doing so proves to be sillier than the monkey man's performance itself.

Competition

It is a truism that human beings compete with one another to survive and that the rules for competition depend on the society in which one lives. "Business" tells the story of one man's fight to survive in an environment that both appreciates his work and disdains it. The public's appreciation of the monkey man's work is evident in the "huge crowds" that show up to buy his whistles and puppets and listen to his music. Government's disdain for his work is evident by the man being arrested on a regular basis for simply trying to survive. The monkey man, then, must craft a strategy for appeasing the demands of government while continuing to do the work that he loves. He accomplishes this by being himself: a performer.

Performing in a courtroom, a place often associated with solemnity and mind-numbing bureaucratic procedures, brings life and laughter to the detective and court clerks, who "[roll] on the floor" with glee at the monkey man's puppet show. It is significant that these two groups of people side with the monkey man, as they are also working people. They stand in contrast to the judge, symbolic of a society's idea of justice, who remains opposed to the monkey man's work. The end of the poem sets up a confrontation between the judge and ordinary people, represented by the monkey man, the court clerks, and the police. This David and Goliath scenario does not need to play itself out in order for readers to sympathize with the monkey man. After all, he is the underdog.

Individualism

Balancing the needs of the state with the desires of the individual is a continuing struggle for modern governments. Cruz demonstrates the absurdity that results when government equally applies rules to citizens regardless of circumstance. By denying a man who is simply trying to make a living his business, the government reveals its inability to represent all the people.

An individual's rights are codified in the first ten amendments to the Constitution of the United States, and in his poem Cruz draws on the sympathy that most people have for the individual when challenging the state. The judge, in enforcing the letter of the law, misses the spirit of the law and elicits readers' contempt.

Style

"Business" is written in short free-verse lines and is almost completely punctuation free. Instead of following a set pattern of stresses or rhymes, as in formal verse, Cruz uses the more relaxed and varied rhythms of everyday conversation, perhaps similar to the voice of Don Arturo, from whom the speaker claims to have heard the story. By keeping his lines short—usually only three to five words—and the vocabulary simple and straightforward, Cruz succeeds in creating an easy tone. Almost every line lacks end punctuation, a technique called enjambing the line, which allows the phrase to runover to the next line. The resulting effect is a flowing, nonstop motion throughout the work. Since this poem's subject matter questions authority (who would judge selling whistles and puppets illegal?), Cruz's refusal to incorporate "proper" punctuation in this poem—and many of his other works—reflects his questioning nature and a tendency to trust his own sense of voice over one determined by someone else.

Historical Context

Cuban Immigration and New York City

The character of Don Arturo is based on a Cuban immigrant and friend of Cruz's who lives in New York City. Cruz wrote many of the poems in *Mainland* while living in New York City in the 1960s and early 1970s. Many of the Cubans who immigrated to the United States during the early 1960s were staunch anticommunists and had family ties in Florida and New York. Many were middle-class government workers, businessmen, professionals, and managers who left Cuba not only because they opposed the revolution but because they wanted to protect their financial assets.

Some of these new arrivals formed groups whose members actively worked for the overthrow of the Castro government. Such groups, including the Insurrectional Jose Marti Movement and the Cuban National Liberation Front, were based in Miami, Florida, and carried out bombings of Cuban interests and associates throughout the United States and Canada. Cubans who immigrated during the mid-1960s to mid-1980s also came for political and economic reasons but tended to be less educated and less skilled than the previous wave of Cuban immigrants. The Mariel boatlift of 1980 alone brought more than 120,000 Cubans to American shores. In the early 1970s, Cuba and the United States explored the possibility of reestablishing ties, but, in 1975, the United States suspended talks when Cuba sent a large number of troops to fight in the Angolan civil war. In 1977, the countries fi-

Topics for Further Study

- Research African folk tales having to do with animals. What is the role of the monkey in such tales? Write a short essay making any connections between how the monkey appears in these tales and how it is used in Cruz's poem.

- Interview a "wise man" in your neighborhood or family, asking him how to be successful in love and business. How do his responses compare to Don Arturo's? What about the responses are wise? Present your findings to the class.

- Do an informal survey of the small businesses in your city or town. How many of these businesses are owned by immigrants or the children of immigrants? Research the relationship between various kinds of businesses, such as corner stores, quick marts, and fast food restaurants, and the people who own them and work in them. Are people of certain ethnic backgrounds over-represented in them? Account for your findings.

- Brainstorm as many ethnic and racial stereotypes related to money and work as possible, and then hold a class discussion on the danger of such stereotypes.

- With your class, make a chart listing the advantages and disadvantages of self-employment. What are some of the qualities needed to be self-employed? How many people in your class envision working for themselves in the future? Discuss possible job opportunities.

nally established special interest sections in their respective capitals.

During this period, John V. Lindsay was New York City's mayor (1966–1974). A reformer, Lindsay tried to pare down government by consolidating administrative agencies and to decentralize authority by creating neighborhood councils. However, the city became a hotbed of tension and unrest as severe rioting rocked its streets in 1964 and again in 1968. The crime rate jumped by 91 percent

Compare & Contrast

- **1970s:** The Cuban Communist Party approves a new socialist constitution, and Fidel Castro is elected president.

  Today: The United States House of Representatives approves a measure allowing the sale of food and medicines to Cuba as American corporations prepare themselves to do business in Cuba if Castro ceases to exercise power.

- **1970s:** Rudolph Giuliani becomes the assistant United States attorney in the office of the Southern District of New York where he takes on drug dealers, organized crime, and white-collar criminals.

  Today: On September 11, 2001, two hijacked jetliners crash into the World Trade Center in lower Manhattan, killing thousands, including hundreds of firefighters and police, and causing massive economic and emotional shock waves that reverberate throughout the country. Giuliani emerges as one of the city's heroes, providing leadership and offering hope.

- **1970s:** One-and-a-half million Puerto Ricans live in the United States.

  Today: More than two-and-a-half million Puerto Ricans live in the United States, with most of them residing in New York City and northern New Jersey.

between 1965 and 1971, leading to the establishment of special homicide, robbery, and burglary squads in the Detective Bureau. In 1971, the Organized Crime Control Bureau was founded to investigate narcotics crimes.

In the late 1960s and early 1970s, New York City lost more than a half million jobs, which seriously eroded its tax base. The unemployment rate skyrocketed and by 1975 the city teetered on bankruptcy, with a deficit of more than three billion dollars. The poor, as always, were disproportionately affected. Rising poverty rates, growing drug use, and protests against American involvement in the Vietnam War all contributed to the public's increasing distrust of government. This distrust escalated in 1972 when a group of men, including former CIA agent James McCord, were arrested in the burglary of the Democratic Party headquarters in the Watergate apartment complex in Washington, D.C. Over the next two years this incident led to more investigations, which found many members of President Nixon's inner circle to be involved with the break-in and ensuing attempted cover-up. Under the threat of impeachment, Nixon himself resigned in 1974.

New York City Culture: 1960s–1970s

Cruz's poetry makes frequent reference to music in general and salsa in particular. The term

"salsa" describes a type of music that originated in the late 1960s as a marketing gimmick by Fania Records to sell a product that was significantly different than the Latin big band sound of the 1950s. The new sound is derived from the Afro-Cuban religious and secular music of island slaves but incorporates genres from other Afro-Caribbean and African-American musical traditions as well. The large number of people immigrating to New York from Cuba and Puerto Rico in the 1940s and 1950s helped to fuel the popularity of salsa music, and many salsa bands include both Cuban and Puerto Rican musicians. The aggressive sound of salsa, improvisation, and combination of rhythms are also distinctly urban and reflect the music's connection to the streets of New York City.

Critical Overview

Though not much has been written critically about the poem "Business," Cruz is considered by critics to be one of the leading contemporary Hispanic-American poets writing today. In his book *The Nuyorican Experience: Literature of the Puerto Rican Minority*, Eugene Mohr comments, "Cruz is, despite his ethnic experience, clearly at home in contemporary American poetry and has established an increasingly solid reputation for himself with critics and serious readers." Martín Espada, a well-known Latino poet, calls Cruz "a dazzling talent considered for many years to be one of the leading Puerto Rican poets in the United States." Some critics highlight Cruz's musical sense of common speech and nontraditional use of punctuation; as Nicolas Kanellos has written in the introduction to Cruz's collection *Rhythm, Content & Flavor*, "When Random House issued the poetic works of a New York Puerto Rican prodigy in *Snaps* (1968), it was fully aware of the originality, power and clarity of vision in the young poet's snapshots of life in the urban ghetto." According to Kanellos, Cruz's editors, by agreeing to publish his poems, were "respectful of Cruz's diction—which was apparently nurtured in black English and popular music—and his irreverence for some of the formalities of grammar and style."

Criticism

Chris Semansky

Semansky is an instructor of English literature and composition. In this essay, Semansky considers "Business" in relation to other Cruz poems.

One can imagine Cruz's poem being performed as a comedy sketch on *Saturday Night Live* or as a scene in a Gene Wilder film. It has all of the ingredients of popular appeal: a playful and clownish everyman fighting established power; a sympathetic public; a buffoon of a judge representing institutional authority; and a punch line that turns on a pun. Underneath the comedic tone, however, lies the truth of the poem, the message Cruz wants readers to take away. This truth can be seen more clearly by examining the poems that accompany "Business" than by considering it alone.

The business of "Business" permeates the other four poems with which it is grouped. These poems, "Atmosphere," "Memory," "Love," and "Music," all function as parables describing how one should live. They are presented as nuggets of wisdom from a sage who has lived the advice he offers. The first poem, "#1 Atmosphere," offers advice on how to make one's own way in the world:

> Don Arturo says:
> You have to know
> what the atmosphere

> *The need to give love, to proactively transform one's environment and to be accountable for one's actions are all embodied in the parable of the 'monkey man.'*

> is creating
> You have to know
> Because if it's good
> You can go somewhere
> and make your own.

This poem is about the necessity of being aware of one's surroundings. Understanding, being sensitive to one's environment, Don Arturo claims, means that people have a better chance of creating their own atmosphere. Although the logic seems anti-materialist in that initially the atmosphere, rather than people, does the creating, it is actually circular. Notice that he does not say, "if it's bad, you can avoid it." Don Arturo's advice is like a New Age affirmation for those looking for a quick fix of positive energy: it's light and fluffy and belabors the obvious. The second poem in the suite, "Memory," carries a warning of sorts.

> Don Arturo says:
> You have to know
> what you once said
> Because it could
> travel in the air
> for years
> And return in different
> clothes
> And then you have to
> buy it.

This poem underscores the importance of accountability to one's words. Don Arturo emphasizes that people must be conscious of what they say and make sure that their words match their intentions. The future acts as a kind of glue, binding a speaker to his or her words. The message here is not to be cavalier with language but to use it appropriately. The verb "buy" to describe the act of being held accountable is significant because it highlights the similarities between responsible behavior

What Do I Read Next?

- Cruz tells the story of Don Arturo, the person behind the character, in "Don Arturo: A Story of Migration," an essay included in his 1982 collection *By Lingual Wholes*.

- "Business" is also included in Cruz's most recent collection of poems, *Maraca: New and Selected Poems, 1966–2000* (2001).

- In 1994, Puerto Rican poet and political activist Martín Espada edited *Poetry Like Bread: Poets of the Political Imagination* from Curbstone Press. The anthology collects poems by activist writers, such as El Salvador's Roque Dalton, Nicaragua's Tomas Borge, Puerto Rico's Clemente Soto Velez, and Cruz.

- *Puerto Rican Voices in English* (1997), edited by Carmen Dolores Hernandez, collects interviews with more than a dozen Puerto Rican writers living in the United States and writing in English. These writers, including Cruz, discuss such topics as the challenge of writing for multiple audiences, cultural adaptation, and literary racism.

- In 1995, Roberto Santiago edited the collection *Boricuas: Influential Puerto Rican Writings—An Anthology*, which contains more than fifty selections of poetry, fiction, plays, essays, monologues, screenplays, and speeches from some of the most powerful voices in Puerto Rican literature, including poems by Cruz.

---

and business practices. The fourth poem in the suite, "Love," dispenses advice indirectly, using the subjunctive, rather than the imperative, mood to get its point across:

> Don Arturo says:
> if you put your hands
> in all the time
> Some day it will fly
> away with your mind.

This is a variation on the warning against falling in love. Don Arturo recommends prudence in matters of the heart, advising readers to be careful of giving themselves to others too often or without discrimination. Emotion will dominate reason, Don Arturo reminds readers, if they let it. However, his last poem in the suite, "Music," seems to suggest just the opposite, to let oneself be carried away by emotion and to live in the moment.

> Don Arturo says:
> There's supposed to
> be more sauce than
> fish
> It's suppose to be
> like riding on a
> horse
> or stepping out
> of the room
> Without a single motion.

Including music in a list of subjects that one needs to know to lead a successful and happy life underscores the significance of music in Hispanic culture. The point of Don Arturo's description is that while playing or listening to music, one needs to become one with it, to merge one's body with the sounds and rhythms. To know how to be in relation to music means to know how to cultivate pleasure from the world.

Cruz underscores the importance of enjoying oneself in "Business." In this poem, all of the values that Don Arturo advocates pursuing in his other poems are evident. The need to give love, to proactively transform one's environment and to be accountable for one's actions are all embodied in the parable of the "monkey man." The world can be a hostile place, full of obstacles the individual must overcome in order to survive. And often, those whose job it is to protect you become your enemies. It is no surprise that the central character in "Business" is a musician who manages to make a living at what he enjoys through persistence, ingenuity, and good will. Rather than being daunted by his thrice-weekly arrests—presumably for petty vending regulations—the musician wins over the very people who hound him: the police. He does this simply by being himself, something he cannot help being, even in the face of such sour-faced authority as the judge.

It is important to note that the character of Don Arturo is based on a friend of Cruz's, featured in his essay "Don Arturo: A Story of Migration." The real Don Arturo, Cruz tells readers, immigrated to the United States in 1926 from Cuba. Cruz relates Arturo's mischievous ways, including his seduction of a minister's wife. When the Great Depression hit, Arturo quit the Christian band he was playing for and became a street musician. Cruz describes the event as follows:

When the market crashed he [Arturo] became a street musician, taking a position outside Macy's and sometimes Gimbels. He played many instruments at the same time, even putting a tambourine on his feet. He sang popular Latin American songs and told jokes. Sometimes he got arrested and he put puppet shows on in the courtroom. The court clerks rolled on the floor.

Cruz's admiration of Arturo is obvious, both in his poems and the essay itself, which serves as the basis for his poems. By writing from material he has already used, Cruz also emulates Arturo, who has learned to survive by his wits. Just as Arturo put on puppet shows both to make a living and, in the courtroom, to escape from the punishment of the law, so too has Cruz reshaped his own material for different audiences. Both Cruz and Arturo exhibit the kind of entrepreneurial zeal and strategic intelligence often associated with immigrants to the United States. They try, they fail, they adapt, and they overcome. In 1981, when Cruz wrote the essay about Arturo, he also wrote another poem, titled simply, "Don Arturo Says," which appeared in his 1989 collection, *Rhythm, Content and Flavor*.

Like some of the other poems, this one also advocates the joys of diving into life, erasing the distinction between the person engaged in the activity and the activity itself. To "disappear" here means to lose all self-consciousness. This is also the only one of the poems in which Don Arturo talks about himself in the first person. However, unlike the other poems, this one is full of nostalgia and melancholy. There is no explicit advice being dispensed, nor warnings proffered. Instead of the folksy wisdom in the other "Don Arturo" poems, there is wistfulness. The elegiac tone also shows Don Arturo's more vulnerable side. He is no longer the avuncular and mischievous raconteur but someone who seems to be practicing his own elegy, mourning his own passing before the fact. In his essay on Arturo, Cruz listens to him recount his life, writing:

> He savors memory like espresso coffee. He calls up his beautiful moments with women like an encyclopedia, though his memory sometimes scatters. The details he gives shine like light bulbs and make bridges with each other.

This last image is telling in that it offers a justification for Cruz's poems about the old man. They function to continue the "bridge" of Don Arturo's memories. Here, Cruz's role as poet is to preserve his friend's stories and the lessons they teach. By acting as cultural historian for the immigrant experience, Cruz keeps alive the lessons of the past. This is the poet's true business.

To survive, newcomers may sometimes break the letter of the law, but perhaps they are showing drive and determination to earn a living in a difficult world."

Source: Chris Semansky, Critical Essay on "Business," in *Poetry for Students*, The Gale Group, 2002.

Michelle Prebilic

Prebilic is an independent author who writes and analyzes children's literature. She holds degrees in psychology and business. In this essay, Prebilic discusses how Victor Hernandez Cruz strives to reconcile the worlds of Puerto Rico and mainland United States in the life of an immigrant or street vendor.

The poem "Business" (*Mainland*), by Victor Hernandez Cruz, exposes the mediocre side of mainland United States. "Business," the third title of a group of five in Cruz's 1973 poetry collection, also includes poems called: "Atmosphere," "Memory," "Love," and "Music." All the poems communicate the sayings of Don Arturo; they all portray universal themes. "Business" portrays the difficulties of an immigrant making a living as a street vendor in a metropolitan city. Cruz, a Puerto Rican, relays the complexities of this business through the trials of a wise, risk-taking businessman.

To fully appreciate Cruz's poem, readers should consider several ideas: Cruz's use of Don Arturo to define setting; the events in Puerto Rican history that brought immigrants, including Cruz, to mainland United States; the audience that Cruz's poetry inspires; the business of street vending; and the symbolism of the monkey man.

Cruz defines the setting of the poem in his introductory line "Don Arturo says." This identification to Arturo lets readers know that the poem refers to a cohesive community with a strong ethnic affiliation. Arturo symbolizes an explicit cultural upbringing, and "Don" means sir, a title formerly attached to the last name of a high-ranking Spaniard. Cruz uses a man he respects and likes to share his ideas through a poem. This act in itself shows the importance of Cruz's topic. During this thirty-four-line free verse poem, readers immediately learn that the speaker is of Spanish birthright.

Consider the events that brought immigrants to mainland United States. In 1951, Puerto Ricans voted to start their own government and to remain a commonwealth of the United States. Puerto Ricans adopted their new constitution in 1952.

Together, Puerto Rico and the U.S. Congress devised an economic-stimulus plan, Operation Bootstrap, to deal with the trade and industry woes of the island. The plan called for U.S. companies to build factories on the island to employ Puerto Rican workers. In return, businesses avoided paying taxes for seventeen years. From 1947 to 1960, the number of factories increased from one hundred to six hundred. By 1955, manufacturing exceeded farming as a contributor to the island's economy. Yet, Operation Bootstrap could not guarantee employment for all Puerto Ricans. Large Puerto Rican communities formed in metropolitan cities like New York and Chicago.

In looking at a snapshot of history, it is imperative that readers understand the influence Puerto Rico had on Cruz's childhood, his proclivity towards writing, and the development of his writing style. In *Contemporary Poets*, Cruz reflects on the journey of his family to the mainland. He explains that his grandfather rolled cigars in Puerto Rico, thus making a living as a tobacconist. When the agricultural system of the island failed due to bad management, it displaced an enormous segment of the interior population. Cruz's family became part of the massive mandatory migration to mainland United States.

Cruz, as quoted in *Contemporary Poets*, remembers staring out a window at the lower east side of Manhattan at the age of five. By age 15 he began to write, feeling a deep impulse to do so. He felt he had to "balance a lot of worlds together . . . feeling and looking at the culture of my parents and the new and modern culture of New York, its architecture, its art, and its fervent intellectual thought." Cruz continues, stating that he believes a poet "deciphers his psychological, emotional, and historical position . . . within the rhythms of his culture, the culture he was born into and the culture which he continuously acquires."

Cruz learned first hand the challenges of migration. Like many other writers, Cruz seems to have captured the spirit of the dislocation that Puerto Rican immigrants felt in the mid-twentieth century. It seems as if Cruz's monkey man deals with dislocation by becoming a street vendor. He sells whistles and puppets, and plays a guitar. People in the crowded shopping areas toss money into his guitar. This somehow breaks the law, so law enforcement repeatedly arrests him. Readers must assume that he either does not have the proper license or does not meet the peddling requirements such as operating within legal hours, paying taxes, or selling at officially authorized locations. Yet, the monkey man continues to do what he knows to earn his living. Establishing this background immediately allows for the readers to settle into the atmosphere typical of immigrant Puerto Ricans as they become a part of mainland United States.

In addition, these historical experiences and beliefs shaped Cruz's writing style significantly as seen in the presentation of "Business." This metropolitan setting validates the experiences of more than two million Puerto Ricans traveling to mainland United States, not to mention the numerous other cultures who can identify with this scenario. The poem offers a simple yet effective insight into the complexities of cultural changes—both in the world of one's birth and the way of life that one continuously acquires. In the poem, an immigrant struggles with both worlds. Born into a society of extreme poverty, this man perhaps developed the persistence to sell his wares against all odds. He survived extreme poverty. Perhaps forced to immigrate to the mainland, he continues to use the same skills, only to be arrested and prosecuted by his new world. This cultural dichotomy may perplex him; however, the character in the poem seems adeptly comfortable with his street vending business.

Next, take into account the popularity of Cruz's poems, his audience. As Pamela Masingale Lewis notes, Cruz's literature "reaches a diverse and large audience. His poems have been translated into five languages." Cruz leads a movement of "Neorican" writers, that is, Puerto Rican writers who have spent "their formative years on the United States mainland . . . write in an idiomatic English influenced by Spanish and Black English and . . . derive mainly from the working class." Their literature examines the reality of life of Puerto Ricans on the mainland and their traditions.

This leads us to examine street vending or peddling. As an established street vendor, the man in the poem finds himself caught between two desires: earning a living and abiding by the law. Cruz establishes this man's resolve—his many arrests do not cause him to stop peddling. Secondly, the court appearance shows this man's plight. As he breaks the law in front of the judge who scorns him, the detectives and court clerks roll on the floor in laughter, indicating that they enjoy his business. Subsequently, they buy his whistles and puppets.

Street vendors continue to meet with this type of complexity today, as Regina Austin presents in *Yale Law Journal*: "the line between the legal and the illegal in the area of economic activity is ephemeral." Laws in the United States largely do not encourage street vending. If a city's regulations do not explicitly ban it, they hamper it by limiting vending licenses, increasing fees, restricting locations, or stipulating business hours, table proportions, or cart design. Why do vendors continue to violate these prescribed regulations? Perhaps those that do it are like "some poor blacks, [for whom] breaking the law is not only a way of life; it is the only way to survive." Austin's article speaks specifically about blacks; however, a poor immigrant of any nationality can certainly use street vending to survive. As Cruz points out in this man's case, the judge, a law-enforcing entity, exclaims "What kind of business is this," to which the man replies that the monkey man sells monkey business.

Why does this man say he is a monkey man? The last matter to bear in mind in analyzing Cruz's symbolic poem is the correlation between the monkey man and the monkey. In literature, the monkey symbolizes play, zaniness, and intelligence. It's the most similar of all mammals to humans. Monkey's love to play, and intelligence is an integral part of play. In fact, monkey behavioral patterns that seem irrational have a reason and a purpose. When monkeys "monkey around," they are learning important survival skills: how to control movements, judge the strength of branches, and fall correctly as they travel. Watching monkeys in their native environments can be amusing, as they seem utterly carefree and zany. They love to play so much that female monkeys can overlook the fact that they have children to nurture. Perhaps Cruz uses the analogy of a monkey to draw on these traits.

In addition, the term "monkey business" means mischief, shenanigans, trouble, and pranks. Therefore, monkey man as an entrepreneur is a fittingly symbolic one. The monkey man appears as if he's playing when he strums his guitar and sells puppets or whistles; yet, like nature's monkey, he's engaging in survival skills. He's doing what it takes to ensure he gets food on the table, just as a mon-

key learns how to fall from a tree. He uses his play intelligently to fetch an income; like that monkey that looks silly, but who is actually testing the strength of a tree branch. In fact, the monkey man does his business so well that he sells whistles and puppets in any environment, even in the court. By this, Cruz implies that through being mischievous, causing trouble, and pulling pranks, the monkey man learns how to survive. The monkey man knows that his business is not selling things, but it is about being who he is, just like the monkey.

Although the United States offers many benefits, it challenges newcomers more than readers may realize. Earning a living may not be easy. Language barriers, immigration status, disparities in income, and multicultural misunderstandings may be but a few things that make the transition to a metropolitan area a difficult one. To survive, newcomers may sometimes break the letter of the law, but perhaps they are showing drive and determination to earn a living in a difficult world. Therefore, through Cruz's monkey man and his business, readers learn to appreciate the complexity of immigration.

Source: Michelle Prebilic, Critical Essay on "Business," in *Poetry for Students*, The Gale Group, 2002.

Sources

Austin, Regina, "An Honest Living: Street Vendors, Municipal Regulation, and the Black Public Sphere," in *Yale Law Journal*, Vol. 103, No. 8, June 1994, pp. 2119–31.

Cruz, Victor Hernández, *By Lingual Wholes*, Momos Press, 1982.

———, *Mainland*, Random House, 1973.

———, *Red Beans*, Coffee House Press, 1991.

———, *Rhythm, Content and Flavor*, Arte Publico Press, 1989.

Espada, Martín, and Juan Flores, "Introduction," in *Callaloo*, Vol. 15, No. 4, 1992, pp. 941–42.

Kanellos, Nicolas, "Introduction," in *Ryhthm, Content and Flavor*, by Victor Hernández Cruz, Arte Publico Press, 1989, pp. 10–11.

Lewis, Pamela Masingale, "Victor Hernández Cruz," in *Dictionary of Literary Biography*, Volume 41: *Afro-American Poets Since 1955*, Gale Research, 1985, pp. 74–84.

Meltzer, Bruce, "Cruz, Victor Hernández," in *Contemporary Poets*, 6th ed., St. James Press, 1996.

Mohr, Eugene V., "Nuyorican Poets," in *The Nuyorican Experience: Literature of the Puerto Rican Minority*, Greenwood Press, 1982, pp. 91–108.

Further Reading

Cruz, Victor Hernandez, Leroy Quintana, and Virgil Suarez, eds., *Paper Dance: 55 Latino Poets*, Persea Books, 2000.
    This anthology of Latino and Latina poets includes work that addresses topics such as cultural displacement, English as a second language, and the relationship between Spanish and English literary traditions.

Gonzalez, Ray, *Currents from the Dancing River: Contemporary Latino Fiction, Nonfiction and Poetry*, Harcourt Brace, 1994.
    This anthology includes excerpts from poems, novels, and memoirs from both well-known and lesser-known Latino works. It features such writers as Cruz, Rafael Campo, and Juan Felipe Herrera.

Jones, Leroi, and Larry Neal, eds., *Black Fire: An Anthology of Afro-American Writing*, William Morrow, 1968.
    This is one of the first anthologies to publish work written by Cruz, who has African as well as Spanish and Indian heritage. It provides a healthy sampling of African-American writing from the 1960s.

Stavans, Ilan, *The Hispanic Condition: The Power of a People*, RAYO, 2001.
    Stavans explores the history and psychology of Hispanic society in the United States, interweaving literary and political references with his personal experience.

Colibrí

Martín Espada
1990

"Colibrí" first appeared in the *Americas Review* and is included in Martín Espada's bilingual second collection *Rebellion Is the Circle of a Lover's Hands*, published in 1990. Espada won the 1989 PEN/Revson Award and the Paterson Poetry Prize for the book. Like his other collections, *Rebellion Is the Circle of a Lover's Hands* gives voice to oppressed peoples, particularly Latinos, and demonstrates a historical awareness of the roots of oppression. Written in four short free-verse stanzas, "Colibrí," which means hummingbird, addresses the colonization by the Spanish of the Taino, the native people who inhabit what is now called Puerto Rico. Setting the poem in Jayuya, a city founded in 1883 and the place of a 1950 uprising, Espada uses crisp imagery and an extended metaphor to connect past to present and to evoke sympathy for the Taino. Espada's father is Puerto Rican and many of his poems address the island's history and its fight for independence.

This poem is a good example of Espada's ability to politicize his subject matter without sounding strident or condescending. He is able to do this by showing rather than telling readers about the Taino's situation. By focusing on the ways in which the Spanish conquered the Taino using language as well as guns, Espada universalizes the Taino's plight, suggesting that oppressed peoples throughout history have endured similar tribulations. The image of hands occurs in poems throughout the collection, particularly the hands of working-class people such as janitors and secretaries.

Martín Espada

Author Biography

Former tenant lawyer, poet, and professor Martín Espada was born in 1957 in Brooklyn, New York, to a Puerto Rican father and a Jewish mother. He received his bachelor of art degree in history at the University of Wisconsin and a juris doctor degree in law from Northeastern University in Boston. Before working as a lawyer and advocate for the renting poor, Espada held jobs as a salesman, clerk, telephone solicitor, gas station attendant, bouncer, and bartender. Although Espada gave up his law career to devote himself full-time to writing and teaching, he did not abandon political activism; he merely changed the means through which he practices it. At a time when most poets have turned inward to explore the nuances of an angst-ridden self, Espada has turned outward, writing about the injustices done to other people and advocating change.

Espada began writing when he was sixteen, as a means of self-discovery and a way of coming to terms with the hostile community in which he lived. His poetry speaks out against poverty and racism while trying to avoid being strident or preachy—a failing of much so-called political poetry. Espada is a staunch advocate for Puerto Rican independence and has supported a number of

other controversial causes, including the case of death-row inmate Mumia Abu-Jamal. Poems such as "Colibrí," from his collection *Rebellion Is the Circle of a Lover's Hands* (1990), show rather than tell about the subjugation of the native people of Puerto Rico through clever metaphors and striking images.

Espada's poetry collections include *The Immigrant Iceboy's Bolero* (1982), with photographs by his father; *Trumpets from the Islands of Their Eviction* (1987); *City of Coughing and Dead Radiators* (1993); *Imagine the Angels of Bread* (1996), which won an American Book Award; and *A Mayan Astronomer in Hell's Kitchen: Poems* (2000). He has also edited a number of collections, including *Poetry Like Bread: Poets of the Political Imagination* (1994) and *El Coro: A Chorus of Latino and Latina Poetry* (1997). In 1998, South End Press released his collection of essays, *Zapata's Disciple*.

Espada has received numerous awards for his work, including the PEN/Voelker Award for Poetry, the Paterson Poetry Prize, two fellowships from the National Endowment for the Arts, a PEN/Revson fellowship, and a Massachusetts Artists Foundation fellowship. He is an associate professor of English at the University of Massachusetts in Amherst.

Poem Summary

First Stanza

"Colibrí" is set in Puerto Rico in the city of Jayuya. The city's name is derived from local Indian Chief Hayuya. Jayuya is tucked into the northern border of Toro Negro Forest Reserve and commands breathtaking views extending to the Atlantic and the Caribbean. Sometimes natives refer to it as "La Capital Indigena," to signify its large population of Taino.

Espada first compares the scattering of the lizards to the way that "green canoes" scattered "before the invader." This is a historical allusion to the 1493 Spanish invasion of the island, which natives called Borinquen.

"Iron and words" refer to guns and language, two of the primary tools the conquerors used to subjugate people. The Spanish named the native Arawak Indians Taino. When Espada writes that the Taino "took life / from the plátanos in the trees," he is describing how this banana-like fruit sustained them. The fruits resemble "multiple green fingers" in their shape and size. The rock carvings refer to the Taino written language, which was in the form of petroglyphs, or symbols, carved in stone.

Second Stanza

In this stanza, Espada tells readers that the Spanish "christened" the hummingbird "colibrí." The word "christened" is significant for its allusion to the Christian practice of baptism. Espada suggests that christening something that is not yours is also an act of appropriation. In this case, the Spanish are appropriating the Indians' land as well as their culture by naming the things of their world. He compares the hummingbird's frantic darting to the racing of the Taino's hearts when they first heard the sound of guns, underscoring the fear the bird and the Indians share. "Hacienda" is Spanish for a large estate, or the main building in such an estate. The bird, and figuratively the Taino, are caught inside the walls of the hacienda.

Third Stanza

In this stanza, Espada extends the comparison between the bird and the Taino, showing how the bird, like the native Taino, becomes paralyzed in the clutches of the Spanish. However, the hand also serves the function of liberator as well as captor, as it can both free and imprison the bird. The image of the hand also echoes the image in the collection's title, as do the carved circles at the end of the first stanza.

Espada describes the hummingbird's native habitat as "a paradise of sky, / a nightfall of singing frogs." The frogs are *coquí*, a local species that lives in trees and is found almost nowhere else in the world.

Fourth Stanza

These two lines provide the punch—some might say the punchline—for the poem. The wish that history might be like hands refers to the preceding image of the hand freeing the bird and, by extension, the Taino, from its, and their, imprisonment. The speaker desires that history could also free people. The tone here is melancholic, as the speaker realizes that history is not like hands.

Espada is outspoken in his desire for Puerto Rican independence. He considers that the United States, like Spain before it, is an occupying force and needs to leave so that the native people can rule themselves.

Topics for Further Study

- Compare and contrast the use of bird imagery in Espada's poem with the bird imagery in Richard Wilbur's poem "The Writer." Discuss the ways in which Wilbur's poem is political, and Espada's poem is personal.

- Research the history of the Spanish occupation of Borinquen beginning in 1493 and construct a chart listing the political "development" of the island. Present your findings to your class.

- Get into groups and develop a dictionary of Taino words that have made it into the English or Spanish language. Make copies and distribute them to your class.

- Research the history of Christopher Columbus's trips to the "new world" and make a chart of popular myths related to his discovery of America. Next to that list, make another one explaining the historical facts relating to the events.

- Research the history of the Taino. How did they get to Borinquen and when? Present your findings to your class.

- Research the history of independence movements in Latin America. Write a short essay on how the Puerto Rican independence movement compares to those of several other countries.

- Christopher Columbus wrote in his journal that Tainos had beautiful tall slender bodies and that the Taino tongue was "gentle, the sweetest in the world, always with a laugh." From a Borinquen's point of view, write diary entries for the first week during which they encountered the Spanish. Take turns reading these out loud to your class.

Themes

Language

One of the primary ways that colonizing powers subjugate a people is through language. The colonizer's act of naming and renaming the world of the colonized forces the less powerful to see themselves through the eyes of the occupiers, rather than through their own eyes. Espada foregrounds the diabolical nature of this practice by listing it along with guns as the primary weapon the Spanish used on the native Borinquens.

Espada provides two examples of renaming, "colibrí" and "Taino." The Spaniards called the native Arawak Taino, and they dubbed the hummingbird *colibrí*. The poem itself extends the metaphor comparing the former to the latter. Ironically, although the final image of the poem is one of liberation, there is no escaping from the circle of the oppressor's language, as it becomes part of the fabric of the way that the oppressed view and experience life. The poem's final image suggests that there can be no real liberation from the Europeans' linguistic colonialism.

History

History has as much, if not more, to do with the present than it does the past, as those who write it do so out of the demands of the present. The rush in the last few decades to rewrite American history taking into account the viewpoints of Native Americans and previously omitted peoples attests to this. Espada's poem can be seen as an attempt to provide another view of Puerto Rico's past by describing its "discovery" and occupation as acts of aggression. The last two lines of the poem—"If only history / were like your hands"—are both a wish and a lament, as they underscore the difficulty of undoing popular thinking about Puerto Rico and righting the injustices of the past.

Nature

Poets often romanticize nature by describing it in Edenic terms, as if it were a place of salvation and innocence. Espada draws on this tradition in "Colibrí" by linking the Taino to the natural world and the Spanish to a fallen world that attempts to dominate nature rather than live in harmony with it. Espada describes the Taino as living off the "plátanos in the trees," and he figuratively links the Taino with the hummingbird, an animal known for its beauty and vulnerability. Both are captives. When the bird is freed, it is released into "a paradise of sky / a nightfall of singing frogs." This line suggests the Taino also need to be freed into such a paradise. There are no predators in Espada's nature, no threats, except for the Spanish interlopers.

Colonialism

At various points in the history of civilization, countries have sought to occupy and annex other countries, often destroying the culture and irrevocably changing the history of those countries. In "Colibrí," Espada shows the effect of Spanish colonization on the Taino. The Spaniards change the Taino way of life, striking fear into them with their "iron and words." By comparing the Taino with the hummingbird, who "darts and bangs / between . . . white walls," Espada emphasizes how the Taino are imprisoned as well, literally and figuratively. Espada underlines the sheer brutality of colonial power with the image of the colibrí's "pure stillness" in the predator's hands.

Style

Metaphor and Simile

Metaphors underscore the similarities between two dissimilar things or ideas. Extended metaphors draw out that comparison. In "Colibrí," Espada develops an extended metaphor by comparing the Taino to the hummingbird. The tenor, or subject, of the comparison is the hummingbird, and the vehicle, or the metaphorical term itself, is the Taino. The third stanza is an example of an implicit metaphor, which is one in which the tenor is not specified but implied. The implied tenor here is the Taino.

In similes, comparison between two different things or ideas is made through the use of the word "like" or "as." Espada begins the poem with a simile when he writes, "the lizards scatter / like a fleet of green canoes / before the invader." This comparison draws attention to the fear of the lizards and the people in the canoes, and to the way in which both physically respond to that fear.

Imagery

"Colibrí" effectively portrays a picture of Taino oppression through its use of concrete imagery. Such imagery describes the world through the five senses. Espada's imagery is primarily visual, although he also includes aural (auditory) and kinesthetic (touch) imagery as well. Examples of visual imagery include the phrases, "fleet of green canoes," "multiple green fingers," and "rock carvings / of eyes and mouths." An example of an aural image is the phrase "hearing / the bellowing god of gunpowder." An example of a kinesthetic image, or one related to body movement or feeling, can be found in the first lines of the third stanza, when the colibrí is "seized in the paralysis / of the prey."

Compare & Contrast

- **1500s:** Juan Ponce de Leon is given a charter by the king of Spain to colonize Borinquen (Puerto Rico).

  Today: Puerto Rico is a commonwealth of the United States, although various groups lobby both for statehood and independence.

- **1500s:** More than fifty thousand Taino Indians live on the island of Borinquen.

- **Today:** Puerto Rico's population is 3.8 million. Europeans, Indians, and Africans have interbred to create a racially mixed people.

- **1500s:** The Spanish explore the world, colonizing numerous lands including what are now Mexico and Peru.

  Today: Spain, its empire long dissolved, is now a member of both the European Community and the North Atlantic Treaty Organization.

Historical Context

History of Puerto Rico

Espada's poem attempts to capture the fear and oppression felt by the Borinquens since the unwelcome arrival of outsiders. About fifty thousand Indians inhabited the island of Boriquen (which means "the great land of the valiant and noble Lord") when Christopher Columbus landed there in 1493. A peaceful people, the Taino were primarily farmers and fishermen living in a well-organized communal society. Columbus named the island "San Juan Bautista," for St. John the Baptist, and the town in which they landed "Puerto Rico" (rich port) because of its wealth of natural resources. The names were later switched when the King of Spain gave Columbus's lieutenant Juan Ponce de Leon a charter to settle the island in 1508. Spanish Conquistadors battled the native Indians, and those not killed were enslaved.

Continuing atrocities by the Spaniards and a smallpox epidemic almost wiped out the entire Taino population in the following decades. The womanless colonizers bred with the surviving Taino women, and, in the 1800s, the European population increased dramatically when Spain awarded land grants to immigrants seeking to settle on the island.

During this time, Puerto Rico's economy changed as sugar and coffee plantations replaced small farms. Puerto Rico became part of the United States after the Spanish-American War (1898–

1902), and in 1917, Puerto Ricans were given U.S. citizenship. Congress refused to grant either statehood or independence to the island but in 1952 gave it "commonwealth" status, meaning that Puerto Ricans have a large degree of local control over government, but the United States retains control over immigration, customs, and defense, and residents do not pay federal income taxes or vote in presidential elections.

By setting the poem in Jayuya, a historical center of Taino civilization, Espada draws on that city's recent revolutionary past. In 1950 Nationalist Party freedom fighters battled the U.S.-trained colonial police and national guard in an attempt to free the island from U.S. control. After learning of government plans to abolish his pro-independence organization, Dr. Pedro Albizu Campos, the party's leader, argued that Puerto Ricans had the right to use whatever means necessary to rid the island of foreign domination. Led by Blanca Canales, a group of party members captured the Jayuya police station and declared the independent Republic of Puerto Rico. Nationalists clashed with government forces in other municipalities as well, including Utuado, Ponce, Mayaguez, Arecibo, Naranjito, Ciales, and Penuelas. Police called in the national guard to crush the uprising, and the government imposed martial law.

In retaking Jayuya, warplane bombs destroyed more than 50 percent of the city, including numerous homes. After U.S. President Harry Truman represented the events in Puerto Rico as a local conflict, nationalists Oscar Collazo and Griselio Torresola attempted to assassinate him in Washington, D.C. However, D.C. police and Truman's bodyguards killed Torresola in a shoot-out and critically wounded Collazo.

The fight for Puerto Rican independence continues today. Espada, who is baffled by the failure of Puerto Rican voters to pass a resolution proclaiming independence, writes in an essay for the *Progressive* that the United States has "greedily exploited the labor and natural resources of the island; established a menacing, strategic military presence; forced English on the public schools and the court system; and repressed the independence movement." Arguing that the island is a colony of the United States, Espada claims that Puerto Rico's commonwealth status "is part of a colonial strategy, an illusory liberalization which has actually perpetuated U.S. control." A more recent clash between nationalists and the United States is over the U.S. Navy's use of the uninhabited Puerto Rican island of Vieques for bombing practice. The moratorium on bombing is set to expire in 2003.

Critical Overview

The bilingual collection in which "Colibrí" appears, *Rebellion Is the Circle of a Lover's Hands*, was awarded the 1989 PEN/Revson Award and garnered a good deal of praise from reviewers. Writing for *Publishers Weekly*, Penny Kaganoff notes, "All the poems are fine, but Espada is at his best in his pieces about the plight of migrant workers and refugees from Central America." Sam Cornish, in a review for *Ploughshares*, calls Espada "talented and promising" and writes, "Espada's work has integrity mingled with an ironic and sometimes bitter well-articulated sense of alienation by class and language." Roger Gilbert underscores Espada's political convictions as well. In the *Partisan Review*, Gilbert writes that Espada's poems are "continually informed by anger at social and economic injustices. This anger gives the book considerable moral urgency."

Arguing that Espada's poems "deserve an audience," Alan Gilbert praises Espada's style in the *Boston Review*, writing that "the individuality of Espada's voice is one to which any attentive reader can respond." Leslie Ullman underscores Espada's gift for narrative in her review for the *Kenyon Review*. Ullman writes, "The poems in this collection

tell their stories and flesh out their characters deftly, without shrillness or rhetoric, and vividly enough to invite the reader into a shared sense of loss." Critic John Bradley lauds the collection in the *Bloomsbury Review* for "the expansive humanity of Espada's vision."

Criticism

Chris Semansky

Semansky is an instructor of English literature and composition. In this essay, Semansky considers Espada's poem as a political poem.

Espada is a political poet at a time when the relevance of both politics and poetry has become significantly challenged in the American popular imagination. He is largely successful not because his politics agree with the poetry-reading public, but because they enliven the art. Espada does not use poetry as a vehicle for his politics; rather, he fuses the two to create work that various readers can appreciate, whether they agree with his political positions or not. "Colibrí" is an example of such a fusion.

Espada titles the poem with the name Spanish colonizers gave to the hummingbirds they found on the island of Borinquen. Doing so highlights the role of language in the poem, asking readers to keep in mind the significance of the term throughout the poem. Whereas less-skilled poets interested in merely "expressing" themselves might simply title the poem "Evil Spanish Conquistadors" and rant about the miscarriage of justice suffered by the native Borinquens, Espada creates a portrait of a tropical paradise. This shows readers the world that Borinquens lost and creates sympathy for the Indians. By showing instead of telling readers what the Spaniards did, Espada avoids the pitfall of appearing to preach, always a danger in poems with explicitly political subject matter.

Noting that much political verse has a "bad name," critic Ray Olson nonetheless praises Espada's poetry, writing in *Booklist* that it is "unsentimental, realistic work that almost never sounds a contestable note." Espada's realism is another way in which the poet establishes credibility for his politics. By realism, Olson means the way in which Espada uses concrete imagery to describe relatively ordinary events such as lizards scattering and hummingbirds darting. These are perfectly plausible descriptions that readers can see and understand; they are not romantic flights of fancy requiring readers to suspend their disbelief. Black activist and poet Amiri Baraka writes in the foreword to *Rebellion Is the Circle of a Lover's Hand*: "Martín Espada's work does not necessitate fantasy as its voice, it illuminates reality. Its truth . . . will make new volumes of Espada's still young work as seriously awaited as the next day." Espada does, however, occasionally lapse into the sentimental, as in his Edenic depictions of the natural world into which the hummingbird is released. Even these lapses, however, have significance for the reader aware of Puerto Rico's rich tropical environment. When reading that the hummingbird is released into "a paradise of sky / a nightfall of singing frogs," such readers would visualize the coquí tree frog, that is ubiquitous on the island, and hear its melodious call.

Espada's success in crafting political poems has as much to do with what he leaves out as what he includes. In his more successful poems such as "Colibrí," Espada puts history rather than himself at the center of the poem and, as Espada critic John R. Keene notes in *MELUS*, "History is the mirror that reflects the interplay of political forces." Too often political poetry overdoses on "I-ness," the compulsion by poets to put their own egos at the center of the universe, to personalize subjects only to trivialize them. By writing about historical subjects that are still relevant today, Espada mines the distance between past and present to allow readers to recognize themselves in history's mirror.

Espada also challenges readers to do their own research, rather than giving them all of the information of an event up front. For readers, this adds to their sense of discovery, and, hence, appreciation of the poem. For example, few readers unfamiliar with Puerto Rico or the independence movement there would grasp the significance of setting the poem in Jayuya, a nationalist stronghold and center for a nationalist uprising in 1950. Similarly, few readers would know that "the rock carvings / of eyes and mouths in perfect circles of amazement" refer to Taino petroglyphs and that these petroglyphs comprise Taino written language. The beauty of this poem is that although it still "works" without the reader knowing these allusions, the poem becomes richer with such knowledge. For example, knowing the significance of the carvings adds irony to the image of the "eyes and mouths / in perfect circles of amazement," for it suggests that the Taino had a kind of foreknowledge of their fate. Being a form of writing, the petroglyphs also stand in stark contrast to the speech of the Spaniards, who literally

> *By writing about historical subjects that are still relevant today, Espada mines the distance between past and present to allow readers to recognize themselves in history's mirror."*

subjugate the natives through their power to name. The mute "amazement" of the carvings echo and underscore the Indians' powerlessness.

The word Taino is derived from one of the initial encounters between the Spaniards and the Indians. When the Spaniards asked, "Who are you?" the Indians simply answered "Taino," which in their language means "good and noble people." This was to distinguish themselves from some of the more hostile tribes, such as the Caribs. That the colonizers would call the Indians "Taino" from then on is ironic, as it contrasts with the Spaniards' brutal and ignoble behavior towards the natives. The Jatibonicu Taino of Puerto Rico are descended from the original twenty-four tribal bands that settled in Puerto Rico (whose ancestors are the Central American Indians and the Arawak Indians of South America), and the colibrí is the sacred totem of the Jatibonicu Taino. The very existence of the Tainos was not proven until the middle of the twentieth century, when scientists and historians began tracing their origins through pottery made only by the Taino. More recently, anthropologists and linguists have been drawn to the Taino language. David Wahayona Campos links the Taino language to the "Arawakan stock stemming from South America," and writes:

> Contrary to what has been thought and taught by some, the Taino language was not completely extinguished. Portions were absorbed over time into the Spanish-speaking Caribbean. Spanish spoken in Boriken retains over 600 Taino words. . . . Among words of indigenous origin are objects, geographical names, personal names as well as flora and fauna. . . . Throughout all the islands, a majority of native trees, fruits and rivers also retain their Taino names.

What Do I Read Next?

- *Imagine the Angels of Bread* (1996) is Espada's sixth book of poems and, like his previous five, has been widely praised by critics. Reviewing the collection for the *Progressive*, Matthew Rothschild notes that Espada "continues to serve up his trademark vignettes of the indignities that working-class and immigrant Americans suffer every day."

- *Puerto Rico Past and Present* (1998), by Ronald Fernandez, Serafin Mendez, and Gail Cueto, is an encyclopedia that provides a useful and broad overview of more than five hundred years of Puerto Rican history and culture.

- In 1995, Ballantine Books published *Boricuas: Influential Puerto Rican Writings—An Anthology*, edited by Roberto Santiago. This anthology contains more than fifty selections of poetry, fiction, plays, essays, monologues, screenplays, and speeches from some of the most powerful voices in Puerto Rican literature. Poems by Espada are included.

- In 1994, Espada edited *Poetry Like Bread: Poets of the Political Imagination*, published by Curbstone Press. The anthology collects poems by activist writers, such as El Salvador's Roque Dalton, Nicaragua's Tomas Borge, and Puerto Rico's Clemente Soto Velez.

By making one of the subjects of his poem Eurolinguistic colonialism, Espada foregrounds the very processes of making history. The fact that the Spaniards colonized the Borinquens, naming them and their world, gives them the "right" to write history. This, along with the mixing of Taino culture and blood over the last five hundred years with the Spanish, African, and French, has made it difficult for people of Taino descent to explore their roots or assert their identity. The very fact that many use the word Taino to identify themselves is proof of colonialism's continuing power and reach. The waning of colonial powers over the last century, however, coupled with the rise of the human rights movement have created a space for just such an exploration of their history. As a result, numerous new histories written from the point of view of subjugated peoples have been published. Espada alludes to this in the last two lines of the poem when he writes, "If only history / were like your hands." As well as echoing the image of the collection's title, this wish is also a statement of possibility, for history is both made through the hard work of people often unacknowledged and written with one's hands.

In supporting Puerto Rican independence, Espada is swimming against the tide of history. The Nationalist Party, the leading voice for independence, has been linked to violence, and nationalists have been engaged in a number of violent acts, including the attempted assassination of President Truman in 1950 and the shooting of five members of the U.S. House of Representatives in 1954. In 1967, Puerto Rico voted to remain a commonwealth, and, in 1993, Governor Pedro Rosselló of the New Progressive party held a plebiscite in which 48 percent of the voters elected to petition the U.S. Congress to retain the commonwealth with enhanced status, 46 percent chose statehood, and just 4 percent chose independence.

Source: Chris Semansky, Critical Essay on "Colibrí," in *Poetry for Students*, The Gale Group, 2002.

Pamela Steed Hill

Hill is the author of a poetry collection, has published widely in literary journals, and is an editor for a university publications department. In the following essay, Hill suggests that the horrors of virtual genocide and destruction of a culture are made all the more poignant by the soft, beautiful imagery and low-key voice that Espada uses to describe them.

Quite often, poets who want to use their creative skills and poetic inspirations to make social or political statements do so in harsh, "loud" language that seems to shout at the reader in anger and protest. Sometimes the words are meant to shock, whether by means of the brutal or explicit subjects they describe or by being the taboo four-letter kind, and the desired results are to rile the reader into feeling what the poet feels, believing what the poet believes. Sometimes these kinds of poems work. Consider, for instance, Allen Ginsberg's much-heralded anthem of the Beat Movement, "Howl," which shocked, outraged, and protested its way into the annals of classic American literature. Since then, many other poets have taken up their pens and used them like axes, chopping through polite, safe protocols to produce works that arouse reactions, both positive and negative. For these writers, the poem is a soapbox—a good place to get vocal and draw a crowd. But one need not always shout to be heard. In "Colibrí," Martín Espada addresses one of the most controversial and maligned historical accounts ever recorded—Columbus's "discoveries" and the subsequent Spanish colonization of New World territories—and he does so with a quiet voice, subtle innuendos, and strikingly beautiful imagery. This kind of poem works too, often better than a loud one.

A bit of historical research and a good understanding of Puerto Rican culture are essential in realizing the full meaning of "Colibrí." While one can read the poem and pick up an accurate notion of its intent from the surface, a much richer appreciation of what Espada is really saying can be found in the work's not-so-visible depths. Why "Jayuya," for example? For hundreds of years this small, relatively unknown town in the center of Puerto Rico has maintained more ties to the original Taino culture than probably any other community on the island; therefore, it is only fitting that Espada chose it to represent what little is left of an entire way of life once the destructive forces of invading armies and colonizers roll through. Comparing the helpless native Taino people in canoes to scattering lizards as they tried to flee from Spanish soldiers is metaphorically brilliant as well as very telling of the fears the natives experienced at the hands of the invaders. A more subtle, but just as troubling, reference is in the lines, "The Spanish conquered with iron and with words: / 'Indio Taino.'" Because Columbus and his explorers mistakenly thought they had reached India when, in fact, they had landed in the Caribbean islands, they attached the word "Indio" to the actual name of the people they encountered. Right away, they gave the native people and their entire culture a new title—half Spanish, of course—whether they wanted it or not. In this way, the European invaders were able to overcome and defeat the original settlers not only "with iron" weapons but also with infiltrating words that signaled the crumbling of one culture beneath the rule of another. Proof of how well the disrespectful moniker stuck is evidenced still today in the common use of the terms "Indio Taino" or "Taino Indians," even by people who can trace ancestry back to the original Tainos. It is also true that many of those people are still offended and angered by the terms.

> *This peaceful, serene moment is hauntingly at odds with the chilling and sorrowful events it symbolizes. But, that is the power of a quiet poem."*

The gentleness of Espada's words reflects the gentleness of the Taino people (most historical writings make this claim), even when the imagery alludes to violence and defeat. He describes the island natives as "the people who took / life from the rain that rushed through the trees," implying a loving and reciprocal relationship with their tropical environment. But the life-giving rain is then compared to "evaporating arrows," suggesting the ineffectiveness of such crude weaponry when confronted with the firearms and cannons of the strangers from Europe. And it was not only the hapless arrows that evaporated at the hands of the Spanish, but the entire Taino culture as well. Known for their artistic abilities with wood and rock carvings, the Tainos typically depicted human faces with wide circles for eyes and mouths. Here, the poet implies that the art reflected the shock and amazement over how swiftly and easily their lives had been forever altered by the unstoppable conquerors.

It is interesting that a poem which laments the atrocities of political history and the usurpation of a people's homeland by dogged explorers is titled for such a tiny, vulnerable creature as the hummingbird. Notice that Espada makes it clear that the animal suffered the same abuse of its name as did the Tainos themselves. The line, "So the hummingbird was christened 'colibrí'" really says, "Here is another example of the Spanish language infiltrating the original Taino." Even so, the little colibrí is a perfect symbol of the people who were just as defenseless against their invaders as a hummingbird would be against nearly any other being, animal or human (if it could be caught, of course). The poem's movement from the distant past to the present is smooth and not intrusive, but it very poignantly ties today's grievous memories to the history that created them. The image of the small bird frantically trying to escape from a place where it does not belong—someone's house, in this case—is made stronger by Espada's reference to its "racing Taino heart." The symbolic link between the colibrí of the present and the Taino people of long ago is one of vulnerability and fear, brought on by the "bellowing god of gunpowder." For the colibrí, this is just a striking metaphor; for the Tainos, it is all too literal.

Using the hummingbird as a symbol for the original inhabitants of Jayuya may be an obvious metaphorical connection in this poem, but there is a deeper meaning as well. The hummingbird was sacred to the Taino people because it is a pollinator—that is, a life giver, something very important in many native cultures. It was not, then, just its small size and seeming helplessness that motivated Espada to use it as the central metaphor but also the irony in knowing its natural inclination to create life, not take it away. It is not necessary to grasp this subtle information in order to *get* the idea in "Colibrí," but its presence is a good example of how a quiet little poem can carry a much more profound and complex message than its conspicuous meaning may reveal. Perhaps other examples are the use of the word "hacienda"—yet another Spanish term—and the mention of the bird's being caught "between the white walls." The latter is conceivably a metaphor for the white Europeans who essentially trapped the worlds they invaded within the confines of their own.

The last full stanza of "Colibrí" contains the poem's softest, most beautiful imagery. And it is not a contradiction to say the descriptions are also the strongest and most provocative. Just as the fraught little hummingbird suddenly "becomes pure stillness," the poem, too, seems to let its social protests and historical accounting quickly fall silent, giving way to the bare artistry of *showing* the reader a scene rather than just telling about it. The simple and thoughtful gesture of the "you" in the poem—who it actually is does not matter—cupping the bird, paralyzed with fear, in gentle hands and setting it free through a window is remarkably vivid and satisfying. One can easily *see* that happening, can readily picture the tiny, stock-still animal, probably hidden within the human hands, suddenly taking flight "into a paradise of sky, / a nightfall of singing frogs." This peaceful, serene moment is hauntingly at odds with the chilling and sorrowful events it symbolizes. But, that is the power of a quiet poem.

Any reader not yet convinced of the punch that "Colibrí" unloads must surely be tempted by the raw understatement of the poem's final line. This is where everything comes together: the scattering lizards, the brutal conquering of the Taino people by the Spanish, the hummingbird's frenzied attempts to escape and its ultimate stillness, the protective hands that set it free. Given all these extraordinary descriptions and the tumultuous history they reference, it is almost anticlimactic to end the poem with such a doleful sentiment as, "If only history / were like your hands." It sounds terribly pathetic, if not whining and weak. Yet, just the opposite is true. This final line implies a final lamentation, one based solely on an impossible condition. "If only" really means *this is not the way it is*, and pointing that out in such a soft, subdued tone is both startling and disturbing. Considering what the sentence means—that the human race has chosen to kill its prey rather than to free it—and the vital importance of its message, one may expect it to be shouted from that proverbial soapbox mentioned earlier. At the very least, should it not cry out in despair? No, not if the intent is to leave the reader uneasy and troubled by its eerie subtlety. As is often the case, presenting something unexpected riles more feelings than simply meeting readers' presumptions. Espada manages to do that throughout "Colibrí" and, in particular, with the last line. His quiet voice is, indeed, despairing, and he need not raise it to be heard.

Source: Pamela Steed Hill, Critical Essay on "Colibrí," in *Poetry for Students*, The Gale Group, 2002.

Sources

Baraka, Amiri, "Foreword," in *Rebellion Is the Circle of a Lover's Hands*, Curbstone Press, 1990.

Bradley, John, Review of *Rebellion Is the Circle of a Lover's Hands*, in *Bloomsbury Review*, March 1991, p. 5.

Campos, David Wahayona, "The Taino Language," in *La Voz del Pueblo Taino*, Vol. 2, No. 3, July/August 1999.

Cornish, Sam, Review of *Rebellion Is the Circle of a Lover's Hands*, in *Ploughshares*, Vol. 17, No. 1, Spring 1991, pp. 229–31.

Espada, Martín, "On the 100th Anniversary of the U.S. Invasion, Puerto Rico Still Deserves Independence," Knight Ridder/Tribune News Service, July 23, 1998.

———, *Rebellion Is the Circle of a Lover's Hands*, Curbstone Press, 1990, p. 34.

Frost, Linda, Review of *Trumpets from the Islands of Their Eviction*, in *Kenyon Review*, Fall 1991, pp. 129–35.

Gilbert, Alan, Review of *Rebellion Is the Circle of a Lover's Hands*, in *Boston Review*, 1991, p. 29.

Gilbert, Roger, Review of *Rebellion Is the Circle of a Lover's Hands*, in *Partisan Review*, Winter 1994, 180–86.

Kaganoff, Penny, Review of *Rebellion Is the Circle of a Lover's Hands*, in *Publishers Weekly*, Vol. 237, No. 41, October 12, 1990, p. 57.

Keene, John R., Review of *City of Coughing and Dead Radiators*, in *MELUS*, Vol. 21, No. 1, Spring 1996, pp. 133–36.

Olson, Ray, Review of *A Mayan Astronomer in Hell's Kitchen*, in *Booklist*, Vol. 96, No. 12, February 15, 2000, p. 1074.

Rothschild, Matthew, Review of *Imagine the Angels of Bread*, in *Progressive*, Vol. 61, No. 1, January 1997, p. 39.

Ullman, Leslie, Review of *Rebellion Is the Circle of a Lover's Hands*, in *Kenyon Review*, Vol. 14, No. 3, Summer 1992, p. 174–88.

Further Reading

Espada, Martín, *Zapata's Disciple*, South End Press, 1998.
    This collection of essays provides detailed information on Espada's personal life and politics, including essays on topics such as the English Only movement, and Puerto Rican independence.

Labrucherie, Roger A., *Puerto Rico, Borinquen Querida*, Imagenes Press, 2001.
    This book consists of a long photographic essay about Puerto Rico. With photographs, paintings, maps, and text, it details Puerto Rico's history, geography, scenery, and culture.

Rouse, Irving, *The Tainos: Rise & Decline of the People Who Greeted Columbus*, Yale University Press, 1993.
    This engaging book tells the story of the Taino people from their ancestral days in South America through their migration to the northern Caribbean islands to their rapid decline at the hands of European colonizers.

Santana, Maria Cristina, *Puerto Rican Newspaper Coverage of the Puerto Rican Independence Party: A Content Analysis of Three Elections*, Garland Publishers, 2000.
    This study explores the struggle of the Puerto Rican Independence Party for serious press coverage in the last three gubernatorial elections. Espada is an ardent supporter of the Puerto Rican independence movement.

Hugh Selwyn Mauberley

Ezra Pound

1920

Ezra Pound's 1920 poem "Hugh Selwyn Mauberley" is a landmark in the career of the great American modernist poet. In the poem, Pound uses two alter egos to discuss the first twelve years of his career, a period during which aesthetic and literary concerns fully engaged Pound's attention. The poem reconstructs literary London of the Edwardian period, recreating the dominant feeling about what literature should be and also describing Pound's own rebellious aesthetic beliefs. The poem also takes us to the catastrophe of the early twentieth century, World War I, and bluntly illustrates its effects on the literary world. The poem then proceeds to an "envoi," or a send-off, and then to five poems told through the eyes of a second alter ego.

In the first section of the poem, Pound portrays himself as "E. P.," a typical turn-of-the-century aesthete, and then in the second he becomes "Mauberley," an aesthete of a different kind. Both E. P. and Mauberley are facets of Pound's own character that, in a sense, the poem is meant to exorcise. After composing this poem, Pound left London for Paris and, soon after, for Italy, where his view of his role as a poet changed dramatically. No longer would his work be primarily concerned with aesthetics; after 1920, he started to concentrate on writing *The Cantos* and on studying politics and economics. "Hugh Selwyn Mauberley" is not just Pound's farewell to London; it is Pound's definitive good-bye to his earlier selves.

Author Biography

Ezra Pound was born October 30, 1885, in Hailey, Idaho. When he was two years old, his parents moved to Wyncote, a suburb of Philadelphia, Pennsylvania, where Ezra's father Homer worked for the U.S. Mint. While in high school, Pound studied Latin, and this study moved him to concentrate on poetry and literary history. He enrolled at the University of Pennsylvania, where he met William Carlos Williams and Hilda Doolittle (both later to become, with Pound, prominent modernist poets). Pound transferred to Hamilton College in New York, graduated from there in 1905, and then returned to the University of Pennsylvania to pursue graduate study in languages, including old English, old French, Provençal, Italian, and Latin. He received his master's degree from the University of Pennsylvania in 1906 and took a job teaching at Wabash College in Indiana. This teaching experience, however, was a disaster for the bohemian Pound, for Indiana society was deeply conservative. He was fired before the school year ended for having a woman in his room without a chaperone.

Disgusted by America's conservatism, Pound resolved to go to Europe to become a poet. He went first to Venice, Italy, where he produced a small book of poems but suffered from poverty. Pound then left for London, England, and quickly became a member of a number of literary circles. Within a few years, Pound became the center of a nascent literary movement, imagism, and through the sheer force of his will also became one of London's most important literary figures. He met Henry James, worked as William Butler Yeats's personal secretary, and gathered around him such writers as Richard Aldington, Wyndham Lewis, and T. S. Eliot. He tirelessly promoted himself and his compatriots from his position as foreign editor of Harriet Monroe's *Poetry* magazine. At this time, Pound was driven by the dictum "make it new." He campaigned against the very Victorian poetry that had initially drawn him to literature. He also incorporated influences into his own work that were new to English-language poetry: the Chinese written character, Japanese Noh drama, Provençal troubadour lays, and medieval Italian forms and themes.

All of this literary ferment came to a dramatic halt in 1914 with the outbreak of World War I. During the war, Pound and his wife Dorothy (a British citizen) were forced to stay in England. Pound's writings from the period of this war barely acknowledge the carnage taking place off England's shores. In

Ezra Pound

1917, Pound began composing what he called his "poem containing history," *The Cantos*, an epic that would take him the rest of his life to finish.

In 1920, after eleven years in London, Pound moved to Paris, France. "Hugh Selwyn Mauberley" served as his farewell to London, the city that had brought him from obscurity to prominence. It was also the last short poem Pound ever wrote. From that time on, all of his poetic efforts were put into *The Cantos*.

In Paris, Pound found that he could not occupy his customary role at the center of the literary world, for another American—Gertrude Stein—already held that position. The drunken, hedonistic ethos of "lost generation" Paris conflicted with Pound's sense of seriousness and mission and after a few years, he relocated again, this time to the small Italian coastal town of Rapallo.

Pound's life grew significantly more difficult and complicated after his move to Italy, for he stopped seeing himself as a poet and began to feel that he was a public intellectual, a sage, a man who should be consulted by world leaders. He began to study history and economics, attempting to discover a solution for the problems of the world. At this time, he also grew increasingly attracted to Italy's fascist leader, Benito Mussolini, and began to manifest a deep anti-Semitism. For twenty years,

Pound continued to write cantos, but he also spoke more and more loudly against Roosevelt, against capitalism, and in favor of fascism.

When the United States joined World War II in 1941, Pound tried to return to his home country but was not allowed to do so. To support himself and his family during the war, Pound volunteered to do radio broadcasts for Italian state radio. In response, the U.S. government indicted Pound for treason in 1943, and, after Italy fell, Pound was arrested, held in a cage near Pisa, and returned to Washington to face trial.

Pound escaped the execution that could have been his fate when the judge found him mentally unfit to face trial, but he was sentenced to an indefinite period in a mental hospital. He spent thirteen years in St. Elizabeth's Hospital in Washington, D.C., refusing to disavow his beliefs. Even incarcerated, he continued to produce poetry, and even won the prestigious Bollingen Library of Congress Award for his 1949 volume *The Pisan Cantos*, composed while Pound was held prisoner by the U.S. Army. Finally, in 1958, Pound was released from the hospital and returned to Italy.

Pound lived the remainder of his life quietly. Settling in Venice, Pound initially continued to work and write, but, in the early 1960s, he fell into a deep depression and an unbreakable silence. Young poets such as Allen Ginsberg visited him, but Pound would not speak. Near the end of his life, largely because of the tireless efforts of his publisher James Laughlin, Pound finally began to enjoy the honors that had been denied him for decades and also began earning enough money from his poetry to live on. He died in Venice in November 1972.

Poem Text

E.P. ODE POUR L'ELECTION DE SON SEPULCHRE

For three years, out of key with his time,
He strove to resuscitate the dead art
Of poetry; to maintain "the sublime"
In the old sense. Wrong from the start—

No, hardly, but seeing he had been born   5
In a half savage country, out of date;
Bent resolutely on wringing lilies from the acorn;
Capaneus; trout for factitious bait;

. . . .
Caught in the unstopped ear;   10
Giving the rocks small lee-way
The chopped seas held him, therefore, that year.

His true Penelope was Flaubert,
He fished by obstinate isles;
Observed the elegance of Circe's hair   15
Rather than the mottoes on sun-dials.

Unaffected by "the march of events,"
He passed from men's memory in *l'an
  trentuniesme*
De son eage; the case presents
No adjunct to the Muses' diadem.   20

II

The age demanded an image
Of its accelerated grimace,
Something for the modern stage,
Not, at any rate, an Attic grace;

Not, not certainly, the obscure reveries   25
Of the inward gaze;
Better mendacities
Than the classics in paraphrase!

The "age demanded" chiefly a mould in plaster,
Made with no loss of time,   30
A prose kinema, not, not assuredly, alabaster
Or the "sculpture" of rhyme.

III

The tea-rose tea-gown, etc.
Supplants the mousseline of Cos,
the pianola "replaces"   35
Sappho's barbitos.

Christ follows Dionysus,
Phallic and ambrosial
Made way for macerations;
Caliban casts out Ariel.   40

All things are a flowing,
Sage Heracleitus says;
But a tawdry cheapness
Shall outlast our days.

Even the Christian beauty   45
Defects—after Samothrace;

We see . . .
Decreed in the market place.

Faun's flesh is not to us,
Nor the saint's vision.   50
We have the press for wafer;
Franchise for circumcision.

All men, in law, are equals.
Free of Pisistratus,
We choose a knave or an eunuch   55
To rule over us.

O bright Apollo,
. . . .
What god, man, or hero
Shall I place a tin wreath upon!   60

IV

These fought in any case,
and some believing,
    pro domo, in any case...

Some quick to arm,
some for adventure,   65
some from fear of weakness,
some from fear of censure,
some for love of slaughter, in imagination,
learning later . . .
some in fear, learning love of slaughter;   70

Died some, pro patria,
        non "dulce" non "et decor". . .
walked eye-deep in hell
believing in old men's lies, then unbelieving
came home, home to a lie,   75
home to many deceits,
home to old and new infamy;
usury age-old and age-thick
and liars in public places.

Daring as never before, wastage as never before.   80
Young blood and high blood,
fair cheeks, and fine bodies;

fortitude as never before

frankness as never before,
disillusions as never told in the days,   85
hysterias, trench confessions,
laughter out of dead bellies.

V

There died a myriad,
and of the best, among them,
For an old bitch gone in the teeth,   90
For a botched civilization,

Charm, smiling at the good mouth,
Quick eyes gone under earth's lid,

For two gross of broken statues,
For a few thousand battered books.   95

YEUX GLAUQUES

Gladstone was still respected,
When John Ruskin produced
"Kings' Treasuries"; Swinburne
And Rossetti still abused.

Fœtid Buchanan lifted up his voice   100
When that faun's head of hers
Became a pastime for
Painters and adulterers.

The Burne-Jones cartons
Have preserved her eyes;   105
Still, at the Tate, they teach
Cophetua to rhapsodize;

Thin like brook-water,
With a vacant gaze.
The English Rubaiyat was still-born   110
In those days.

The thin, clear gaze, the same
Still darts out faunlike from the half-ruin'd face,
Questing and passive. . . .
"Ah, poor Jenny's case" . . .   115

Bewildered that a world
Shows no surprise

At her last maquero's
Adulteries.

"SIENA MI FE'; DISFECEMI MAREMMA"

Among the pickled fœtuses and bottled bones,   120
Engaged in perfecting the catalogue,
I found the last scion of the
Senatorial families of Strasbourg, Monsieur Verog.

For two hours he talked of Galliffet;
Of Dowson; of the Rhymers' Club;   125
Told me how Johnson (Lionel) died
By falling from a high stool in a pub . . .

But showed no trace of alcohol
At the autopsy, privately performed—
Tissue preserved—the pure mind   130
Arose toward Newman as the whiskey warmed.

Dowson found harlots cheaper than hotels;
Headlam for uplift; Image impartially imbued
With raptures for Bacchus, Terpsichore and the
        Church.
So spoke the author of "The Dorian Mood,"   135

M. Verog, out of step with the decade,
Detached from his contemporaries,
Neglected by the young,
Because of these reveries.

BRENNBAUM

The skylike limpid eyes,   140
The circular infant's face,

The stiffness from spats to collar
Never relaxing into grace;

The heavy memories of Horeb, Sinai and the forty
        years,
Showed only when the daylight fell   145
Level across the face
Of Brennbaum "The Impeccable."

MR. NIXON

In the cream gilded cabin of his steam yacht
Mr. Nixon advised me kindly, to advance with
        fewer
Dangers of delay. "Consider   150
        "Carefully the reviewer.

"I was as poor as you are;
"When I began I got, of course,
"Advance on royalties, fifty at first," said Mr.
        Nixon,
"Follow me, and take a column,   155
"Even if you have to work free.

"Butter reviewers. From fifty to three hundred
"I rose in eighteen months;
"The hardest nut I had to crack
"Was Dr. Dundas.   160

"I never mentioned a man but with the view
"Of selling my own works.
"The tip's a good one, as for literature
"It gives no man a sinecure.

"And no one knows, at sight, a masterpiece.   165
"And give up verse, my boy,
"There's nothing in it."

                    * * * *

Likewise a friend of Blougram's once advised me:
Don't kick against the pricks,
Accept opinion. The "Nineties" tried your game   170
And died, there's nothing in it.

X

Beneath the sagging roof
The stylist has taken shelter,
Unpaid, uncelebrated,
At last from the world's welter   175

Nature receives him;
With a placid and uneducated mistress
He exercises his talents
And the soil meets his distress.

The haven from sophistications and contentions   180
Leaks through its thatch;
He offers succulent cooking;
The door has a creaking latch.

XI

"Conservatrix of Milésien"
Habits of mind and feeling,   185
Possibly. But in Ealing
With the most bank-clerkly of Englishmen?

No, "Milesian" is an exaggeration.
No instinct has survived in her
Older than those her grandmother   190
Told her would fit her station.

XII

"Daphne with her thighs in bark
"Stretches toward me her leafy hands,"—
Subjectively. In the stuffed-satin drawing-room
I await The Lady Valentine's commands,   195

Knowing my coat has never been
Of precisely the fashion
To stimulate, in her,
A durable passion;

Doubtful, somewhat, of the value   200
Of Well-gowned approbation
Of literary effort,
But never of The Lady Valentine's vocation:

Poetry, her border of ideas,
The edge, uncertain, but a means of blending   205
With other strata
Where the lower and higher have ending;

A hook to catch the Lady Jane's attention,
A modulation toward the theatre,
Also, in the case of revolution,   210
A possible friend and comforter.

* * * *

Conduct, on the other hand, the soul
"Which the highest cultures have nourished"
To Fleet St. where
Dr. Johnson flourished;   215

Besides this thoroughfare
The sale of half-hose has

Long since superseded the cultivation
Of Pierian roses.

ENVOI (1919)

Go, dumb-born book,   220
Tell her that sang me once that song of Lawes:
Hadst thou but song
As thou has subjects known,
Then were there cause in thee that should condone
Even my faults that heavy upon me lie,   225
And build her glories their longevity.

Tell her that sheds
Such treasure in the air,
Recking naught else but that her graces give
Life to the moment,   230
I would bid them live
As roses might, in magic amber laid,
Red overwrought with orange and all made
One substance and one colour
Braving time.   235

Tell her that goes
With song upon her lips
But sings not out the song, nor knows
The maker of it, some other mouth,
May be as fair as hers,   240
Might, in new ages, gain her worshippers,
When our two dusts with Waller's shall be laid,
Sifting on siftings in oblivion,
Till change hath broken down
All things save Beauty alone.   245

MAUBERLEY (1920)

"Vacuos exercet in aera morsus."

Turned from the "eau-forte
Par Jacquemart"
To the strait head
Of Messalina: 250

"His true Penelope
Was Flaubert,"
And his tool
The engraver's.

Firmness,   255
Not the full smile,
His art, but an art
In profile;

Colourless
Pier Francesca,   260
Pisanello lacking the skill
To forge Achaia.

II

"Qu'est ce qu'ils savent de l'amour, et qu'est ce
*   qu'ils peuvent com-*
prendre?
*   S'ils ne comprennent pas la poésie, s'ils ne*   265
*   sentent pas la musique,*
qu'est ce qu'ils peuvent comprendre de cette
*   passion en comparaison*
avec laquelle la rose est grossière et le parfum des
*   violettes un*
tonnerre?" CAID ALI

For three years, diabolus in the scale,
He drank ambrosia,   270
All passes, ANANGKE prevails,
Came end, at last, to that Arcadia.

He had moved amid her phantasmagoria,
Amid her galaxies,
NUKTIS'AGALMA   275

* * * *

Drifted . . . drifted precipitate
Asking time to be rid of . . .
Of his bewilderment; to designate
His new found orchid. . . .

To be certain . . . certain . . .   280
(Amid ærial flowers) . . . time for arrangements—
Drifted on
To the final estrangement;

Unable in the supervening blankness
To sift TO AGATHON from the chaff   285

Until he found his sieve . . .
Ultimately, his seismograph:

—Given that is his "fundamental passion,"
This urge to convey the relation
Of eye-lid and cheek-bone   290
By verbal manifestation;

To present the series
Of curious heads in medallion—

He had passed, inconscient, full gaze,
The wide-banded irides   295
And botticellian sprays implied
In their diastasis;

Which anæsthesis, noted a year late,
And weighed, revealed his great affect,
(Orchid), mandate   300
Of Eros, a retrospect.

* * * *

Mouths biting empty air,
The still stone dogs,
Caught in metamorphosis, were
Left him as epilogues.   305

"THE AGE DEMANDED"

For this agility chance found
Him of all men, unfit

As the red-beaked steeds of
The Cytheræan for a chain bit.
                                                      310
The glow of porcelain
Brought no reforming sense
To his perception
Of the social inconsequence.

Thus, if her colour
Came against his gaze,   315
Tempered as if
It were through a perfect glaze

He made no immediate application
Of this to relation of the state
To the individual, the month was more temperate   320
Because this beauty had been.

The coral isle, the lion-coloured sand
Burst in upon the porcelain revery:
Impetuous troubling
Of his imagery.   325

Mildness, amid the neo-Nietzschean clatter,
His sense of graduations,
Quite out of place amid
Resistance to current exacerbations,
                                                      330
Invitation, mere invitation to perceptivity
Gradually led him to the isolation
Which these presents place
Under a more tolerant, perhaps, examination.

By constant elimination
The manifest universe   335
Yielded an armour
Against utter consternation,

A Minoan undulation,
Seen, we admit, amid ambrosial circumstances
Strengthened him against   340
The discouraging doctrine of chances,

And his desire for survival,
Faint in the most strenuous moods,
Became an Olympian *apathein*
In the presence of selected perceptions.   345

A pale gold, in the aforesaid pattern,
The unexpected palms
Destroying, certainly, the artist's urge,
Left him delighted with the imaginary
Audition of the phantasmal sea-surge,   350

Incapable of the least utterance or composition,
Emendation, conservation of the "better tradition,"
Refinement of medium, elimination of superfluities,
August attraction or concentration.
                                                      355
Nothing, in brief, but maudlin confession,
Irresponse to human aggression,
Amid the precipitation, down-float
Of insubstantial manna,
Lifting the faint susurrus
Of his subjective hosannah.   360

Ultimate affronts to
Human redundancies;

Non-esteem of self-styled "his betters"
Leading, as he well knew,
To his final   365
Exclusion from the world of letters.

IV

Scattered Moluccas
Not knowing, day to day,
The first day's end, in the next noon;
The placid water   370
Unbroken by the Simoon;

Thick foliage
Placid beneath warm suns,
Tawn fore-shores
Washed in the cobalt of oblivions;   375

Or through dawn-mist
The grey and rose

Of the juridical
Flamingoes;

A consciousness disjunct,   380
Being but this overblotted
Series
Of intermittences;

Coracle of Pacific voyages,
The unforecasted beach;   385
Then on an oar
Read this:

"I was
"And I no more exist;
"Here drifted   390
"An hedonist."

MEDALLION

Luini in porcelain!
The grand piano
Utters a profane
Protest with her clear soprano.   395

The sleek head emerges
From the gold-yellow frock
As Anadyomene in the opening
Pages of Reinach.

Honey-red, closing the face-oval,   400
A basket-work of braids which seem as if they
          were
Spun in King Minos' hall
From metal, or intractable amber,

The face-oval beneath the glaze,
Bright in its suave bounding-line, as,   405
Beneath half-watt rays,
The eyes turn topaz.

Poem Summary

E.P. Ode pour l'election de son sepulchre

The first section of this long sequence introduces the reader to almost all of the themes and content of "Hugh Selwyn Mauberley." The displacement of Pound's own self into a persona, the allusions to literary history, the foreign phrases: all of these typical Poundian elements appear in this first poem.

The section's title means "E. P. Ode for the Selection of His Tomb" (an allusion to the French poet Ronsard) and this section is, in a sense, a eulogy for "E. P.," Pound's aesthete alter ego. Written like most of "Hugh Selwyn Mauberley" in quatrains (four-line stanzas), this section tells of E. P., who "strove to resuscitate the dead art / Of poetry" by means of resurrecting the old idea of "'the sublime'." The poem's subject is clearly based on

Pound himself, "born / In a half savage country" (Pound was born in Idaho). In this section, E. P. is an aspiring artist, admiring Flaubert (who, famously, pursued "le mot juste," or the exact word, and sought to create an art that was all style and no content) and "unaffected by 'the march of events.'" The portrait of E. P. is of an erudite, well-educated, classically-steeped aesthete: the very model of the late Victorian poet. Yet we already know that this E. P. will die, for he "passed from men's memory" in his thirty-first year (the French quote is from Pound's idol Francois Villon, and the reference is to the profound change in Pound's poetry that occurred in his thirty-first year).

II

The second section moves away from the subject of Pound himself and attempts to describe the artistic scene in London in the early 1900s. "The age demanded," Pound tells us, merely images; the age will settle for "mendacities" (lies) rather than the "classics in paraphrase" (this reference is to the hostility that greeted Pound's loose translation of Sextus Propertius's Latin lyric poems). Many art lovers in London in the 1910s were interested in art that was outwardly attractive but not deeply beautiful, immediately pleasing but not enduringly rewarding. Contrasting a "prose kinema" (i.e., versions of primitive movies told in literature) to alabaster (one of the most beautiful materials used in classical sculpture), Pound asserts that "the age demanded" the former. One of the primary themes of "Hugh Selwyn Mauberley" is the difference between art that aspires only to outer beauty and art that aims at profundity. In the early poems, Pound portrays E. P. as a figure only too happy to pursue shallowness in art and the cheap reproduction of what has worked before.

III

In the third section, Pound details objects that "tasteful" people appreciated in the 1910s. Much of this section is simply contrast: Pound contrasts a typical artifact of Edwardian London with a legendary classical object and wants the reader to understand the cheapness of the former. He contrasts a "tea-rose tea-gown" with the legendary gauzy fabric produced by the Greek island of Cos and the pianola (a player-piano) with the legendary lyre on which the Greek poet Sappho composed her verse.

As the section progresses, Pound begins to forward some explanations for this "tawdry cheapness" that characterizes his age. Capitalism and Christianity, he feels, have eaten away at the greatness and authenticity of classical culture. He compares the "maceration" (wasting away of the body, as by extreme fasting) of Christ's body in the communion sacrament to the festivals of wine and music that honored the Greek god Dionysus, and states that Caliban (the savage slave in Shakespeare's *Tempest*) has replaced Ariel (a fairy in the same play). In the fourth stanza Pound states that "beauty" in ancient Greek, is "decreed in the market place." This section bemoans the cheapness that capitalism and the melodrama of Christianity have brought to culture.

IV

The fourth section takes readers from the parlors of early twentieth-century London to the muddy battlefields of World War I. This section's main thrust is that the slaughter of the war was perpetuated by lies and by the intentional deceits perpetrated by politicians and the wealthy. Focusing on why young men would volunteer to fight, Pound identifies several varieties of self-delusion. Some of the men fought "pro domo," or "for home"; some fought because they sought adventure; some because they wanted glory; some because they feared ridicule; and some just because they were disposed to violence. Nowhere in this poem does Pound mention the kinds of soldiers that politicians and generals talk about: young men who are willing to give up their lives for abstract concepts defined and defended by those in power.

After listing the reasons some went to war, Pound describes the war's effects. He alludes to Horace's famous line about patriotism, "dulce et decorum est pro patria mori" (sweet and fitting it is to die for one's country) and angrily denies it: "non 'dulce' non 'et decor'. . . / walked eye-deep in hell." Pound tersely illustrates the conditions of trench warfare and angrily attacks the "old men's lies" that caused so many to die.

V

Although it is short, this section may be Pound's most well-known from this poem. In its eight lines, Pound bitterly states that there was no point to the war, that even if the war was, as the "old men" of section IV said, a sacred effort to defend civilization as we know it, civilization's defense was not worth all of those deaths. In the end, Pound says, "a myriad" died "For an old [b——] gone in the teeth, / For a botched civilization." Especially surprising is Pound's verdict that art is not worth defending with young men's lives: he boils down the aesthetic heritage of section II to "two

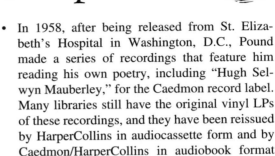

Media Adaptations

- In 1958, after being released from St. Elizabeth's Hospital in Washington, D.C., Pound made a series of recordings that feature him reading his own poetry, including "Hugh Selwyn Mauberley," for the Caedmon record label. Many libraries still have the original vinyl LPs of these recordings, and they have been reissued by HarperCollins in audiocassette form and by Caedmon/HarperCollins in audiobook format (2001).

gross of broken statues . . . a few thousand battered books." At this point in the poem, Pound the narrator can clearly be seen to disagree with E. P., who presumably would hold art as being the most valuable thing in the world, very much worth defending with one's life.

Yeux glauques

The subject of "Yeux glaugues" ("grey eyes") is the artistic movement known as the Pre-Raphaelites. These artists—led by Edward Burne-Jones, Dante Gabriel Rossetti, and Rossetti's sister Christina—named themselves after the period before the Italian Renaissance painter Raphael became dominant. They favored a shimmering, detailed, highly emotional presentation of their subject matter, such as is present in Burne-Jones's painting *King Cophetua and the Beggar-Maid*.

This section describes the hypocritical relationship between English politics of the late Victorian period and Pre-Raphaelite art. Prime Minister Gladstone and the art reviewer Robert Buchanan represent the conservative Victorian culture that disliked Pre-Raphaelite art and condemned its lack of morality. Pound viewed Gladstone and Buchanan as comics but feels they were still very harmful in their own time. And although Pound sympathized with the Pre-Raphaelites (and certainly E. P. would have found them kindred spirits), he felt that such Pre-Raphaelite art as Burne-Jones's aforementioned painting did not sufficiently confront social conditions. Such art aestheticized poverty while Pound would have had them attack the conditions that cause poverty.

"Siena mi Fe'; Disfecemi Maremma"

The title of this section comes from Dante's *Purgatorio*; it means "Siena Made Me; Maremma Unmade Me." This quote was spoken by "La Pia dei Tolomei," who was murdered by her husband in the swampy Maremma region. Rossetti painted her. This section presents a number of anecdotes of the aestheticists whom E. P. admires. While the previous section focused on the visual arts and the relation between politics and painting, this section discusses poetry and, in particular, the "Rhymers' Club" of poets of the 1890s. Lionel Johnson was the central figure of this group (Pound edited a collection of his verse during his early days in London), and Pound's friend and mentor William Butler Yeats also was a member. John Espey, an early scholar of this poem, identifies M. Verog as Victor Plarr, who was librarian of the Royal College of Surgeons in 1909 (when Pound first came to London). This section is suffused with images of decay, of unnatural preservation, and of tawdriness.

Brennbaum

This short section is generally regarded as an early manifestation of Pound's growing anti-Semitism. "Brennbaum" is a figure for Max Beerbohm, a Jewish artist active in London in the 1910s, whom T. S. Eliot also caricatured.

Mr. Nixon

One of Pound's favorite stories to tell was of his meeting with Henry James soon after Pound arrived in London. James at the time was unquestionably the leading figure in American literature, and, in "Mr. Nixon," Pound provides a short, satirical portrait of James's advice to him. Some critics feel that Mr. Nixon is also a representation of Arnold Bennett, an important figure in the English literary scene in the early 1900s whose practical and capitalistic approach to art Pound would have reviled. At the same time, this section is a parody of one of James's own stories, "The Advice of the Master." The primary thrust of this section is to present another kind of figure from London's literary scene of the early 1900s, the practical-minded, pretentious, self-appointed advisor to a young writer.

X

This short section, according to scholar Christine Froula, is based on an interlude in the life of Ford Madox Ford, a novelist active in London at the time and a friend of Pound's. Contrasting with the well-fed, self-satisfied Mr. Nixon is the starving artist of this section, who returns to his cabin with its "sagging roof" and "creaking latch" where he and his "placid and uneducated mistress" enjoy each other's company.

XI

Like section X, this poem is a subtle description of sexual behavior of the time. The bohemian lovers become the proper woman and the "Conservatrix of Milésien." This obscure allusion is to the lost ancient Greek erotic text, the *Milesian Tales*. Broken up into two short stanzas, this section describes a "bank-clerkly" Englishman, presumably shy and sexually inexperienced, about to have a rendezvous with his lover, whose own sexual attitudes are based on her grandmother's advice about what is proper for her station.

XII

This section illustrates the literary salon culture in which Pound refused to take part. The salons, generally led by women, were a development of the eighteenth century, when upper-middle-class women cultivated an appreciation for art. In this poem the "I" goes to the home of the Lady Valentine, the *salonniere*, to seek her approval for his verse. The narrator here is nervous about frivolous things such as his coat and his appearance, which Pound emphasizes to illustrate how salon society was primarily concerned with appearances, social niceties, and the like, rather than the value of art. The end of the section, contrasting the sale of "half-hose" (stockings) with "Pierian roses," alludes to Sappho's line about Pierian roses and again indicates how Pound felt that literary salons were not really concerned with genuine evaluation of art.

Envoi (1919)

An "envoi" is a send-off; often it is an author's final word to his or her literary composition, wishing it well as it goes to be appreciated by the public. This envoi is a send-off in a number of ways: it is the poem's farewell to the character of E. P.; it is an imitation of the Renaissance poem "Go, Lovely Rose" by Thomas Campion; and it says a definitive goodbye to the aestheticist verse of E. P. and the Victorian period. The poem is remarkably accomplished both in its imitation of Campion's poem and in its sophisticated use of musical rhythms. Pound argued for a meter that was based on the musical phrase, and "Envoi" clearly embodies this, especially when compared to the short, irregular, and often forced tempos of the earlier sections of "Hugh Selwyn Mauberley."

Mauberley (1920)

In this section, Pound introduces a new character, "Mauberley." Mauberley is an aesthete like E. P. but less earnest, less naive, and less desirous of joining the literary circles of his time. However, he is no more sophisticated than was E. P. This first poem portrays Mauberley as another kind of aesthete, one for whom art is engravings and etchings. Pound also introduces the motif of the medallion here with the allusion to Pisanello, an Italian Renaissance artist who struck medals.

II

This long and complex section illustrates how Mauberley's growing fascination with aestheticism prevents him from reaching a sexual connection with a woman. Pound was fascinated with the relationship between creative energy and sexual energy, and developed a number of spurious theories about sex and creativity. In this section, Mauberley's fascination with the bric-a-brac of the aesthetic life (ambrosia, orchids) and his immersion in cultural heritage render him unable to relate on an immediate physical level with a woman.

"The Age Demanded"

"The Age Demanded" puts the reader deeply into the head of Mauberley, who is lapsing into solipsism (a theory holding that the self is the only existent thing). The Latinate words of this section and its long lines contrast with the short lines and more concrete diction of earlier sections and underscore Mauberley's retreat into his own head. As Mauberley develops an ever-finer aesthetic sense, he begins to lose touch with the outside world. "Beauty," as in line 321, could make his month more "temperate." Mauberley is retreating into isolation; "By constant elimination" of the outside world, "The manifest universe" of aesthetic refinement "Yielded an armour / Against utter consternation." As he further develops his artistic sensibility, Mauberley becomes less and less capable of creating original art. Pound notes in the later stanzas of this section that this development will lead "To his final / Exclusion from the world of letters."

IV

Although it is not explicitly mentioned, the image underlying this whole section is that of the lotus-eaters of Homer's *Odyssey*, in which many of Odysseus's sailors are lured onto an island where they learn to eat the fruit of the lotus. This fruit is like a drug and makes the sailors never want to leave the island. Mauberley's drift into aesthetic reverie, Pound suggests, is like the surrender of the sailors to the fruit of the lotus. The section is dominated by images of warm places (Molucca, the Simoon winds of the African deserts) and islands (a "coracle" is a small boat). The section ends with Mauberley's possible end: "'I was / And I no more exist; / Here drifted / An hedonist'."

Medallion

Like "Envoi," "Medallion" completes one of the poem's sections and is therefore doubly complicated. Most of the sections either observe E. P./Mauberley or are in the voice of the character; "Envoi" and "Medallion," by contrast, might be examples of their own work, or might be examples of Pound's work as influenced by them, or might be something else entirely. Scholar Christine Froula argues that "whereas the 'Envoi' represents the lyric mode, 'Medallion' represents 'Imagistic' poetics." ("Imagism" was a school of verse headed by Pound in the mid-1910s.) But Jo Brantley Berryman, another critic, feels that "Medallion" is actually the voice of the contemporary Pound because the poem exhibits characteristics of the Vorticist movement. The Vorticist movement was a literary/artistic movement in London that took place around 1915–1917. The main instigators were Pound and Wyndham Lewis, who published a journal called *BLAST*. The movement was much like Imagism but valued art that was more intense, violent, and powerful.

"Medallion" is an attempt "To present the series / Of curious heads in medallion," in the words of an earlier section, and, unlike the rest of the sections here, "Medallion" follows imagist dogma: it presents images, but it does not comment. In many ways, "Medallion" is the most accomplished and sophisticated poem that Mauberley could have produced, and it is indeed a fine poem from a sure hand with imagery. However, it is bloodless and irrelevant. Mauberley's careful cultivation of his aesthetic sensibilities rendered him unable to create, and this limits his verse's importance. "Medallion" shows that Mauberley's aesthetic sensibilities are indeed very sharp, but at the same time the section leaves the reader unsure as to its relevance. We understand why Pound felt that he had to leave this kind of aestheticism behind when he left London, especially because he wanted his poetry to become more, not less, socially involved.

Themes

Aestheticism

"Aestheticism" was the nineteenth-century term for the desire to live one's life completely in pursuit of aesthetic beauty. The "aesthete," or one who lived an aestheticist life, disdained the world as a fallen, brutal, ugly place. Only in art could the aestheticist find solace. Aesthetes spent their lives attempting to refine their own aesthetic taste, to be able to make finer and finer distinctions between the beautiful and the ugly. In the end, aesthetes dreamed of surrounding themselves with beauty.

In the mid-Victorian period, aestheticism gained a new popularity among the upper middle classes. An Oxford scholar named Walter Pater, active in the mid-nineteenth century, has become the very emblem of aestheticism. His book *The Renaissance* is a series of essays on Italian Renaissance painters, but many of the essays stray from scholarship toward simple appreciation and even reverie—especially in his essay on da Vinci's *Mona Lisa*. "All art," Pater once said, "aspires toward the condition of music," by which Pater intended to say that the aesthetic experience at its most pure is without content or themes. It is intoxicating, it simply carries one away.

Inspired by Pater and by his followers, many of London's important literary figures of the 1880s and 1890s adopted aestheticist ideas and poses. The Pre-Raphaelites attempted to bring art back to medieval times, but in reality their art was unlike medieval art. Instead, it is shimmering, complicated, ravishing, and highly romantic. The Pre-Raphaelites also wrote poetry, and their verse concentrated primarily on sensual pleasures. Dante Gabriel Rossetti, Christina Rossetti, and Algernon Charles Swinburne are the best-known of the Pre-Raphaelite or, as they later came to be called, "decadent" poets. Their poems were caught up in the beauty and complexity of language, and often piled on adjective after adjective in an attempt to make language carry the weight of sensory experience.

Eventually the aesthetes or decadents became parodies of themselves. Eschewing seriousness, social commitment, or any kind of relevance whatsoever, decadent literature became the verbal equivalent of opium for many readers: a stimulant for sensory pleasure and a spur to "drop out" of society.

The ultimate expression of decadent or aestheticist literature is J. K. Huysmans's book *Against the Grain*, which tells of a wealthy Frenchman, des Esseintes, who spends his life insulating himself from the world and searching for the rarest, most refined sensory pleasures possible. He orders strange plants from all over the world and fills his house with them. He spends weeks locked in his overstuffed basement sampling the liqueurs of the world. In becoming decadent, aestheticism moved from being simple appreciation for good art and became a way of turning one's back on the world. In "Hugh Selwyn Mauberley," Pound sketches out a portrait of such decadents, ridiculing their shallowness and suggesting that literature must be involved in the world or risk utter irrelevance.

World War I

World War I was a cataclysmic event in Pound's early career, although he barely mentioned it while the war was taking place in either his correspondence or his literary work. Imagism's harsh attacks on late Victorian poetry and the frankly violent language of the Vorticist movement headed by Pound seemed ridiculous when the real slaughter began. Eventually and inevitably, Pound lost friends in the conflict. He even wrote a book about one of these friends, a French sculptor named Henri Gaudier-Brzeska, who had carved a "Hieratic Head of Ezra Pound" out of a discarded chunk of marble Pound found for him under a London bridge.

It was not until the publication of "Hugh Selwyn Mauberley" in 1920 that Pound finally confronted the war in his writing. Pound's verdict on the war's meaning was blunt. He condemns the rhetoric used by leaders to inspire young men to fight and die. He conjures up terse, memorable images for death more effective than paragraphs of long-winded prose. He determines, memorably, that the civilization for which these men were fighting consisted of nothing more than "broken statues" and "battered books." Nothing justified war for Pound. War was the ultimate evil, and throughout his life Pound tried to identify war's deepest causes and bring them to public light. Pound came to the conclusion that wars occur because wealthy peoples' financial interests benefit from war: banks, arms manufacturers and dealers, and politicians all benefit when a country must go to war. Sadly, though, beginning in the 1930s, Pound brought this insight to a disturbing conclusion when he began arguing that Jews were behind most war profiteering and decided that Mussolini's Italy was a state that would never contribute to the causes of war.

Style

Point of View

The most enduringly difficult aspect of "Hugh Selwyn Mauberley" is the maddening way that Pound creates two alter egos. These alter egos may be aspects of himself but to what extent? What in them does he admire, what in them does he wish us to condemn, what of himself does he unconsciously include? E. P., one of the alter egos, even has Pound's own initials—is he an earlier version of Pound, accurately portrayed, or is he (like James Joyce's character Stephen Dedalus) a satirized version of some of the author's old traits?

E. P. is the first alter ego. We learn this from the fact that the first poem is called "E.P. Ode pour l'election de son sepulchre," or "E.P. Ode for the Selection of His Tomb." E. P. is clearly the "he" of this first poem, a young poet who came to Europe from his own "half-savage country" and wanted to "resuscitate" the art of poetry and the old-style "sublime." The imagery of the poem presents E. P. as an aesthete, contemplating "the elegance of Circe's hair" while history passes him by. Most of the poems of the E. P. section of "Hugh Selwyn Mauberley" show snapshots of late Victorian London and its literary scene; E. P. is either absent or his presence barely registers (much as Pound seems to think is the case with aesthetes in general). However, throughout the poem, he observes everything that is going on around himself. But a knowledge of Pound's own life shows that E. P. and Pound have much in common: acquaintances, artistic tastes, life experiences.

Mauberley is a different matter. He almost literally fades out of the poems as he refines his aesthetic tastes even more. Pound often uses the image of a medallion throughout the five poems of the Mauberley sequence, alluding to Pound's own fascination with Pisanello, with coinage, and "mould in plaster" that "the age demanded" in the second poem of the E. P. sequence. Like the profile on a medallion or a coin, Mauberley is only seen in half-view; he is never fully there. Mauberley is a different kind of aesthete than E. P. While E. P. will follow the sirens, Mauberley will lose himself in the sensual pleasures of the land of the lotus-eaters. E. P. exists in the world but does nothing of importance in it, while Mauberley, a man of admittedly more refined aesthetic sensibilities, runs the risk of just fading out as he melts into his sensual pleasures.

Topics for Further Study

- How did various writers respond to World War I? Compare and contrast the works of two writers of the time. Examples are the poems of Rupert Brooke and Siegfried Sassoon and novels such as Erich Maria Remarque's *All Quiet on the Western Front* and Ernest Hemingway's *A Farewell to Arms.*

- Although he stayed in London for most of World War I and did not take part in it, a much older Ezra Pound lived in Italy throughout World War II and wrote and performed radio broadcasts for Mussolini's state radio network. For this act, he was indicted for treason in 1943. Research the "case of Ezra Pound" and write an essay about his life during World War II. How did his writings from World War II compare and contrast with his writings from World War I?

- Pound's "Hugh Selwyn Mauberly" takes place largely in a London that is long gone. It is hard to imagine what daily life was like in that city in 1909, when Pound first moved there. Research the details of daily life in London in 1909 and write an essay about it. How did people move around the city? How was the nation governed? What were the popular pastimes? How did people find out about world events?

- In 1914, Pound edited a collection of poems that he called *Des Imagistes*, or "some imagists." He created the imagist movement, wrote its manifestos, and recruited the poets who took part in this literary group. Research the imagists and prepare a speech about them. Who were they? What were the "rules" of the school? What group did Pound found after he grew tired of imagism? Who took over the movement?

Allusion

Allusions (implied or indirect reference) to dozens of sources fill "Hugh Selwyn Mauberley." Whole books have been written tracking down all of Pound's allusions, but it is possible to understand the essential message of the poem with the explanation of just a few of them. Most of the allusions fall into two categories: allusions to the classical world and allusions to the aesthetic/decadent worlds.

Most important, probably, are the allusions to classical civilization, for at this point in his career Pound was searching for a way to use classical civilization as a way to understand the modern world. On a basic level, E. P. and Mauberley represent two types of Odysseus's companions from Homer's *Odyssey*: E. P., the sailors lured by the sirens, and Mauberley, the sailors who stay on the island of the lotus-eaters. But these are by no means the only classical allusions. The poem begins with an epigram by the Carthaginian poet Nemesianus, and in the first poem Pound also alludes to the *Odyssey* three times, the muses, and one of the "Seven against Thebes" from Sophocles's play. The rest of the poem continues to allude to the Greeks and Romans, referring to "an Attic grace," "the mousseline of Cos," Samothrace, Pisistratus, Horace, and many others, in the first few poems alone. There is no unifying structure to the allusions; Pound saw the classical world as still being alive and relevant, and the poem shows how both E. P. and Mauberley felt the same.

The allusions to the late 1800s and early 1900s in London are much more specific and less accessible to the nonspecialist. "Mr. Nixon," for instance, alludes to authors Arnold Bennett and Henry James, and "Yeux glauques" alludes to Victorian politicians Robert Buchanan and Prime Minister William Gladstone and writers John Ruskin and Dante Gabriel Rossetti. Some of the allusions are plain; others, such as Brennbaum, are disguised.

Historical Context

World War I

Pound's poem provides a number of brief vignettes and portraits of literary London in the 1890s and 1900s. The frivolity of these times, though, becomes patent when the poem abruptly moves to a discussion of the unthinkable catastrophe that became known as World War I. In the years leading up to World War I, the London literary scene fragmented into ever-smaller feuding movements, all based on minute distinctions in aesthetics. Because of what they saw as their daring in challenging the morality of the Victorian age, modernist writers found themselves cast in the roles of rebels, pariahs, even dangerous men and women. Such writers as Ezra Pound and Wyndham Lewis even began to believe their own hype about being dangerous to society.

The coming of World War I, though, fulfilled the modernist predictions of a coming fragmentation and destruction beyond anything they could have imagined. The war itself came upon an unsuspecting Europe almost in a way that the modernists might have envisioned, for it was society's faith in its own structures that ended up destroying it. Specifically, the complicated network of alliances dividing Europe into two moderately hostile camps (one consisting largely of democracies such as Great Britain and France, the other consisting of monarchies or dictatorships such as Germany and the Austro-Hungarian Empire, but even these categories had exceptions—Czarist Russia fought on the side of the democracies) became not a means of stability but the mechanism of Europe's destruction.

The war began when the Serbian rebel Gavrilo Princip assassinated the Austro-Hungarian archduke Franz Ferdinand in Sarajevo in 1914. Austria-Hungary sought reprisals against Serbia, the Russians came to the Serbian defense, the Germans came to the assistance of the Austro-Hungarians, and Eastern Europe was at war. At the same time, the Germans took this opportunity to try out a plan they had been developing for years. The German strategic command had worked out a way to march across Belgium and northeastern France and take Paris in six weeks, and in 1914 they attempted to do just this. The plan bogged down, though, and soon the English came to the assistance of the French and Belgians. Pushing the Germans back from the very suburbs of Paris, the Allied forces managed to save the French nation, but the armies soon found themselves waging trench warfare in the forests and fens of northern France and Belgium. Millions died in futile attempts to move the line forward a few yards. Among these were a number of modernist artists and writers, including the French sculptor Henri Gaudier-Brzeska, a friend of Ezra Pound's.

The tone of excitement about violence that characterized early modernist writing disappeared after the war, for the writers who exalted in the promise of destruction were utterly numbed by the effects of real destruction. Although the soldier-writers like Rupert Brooke and Siegfried Sassoon have left readers with vivid, horrifying

Compare & Contrast

- **1920s:** Calvin Coolidge is elected President of the United States. After Woodrow Wilson—an intellectual who tried to persuade the reluctant, isolationist United States to join the League of Nations—Coolidge is a drastic change. While Wilson was cerebral and visionary, Coolidge is practical and bourgeois. Advancing U.S. business interests is his primary concern.

  Today: In the election to succeed, U.S. President Bill Clinton, Vice President Al Gore, and Texas Governor George W. Bush face-off. After the closest election in American history, the Supreme Court declares Bush the winner.

- **1920s:** The aftereffects of World War I continue to resonate in defeated Germany. Because of its need to pay off massive war reparations, the German government simply prints more money. The effect is massive inflation, so much so that in the 1920s German shoppers must bring wheelbarrows full of cash in order to do their grocery shopping.

  Today: After almost eight years of continuous record economic expansion, the U.S. economy begins to slow down. Large corporations decree massive layoffs, and small companies simply go out of business. A terrorist attack on September 11, 2001, only exacerbates the economic troubles, putting the airlines in particular at risk.

- **1920s:** Theaters dedicated exclusively to the exhibition of motion pictures spring up around the United States. This new form of entertainment proves to be surprisingly popular, so much so that a number of performers become internationally famous. Some industry experts predict that within twenty years, motion pictures will have simultaneous soundtracks.

  Today: The film industry is perhaps America's most powerful export. American film stars such as Tom Cruise and John Travolta are more recognizable than the leaders of most nations. And although Congress continues to grumble about violent, antisocial, or sexual content in Hollywood films, the major studios are able to avoid federal regulation by policing themselves.

- **1920s:** The Nineteenth Amendment to the U.S. Constitution, giving women the right to vote, is ratified. For the first time in U.S. history, women can have a direct say in the governance of the nation.

  Today: In the Presidential election of 2000, numerous voting irregularities in states such as Florida may have determined the outcome. As a result of the contested election, many commentators and even some politicians begin arguing that the Constitutional prohibition against convicted felons voting be eliminated.

- **1920s:** The first Red Scare (a public hysteria, led by politicians and business leaders, about the presence of communists in America) reaches its climax, and Attorney General A. Mitchell Palmer stages raids in thirty-three cities without search warrants to seek communists. Four thousand people are jailed and denied counsel, and more than five hundred are deported, as the labor leader Emma Goldman was in 1919.

  Today: After the terrorist attack on September 11, 2001, thousands of U.S. residents of Arab or Middle Eastern descent are detained without charge. Almost six thousand people are rounded up in the Justice Department's search for collaborators.

---

pictures of combat, perhaps the most enduring modernist imagery of the war is contained in two poems: Eliot's "The Waste Land" and Pound's "Hugh Selwyn Mauberley." Pound's poem addresses the war directly, stating "There died a myriad, / and of the best, among them, / For an old bitch gone in the teeth, / For a botched civilization."

Critical Overview

"Hugh Selwyn Mauberley" was originally published by the small private press of John Rodker, a printer who specialized in expensive, finely made editions of books by modernist authors. At the time, Pound was often issuing his works twice in quick succession—once with small publishers such as Rodker, who would sell books to collectors and devoted fans of Pound's, and again with trade literary publishers such as Alfred A. Knopf or Farrar and Rinehart, whose books were sold in bookstores and purchased by a broader group of readers. As a result, it is important to keep in mind that early readers and reviewers are often responding to two different presentations of the poem, for "Hugh Selwyn Mauberley" appears quite different when printed on fine paper, accompanied by illustrations, and bound in hand-tooled leather versus when it is printed on inexpensive paper and machine bound.

The earliest reviewers read the Rodker edition and were often swayed by the poem's classy, or very established, face in that version. An anonymous reviewer in the *Times Literary Supplement* (reprinted in Eric Homberger's book *Ezra Pound: The Critical Heritage*) in July 1920 remarks on the "beautifully printed book" but finds the poems "needlessly obscure." The reviewer notes that the book "has no wish to appeal to more than a small circle of readers." The poems, the reviewer continues, seem to be both courting and hostile to readers; however, they have a "mathematical charm."

Other contemporary reviewers caught the acerbic tone of the poem but, as with the *Times Literary Supplement* writer, felt that Pound was unnecessarily obscure. Writing in the *New Age* (as reprinted and quoted from *Ezra Pound: The Critical Heritage*) in 1922, Edwin Muir wished that "the condemnation of our age which is implicitly damning in this book had been explicitly so." Muir was impressed by Pound's refusal to slip into "rhetoric"; his scorn "is so great that it does not even express itself." However, Muir felt that the poem simply pronounces the end of the possibility of poetry: "the tragedy," Muir says, "is that an artist here tells us that art is no longer possible, and that the only thing we can utter now is our desperation and our contempt." In January 1922, John Peale Bishop of *Vanity Fair* (also reprinted in *Ezra Pound: The Critical Heritage*) compared Mauberley unfavorably to a contemporary's work, stating that the poems are "elliptical, coolly wrought, delicately pointed satires,

but there is nothing here so poignant as the poems of T. S. Eliot in a similar genre."

As Pound's fame grew and critics began to look at "Hugh Selwyn Mauberley" not simply as an isolated poem but as a moment in a long career, judgements on it grew more sophisticated and more accepting. In 1928, T. S. Eliot wrote in the introduction for an English edition of Pound's selected poems that "Hugh Selwyn Mauberley" was "a great poem . . . I know very well that the apparent roughness and naivete of the verse and rhyming of 'Hugh Selwyn Mauberley' are inevitably the result of many years of hard work." Other critics of the day are similarly favorable. Maxwell Bodenheim, writing for the *Dial* (reprinted in *Ezra Pound: The Critical Heritage*), found the two war poems to be "the most condensed and deftly sardonic account of the war and its causes that has so far appeared."

In his 1932 book *New Bearings in English Poetry*, the eminent British critic F. R. Leavis took Eliot's judgments and refines them, arguing that "the verse is extraordinarily subtle, and its subtlety is the subtlety of the sensibility that it expresses." After describing the individual poems, Leavis concludes that "the whole is great poetry, at once traditional and original. Mr. Pound's standing as a poet rests upon it and rests securely." However, this was faint praise; Leavis believed that Pound's earlier work was substandard, and that *The Cantos* were simply obscure and sloppy.

The first full-length study of Ezra Pound's work appeared in 1951 from an emerging Canadian scholar. Hugh Kenner placed Pound, not Eliot or Joyce, at the center of the movement. In his book, Kenner states unequivocally that "had not a single Canto been finished, ['Hugh Selwyn Mauberley'] dispels any doubt of Pound's being a major poet." But Kenner also argues with Leavis explicitly, denying that "Hugh Selwyn Mauberley" is the high-water mark in Pound's career and insisting instead that the poem simply sets the stage for the much greater and more important *The Cantos* (which Kenner definitively explains in his 1973 volume, *The Pound Era*).

After Kenner, dozens of critics began writing on Pound, and two scholars produced book-length studies of "Hugh Selwyn Mauberley." John Espey's *Ezra Pound's "Mauberley": A Study in Composition* is an "experiment," in Espey's words,

focused on the question of how effective the traditional academic method of attack, with its full panoply of textual collation, identification of sources, and historical method, would prove when used in analysing a piece of contemporary poetry.

Its purpose is less to judge the value or importance of "Hugh Selwyn Mauberley" than to judge the viability of academic criticism. A later study, Jo Brantley Berryman's *Circe's Craft: Ezra Pound's "Hugh Selwyn Mauberley,"* is intended to use a greater knowledge of Pound's early readings and aesthetic beliefs to shed light on the meaning of the poem.

More recent criticism of Pound has generally focused on the prose and *The Cantos*, but scholars still continue to put "Hugh Selwyn Mauberley" in context as a number of different interpretations of Pound's ultimate importance compete with each other. If *The Cantos* fail because of their ultimately fascist meaning, what does that mean for "Hugh Selwyn Mauberley"? Is the poem a more perceptive analysis of late Victorian aestheticism than readers realize? Are E. P. and Mauberley ironic versions of Pound himself, or are they creatures that "the age demanded" and that Pound is ridiculing? These and other questions about gender, sexuality, war, and aestheticism dominate current studies of the poem.

Criticism

Greg Barnhisel

Barnhisel directs the Writing Center at the University of Southern California in Los Angeles. In this essay, Barnhisel discusses the use of the image of the medallion in the second half of Pound's poem and how it prefigures Pound's later interests in the confluence of economics and literature.

In his 1928 introduction to the *Selected Poems* of Ezra Pound, T. S. Eliot writes that "I am sure of 'Hugh Selwyn Mauberley,' whatever else I am sure of." "Hugh Selwyn Mauberley" is generally seen as the poem that takes Pound from his early adventures in poetry to his mature lifelong endeavor of *The Cantos*. Admirers of Pound's epic poem praise "Hugh Selwyn Mauberley" as a prefiguration of the methods and subject matter of *The Cantos*, while critics who see *The Cantos* as a failure laud "Hugh Selwyn Mauberley" for its traces of imagism, Vorticism, and Pound's other early obsessions. Almost all critics, though, admire "Hugh Selwyn Mauberley" as perhaps Pound's most purely successful creation.

> *And for the later Pound, obsessed with money and the machinations of power, coinage itself was also one of these combinations of material fact, power, and symbolic value."*

Much of the commentary on "Hugh Selwyn Mauberley" centers on the personae Pound constructs in the poem. E. P. and Mauberley represent two types of aesthete and, most critics agree, also represent two aspects of Pound himself that he wished to exorcise. E. P. is callow and immature, a follower, a hanger-on to the literary scene of early 1900s London. He latches onto people such as Mr. Nixon, the Lady Valentine, and Monsieur Verog but ultimately creates nothing of any importance. Mauberley, by contrast, is an older and more self-assured E. P. His aesthetic sense is more refined, but at the same time, he is more separated from the world, desiring more to observe and appreciate rather than to interact. It is telling that the poet compares E. P. to a sailor lured by a siren (i.e., one who wants contact) and Mauberley to a lotus-eater (i.e., one who wants to be alone with his objects).

In addition to being equated to a lotus-eater, Mauberley is repeatedly associated with a "medallion." The medallion—its appearance and the process of its creation—are both indicative of Mauberley's aesthetic tastes, but at the same time, the use of the medallion indicates that Mauberley's taste in objects was a stage that led, later, to Pound's own taste. In the 1910s, Pound went through a series of aesthetic incarnations, moving from the caped Swinburnian decadent to the austere imagist to the blustering Vorticist to, ultimately, his final incarnation as the man who tells the "tale of the tribe," as he called *The Cantos*.

Driving that evolution was a belief that energy, meaning, and aesthetic power could all be concentrated in a single thing. At times, that "thing" was a particular artwork (such as the mosaic in the

What Do I Read Next?

- After finishing "Hugh Selwyn Mauberley," Pound stopped writing short poems and focused his literary attention almost exclusively on *The Cantos*, a series of longer poems that he ultimately finished in the late 1960s. The poems are difficult and at times obscure.

- Perhaps a more immediately rewarding Pound book would be his *ABC of Reading*, a sort of textbook/literary manifesto that Pound first published in 1934.

- A movement that was dissimilar to modernism in its formal features but provided many modernist writers with a model of artistic rebellion was the so-called "decadent" movement of the 1890s. One of the best-known decadent writers was the Anglo-Irish poet and playwright Oscar Wilde, whose *Importance of Being Earnest* (1895) and "Ballad of Reading Gaol" (1898) are hallmarks of the decadent movement.

- In France, literary decadence also took hold. Among dozens of other writers, the novelist J. K. Huysmans stands out. Read Huysmans's *Against the Grain* (1894) for an idea of the nature of French decadent literature.

- World War I was the central historical event affecting modernism. Paul Fussel's study *The Great War and Modern Memory* (1977) provides a detailed and often moving discussion of this war and its effects on contemporaries.

church on the island of Torcello, near Venice, or the relief medallions of Sigismondo and Isotta Malatesta in the church of San Francesco in Rimini); at times, that "thing" was a "luminous detail" of history. For years, influenced by the scholar Ernest Fenollosa, Pound pursued the (ultimately incorrect) theory that the Chinese written character was a unique combination of the sign for and picture of an object. Sometimes this combination was a person, a "factive personality" in Pound's

terms, a man who embodied the spirit of a time and place and single-handedly sought to fuse the artificially sundered strains of power and politics and art. And for the later Pound, obsessed with money and the machinations of power, coinage itself was also one of these combinations of material fact, power, and symbolic value. The images of medallions that recur in the "Mauberley" section of "Hugh Selwyn Mauberley" are another example of Pound's preoccupation with coins. Their meaning in the poem is just a stage in the development of Pound's thought about the conjunction of aesthetics and politics.

The first section is dominated by images of different kinds of artistic production but focuses on the art of the engraver. The poem begins "Turned from the 'eau-forte / Par Jacquemart' / To the strait head / Of Messalina," a confusing batch of images. "Eau-forte" means "strong water" and is the French term for an etching (a type of print that uses acid to make the image); Jules Jacquemart was a Parisian artist who did an etching of the French poet Theophile Gautier. But, the unnamed subject of the verb "turned," a subject that we can assume is Mauberley, has left the aestheticism of Gautier and the art of the etcher behind for the "strait head of Messalina," a reference to the Roman emperor Claudius's wife whose head appeared on Roman coins of the first century A.D. Like E. P., Mauberley's "'true Penelope / Was Flaubert,'" indicating his essential aestheticism, but Mauberley grounds his art in the concrete: "his tool / The engraver's." Mauberley's art is "colorless," "not the full smile," "an art / In profile." In other words, Mauberley's art is incomplete, lifeless. The poem ends with an implicit comparison of the engraver's art to the craft of the ironworker: "Pisanello [an Italian carver who made medallions] lacking the skill / To forge Achaia [ancient Greece]."

The incomplete art of the engraver, the art in profile, is paralleled to Mauberley's own life in the second poem, which is (in the words of Christine Froula in *A Guide to Ezra Pound's "Selected Poems,"*) "a fable of Mauberley's uncomprehending response to the urgings of Eros." Mauberley's response to the woman's advances is stiff, jerky, nonrhythmic, much like the rhythm of the poem itself. The erotic drives of the woman are incomprehensible to Mauberley, whose "fundamental passion" is for art: he wants to describe her, to present "the series / Of curious heads in medallion." Unable to respond to her as a woman, Mauberley is metaphorically turned to stone. Unlike in the E. P. section, the Greek phrases here are rendered in phonetic translation rather than in the Attic script—like a medallion carving in profile, the Greek is rendered only partially faithful to the original.

The third poem, "The Age Demanded," moves us from the private to the public. Criticizing Mauberley's ultimate irrelevance, the poet notes, "The glow of porcelain / Brought no reforming sense / To his perception / Of the social inconsequence." (The reference to "the glow of porcelain" alludes, as well, to another school of artists, the della Robbia family of Renaissance Florence who made medallion-shaped, glazed terra-cotta sculptures that were placed over doorways and over wall altars.) Mauberley has retreated into aestheticism, into antiquarianism, and as a result, suffers "social inconsequence," or an ultimate irrelevance to society. In the poem, Mauberley's perceptions are filtered through his preoccupations with art. He sees women not as they are but as they might be portrayed in an engraving or a porcelain representation. Mauberley's aestheticism, moreover, has made him incapable of even creating art any more. All he can do is appreciate art, evaluate it, eat the lotuses; he is "incapable of the least utterance or composition."

"Medallion," the final section of the Mauberley sequence and of "Hugh Selwyn Mauberley" as a whole, has generated some critical controversy. Is this poem Mauberley's own? Is Pound trying to indicate the kind of verse that Mauberley might write? Or is this poem a production of the narrator, or of Pound himself? Is it a good poem or a bad poem? "Critical opinions over the past several decades," writes Jo Brantley Berryman (writing in *Circe's Craft: Ezra Pound's "Hugh Selwyn Mauberley"*) in her study of "Hugh Selwyn Mauberley," "have agreed in assigning 'Medallion' to Mauberley." However, Berryman argues that Pound himself speaks in "Medallion." Basing her argument on Pound's Vorticist dogma, she states that "Medallion" "can be vindicated and identified as Pound's own poem." The poem, she continues, illustrates the Vorticist preference for "hardness of outline," sharpness, gauntness, and austerity.

In this, of course, it is like a medallion or a coin, and thus it represents a link between Mauberley's characteristics (antiquarianism, lifelessness) and Pound's interest in the luminous detail or the node of power. The poem is stripped of all unnecessary words and attempts simply to construct a luminous image of a woman's face. Returning to the second poem of the Mauberley sequence, this poem

can be seen as what Mauberley is seeking to create when the real woman is trying to connect with him: "This urge," the poet says, "to convey the relation / Of eye-lid and cheek-bone / By verbal manifestation." "Medallion" accomplishes this. But, at the same time, the poem condemns the living woman it describes to the dusty pages of archaeology—specifically, of the archaeological writings of Solomon Reinach, alluded to in the eighth line. This musician, her sensual face, the heat of the room, the sound of her voice and of the piano, are transformed into a static, lifeless medallion through the intervention of Mauberley. They are beautiful, the description accomplished, but the fact is that they are devoid of inspiration ("inspiration" deriving from the Greek term for "to blow life into something"). Even the eyes, the seats of life, "turn topaz." Life becomes stone.

In later years, Pound's own thoughts on economics began to reflect just such ideas about medallions, coins, and the like. Pound viewed purchasing power as a dynamic thing. Money was simply a flawed representation of purchasing power, he felt, and should not be admired or valued for itself. In the 1920s and 1930s, Pound developed a quite complicated theory about banks and their control over purchasing power. Money, initially used as simply a marker or a symbol, becomes itself value, and eventually, banks are able to create money out of money by charging interest on credit. This, for Pound, was an abomination, for one should not be able to create value out of nothing—this perverted the idea that all value was in the end based in human effort. The coin "petrifies," or turns to stone, the dynamic nature of purchasing power and allows an essentially free entity to be captured and owned. Even more than being lifeless, it petrifies life itself, taking purchasing power and turning it into an object. Similarly, Mauberley's medallions are valuable things, desirable and well-crafted, but lifeless. "Hugh Selwyn Mauberley" is not only a stylistic indication of where Pound has been and where he will eventually go; the poem also contains a structure of symbols and images that will make sense only in the light of Pound's later beliefs and writings.

Source: Greg Barnhisel, Critical Essay on "Hugh Selwyn Mauberley," in *Poetry for Students*, The Gale Group, 2002.

Hugh Witemeyer

In the following essay excerpt, Witemeyer examines the artist portraits Pound creates as an "aesthetic heritage for Mauberley."

The first major work in which Pound expresses this embittered social vision is *Hugh Selwyn Mauberley* (1920). Pound wrote the sequence as a poetic farewell to London on the eve of his departure for Paris. In it, he adumbrates the reasons why, after a residence of twelve years, he no longer finds England congenial to art and artists.

His analysis is complex and uncompromising. To begin with, his formidable style makes few concessions to the common reader. Those tackling the poem for the first time may well come away with little more than a general impression of angry urgency and bitter irony. A major source of difficulty is the extreme condensation of the images and allusions, which often imply discursive arguments made elsewhere in Pound's writings but not repeated here. In the absence of an easily identifiable central speaker or *persona*, another problem lies in gauging the point of view and tone of voice of the various sections of the sequence. The reader is forced to construe unfamiliar, heterogeneous materials juxtaposed according to a logic that is not immediately apparent. It is as though the imagistic technique of "In a Station of the Metro" had fissioned.

To bring the *Mauberley* sequence under control, each reader must make a set of personal hermeneutic decisions about the meaning and connection of its various elements. Here is one set of choices that may prove helpful. In its first twelve sections, the sequence analyzes the false values of modern civilization by showing their effects upon the market for art and upon the careers of a series of minor artists. As in many of his earlier poems, Pound takes the *vida* of the secondary artist to be a valid index of the general culture of his society. The poem is by no means a neo-romantic *"Kunstlerroman"* (novel of the education of the artist) in verse, however. Ironically, the title character, a fictive poet named Hugh Selwyn Mauberley, does not even appear until the second part of the sequence, beginning with "Mauberley 1920." Instead of spotlighting a protagonist, the first part of the poem presents a critique of "the age" and shows its effects upon the lives and works of other English artists, from the mid-Victorian period on.

These portraits provide an aesthetic heritage for Mauberley and a glance at some contemporary careers with which his may be compared. The voice that knits the sequence is the flexible voice of Pound himself, speaking in various tones of irony, rage, detachment and impersonal sympathy; but the voice does not build up a *persona* or generate an illusion of dramatic character. There are moments of lyric affirmation, especially in the "Envoi" and "Medallion," but the predominant tone is diagnostic, ironic, and satiric.

Pound's criticism is two-edged. First, he condemns the philistine priorities of a society which values money more than life, profit more than beauty. Secondly, he criticizes modern artists themselves for their escapist responses to the pressures of the age, for either giving up or taking refuge in a hedonistic aestheticism. In other words, *Mauberley* is an extended case study of what happens when, as Eliot put it, the doctrine of "Art for Art's sake" is challenged by the demand that art "be instrumental to social purposes."

After the opening "Ode," sections II–V present Pound's critique of British values in an era of "tawdry cheapness." In art, the age demands a prettified image of itself, a "mould in plaster" or a photographically realistic drama and fiction which are endlessly replicable for a mass market. When beauty (TO KALON) is "decreed in the market place," art becomes mechanical; the pianola which "replaces" Sappho's barbitos or lyre symbolizes this decline. In politics, a mechanical democracy of electoral franchise and mass-circulation newspapers displaces a traditional religious sense of community and chooses corrupt or ineffectual leaders. Aesthetic and political ideals "defect" and turn into hollow mockeries.

The Great War of 1914–18 was the logical outcome of this displacement of life values by money values. Those who went to battle out of patriotic idealism returned with no illusions:

> believing in old men's lies, then unbelieving
> came home, home to a lie,
> home to many deceits,
> home to old lies and new infamy;
> usury age-old and age-thick
> and liars in public places.

The Social-Credit conspiracy-theory of the economic and political causes of the war underpins these bitter lines, which mark the first appearance of the term *usury* in Pound's poetry.

Pound traces the philistine phase of modern British society back some seventy-five years, to the Pre-Raphaelite controversies of the mid-Victorian period. Much of *Mauberley* is devoted to showing how different artists have responded to economic and social pressures during this period. Pound does not let his sympathy for the artists' cause prevent him from making an unsentimental diagnosis of the flaws in their will and their aesthetic views. After all, "the age" is not wholly to blame if its minor talents do not succeed.

Mauberley's gallery of impaired, failed, and compromised artists begins with the *"E.P."* of the opening ode, a version of Pound himself in the years just after his arrival in London. Well-meaning but immobilized by the dated cultural baggage of his provincial American upbringing, *"E.P."* fails to modernize his style and falls behind, trapped in the contemplation of an old-fashioned ideal of beauty.

The gallery resumes in *"Yeux Glauques"* and proceeds in roughly chronological order, from Ruskin, Rossetti, Swinburne and Burne-Jones, to the Rhymers of the Nineties (Lionel Johnson, Ernest Dowson), to Max Beerbohm (*"Brennbaum"*), Arnold Bennett (*"Mr. Nixon"*) and Ford Madox Ford ("the stylist"). In Sections XI and XII, the focus shifts from the artists to their audience, as Pound satirizes bourgeois, aristocratic and popular representatives of modern public taste. If the economic and social demands of the age induce escapism or compromise among artists, among consumers of the arts they erase all notions of patronage based upon aesthetic merit.

The second part of the sequence, beginning with *"Mauberley 1920"*, traces the effect of these forces upon the career of a fictive English poet. Hugh Selwyn Mauberley is not modelled upon any identifiable, historical individual. Rather, he is a type of the aesthete. Mauberley begins as an Imagist poet but declines, under the pressures of the age, into hedonistic impressionism.

Mauberley starts out as an admirer of the Parnassian poetry of Théophile Gautier in *Emaux et Camées*. (The "eau-forte / Par Jacquemart" is the engraved portrait bust of Gautier on the frontispiece of the 1881 edition. With this allusion, the poem is also declaring its own aesthetic allegiances, for Gautier's quatrains are one model for those of *Mauberley* itself.) The connoisseur admires engravings, coins, medallions, relief sculpture and the linear style of Italian Renaissance portraiture. With Flaubertian precision, he models his own imagistic poetry upon this lapidary visual art. Indeed, the "Medallion" which closes the entire poem should probably be read as a work by Mauberley himself, a typical profile portrait in "sculpted" rhyme of a beautiful woman singing. (The "Envoi" offers a more melodic treatment of the same subject).

After three productive years, however, Mauberley's talent recedes into silence. He misses

> *The reader is forced to construe unfamiliar, heterogeneous materials juxtaposed according to a logic that is not immediately apparent."*

an opportunity for love because he simply lacks erotic desire. (For Pound, as the French epigraph from "Caid Ali" suggests, eros and creativity are different manifestations of the same energy.) Mauberley's response to the age is not to yield to its demands but to withdraw into a private, subjective world of "selected impressions," rare and exquisite apperceptions of beauty passively received but not returned to the world as art.

> A pale gold, in the aforesaid pattern,
> The unexpected palms
> Destroying, certainly, the artist's urge,
> Left him delighted with the imaginary
> Audition of the phantasmal sea-surge.

Mauberley drifts into psychic isolation or solipsism, depicted as a tropical lotos-land where he need do nothing but enjoy the "overblotted / Series / Of intermittences" which now constitutes his consciousness. His poetic quest is over. Like one of the failed crewmen of Odysseus, he leaves an engraved oar (his "Medallion") to commemorate his passing.

With this bleak critique of the modern poet's dilemma, Pound himself ceased to write minor poetry. He did not lapse out like Mauberley, but turned his considerable energies to his epic. After 1921, all of Pound's serious, original poetry went into *The Cantos*. But his conception of that project had changed since the palmy days of his novitiate. After writing *Propertius* and *Mauberley*, he was convinced that only a huge, indigestible poem would stick in the craw of a monstrous, all-consuming age. Into that poem he would put what needed saving. Few might read it, yet only thus could he continue to serve both art and society.

Source: Hugh Witemeyer, "Early Poetry: 1908–1920," in *The Cambridge Companion to Ezra Pound*, edited by Ira B. Nadel, Cambridge University Press, 1999, pp. 43–58.

Thomas F. Grieve

In the following excerpt, Grieve details some of the critical observations that have been made about Pound's poem.

It might be best, given all the vexed and vexing discussion that has surrounded Ezra Pound's *Hugh Selwyn Mauberley*, to begin with some simple observations. After briefly making these, I would like, less briefly I'm afraid, to draw out their implications for a reading of Pound's poem and for some perspective on the critical debate that has engulfed it for some seventy years. Whether we agree or not with A. L. French's assessment that "*Mauberley* has never really caught on," the poem has certainly caught many a reader up in its accomplishments and demands, and threatens to continue doing so. The success of *Mauberley* in stirring up strife among its commentators is due in large part, I believe, to its being a unique sort of poem—a "homage," to borrow the designation that Pound applied to its companion piece, *Homage to Sextus Propertius*. Understood as a homage—which, as we will see, is the particular form taken by the confrontation Pound stages between tradition and the individual talent—*Mauberley* exhibits both internal coherence and the consistent line of development of Pound's pre-*Cantos* poetics.

First, then, and, on the surface at least, most simply, *Mauberley* exploits the conventions of the dramatic monologue. "Exploits" is a better word here than "adapts" or "works within" because it draws attention to the deliberate violence that the poem enacts upon these conventions and the pervasively (and, some might say, perversely) self-conscious and self-aggrandizing irony observable in this relentless unsettling. As well, "exploits" seems a more appropriate term to identify the poem's ambitious play with various normative expectations that come with the genre, expectations regarding consistency of tone and voice, the identity of the speaker and interlocutor, and a generally perspicuous orderliness of discourse, narrative and context. Of course, Pound had exploited the monologue and unsettled its conventions long before *Mauberley*. It could well be argued, based on the evidence of many of the poems in *Personae* that precede it, that he had made a career of doing just this. The adaptations of Browning's form in such performances as "Cino," "Marvoil," or "Piere Vidal Old," or the hybridization of translation and monologue in "The Seafarer," "Exile's Letter," and *Homage to Sextus Propertius*, are different in degree but not in kind from the radical formal experiment of *Mauberley*. Pound had practiced these scales long enough to earn the right to improvise.

Second, *Mauberley* is a love song, by which I mean it places itself, again deliberately and with a fine ironic gusto, in the tradition of courtly love. Circe and the Sirens, pre-Raphaelite muses and Edwardian patronesses, Penelope and Messalina, singers and models, and, as John Espey was so patient to explain, the sexual innuendo of irides and orchids, lilies and acorns—these are not empty allusions, one time name-dropping as French would have it, but concomitants in a complex structure of genre markers in Pound's play on the stock euphemisms of this convention. This tradition had been an obsessive concern and the dominant theme of Pound's early verse and translations. The pre-*Mauberley* poetry covers the spectrum: from the mawkish and lugubrious posturing of so much of the *Exultations* (1909) and *Canzoni* (1911) volumes, through the gentle ironies of *Riposte*'s "Silet" and "Portrait d'une Femme" (1912), to the indecorous satire of "Tenzone," "The Garden" and "The Garret" (1913), and the vitriolic barbs of *Lustra*'s epigrams (1916). Pound's translations from this period rarely stray from the theme, a consistency not surprising given his preoccupation with the Troubadours and Cavalcanti. The imagist poet, presumably, can practice "direct treatment" in his presentation of any subject, but more often than not the terse products of Pound's contribution to the movement—"In a Station of the Metro," say, or "Liu Ch'e"—fasten on courtly love. This is the ground that Pound cultivates for the reticent regret of such poems, as it is for the sustained brio of the *Homage to Sextus Propertius*. If the amorous exploits he patched together out of Propertius's opus are questionably courtly, it is clearly the purchase that Propertius gave him on the theme that attracted him. Just as *Mauberley* represents a sort of completion of Pound's project in transforming the monologue, so too it is a consummation of his efforts to put the courtly love tradition to use in modern poetry in a way that is not maudlin, trite or merely cynical. What is crucial is that all these resuscitations of the dramatic monologue and the courtly love lyric not be reduced to either the imitative or the parodic. From very early on, at least from *Canzoni*'s "Und Drang" (1911), Pound had worked to realize the precarious equilibrium between preservation and rejection, affirmation and denial, self-defense and self-indictment that characterizes the homage registered in *Mauberley*.

Third, *Mauberley* is a poem including history. If this history is both real and fabricated, public and private, actual and literary, in being such it is representative of a consistent tension in Pound's early poetry and directs us to see *Mauberley* as a culmination of his decade-long effort to free his poetry from the constraints of lyric utterance and to stake out some middle ground between a subjective and an objective poetics. The poles of this opposition were personified for Pound by his two early masters, Yeats and Browning, and it is instructive to read his early work as a sort of dialogue between these two influences as he answers his Yeatsian exercises in autobiographical mask-making with Browningesque excursions into "objective" history. "Near Perigord" (1915) is the most interesting instance before *Mauberley* of Pound dramatizing the rival claims of the two poetics in a single poem, and "Three Cantos" (1917) is a revealing exhibition of Pound's failure to turn his "phantastikon" to objective account. This failure instigated not only the lengthy project of revision on the early cantos, but the catharsis and exorcism undertaken in the homages of *Propertius* and *Mauberley*.

Fourth, *Mauberley* is a surface. By this I mean, and I think that Pound meant, that it is a poem more concerned with registering tone, attitude and treatment through its multiple voicings than with investigating the inner life of its protagonist. *Mauberley* does not present a personality or in-depth psychology; it presents an indictment, which is at times inextricable from a self-indictment, through a mode that I am calling a homage and that Pound was later to explain (in the 1934 essay, "Date Line") as "Criticism by exercise in the style of a given period". I also mean that *Mauberley* is a work of art that, as the work of Marjorie Perloff, Reed Way Dasenbrock and Vincent Sherry has helped us to see, is true to its vorticist aesthetic foundations in drawing attention to its constructedness, to its "surface," to its experimentation with form in order to display the creative energies of the maker through the "composition" and "arrangement" of that art's materials. In this case, the materials are not "shapes, or planes, or colours", nor are they "masses in relation"; they are the verbal textures and tonalities of the various homages that, from part to part, compose the poem's "surface." Whether this surface is "mere" or "thin," terms that Pound applied to his technical accomplishment in *Mauberley* in moments of self-deprecation in his letters, and which unsympathetic critics have been only too quick to fasten on, is another story. R. P. Blackmur was the first

> *Mauberley is a love song, by which I mean it places itself, again deliberately and with a fine ironic gusto, in the tradition of courtly love."*

of the persuasion (and I doubt whether Donald Davie will be the last) that *Mauberley*'s display of craft and "workmanship" is at the expense of substance, which for him is merely "commonplace" and "conventional". His assessment—that "the poem flows into the medium and is lost in it, like water in sand"—was delivered in a memorable enough simile to convince a number of later detractors who did not take the trouble to see that *Mauberley*'s hard and highly polished surface is, among other things, a mirror that reveals the limitations of the presuppositions and conventional expectations that are brought to it. Such dichotomizing of surface and substance, treatment and subject, outer and inner, which always privileges the latter term in an oversimplified opposition, is a commonplace in the criticism, not only of *Mauberley*, but of Pound's work as a whole. "I believe in technique as the test of man's sincerity," Pound had the temerity to announce to an audience complacent in the belief that sincerity was a matter of unproblematized authenticity of utterance, of confessional self-exposure, or of sententious moralizing. Perhaps he is still paying the price, not just for saying it, but for writing poetry out of this belief.

Source: Thomas F. Grieve, "Pound's Other Homage: 'Hugh Selwyn Mauberley,'" in *Paideuma*, Vol. 27, No. 1, Spring 1998, pp. 9–30.

E. San Juan Jr.

In the following essay, San Juan advocates focusing on the end results of Mauberley, *rather than the means used to achieve those ends.*

Conceived as a poem with formal parts so unified as to subserve the whole—complete and possessing a certain magnitude—Pound's *Hugh*

Selwyn Mauberley reveals its virtues and powers in the style—the devices of representation—by which the poet is able to "imitate" or render in expressive form the subtle, refined workings of a unique sensibility. Our idea of the sensibility to which we attribute the nuances of attitudes and feelings, the antinomies of imaginative logic, articulated in the poem is of course an inference which depends on our grasp of the structure of the poem itself. For Pound, sensibility is a method of transfiguring personae or masks in order to actualize a complex harmony of vision. In *Mauberley*, the speaking voice syncopates in fugal arrangement the splenetic, the maudlin, the serious, and the sublime. Style accordingly conforms in texture and tone—confessional, ironic, pompous, banal—to the shifts of personalities that one will observe as the main cause, the primary rationale, for the intricate variety and the highly allusive, elliptical mode of representation in the poem.

Critical opinion concerning the formal organization of *Mauberley* has in general been diffuse, impressionistic, or ingeniously assured—in any case, unable to define cogently the formal unity of the multiple elements contained within the architectonic rhythm of the whole utterance. While there is agreement about the themes of aesthetic revolt, the polemic of self-justification, and the rhetoric of elegant irony, we still lack a clear and precise elucidation of the organizing principle behind the poem. F. R. Leavis' comments, for example, betray a simplistic opacity: "The poems together form one poem, a representative experience of life—tragedy, comedy, pathos, and irony." In his synoptic gloss, Leavis fails to distinguish the speaker of the first poem from that of the rest. Hugh Kenner, by contrast, is infinitely suggestive about Pound's impersonality: his style is "an effacement of the personal accidents of the perceiving medium in the interests of accurate registration of moeurs contemporaines." But his actual explication fails to yield the total pattern and orchestration of the various motifs and topics. I suggest that the limitations of modern exegeses of *Mauberley* stem from the approaches and procedures used to determine the informing motivations of the poem by emphasizing language and its symbolic resources to the neglect of the ends or purposes for which language is only a means.

Pound him\self demanded a refocusing of attention on the underlying forces that determine poetic structure or, in his terminology, "major form." He implicitly stresses the primacy of ends, controlling intentions, in the creative process:

Any work of art is a compound of freedom and order. It is perfectly obvious that art hangs between chaos on the one side and mechanics on the other. A pedantic insistence upon detail tends to drive out "major form." A firm hold on major form makes for a freedom of detail. In painting men intent on minutiae gradually lost the sense of form and form-combination. An attempt to restore this sense is branded as "revolution." It is revolution in the philological sense of the term.

By "major form" Pound means exactly the shaping principle which measures and adjusts the possibilities of material and technique toward the realization of an intelligible form. In interpreting *Mauberley*, our concern should be with the kind of action or activity—Aristotle's *praxis* includes doings, thoughts, feelings in dynamic suspension—the poem seeks to present by means appropriate to the attainment of that end.

Our concern, in short, would be with "major form." Explicating the poem on the basis of its organizing principle, of the thematic argument which determines the dialectic interplay of incidents, character, thought, and linguistic properties crystallized in style, we would then formulate the meaning of the poem from the inside, as it were, since our knowledge of what the poet's ends are would tell us by inference the means which he employed to accomplish his ends. These propositions about critical method will make sense only as they show pragmatic efficacy in the process of textual analysis.

Mauberley consists of two parts: the first part, with thirteen sections, projects the negative milieu of the artist by mock-elegy, condensed report, and satiric editorializing; by retrospect, direct monologue, and other means. The concluding poem, "Envoi," may be unquestionably assigned to the persona nearly coinciding with Pound, assuming that the work is partly autobiographical. But I propose that the different personae here be deemed functions of Pound's sensibility; and despite the short-circuiting nexus or asyndetons in syntax and thought, each persona is never exactly equivalent to the poet's mind in its isolation and integral place in the sequence. The totality of the poem may be considered identical with a process of awareness occurring in Pound's mind. In this sense "Envoi" with its rich lyrical cadence affirms a part of the ideal poetic self whose orientation is not toward the Pre-Raphaelite earthly paradise, to recollected scenes in his life, but to the complementing and reconciling possibilities of the future. The address to "dumb-born" (because mutely renouncing) artifice—the bulk of the poem—descants on the *sic transit* idea with triumphant confidence that time and change will prove "Beauty's" immortality.

Like the first poem, presumably E. P.'s "election" or choice of his tomb, "Envoi" confronts the finitude of existence and looks backward, prophetic in adventurousness. But unlike the mock-elegy of the "Ode," which condemns the poet in terms of the past without any hope of appeal, "Envoi" asserts the power of the poet to resurrect the splendid past and reinstate by alchemical magic what time has destroyed in the realm of eternal permanence: "Giving life to the moment,"

> I would bid them live
> As roses might, in magic amber laid,
> Red overwrought with orange and all made
> One substance and one colour
> Braving time.

And the third stanza accepts the future with qualification: "Till change hath broken down / All things save Beauty alone." Within this tight contrastive frame, between the varyingly ironic and pathetic assessment of the poet's heroic aspirations in the "Ode'" and the intimate, cantabile praise of beauty ("her" may refer to integrity, the glorious past, beauty, and England), the ten poems fall in a deliberate sequence whose development leads toward the *peripeteia*, the hypothetical twist, of the "Envoi." In this last section, the poet, cognizing the degenerate times, reverses his fortune by passionately affirming the metempsychosis of experience into vision. The second part of the poem entitled "Mauberley" may be designated as the exploration of conscience, the elaborate plight of identification: the speaker recognizes at last that Mauberley, with his cult of *"l'art pour l'art"* (theory and practice now being delineated in a quasi-narrative manner), has caused his own downfall. "Medallion," the epilogue vindicating his private if passive strength, counterpoints "Envoi" by a successful confrontation of "the face-oval" (the oval being an image of completion or perfection) and a dazzling lucidity transcending the flux of sensual, chaotic experience.

Turning now to the stages of establishing the situation in part one for a character like Mauberley who composes the twelve poems, I would like to trace Pound's ventriloquism—the constant incommensurability of leading motives and surface complexity—as a method of characterizing his persona. In the first poem, as Pound testified, we perceive Mauberley trying to get rid of the poet—a fragment trying to eschew the whole psyche. A certain duplicity, a mixture of condescending praise— "wringing lilies from the acorn"—and restrained, unresolved scorn may be observed in this passage:

> *In interpreting Mauberley, our concern should be with the kind of action or activity— Aristotle's praxis includes doings, thoughts, feelings in dynamic suspension—the poem seeks to present by means appropriate to the attainment of that end."*

> His true Penelope was Flaubert,
> He fished by obstinate isles;
> Observed the elegance of Circe's hair
> Rather than mottoes on sun-dials.

Note the verbs of motivation in context: "strove," "bent resolutely," and "fished," with positive accent laid on the intensive effort giving vital thrust and pressure to the career and poetic vocation which is the object of mourning. Ronsard, Villon, and Flaubert exemplify the creative agents redeeming the apparent failure of the poet to realize the ambition of transforming the tastes of a historical period by cultural discipline. But Pound's death, Mauberley (construing him as the funeral orator) suggests, bears heroic justification. Later the "Envoi's" melodic and delicate speech of farewell will transubstantiate the "Ode's" epigrammatic terseness.

I submit that Mauberley's "juridicial" pronouncement on Pound presents an ambiguous "case": he admires and yet censures, by turns lamenting and casuistic. He thus creates a curious "bastard" genre that violates the elegiac form by ramified yet conscientiously accurate and compact descriptions of the ordeals Pound has undergone for the sake of preserving his integrity and his exemplary ideal of cultural engagement. The siren song of surrender and escape to the ivory tower beguiles and chastens at the same time: Circe counsels the pursuit of knowledge when he conveys to Odysseus the importance of communicating with Tiresias, as *Cantos* I and XLVII indicate. Such active passion lurking behind the scrupulous gravity of the poet demonstrates itself in the pure, absolute devotion in the "Envoi" and, by empathy, in the trancelike elevation of "Medallion."

After disclosing his ambivalent but comprehensible attitude to the "dead" and buried self, the whole poet embracing the dualities of self and the world, Mauberley proceeds to place the celebrated figure in relation to his milieu: the "age" demanded exactly the opposite of what Pound intended to achieve. It wanted not "the obscure reveries / Of the inward gaze" but "chiefly a mould in plaster," a mass-manufactured icon for gratifying its narcissistic impulse and death-drive. Poem II identifies the denied offering: the static harmony of truthful, objective synthesis. It accounts also for the futility of the poet's existence: his works "still-born," he becomes useless, later associated with the image of "pickled foetuses."

With a notion of the radical disparity between the poet's conception of the ideal and the epoch's need for "an image / Of its accelerated grimace," Mauberley elaborates on the massive corruption of the body politic and the exorbitant decay of ritual, the commercialized vulgarity of the middle class subverting Attic grace and "ambrosial" Dionysus. The philistine public has ruined tradition, profaned Eros and the mysteries, and annihilated any hope for a transvaluation of norms:

> All things are a flowing,
> Sage Heracleitus says;
> But a tawdry cheapness
> Shall outlast our days.

The flowing image of reality is fully evoked in Mauberley's drifting and drowning in the second part. But now Mauberley parodies Pindar's invocation: instead of bestowing a wreath on Olympic heroes, Mauberley registers the deplorable decay of honor and virtue in his milieu. Less a jubilant praiser than a mordant mourner, he criticizes the age in sharply juxtaposed contrasting imagery. Poem III seeks to assign responsibility for the poet's passage "from men's memory"—the phrase itself being a non-committal remark. In context, the passage signifies a temporal and spatial departure in a quest-pilgrimage to the past, later projected in Mauberley's drift to solipsistic ecstasy in part two. In cinematic montage, Poems II to XII seek to diagnose the malady and explain the death of the poet by attributing the cause to the convergence of time and place to which fate has consigned him.

Poem IV locates corruption and denounces the perversion of ideals embodied in the sanctity of the homeland by the sacrifice of lives in meaningless mass-slaughter. The allusions to Cicero and Horace point to the discrepancy between past and present: the present is witness to the inane confusion of motives, the desecration of qualities (the fortitude and frankness of youthful combatants) exacted by the crisis. Hence the age with its fraud and avarice ultimately gets what it deserves: "laughter out of dead bellies." Yet Mauberley does not descend into hell (the Homeric motif) simply because he is in hell. He remains the unflinching if Mephistophelian observer of reality, austerely bitter but not savagely cynical. Here one discerns an elegiac homage, a truncated bucolic inspired by Bion, whose intensity is measured by the indignant response to the visible survivor—in effect, Poem V attacks the equivocal mourner in Poem I and converts Mauberley from a grudging obituarist to an outraged spirit instigating revolt by incantatory repetitions—his remedy for the absence of ritual, Yeats's "custom and ceremony." The balance is restored: the kind of death acknowledged here, though futile, redeems Pound's "death" from ignominy or innocuous obscurity:

> There died a myriad,
> And of the best, among them,
> For an old bitch gone in the teeth,
> For a botched civilization,
> Charm, smiling at the good mouth,
> Quick eyes gone under earth's lid.

Poems VI to XII, with swift incisive rhythms and sensitive transcriptions, render a plot-like continuum: from retrospective portrayal of the Nineties and the Pre-Raphaelites, then a gradual transit to the present via the interview with Mr. Nixon, a visit to the "stylist," and witty sizing-up of sophisticated females in Poems X and XI. Poem XII ushers us into a drawing-room as setting from which Mauberley launches his tempered indictment of the genteel but debased elite: Lady Valentine's heart seems made up of papier-mâché. On the whole, this section prepares us for Pound's "Envoi" which may be considered as the authentic, noble heritage the dead poet bequeaths to his contemporary apologist-arbiter Mauberley. Clarification of this movement will further disclose the probability of the "Envoi" appearing at this point in the sequence as an eloquent reversal of what the "age" would expect despite the hostile tenor of the previous forensic quatrains.

Yet Mauberley's true sympathy—for the dead Pound (a persona within the poem), not for society—chooses the last two stanzas of Poem XII as the epiphanic contact between the soul and its paradisal repose: the Augustan poise of Dr. Johnson's culture. Charting the sordid plight of the artists from "Yeux Glauques" up to the "stylist" cultivating his own garden so to speak, Mauberley nonetheless halts that merciless, self-chastising exposure of the artist's vanity in order to pay sincere tribute to the dead poet—his real total self—by evoking "Pierian roses" and introducing the matrix of music-flower-love motifs which integrate the second part.

Poems VI to IX present concrete dramatic situations in stylized patterns, the persons and their surroundings contrived to illustrate those who compromised with the age and those who persisted in intransigent defiance. These scenes also serve to distill emotions recollected in tranquil review affording sardonic and aphoristic violence of notation. Spiritual discipline is exercised in achieving balance, a "perspective by incongruity" yielding comic innuendo, as for instance: Lionel Johnson's "pure mind / Arose toward Newman as the whiskey warmed" or "Dowson found harlots cheaper than hotels."

In Poems IV and V, the demands of the age receive exaggerated and abusive response in the loss of innocence and potentiality, a cataclysmic holocaust reducing all human purpose into dust. A reversal of the idea that piety and mores always prevail occurs here. Mauberley painstakingly discovers in disillusionment the vain delusive cause which mocks the value of sacrifice and deprives life of all sacramental import. To withdraw into memory seems the only alternative out of the impasse (later merging into "apathein," impassivity), the intractable mood of nihilism, in Poem V. With "Yeux Glauques," Mauberley strives to resurrect those "quick eyes" swallowed by war's ruins.

Poem VI incorporates in the figure of the female victim the larger scheme of transformation in the whole poem. The Muse here becomes a prostitute: art, represented by Ruskin, Swinburne and the Pre-Raphaelites, has already entered its dying phase at the apotheosis of the pandering bourgeoisie. For the puritanical prudes of Victorian England, beauty smacked of obscene pagan deviations:

> Foetid Buchanan lifted up his voice
> When that faun's head of hers
> Became a pastime for
> Painters and adulterers.

Yet Burne-Jone's painting, levelling the ranks of king and beggar-maid, has ably transfixed an orgiastic moment which defies mutability and fashionable canons of taste. Now, however, the beautiful features of the Pre-Raphaelite model (Elizabeth Sid-

dal) seem artificially fragile, destitute: "Thin like brook-water, / With a vacant gaze." Her luminous eyes still search for a sympathetic or possessive gaze, such as the mesmerized Mauberley's in "Medallion." But there, of course, the rapturous vision explodes so powerfully as to dissolve the firm, "suave bounding-line" and immediately impose self-transcendence. Despite the oppressive indifference of the audience, Mauberley preserves a suspicious distance and reveals the fidelity and sincerity of art in the person of an animated fiction. Thus the persona Mauberley energizes another persona, Jenny the pure unfortunate, liberating the aesthetic vision from the stasis of memory and incarnating its presence in the vivifying context of secular betrayal:

> The thin, clear gaze, the same
> Still darts out faunlike from the half-ruin'd face,
> Questing and passive....
> "Ah, poor Jenny's case" …
>
> Bewildered that a world
> Shows no surprise
> At her last maquero's
> Adulteries.

Indignant but cautious, aware of the great propensity for sentimentalism in his subject, Mauberley handles language with ascetic and economical finesse. He does not really believe that Jenny's status is hopeless and beyond rectification. His tone and mode of representing her decline obviously deride the age for its hypocritical rectitude; amidst all indignities, Jenny's beauty remains unblemished, radiant. The pathos of her situation assumes allegorical significance in the quotation heading Poem VII: in Dante's Purgatory, Pia de' Tolomei's flat statement of birth- and death-place attests to a possible salvaging of which Pound's "Envoi" is the prophetic affirmation.

Poem VII resumes the elegiac but detached, condensed critique of a hermetic aestheticism founded of Flaubert's code of *le mot juste* and the anti-bourgeois policy of the French Symbolistes. If eunuchs and maqueros ruin the vital erotic union between man and woman (by extension, between artists and the Muse), they also disrupt the continuity of a viable tradition. Paralyzing deracination afflicts Verog's existence:

> Among the pickled foetuses and bottled bones,
> Engaged in perfecting the catalogue,
> I found the last scion of the
> Senatorial families of Strasbourg, Monsieur Verog.

In a recollection within the framework of nostalgic recall, Verog imparts information about the last days of the Rhymers: Dowson's dissipation,

Lionel Johnson's fall, etc. His reminiscences, re-fracted through splintered immediacies of detail, give proof of the arbitrary, shifting *modus vivendi* that the Nineties adopted amidst universal anarchy and disorder. Lumping Bacchus, Terpsichore and the Church, they pursued a Paterian goal of attaining organic beatitude. Intoxicated by alcohol and hashish, Dowson succumbed to his "artificial paradise"; in part two, Mauberley sails toward his occult mirage, an island of spices, but drowns in the process. Aesthetics, exemplified by Pound's assimilation of "influences", appears to be the only hope for restoring a sacramental ambience to the industrial, dehumanized atmosphere of the years circa World War I. With the public's rejection of the "inward gaze," we find Mauberley defining the estranged distinction of the gentleman-scholar:

M. Verog, out of step with the decade,
Detached from his contemporaries,
Neglected by the young,
Because of these reveries.

Where Poem VII conveyed Mauberley's imitation of Verog's conversation, the next poem "Brennbaum" renders with impressionistic vigor the countenance of a ludicrous "clerk," or connoisseur-intellectual. Infantile and lugubrious stiffness in conformity with orthodox norms blights Brennbaum "The Impeccable." His subservience to the rule of prudence and punctilio undermines memory and repudiates genealogy. Thus Brennbaum appears as Mauberley's nemesis in so far as Brennbaum represents the futility of looking backward, the vapid past signified by his ignoring Mt. Horeb (life-renewing water gushing from the rock) and Sinai, and the mechanical efficiency of mere formal correctness:

The skylike limpid eyes,
The circular infant's face,
The stiffness from spats to collar
Never relaxing into grace;

The heavy memories of Horeb, Sinai and the forty years,
Showed only when the daylight fell
Level across the face
Of Brennbaum "The Impeccable."

Mauberley's act of describing what is basically the studied shape of a cadaver, anticipated by the preceding "pickled foetuses and bottled bones," constitutes a severe epitaph for Brennbaum. Contrasting with the eulogistic overtones of Poem I, "Brennbaum" factually states what is left of a human being. Anesthetized by empty decorum, Brennbaum's substance reflects his unhonored origin and the tenebrous exodus and liberation of the tribe left unheeded by his public self.

Another case of a death-in-life existence is dramatized in Poem IX, where Mr. Nixon advises compromise in a smugly opportunistic expertise. Selfish Mr. Nixon, however, is seriously limited by his surroundings; he looms as the anti-Odysseus (a composite of worldly, complacent citizens) who negates all the values Mauberley upholds in his twin role of ironist and annalist:

"I never mentioned a man but with the view
"Of selling my own works.
"The tip's a good one, as for literature
"It gives no man a sinecure.

"And no one knows, at sight, a masterpiece.
"And give up verse, my boy,
"There's nothing in it."

Mr. Nixon's coaxing and proverbial rhetoric, though ultimately intended to purge suicidal ambitions, aims to persuade Mauberley to sacrifice his life for the glory of the bitch goddess Success. Mauberley, however, recalls Bloughram and the anti-pastoral equations and imperatives of Victorian evangelists. He recalls the aesthetes whose deaths burlesque those of the soldiers in Poems IV and V. The Rhymers and the Pre-Raphaelites served a spiritual ideal—"the thin, clear gaze" of Venus in her temporal revelations—that was once immanent but is now hardly perceptible.

The next three poems attempt to effect a reincarnation of beauty (Venus) in a female figure only to end in the resigned news that the sale of "half-hose" has superseded the appreciation of art in the city. As an answer to Mr. Nixon's double-edged program—to save one's life by violating one's integrity—Mauberley allies himself with the impoverished "stylist" who has retreated to the country. But Poem X is not less ambiguous, no more pro- or anti-art, as the first poem if one notes the allowance of positive gifts to the "stylist" and recognizes his incapacity to conduct a harmonious transaction or rapport with his society. Nonetheless, his talent and gusto flourish by coalescing with nature's self-renewing life:

Nature receives him;
With a placid and uneducated mistress
He exercises his talents
And the soil meets his distress.

The haven from sophistications and contentions
Leaks through its thatch;
He offers succulent cooking;
The door has a creaking latch.

But what then is the "placid and uneducated mistress" doing if the stylist manages household affairs? The next two poems show Mauberley's discriminating insight into the fate of art as personified by female personages or acquaintances.

By the evidence of Poem X, Mauberley conceives of Nature as generous and patronizing, set beside which the stylist's companion is an ineffectual mistress. Certainly it is difficult to envisage this mistress as one of the metamorphosed forms of Sappho or Penelope, let alone Circe. Yet she is one of the representatives of the generative, erotic force in *Mauberley*. Although the house is wretchedly falling apart, the stylist is happy and at peace with his environment. If his proper function is to observe "the elegance of Circe's hair" like Pound's in Poem I, then he is temporarily defunct. But Circe is concealed nowhere; the fault is not his, perhaps. In Poem XI, Mauberley hardly suspects the wife-mistress of "the most bank-clerkly of Englishmen" to be one of her profane re-incarnations. In "habits of mind and feeling," she scarcely evokes the fabled seductiveness of the archetypal goddess. To call her "Conservatrix of Milesien" would be an insinuating joke if not forthright anachronism; her "tea-gown" and her alliance with the commercial class betoken her low pedigree.

In Poem XII, Mauberley projects himself in a drawing-room where amid the insipid and pretentious crowd he suffers an eclipsed consciousness:

"Daphne with her thighs in bark
Stretches toward me her leafy hands,"—
Subjectively. In the stuffed-satin drawing-room
I await The Lady Valentine's commands,

Knowing my coat has never been
Of precisely the fashion
To stimulate, in her,
A durable passion;

(Note the repeated "bass" beat of aesthetic stasis in frozen Daphne/laurel tree, "tin wreath" of Poem III, metallic flowers, pickled foetuses, porcelain images, etc.) Mauberley experiences an illusory triumph: he imagines Daphne the legendary nymph stretching out a laurelled crown. But that happens "Subjectively," he bravely confesses. In truth he apprehends his actual circumstance with self-deprecatory reference to his non-dandiacal appearance, his nondescript clothes being a natural consequence of his loathing for frills or fustian:

Doubtful, somewhat, of the value
Of well-gowned approbation
Of literary effort,
But never of The Lady Valentine's vocation:

Mauberley sees the Lady Valentine as a powerful authority who, like Circe, can accomplish her sinister designs by exploiting the thaumaturgy of art. Lady Valentine also functions here as mock-

Muse to the poet-Pierrot (Petrushka in Stravinsky's ballet). Defensive and shrewdly realistic, Mauberley would seize this opportunity for his own advancement: for promoting a dubious liaison or ingratiating himself into theater business. Throughout the sequence, Mauberley's sexual prowess is sublimated into Latin ribaldry and etymological punning—as Espey has shown—to fulfill Venus' mandate. In revolution or in any emergency, Lady Valentine would be a refuge, a possible "comforter." Mauberley's physical self as free agent accepts the circumscribed realm of action imposed by a degenerate milieu. But if he can perceive the possibility of living in another manner—the stylist and the dead Pound of the "Ode" offer alternatives—it is because he has a virile spirit capable of epic dignity and tragic purposiveness, a spirit which does not share the mood of resigned futility and his later castrating numbness, nor participate in the body's commitments. Yet his "soul" sent on a journey to an Augustan haven of the imagination only intensifies his awareness that such a haven cannot be found anywhere today:

Conduct, on the other hand, the soul
"Which the highest cultures have nourished"
To Fleet St. where
Dr. Johnson flourished;

Beside this thoroughfare
The sale of half-hose has
Long since superseded the cultivation
Of Pierian roses.

We encountered this "ubi sunt" motif before in Poem III where we learned that the discordant "pianola" has overthrown Sappho's lure. Cheap imitations flood the market. Nourishment of sensibility is succeeded by "macerations"; the memory of Dr. Johnson's (like Lionel Johnson's) career receives the discounting pun in "Fleet Street"—for fleeting time spoils the genuine artifice and dissolves sensations into phantasmagoria—as part two exhibits. Perhaps the anatomical connotation of "half-hose" escapes the diffident but restrained Mauberley. He forgets the ubiquity of those roses in the "tea-rose" of Poem III; his temperament favors only the precious, rarefied luxuries: "The thin, clear gaze, the same / Still darts out faunlike from the half-ruin'd face." Contrast further Pieria, seat of the worship of the Muses, with Ealing where the lady curator of Milesian ware languishes in chill respectability.

Comparing the amorous "Envoi" and the chiselled strophes of the first part, we note that except for the change in cadence and texture there exists between them a unity of focus on an idealized past (Mauberley celebrated the Pre-Raphaelite model; Pound casts his challenging valedictory in Waller's mold) and in a dualistic notion of existence as comprised by perishable flesh and undying spirit, the spirit able to preserve in art the lineaments of fleshly beauty. Two or three lines uttered by Mauberley may be orchestrated with the climactic bravura of "Envoi":

> The thin, clear gaze, the same
> Still darts out faunlike from the half-ruin'd face,
> Questing and passive …
> (Poem VI)

> "Daphne with her thighs in bark
> "Stretches toward me her leafy hands,"—
> (Poem XII)

> Young blood and high blood,
> Fair cheeks, and fine bodies;
> (Poem IV)

The thirteenth poem, instead of enacting a disproof of Mauberley's sentiments, offers him a finely-controlled modulation into Pound's voice. It is as if the poet, whose death occasioned the memorial in Poem I, were resuscitated by the enigmatic verbal magic of Poems II to XII—both the dissonant and the mellifluous—while Mauberley, in speculative and abstracted vigil over his corpse, muses on the whys and wherefores of the artist's ordeal in this mercantile, inimical world. Can one then plausibly construe the "Envoi" as the envoy/embassy of Pound (The dead poet's ghost) speaking with the oracular gestures of hindsight and foresight?

In the second part entitled "Mauberley," Pound vigorously turns the tables over and maneuvers the situation so that Mauberley assumes the role of partisan and accomplice, and alter ego with his flawed consciousness. In a condensed and telescoped summation of Mauberley's struggles, this second part modifies and enhances by specific demonstration the attitudes supporting the manner of expression in the first part. Messalina, her licentious urge curbed by her rigorously defined head, supplants Circe; Mauberley, to the speaker Pound (tagged here as the persona), also regards Flaubert "His true Penelope." Kins or brothers by elective affinity, Mauberley and Pound share many interests in common. But Mauberley is distinguished by the kind of art-form he has chosen to concentrate on (announced in Poem I):

> Firmness,
> Not the full smile,
> His art, but an art
> In profile;

The laconic characterization hits the bull's-eye: Mauberley himself has fearfully turned sideways and avoided the full gaze of the female sex: Lady Valentine, the "Conservatrix," and the stylist's mistress. With his satiric craft, however, he was able to depict Brennbaum's countenance: "The skylike limpid eyes, / The circular infant's face"— but then Brennbaum turned out to be a frigid corpse. After Poem II where he indirectly refuses to indulge the age's egocentric delight in beholding its grimace, he is stunned by the impact of war's grotesque testimony: "Charm, smiling at the good mouth, / Quick eyes gone under earth's lid" (Poem V of part one). Brutalized by the ignoble present, he recoils to the past and for a moment he can contemplate directly not Circe's hair but the Pre-Raphaelite nymph, her eyes "Thin like brook-water, / With a vacant gaze." And he records his sympathy and sad impotence in yoking polished loveliness and carnal corruption together:

> The thin, clear gaze, the same
> Still darts out faunlike from the half-ruin'd face,
> Questing and passive…
> "Ah, poor Jenny's case"…

This inclination to retreat into an idealized past and witness amid insidious decay the last desperate gasp of the adored Muse (an eclipsed Medusa/Circe/Venus type) seems to have caused Mauberley's "anaesthesis" and his slow disintegration in cosmic nirvana. Poems II, III, and IV in the second part relate the progressive extinction of Mauberley's spirit. The epigraph at the head of Poem II, signed by Caid Ali (Pound masquerading as a persona stepping out of an exotic Oriental utopia, or out of the *Rubaiyat*), functions as Pound's flamboyant tribute to his moribund proxy. If Mauberley's passion is too mystical as to be incomprehensible to ordinary mortals, then—Caid Ali (Pound's persona within a persona) implies—whatever feeling or attitude we may have toward Mauberley's earthly vicissitudes will fail to correspond with the real worth of the motives or purposes that have governed his spirit. Fatality has "translated" Mauberley into the empyrean of dreamy necessity, somewhat analogous to Baudelaire's artificial paradise (duly authenticated in *Canto* LXXVI):

> For three years, diabolus in the scale,
> He drank ambrosia,
> All passes, ANANGKE prevails,
> Came end, at last, to that Arcadia.

> He had moved amid her phantasmagoria,
> Amid her galaxies,
> NUKTIS 'AGALMA

Is beauty then a deceitful and traumatic hallucination? The experience is valid nonetheless as an example of what "the obscure reveries / Of the inward gaze" can generate. Drifting away from time, Mauberley with his "orchid" as the possessed grail finally reaches "the final estrangement." The erotic associations of orchid-iris-mouth-eyes cluster of images combine with allusions to Hesper, Arcadia, flamingo, thunder, etc., to produce a consistent unifying theme of Eros-in-action throughout the poem. Indeed, the mandate of Eros requires Mauberley's introspective recollection and subtle conjuring: for instance, the perception of "The thin, clear gaze." Obeying such a mandate, he becomes "inconscient" to the phenomena of normal life. He does not need a "sieve" to sift beauty from chaos—in "Envoi," Pound described the "siftings on siftings in oblivion" as ultimately a refining technique. What Mauberley needs is a "seismograph," an inner equipment, fit for his experiment whereby *aesthesis* evolves into "anaesthesis":

—Given that is his "fundamental passion,"
This urge to convey the relation
Of eye-lid and cheek-bone
By verbal manifestations;

To present the series
Of curious heads in medallion—

Mauberley as engraver concerns himself with anatomy. Somehow his knowledge or technique fails to reconcile "eye-lid and cheek-bone"—objective perception—with "aerial flowers," his "orchid": organic sensations, physiological vibrations. Thus Pound's oblique judgment of the simultaneous victory and defeat of his enterprise is foregrounded in an Ovidian tableau:

Mouths biting empty air,
The still stone dogs,
Caught in metamorphosis, were
Left him as epilogues.

Transfixed in this posture, the dogs accompanying the hunt are freed from their violent biological urge. Yet such freedom manifests the impotence, the vitiating inability, of mere animal existence to satisfy man's infinite desires.

Poem III centers on Mauberley's rejection of the age's demands, thus confirming his sympathy for Pound the dead persona-poet in the "Ode." Chance found Mauberley and his unctuous vanity unfit for fulfilling any civic responsibility: his mind is all focused on "The glow of porcelain," the vibrant color of his model's beauty reflected in "a perfect glaze," a translucent veil: to him "the month was more temperate / Because this beauty had been." Inner mood dictates outer climate. But just

as in Poem XII in part one, Mauberley suffers from a worsening imbalance: his will to inhabit Arcadia heightens the conflict between *Anangke* and the "manifest universe" and his confessed "diastasis" (separation) from all life, ignoring the erotic or sexual ("The wide-banded irides / And botticellian sprays."). His psychic malady is suggested:

The coral isle, the lion-coloured sand
Burst in upon the porcelain revery:
Impetuous troubling
Of his imagery.

Exclusion of everything alien to his sensibility induces "the imaginary / Audition of the phantasmal sea-surge," linking up with the earlier signal of "Minoan undulation … amid ambrosial circumstances." "Olympian *apathein*" postulates the antithesis to Dionysian celebration and loss of self which accompanies creation; art as icon mediates between the spiritual and the sensual, mobilizing knowledge into action. The deterioration of Mauberley's ego increases with the coagulated sounds of the polysyllabic diction toward the close of Poem III:

Incapable of the least utterance or composition,
Emendation, conservation of the "better tradition,"
Refinement of medium, elimination of superfluities,
August attraction or concentration.

In spite of Pound's sensitive appreciation of Mauberley's delirious union with deity ("subjective hossanah") in the context of a depraved world, he maintains ironic distance throughout with fastidious quotation marks and subdued parodic touches in such phrases as "insubstantial manna," in sly idiom or parenthetical asides.

Poem IV represents Mauberley's death by the metaphoric vehicle of an aborted voyage cursed and waylaid by the constellation of Hesperus (Beauty). Elpenor's image, the voluptuary aspect of the heroic Odysseus, hovers over the last stanza which discharges Mauberley's barren epitaph on a defunct oar:

"I was
"And I no more exist;
"Here drifted
"An hedonist."

With "consciousness disjunct," Mauberley attains a kind of supernatural insight into transcendence with the vividly pigmented landscape of his tropic paradise. Associations with Daphne, rose, water, Pindar's wreath, aereal flowers, faun's flesh, oar and foam substantiate the regenerative implications of Mauberley's last glimpses of the world, a world half-dreamt and half-real:

Thick foliage
Placid beneath warm suns,
Tawn fore-shores
Washed in the cobalt of oblivions;
Or through dawn-mist
The grey and rose
Of the juridical
Flamingoes;

The grey and rose flamingoes seem to render a judgment on Mauberley's struggles, a verdict cancelling the drowning utterance of the "hedonist" inscribed on a drifting oar. But just as Poems II to XII of the first part delivered over the poet's corpse, miraculously revived the poet so that he could sing his "Envoi," so here Poems I to IV succeed in effect, summoning the spirit of the drowned Mauberley back to life in order to recite "Medallion," his true "epilogue" and his humble "adjunct to the Muses' diadem."

Conceived as an epitaph as well as a last will and testament, "Medallion" aptly illuminates the surface complexity, the overall pattern, of the poem. The principle of coherence in the poem lies in the process involving the transfiguration of Venus Anadyomene's face, seen in a reproduction, into a dazzling vision. The depth of Mauberley's inward gaze has succeeded in embodying beauty in a medium perfectly indivisible with the content of his intuition: the verbal medallion redeems the second part just as "Envoi" redeems the whole of the poem. Plunged in "porcelain revery," Mauberley insulates himself against the "profane intrusions" of the blasphemous hollow world. Avoiding direct confrontation with reality, Mauberley sought only the profile; but now nature, in her guise of Anadyomene the goddess of fertility and love, forces him to look straight and recognize that art draws its energy and life-enhancing *virtù* (the emphasis on light accords with Pound's concept of paradise in the later *Cantos*) from the erotic experience itself which lies at the core of the imagination.

In his essay on "Cavalcanti," Pound writes: "The Greek aesthetic would seem to consist wholly in plastic, or in plastic moving toward coitus…" That truth Mauberley has sought to obscure by pure aestheticism and timorous pride, but now this truth asserts itself. "Medallion" embodies this slow awakening into the mystery, the artifact becoming a vessel of the sublime:

The sleek head emerges
From the gold-yellow frock
As Anadyomene in the opening
Pages of Reinach.

Honey-red, closing the face-oval,
A basket-work of braids which seem as if they were
Spun in King Minos' hall
From metal, or intractable amber;

The face-oval beneath the glaze,
Bright in its suave bounding-line, as,
Beneath half-watt rays,
The eyes turn topaz.

(Note the affinity between the "Envoi's" "in magic amber laid" and the phrase "intractable amber" in "Medallion.") All the other disgraced female personages in the poem, in particular the Pre-Raphaelite Muse with her "clear gaze," merge with the oval face and luminous eyes of sea-borne Aphrodite (Anadyomene: literally, "birth foam"). "Topaz," usually transparent yellowish mineral, continues and amplifies "glaucous eyes" of the Muse-Siddall-Jenny-harlot constellation in the first part. The Sirens, Circe, Penelope, Messalina, Venus, and the courted virgin in "Envoi" (Circe's hair finds analogue in the "basket-work of braids" in "Medallion") blend into the radiant image of Venus arrested yet hauntingly moving in Mauberley's verbal artifice. The poetic "Medallion" then provides a foundation in experience and myth for the dominant action symbolized in the two parts of the whole poem.

For the action imitated by *Mauberley* is essentially the tragic experience of death metaphoric and literal after the loss of psychic equilibrium, conducing to an inquiry by turns comic, satiric, serious, and detached, into motives and ideals in the context of a civilization which has victimized the bearers of the life-sustaining vision of mystery. Poem I states the death of the clairvoyant poet; Poems II to XII survey past and present to define Mauberley's anger, doubts, and despair. Poem XIII, a lyrical affirmation of the spirit, may have inspired Mauberley's "Medallion" since both poems dramatize metamorphosis and exaltation by art. Poems I to IV in the second part recount Mauberley's fortunes, with a reversal effected in "Medallion."

Celebrating the symbolic death and rebirth through art of two poets in a reflexive mode, the whole sequence of *Mauberley* may be seen from one point of view as an extended epitaph to the tombstone of art at a specific time and place: England circa 1918–20. Exorcising demonic skepticism, it functions as a cathartic consolation for the speaker-elegist whose technique, resisting the temptations of the lotus-life ascribed to the exiled Mauberley as well as to the successful literati, changes completely our expectations of the conventional elegy by its problematic orientation. Although the power of nature and pagan cults determine the sympathetic response of the speaker to the poet's predicament, the manner of elucidating death alternately depends on the human resources of rhetoric, calculated irony, recollection, music, intuitive learning, insights, etc.—in short, the complete ensemble of faculties harnessed against the human condition of finitude and contingency. Oscillating between the polarities of "faun's flesh" and "saint's vision," the whole poem evolves as a new species of "ode," neither Pindaric nor Horatian; at first subverting the sublime and elegiac, then developing into a sustained counterpoint between past and present in order to resolve the tension of the predicament (bondage by Circe/art) in the first poem. After showing how civilization drives men to senseless death in war and hinting the prospect of a bleak future, Mauberley is left with no other choice but to seek refuge in the pathetic relics of memory. If he acquiesces to a mediating position in Poem XII, he still implicitly subscribes to the premise of a sharp disparity between, say, neo-classic urbanity and the vulgar materialism of the present.

With "Envoi," Pound himself shifts the modality of expression to pure lyrical assertion of art's transcending life. In the second part of the poem, such a transcendence is projected as immanent in Mauberley's "porcelain revery" which fuses vision and artifice together. The second part functions as the validating framework of the first part, for here Mauberley's character is drawn in terms of his behavior, his decisions, which are needed to clarify his utterance of Poems I and XII of the first part. Pound traces Mauberley's career after the first part has furnished us by suggestion and implication all we want to know (from Mauberley himself) of his "contacts" or crucial experiences, his thoughts and feelings about them. It remains for the poet to give an objective accounting, a graphic résumé, of Mauberley's endeavors to pursue his vocation amidst the perils of the market and the drawing room. But he would not remain for long in society: the exile-death wish motif is announced in the poem's epigraph, a quotation from Eclogue IV of Nemesianus, a counterpart to the sportsman-scholar of the *Rubaiyat*.

Withdrawing from any profound involvement with the issues of his age, Mauberley proceeds to commit the error of the inveterate pleasure-seeker: he elevates the means—sensual experience—into an end. He therefore condemns himself to exhaustion, abandoning the aesthetic imperative of justifying his own thoughts and feelings. Paradoxically, sensuality leads to "anaesthesis"; but this detach-ment does not yield any knowledge or insight of an informing purpose—except "Medallion." With "Medallion," his scrupulous indulgence of the senses may be thought redeemed because of his having experienced (for he has been by training and disposition prepared for this and has indeed practically brought it about) an illumination equal to the degree of his devotion and talent. One cannot legitimately expect anything more from Mauberley at this point, given his character and the conditions of his existence. The nature of the action imitated by *Hugh Selwyn Mauberley* is then organized around the idea of life's affirmation by art as achieved in the tragi-comic quest of a hero assuming varied personae—his ethos in the mode of disclosing its formal wholeness—according to the tensions and resolutions of his agonizing, incandescent consciousness.

Source: E. San Juan Jr., "Ezra Pound's Craftsmanship: An Interpretation of 'Hugh Selwyn Mauberley,'" in *Critics on Ezra Pound*, edited by E. San Juan Jr., University of Miami Press, 1972, pp. 106–24.

Sources

Berryman, Jo Brantley, *Circe's Craft: Ezra Pound's "Hugh Selwyn Mauberley,"* UMI Research Press, 1983.

Eliot, T. S., "Introduction," in *Selected Poems*, by Ezra Pound, Faber & Faber, 1928.

Espey, John, *Ezra Pound's "Mauberley": A Study in Composition*, University of California Press, 1955.

Froula, Christine, *A Guide to Ezra Pound's "Selected Poems,"* New Directions Publishing Corporation, 1983.

Homberger, Eric, ed., *Ezra Pound: The Critical Heritage*, Routledge and Kegan Paul, 1972.

Kenner, Hugh, *The Poetry of Ezra Pound*, University of Nebraska Press, 1985.

Leavis, F. R., *New Bearings in English Poetry*, Chatto and Windus, 1932.

Pater, Walter, *The Renaissance*, World's Classics, 1998.

Further Reading

Brooker, Peter, *A Student's Guide to the Selected Poems of Ezra Pound*, Faber and Faber, 1979.
    Like Christine Froula's book, this critical resource is less a study of Pound than a guide to the references and allusions of the poems collected in Pound's *Selected Poems* anthology.

Carpenter, Humphrey, *A Serious Character: The Life of Ezra Pound*, Houghton Mifflin, 1988.

> Of the dozen or so biographies of Pound, Carpenter's is the most thorough and least ideologically driven.

Kenner, Hugh, *The Pound Era*, University of California Press, 1973.

> Kenner's book magisterially surveys Pound's entire career. Although the majority of the book is concerned with Pound's *The Cantos*, Kenner discusses "Hugh Selwyn Mauberley" extensively, including its influences and its place in Pound's career as a whole.

Sutton, Walter, *Ezra Pound: A Collection of Critical Essays*, Prentice-Hall, 1963.

> Sutton provides a good introduction to critical thought on Pound. This anthology includes essays from a number of important literary critics and spans all of Pound's work and almost his entire career.

Witemeyer, Hugh, *The Poetry of Ezra Pound: Forms and Renewal 1908–1920*, University of California Press, 1969.

> After Kenner, Witemeyer is probably the leading Ezra Pound scholar in the world. Witemeyer, moreover, tends to ground his studies in the particulars of Pound's life and contacts, while Kenner is much more interested in larger cultural trends. This book contains an excellent chapter on "Hugh Selwyn Mauberley" that draws parallels between the poem and James Joyce's great novel *Ulysses*.

I Stop Writing the Poem

Tess Gallagher
1992

"I Stop Writing the Poem" is written as if Tess Gallagher were talking to herself in an attempt to console the pain she is feeling at the loss of her husband, Raymond Carver, the famed short story author. The poem is as much about their relationship as it is about Gallagher's sense of loss. In fact, the entire collection in which this poem is included, *Moon Crossing Bridge* (an American Library Association Notable Book in poetry, 1993), is about the life and love of Gallagher and Carver, as seen through Gallagher's mourning.

Gallagher wrote an essay in 1984, which she called "The Poem as a Reservoir for Grief." In the essay, she refers to her belief that poems are the best way to confront grief. The essay was written several years before Carver died and before Gallagher began writing her way through her sorrow. However, in an interview with Katie Bolick for the *Atlantic Monthly*, Gallagher says, "although I didn't know it at the time, much of what I was writing in that essay was preparatory to those poems" in *Moon Crossing Bridge*. In the same *Atlantic Monthly* article, she continues, "that book was written partly in order to sustain the grieving process long enough for me to absorb the loss." She says she realized through writing her poems for this collection, "all the different inflections in the process of grieving." She further describes the process of writing this group of poems as "discovering a form" that she could use to "move *with* the experience."

In a review of *Moon Crossing Bridge* in *Publishers Weekly*, some of the poems in this collection

Tess Gallagher

are described as affecting the reader "more because of what lies behind them than because of what shows through." This sentiment sums up "I Stop Writing the Poem," in which Gallagher writes about continuing the mundane chores of life while the reader feels the grief behind the ordinariness of these activities.

Author Biography

Tess Gallagher was born on July 21, 1943, in Port Angeles, Washington, to Leslie (a logger and long-shoreman) and Georgia Bond. Gallagher received her bachelor's and master's degrees in English from the University of Washington, where she studied poetry under the guidance of Theodore Roethke, a National Book Award-winning poet. She went on to earn a master of fine arts degree in poetry from the University of Iowa in 1974.

While she was teaching English at St. Lawrence University in New York, Gallagher published her first collection of poems, *Stepping Outside* (1974). The following year, she began teaching creative writing at Kirkland College, also in New York, and would eventually publish her second collection, *Instructions to the Double* (1976), which is

often referred to as her best-known work. She would go on to publish six more poetry collections, as well as teach at various other colleges, and marry three times before publishing her book *Moon Crossing Bridge* in which "I Stop Writing the Poem" (1992) appears. This entire collection is devoted to Raymond Carver, the well known short-story writer, with whom Gallagher lived and whom she married shortly before Carver's death.

Gallagher's other publications include *Owl-Spirit Dwelling* (1997), a collection of poems; *At the Owl Woman Saloon* (1997), a collection of stories about living in the Pacific Northwest; *My Black Horse* (2000), a poetry collection introduced by an essay written by Gallagher that details events in her childhood; and *Soul Barnacles: Ten More Years with Ray* (2001), in which Gallagher relates some of the more interesting moments she shared with her famous husband.

Gallagher has also written two screenplays, one of them with Carver. She also conferred with Robert Altman for his 1993 film adaptation of Carver's short-story collection called *Short Cuts*.

Equally comfortable writing poetry and prose, Gallagher compared the two forms in an interview for the *Atlantic Monthly*. If writing poems, she said, is like "deep-sea diving," then "writing fiction is foraging." She has won several awards for both styles of writing, including two from the National Endowment for the Arts (1976 and 1981), another from the Guggenheim Foundation (1978–1979), and several Governor's awards from the state of Washington (1984, 1986, and 1987). She lives in her hometown of Port Angeles, where she writes (with the same special pen she has had since the publication of her second collection of poetry) from her Sky House, a home she designed and built for herself.

Poem Text

to fold the clothes. No matter who lives
or who dies, I'm still a woman.
I'll always have plenty to do.
I bring the arms of his shirt
together. Nothing can stop   5
our tenderness. I'll get back
to the poem. I'll get back to being
a woman. But for now
there's a shirt, a giant shirt
in my hands, and somewhere a small girl   10
standing next to her mother
watching to see how it's done.

Poem Summary

Lines 1–2

The way "I Stop Writing the Poem" is written, the title works as the first line, with the actual first line completing the sentence that the title began. In setting the poem up in this manner, the author emphasizes the reason behind why she has stopped writing. The reader of the poem is forced to go back and reread the title, so that there is a full understanding that something very serious has disturbed the poet's life. Upon rereading the title and the phrase that follows in the first line, the reader is struck with both the ordinariness of the action of folding clothes as well as the seeming absurdity of a poet interrupting her writing in order to take care of laundry chores. Readers also note that the title is ironic because obviously she has not stopped writing poems.

The second half of the first line offers a hint as to the real reason behind the poet's suspending her art. The phrase "no matter who lives" ends the first line without punctuation, leading the reader to believe that a counter-statement is about to be given, which it is, in the second line. The speaker is now assumed to be the one who continues to live, and the reader can deduce from all that has already been written that someone close to the speaker has died. However, the last phrase on the second line is a bit ambiguous as well as somewhat misleading. Gallagher writes, "I'm still a woman." Is she referring here to the chore of ironing? Or is something else going on with this statement? She may be suggesting another aspect of loss that a woman might feel upon losing her husband. Implied in this phrase is the sense of her husband having taken a part of her with him. At this point in the poem, the reader can only guess at the obscured meaning.

Line 3

In the third line, Gallagher clears up the mystery of the second line. She ties together her statement of being a woman together with the household chores she finds herself compelled to do. On first reading, it seems as if the speaker cleans the house and does the laundry to keep herself busy enough not to get lost in her oppressive moods. This could be partly true. Physical action can dispel certain aspects of depression. However, is this all that Gallagher is saying here? Or is she speaking in an ironic tone? Through her use of irony, she might be trying to fool herself. Someone might use busy work to keep them from thinking, but eventually that person will tire of the activity and have to sit

Media Adaptations

- Gallagher has made several audio tapes. Two of them were produced by American Audio Prose Library and can be downloaded from the Amazon bookseller web site. Their titles are *An Interview with Tess Gallagher* (1994) and *Tess Gallagher Reads: Prose and Poetry from the "Lover of Horses," "Moon Crossing Bridge," "Portable Kisses," "Amplitude"* (1994).

down. Gallagher knows this because she is a poet and is used to writing about her experiences. She might be temporarily at a loss of poetic expression, but that does not mean that she has stopped thinking. As a poetess, a major part of her normal activity is to write and think. All the other activities are substitutes, and she is aware of this. So no matter how busy she keeps herself, she is always conscious of the reason behind her focused attention on the trivial things of life.

Lines 4–6

The image of line four is a return to the clothing that the speaker is folding. This is no ordinary piece of laundry. The shirt is (or was) his shirt. It embodies him. It contains his smells and a memory of his shape. Following his death, it becomes him, in spirit. The reader can imagine the speaker's gaze as she looks at the shirt. Her eyes are fixed on it in a way that goes beyond her seeing the material, the buttons, the collar and sleeves. Also implied in this image is the way the speaker handles the shirt. Her hands touch it as if it were alive. She writes: "I bring the arms of his shirt / together." This break in the line offers a double image. At first it sounds as if she is folding the shirt. However, Gallagher imbues this image with a deeper meaning. Is she folding the shirt, or is she wrapping the arms of the shirt around her, as if in an embrace? The phrase following this image is Gallagher's statement that "Nothing can stop / our tenderness," which reinforces the likelihood that the speaker has either wrapped the shirt's arms around her or, in the least, thought about doing so, remembering how he had once worn the shirt while hugging her. The "nothing" she is referring to could be interpreted as the speaker implying that even death will not stop them from being close to one another. The previous use of the word "together" emphasizes their union, both before and after his death.

Lines 7

In these lines, Gallagher somewhat contradicts herself. Here she states, "I'll get back to being / a woman." In line two she had already said she was "still a woman." Is she confused? Well, maybe she is not confused. Maybe she is just trying to convince herself. She is definitely struggling with the concept, though. Did death rob her of some underlying concept of herself by taking away the man she loved? She knows that she is having trouble expressing herself through poetry, so death has stripped her of at least one of her basic perceptions of herself.

If poetry is gone, what else might have been taken? The speaker touches on this issue as if she is only slightly aware of the complications of loss. It is not only that someone she has loved is gone. There are pieces of her missing also. She is aware of this, but she does not want to think about it for too long. It is too frightening at this point in her mourning. The emotions are too raw. She has enough to do to keep herself from missing him. She is not yet ready to face all the missing pieces of her own selfhood. At times as powerful as those that she is facing, emotions rise and fall without much reason. In the beginning of the poem, she might have felt stronger. As she was beginning the laundry, she might have seen the clothes just as pieces of material. Possibly, as she picked up his shirt, her confidence waned. All the memories and the pain came rushing in on her. At that moment, she began questioning if she really could claim that she was "still a woman."

Lines 8–10

"But for now / there's a shirt," Gallagher writes, taking the reader back to the first line, again, turning the emotions away from the memories of who used to wear the shirt, making the shirt just an object that needs cleaning and folding. Then she adds a new dimension. This shirt is huge, "a giant shirt." Why does she mention the size? Carver was a large man, but these words seem to imply more than that. By citing the enormous size of the shirt, Gallagher could be reflecting on the depth of her pain, the vast sense of her loss. Then, she ends line

ten with the concept of a "small girl," juxtaposing the huge dimension of the shirt with the diminutive size of the girl. She is also contrasting the former mention (and questioning) of the idea of woman with the image of a small child. In doing so, Gallagher exposes her inner feelings. She is a woman old enough to have lived with a man, and yet, at the moment of this poem, she feels like a child. She is confused and frightened. She feels weak and, therefore, vulnerable. Just as the little girl is no match for the giant shirt, the speaker believes that she is no match for the emotions she is experiencing.

Lines 11–12

In the last two lines of the poem, Gallagher weaves together a double image. She has the small girl "standing next to her mother," implying that the child is watching her mother do the laundry, fold the clothes. Of course, this is too simple a meaning for these closing lines. The child is obviously the speaker, feeling as a child, possibly turning to her mother, who may have also lived through the death of her husband. At least, this is what is implied. There is something that the mother has endured that has given her a strength that the speaker hopes to learn from her. If the speaker feels that she has lost "being a woman," then the natural place for her to turn would be to her mother, who was the first woman that she knew.

Themes

Loss

Not only the single poem "I Stop Writing the Poem" but the entire collection from which this poem was taken deals with loss. In questioning whether or not the speaker is still a woman, the poet is also concerned with a loss of identity. It could be argued that the speaker had created a large portion of her sense of identity through her relationship with her husband. Even if the reader has no idea about the background of the poet and her relationship with Raymond Carver, in most relationships when one member of that relationship dies, the surviving partner must reestablish himself or herself in terms of being a single person. The dreams they might have created together for the future no longer can survive. The person left behind in a relationship must create new dreams to follow, which entails creating a new reality, a new identity. So, the immediate loss might be felt as a loss of a friend or partner, but, upon deeper inspection, it is as if one has also lost a part of oneself.

The speaker's initial statement, referred to in the title of the poem, suggests that she has also lost her creativity. She is incapable of putting her feelings into a poem, and so her poetry has stopped. The emotions are too large for her to comprehend. She has lost her capacity to see the wholeness of her experience and capture it in a poem (although, she has, ironically, done just that by writing the poem).

Strength and Weakness

Throughout this short poem, the speaker expresses both her weaknesses and her strengths. She has the strength to work. She knows that if she does not work, she will become consumed by her emotions. However, in stating that she will also find things to do, she contradicts the initial sentiment of this poem, which is that she has stopped writing. She is not yet strong enough to embrace and examine the emotions that she is experiencing. Her creativity is blocked by her mental state, which she expresses as being vulnerable.

As the poem continues, the speaker demonstrates strength in her statement "Nothing can stop / our tenderness." She defies death in this way, taking a stand that despite her husband's passing, she will find some way to remember their embraces, to remember the love that she shared with him. She will not let death take away her memories of him. She also realizes that despite the weakness she is feeling at the moment, she is strong enough to know eventually she will regain her strength. She will one day get back to a stronger position in which she will be capable of writing. She also demonstrates her strength by knowing that even if she has lost her prior definitions of who she is as a woman, she will discover new definitions.

At the end of the poem, the speaker also demonstrates both her strength and weakness. She feels like a small child who does not know how to go on living. She feels lost and confused. Her strength comes through in the fact that she knows where to go to regain her confidence. She will not remain ignorant of life's lessons. She knows that she needs a mentor, and she is willing to find someone who will lead her out of her misery.

Womanhood

Gallagher explores the sense of womanhood in this poem in various ways. She uses female language in the sense that she exposes her emotions

Topics for Further Study

- Critics have found that some of the poems collected in Gallagher's *Moon Crossing Bridge* to be overly sentimental, a negative attribute as they see it. Research the criticism of sentimentality in writing. What does it mean? Find poems in the collection that you think contain this characteristic and compare them to "I Stop Writing the Poem." Which style do you find more appealing? Why?

- If you have experienced a great loss, take that experience and write a poem about it. Use a strong but ordinary image in your daily life as a metaphor through which you come to terms with that loss.

- Some theorists believe that our common language is dominated by male-oriented vocabulary. Phrases such as "the war on poverty," using a reference to battle, or purely rational expressions that eliminate emotions are defined as male language. Write a speech on a specific topic of your choice, first as if it were written by a woman and then as if written by a man. Then, analyze the two speeches and prepare a short report on the difficulties you may have encountered in writing them, as well as a brief study of the differences in word choices.

- Research the concept of death as professed by various world religions. Look for diversity in your search by reading about philosophies held by Christians, Jews, Buddhists, and Hindus, as well as indigenous beliefs found in Native American cultures, African tribal beliefs, or tribes in New Guinea or Australia. Outline your findings in a detailed paper.

in this poem through the language of a traditional female environment. At a moment in her life when she is confused by a definition of what it means to be a woman in general, or what it means to be a specific woman (namely Tess Gallagher, the poet and wife), she turns to the traditional images of woman as homemaker. Although she has lost her husband, she continues to care for his clothes. By using the image of the speaker as a young child watching her mother also taking care of a home, she reinforces this traditional role of womanhood.

Gallagher does not, however, imply that home-making is the only role for women. She is a writer who has learned not only to express her emotions through poetry but has also earned her living doing so. She is a contemporary woman who works both inside and outside of the home. The fact that she has lost her ability to write poetry is shocking, in the same way that the loss of her role of wife is distressing. She had identified her sense of the feminine through both her poetry and her love of her husband. Having lost both, she has trouble identifying what it is inside of her that now makes her a woman. It is in an attempt to find a new definition of womanhood that she turns back to the basic, traditional role.

Relationships

There are many different types of relationships embedded in this poem. First, there is the most obvious, the relationship of the speaker with the person in her life who has died. She must remember their connections even though the memories are now painful. She must also redefine their relationship on new terms. Although he is not physically present in her life, she needs to find some way to include him in her present situation.

There is also the relationship between the speaker and her sense of self, including her connection to the outside world in terms of her having to adjust to the role of widow. On a physical and psychological level there is a need for her to redefine her relationship to womanhood. She is not the same woman she was while her husband lived. She is alone. She does not have her lover to reflect back to her the concept of femininity. On a spiritual and creative level, she must also come to terms with her relationship to her work. She formerly defined herself as a poet. Since she finds that she cannot write, she must discover a way to relate to her creative self that will allow her form of expression to flow out of her.

Finally, she also mentions her interactions with her mother. She first visits her mother by returning to the relationship that they once had, while she was still a child. However, things have changed. The speaker implies that now the mother and daughter share a new experience. It is possible that both have lived through the death of a loved one. This newly shared experience now means that the daughter and mother must also redefine their relationship.

Death

Although the theme of loss and the theme of death are closely related, there are some contrasts. Death is permanent. There is no hope of that which is lost returning. The speaker senses that the loss of her creativity and expression, as well as her sense of being a woman, will eventually return, even if they are altered by the experience. However, her husband is gone forever. All that remains are the abstractions of him: the speaker's memories of him, his clothes, and the feelings of his embrace and tenderness. There may be a pause in her writing, but his departure is forever.

Style

Irony

The irony in Gallagher's poem begins with the title. She obviously has not stopped writing the poem since she has produced one. There is also subtle irony in the overall tone of this poem. The speaker waivers back and forth between indicating that she is doing well despite the trauma obvious to her and her reader and that she is suffering. In this way, Gallagher uses irony by choosing words that sometimes suggest meanings opposed to her thoughts. Examples of this are her reference to "I'm still a woman," which she later admits was not correct by stating, "I'll get back to being a woman." She also writes, "No matter who lives / or who dies," which also contains a touch of irony, because she would not be having trouble writing a poem if it did not matter that she experienced the death of a loved one. Another example is offered in her statement, "I'll always have plenty to do." Here, the speaker is trying to convince herself that doing the laundry will take the place of writing poetry.

Form

Gallagher's poem has no formal structure in either meter or rhyming pattern. Her form is fluid and reads like a lyric verse or like free verse in that it expresses a single emotion in a style that reads almost as prose. There is a rhythm in her poem, but it is imposed not by a set number of beats per line but rather by the arrangement of words often constructed in enjambments, such as the title of the poem running into the first line of the poem and the first line then running into the second line, and so on. In other words, the line stops before the thought is completed. For example:

> I bring the arms of his shirt
> together. Nothing can stop
> our tenderness. I'll get back
> to the poem. I'll get back to being

There are also echoes present in her poem in the repetition of certain words. The word "woman" is repeated (line two and line eight) as well as the phrase "I'll get back to" (line six and line seven). The word "shirt" is repeated three times. In using an echo, the writer emphasizes the importance of the word. The emphasis on the word "shirt" reminds the reader that the shirt is all that the poet has left of her husband. The shirt is empty now, also emphasizing her loss. By repeating the phrase "I'll get back," Gallagher implies she knows she is not where she wants to be. The word "woman" is emphasized because Gallagher is struggling to redefine what it means to be a woman in her new state of widowhood.

Images

The strength of Gallagher's poem is based on the images she creates. These images are both physical ones that the reader can visualize, such as the woman folding laundry, as well as more abstract or emotional images, such as the image of the pain the woman is suffering while she folds the shirt of her dead husband. In creating these images Gallagher touches upon universal themes, pictures to which many readers can relate. Anyone who has suffered a loss probably has little trouble imagining what the speaker of the poem is feeling when she envisions the arms of the shirt wrapping around her. The material things left behind remind the bereaved person of the precious moments he or she once shared with the person who is now gone.

Gallagher's images are simple on the surface. They take on complexity as the poet moves forward in her writing. The woman doing the laundry becomes a woman in pain, a woman suffering a loss, a woman who is confused and vulnerable like a child. The picture of the woman folding the shirt is carried through the entire poem and finally transferred to an image of the woman's mother folding a shirt. At this point, the image is not only transferred, it is transformed to take on not so much a woman completing some mundane household chore but rather a woman coming to terms with death.

Historical Context

Raymond Carver

Raymond Carver (1938–1988) was a famed American short-story writer and poet. Gallagher met Carver at a writer's workshop in Iowa, and they began a friendship that would last a decade and would color both Gallagher's life and her writing.

Before meeting Gallagher, Carver had turned to alcohol to ease the distress of a failed marriage, several unfulfilling jobs, and a lack of the kind of success in writing that he was craving. In 1977, Carver quit drinking and coincidently met Gallagher. They lived and worked together for ten years. A few months before he died of cancer, Carver and Gallagher were married.

As a cultural figure, a famous writer, and a lover and friend, Carver significantly influenced Gallagher. His writing, which has been credited with bringing the short story back into American literary culture, became more focused and more widely read during the time of his relationship with Gallagher. His stories contain ordinary people doing ordinary things, but his writing style was anything but ordinary and has become a model for most contemporary short story writers. His short story "Cathedral" is considered a classic work.

Carver began his writing career as a poet, but it was through his association with Gallagher that he returned to poetry in his last years. Gallagher was responsible for collecting his poetry and finding a publisher. His *All of Us* was finally set to print in 2000.

In her book *Soul Barnacles: Ten More Years with Ray* (2000), Gallagher makes a reference to the poems contained in *Moon Crossing Bridge*. She writes that this collection was "the first stage in the reintegration of Ray into my inner life.... The cargo of those poems forged a word-bridge across which I felt I could move back and forth to Ray." Although the poems in this collection helped Gallagher invent a new way to communicate with Carver, she also realized that she would never again enjoy "the reciprocal nourishment, the almost intrapsychic way Ray and I had collaborated and inspired each other."

Since Carver's death, Gallagher has taught a course on his works at Whitman College in Walla Walla, Washington. She also helped to bring together the book *Carver Country: The World of Raymond Carver* (1994), a collection of his works together with photographs of the environment that inspired his stories. Gallagher collaborated with filmmaker Robert Altman on a 1993 movie called *Short Cuts* based on Carver's short stories.

L'Ecriture Feminine

The term *l'ecriture feminine* was coined by French playwright and feminine theorist Helene Cixous in the 1970s to encourage women to find a new form of language not driven by male-oriented vocabulary, style, and subject matter. The theory has influenced the study of literature, especially that written by women during the past thirty years.

This theory has yet to find a clear definition, but it relates to the role of women's voices. Cixous defines this term as the process and journey a woman takes in order to write. She encourages women to ask themselves questions, such as how do they react to situations differently than men? Then she suggests women try to figure out why men and women react differently. What can women learn from an analysis of these differences? Through this process, Cixous believes that women will come to a different kind of writing, one that comes from their personal experiences rather than trying to duplicate experiences men have. She refers to this process as writing from the body. This type of writing is not limited to women, but it does come forth more from the emotions and the subconscious, typically female-oriented sources of strength. By creating this language, she and other feminists hope that women's reactions to life's experiences as expressed in their creative works will take on a legitimacy that has heretofore been relegated mainly to male artists.

In trying to grasp the concept of *l'ecriture feminine*, some colleges offer literature courses that look at definitive works by women writers. Authors most often studied include Kate Chopin (*The Awakening*, 1899); Virginia Woolf (*To the Lighthouse*, 1927); Adrienne Rich (*Diving into the Wreck: Poems 1971–1972*, 1973 and *The Dream of a Common Language: Poems 1974–1977*, 1978); and Toni Morrison (*Sula*, 1982).

Confessional Literature of the 1980s and 1990s

The influence of the feminist movement of the 1960s was eventually felt in the literature that women published in the 1980s and 1990s. Literature written by women was often eclipsed by works written by men in college courses prior to the 1960s. As women gained a more powerful voice and a more liberal standing in the major publishing houses, their works eventually made it to bookstores in increasing numbers.

More personal as well as more confessional, the literature of women writing during these two decades often reflected the inner life, or the emotions, that the female author had experienced. Some theorists point out the very obvious appearance of the narrator in the form of the pronoun *I* that appeared in the very popular memoirs of that period, as well as in fiction, essays, and poetry. Poets who wrote in the earlier part of the twentieth century and who influenced this type of writing in more recent years include Anne Sexton, Lucille Clifton, and Rita Dove.

Critical Overview

Most literary critics agree that Gallagher's *Moon Crossing Bridge*, the collection from which "I Stop Writing the Poem" is taken, was a difficult project to undertake. The emotions entailed in pursuing the grief and sense of loss after experiencing the death of a loved one are often so overwhelming that there can be a tendency for the author to become excessively sentimental. Although critics have found that flaw in some of the poems in Gallagher's collection, most have also found gems. There were, in fact, so many gems, that the American Library Association named the collection their 1993 Notable Book in poetry.

In spite of the flaws, several literary magazines responded to this collection favorably, commending the collection for its lyrical style, one of Gallagher's strongest expressive forms. A reviewer in *Publishers Weekly* writes that the best poems in this collection "evoke the ambiguous life of the survivor," who must find some way to continue along her own path and "go on charting a life." Likewise, Margaret K. Powell, writing in *Library Journal*, concludes that despite the difficulty in finding the correct language to convey her feelings, Gallagher creates "a luminous and important book that well repays careful attention."

In a review for *Choice*, H. Susskind finds that the whole collection reads like "one long elegy. As such, it takes its place among the very best." Anthony Flinn, a reviewer for the *Seattle Times*, describes Gallagher's writing in this way: "Never morose, sentimental or embittered, Gallagher opens herself to the intricate miseries and mysteries of love in poems that are worthy of the Pulitzer Prize." Flinn later notes, "much of the beauty in these poems comes from their heroism." He believes that Gallagher wrote this collection by exploring "her loss with such exquisite care that she reveals the very viscera of love."

Criticism

Joyce Hart

Hart has degrees in English literature and creative writing and is a published writer of literary themes. In this essay, Hart studies Gallagher's poem in light of the poet's own reflections that it was written to help her form a new language.

Tess Gallagher and short-story writer and poet Raymond Carver were intricately linked not only as husband and wife but also as colleagues, helping one another bring forth their artistic expressions. When Carver died, Gallagher fell into a six-month silence in terms of her creative writing. When the silence was broken, she returned to poetry, slowly forming a new voice. The creation of this new voice, the author claims, was captured in her poems collected in *Moon Crossing Bridge*, which includes "I Stop Writing the Poem." Studying what Gallagher was trying to do in this collection gives the reader an opportunity to rethink the images and language contained in her work and thus come to a more valued understanding of the poem.

The first and probably most natural impression one might take upon reading Gallagher's poem "I Stop Writing the Poem" is that the speaker is struggling over the loss of a loved one, that the poet wrote the poem to help her get over the pain of death. According to Gallagher in her book *Soul Barnacles: Ten More Years with Ray*, that was indeed part of the process. She emphasizes this point in her memoir with her statement that she visited Carver's grave every day for two and a half years. The loss must have been devastating for her. However, she elaborates further, writing that most people mistakenly defined all the poems in *Moon Crossing Bridge* "as simply artifacts of mourning." Gallagher clarifies her actual intent for writing these poems by stating, "These poems [were written as] the replenishment of self, and of the beloved, to fertile inner ground." In other words, Gallagher was searching through her writing for a

> *In remembering his physicality—his arms around her, the feeling of his body close to hers—she begins to realize that even in death, he is not so far away."*

new form or a new language with which she could continue communicating with herself, her emotions, and Carver despite the fact that he was gone. "The poems melded what had been parted," she writes, "as the new form took hold, the distance between us dissolved."

So, what does Gallagher mean when she says she wanted to create a new form of language, and how does this language dissolve the distance between the lovers, one of whom no longer exists on the physical plane? Gallagher gives the reader a hint of the first step in her process in the opening lines of the poem "I Stop Writing the Poem," in which the speaker stops writing in order to take care of mundane household chores. By stopping her writing and moving on to an everyday kind of task, the speaker has changed her focus from the abstract process of creativity to the more physical aspects of daily life. Gallagher does not write that she takes a break from her writing or that she pauses, both of which connote that a return is inevitable; rather, she uses the word "stopped," which, of course, conveys a cessation or discontinuance. In choosing the word "stopped," Gallagher creates a gap between the worlds of the imagination and the corporeal. She implies that one world must end before the other can begin. There is no bridge connecting the two.

This is the same feeling she experienced when Carver died. The physical world and the unknown world to which he departed appeared to her as being disconnected. In life, the lovers identified one another through physicality, but upon death, his body decayed, and, therefore, the lovers no longer could communicate, or that is what she believed at first. In the same way as the act of writing a poem

What Do I Read Next?

- Gallagher wrote a collection of essays on the art of poetry. To gain a deeper understanding of her philosophy of poetry and writing, read *Concert of Tenses: Essays on Poetry* (1986).

- *No More Masks: An Anthology of Twentieth-Century American Women Poets* (1993) offers the reader a wide expanse of writing through which the transitional changes of language can be explored. This collection contains over one hundred poets, including the works of Rita Dove and Anne Sexton.

- Anne Sexton's *The Complete Poems* (1999) demonstrates the progression of women's language through the years and the writing of a single author. Sexton's poetry centers on the personal issues of her life. Her language is honest, and she writes with unusual courage.

- Rita Dove, a U.S. poet laureate (1993–1995), writes about the daily lives of ordinary people in accessible language in *Selected Poems* (1999). She explores the loves and hopes of the people around her and thus touches on universal themes to which anyone can relate.

- In *Dream of a Common Language: Poems 1974–1977* (reprint, 1993), Adrienne Rich, acclaimed as one of the most influential female American poets, explores language as she looks for a more feminist vocabulary and form of expression in her writing.

- Lucille Clifton makes reading poetry fun. In her *Good Woman: Poems and a Memoir 1969–1980* (1989), she writes about topics as diverse as eccentric family members and matters of spirituality. Her language is carefully chosen to give a feminine slant to her poems.

- *Sula* (1989), a novel by Nobel and Pulitzer Prize–winning author Toni Morrison, not only tells a fascinating story about people living in a small Midwestern town but also conveys a unique language. The book is especially useful for a study in the art of using vocabulary to create fresh images.

- Raymond Carver's *Cathedral* (reissued in 1989) contains his most famous short story (for which the collection is named), as well as eleven other classics. For a stunning insight into the genius of this writer, this book is a good place to start.

- Carver's poems were collected in his *All of Us: Collected Poems* (2000). This collection provides a good sample for comparing Carver's poetry to Gallagher's.

- *The Newly Born Woman* (1986), by Helene Cixous and Catherine Clement, is a landmark feminist text, exploring the concept of *l'ecriture feminine* (the ways in which women's language and writing is shaped by their sexuality).

is separated from the performance of chores, so too are the two lovers separated by death. These are the impressions given in the beginning of Gallagher's poem, reflecting the initial understanding she must have had upon losing her husband.

With the poem out of her mind, the speaker focuses on the tangible. She leaves her writing to go do the laundry. However, despite the fact that she has stopped writing, the speaker has not stopped thinking about her loss, nor has she stopped feeling the pain. She soon realizes that delving into the world of the ordinary does not relieve her. Although she conceives that the world of her imagination is unconnected to the world of the ordinary, she finds that the same concept does not apply to her sense of self.

The poet has been marked by the loss of her husband, and, no matter what she does, the memory of his death lingers in her thoughts. It affects everything she does, no matter how mundane the task. Anger rises in her as she attempts to ignore her feelings. "No matter who lives / or who dies, I'm still a woman," Gallagher writes. The speaker is angry that her lover is not there but pretends that it does not really matter. She then tries to grab onto a stable definition of herself. In using the phrase "I'm still a woman," she implies she is unaffected by the death. She was a woman before he died, and she remains a woman after his death. The next line in the poem declares, "I'll always have plenty to do." This, too, is written in a somewhat angry, or defiant, tone. So what if he is gone and I cannot do the things we used to do together, the speaker seems to be saying. Buried beneath this phrase is also the declaration that the poet does not really mind that she had to stop writing—there are always other things to do, like laundry. However, immediately following these lines, the speaker takes on a different attitude.

While folding her husband's shirt, the speaker softens her tenor. As she brings the arms of the shirt together (a symbolic representation of bringing their two worlds together), she begins the process of building a bridge. In remembering his physical-ity—his arms around her, the feeling of his body close to hers—she begins to realize that even in death, he is not so far away. The memories of his touch are safely stored in her thoughts and on her skin. Upon this realization, she states, "Nothing can stop / our tenderness."

Immediately following this thought, Gallagher inserts the lines: "I'll get back / to the poem. I'll get back to being / a woman." In creating a link to her husband, the speaker suddenly understands that she can also create a link between her former self and the self she has become. She now senses that she can build a connection between the poet that she was before his death and the poet who is to come. Likewise, she comprehends that she can also create a link between the woman she was when Carver loved her and the woman she has become since his departure. In stating that she will "get back," she is saying that even if at that moment she has not quite figured out how to do it, somewhere deep inside of her, she feels it is possible.

Although the speaker realizes that she must find some way to connect the different aspects of herself, she remains focused on completing her chores. She is not yet capable of returning to her poem. Instead, she holds the shirt before her and notices how big it is. In contrast to the size of the shirt (as well as the size of the problem she is deal-ing with), she feels small. In the sense of her di-minished form, the speaker returns to her childhood. By doing so, crossing from the present moment of womanhood to that of the past, she completes

another step in the process of creating a new form for herself. Establishing a link between the pre-sent and the past is not as difficult for her as build-ing a bridge to the future. In her time of need, she easily crosses over to her youth to be comforted and guided by her mother. Although the image that Gallagher presents, that of a "small girl / standing next to her mother," the "watching" she does is not done through the eyes of the young child. The speaker looks at her mother through a newly achieved, heightened awareness of suffer-ing. The poem implies the speaker knows the mother has suffered, too. When she looks at her mother, she is watching to see how her mother created a bridge, how her mother found a way through the suffering, how her mother recreated herself.

In reading the poem in this way, it is easier to understand what Gallagher means about creating a new language, a new form, in order to meld what had been parted. She found a way to see the worlds of abstraction and concreteness, as well as the worlds of the living and the dead, as two aspects of one thing. Routine chores, such as doing the laundry, she decides, can inspire the poet in her as much as a meditation at dawn inspires her. A hus-band who has passed on to a spiritual state can still love and encourage her. If these worlds can be bridged, then Gallagher realizes through the poem that maybe all the worlds she once thought to be estranged can also come together. She does not have to give up either her writing or her definition of womanhood. The world of her past is intertwined with who she is now in the midst of her suffering, and who she will soon become.

Source: Joyce Hart, Critical Essay on "I Stop Writing the Poem," in *Poetry for Students*, The Gale Group, 2002.

Adrian Blevins

Blevins teaches writing courses at Roanoke College. In this essay, Blevins suggests that Gal-lagher's poem ultimately fails because Gallagher "does not sufficiently enhance her discursive statements with images and other figures of speech or with unexpected shifts in sentence type and syntax."

Poetry, like all forms of art, is so fully con-structed out of a marriage between content and form that it is impossible to talk about a poem's subject without investigating its technique. Tess Gallagher's "I Stop Writing the Poem" explores the conflict between domestic labor and literary work in discursive lines that are completely free of im-

> *The poem's lyric strategy of condensing language—of saying a good bit in a small artistic space—can be seen in its first lines."*

ages and other figures of speech. While the poem's content is interesting because it is shyly ironic, suggesting that the domestic work that is the poem's central action is a woman's "true" work while simultaneously suggesting that a woman poet's writing is also important and "true," the poem ultimately fails because it does not complicate or enrich its content with its form. In other words, because Gallagher does not sufficiently enhance her discursive statements with images and other figures of speech or with unexpected shifts in sentence type and syntax, she fails to make her poem as energetic—and therefore convincing—as it could be.

By saying that even a literary woman's work must include laundry and by subtlety celebrating domestic labor in lines that imply a sensual relationship between the speaker and the shirt she's folding, Gallagher explores old ideas about the division of labor in American households. "I Stop Writing the Poem" comes very close to suggesting that laundry is more important to a woman's emotional life than poetry, and therefore teeters on the edge of violating politically correct constructs about the kind of work women should do. Yet, because the poem is *a poem* (and not a folded shirt), "I Stop Writing the Poem" does suggest that it is appropriate for women to write. That a twelve-line poem could produce such ambiguity at the content level is impressive. Yet "I Stop Writing the Poem" pushes the boundaries of the flat, discursive line. The questions the poem forces readers to ask about the ways discursive statements in poetry risk both monotony and emotional barrenness if they are not countered with images and other figures of speech or with surprising shifts in sentence type and syntax systems ultimately reveals that complex content will never alone a poem make.

The poem's lyric strategy of condensing language—of saying a good bit in a small artistic

space—can be seen in its first lines. "I Stop Writing the Poem" begins when the speaker tells readers that she stops writing to fold clothes. In other words, by the time one has read the poem's title and its first line, one is immediately located in a central activity and conflict. Readers understand that the speaker is straddling two kinds of work, and, furthermore, that the domestic work of doing laundry seems to be taking precedence, for the time being, over the literary work of poem writing. The poem's second sentence—"No matter who lives / or who dies, I'm still a woman"—suggests that being a woman automatically involves "[folding] the clothes." But the poem's third sentence, "I'll always have plenty to do," obscures that idea by moving the poem's focus away from the particular work of laundry to the general idea of how busy women are. In other words, "I Stop Writing the Poem" very quickly moves readers from its title, which stops the action of writing, to three lines that locate the speaker in the act of folding clothes, to more general statements about what it means to be a woman. In this way, Gallagher reveals the effectiveness of lyric condensation.

When the poem returns to the action of laundry in "I bring the arms of his shirt / together," one finds the poem's emotional center. The personal pronoun "his" in this line is significant, since it reveals that the speaker is folding a man's shirt, rather than her own or a child's. If "I Stop Writing the Poem" can be said to have any emotional heat, it must be located here, in the way Gallagher *sensualizes* the folding of a man's shirt in "Nothing can stop / our tenderness." This line reveals an emotional motivation for the speaker's shirt folding, further complicating the idea of what it means to be a woman. Although the speaker is only folding a shirt, her feelings about the person who wears the shirt seep into the poem in her description of this action, suggesting that doing the laundry evokes "tenderness," if not love. This line also helps readers realize that it is not just laundry that compels the speaker to stop writing. It is, rather, the "giant shirt / in [her] hands," and, further, the man who wears it.

The poem's complexity becomes more apparent when it moves away from the speaker's shirt folding in the next sentence to statements that further complicate the speaker's stance about the work she is doing. The speaker says: "I'll get back / to the poem. I'll get back to being / a woman." The idea that being a woman *really* involves writing contradicts what the speaker says in her first two lines and thereby reveals the poem's irony: the speaker seems here to be suggesting that being a woman means both doing the laundry and writing. Thus, "I Stop Writing the Poem" straddles the fence between traditional notions of women's work and more contemporary attitudes.

Yet, if the poem has been in the act of exploring the conflict between the two kinds of labor that are demanding the speaker's attention, suggesting that both kinds of work are "suitable" for a woman, the poem chooses, "for now," the work of laundry, resting on the idea that the "tenderness" between the speaker's hands and the unnamed man's shirt is a kind of sensuality. The poem chooses to celebrate domestic work. That choice is reinforced in the poem's last sentence, which moves readers out of the speaker's particular act to an imagined scene in which "a small girl / [is] standing next to her mother / watching to see how it's done." This statement could suggest that girls learn how to do the laundry by watching their mothers do it, but because the pronoun "it" is grammatically ambiguous, the statement could also be suggesting that girls learn how to be women by watching their mothers do everything they do. Yet, because the speaker imagines a girl watching her mother do the laundry, rather than watching her write a poem, "I Stop Writing the Poem" does seem to favor domestic work over literary.

However, the poem's final irony is the poem itself. Although the poem itself chooses laundry over writing, the poem does get written, suggesting that the speaker did forsake laundry for writing at some point. It can be said that "I Stop Writing the Poem" ultimately straddles the conflict between a life in the domestic realm and a life of letters—celebrating the potential "tenderness" of domestic work in a speech act that is not domestic but literary. That the poem could commingle such opposing forms of work without choosing one over the other saves it from being overly agenda driven at the content level.

Despite its complexities at this level, "I Stop Writing the Poem" is technically barren, since it fails, in the end, to violate the pattern established by the discursive line with image and other figures of speech or sentence and syntax systems. The poem enjambs its title with its first line. This strategy helps the speaker express the poem's central conflict immediately and reveals that the poem is going to be constructed out of plain-style, discursive statements and hard enjambments. A generally enjambed lineation will increase a poem's

speed and power to surprise; certainly, there is excitement and suspense in lines that do not end at grammatically foreseeable places. To avoid the risk of monotony—an especially potential risk in discursive poems that do not rely on images—any pattern that is established in a poem will need to be violated or complicated in some way. The hard enjambments between the poem's title and first line and between the poem's first line and its second are countered by three end-stopped lines. These lines, since they violate the expected pattern of hard enjambment, take on special weight. Notice how much longer one rests on the end-stopped lines ending in "woman" and "do" than on lines like "I'll get back to being / a woman" and "But for now / there's a shirt." Gallagher's ability to counter her hard enjambments with strategically placed end-stopped lines does enrich her poem's rhythmical power.

It is odd, then, that Gallagher does not choose to vary her discursive strategy at all. The poem's discursive approach is established early on: the enjambed title and first line construct a basic statement—"I Stop Writing the Poem / to fold the clothes." This statement is followed up with seven very similar statements. "No matter who lives / or who dies" shares the tone and simple sentence structure of "I Stop Writing the Poem / to fold the clothes," which shares the tone and simple sentence structure of "I'll always have plenty to do." It is important to note—again—that there are no images or other figures of speech in these statements. The poem's final four lines, constructing the last sentence, is the only compound sentence in "I Stop Writing." So, while Gallagher juxtaposes end-stopped lines with enjambed lines in "I Stop Writing the Poem" and so avoids monotony at the end of the line, she fails to violate the discursive strategy with images and other figures of speech or different sentence and syntax systems. This oversight ultimately undermines the poem's power to convince and enlighten, since it drains the energy out of the poem's subject-level complexity by maiming the marriage between content and form.

"I Stop Writing the Poem" fails to persuade that choosing domestic work over literary work is a good idea because Gallagher was either unwilling or unable to use the many formal techniques available to her. If the speaker had chosen to keep writing rather than fold a shirt, maybe she would have found a way to make a complex statement about the nature of women's work aesthetically pleasing as well as rhetorically interesting.

Source: Adrian Blevins, Critical Essay on "I Stop Writing the Poem," in *Poetry for Students*, The Gale Group, 2002.

Sources

Bolick, Katie, "A Conversation with Tess Gallagher," in *The Atlantic Online*, http://www.theatlantic.com/unbound/factfict/gallaghe.htm (July 10, 1997; last accessed: March 19, 2002).

Flinn, Anthony, "A Poet Builds a Bridge over Her Gulf of Grief," in *Seattle Times*, July 5, 1992, p. L2.

Gallagher, Tess, *Soul Barnacles: Ten More Years with Ray*, edited by Greg Simon, University of Michigan Press, 2000, pp. 228–29.

Powell, Margaret K., Review of *Moon Crossing Bridge*, in *Library Journal*, March 15, 1992.

Review of *Moon Crossing Bridge*, in *Publishers Weekly*, Vol. 239, No. 8, February 10, 1992, p. 75.

Susskind, H., Review of *Moon Crossing Bridge*, in *Choice*, September 1992.

Further Reading

Cixous, Helene, *Three Steps on the Ladder of Writing*, Columbia University Press, 1994.
  This book is not light reading; however, it is refreshing material for anyone interested in developing their art of writing. Cixous, a playwright as well as a feminist theorist, does not present theories filled with academic jargon. She takes her thoughts and applies them to her own writing, giving other writers deeper insights into their own art.

Elgin, Suzette Haden, *Native Tongue*, Feminist Press, 2001.
  Elgin's science fiction thriller takes on the topic of the power of language. The setting is the twenty-second century, during which time women's legal rights have been repealed. Most of the female population are bred to become linguists and translators. In an attempt to win their freedom, they create a new language. This book won critical praise when first published in the 1980s.

Lewis, C. S., *A Grief Observed*, Harper, 2001.
  C. S. Lewis, the famed British author, fell in love late in life and later lost his wife to cancer. In this book, he discusses how humbling this experience was. This book is an excellent view from a male perspective on the loss of a loved one.

Richard-Allerdyce, Diane, *Anaïs Nin and the Remaking of Self: Gender, Modernism, and Narrative Identity*, Northern Illinois University Press, 1997.
  Richard-Allerdyce traces the development of Nin's theories of gender and the creative self through her experimental writing. Nin is considered one of the earliest women writers who tried to find a feminine language form.

Rinpoche, Sogyal, *The Tibetan Book of Living and Dying*, Harper, 1994.
  Offering a different understanding of death, Rinpoche has translated many of the Buddhist beliefs about life, death, and the hereafter. Also contained in this book is a survey of the concept of death as taught by all the other major religions.

Merlin Enthralled

Richard Wilbur
1956

"Merlin Enthralled" is from Richard Wilbur's 1956 poetry collection *Things of This World*, a book that was awarded both a Pulitzer Prize and a National Book Award. The poem offers a new look at the ancient legend of Merlin, the magician who served as counselor to the legendary King Arthur of England. The episode that Wilbur recounts is from the end of Merlin's life when he falls under a spell cast by Niniane, a sorceress who lulls him to sleep. In most versions, this story ends with Merlin trapped within a tree or cave or tomb where he slowly wastes away in an agonizing death, but, in Wilbur's poem, Merlin lies peacefully beside a lake, becoming one with nature as he dies.

Among this poem's noteworthy aspects is the way it modernizes a traditional story dating back almost a millennium. Arthur, Gawen, and the other knights, who have stood for centuries as figures of military force, are shown to be almost childlike when they cannot find Merlin, while the sorcerer himself seems to be released, rather than captured, by Niniane (the medieval sense of the word "enthrall" entailed holding one in slavery). Wilbur's use of formal elements of rhyme and meter links this work with centuries of poetic tradition, but he uses enough verbal flexibility to make this formal structure nearly inconspicuous. "Merlin Enthralled" is generally considered to be one of the best of Richard Wilbur's early poems, a standout in a career that has lasted for more than fifty years.

Richard Wilbur

Author Biography

Richard Purdy Wilbur was born March 1, 1921, in New York, New York, into a family of writers and artists. His mother's father and grandfather were newspaper editors, and Wilbur's father was a commercial artist in New York. When Wilbur entered Amherst College in 1938, he studied to become a newspaper editor himself, spending summers travelling the country in boxcars. In college, his writing was mostly prose, with a focus on essays and editorials. After graduation, he served in Europe during World War II, and his intimate experience with the horrors of war caused him to change his career goal, leading Wilbur to appreciate the subtleties of poetry. The idea that poetry is a way of making order out of a chaotic situation can be seen in his early postwar poems. His first book of poetry, *The Beautiful Changes and Other Poems*, was published in 1947, the same year that he received his master of arts degree from Harvard University in Cambridge, Massachusetts.

It took Wilbur just a short time to gain a reputation as a poet. Throughout the 1940s and 1950s, he won major literary prizes, establishing a pattern of recognition from his peers that has continued throughout his career as a writer. A small sampling of these honors include Guggen-

heim fellowships in 1952 and 1963, the Harriet Monroe Memorial Prize from *Poetry* magazine in 1948 and 1978, the Pulitzer Prize for poetry in 1957 and 1989, and a Gold Medal for Poetry from the American Academy and Institute of Arts and Letters in 1991.

In addition to his career as a poet and teacher, Wilbur has earned praise as a translator. His translations of the plays *Tartuffe* and *The Misanthrope*—both written by seventeenth-century French playwright Molière—were produced in 1955 and 1964, respectively, and have become standard translations of these plays when they are studied in English today. He has published other translations of plays by Molière as well as plays by Voltaire and Jean Racine and poetry by Charles Baudelaire. He has also written several children's books, including some that he himself illustrated.

In 1987, the Congress of the United States recognized Wilbur's long, distinguished career by appointing him poet laureate. After serving in that position for a year, he resumed writing and lecturing. His book of poetry, *Mayflies: New Poems and Translations*, was published in 2000. He lives in Cummington, Massachusetts.

Poem Text

In a while they rose and went out aimlessly riding,
Leaving their drained cups on the table round.
Merlin, Merlin, their hearts cried, where are you
    hiding?
In all the world was no unnatural sound.

Mystery watched them riding glade by glade;   5
They saw it darkle from under leafy brows;
But leaves were all its voice, and squirrels made
An alien fracas in the ancient boughs.

Once by a lake-edge something made them stop.
Yet what they found was the thumping of a frog,   10
Bugs skating on the shut water-top,
Some hairlike algae bleaching on a log.

Gawen thought for a moment that he heard
A whitehorn breathe *Niniane*. That Siren's daughter
Rose in a fort of dreams and spoke the word   15
Sleep, her voice like dark diving water;

And Merlin slept, who had imagined her
Of water-sounds and the deep unsoundable swell
A creature to bewitch a sorcerer,
And lay there now within her towering spell.   20

Slowly the shapes of searching men and horses
Escaped him as he dreamt on that high bed:
History died; he gathered in its forces;
The mists of time condensed in the still head

    25

Until his mind, as clear as mountain water,
Went raveling toward the deep transparent dream
Who bade him sleep. And then the Siren's
    daughter
Received him as the sea receives a stream.

Fate would be fated; dreams desire to sleep.
This the forsaken will not understand.   30
Arthur upon the road began to weep
And said to Gawen *Remember when this hand*

Once haled a sword from stone; now no less strong
It cannot dream of such a thing to do.
Their mail grew quainter as they clopped along.   35
The sky became a still and woven blue.

Media Adaptations

- "Merlin Enthralled" is included on the 1969 Caedmon record album *Richard Wilbur Reading His Poetry*. It was also published by Harper-Collins in audiocassette format.

Poem Summary

Lines 1–4

At the start of "Merlin Enthralled," the knights of the Round Table are already aware of Merlin's disappearance. The first few words, "after a while," indicate that they have waited for some word of him or for someone to lead them into action. The fact that they have no clue about where to begin looking is made clear in the first line, which specifies that they are "aimlessly riding." The reference to their "drained cups" shows that the knights have held off their search until their drinks were finished. In line four, the lack of any "unnatural sound" presents readers with a paradox. If "unnatural" is taken to be a bad or threatening thing, the sort of mischief an evil sorcerer might perpetrate, then its lack is a good thing, but if Merlin himself is considered something different than nature, then the lack of unnatural sound might indicate that he is dead.

Lines 5–8

In line five "mystery" is personified. The word is usually used to describe a mood, but Wilbur gives it human characteristics. It watches the way a person would watch, and it "darkle[s]," which is the action of making things dark or mysterious. In line seven "mystery" is said to have a voice, which is the sound of the wind through the leaves. Line eight describes the squirrels as making an "alien" sound as they chase each other. They are contrasted with the "ancient" trees that are solid, still, and steady.

Lines 9–12

The third stanza refers back to the distorted reality frequently implied throughout the poem. Wilbur does not describe for readers what it is that might have made the knights stop, or what they felt that made them suspect that Merlin might be near the edge of the lake. Instead, the poem describes this feeling in line nine with the vague word "something." Stopping and being still for once, the knights pay attention to the small things of nature that they might ordinarily be too busy to notice, such as frogs and insects. Line eleven describes the bugs skating on top of the water and states that the top of the water is "shut," as though nothing could penetrate it. In line twelve, the sun is described as hot enough to dry out algae on a log.

Lines 13–16

Niniane is revealed in the fourth stanza. As with other aspects of the poem, her presence is implied rather than directly explained. The knights do not directly encounter Niniane, nor are they told that she is behind Merlin's disappearance. Instead, one knight, Gawen, *thinks* that he hears a white-horn deer say her name, but he is not sure. Wilbur goes on to directly explain Niniane's actions, leaving a question about whether the details in stanzas four and five represent what really happened or if they are just what Gawen imagines.

Lines 17–20

This stanza expresses Niniane's complete control over Merlin. In line nineteen, Wilbur states that Merlin has been "bewitched" by Niniane. There is some indication he is under the power of a more potent magician than himself, particularly in line twenty. Line eighteen plays off two definitions of the word "sound": the first is the common use of the term to refer to things that can be heard audibly, while the second hints at the old English word "sund," meaning "to swim," which is interpreted in modern language as a "sound" referring to an inlet of water.

Lines 21–24

The sixth stanza shows Merlin slowly losing consciousness of the world around him. In the first two lines of this stanza, death is presented physically. Shapes "escape" from him as if they are moving away from him, when actually his mind is moving away from reality. In the second two lines, death is presented in terms of time. As Merlin dies, history dies, taking him with it. Line twenty-four explains death as a gathering of "the mists of time," joining the physical metaphor—time as a mist that becomes increasingly solid—to the temporal metaphor of time's end as death.

Lines 25–28

This stanza joins together Merlin's thoughts with the thoughts Niniane wants him to think, and it also introduces the symbolism of water. Line twenty-five uses "mountain water" to express how clear his thoughts are when he gives in to the sorceress's spell. The verb "raveling" in line twenty-six is a unique one in that its meanings include opposite definitions: it can mean "to become entangled or confused," but it can also mean "to untangle." Here Wilbur uses it in a deliberately unclear context so that either definition may apply. Calling the dream "deep" and "transparent" in line twenty-six draws a relationship between dreaming and water. This relationship is punctuated in line twenty-eight, in which the relationship between Merlin and Niniane is metaphorically compared to that of a river to the sea. The break between lines twenty-six and twenty-seven draws attention to the unusual time sequence. A dream usually does not exist until one is asleep, and so it could not have called out to Merlin ("bade" him) to sleep, except in the strange mix between reality and magic that Wilbur has created in this poem.

Lines 29–32

Line twenty-nine presents two ideas that challenge the reader's sense of reality: fate (an abstract concept itself) is said to wish fate, and dreams (a product of sleep) are said to wish sleep for themselves. The poem uses complex language. In line thirty, the word "forsaken" implies that these impossible situations make sense to those, like Merlin, who have not been abandoned. In doing so, it turns readers' sympathies around. Merlin, who may have once seemed victimized by Niniane, seems fortunate to be joined with her, while Arthur, the powerful king, seems helpless and confused. This stanza ends with Arthur mentioning his hand, drawing attention to his physical power as well as his power as the reigning king.

Lines 33–36

The word "hale," used in line thirty-three, means both physical might and also, in old English, to pull or drag. The reference here is to the legend of Arthur pulling the sword Excalibur out of a stone when no one else could, proving himself the person fit to rule England as its king. Arthur points out that although he has lost none of the physical strength he had when he performed that feat in his youth, he still could not do it now. Mentioning Arthur's sadness and his realization that his power is gone in such close proximity to the death of Merlin shows readers that Arthur senses Merlin has gone from the world, even though he has not seen him die. The "woven" blue of the sky at the end of the poem refers to the ancient tapestries that would be woven with scenes from the Arthurian legends.

Themes

Mortality

This poem deals with the death of Merlin, the legendary sorcerer from the court of King Arthur. Because Merlin was known for his magical powers, it is a bit of a surprise that he could die at all. More surprising than that is the fact that he dies willingly, accepting death as a release from his responsibilities.

Merlin's death is represented here as a form of sleep, as mentioned in stanzas five and seven. The poem does not explicitly say that he dies, but it is implied in the way that the magician's consciousness slips away from him. The shapes of the searching men "escape" him as he loses awareness of the world. At the same time, "the mists of time condensed in the still head," implying with his motionlessness and with the stopping of time that this is not a sleep from which he will ever emerge. The most definitive clue that Merlin is dead comes from the reaction of his comrades—especially King Arthur, who apparently senses the loss of the magic that once enabled him to pull Excalibur from the stone in which it was embedded.

The fact that Merlin goes willingly to his death can be inferred from the poem's references to Niniane as the siren's daughter who has bewitched him. Readers might interpret this to mean that Merlin has been tricked into accepting death, but, whether his infatuation with Niniane is natural or unnatural, he still dies peacefully. When line thirty says "this the forsaken will not understand," it implies that

Merlin, who has been accepted by Niniane (and is therefore not one of the forsaken), has knowledge that makes his death acceptable to him, even though readers and his peers in the poem might find it something against which to fight.

Mourning

Because of the magical nature of the events related in this poem, Merlin's friends do not react to his death the way that they might in real life. This is established from the start when the knights rise up from the Round Table and go looking for Merlin. No explanation is given for why they did not move earlier or why they suddenly know it is the right time to act. Readers are presented with a magical, intuitive relationship between Merlin and the knights. The knights' concern is evident in the third line when they "cried" his name, as if these knights who are masters of their world are panicked when they think of losing him. Riding out through the forest to find him, they are hypersensitive to the sounds and motions around them, which gives another clue to just how frightened they are at the thought of losing him.

Of all of Merlin's associates, though, it is King Arthur who mourns Merlin most intensely and most directly. Merlin was Arthur's guardian all his life, taking him away into hiding soon after his birth and then returning him to rule Britain when the time was right. When Merlin dies, Arthur does not see any evidence of his death, yet still he stops riding to weep. Like the others, he senses the loss of his friend and mentor. Telling Gawen that his hand is still as strong as it was long ago but that he would not now be able to pull the sword from the stone is his admission that the loss of Merlin's magic has left him vulnerable. The fact that their armor became "quainter," or more old-fashioned, as they rode along, gives an added dimension to the knights' mourning, indicating that Merlin's death has made them somewhat self-conscious of their own eventual deaths.

Motion

Wilbur connects the concepts of time and motion, saying time and history come to an end as Merlin stops moving. It begins with meaningless action—aimless wandering—which follows after the passage of an indefinite "while." As the knights ride through the forest, they are aware of the slightest motions, such as the actions of frog or bugs, to such an extent that when squirrels chase each other, it is described as an "alien fracas." The exact moment of Merlin's death is presented as a conden-

Topics for Further Study

- Just a few years after "Merlin Enthralled" was first published, the administration of President John Kennedy came to be called "Camelot" after the court of King Arthur. Research Kennedy's presidency and identify the similarities to Arthur's Round Table.

- Modern tales of sorcery, most notably J. R. R. Tolkien's *Lord of the Rings* novels and J. K. Rowling's books about the young wizard named Harry Potter, use ideas about magic that derive from Arthurian legend. Read one of these books and note which ideas about magic might have come from the centuries-old stories about Merlin.

- What kind of music might the siren's daughter have used to enchant Merlin? Research and write an essay on the instruments of the Middle Ages and the sort of songs that might have been played on them.

- Find a source that gives a different account of Merlin's death than that in "Merlin Enthralled." Write a paper that briefly describes the other version and then explain which version you think is more likely and why.

- If you have ever had an older mentor who disappeared from your life suddenly, the way that Merlin disappears from Arthur's, write an essay or poem about him or her, the cause of his or her disappearance from your life, and how his or her disappearance affected you.

- Merlin is lulled to sleep beside a lake where he goes unnoticed by the people looking for him. Take a camera to a nearby body of water and bring back a picture of a place you think might have been the sort of spot where Merlin would have died. Explain the picture to your classmates.

sation of the "mists of time" as they change from a drifting vapor to a motionless solid. In the poem's final line, as the scene of King Arthur and his knights freezes like an old picture on a tapestry, the sky itself becomes "still" and "woven," indicating that this moment is stopped forever, while at the same time it has become part of the rich and complex weave of history.

Delusion

Much of the action in this poem depends upon the power of sorcery to delude people, just as much of the poetic effect depends upon keeping readers uncertain of the difference between delusion and reality. The knights set out on their quest with the impression that Merlin is hiding from them. In their search, "something" makes them stop. Although they cannot see him, they have a feeling they have found Merlin, and since he is able to see them, it is clear that Niniane's sorcery has hidden him from their view. At that point, Gawen has a feeling of Niniane's involvement in the disappearance of Merlin, a feeling that seems to come from a whitehorn deer. The poem does not specify whether Gawen's suspicion is real or delusional.

The poem is just as vague about how much of Merlin's experience is a delusion. He feels that he is sleeping, that Niniane is just a figment of his imagination, and that he is dreaming that she is "receiving" him as the vision of his friends in the real world slip away. These impressions are of course what she would want to bewitch him into believing. A good case can be made for interpreting this as her way of making Merlin cooperate as she lures him to his death.

Style

Quatrain

A quatrain is a stanza of a poem that is written with four lines. Usually these lines will have a similar number of syllables, giving the poem an even look and a well-rounded feel when it is recited. It is the most common and most recognizable form of English poetry, allowing poets to use symmetrical rhyme schemes of AABB or ABAB. For a poem like "Merlin Enthralled," the quatrain allows for short stanzas that lend themselves to quick and frequent changes of scene and point of view. Even though the focus of the poem changes frequently, these transitions are smoothed over by the fact that the traditional quatrain structure is familiar to most readers. In addition, its geometric density gives readers a sense of stability that might have been lost by the poem's uneven, mysterious sense of what is real and what is illusion.

Rhyme

Rhyming poems use words that sound either identical or at least very similar in parallel positions, usually at the ends of lines. "Merlin Enthralled" has a strict rhyme scheme from which it never diverts: the last words of every first and third line in each stanza rhyme, as do the last words of every second and fourth line. In the majority of cases, rhymes are simple, with single-syllable words that sound alike matched together, such as "frog" and "log" or "swell" and "spell," although there are also cases, like "riding" and "hiding" and "horses" and "forces," in which both syllables of two-syllable words sound alike. The furthest deviations from this strict rhyme scheme occur when the poem uses multisyllabic words that only rhyme on the last syllable. He does this in the fifth stanza, rhyming "imagined her" with "sorcerer," and in the eighth stanza, where "understand" is rhymed with "when this hand."

The use of a strict rhyme scheme is unusual in twentieth-century poetry, a time when most acclaimed poets produced work in free verse (poetry that does not use rhymes) or used rhyme more freely, allowing similarities in a few sounds in the two rhyming words to stand for a loose but acceptable rhyme. One criticism of strict rhyme is that it limits the words, and by extension the meanings, a poet can choose from in specific places in their poems. In the case of "Merlin Enthralled," though, the strict rhyme scheme resembles the structures of traditional verses. Since Wilbur's theme is traditional, this similarity seems appropriate.

In Medias Res

In Medias Res is a Latin term meaning "in the middle of things." It refers to artistic works that, like "Merlin Enthralled," begin mid-action, when the story being told has already begun for the characters. Such works often use flashbacks to bring readers up-to-date with what has happened in the story so far. Wilbur, however, focuses on the action at hand, leaving unanswered the questions of how the knights of the Round Table knew that Merlin had disappeared and why they waited to begin searching for him. These questions are never fully answered, although the style that the rest of the poem takes hints at part of the explanation. Much that these knights do is intuitive, such as stopping at the side of the lake, Gawen believing he hears Niniane's name, and Arthur understanding as he rides along the road that he has lost the magical power of his friend and ally. Readers can reasonably believe the knights might subconsciously understand what they have to do, even if they do not have a particular reason for jumping up from the table at that particular time. If this explanation is satisfactory enough to keep readers from dwelling on the missing pieces, then the poem works. What the poem gains from beginning *in medias res* is that it makes its readers feel as though they are joining a longer work already in progress, reminding them that it is just a small moment in the overall legend of Camelot.

Point of View

Point of view refers to the consciousness from which a story is being told. Often the point of view of a literary work will be that of one of the characters involved in the action, although authors sometimes use an "omniscient" point of view, which can give information known to none of the characters. The point of view for "Merlin Enthralled" shifts freely and in some cases is unidentifiable.

Often a poem's point of view is assumed to be that of the person or persons being discussed at the time. For instance, it is probably the knights of the Round Table who believe that "in all the world was no unnatural sound" and that the squirrels in the trees made "an alien fracas," although the knights themselves might not have phrased their experiences with those words. The fifth stanza describes Merlin but uses the phrase "a creature to bewitch a sorcerer" to describe Niniane: although the focus of this stanza is on Merlin, this particular phrase is probably not from Merlin's point of view but is instead the poem's narrator commenting directly on Niniane. The seventh and eighth stanzas clearly present the situation from Merlin's point of view, raising the possibility that he sees the situation unclearly because Niniane has a spell on him, that his death is not as calm and liberating as he might think it is.

The first two lines of stanza eight and the last two of stanza nine give an omniscient view of the characters from philosophical and historical perspectives. These lines are interrupted by a brief but powerful direct quote from King Arthur, who understands that Merlin has died as well as the significance of his death.

Historical Context

Arthurian Legend

There is no accurate historical record clearly pointing to the "King Arthur" described in the leg-

ends of Camelot. Legends about a ruler named "Arthwyr" circulated around the British Isles beginning in the sixth century, but at that time there were dozens of kingdoms in what is now known as England, and, with no written records, it is difficult to verify any relationship between historical figures and the Arthur of legend. The matter is further complicated by the supernatural elements concerning sorcery that the legend has accumulated over the centuries, raising doubts about any claim of authenticity.

Of the various claims to a historically accurate King Arthur, the one that has had the most influence is that of Geoffrey of Monmouth (c. 1100–1154). At a time when little was known about English history, Geoffrey published a text in 1136 called *History of the Kings of England*, which traces the country's ruling government from 1100 B.C. to 689 A.D., giving England a legitimate background to match those of the Roman and Greek empires. It is difficult to tell where reality and Geoffrey's version of reality part company. The Arthurian legends, as they are discussed today—with Arthur, Merlin, Niniane, the Round Table, and the Quest for the Holy Grail—are mostly based on Geoffrey's version of stories that had existed for at least five hundred years.

History of the Kings of England identifies the legendary Arthur as the son of Uther Pendragon, saying he was born to Ygerna, the wife of Gorlois, the Duke of Cornwall. In Geoffrey's version, there was tension between Uther and Gorlois after Uther showed interest in Ygerna. Gorlois sealed his castle against an attack, but Merlin cast a magic spell that made Uther look like Gorlois, gaining him entry into the castle and into Ygerna's bed. When Arthur was born, Merlin took the infant into hiding.

Merlin was a more recent addition to the oral legends of King Arthur, with records of him tracing only to the tenth century. He was called "Myrddin" in earlier accounts, but Geoffrey of Monmouth is said to have changed the spelling of his name because he thought the traditional form sounded too much like the French word *merde*, meaning excrement. In Geoffrey's history, Merlin not only arranged for the young king's birth but also for the competition which gained him the throne. After Uther's death, it was decided that the one who could pull an enchanted sword out of a stone was the one destined to rule England, a challenge which Merlin made sure Arthur would win.

As with all aspects of the legend, there are different accounts of how Merlin met his end. The

Compare & Contrast

- **500s:** Britain is fractured by competing king-doms and beset by Saxon invaders. Britain's rulers briefly unite to drive back the Saxons, but the island is ultimately overrun and settled by the foreigners.

  1950s: Britain is considered a venerable, estab-lished civilization. Americans consider it the "old world," with dated political practices such as colonies and a monarchy.

  Today: The last of the British colonies in Africa received its independence in the 1960s, and the British Royal Family has only symbolic power.

- **500s:** The identity of the actual King Arthur, if there was one at all, is unclear because written records are scarce and communication between different countries is almost nonexistent.

  1950s: Television increases in popularity through-out the decade, allowing politicians to communi-cate directly with the general population.

  Today: Politicians still speak directly to the public via television, but educated viewers are wary of image manipulation.

- **500s:** International conflicts are fought with swords and maces; legend tells of magical pow-ers wielded by magicians such as Merlin and Niniane.

  1950s: After the decimation of Hiroshima and Nagasaki in Japan at the end of World War II, people across the world lived in fear of the de-structive power of atomic bombs and hydrogen bombs.

  Today: Nuclear bombs are many times more powerful than they were when they first were developed, but they are not used in conflict. Mil-itary reliance is on improvements in fighter jets, submarines, tanks, artillery, intelligence, and stratagem.

---

woman referred to as Niniane in "Merlin En-thralled" has also been known as Nineve, Nimue, Nyneve, or simply as "the Lady of the Lake," al-though in most stories she is just one of several to hold this position. In Geoffrey's history, Mer-lin accompanies a wounded Arthur at the end of his life to Avalon, the mystic isle. Other versions of the story, closer to Wilbur's, say that Merlin fell in love with Niniane and taught her the se-crets of magic, whereupon she enslaved him, al-ternately, in a glass tower, a cave, a tree, or the tomb of two lovers. Different sources view her morality differently. In *Estoire de Merlin*, a me-dieval French vulgate text, she loves Merlin so much she seals him in a tower to keep him to her-self. Sir Thomas Malory's 1485 text *Le Morte d'Arthur* has her aiding Arthur several times af-ter she imprisons Merlin. At the other extreme, the nineteenth-century poet Alfred, Lord Ten-nyson, who wrote extensively about the legends of King Arthur, presented Naniane as an evil and malicious witch.

The 1950s

In 1956, when Wilbur first published this poem, the American political scene was characterized by a notable lack of dynamic or inspiring leaders. That year, Dwight Eisenhower, a sixty-six-year-old for-mer general who made his reputation by com-manding the Allied forces during World War II, was reelected to the presidency for a second term, despite failing health. Although Eisenhower was personally popular, the officials serving under him were generally bland, anonymous bureaucrats. In particular, Eisenhower's vice president, Richard Nixon, seemed to represent the mood of the time: a capable functionary with a brilliance for interna-tional diplomacy, Nixon was widely disliked and distrusted by many of the American people (he was later elected to the presidency and forced to resign under a cloud of scandal). At the time, the central political issue was the rivalry between the United States and the Soviet Union. Each of these super-powers monitored the other's support among coun-tries around the world, carefully watching the balance of power in a conflict that came to be called "the Cold War" ("cold" because, despite the tensions and the stakes involved, there was no direct fighting between the two sides).

The government was an active force in everyday life, investigating citizens who were thought to be sympathetic to communists. Television, in the mean time, had reached its second phase of development. After the end of the war in 1945, television quickly became a widespread consumer product, and broadcasters, unprepared for its immense popularity, scheduled shows that were little more than filmed stage acts. By the late 1950s, though, networks were developing original programming, and they found that original fantasy and adventure shows were perfect for the medium. Shows about legendary characters like the Lone Ranger and Tarzan and Robin Hood suited television's half-hour, segmented format, and these shows in turn affected public tastes. When "Merlin Enthralled" was published, the country was ready for a heroic figure.

A few years later, in 1960, Robert F. Kennedy was elected to the presidency, defeating Nixon. Young, handsome, and married to a smart and fashionable wife, Kennedy provided the country with a new identity. That year the musical *Camelot* opened on Broadway and political commentators quickly compared King Arthur's Round Table to Kennedy's administration. To this day, "Camelot" is used in American journalism to refer to the Kennedy administration as often as it is to refer to the rule of Arthur.

Critical Overview

Critics have had opposing views about Richard Wilbur's poetry since the start of his career, mostly disagreeing about the success of his style. Other poets who appeared in the 1940s and 1950s flaunted tradition and tried to impress readers with originality. Wilbur, on the other hand, always worked within conventional forms. Even the critics who found his work sterile and thought that he sacrificed meaning for the sake of style commended his work for its craftsmanship. As John B. Hougen explains it in his book *Ecstasy Within Discipline: The Poetry of Richard Wilbur*: "It is no doubt Wilbur's reliance on traditional poetic forms in an era when they were out of fashion that muted the praise of his work in some quarters and in others gave rise to blatantly negative criticism." The critics who found Wilbur's work too stiff and for-

Merlin reading

mal did not see that his experiments within formality were just as daring as those by poets who flaunted formal rules.

One review from 1956, written by Horace Gregory, praises Wilbur's talent while at the same time represents him as a writer of his time. In "The Poetry of Suburbia" published in *Partisan Review*, Gregory identifies Wilbur's place among other contemporary poets but says that, like many of them, he has nothing very new to offer the world. He compares Wilbur's poetry to the kind of "magazine verse" that was published in the *New Yorker* forty years earlier: light, witty verse that was popular in the growing suburbs precisely because it was so insubstantial. He compares particular poems from *Things of the World* to forgotten works by T. S. Eliot and Phelps Putnam, noting that, "In contrast to Putnam's, Wilbur's poem is overdressed and a shade pretentious—and his phrase, 'God keep me a damned fool,' rings false, false because Wilbur seems so expert at contriving certain of his lines."

Even though some critics find Wilbur to be a poet with limited imagination, he has always had ardent supporters among critics and fellow poets. The book in which "Merlin Enthralled" was published, *Things of the World*, won both a Pulitzer Prize and a National Book Award for the year it was published, just a few of the dozens of awards

> *Wilbur draws an association between love and time that goes beyond any consideration of who has what power of enchantment over whom, and highlights the power that human affection has to make the world start and stop."*

presented to Wilbur throughout his long career. He is such an influential writer that a book-length study of his poetry was published in 1967, just twenty years after the publication of Wilbur's first collection. In his book *Richard Wilbur*, Donald L. Hill analyzes "Merlin Enthralled," finding it to be "beyond a doubt one of his finest poems." Lauding it for being able to say things often left unsaid, Hill concludes his analysis by noting that "there is a spaciousness about the poem, a fullness of expression and a harmony among the parts, that are the marks of a masterpiece." While Hill is generally favorable to Wilbur's work, such ardent praise for an individual piece is rare.

Over the years, Wilbur became established as one of America's most accomplished poets and one of the most reliable. The old controversy about his formal style masking a lack of spirit faded as critics accepted him on his own terms. By the time his *New and Collected Poems* was published in 1989, several of Wilbur's translations of French dramas had been performed on Broadway and had become standard English-language versions; he had published over twenty books of poetry, children's verse, and literary criticism; and he had served as the poet laureate of the United States.

Criticism

David Kelly

Kelly is an instructor of creative writing and literature at Oakton Community College. In this

essay, Kelly examines "Merlin Enthralled" as an independent work which can be understood and appreciated with little knowledge of Arthurian legend.

Arthurian legend is so old that there is no way of verifying the truth of any of it. It would be silly for a literary critic to say that one author is lying or mistaken because his or her version of the story does not match a version that some other author previously made up. In his poem "Merlin Enthralled," Richard Wilbur tells a story that has often been told over the last thousand years or so. It may help readers somewhat to understand how Wilbur's version relates to other versions—to the original source recorded in the twelfth century by Geoffrey of Monmouth, or Alfred, Lord Tennyson's version, or Edgar Arlington Robinson's version—but such a literary exploration would probably do as much to confuse the issue as it does to clarify it. Naturally, the subsequent versions are different from one another, and the various authors knew what their predecessors had to say, and they built upon the past. What seems even more interesting is to see how Wilbur's poem can stand by itself, without reference to the past. This is, at heart, a story about love and sacrifice, regardless of what the ancient Saxons or the historians who study them might think. It can be used as a lesson in social history, but Wilbur's style is more focused on the psychology of mid-twentieth century America.

"Merlin Enthralled" has three main characters: Arthur, Gawen, and Merlin. A fourth, Niniane, is mentioned, but the closest she comes to actually appearing in the poem is when it is pointed out that she "receives" Merlin—a verb that has no specific action associated with it, making her presence indistinct. Of the three characters, it is Merlin, the one named in the poem's title, who has the least to do here. He just wants to lie down and go to sleep in his lady's arms, or at least her good graces. Arthur has the most touching observation of the poem when he finally speaks at the end. It could almost be said that this poem is told from the point of view of Gawen, a knight who shows no particular characteristics beyond the fact that he is an observer.

To some degree, Gawen's lack of personality can be seen as the very point the poem is making. He does not function as an individual here, but rather as a representative of the entire assembly of knights of the Round Table. Wilbur could easily have said "one of the knights" in place of Gawen's name, with little change in the overall effect. The

What Do I Read Next?

- This poem, originally from the 1956 collection *Things of This World*, is included in Richard Wilbur's *New and Collected Poems*, published by Harcourt Brace Jovanovich in 1988.

- The story of Merlin's life, from childhood to death, is the subject of a series by popular novelist Mary Stewart: *The Crystal Cave* (1970), *The Hollow Hills* (1973), *The Last Enchantment* (1979), and *The Wicked Day* (1983).

- Alfred, Lord Tennyson wrote several books of poetry about the legends of King Arthur, including the book-length poem *Idylls of the King*. This 1885 book includes "Merlin and Vivien," a version of the story told in "Merlin Enthralled."

- One of the most readable recent versions of the Arthurian legend was written by author John Steinbeck, who based his book *The Acts of King Arthur and His Noble Knights* (1976) on the writings of fifteenth-century English scholar Sir Thomas Malory.

- Over the course of his long career, Wilbur has given dozens of interviews. Many can be found on the Internet. Some of the best were collected by William Butts in the 1990 book *Conversations with Richard Wilbur*, published by the University of Mississippi Press.

- If Richard Wilbur were not a poet, he would still be known for his work as a translator, especially for his translations of the comedies of seventeenth-century French playwright Molière. His translations of Molière's plays *The Misanthrope* and *Tartuffe* were done in the 1960s and published in one volume in 1991 by Harvest Books.

- Another fascinating achievement in translation is Wilbur's 1980 translation of the collection *A Part of Speech* by Pulitzer Prize–winning Russian poet Joseph Brodsky.

- Geoffrey of Monmouth's 1136 history has been published in a 1981 Penguin edition titled *The History of the Kings of Britain*, which includes a comprehensive introduction and notes. Monmouth's book provides one of the first written histories of both King Arthur and Merlin, though scholarly opinion holds that Monmouth's work is largely fiction.

- Thomas Malory's *Le Morte d'Arthur*, first published in 1485, is one of the most popular sources for tales of the Arthur legend. It has been published in many different editions, including an illustrated hardback edition published in 2000.

---

only difference is that poetry is stronger when it is specific rather than vague, and so the use of a particular name helps establish the reality of the world in which these characters live.

It does not matter whether the character called Gawen here speaks for one or many; what does matter is that this poem is about observers, not participants. In this way it is solidly a twentieth century, postmodern work, as concerned with the fact that someone is there to witness the story as it is with the story itself. To add to this, the historical associations Gawen has might add some nuances, but it would also add complications that would obscure Wilbur's view of the world.

The knights—and Gawen, of course—stand in for the readers of the poem. It starts with them leaving the comforts of their chambers but not so abruptly that they would leave their drinks half-finished. They are plunged into a new situation, aimlessly searching, not seeing what is in front of them but only what is not: Merlin. Like the readers, the knights settle into this new situation after a short time—a stanza or two—and start to understand the world in which they find themselves. It is a world of mystery, a world where the things of nature live their lives generally unnoticed. In short, this poem is doing what most nature poetry does—drawing readers' attention to the world that they regularly take for granted.

After a short while as a nature poem, "Merlin Enthralled" shifts its focus, becoming a love poem. Again it is not important to know the precedents for the Merlin/Niniane affair so much as it is important to read the clues Wilbur gives and to understand what he has to say about love. Merlin may submit to a spell that has been cast upon him because Niniane is powerful enough to make him love her, or he may allow himself to fall under her power because of his natural love. With love, it is always difficult to distinguish just how voluntary enthrallment is. Wilbur *could* have been more clear on this point if he had wanted to be. For instance, if Niniane were called a "siren," it would be likely that she means to lure Merlin to his destruction, but the poem specifically refers to her twice as a "Siren's daughter." Readers are left to figure out for themselves whether the daughter of a siren would be more or less reckless and mischievous than a real siren. Merlin's apparent happiness about being "received" by Niniane smacks equally of sorcery and love.

Unclear about the cause of love, of whether it is freedom or manipulation, the poem is in fact fairly direct in showing love's results. This enchantment takes Merlin away from his friends. Unlike other versions of this story, "Merlin Enthralled" does not specify whether Merlin is murdered or just forever hidden away somewhere in a deep sleep. These each have their symbolic significance, but none applies here. What is important here is that enchantment, or love, might leave Merlin contented with his fate, but it leaves his comrades feeling abandoned.

This is a point made most directly at the end, when King Arthur, sensing that Merlin has left for good, knows he no longer has access to the magic that gave him the power to pull Excalibur from its stone, establishing his right to the throne of England. In a literal sense, Arthur is right: no Merlin equals no magic, leaving Arthur and his knights on their own to cope as humans. As in the rest of the poem, however, Wilbur is not concerned here with the natural limits of magic so much as with the emotional story behind what transpires. There is no hint that Arthur, having reigned for years at that point, would be left vulnerable by the loss of Merlin. It is sadness, not fear, that weighs upon Arthur in the end.

All of this can be explained in psychological, non-magical, terms: Merlin's submission to Niniane, the knights' panic about losing an important court figure, their discovery of the complexities of nature once they actually look at the world, and

Arthur's sorrow over losing a close friend and advisor. The magical part of the poem is poetic, not supernatural, magic. Wilbur draws an association between love and time that goes beyond any consideration of who has what power of enchantment over whom, and highlights the power that human affection has to make the world start and stop.

Time stops for Merlin, just as time starts for the knights at the moment that they lose him. Amid all of the motion and commotion of the search, the darkling leaves and the fracas of nature going about its business, he lies silent and still, and "the mists of time condensed in the still head." Though this figure of speech strongly implies death, it does not explicitly say it; it only says that motion ceased. Regardless of what Merlin's fate might be, it is outside of the bonds of time as far as the knights are concerned, and, by extension, as far as readers are concerned. While Wilbur uses the condensation of the mists of time to signify Merlin's disappearance, though, he also uses the passage of time to mark how his disappearance affects those who care for him. They become relics almost immediately: their armor becomes "quainter" and the sky above them turns into the sort of woven tapestry that modern readers associate with medieval stories. The implication here is that love takes one outside of time, as it does for Merlin when he joins Niniane, and also that the lack of love, which Arthur and Gawen and the rest of the knights feel upon the loss of their friend, can make one old and worn, on the way to quick obsolescence.

It can be quite tempting to take a poem like "Merlin Enthralled" and see how it compares to other versions of the Merlin story, but this is a thoroughly modern work that has much to say even without outside references. The story is as magical as it has ever been, but Wilbur's version relies mostly on the magic of human interaction. The story here is not about the enchantment of magical spells but about the enchantment of lovers and friends and the ways in which that basic human function affects people as time goes by.

Source: David Kelly, Critical Essay on "Merlin Enthralled" in *Poetry for Students*, The Gale Group, 2002.

Sources

Gregory, Horace, "The Poetry of Suburbia," in *Partisan Review*, Fall 1956, pp. 545–53.

Harris, Peter, "Forty Years of Richard Wilbur: The Loving Work of an Equilibrist," in *Virginia Quarterly Review*, Summer 1990, pp. 412–25.

Hecht, Anthony, Review of *New and Selected Poems*, in *New Republic*, May 16, 1988, pp. 23–32.

Hill, Donald L., *Richard Wilbur*, Twayne Publishers, 1967, pp. 118–20.

Hougen, John B., *Ecstasy Within Discipline: The Poetry of Richard Wilbur*, Scholars Press, 1995, pp. 3–23.

Further Reading

Goodrich, Norma Lorre, *King Arthur*, Franklin Watts, 1986.
   King Arthur offers an in-depth scholarly look at the Arthurian legends with the intention of separating reality from myth.

Littleton, C. Scott, and Linda A. Malcor, *From Scythia to Camelot: A Radical Reassessment of the Legends of King Arthur, the Knights of the Round Table, and the Holy Grail*, Garland Publishers, 2000.
   This book traces Arthurian legends beyond British history to Russian and Ukranian roots and serves as a fascinating example of folklore detection.

Scott, Nathan A., *Visions of Presence in Modern American Poetry*, Johns Hopkins University Press, 1993.
   Scott looks at the sense of "reality" in the poetry of several contemporary poets, including Wilbur, in order to refute the theory that poetry is a thing of words unconnected to an objective world experience.

Snyder, Christopher A., *An Age of Tyrants: Britain and the Britons, A.D. 400–600*, Pennsylvania State University Press, 1998.
   Snyder presents serious and direct historical exploration of the time when Arthur was supposed to have lived, as well as an appendix linking Arthurian legend to the known facts.

Much Madness Is Divinest Sense

Emily Dickinson

1890

The date that "Much Madness Is Divinest Sense" was written has been guessed as 1862, but nobody knows for sure because the poem was not published until almost thirty years later, in 1890, after Dickinson's death. Her poetry was first introduced to the public through the efforts of friends and relatives who discovered her poems, corrected her punctuation, designated titles, and modified some of Dickinson's meanings so as not to offend her audience. It was more than forty years before her original poems were handed over to the United States Library of Congress, where they were thoroughly examined and Dickinson's original versions were restored. The only editing that was done for the later publications was to assign location numbers to each full piece as well as to every poem fragment. "Much Madness" was given the number *435*.

"Much Madness Is Divinest Sense" was published in Dickinson's first collection, which was simply called *Poems* (1890). This poem stands wide open to a variety of interpretations. It can be said to represent her sense of humor, or rebellion, as well as her sense of frustration as an intelligent female living in a world that was dominated by dictatorial males. The poem can also reflect her anger, for although she was described as quiet spoken and demure, Dickinson did not hold back her strongest sentiments when it came to writing them. Read in another view, the poem could be taken to express Dickinson's fear of literal madness.

The poem is deceptively brief and at first glance appears simple. However, within its eight

lines is hidden a universal theme that runs so deep that more than a hundred years later its significance is still fresh, its impact is still sharp, and its expressed emotion is still controversial. This poem is so contemporary that Robert Hass, former United States poet laureate (1995–1997), chose to read "Much Madness Is Divinest Sense" to President and Mrs. Clinton at a celebratory meeting in the White House in 1998.

Author Biography

Emily Dickinson was born in Amherst, Massachusetts, on December 10, 1830, the second daughter of Edward and Emily (Norcross) Dickinson. Her family was well established in the community, her grandfather having been one of the founders of Amherst College and her father having served in both state and federal Congresses. For most of her life, however, Dickinson shunned public life, preferring to detach herself from society and focus, instead, on her writing.

As a child, Dickinson was educated at home, mostly under the guidance of her father, who heavily censored her subject matter in fear that some books might lead her away from his religious beliefs, which he demanded that his daughter accept without argument. Her father must have been torn between recognizing her intellectual curiosity and wanting to control her thoughts, for he bought her books, then hid them after showing them to her, telling her he was concerned that the books might shake her thoughts.

Although Dickinson went on to attend both the Amherst Academy and Hadley Female Seminary (present-day Mount Holyoke College), she did not receive a degree. Her accomplishments in school, however, were famous; her intelligence, her imagination, and her ability to write dazzled many of her teachers. Shortly upon completing her first year of college in 1848, she returned to her family home and remained there until her death, venturing out for only occasional trips.

Although Dickinson seldom left the confines of her father's home and infrequently responded to visitors, she did chance to meet two men, in particular, who would greatly influence her. First there was the Reverend Charles Wadsworth, whom many Dickinson biographers believe inspired her intellectually. Some critics have speculated that Wadsworth was the focal point of many of Dickinson's poems.

Emily Dickinson

The other man who influenced her was Thomas Wentworth Higginson, a literary editor and essayist who had written an article in the April 1862 *Atlantic Monthly* that offered advice for young poets. After reading Higginson's essay, Dickinson began sending poems to him, asking him to evaluate her writing. Higginson was gentle in his suggestions, and he advised her not to publish. Ironically, Higginson would, after Dickinson's death, become instrumental in publishing her first collection.

As she grew older, Dickinson withdrew even further from society and devoted the rest of her life to improving her art. She wrote prolifically. In 1862 alone, it is believed that she wrote a total of 366 poems. Her later poems reflect an examination of the personal self, especially in terms of her emotions, and of the greater concept of self, her soul. Her more mature writing also explores the universal themes of death, knowledge, and immortality.

Dickinson saw less then ten poems published in her lifetime. Her first collection, *Poems*, was published in 1890. "Much Madness Is Divinest Sense" appeared in this collection. The following year, a second collection, *Poems, Second Series* was published. Both collections were reprinted several times due to popular demand. The first publications of both collections were also heavily edited, so the poems would appear more conventional and pleasing to a general audience.

On May 15, 1886, Dickinson died of Bright's disease. She was buried in Amherst.

Poem Text

Much Madness is divinest Sense—
To a discerning Eye—
Much Sense—the starkest Madness—
'Tis the Majority
In this, as All, prevail—   5
Assent—and you are sane—
Demur—you're straightway dangerous—
And handled with a Chain—

Poem Summary

Line 1

Dickinson's poem, "Much Madness Is Divinest Sense," opens with a statement that immediately demands the reader's attention. Dickinson employs her ironic, or contradictory, wit to the full text of this poem, beginning with the paradox in the first line. Questions that may arise with the first two words in this line might concern what she means by "madness." Is Dickinson referring to insanity or anger? To complicate matters, Dickinson throws the reader off by adding the surprising two words at the end of this line, juxtaposing the first impressions with a contradictory second one. The reader might wonder if Dickinson is serious or if she is poking fun at someone or something. Is she enjoying her madness? Is she using madness to rise above a situation in which she feels uncomfortable or trapped? How can madness make sense? And why "divinest Sense?" Does she mean divine in the sense of being godly, or is she referring to something that is merely delightful?

Note the alliteration in this line. There is the double *m* in "much madness," and the *s* at the end of the words "madness," "is," and "divinest." Also, the word, "Sense," has *s* at both the beginning and the end. So this initial line is not only catchy for its contradictory or rebellious twist in meaning, but the use of alliteration makes the line fun to read with the tongue slipping over all the *s* sounds.

Line 2

The word "discerning" in the second line can be understood in a variety of ways. Discerning can

mean discriminating in the sense of being cautious; or it can mean astute, or wise. It can also mean sensitive or even shrewd. Depending on the reader's experience with, or attitude toward, madness, the poem can turn on the word "discerning." The reader can interpret this poem as sarcastic, judgmental, or playful. Like all good literature, Dickinson's poem offers space in which the reader can move around, bringing his or her emotions to the work and enjoying it not only through the author's view of life but on a personal level as well.

Line 3

In the third line, Dickinson almost completely turns the first line on its head, placing what was first last and vice versa. Again the line uses alliteration, with *s* appearing five times. And again there is ambiguity here, this time present in the word "starkest." Does the poet mean bleak, harsh, or desolate? Or is she making reference to a sense of completeness? She can also be suggesting the adjective, plain.

By twisting the phrases around between lines one and three, Dickinson may simply be emphasizing her opening statement. She may also be saying that it does not take a lot of madness to make sense because even the starkest madness is understandable. However, she is stating that too much sense is the harshest madness of all.

With this line, there arises another question. What does she mean by "Sense?" Is this common sense? Is she implying sanity or rationality? These questions about the meaning of "Sense," to which she is referring, actually make up the core of the whole poem. It is upon a definition of "Sense" that the poem is written, is it not? Does not the poet want the reader to think about who defines that which is referred to as sense?

Lines 4–5

It is lines four and five that offer a possible answer to these questions, in part, at least. "'Tis the majority" who defines sanity and sense. This does not mean that their definition is correct. Dickinson is only implying that since the majority has the rule, "as All," their definition is that which "prevails." This might lead the reader's thoughts to the question: What if madness was in the majority? Then, the next question might be, What is madness?

Line 6

The word "Assent" implies abiding by or, in more oppressive terms, acquiescing. If the reader is familiar with details in Dickinson's life, such as her domineering father and the small-town pressures of Christian conversion that Dickinson experienced in Amherst during her time, this word takes on stronger emotions. Dickinson was torn between her natural shyness, her sensitivity, and her innate sense of rebellion. Understanding these variant forces in her life helps the reader to appreciate the weight of the contradictions and emotional battles that she confronted. To give in to the dominant forces was to be declared sane, safe, and proper. If she assented, more than likely, she was also left alone, something that she craved.

This conflict is a universal one. It defines the relationship between parents and children; families and villages; tribes and states. To go along with the majority is to find peace, at least in some situations, but it is not always a comfortable peace. It is sometimes a peace that comes at a high price, the price of one's own private sanity.

Line 7

The use of the word "Demur" is fascinating. The word means to object, or protest. However, spelled with an additional *e*, "demure," the word takes on nearly the opposite meaning of modest, or shy. "Demure" is a word that is often used in describing Dickinson's personality. In the seventh line, however, she uses the word in contrast with "Assent."

Immediately after using this word, she inserts a dash, which is sharp and pointed, almost weapon-like. If a person opposes the majority, he or she is held at bay, because to protest is to be more than just wrong, it is to be dangerous. The adjective that she uses in this line, "straightway," reflects back to the straight form of the dash that precedes it; and it implies immediacy: no trial by peers, no justification. Whoever balks at the majority rule will be considered worse than a traitor. They will be denied any rights and quickly taken away. It is also interesting that when the language in line six (in which Dickinson mentions sanity) is compared to line seven, the latter is written with much more interesting words. This gives the reader a hint that Dickinson might enjoy leaning toward madness.

Line 8

Line eight suggests that not only will the objector be declared insane and taken away, he or she will either be confined with chains or beaten with them. The word "handled" is again a bit ambiguous, but the sentiment is very clear: either all freedoms will cease to exist, or the perpetrator will feel pain. Whether chained or beaten, the picture is not

Media Adaptations

- There is a wide selection of audiotapes, recorded by various artists, of Dickinson's poetry. Julie Harris reads from Dickinson's poetry and letters in a tape called *Emily Dickinson—Self-Portrait*. Harris won a Tony Award in 1977 for her portrayal of Dickinson in the one-woman play *The Belle of Amherst*.

very pleasant. It is so unpleasant that the poem suggests that one should take very seriously the attitude of madness, because the consequences can be severe.

Themes

Madness Versus Sanity

The main, or at least most obvious, theme of this poem deals with the argument over the definition of sanity and its opposite, madness. Sanity is an ambiguous term. It takes on its definition from its surroundings. What is considered sane in one society might be defined as crazy in another. The passage of time also alters the definition.

Dickinson is also correct in pointing out that the majority classifies what is sane and what is not. In any group, rules of conduct are determined by the majority. Deviation from this standard cannot be tolerated if the majority of the group is to "prevail." In some way, those who object must be ostracized or else they will threaten the group's goals. Although the words "sanity" and "madness" have definite meanings recognized by modern readers, in Dickinson's time, these concepts were often used when discussing women's rights or the attempts to suppress them.

Individuality

The individual versus the group is a perpetual battle for balance. For the creative spirit to expand and explore, the individual must be given the

Topics for Further Study

- Find a complete collection of Dickinson's poems that contains a subject or category classification of her poetry. Choose at least five poems that could be interpreted as focusing on issues of self, identity, oppression, or some other topic that could be taken as a feminist concern. Write a paper as if you were a feminist theorist studying these particular poems.

- The treatment of those who were deemed insane was a topic often discussed during the nineteenth century. Research the history of the asylums that existed in the United States during this time period, especially those in New England, focusing mainly on the female population that inhabited these institutions. What was the most significant malady? What were the treatments?

- The film *Beautiful Dreamer* (1991) captures a portion of the lives of Dr. Maurice Burke and Walt Whitman as they come together in an attempt to look at insanity in a new and creative way. Watch this movie, then watch *One Flew Over the Cuckoo's Nest*, another movie that deals with people who have been deemed insane. Compare the themes in these two movies. After watching both videos, write your own poem dealing with some aspect of madness and sanity.

- Dickinson wrote hundreds of letters in her lifetime. In most of these letters, she included one or more poems. Pretend that you are Dickinson and that you have sent a poem to one of your closest friends. Make up a letter to go with this poem. Expand on Dickinson's ideas of how the definitions of sanity and madness are somewhat arbitrary concepts. Go deeper into her feelings of suppression in regards to her sense of individuality.

freedom to think differently from the traditions of the group. Innovations occur when imagination is unconfined.

This said, it is easy to understand Dickinson's concerns for the needs of the individual. She was an artist and therefore had a unique way of thinking. The pressures on her to conform were powerful. Not only was her voice out of place in her community but also her era. For her to be confined to the manners of the women who surrounded her would be akin to a spiritual death. Though the majority prevailed, she had the strength of her individuality to help her maintain her vision, but it is likely that she was often told how dangerous it was.

Rebellion

An implied theme of this poem is rebellion. Although Dickinson does not discuss whether she rebelled against the majority rule, the reader can infer that she is at least thinking about it. If she has contemplated the concepts behind the ambiguity of madness and sanity, then she has most likely considered going against the rules of the majority. From her opening statement that madness is divine, the reader can infer that Dickinson prefers madness to the strictures of sanity. She wrote in some of her letters that she rebelled against the religious conversions that most of her peers were going through—the rebellious spirit was definitely available to her. She also went against her father's wishes by reading books other than the Bible. To conclude that, in this poem, she was a willing partner to those who "demur" does not require a great leap of assumption.

Feminism

Another implied theme, it can be argued, is a sense of early feminism. Although it is never mentioned in this poem, a feminist reading of the poem can relate it to writings by other women of Dickinson's time as well as contemporary female authors who discuss oppression in terms of madness. In male-dominated societies like the one in which Dickinson lived, the majority rule was in the hands of men, whether they were in the majority or not. Men were the lawmakers and thus represented the majority. They defined what was considered sane. To rise against their oppression and demand a voice is a feminist theme.

Style

Ambiguity

Dickinson's poems often employ ambiguity. Most accomplished writers realize that to allow ambiguity to exist in their works is to invite the reader to come to their own conclusions about the meaning of the work. In this way, the reader takes part in the writing. The story or the poem is not just the author's experience—it is also a mirror reflecting the reader's life. Dickinson was aware of this, and her ability to leave things unexplained is a mark of high literary capability and understanding. In this poem, Dickinson uses many words that are ambiguous in meaning, such as "madness," "Sense," "divinest," "discerning," and "starkest."

Suggestion

Suggestion goes hand in hand with ambiguity. By using ambiguous words, Dickinson sets up an environment in which she can point to situations without completely stating them. In "Much Madness Is Divinest Sense," there is the suggestion of rebellion, although Dickinson never comes straight out and declares it. There is also the suggestion of feminism, even if she was not thinking in those terms. She was aware of the limitations imposed on her because she was female, but she never mentions this outright. The reader might also infer that she herself leans toward those who think in terms of madness, as she grants them a benefit of the divine.

Alliteration

One of the most prevalent poetic forms that Dickinson uses in this poem is that of alliteration, the repetition of consonants. The *s* is the letter she uses most frequently for this effect. Actually, it is used in every line except for the last one. In doing this, Dickinson sets up a particular sound that is not broken until the last line, thus calling attention to the conclusion of the poem. The sound of *s* is soft and slippery, so the reader moves along the poem rather smoothly until the final moment. The last line is more straightforward and blunt, with the lack of alliteration and the sound of *s* creating the illusion of harshness and punishment.

Rhyme

There is only one official rhyme in this poem. It occurs in lines six and eight with the words "sane" and "Chain." As the only rhyme, it brings attention to itself. There's an interesting connection between these two words. Dickinson appears to be emphasizing that it is those who declare themselves sane who will administer the chains. By doing this, she ties together the last three lines of the poem with the image of the oppressed and the oppressor.

Tone

Because she uses ambiguous words in this poem, it is difficult to determine the tone that Dickinson intended for "Much Madness Is Divinest Sense." Is she being cynical or humorous; is she depressed? Or is she writing these words because she has figured out the system and wants to pass the news along? Is she celebrating madness? Is she exposing the nonsense of those who claim to know what sanity is? The last line is rather disheartening with its image of the chain, but Dickinson could be ridiculing the oppressor. She could be telling them that despite their use of restraining devices, she is still free. After all, there is her reference to the divine in the first line. Also, regardless of the threats of the majority, Dickinson was able to write this poem, proving that their attempts to control her thoughts have failed.

Historical Context

Civil War

While Dickinson wrote this poem, chances are the Civil War was in progress. She never mentions this war in her poems; however, in her letters to Thomas Wentworth Higginson, she comes in contact with the effects of battle. She wrote quite often to Higginson, including during the time that he served in the war. She also corresponded with him after he was injured, while he was in the hospital, so she was aware of the pain and suffering on a somewhat personal level.

Calvinism and Transcendentalism

Calvinism was the dominant religion in New England in Dickinson's time. The Calvinists believed in a church-dominated society, the absolute sovereignty of God's will, and punishment for sins. They emphasized materialism and logic, from which the Puritan ethic of hard work is derived. They also believed that salvation only came through faith in God, and if chosen by God, one could not resist. This religion promoted the group over the individual, and concrete reality over imagination or intuition. At a certain point in the young adult's life, a statement of conversion to these beliefs was common practice.

Dickinson, in her letters and her poetry, makes allusions to these Calvinist beliefs, as well as her rebellion against them. She refused to convert. Her concepts of God did not match those of the church, despite her father's efforts to convince Dickinson—her father was an orthodox Calvinist.

Instead, Dickinson turned to nature and her own instincts and intuitions about the sacredness of this life. Most critics agree that she was influenced by

Compare & Contrast

- **1800s:** The first women's rights convention is held in Seneca Falls, New York. Several years later, in Rochester, Susan B. Anthony registers and votes, stating that the 14th amendment gives her that right. Several days later she is arrested. At her trial, the judge does not allow her to testify on her own behalf, dismisses the jury, rules her guilty, and fines her $100, which she does not pay.

  1900s: The Equal Rights Amendment bans sex discrimination in employment and education. Shortly after, Shirley Chisholm becomes the first black American to run for president. In 1974, Ella Grasso becomes the first woman governor.

  Today: The women's rights movement has spread internationally, with United States women supporting causes in China, India, Africa, Afghanistan, and other countries. Women in Congress are still outnumbered: 9 out of 100 are women senators, 47 out of 436 are representatives.

- **1800s:** The Civil War frees slaves, but more than 600 thousand people are killed in the battles.

  1900s: During the twentieth century, America becomes involved in five separate wars, World War I, World War II, and the Vietnam, Korean, and Gulf Wars, with a total of more than 200 thousand casualties.

  Today: The twenty-first century begins with an unexpected attack by terrorists on the World Trade Center in New York and the Pentagon in Washington, D.C. This attack precipitates the United States declaration of war on terrorism. Initial casualties in America are more than 3,000. International casualties are yet unknown.

- **1800s:** The most prominent literary movements in the United States include the romantics and the transcendentalists.

  1900s: As this century opens, realism gives way to a modernist movement in which experimentation is promoted. Writers such as Hilda Doolittle, e. e. cummings, Ezra Pound, and William Faulkner are associated with this period.

  Today: Postmodernism spreads outside the confines of literature and is defined in general terms of non-realism and the nontraditional. Authors associated with this movement include Don DeLillo, Thomas Pynchon, John Barth, and Toni Morrison, among others.

Ralph Waldo Emerson (1803–1882), an essayist, philosopher, and poet, who proposed an alternative philosophy. Emerson helped found the transcendentalist movement. Transcendentalists believed that answers about this reality could be found by the individual in quiet meditations on nature. They promoted the individual and self-reliance. Emerson also encouraged everyone, especially those inclined to write, to live a hermit's life, to withdraw from society in order not to be contaminated with the materialism and professed logic of the group.

Suffrage

The United States women's suffrage movement began in the middle of the nineteenth century in the northeastern states. Women, such as Lucretia Mott and Lucy Stone, discovered that when they spoke out for such reforms as the antislavery and temperance movements, they were told they had no voice. This attempt to silence them inspired the women to organize.

These early feminists, meeting for the first time as a group at the Seneca Falls Convention, held in New York State on July 20, 1848, made many demands for improvements in their status, the most controversial of all being the right to vote. At that time, they were more concerned with social, economic, legal, and educational issues. After the Civil War, when the Fifteenth Amendment offered suffrage only to black men, the suffrage movement went into crisis, as some women in the movement refused to support the new amendment, demanding that women be included. This caused a schism in the movement.

It was during this time, in 1869, that the National Woman Suffrage Association (NWSA), headed by Elizabeth Cady Stanton and Susan B. Anthony, was created. One of its main focuses was a demand for a Sixteenth Amendment, which would give women the right to vote. This suffrage group became more radical, more vocal, and, therefore, more visible, thus addressing their issues to a wider audience of women. The more conservative organization, the American Woman Suffrage Association (AWSA), founded that same year, included Thomas Wentworth Higginson among its supporters, the essayist with whom Dickinson maintained a lifetime correspondence.

In 1890, four years after Dickinson's death and the same year that her first book of poems was published, the two segments of the movement reunited into the National American Woman Suffrage Association (NAWSA). Elizabeth Cady Stanton was elected president and Susan B. Anthony, vice president. It was decided at this point that the movement should drop all other issues and focus their efforts on recruiting new members and winning the right to vote. However, women's right to vote would not be won until 1920 with the nineteenth amendment.

Literature and Literary Movements

Literature that was available during Dickinson's time and that influenced her included the works of William Shakespeare, John Keats, Helen Hunt Jackson, Robert and Elizabeth Barrett Browning, and probably Ralph Waldo Emerson. Although Walt Whitman was her contemporary, she was dissuaded from reading him because his writing was said to be disgraceful. Dickinson also read the Bible.

Literary movements during the nineteenth century in America included the romantic movement, which reached the United States around the year 1820. This movement provided a tool with which authors attempted to create a distinctive American voice. The romantics viewed nature and art as more important than science. Self-awareness was promoted as a way of understanding the universe. Previous to this movement, a focus on self was considered selfish, a word that was imbued with a derogatory tone. William Wordsworth and Samuel Taylor Coleridge were two of the more dominant writers associated with the Romantics.

The romantic movement is closely associated with the transcendentalists, among whom were found Ralph Waldo Emerson and Henry David Thoreau. Unlike many other movements, the transcendentalists insisted on and promoted the individual, to the point that they made no rules for, or definitions of, their movement. They encouraged unconventional thought, believing that to fall into the traps of accepted conventions was dangerous. Other authors influenced by the transcendentalists were Edgar Allan Poe, Herman Melville, and Mark Twain.

In sharp contrast to the transcendentalists were the poets who are often referred to as the Brahmin Poets, most of whom were also Harvard professors. These poets were heavily influenced by European literature, which caused their philosophies and writings to be much more conservative than the Transcendentalists. The most prominent writers in this group included Henry Wadsworth Longfellow, Oliver Wendell Holmes, and James Russell Lowell.

Critical Overview

Although there is little direct criticism of "Much Madness Is Divinest Sense," the range of comments over the years signifies how Dickinson's reputation as a poet has grown. *The Recognition of Emily Dickinson*, edited by Caesar R. Blake and Carlton F. Wells, contains many critical essays on the writing of Dickinson in general, which collectively demonstrate the increased appreciation of her writing over time. It begins with Thomas Wentworth Higginson, who writes, in the preface to Dickinson's first published collection in 1890:

> the verses of Emily Dickinson belong emphatically to what Emerson has long since called 'the Poetry of the Portfolio,'—something produced absolutely without the thought of publication, and solely by way of the expression of the writer's own mind.

Higginson believed that it was because of this attitude that Dickinson had the freedom of "daring thoughts." Three years after the publication of this collection, Arlo Bates, a novelist and editor of a Boston newspaper, writes that "there is hardly a line in the entire volume and certainly not a stanza, which cannot be objected to upon the score of technical imperfection." He softens his criticism by then adding that there also was hardly a line, "which fails to throw out some gleam of genuine original power, of imagination, and of real emotional thought."

Jumping ahead to the twentieth century, Pulitzer Prize-winning poet Conrad Aiken, who edited some of Dickinson's poems, had this to say about her writing:

Once one adjusts oneself to the spinsterly angularity of the [poetic] mode, its lack of eloquence or rhetorical speed, its naive and often prosaic directness, one discovers felicities of thought and phrase on every page. The magic is terse and sure.

Archibald MacLeish, a well-known, American, Pulitzer Prize-winning poet, offered his evaluation of Dickinson's poetry as it was studied in the 1960s. He writes that Dickinson was one of the most important modern poets, despite the fact that "her forms are among the simplest of which the English language is capable." These remarks were not meant to be derogatory. Rather, he continues, saying form for Dickinson was not the basis of her poems. "In Emily's poems, however, things are otherwise arranged." He then praises Dickinson for her imagery, not the kind of images that are visible through the eye but rather the mental images that she constructs to represent abstract feelings. To make his comments clearer, MacLeish uses, as an example, a line from Dickinson: "that white sustenance / despair." He refers to this ability of hers to make abstraction appear in picture form as images that are presented "directly to the imagination by the suggestion of words." MacLeish ends by calling Dickinson's tone "wholly spontaneous" and writes that "it is the voice rather than the form which supplies the key to her work." Her voice is particular to her, "and when that particular voice is Emily Dickinson's at her most particular best they [the poems] can be very great poetry indeed."

More recently, novelist Joyce Carol Oates has written several articles about Dickinson's poetry. In her "'*Soul at the White Heat*': The Romance of Emily Dickinson's Poetry," published in *Critical Inquiry*, Oates writes:

No one who has read even a few of Dickinson's extraordinary poems can fail to sense the heroic nature of this poet's quest. It is riddlesome, obsessive, haunting, very often frustrating . . . but above all heroic.

Oates continues that Dickinson's poetry reflects the poet's attempts "to realize the soul," which, according to Oates, "is nothing less than the attempt to create a poetry of transcendence—the kind that outlives its human habitation and its name." Oates praises the poet's ability to explore not only what is known but also what is unconscious, which Dickinson exposes through "contradictory forces . . . held in suspension." It is through Dickinson's poetry that readers gain "a heightened sense of the mind's uncharted possibilities," Oates writes. "Here is an American artist of words as inexhaustible as Shakespeare, as ingeniously skillful in her craft as Yeats, a poet whom we can set with confidence beside the greatest poets of modern times."

Criticism

Joyce Hart

Hart has degrees in English literature and creative writing and is a published writer of literary themes. In this essay, Hart ponders the inspiration behind Dickinson's poem in an attempt to identify the allusion to madness.

Many literary critics and literary historians believe that Ralph Waldo Emerson influenced Dickinson. Knowing even the vaguest details of Dickinson's reclusive life reinforces this conclusion, as Emerson encouraged a pulling into oneself by limiting social contacts. Emerson also, as espoused in his essay "Self-Reliance," advocated individualism. Reading Dickinson's poem "Much Madness Is Divinest Sense," with Emerson's writing in mind, influences the reader to interpret this poem in a way that might illustrate a rebellious nature in Dickinson. Between the lines, the reader can envision a young poet who is determined to defy the majority rule and is willing to fight for her individuality. However, when this poem is read with some of Dickinson's own works in mind, the analysis takes on a different tone. Could it be literal madness that Dickinson is referring to and not just a general allusion to society's labeling a nonconformist as being mad? In other words, was Dickinson afraid that she might have a mental illness? Was she afraid of going insane? If this is true, is the emotion behind this poem fear rather than rebellion?

The Complete Poems of Emily Dickinson (1950), edited by Thomas H. Johnson, contains a subject index in the back pages. A thorough search of this index results in no mention of words such as rebellion, individuality, or self-reliance. Yet these are the concepts that Dickinson supposedly learned from reading Emerson, and these are the themes that a reader could easily conclude are emphasized in Dickinson's poem "Much Madness Is Divinest Sense."

Emerson also wrote that a person should trust their own thoughts. The problem, he believed, was that people who took the time to listen to their thoughts, often forgot them, or worse, were coerced out of them once they left the confines and privacy of their home and went out into society. Society, for its own benefit, seeks conformity. Society has an aversion, he wrote, to free thinkers and creators, as it maintains its power through regulated custom. Society functions on naming things, Emerson believed. The things that society deemed bad were not necessarily inherently evil; it was, after all, just a name applied to something that society feared would cause trouble for the majority. In Emerson's mind, the only bad things in life were whatever denied him the right to believe in, and think for, himself.

By taking these concepts of Emerson's and applying them as a background for Dickinson's poem, the reader will find an almost perfect match. Dickinson's poem implies the same sentiments. For instance, Dickinson writes that the majority defines the term "madness" and judges it to be wrong. The majority dictates the rules, and those rules demand conformity. To go against the majority means the perpetrator will be punished. In other words, to be a self-thinker means to be eventually locked up in chains. Is it no wonder that, as Emerson wrote, the conformist has a much easier road?

However, Dickinson's poem takes up the issue of madness. Why does she use this word? Although Emerson mentions that taking the road of the nonconformist may not be easy, he does not refer to madness as a consequence.

Returning to the subject index of the collection of Dickinson's poems, one finds many references to madness. The word "madness" itself is listed, as well as references to a haunted brain, a cleaving in the brain, and a funeral in the brain. Subject listings under "soul" include storms within the soul, a numbness of the soul, and a paralysis of the soul. With much more emphasis in Dickinson's writing on the subject of mental strain as opposed to individuality or self-reliance, the true theme of this poem may well be the fear the author had of being deemed mad.

Dickinson's references to madness appear in several of her poems. In her poem "It Struck Me—Every Day—" (number 362), she discusses a storm that both appears to be present every day and yet is still fresh. She writes that the storm burned her in the night, "It blistered to My Dream—." She also mentions that she thought the storm would be brief, "But Nature lost the Date of This— / and left it in the Sky—." The storm creeps up on her during the

> *She then goes on to explain that after feeling her brain break apart, she tried to fix it, much like she had earlier tried to fix the strings of her soul. She was, again, unsuccessful."*

day. Each day she thinks she is rid of it, but suddenly it flashes through the clouds. It builds up in intensity until it is like a fire that burns her when she sleeps. This is one example that could prove that Dickinson struggled with a sense of mental imbalance in her life.

In her poem, "We Grow Accustomed to the Dark—" (number 419), Dickinson first refers to how eyes adjust to the dark after stepping out of a lighted room. Then she moves to another concept of darkness, "And so of larger—Darknesses— / Those Evenings of the Brain—," when she can find no light within. She continues her thoughts by stating that eventually, even the brain can adjust to the darkness within, "And Life steps almost straight." In this poem, it sounds as if she has grown accustomed to going in and out of some kind of mental problem. There are moments when she feels lost in the darkness but has learned to cope with it. She does not say, however, that she found a light. She only states that her brain "Adjusts itself to Midnight—."

One of her more popular poems, "I Felt a Funeral, in My Brain" (number 280), deals with the sense of madness quite directly. Dickinson describes a falling into madness in this poem. She writes, "My Mind was going numb—," then relates, "a Plank in Reason, broke, / And I dropped down, and down—." The straightforward mention of "reason" suffering some kind of misfortune makes it hard not to conclude that Dickinson is specifically referring to some kind of madness. She is not using a metaphor of a storm in this poem. She is openly declaring that she felt as if something in her brain had died.

Again in 1862, Dickinson wrote a poem that begins "The first Day's Night had come—" (number

What Do I Read Next?

- Edgar Allan Poe's *Complete Stories and Poems of Edgar Allan Poe* (1966) contains the short story "The System of Doctor Tarr and Professor Fether" in which a young man finds himself invited to a dinner party at a state institution for the insane. During the course of the meal, the so-called keepers of the institution tell the guest about the procedures of imprisonment that must be maintained to keep the insane people under control. As the dinner proceeds, the guest starts questioning the sanity of the keepers themselves. Poe explores the thin line between sanity and madness, a topic that nineteenth-century society found fascinating.

- Ralph Waldo Emerson's essays were one of the great influences in Dickinson's life. *Self-Reliance: The Wisdom of Ralph Waldo Emerson as Inspiration for Daily Living* (1991) contains some of Emerson's best essays, including "Self-Reliance," "The Over-Soul," and "Spiritual Laws."

- Michel Foucault is a French philosopher who focuses on social evolution. In *Madness and Civilization: A History of Insanity in the Age of Reason* (1988), he expresses his thoughts on the history of how civilizations have dealt with insanity. Beginning in 1500, when the insane were simply considered eccentric, to the nineteenth century when asylums were in vogue, this book offers the reader a glimpse into the ever-changing role of people whose thoughts and/or behavior fell outside the boundaries of what was considered sane.

- Charlotte Perkins Gilman first published the novella "The Yellow Wallpaper" in 1899. In this tale, she creates a narrator who is oppressed by her husband and who finds her freedom only by escaping into insanity. This story, which can be found in *The Yellow Wallpaper and Other Sto-*

ries (1989) published by Bantam Classics, has become a symbol of oppressed women in every age, despite the fact that it was written in the early part of the nineteenth century.

- Edited by Diana Scott, *Bread and Roses: An Anthology of 19th–20th Century Poetry by Women Writers* (1983) is a collection that contains representative women poets from both Britain and the United States. This anthology offers a rare opportunity to gain an overall view of the women who were writing during both centuries as well as the topics that concerned them.

- Sylvia Plath was a poet who, in the 1950s, openly dealt with issues in her personal life, such as her depression, family relationships, individuality, rebellion, and sexuality. In addition to her poetry, Plath wrote an autobiographical novel in 1963, *The Bell Jar*, in which she tells the story of a young woman's mental breakdown.

- In the 1970s, Sandra M. Gilbert and Susan Gubar published their groundbreaking volume of feminist literary criticism, *The Madwoman in the Attic: The Woman Writer and the Nineteenth-Century Imagination*. In this book, Gilbert and Gubar offer critical studies of Jane Austen, Mary Shelley, Charlotte Brönte, and other notable women novelists of the era. Perhaps more importantly, they also challenge prevailing thoughts about female creativity and offer some startling new insights that revolutionized literary criticism about women. The book was reprinted by Yale University Press in 2000.

- Dickinson's poetry is often compared to that of one of her contemporaries, Walt Whitman. Walt Whitman's *Leaves of Grass*, first published in 1855, is a good place to start for such a comparison because it helps to illustrate the different outlooks of the time period.

410), in which she talks about her soul being unable to sing. She tries to fix the soul's strings, but the next day is so horrible that she loses her sight. When she reflects on that day, which she refers to having happened several years prior, she states that she is still a bit confused about it all.

> and Something's odd—within—
> that person that I was—
> and this One—do not feel the same—
> could it be Madness—this?

Although she believed in Emerson's philosophy of life and took to heart his suggestions of living a secluded life and fighting for the right to think original thoughts, Dickinson's poetry makes it obvious too that she suffered more than just the humiliation and frustration of fighting for her individuality. Her huge collection of poems, as well as the letters that she wrote, is testament to her creativity and insight. Taking into account the times in which she lived and the domineering father that she had, there is little argument about the courage that she must have had to fight conformity. This does not, however, mean that she did not suffer. Upon reading Emerson, she might have even suffered more, as suggested in another poem.

In 1864, she wrote "A Door Just Opened on a Street" (number 953) in which she describes a type of awakening. The image present in the poem is that of the speaker walking, lost somewhere, when suddenly as she passes a house, the door opens to her. While the door is ajar, the speaker enjoys "an instant's Width of Warmth disclosed— / and Wealth—and Company." Unfortunately, just as suddenly, the door closes, and because of this experience, the speaker now suffers doubly. She is not only lost but she is also experiencing misery. In this poem, Dickinson seems to imply that when she was lost, at least that was all that was on her mind. She was trying to find her way. However, when the door opened, she saw that someone was living in a manner that was quite different from hers. That way of living exuded warmth. For a brief second, she felt that she had found something or someone with whom she could share her thoughts. It was far better not knowing that such a way of life existed for it made her feel even more lost when she had to go back to her way of life.

Taking a small leap of conjecture, one could conclude that in some ways, reading Emerson made Dickinson's life even more miserable than before. Prior to having her mind opened by his words, Dickinson might not have thought about rebelling against the majority. She might not have taken so seriously his instructions that people should explore their own thoughts and trust their intuitions. Once she did read his thoughts, however, she could not forget them. Although his words might have opened up her mind, they also might have confused her, for she had very few supports available to her to reinforce her way of thinking.

Another poem, referred to as "I Felt a Cleaving in My Mind—" (number 937), was also written in 1864. The cleaving that Dickinson felt was "As if my Brain had split—." She then goes on to explain that after feeling her brain break apart, she tried to fix it, much like she had earlier tried to fix the strings of her soul. She was, again, unsuccessful. "The thought behind, I strove to join / Unto the thought before—," she writes, but everything unraveled. In her attempt to understand some unnamed concept, Dickinson, in this poem, tells the reader that she could not match what she had once believed with some new information that she has received. Her thoughts are jumbled. They no longer make sense. She cannot find any connection between them.

Returning to the original poem, "Much Madness," after reading Dickinson's meditations of her feelings of being lost, of her brain suffering a funeral, or being torn apart, much more depth is added to the interpretation. It is hard to maintain that Dickinson was making some general reference to a cultural madness. The subject of madness is very serious for the author. Whether she officially suffered from mental illness is not important; that she suffered is. Her adjacent poems make it very clear that she was frightened at times, that she was miserable, and that she sometimes felt she had lost the voice of her soul and might truly go mad.

Source: Joyce Hart, Critical Essay on "Much Madness Is Divinest Sense," in *Poetry for Students*, The Gale Group, 2002.

Beth Kattelman

Kattelman holds a Ph.D. in theatre from Ohio State University. In this essay, Kattelman discusses how Dickinson's poem can be best understood by studying both the structure of text and the poet's life.

The magic of poetry is that it packs a great deal of meaning into very few, well-chosen words. The greatest of poets are experts at manipulating word choice and syntax to convey an entire world of images and concepts. Emily Dickinson was among these masters. She was able to compress numerous images and ideas into a few short lines, thus creating some very powerful, but also very cryptic poems. Her economy of expression produced some

> *Instead of standing as a casual observation of the insanity of society's norms, it becomes a personal declaration of the wisdom that comes from following one's own convictions."*

wonderful poetry but also created a unique challenge for the reader. The brevity of her poems can make it difficult to glean her intention. To gain the most complete understanding of a Dickinson poem, it is useful to analyze it in more than one way. By looking specifically at the text itself, a reader can gain one level of meaning. The use of punctuation, capitalization, meter, etc., all provide clues as to what the poet is "trying to say." To gain an additional level of meaning, one can examine the poem in relation to the poet's life. Even though there may not be a direct correlation to events that were occurring, an added layer of understanding can be obtained. "Much Madness Is Divinest Sense" is an excellent example of a poem whose meaning can be revealed through a combination of these two types of analyses. Upon first reading, the poem conveys a sense of irony and defiance. Here is a soul that rebukes the notion of "common sense" and is able to see a larger truth. The speaker of the poem recognizes the "insanity of sanity." While this is definitely an aspect of the poem, this surface reading does not transmit all of the subtle nuances of meaning that can be found within these eight lines. By combining what can be gleaned from the text itself with information known about Dickinson's life, a reader can gain a deeper understanding of the poem. Many critics agree that this technique can actually produce a more specific meaning from each poem. As Cristanne Miller notes in her book *Emily Dickinson: A Poet's Grammar,*

> The poet's metaphors and extended analogies, her peculiar brevity, lack of normal punctuation, irregular manipulation of grammar, syntax, and word combination all invite multiple, non-referential interpretations of what she means. Tempering this multiplicity with a historical understanding of the poet's life and

the language theories and practice available to her focuses the possibilities of meaning.

"Much Madness Is Divinest Sense" contains many of the typical textual elements used throughout Dickinson's poetry, including a strange pattern of capitalization, wordplay, alliteration, and liberal use of the dash as punctuation. Each textual element has a specific effect on the reader, pushing him closer to the intended impact of the entire poem. For example, capitalizing words such as "Sense," "Majority," and "All" personifies them. They move from the category of "what" into the category of "who." Once capitalized, the words gain specificity, now strongly referring to the people behind the concepts. Instead of any "majority," it is the ultimate "Majority" who are represented in the poem. Capitalization of the word "Eye" in the second line emphasizes a pun on the pronoun "I." When Dickinson writes, "To a discerning Eye," it is specifically the speaker of the poem to which she refers. The speaker is the "discerning I"; she is the one able to recognize the absurdity of blindly following society's dictates. A similar wordplay occurs in the fifth line of the poem with the capitalization of the word "All." Here again, this personified word can be replaced with a pronoun: "I'll." So, the speaker of the poem proclaims, "I'll prevail," reemphasizing the righteousness of following one's own dictates and not giving in to societal pressure. Capitalization in the poem also helps to emphasize the important words, and points out the contrast that Dickinson presents. The terms "Much Madness," "Sense," "Much Sense," and "Madness" draw the reader's focus and emphasize the juxtaposition of these contrasting notions.

The primary punctuation mark found in "Much Madness Is Divinest Sense" is the dash. This is in keeping with Dickinson's preferred style of the time. Earlier in her career, she was fond of using exclamation marks to add emphasis to her words. Eventually she shifted away from this practice, however, and replaced it with a liberal usage of the dash. In her essay, "Emily Dickinson's Volcanic Punctuation," Kamilla Denman notes this phenomenon,

> By 1862, the exclamation mark is increasingly rare. In this period, Dickinson becomes anarchic in her use of the dash, both in terms of its replacement of almost every other mark of punctuation and in its placement between almost every one of the parts of speech.

These dashes serve to break Dickinson's words into small "packets" of words, each of which can be scrutinized individually and then combined to unveil a broader meaning. They also provide a strong visual element that controls the poem's rhythm. Some critics have presumed that Dickinson's use of the dash is an indication of her tortured mental state, while others see it as a strategy of defiance. She refused to give in to the traditional use of punctuation, thus confounding those whose tastes run toward the conventional. While a strong case could be made for either argument, the latter is certainly in keeping with the spirit of this particular poem. Dickinson not only writes a poem about defying the norms of society but also practices this defiance within the poem by creating her own use of the dash.

Now that the textual elements have provided some insights into this poem, what can be learned by relating the poem to Dickinson's life? First, of course, it is necessary to have some knowledge of the poet's biography. Little is known about Dickinson's day-to-day existence, but some major facts about the poet can shed some light on the poem at hand. It is well known that Dickinson was reclusive. While many poets and artists have been known to retreat into his/her "own world," Dickinson took her retreat to pathological extremes. As Harold Bloom notes, "We know that Dickinson began, in her twenties, a gradual retreat into the confines of the Homestead, the house in which she was born, until for the last fifteen years of her life. She did not leave its grounds and saw no one but her brother and sister." When one keeps these facts about Dickinson's existence in mind a deeper understanding of "Much Madness Is Divinest Sense" surfaces. The poem takes on a strong element of paranoia. Instead of standing as a casual observation of the insanity of society's norms, it becomes a personal declaration of the wisdom that comes from following one's own convictions. The poem carries a different meaning than if a rebel who was publicly espousing antiestablishment ideas had written it. It is much more subtle and contains a message of passive resistance.

Particular episodes from Dickinson's life also provide added information about what she might have been using this poem to convey. The poem moves from a private sphere to a public sphere and can be read as an indication of how Dickinson came to her strong need for seclusion. As a child, Dickinson would avoid doing things she considered unpleasant by physically locking herself up. As Donna Dickenson notes in her book *Emily Dickinson*, "In youth, Dickinson defied her father's insistence that she attend church by the simple ploy of locking herself up in the cellar." This was her power. Dickinson chose to lock herself away rather than allowing society (or her father) to control her

thoughts and actions. Instead of giving in to expected behavior, she defied the norms and withdrew from "the game." She had her own strong beliefs and refused to give in to the coercion of society. She was aware of the consequences of being different and chose to avoid the same by locking herself away. Through these actions she deprived society of the opportunity to force her to conform. She would not be "handled with a Chain." Instead, she would choose her own path and create her own reality. Of course, the irony here is that, although Dickinson was not literally imprisoned, she became figuratively imprisoned through her own, self-imposed seclusion.

Emily Dickinson was an accomplished poet whose brilliance, unfortunately, was never recognized within her lifetime. With just a few lines, she was able to create an entire tapestry of ideas. "Much Madness Is Divinest Sense" is an excellent example of the numerous layers of meaning that can be contained in eight brief lines. In this poem, she puts forth a philosophical premise, creates interest through use of meter, capitalization, wordplay, and alliteration and provides insight into her own life and beliefs. The poem's text and Dickinson's biography reflexively illuminate one another. There has been some debate among critics as to whether a poet's biography should influence a poem's interpretation or meaning. Many believe that a poem should be considered a stand-alone text and that biographical elements from a poet's life should not influence the interpretation. Most scholars of Dickinson, however, take the opposing view. They see her life as fundamental to the understanding of her work. A combination of these two critical views provides the greatest opportunity for the appreciation and explication of Dickinson's poetry, however. There is no reason one should choose one technique over the other. Any clues that can shed light upon a poem should be considered useful, whether they are episodes from the poet's life, or elements contained within the text itself. Pairing these interpretive techniques provides the most complete understanding of "Much Madness Is Divinest Sense" and of the other poems in Dickinson's body of work.

Source: Beth Kattelman, Critical Essay on "Much Madness Is Divinest Sense," in *Poetry for Students*, The Gale Group, 2002.

Deneka Candace MacDonald

MacDonald is an instructor of English Literature and media studies. In this essay, MacDonald considers Emily Dickinson's poem in terms of the

> *Literally seen as a possible madwoman in her own attic by some, the subject of madness and the perception of insanity was something that was a personal issue to the reclusive author.*"

historical context of the period as well as the notion of the individual versus the majority.

A woman who experienced a difficult relationship with the outside world, Emily Dickinson wrote countless poems on the themes of madness, religion, and marginalization. "Much Madness Is Divinest Sense" is one of the more disturbing among these because of the dark imagery of confinement and fear found within the short eight-line poem.

The poem begins: "Much Madness is divinest Sense— / To a discerning Eye—" indicating not only that madness itself is the subject of this poem but that Dickinson sees a divide between what society accepts as "common sense" and what social norm dictates as a stigmatized label (madness). Indeed, transcendentalists of the period (for example, Henry David Thoreau and Emerson, whom we know Dickinson read) rejected the "normalizing" policies of the majority and instead argued that there was a divine or transcendent wisdom available through nature that the majority might miss. Thus, Thoreau, when imprisoned for civil disobedience, famously retorts in response to Emerson's question "What are you doing in here?" "The question is, what are you doing out there?" Certainly, at the time that Dickinson wrote "Much Madness Is Divinest Sense," the issue of madness versus sanity, or the individual versus the majority, was a pressing social concern in the United States. In addition, the Civil War (a war that was to cost the lives of thousands Americans and devastate the South) had begun in 1861. One reading of Dickinson's poem, therefore, must take into account the fact that, as Beth Maclay Doriani (in *Emily Dickinson: A Daughter of Prophecy*) and others have suggested:

Dickinson's poetry should be seen as part of the range of response to the Civil War offered by contemporary writers. Her verse, emerging from an era that was questioning the purity of the nation, certainly challenges audiences to consider their spiritual groundings.

Many people in the North questioned the sanity of pursuing the war itself. At the same time, many Southerners and Northerners would have accepted (as a matter of common sense) that slavery was necessary for the economy of the South. Only the "madness" of a higher "divine sense" would have suggested that the morally correct action was to free the slaves. Dickinson, however, clearly was not limiting her critique to the Civil War. She was also responding to the slavery that was forced on dissenters. Having chosen to remain single, live in seclusion, and find solace in the written word, she herself certainly represented one form of dissent against a majority opinion which stipulated that women should marry and lead lives for the benefit and entertainment of men.

While it is not always purposeful to discuss the author in terms of the art (as has been historically debated by such acclaimed scholars as Rolande Barthes, J. K. Wimsat, and Monroe C. Beardsley), in the case of Emily Dickinson, one must consider her own undeniable presence in her poetry. Indeed, Thomas Wentworth Higginson notes, in *The Recognition of Emily Dickinson* "[her] work, that is, of persons who wrote for the relief of their own minds, and without thought of publication . . . will have at least the merit of perfect freedom." Higginson, the man largely responsible for the first serious attention to Dickinson's poetry, argues that Dickinson's work has "perfect freedom" because she wrote for herself, rather than the scrupulous eye of the public or critic. Thus, her work often exudes an honesty that cannot be found elsewhere. Bliss Carmen, too, notes her unique "untarnished expression," in *A Note on Emily Dickinson*, in 1896, stating that "She borrowed from no one; she was never commonplace. . . . The region of her brooding was that sequestered domain where our profoundest convictions have origin." Further, the fact that Emily Dickinson was a recluse who lived most of her life indoors, confined to her father's estate, has much bearing on the remarkable quality of her poetry. As Higginson notes:

> In [the case] . . . of mental conflict, we can only wonder at the gift of vivid imagination by which this recluse woman can delineate, by a few touches, the very crises of a lyric mental struggle.

Dickinson's own idiosyncratic life choice almost certainly seemed madness, possibly even dangerous, to a majority of Americans. Literally seen as a possible madwoman in her own attic by some, the subject of madness and the perception of insanity was something that was a personal issue to the reclusive author. That is not to suggest that Dickinson herself was mad; she was not. However, social perceptions of a woman who willingly shut herself up in her father's house for all of her adult life were not always kind.

The late nineteenth century was a time when the social and cultural history of both madness and insanity was being severely questioned. Indeed, the trope of the sane/mad inversion reached its literary apogee in this period; by the 1860s, there was widespread psychiatric and public condemnation of chaining or restraining insane patients, something Dickinson specifically refers to in the final line of the poem: "And handled with a Chain—." However, while Dickinson's reference to chaining can obviously be seen to refer to the inhumane treatment of the insane or the "mad," it also, of course, conjures up images of slavery. Undoubtedly, dangerous slaves (those who refused to assent to their slavery), were shackled and frequently resold in the deep South. Dickinson recognizes that her own dissent, and indeed the dissent of any minority, may lead to similar treatment—chaining and silencing—so that "the Majority / In This, as All, prevail—." Thus, the tone of the poem is grim, suggesting the futility of resistance or dissent.

The opening lines of Dickinson's poem make two interesting suggestions: first, that there is a difference in the degree of madness that is acceptable, and second, coupling "Madness" (capital "M") with "Divinest" suggests not only that Madness is an important issue, but also that it is connected with the divine on some level. Moreover, it is significant that Dickinson chooses to write "Much Madness" instead of simply "Madness." Thus Dickinson becomes the "discerning Eye" who sees the sense in what the "Majority" has otherwise stigmatized as madness. Clearly, Dickinson plays upon the word "Eye," also seen as "I"; she is able to "discern" (to comprehend) the "Madness" both with her physical eyes and with her person.

Dickinson's difficult and often confusing relationship with God is well documented among scholarly discourse and is recognizable in Dickinson's own letters to friends. Mary Augusta Jordon notes that early on, Dickinson writes: "my mother does not care for thought, and father, too busy with his briefs to notice what we do. . . . They are reli-gious, except me." Because it is known that Emily Dickinson had read Emerson's essays, one must pay attention to the fact that there is a difference between the "divine" of traditional Christianity and the "divine" spoken of by the transcendentalists who emphasized personal experience and the role of nature in revealing "truth." On the one hand, Dickinson clearly mistrusted God and the divine, as is evidenced in many of her religious poems. Her poetry, therefore, is often rich with jeering irony and sarcasm. Others, however, are convinced that she was prophetic through her poetry.

One Dickinson scholar, Beth Maclay Doriani, insists that Emily Dickinson revised the convention of faith and expressed these visions, often with the intention of undermining them, through her poetry. In discussing Dickinson's religious poems, she argues that they "serve as powerful reminders of the mysteriousness of life, death, and God; they call their readers to consider what lies beyond the visible world." Indeed, the lines "Much Madness is divinest Sense— / To a discerning Eye— / Much Sense— the starkest Madness— / 'Tis the Majority" invoke images of the mystery associated with mental illness and conjure further vividly distinct pictures, as Doriani notes. Particularly, in this poem, Doriani argues that Dickinson "expresses the traditional idea of prophetic ecstasy or 'madness' as yielding divine truth . . . [giving] the lines [a] . . . distinctive emotional impulse." Consequently, the "discerning Eye" (I) of the poem is the "Majority" of social and cultural influence/opinion who have the power to label behavior "normal" or "mad." But the poem also questions madness itself—questions whether the invisibility of the label "madness," the unknowable quality of madness, is perhaps closer to the divine: "Much Madness" coupled later with "Much Sense" furthers this notion and also alludes to the notion of a "common sense" that is being ignored.

Finally, the poem displays an anger toward (mental/social) conflict, madness, and struggle. The anger is ambiguous at times: "Much Madness is divinest Sense—"; and more overt at others: "Demur—you're straightway dangerous— / And handled with a Chain." As with most Dickinson poems, the motifs addressed in this poem are brief—the problematic notions associated with these social issues are teasingly short in description, always leaving the reader hungry for further thought. However, if her choice of language is slight, it is also clever and hard-hitting. The simplicity of her poems brush these larger issues—in this case, of patriarchal power, of the treatment of the insane, of the possible association with divine wisdom and a relationship with God—but they brush them enough that one contemplates the idea long after the lines have been read. She uses capital letters to indicate which words hold the most importance, such as Much, Madness, Sense, Eye, Majority, Assent, Demur, Chain. Each word she chooses carefully to have an impact far beyond the simplicity of the word itself. Dickinson addresses some of the most controversial issues of the nineteenth century and, indeed, in the current one. In this, Dickinson is truly genius.

Source: Deneka Candace MacDonald, Critical Essay on "Much Madness Is Divinest Sense," in *Poetry for Students*, The Gale Group, 2002.

Sources

Aiken, Conrad, "Emily Dickinson," in *The Recognition of Emily Dickinson: Selected Criticism since 1890*, edited by Caesar R. Blake and Carlton F. Wells, University of Michigan Press, 1964.

Bates, Arlo, "Miss Dickinson's Poems," in *The Recognition of Emily Dickinson: Selected Criticism since 1890*, edited by Caesar R. Blake and Carlton F. Wells, University of Michigan Press, 1964.

Bloom, Harold, *Emily Dickinson*, Chelsea House, 1999, p. 11.

Carmen, Bliss, "A Note on Emily Dickinson," in *The Recognition of Emily Dickinson: Selected Criticism since 1890*, edited by Caesar R. Blake and Carlton F. Wells, University of Michigan, 1964, p. 63.

Denman, Kamilla, "Emily Dickinson's Volcanic Punctuation," in *Emily Dickinson: A Collection of Critical Essays*, edited by Judith Farr, Prentice Hall, 1996, p. 196.

Dickenson, Donna, *Emily Dickinson*, Berg Publishers, 1985, p. 80.

Dickinson, Emily, *The Complete Poems of Emily Dickinson*, edited by Thomas H. Johnson, Little, Brown & Co., 1960.

Doriani, Beth Maclay, *Emily Dickinson: A Daughter of Prophecy*, University of Massachusetts, 1996, pp. 8, 110.

Higginson, Thomas Wentworth, "Preface to *Poems by Emily Dickinson (1890),*" in *The Recognition of Emily Dickinson: Selected Criticism since 1890*, edited by Caesar R. Blake and Carlton F. Wells, University of Michigan Press, 1964, pp. 3, 11–12.

Johnson, Thomas H., ed., *The Complete Poems of Emily Dickinson*, Little, Brown & Co., 1960.

Jordon, Mary Augusta, "Emily Dickinson's Letters," in *The Recognition of Emily Dickinson: Selected Criticism since 1890*, edited by Caesar R. Blake, and Carlton F. Wells, University of Michigan Press, 1964, p. 59.

MacLeish, Archibald, "The Private World," in *The Recognition of Emily Dickinson: Selected Criticism since 1890*, edited by Caesar R. Blake and Carlton F. Wells, University of Michigan Press, 1964.

Miller, Cristanne, *Emily Dickinson: A Poet's Grammar*, Harvard University Press, 1987, p. 2.

Oates, Joyce Carol, "'*Soul at the White Heat*': The Romance of Emily Dickinson's Poetry," in *Critical Inquiry*, Summer 1987.

Further Reading

Dickinson, Emily, *Emily Dickinson Poems: First and Second Series*, edited by Thomas Wentworth Higginson and Mabel Loomis Tood, The World Publishing Company, 1992.
> With a total of 1,775 poems, this is an authoritative collection of all her work. The poems are thoughtfully categorized and ordered.

Dickinson, Emily, *Open Me Carefully: Emily Dickinson's Intimate Letters to Susan Huntington Dickinson*, edited by Ellen Louise Hart and Martha Nell Smith, Paris Press, 1998.
> This book contains the personal letters that Dickinson sent to her sister-in-law. The letters have been described as, at times, fierce and erotic. Susan was one of Dickinson's rare friends as well as one of her most valued readers of her poetry.

Farr, Judith, ed., *Emily Dickinson: A Collection of Critical Essays*, Prentice Hall, 1995.
> This book provides a wider vision of what the critics have to say about Dickinson's work. Whether you agree or disagree with their conclusions, the studies of her work offer different ways of reading her poetry.

Fuller, Jamie, *The Diary of Emily Dickinson: A Novel*, St. Martin's Press, 1996.
> This fictional work supposedly contains reprints from a private diary that Dickinson kept between March 1867 and April 1868. The diary, which cast some light on Dickinson's private life, was said to have been found in a wall of her family home during renovations in 1916.

Liebling, Jerome, Christopher Benfy, and Polly Longsworth, *The Dickinsons of Amherst*, University Press of New England, 2001.
> This is a collection of photographs that capture the buildings and landscape of Dickinson's world. The book contains more than a hundred pictures, including portraits of the Dickinson family. The book also includes essays by Dickinson scholars.

Sewall, Richard Benson, *The Life of Emily Dickinson*, Harvard University Press, 1994.
> First published in 1974, this book won the National Book Award. It is the first biography of Dickinson to rely on factual information, instead of on hearsay or speculation, and, as such, remains the definitive study of the poet and her work.

My Father's Song

Simon Ortiz

1976

Ortiz's poetry first appeared in 1969 in the *South Dakota Review*'s special Indian issue, "The American Indian Speaks." Since that time, Ortiz has been critically acclaimed as among the best of the contemporary Native-American poets, a recognition that extends to Indian circles. While the Native-American oral tradition, which includes song and prayer, has generally been unchronicled, contemporary American Indians such as Ortiz are creating a canon of prose and poetry that draws on this tradition.

Ortiz's poetry, including "My Father's Song," which was first published in 1976 in *Going for the Rain*, is strongly narrative. Ortiz has defended his style, stating, "Indians always tell a story. The only way to continue is to tell a story." This particular poem "continues" by remembering a moment in which his father passed on to him the reverence for the earth and for its living creatures. The language is deceptively simple and conversational, presenting images with full significance. Ortiz has said, "I try to listen to the voices of the people back home and use their sounds to direct my composition." The impulse for "My Father's Song" is the desire to hear his father's voice, engendered by his own need to "say things." In addition to this active practice of the oral traditions of his people and the basic philosophy they represent, Ortiz works to present in his poetry the specifics of his life as a Native American in such a way that the poems can achieve a more universal significance. In other words, the value of his poetry is not in presenting the life of the Native

Simon Ortiz

American as a cultural artifact, but in presenting the life of the Native American as one version of a contemporary American life.

Author Biography

Simon J. Ortiz was born in 1941, at the Pueblo of Acoma, near Albuquerque, New Mexico, the son of Joe L. Ortiz and Mamie Toribio Ortiz. Ortiz attended Grants High School in Grants, New Mexico, and then he worked briefly in the uranium mines and processing plants of the Grants Ambrosia Lake area. Ortiz then attended Fort Lewis College, where he became interested in drama and English studies. A leader of the Indian Student Organization, Ortiz became involved in issues of fair treatment for native peoples. Ortiz enlisted in the U.S. Army in 1963, after which he attended the University of New Mexico at Albuquerque. He received a master's of fine art degree from the University of Iowa in 1969. Ortiz taught writing and American Indian literature at various colleges and universities, including San Diego State University, the Institute of American Arts in Santa Fe, and the University of New Mexico. In December 1981, Ortiz married Marlene Foster, and in the following

years, they had three children, Raho, Rainy, and Sara. They divorced in 1984. Since 1982, Ortiz has been the consulting editor of the Pueblo of Acoma Press, and, in 1989, he became First Lieutenant Governor for Acoma Pueblo in New Mexico.

Poem Text

Wanting to say things,
I miss my father tonight.
His voice, the slight catch,
the depth from his thin chest,
the tremble of emotion   5
in something he has just said
to his son, his song:

We planted corn one Spring at Acu—
we planted several times
But this one particular time   10
I remember the soft damp sand
in my hand.

My father had stopped at one point
to show me an overturned furrow;
the plowshare had unearthed   15
the burrow nest of a mouse
in the soft moist sand.

Very gently, he scooped tiny pink animals
into the palm of his hand
and told me to touch them.   20
We took them to the edge
of the field and put them in the shade
of a sand moist clod.

I remember the very softness
of cool and warm sand and tiny alive mice   25
and my father saying things.

Poem Summary

Lines 1–6

It seems at first that the speaker is missing his father because he expresses a wish to say things to him. However, in line 3, it becomes apparent that it is his father's voice the son misses. He remembers it as a physical thing coming from his father's body. His father's voice becomes through the image of his "chest" a solid physical entity stronger than that "thin chest."

Line 7

This line provides a powerful transition between the two stanzas. The father's voice in the first stanza is speaking to his son, and what is to follow is the persona's "song" to his father, the poem that tells the story developed out of the memories. The two words, however, "son" and "song," by their closeness to one another in sound and sight, communicate that the persona himself understands that he is, in a way, his father's "song" by being his "son."

Lines 8–10

The storytelling technique of repetition functions in an almost incantatory fashion here to lead readers into a place where memory is real. Lines 8 and 9 both begin "We planted," and lines 9 and 10 play on the word "time."

It is characteristic of the oral storytelling mode that the teller talk his or her way into the tale, not leaving out the steps to getting there. Western storytelling, in contrast, generally values a more finished story product. Readers follow the persona in this poem through the general statement of line 8, to an explanation that this planting was one of many plantings, finally closing in on the one particular story or memory he wants to relate.

Lines 11–12

There is a digression here, as there often is in the rhythms of natural conversation. The persona is telling the story to the reader in line 11 but almost addressing his comment to his father in line 12. The rhymed couplet at the conclusion of the stanza emphasizes the tactile image of the sand.

Lines 13–17

The image of the sand brings the persona to the beginning point of the story, which is signalled by the stanza break. The father bends over the sand, pointing out to his son a place where the plow has overturned a nest of mice. The assonance of the vowel sounds of "overturned furrow," "unearthed," and "burrow," as well as the rhyme of "furrow/burrow," draw together the strands of this image that is spread over three lines. The effect is of patience, as the father clearly has with his son and the nest of mice and of focus, which is required for anyone to pay such close attention to tiny mice while plowing—or even to a child while doing adult work. The image of the sand, which houses the nest, closes this stanza and parallels the closing image of sand in the son's hand in the final line of the second stanza.

Lines 18–23

In a gesture that contrasts with the strong hand necessary to plow a field, the father lifts the surprise of these small creatures for his son "to touch."

Media Adaptations

- In 1993, Audio Literature of Berkeley, California, released *A Circle of Nations: Voices and Visions of American Indians*, an audiocassette of Ortiz and Joy Harjo reading from their work.

It is interesting to note that it is not enough for the father that the son see these animals; he directs him to touch the mice so that he can feel the life even in something so small. The carefulness of this small gesture is then enlarged upon as the father and the son together move the little animals out of harm's way, out of the hot sun which would scorch them, and back under a clod of cool sand at "the edge / of the field." It is again the physical memory of the sand that closes this stanza.

Lines 24–25

Line 24 characterizes the memory the persona has just related, referring to the gesture of the father, his gentleness toward the mice and to his son. The "softness" from this line moves forward to the tactile image of "cool" and "warm" and movement remembered in the son's experience of touching the mice.

Line 26

The effect of "softness" in the opening line of the fifth stanza is felt in this closing line as well, through the poet's careful lineation into the statement "I remember," then into the tactile image of mice, and finally into remembering the "softness" of the father's voice.

The poem comes full circle here, and the reader realizes with the poet that it is the voice of his father teaching him—"saying things" about tiny baby mice, about the importance of protecting little animals—that he misses. The tradition of passing on stories, information, about life from one generation to the next is the focus here. While it is typical Native-American oral tradition, hence the emphasis on the father's voice, Ortiz enlarges upon this tradition in his poem. He is not merely relating what he knows to a generation that comes after him, he is presenting the tradition as a valuable lifestyle for everyone.

The poem communicates the understanding that even in the midst of busy adult life with its purposeful action, there must be time to honor even the smallest manifestations of life, even those that innocently get in the way. Ortiz the poet has effectively become the song his father sang to him, which he sings to the reader in this poem.

Themes

Language

Phrases such as "actions speak louder than words" highlight the notion that to be credible language must be accompanied by corresponding behavior. Ortiz's poem underscores this point. Although the speaker opens the poem by saying that he misses his father's voice, he does not say that he misses *what* his father says. Rather, Ortiz emphasizes the physical qualities of voice such as "the slight catch" and "the tremble of emotion" when his father speaks. What he really misses is his father's presence, the way in which he interacted with him. By describing his memory of his father showing him the overturned furrow and placing newborn mice in his hands, Ortiz highlights behavior, not words. The link between the speaker's longing "to say things" and missing his father expresses the link between desire and creativity, for Ortiz does "say things" by the act of writing the poem.

Teaching

The relationship between parents and children is also one between teachers and students. Parents teach their children through example and explanation about the world and themselves. Ortiz describes one such experience, in which his father teaches him compassion for all living things by moving vulnerable newborn mice to a safer place. By first placing the mice in his son's hands, the father bonds the animals to his child. Significantly, it's the tactile sensation that the speaker remembers and not the words that his father says. That the memory is so powerful that Ortiz writes about it years later suggests that his father's lesson was learned. Ortiz keeps his father's memory alive by making it into a poem. Ortiz comes from a culture with an oral tradition, and one means of passing down information about your family and people is by making it into a story which you tell to others

His father's song, ironically, isn't a song at all but an event in which the father teaches the son a lesson about life. Ortiz uses singing, in this sense, figuratively. Songs by definition include music and sometimes words. However, the speaker's father does not sing in the poem. Instead, he shows his son an "overturned furrow" and places newborn mice in his hands.

Nature

The Acoma people are tied to the land, and Ortiz himself has commented that every aspect of his life is related to the natural world. "My Father's Song" underscores this relationship, emphasizing that one's own identity and purpose depends on an understanding of nature's processes and humans' relationship to other living beings. By choosing the incident of corn planting at Acu to figuratively describe his father's song, Ortiz zeroes in on that incident's significance. The feel of the "soft damp sand" and the "tiny pink animals" in his hand and the sight of the overturned furrow reinforce the connection between his own body and the earth's. Just as the tiny newborn mice need to be protected and nurtured in order to live, so too does the memory of Ortiz's father.

Poetry

Teachers of poetry and fiction are fond of telling their students that good writing *shows* readers something rather than *tells* them about it. Ortiz's poem follows this advice in both form and content. His father shows him the beauty and preciousness of living beings by placing the mice into his hands, just as Ortiz the poet shows readers his love for his father through description rather than explanation. The concrete images he chooses such as "sand moist clod" and "tiny alive mice" provide readers with a detailed image that sticks in their minds long after they've finished the poem.

Style

"My Father's Song" takes the shape of a simple first person childhood memory story. It is structured into five stanzas of varying length. The syntax is conversational, with the punctuation simply marking pauses and stops.

The poem is framed by the first two lines, "Wanting to say things, / I miss my father tonight," and the concluding stanza, which begins "I remember. . ." and ends with "and my father saying things." In between are memories, each stanza bringing the memory to a solid physical reality of "the soft damp sand," "the soft moist sand," and "a sand moist clod."

In the first stanza, there is the physical memory of the voice moving out of his father's "thin chest." The second stanza is the memory of the specific activity of planting corn. The memory deepens in the third stanza, with the discovery of a nest of mice. The fourth stanza focuses the memory more closely by the appearance of the "tiny pink animals." The final stanza connects this memory back to the father's voice.

Historical Context

Native-American History: 1960s–1970s

During the late 1960s and early 1970s in America many oppressed groups, including African Americans and women, protested economic and social inequality and demanded greater representation. This was a time of idealism and youthful enthusiasm, when a just future for all seemed possible. By the mid-1970s, Americans had developed a hardened cynicism, born from their failure in Vietnam and the debacle of Watergate.

Around the time when Ortiz was writing the poems that appeared in *Going for the Rain* (1976), Native Americans were rebelling against centuries of oppression by the United States government. Then, as now, most Native Americans lived on impoverished reservations, their land and many of their traditions taken from over a few hundred years by European colonizers. In 1969, a group of Native-American activists occupied vacant Alcatraz Island, off the coast of San Francisco, for eighteen months. The group demanded that a cultural and educational center for Native Americans be built on Alcatraz, formerly the site of a federal prison.

In 1972, another group of activists led a march to Washington, D.C., to publicize the numerous treaties between the United States government and various Native-American tribes that had been broken. They called this march "The Trail of Broken Treaties," alluding to the forced migration of the Cherokee Indians from the eastern United States in 1838–1939 called "The Trail of Tears." Once in Washington, they occupied the offices of the Bureau of Indian Affairs for a week.

A more radical group of activists, the American Indian Movement, seized the village of

Topics for Further Study

- Research the Acoma Pueblo Indians and prepare a presentation for your class. Include a simple map detailing where the Acoma have lived. What is their relationship to nature, language, and community?

- Write a poem about one event that characterizes your own relationship to your mother or father; then, read it to your class.

- Watch and compare Westerns released in the 1940s and 1950s with those released in the 1980s and 1990s. What differences do you notice between how Native Americans are represented and how do you account for these differences?

- Rewrite Ortiz's poem from the point of view of the father. How does this change the themes and the meaning of the poem?

- The speaker of the poem says that he wants "to say things" and that he remembers his father "saying things," yet such things are never mentioned. Rewrite the poem using dialogue instead of reported action. Does this diminish the impact of the poem? How or how not?

- Research the language of the Acoma and prepare a short list of vocabulary with a pronunciation guide for your class. Include the following words from the poem: voice, corn, sand, father, hand, mice, sand, alive, damp, time.

- In pairs, dramatize the poem, taking as many liberties with the "script" as you deem necessary. One person plays the father, one the son. Perform your interpretations for the class and then discuss variations.

Wounded Knee, South Dakota, in 1973 to protest the collusion between the government and what they claimed was a corrupt tribal leadership. The federal government agreed to negotiate with the Indians after 71 days, but they refused to reopen treaty negotiations. Two AIM leaders, Russell

Compare
&
Contrast

- **1970s:** The Indian unemployment rate is 10 times the national average, and 40 percent of the Native-American population live below the poverty line.

  Today: Half the total Native-American workforce remains unemployed, and nearly one-third live in poverty compared to 13 percent of the total U.S. population.

- **1970s:** Native-American life expectancy is just 44 years, a third less than that of the average American.

  Today: Life expectancy for Native Americans remains virtually unchanged.

- **1970s:** The American Indian Movement leads urban Indians, traditionalists, and young Indians along the "Trail of Broken Treaties" to Washington, D.C., seizes the offices of the Bureau of Indian Affairs in Washington, D.C., and occupies them for a week in order to dramatize Indian grievances.

  Today: Most Native Americans maintain an uneasy relationship with the BIA, which is responsible for managing Indian affairs, claiming that the BIA restricts their freedom and continues to demonstrate a paternalistic attitude towards Native Americans.

Means and Dennis Banks, were arrested and indicted for their part in the siege. These actions gave Native Americans across the country courage to battle the federal government, and many tribes took the federal government to court in an attempt to reclaim land and demand enforcement of treaties. The Sioux, for example, sued to reclaim 1.3 million acres of land in Black Hills, South Dakota, and the Passamaquoddy and Penobscot tribes in Maine won a $37 million dollar settlement from the United States government.

Native American Publishing

In the 1960s and 1970s, many Native-American authors published their writing to public acclaim. Kiowa Indian N. Scott Momaday's novel *House Made of Dawn* won the Pulitzer Prize for fiction in 1969. In 1971, Ortiz published a chapbook of poems, *Naked in the Wind*, followed by *Going for the Rain* (1976), and *A Good Journey* (1977). This was also the year that Laguna Pueblo writer Leslie Marmon Silko published her startling first novel, *Ceremony*. Other important novels of this period include Blackfeet Indian James Welch's *Winter in the Blood* (1974) and *Riding the Earthboy 40* (1976).

Over the next few decades, numerous Native-American poets and fiction writers gained an au-

dience for their writing. Some of the most important include poets Joy Harjo, a Muskogee Creek; Adrian Louis, a member of the Paiute tribe; and much-lauded novelist Sherman Alexie, a member of the Coeur d'Alene tribe. Writing in the late 1980s in *I Tell You Now: Autobiographical Essays by Native American Writers*, Ortiz himself notes:

> It has been only a little more than twenty years since Indian writers began to write and publish extensively, but we are writing and publishing more and more; we can only go forward. . . . we persist and insist in living, believing, hoping, loving, speaking, and writing as Indians.

Critical Overview

Andrea-Bess Baxter extols the 1991 publication of *Woven Stone*, which includes "My Father's Song," as "a testament to Simon Ortiz's influential career." Baxter emphasizes the importance of this volume as a collection of previously published poetic works that "use oral histories, narratives, and stories" and are based on "memories of a traditional upbringing at Acoma Pueblo, New Mexico," intertwined with contemporary experiences. She notes Ortiz's clear commitment to "native survival and endurance," but contends that "Ortiz's gift lies in making us aware of our own personal responsibility." This manifests itself powerfully in the simple story told in "My Father's Song."

Many critics see Ortiz's work as part of a contemporary Native-American renaissance. Ortiz himself has suggested that such a critical evaluation denies the ongoing oral tradition intrinsic to Native-American culture. He has discussed the oral tradition of Native Americans as "not merely a simple matter of speaking and listening, but living that process." "My Father's Song" embodies this philosophy.

Willard Gingerich indicates that the oral tradition and the voice of Ortiz's father are inextricably linked, so that "There is first his father . . . and there is the private song of that voice." Gingerich indicates that "we touch here the sacred core of what oral tradition means to those who carry it, not only in the grand affairs of religion and culture, but in the small, everyday acts of family life." In fact, Ortiz's poetic language springs from "the language and tones of his own background." He has indicated that "his formations with regards to language was . . . the way [the Acoma] spoke," and that it is listening to the voices of his people that directs the composition of his work.

Nevertheless, the authenticity of his composition is not consistently appreciated by critics. Harold Jaffe, for example, has expressed concern for what he views as the problematic syntax in Ortiz's work that seems "fractionally off, as if the English were adapted from another language." Gingerich, however, notes Ortiz's "remarkable transparency of language whose range and freshness is worth serious attention . . . [calling to mind] the conversational rhythms of Ezra Pound." But more than that, Gingerich claims, the voices of people in Ortiz's work establish "a new rhythm to English poetry." And as Ortiz himself says, "A new rhythm is a new idea."

Indeed, many may overlook the impact of Ortiz's work on the literary tradition of English poetry. There is a tendency to mistakenly read Ortiz as an example of a Native-American writer, or even read him almost anthropologically to find significance in his poems as cultural artifacts which tell about life as a Native American at the end of the twentieth century. But as Gingerich has said, just to be Native American does not ensure a writer of a place in any literary tradition, Native American or otherwise. In fact, although Geary Hobson points out that Ortiz's primary concern in his poetry is with both the history and contemporary circumstances of his own Acoma Pueblo Indian heritage, Ortiz asserts that he writes as an ordinary human being. Even so, Karl Kroeber insists that "there is no such thing as ordinary experience" and ultimately "My Father's Song" stands as testament to the fact that very particular expressions of human experience transform the ordinary into the universal.

Criticism

Chris Semansky

Semansky is an instructor of English literature and composition. In this essay, Semansky considers the relationship between purpose and language in Ortiz's poem.

Most poets claim that their writing arises out of a necessity, that they have no choice but to write. Some see the act of composing poems as therapeutic, while others believe such a notion is heretical to the very idea of art. Other poets compare writing poems with building something well and derive satisfaction from perfecting their craft, while some consider writing a means of intellectual exploration. Still others use poetry as a means of political protest and view their work as a way to effect social change. A driving force behind the writing of many Native-American poets, such as Ortiz, is the desire to share the history of their people. "My Father's Song" is an example of such a desire.

If it were written by another poet, Ortiz's poem might be considered yet one more of the many "workshop" poems pumped out every year by aspiring writers in creative writing programs across the country. Such poems typically recount some seemingly inconsequential experience of the speaker, who is indistinguishable from the author. According to Greg Kuzma, who criticized the workshop poem in his essay "The Catastrophe of Creative Writing," these poems lack "a sense of necessity or urgency." While Ortiz's poem certainly contains markers of the workshop poem, such as the reliance on the "I" and the description of a seemingly trivial event, his purpose is larger than merely asserting the importance of the self or wallowing in the past. The remembering "I" in Ortiz's poem does not merely put the experience at Acu out there for readers to ooh and ahh at but to explain the process through which the Acoma Pueblo Indians pass down their own culture.

> *All of this preparation is necessary for the individual before he sets out on his journey through life, before he wins the right to bring back the rain to his people.*"

The transmission of cultural knowledge is one of the primary themes of *Going for the Rain*. The collection is structured as a four-part cycle detailing elements of a Pueblo rain ritual. These elements include "Preparation," "Leaving," "Returning," and "The Rain Falls." "My Father's Song" is included in the "Preparation" section, with other poems addressing Native American creation myths, fatherhood, survival, and language. In the prologue, Ortiz describes the act of preparation as follows:

> A man makes his prayers; he sings his songs. He considers all that is important and special to him, his home, children, his language, the self that he is. He must make spiritual and physical preparation before anything else. Only then does anything begin.

Images of preparation and training appear throughout many of the poems in this section and in "My Father's Song." Planting corn, for example, shows the son the importance of the land to one's survival, and protecting the newborn mice shows the son the value of all living things, the interconnectedness of all life. These acts prepare the boy to be a man, giving him the tools required to lead a productive and meaningful life. These acts also help the boy to develop a sense of identity, as the lessons he learns are vital to the values of the Acoma people. All of this preparation is necessary for the individual before he sets out on his journey through life, before he wins the right to bring back the rain to his people. In an interview published in *Survival This Way: Interviews with American Indians*, Ortiz underscores the importance of land, of place, in constructing an identity:

> I can't really see any value in not knowing a place. You have to have it. Otherwise you are drifting. You remain at loose ends and you're always searching without ever knowing where you are or what you're coming to. I guess the background, the heritage of

Native American people at least offers this opportunity to have a *place*.

This kind of earnestness, this seemingly simple approach to life is at odds with the often densely ironic and allusive poetry practiced by today's poets. And though Ortiz's poem purports to describe actual events, it is not confessional poetry, at least not in the way that term is conventionally used to describe poetry that concerns itself with exposing the lurid details of its speakers, often relating to sex, drugs, or mental instability. Ortiz's poetry is a poetry of celebration, of lightness and hope. His voice is not singular and his poems don't set out to prove how the speaker is unique, original, or different from others. Rather, it is a communal voice, determined to show the love that all boys have for their fathers and how they remember them. In this way, the poem also represents an idealized relationship. In the *Dictionary of Literary Biography*, critic Marie M. Schein notes that the poems in *Going for the Rain* emphasize:

> the essential values that constitute the foundation of Ortiz's poetry; the belief in transmitting the gift of culture to the children, the importance of language and words, the respect for nature and for elders, and the harmony of the botanic, animal, and human worlds.

By packing all of these themes into his narrative poems, Ortiz creates a kind of moral urgency that seems neither moral nor urgent. His quiet voice and selection of details that show rather than tell the reader these values, give his words an easy, natural quality, as if he's merely reminding readers what they have always known. Ortiz's audience is not only other Native Americans. His stories of Acoma people and their culture are also meant to inform those unfamiliar with the Acoma way of life in particular, and the Native American experience in general. In this way, his poems serve an educational purpose. His book, after all, was published in Harper & Row's Native American publishing program. Categorizing his work as "Native-American Poetry" rather than simply "poetry" at a time when there were very few Native-American writers signed to large publishing houses gave Ortiz's work a kind of exotic appeal. His poems became representative of the Indian experience.

By writing narrative poetry, Ortiz also taps into the universal significance of storytelling to all human cultures. Schein notes that when asked to explain why he writes, Ortiz said: "Because Indians always tell a story. The only way to continue is to tell a story." The stories of the Acoma are different in their particulars than the stories of other cultures, but they share the same drive to make sense of life, nature, and the future as other cultures.

The irony of Ortiz's poetry is that he adapts the oral tradition to tell his stories in print and in English. But this too is a survival strategy, as it helps to preserve the culture of a people who increasingly use English more and Acoma less. In *Speaking for the Generations: Native Writers on Writing*, Ortiz notes:

> Using the English language is a dilemma and pretty scary sometimes, because it means letting one's mind willfully—although with soul and heart in shaky hand, literally—into the Western cultural and intellectual context, a condition and circumstance that one usually avoids at all costs on most occasions.

However, it is also the best and surest way to reach the widest audience possible. Poems such as "My Father's Song" are important because they provide the reading public with insight into the traditions and culture of a people who have historically been neglected, demonized, and ignored. The real language in evidence in Ortiz's poem is the language of compassion and of hope, a language desired by all, though not always accessible to all. Ortiz, as poet and voice of the Acoma, is also like the shiwana (rainmakers) in the song that opens his collection. His poems are his prayers and his hope.

Source: Chris Semansky, Critical Essay on "My Father's Song," in *Poetry for Students*, The Gale Group, 2002.

David Kelly

Kelly is an instructor of creative writing and literature at Oakton Community College. In this essay, Kelly examines Ortiz's achievement in making readers recognize the father's "song" while avoiding references to music or words.

In "My Father's Song," poet Simon J. Ortiz accomplishes a very difficult task. The poem manages to render a nonverbal experience in printed words. This is something that poems usually try to do, but "My Father's Song" does so by pointing to the connection between experience and song while avoiding any direct reference to music. On the face of it, this is as hollow as using only colors to explain how language works, but Ortiz somehow succeeds. He leaves his readers feeling how they might after actually hearing a song that the speaker's father taught him, but this illusion is just the sign of his skill as a poet. Actually, the father's words are reproduced nowhere in the poem, and only a few of his actions are referred to di-

What Do I Read Next?

- *Going for the Rain: Poems by Simon J. Ortiz*, published in 1976, contains many of Ortiz's most anthologized poems, including "My Father's Song" and "Hunger in New York City."

- *Fight Back: For the Sake of the People, for the Sake of the Land*, published in 1980, contains prose and poetry by Ortiz. Ortiz focuses on Grants, New Mexico, and the surrounding communities, detailing the exploitation of the land and the people from the Spanish conquistadors and missionaries to contemporary lumber, railroad, and mining companies.

- N. Scott Momaday's *The Way to Rainy Mountain* (1976) details Momaday's journey to find out about his people, the Kiowa. The book combines poetry, fiction, history, and meditation, and weaves Kiowa mythology with the legends and memories of Momaday's own family.

- *The People Named the Chippewa: Narrative Histories* (1984), by critic and novelist Gerald Vizenor, collects essays, mythological tales, and personal interviews to bring to life the Native-American people known by three names: the Chippewa; the Ojibwa; and, what they call themselves, the Anishinabe.

- Sherman Alexie's *Reservation Blues* (1995) tells the story of blues musician Robert Johnson, who returns from the dead and appears on the Spokane Reservation in eastern Washington. Alexie is widely considered to be one of the leading Native-American novelists writing today.

rectly. Ortiz redefines the word "song" to include manners and attitudes that his father passed along to him, broadening readers' perceptions of what might be considered music in the same way that deliberate, precise action is sometimes figuratively referred to as "poetic."

Ortiz was raised in the tradition of the Acoma tribe of New Mexico. The Acoma had no written

> *The father's song is both the way that he handled the situation in the cornfield and also the person that the speaker of the poem grew up to be."*

language throughout most of their history, although they have always had a rich culture, which has been carried on from one generation to the next through oral storytelling. This influence is seen throughout Ortiz's poetry, to such a strong extent that it even seems a little too overly simple to draw attention to the many obvious storytelling elements in his poems. He does see the act of telling a story to be more significant and wide-ranging than just a transcription of events, as he has discussed frequently when talking about his work. In a 1985 interview, for instance, Ortiz addressed how the oral storytelling tradition of the Acoma affects those who have been raised within the tribe:

> The oral tradition is not just speaking and listening... [I]t obviously includes everything within it, whether or not it's spoken about or acted out, or worked out, or how people respond to each other personally and socially.

To capture this sense of a world without writing, Ortiz's poetry has to show examples of the Acoma worldview in action. The "song" that the poem's speaker ascribes to his father in this poem is actually a feeling, caused by the father's behavior, which has a song-like effect on the poem's speaker.

This sense of "telling" and "song" that is unfamiliar to European sensibilities is indicated in the way that the poem uses the gangling phrase "saying things." In the first line, the speaker is struggling to "say things," apparently unsuccessfully—he is a poet whose words fail him, and the frustration of this situation is what brings a particular memory of his father to mind. Throughout the poem, the father's words are never directly presented to the reader. His voice is described in the first stanza after it has already come and gone, with a reference to "something he has just said"; and in line 20 the poem

mentions him telling the son something, but it does not render his exact words. The absence of direct quotation becomes conspicuous at the end, when the poem repeats the idea from the first line, using the similar phrase "saying things." Readers are forced to broaden their understanding of what it means to "say" when they see that the father has not actually said anything, at least not in the traditional sense. The poet's failure to say things, contrasted with the father's nonverbal success at it, leads to the conclusion that "saying things" is not as dependent on words as one might at first assume.

The father's song takes a different form than what readers ordinarily understand a song to be. This is emphasized in the poem by the way that this particular story of this particular day is introduced. In line 7, the poem uses the word "son" as if it is an unsuccessful, truncated attempt to say the word "song," which is spelled the same except for one final letter. The staccato, one-syllable words of the phrase "his son, his song" could give the impression of the poem's speaker stammering, choking on the expression the first time before completing it, leading to the conclusion that the two similar words are really the same thing. This structure certainly compels readers to look at how close these two words are, and doing so draws attention to how close they are in concept. Then, after "son" and "song" are united in this way, a third element is added. At the end of line 7, the colon indicates that what follows, the story of the mice in the cornfield, *is* the song and is also, then, by extension, related to the word "son." The poem's central event is therefore more than just something that happened once to the poet, it is in fact a part of his identity. The father's song is both the way that he handled the situation in the cornfield and also the person that the speaker of the poem grew up to be.

Much of this poem's power is derived from Ortiz's use of repetition. This would be true, of course, of any poem, where important points are emphasized by making readers feel the strange familiarity of having seen them before, but it is a technique that is especially important for a poem like "My Father's Song" where, as in a song, the main point comes from its mood, not its ideas. Ortiz ties the elements of this brief poem together with indistinct echoes.

There are echoes of metaphor, which are likely to have an impact on readers whether they are conscious of them or not. Of these, the most obvious is the one of planting seeds for future growth. The story this poem tells takes place when they are planting corn in spring, the traditional time of fertility. In fact, the author adds an extra line to point out "we planted several times," which shows this family's continual togetherness and also puts emphasis on the family's interest in growth. The symbolic connection between planting corn and the lesson that the father gives his son is easy enough to recognize, especially in light of the poem's circular shape: starting with the son wanting to say things and ending with the memory of the father saying things is just another way to say that the father planted the idea of oral tradition in the son's head, for future harvest. The fact that the mice are babies is symbolic enough of growth in and of itself, but the poet ties this symbol to the other one of cultivating corn by having the father place the baby mice in the soil, like seeds.

There are also echoes in the ways that Ortiz returns to one specific image at the end of every stanza in the poem's flashback story. In line 11, he refers to the memory of "the soft damp sand"; in line 17, the mice are found in "the soft moist sand"; in line 23, the father puts the baby mice into the shade next to "a sand moist clod." All of these physical images of sand are tied up in the poem's last stanza, where the reference is to "the very softness / of cool and warm sand and tiny alive mice." Earth and infants combine to capture the speaker's feelings about his father's song. The poem is tied together by the feel of sand, in some places cool and in some warm, but always soft and nurturing, reflecting its theme of how he learned from his father without words.

One final way that repetition is used to hold this poem together is in Ortiz's use of recurring sounds. There is only one direct instance of rhyming at the end of lines, at the end of the second stanza where he pairs "sand" with "hand." In addition to that, he uses some near rhymes, such as "catch" and "chest" in the first stanza and even "time" and "times" in the second: though the latter is not technically an instance of rhyme, it is definitely a case where two words sound similar, and so it serves the purpose of rhyme, which is to give the poem a sense of interconnectedness. The poem's most clever use of repeated sounds occurs in its middle stanza, where "furrow," at the end of line 14, is echoed by "burrow" in the middle of line 16, and they are surrounded by "show" and "plow[share]," which are not related by sound as much as they are by their visual presence. These subtle touches are useful for letting any poem show

that an author's hand is firmly in control, but they are especially significant in a poem about a writer finding a faint, barely recognizable trace from his past repeated in such a subtle way that he can hardly believe that the connection between past and present is real.

It is through his subtle use of repetition, to such a degree that most readers are not aware of his command of technique until attention is given to them, that Ortiz is able to raise the idea of a "song" without being too specific about how the elements of singing might relate his father's thoughts and actions. Though it is not a traditional song, the father's handling of this situation is nonetheless recognizable as a song of some kind. It has musical elements in its repetition, and the artistic elements that characterize nonverbal communication in the way that it touches on universal truths. The various parts and the whole all fit together with a mathematical precision, all steering toward the one main idea of raising seeds, or mice, or cultural identity, out of the sand beneath one's feet.

The poem's greatest mystery is that it is about the oral tradition, and it is called a song, but the singer is silent throughout it. The father's words are obscured by the author's summary of what he said, so that readers experience what happened without seeing much of how he behaved. Action has priority over any one person in the world of this poem: this could be a sign of the relative insignificance of individuals, or it could be a sign that the speaker of the poem is so secure with the memory of his father that he takes it for granted. In either case, "My Father's Song" gives readers with European-based sensibilities a rare opportunity to experience how life looks from the perspective of one of the many world cultures that developed to maturity without the use of written language.

Source: David Kelly, Critical Essay on "My Father's Song," in *Poetry for Students*, The Gale Group, 2002.

Sources

Baxter, Andrea-Bess, Review of "Woven Stone," in *Western American Literature*, Vol. XXVIII, No. 2, August 1993, pp. 162–63.

Bruchac, Joseph, *Survival This Way: Interviews with American Indian Poets*, Sun Tracks and University of Arizona Press, 1987, pp. 211–29.

Coltelli, Laura, "Simon Ortiz," in *Winged Words: American Indian Writers Speak*, University of Nebraska Press, 1990, p. 104.

Gingerich, Willard, "The Old Voices of Acoma: Simon Ortiz's Mythic Indigenism," in *Southwest Review*, Vol. 64, No. 1, Winter 1979, pp. 18–30.

Hobson, Geary, Review of "A Good Journey," in *Western American Literature*, Vol. XIV, No. 1, May 1979, pp. 87–89.

Jaffe, Harold, "Speaking Memory," in *Nation*, Vol. 234, No. 13, April 3, 1982, pp. 406–08.

Kroeber, Karl, Review of "Howbah Indians," in *Western American Literature*, Vol. XIII, No. 3, November 1978, pp. 280–81.

Kuzma, Greg, "The Catastrophe of Creative Writing," in *Poetry*, No. 148, 1986, p. 349.

Meredith, Howard, Book Reviews, in *World Literature Today*, Vol. 72, No. 3, Summer 1998, p. 665.

Ortiz, Simon, *Going for the Rain*, Harper & Row, 1976.

Ortiz, Simon, ed., *Speaking for the Generations: Native Writers on Writing*, University of Arizona Press, 1998.

Peters, Robert, *Hunting the Snark*, Paragon House, 1989.

Schein, Marie M., "Simon Ortiz," in *Dictionary of Literary Biography*, Volume 120: *American Poets Since World War II, Third Series*, edited by R. S. Gwynn, Gale Research, 1992, pp. 231–34.

Swann, Brian, and Arnold Krupat, eds., *I Tell You Now: Autobiographical Essays by Native American Writers*, University of Nebraska Press, 1987, pp. 185–94.

Further Reading

Allen, Paula Gunn, ed., *Studies in American Indian Literature: Critical Essays and Course Designs*, Modern Language Association of America, 1983.
  Allen offers not only insightful essays on Native-American writers but suggestions on how to design courses in Native-American literature. Sample syllabi are included.

Niatum, Duane, ed., *Harper's Anthology of 20th Century Native American Poetry*, Harper, 1988.
  This collection contains more than 350 pages of poetry from some of the leading voices in Native-American poetry, including that of Ortiz.

Smith, Paul Chaat, and Robert Allen Warrior, *Like a Hurricane: The Indian Movement from Alcatraz to Wounded Knee*, New Press, 1996.
  This engaging collection of documents chronicles the turbulent years from 1969, when members of the American Indian Movement took over Alcatraz Island, to 1973, when AIM sympathizers held off federal agents for eight weeks at Wounded Knee, South Dakota.

Wiget, Andrew, *Simon Ortiz*, Boise State University Press, 1986.
  Wiget's critical biography is indispensable for scholars of Ortiz's writing. Wiget's accessible study makes connections between Ortiz's life and work, while providing intelligent readings of individual stories and poems.

Reunions with a Ghost

Ai

1991

Since the publication of her first book, *Cruelty*, in 1973, Ai has established a reputation for writing poems that express the cruel way that people in close relationships behave toward each other. Her poems are uninhibited in their presentation of sex, death, and the darker side of human desire. Often they are narrated by troubled, anonymous speakers, sometimes poor people or those who are otherwise on the margins of society. Ai does not shrink from expressing unsavory and shocking truths; she presents the difficult emotions and destructive acts of her speakers without condemning them.

"Reunions with a Ghost" first appeared in Ai's fourth collection of poetry, *Fate*, which was published in 1991. The speaker of the poem is an anonymous woman who tells of her troubled relationship with the man she is in love with. It focuses on a particular incident that begins in disillusionment on the part of the woman, progresses to an act of lovemaking, and culminates in what appears to be the couple's final separation, although other interpretations might be possible. The emotions expressed range from contempt to love, passion, sadness, and puzzlement; the poem reveals the difficulty that men and women have in forming a successful intimate partnership. Although Ai's ethnic heritage is African American, Asian, and Native American, there is little in this poem that indicates the ethnicity of the two people involved. In that sense the poem is universal in the way it depicts hope, disillusionment, desire, reconciliation, and separation.

Ai

Author Biography

Ai was born Florence Anthony on October 21, 1947, in Albany, Texas. Her father was Japanese, and her mother (who was not married to him) was a mixture of Choctaw Indian, southern Cheyenne, African American, Dutch, and Irish. Ai was raised as a Catholic by her mother, and she and her half-sister attended Catholic school until seventh grade. She recalls that when she was a child, her family was very poor, and her stepfather, Sutton Haynes, needed to borrow money so he could buy food for the family. After living for a period in San Francisco and Los Angeles, the family moved to Tucson, Arizona, in 1961, when Ai was fourteen. By that age, she had discovered through a poetry competition at school that she could write poetry. Her earliest poems were all imitations of Edgar Allen Poe, to whose work she had been introduced at school.

After graduating from high school, Ai attended the University of Arizona, where she continued to write poetry. It was there that she changed her name to Ai, which is the Japanese word for love. It was also at the University of Arizona that she met the poet Galway Kinnell, when he gave a reading. Ai sent some of her poems to Kinnell for his com-

ments, and he encouraged her to apply to the writing program at the University of California at Irvine. After graduating in 1969, with a bachelor of arts degree in Japanese language and literature, Ai did indeed go on to graduate school at Irvine. It was during her graduate career that she decided that she wanted to write in the language of the common person, and her goal was to make her work as accessible as possible. She received a master of fine arts degree from the University of California, Irvine, in 1971. During her second year at Irvine, Kinnell showed her poems to an editor at Houghton Mifflin, and the result was her first book, *Cruelty*, published in 1973.

Recognition for Ai's work came quickly. She was a Guggenheim fellow in 1975, and a Radcliffe (now Bunting) Institute fellow in the same year. She was awarded a Massachusetts Arts and Humanities fellowship in 1976, and was visiting poet at Wayne State University 1977–1978. A second volume of poems, *Killing Floor*, followed in 1979. This volume was chosen as the 1978 Lamont Poetry Selection of the Academy of American Poets.

Ai's third collection of poems was *Sin* (1986), which won the American Book Award, and this was followed by a fourth collection, *Fate*, in 1991. In 1993, her fifth collection, *Greed*, was published by Norton, as was *Vice: New and Selected Poems*, in 1999. *Vice* was a collection of previous work along with seventeen new poems, and it won the 1999 National Book Award for Poetry.

Ai was writer-in-residence at Arizona State University from 1988 to 1989, and visiting associate professor, 1996–1997, at the University of Colorado at Boulder. In 1999, she became a tenured professor at Oklahoma State University.

Poem Summary

The first line of "Reunions with a Ghost" refers to the first night of God's creation being too weak, an obscure idea that quickly turns in lines 2 and 3 into a concrete image of a woman in a cobalt blue dress falling on her back.

Line 4 introduces the speaker of the poem for the first time, and she reveals that she is the woman referred to in the earlier lines. She also says that she survived the fall, although what she is referring to is not stated. It then becomes apparent that the speaker is addressing someone, a man, who is her boyfriend, lover, or husband. It is clear that she was at some point in love with him. She was prepared to make sacrifices and put his needs above her own ("I lived for you"). Apparently she is still doing so, since the next line (6) is in the present tense, indicating that the relationship is still in existence. However, the speaker's anger and dissatisfaction with her partner are clear, as she accuses him of not caring about whatever sacrifices she makes for him. Then she complains that he is drunk again, which appears to be a common occurrence, and is lost in a world of his own, turned in on himself.

In line 8, the speaker summarizes the way her lover complains about his own life. He believes that no one's troubles are as bad as his own. Apparently to demonstrate his misfortune, he unzips his pants to show her the scar on his thigh. The scar is a visible reminder of the injury he received when he was hit by a train at the age of ten. The man talks about the incident with wonder, but also with a contempt that is aimed at himself. He feels guilty because he was not killed in the accident. He thinks he deserved to die.

The speaker of the poem kneels and touches the scar as the man stands in front of her with his eyes closed. His pants and underwear are now at his ankles. The woman slides her hand up his thigh and touches the scar. This is a sexual overture. The man shivers and grabs her by the hair. They kiss and make passionate love on the floor, although the speaker comments that metaphorically speaking they never touch the floor. It is as if they are borne aloft by the ecstasy of the lovemaking.

When their sexual intercourse is over, the speaker says that nothing has changed between them, and she wonders about the nature of their relationship, which seems to puzzle her. Is it love or friendship that "pins us down / until we give in?" She seems to be asking what is it that continually draws them together in a sexual relationship. Whatever union and intimacy they gain during sex does not last, the speaker says. Afterwards they quickly retreat to the safety of their own separate lives.

In line 35, the woman says that her lover is now sober once more, following the sex. He dresses and sits watching her putting on her makeup. They go outside and kiss goodbye. The man departs, carrying whatever it is that haunts him and makes his life turbulent ("arm in arm with your demon").

The speaker reflects that she has once more endured the ordeal of loving, by which she seems to mean not sex but the intimacy of relationship. She feels sane and wise as she watches her lover walk off. Then he turns back, and she sees in his eyes a

look of acceptance and recognition. He appears to be certain that they will meet again "from time to time," although the word the speaker gives to him is not "meet" but "collide." This suggests that he is aware that any encounter between them, whether sexual or otherwise, is going to be stormy.

But it appears that the speaker has something else in mind. The emphatic repetition of "Yes. Yes," regarding the farewell she gave him suggests that she meant this as a final parting, even though he appears to believe something else.

Themes

Love and Sex

The main theme of the poem is the failure of love. The title hints at the story that unfolds, much of which is not stated explicitly but lies under the surface. "Reunions" suggests that in the relationship between this couple, there is a pattern of partings and reunions. The word "ghost" possibly refers to the man, who is only a ghost of what the woman once thought him to be (perhaps when she first fell in love with him). "Ghost" may also refer to the relationship itself, which is just a shadow of what it once was and continues in spite of the fact that, at least from the woman's point of view, there is no rationale for its continued existence.

Perhaps the theme might also be described as the hostility of intimacy, since although the word *love* is used, it does not seem to characterize the relationship, at least as it exists in the time frame in which the poem takes place. The woman seems to have only contempt for her drunken, complaining lover, with his self-pitying attitude and his demand for sympathy. However, she does show love in one particular gesture, and that is when she touches the scar that for the man is the visible sign of the fact that the world (so he appears to believe) has not dealt with him fairly. This is an act of acceptance on the part of the woman. It seems to say that she accepts him for what he is, and perhaps by doing that she seeks to make him whole once more, for there is no doubt that she loved him once, since she says as much. As she touches the scar, he shivers, as if she has indeed touched a vital core of him; she has reached him where his pain lies deepest. The man is obviously a wounded personality, riddled with guilt over something that happened in his childhood that was probably not his fault and over which he had no control. No doubt that guilt is

Topics for Further Study

- What are the underlying roles that the man and the woman in "Reunions with a Ghost" expect each other to play? Are these typical or atypical gender roles? Do the characters fulfill the roles or do they rebel against them?

- Write a paragraph describing how the woman reveals her character during the course of the poem. What sort of woman is she? How would you describe the character of the man, as seen through the woman's eyes?

- What does the speaker mean when she says, "I have come through the ordeal of loving once again?" What do you think she has learned?

- Is the mental and emotional makeup of men inherently different from that of women, or are the differences purely a result of social conditioning?

- Write a free verse poem from the point of view of the man in "Reunions with a Ghost," describing the same incident. Remember that people can remember and interpret the same events in very different ways.

deeply embedded in him, giving him low self-esteem and chronic insecurity.

But the impression the poem gives is that this gesture of touching the scar is something of a ritual between them: he whines about his circumstances, she comforts, consoles, and touches. They make love and all is healed for a short while. But then the troubles start again. This is certainly what happens in the sexual act described in the poem. Sex is just an escape, a temporary mask that covers the sadness at the heart of this relationship, which has reached a point at which it cannot continue any longer (although the man has yet to realize this). At least the physical act of sex provides some temporary exhilaration for this troubled couple, freeing them from their usual boundaries ("we just go on and on tumbling through space"), but even in this there is disappointment. The two "bits of stardust," an image that suggests that their cop-

ulation is lifting them into some exalted, cosmic realm, is immediately undercut by the phrase "shed no light." The mechanical nature of the act becomes apparent in the impersonal "it's finished," as if an involuntary physical spasm or process has simply played itself out. The description of their sexual act, as well as the prelude to it, suggests that it is not an outgrowth of a healthy love relationship, but something indulged in out of habit and necessity. The intimacy it provides is illusory; it changes nothing, as the woman explicitly states: "Nothing's different, nothing." This is also obliquely suggested in the previous line, "our descent, our falling in place," which describes the end of their lovemaking. The phrase "falling in place" puts in mind "running in place," an activity in which a person may expend a lot of energy but not actually go anywhere. The retreat into private, separate selfhood that follows is simply the final nail in the coffin. (There must have been many hammered in before this last one.)

All that remains to be said after this final failure of intimacy is goodbye, but even in that simple act this couple cannot communicate. Although the woman is clear in her own mind that she meant it when she said goodbye, the man appears certain that there will be more meetings, more "collisions," between them.

Style

Language

The poem is in the form of one long, unrhymed verse paragraph, and the diction (the words and phrases used) is largely the language of common speech. Most of it is literal description, although there is also some figurative language, as when the lovers are compared to stardust tumbling through space. The major cluster of images in the poem comes in the first four lines:

> The first night God created was too weak;
> it fell down on its back,
> a woman in a cobalt blue dress.
> I was that woman and I didn't die.

These lines may appear puzzling, and they do not permit a definitive explanation. The God who creates the first night is presumably an allusion to the book of Genesis, in which on the first day of creation God separates the light from the darkness, calling the light Day and the darkness Night. In the poem, the night is "too weak," falls down, and is then metaphorically equated with a woman who is then revealed to be the speaker of the poem. The woman falling on her back is an image of sexual surrender as well as simple weakness. Perhaps the allusion to God and the first night hints at night as the feminine realm, which is overwhelmed by the "day world" of masculine consciousness, but this is not really necessary for an understanding of the poem.

Historical Context

Ethnic Diversity

When "Reunions with a Ghost" was published in 1991, the American literary, social, and political landscape was marked by the need to express the ethnic diversity of the nation. Each ethnic group, whether African American, Asian American, or any other people of color, sought to affirm their own identity, in distinction from the dominant white culture that has tended to marginalize all voices other than its own. Feminists and gays also played a part in this explosion of diversity and multiculturalism, whether based on ethnicity, gender, or sexual orientation. This movement began in the 1960s and has gathered force in each succeeding decade.

Ai, who is half-Asian, part African American, and part Native American, as well as possessing some European blood, has been in a unique position to express the multicultural experience, to say what it is like to be a person of mixed race in contemporary America. Literary scholars and theorists refer to this as the attempt to create a discourse that empowers oppressed peoples. However, it is not a role that Ai has embraced. She says that she does not write as a black person or as a member of any other minority. Some black and feminist writers have criticized her for this, but she insists that she does not want her work to be catalogued in this way. She prefers to create poems that are universal in their meanings.

Changing Roles in Relationships

There is no racial element in "Reunions with a Ghost," since the ethnicity of the two people is not stated. But the poem does reflect difficulties in intimate relationships between men and women that were particularly apparent in 1990s America, and which continue to the present day. A frequently quoted statistic indicates that half of all recent marriages in the United States are likely to end in divorce, and in the 1990s, the United States

had the highest divorce rate in the world. The divorce statistics are related to wider social changes that have been going on since the 1960s. During that time, the number of women in the workforce increased dramatically, and this played a large part in breaking down traditional ideas about the roles of men and women in marriage. In the 1950s family, the role of the husband was to earn money to keep the family, whereas the wife looked after the home and raised the children. But a survey in 1994 showed that less than one person in four agreed that these were still the appropriate roles for men and women. In the absence of generally agreed upon roles for the sexes in close relationships, many couples found that they had to negotiate their own way to a successful partnership. The negotiation might have to cover everything from who pays for the dinner date to whose career is given priority and who does the majority of the housework and childcare. Although this has led to many new ideas about how to create successful partnerships that are in keeping with the temper of the times, it has also led to much unhappiness and failure.

The difficulties in relationships between men and women, and the need for new understanding, were reflected in popular culture. In the early 1990s, there were a number of best-selling books that sought to educate people about the differences between the way men and women think, feel, and behave. These included *You Just Don't Understand* (1991), by sociolinguist Deborah Tannen, which explained the difference in conversational styles adopted by men and women and how failure to recognize the differences leads to miscommunication. Another popular book was *Men Are from Mars, Women Are from Venus* (1992), by John Gray, which argued that couples must acknowledge and accept the differences between men and women before they can develop happier relationships.

Critical Overview

"Reunions with a Ghost" was first published in Ai's fourth collection of poetry, *Fate* (1991), where it was overshadowed by the new direction that the poet's work was taking. Most of the poems in *Fate* are dramatic monologues written from the point of view of famous figures in American culture, such as General Custer, Lenny Bruce, Jimmy Hoffa, and James Dean, and it was those poems that tended to catch the attention of reviewers. They stand in contrast to the narrator of "Reunions with a Ghost," who is an unnamed, ordinary woman, not an icon of American culture. In this respect, "Reunions with a Ghost" is closer to Ai's earlier work, in books such as *Cruelty* (1973) and *Killing Floor* (1979), which contain many poems written from the point of view of anonymous narrators who endure difficult lives.

Reviewers expressed reservations about the effectiveness of many of the dramatic monologues of the famous in *Fate*, and Penny Kaganoff, in *Publishers Weekly*, felt that "obscure lives make better material, as in 'Reunions with a Ghost,' a love poem that effortlessly and beautifully finds a resolution without enduring a full-blown socio-cultural exposition." In a favorable review of *Fate*, Rochelle Ratner, in *Library Journal*, commented that "male and female characters are equally pitiful, yet the poet's strength rests in her ability to avoid wallowing in sympathy for them."

"Reunions with a Ghost" was one of ten poems from the sixteen in *Fate* that Ai selected to be reprinted in *Vice: New and Selected Poems* in 1997, suggesting that it may prove to be one of her more enduring poems.

Criticism

Bryan Aubrey

Aubrey holds a Ph.D. in English and has published many articles on twentieth-century literature. In this essay, Aubrey interprets Ai's poem as one of the most tender poems in all of her work, an affirmation of the power of love, even the flawed love of two imperfect people.

The depiction of intimate relationships between men and women at one crucial moment of revelation is an important element in Ai's work, particularly in her first book, *Cruelty* (1973), as well as in "Reunions with a Ghost." Frequently, this moment is not a comfortable one, either for the protagonists or the reader. Ai's vision is tough and unsentimental; the speakers of these poems refuse to put on an acceptable social mask; they reveal the unvarnished, sometimes brutal truth as they experience it. The images employed are often raw and violent. They show the dark and dangerous impulses that dwell in the human psyche and which rise to the fore when a crisis erupts in personal relations. Often, the only way for the

characters to grasp at some kind of union or intimacy is through sex, and the poems emphasize the down-to-earth, unromantic physicality of the sexual act. ("I'll pull, you push, we'll tear each other apart" is how it is expressed in "Twenty-Year Marriage.") Sex may also simply be a brutal act involving dominance and submission, as in "Recapture," narrated from the male point of view, in which a woman tries to escape from a man but he captures her and beats her. She does not resist, and the result is a violent and coerced coupling that hints at some kind of reconciliation, but entirely on the man's terms:

> Going back, you stumble against me
> and I grab your wrist, pulling you down.
> Come on, [b——] of my love, while it is still easy.

In an interview with Lawrence Kearney and Michael Cuddihy (in *American Poetry Observed*, edited by Joe David Bellamy), Ai highlighted an important aspect of these poems, which might otherwise be missed:

> The distinction between my "sex-and-violence" poems and others you might read is that in mine the characters love each other. The poems are not hate poems. A lot of women's poetry approaches the theme of trouble between men and women in terms of hatred, I think, or "giving it to the man" in the same way that men have given it to women—and I never wrote from that point of view.

The first title Ai considered for *Cruelty* was "Wheel in a Ditch," which conveyed the idea of people who are stuck in a metaphorical ditch in their lives, unable to pull themselves out and move forward. Yet Ai also said that what she was striving for in all her poems was "transcendence. . . . no matter what the characters go through, no matter what their end, they mean to live."

Sometimes transcendence refers simply to the characters' attempts to overcome the oppressive, tragic nature of their circumstances and affirm who they are, or who they believe themselves to be, even if their self-identity might be considered morally unacceptable by society. In the poems about intimate relationships, the transcendence sometimes hinted at is of a kind that would lift the characters out of the messy complexity of their relationships in which conflicting individual wills and desires continually collide. This kind of transcendence can be found, for example, in "Twenty-Year Marriage" in which the speaker craves that she and her husband will be able to shake off the accumulated boredom of twenty years together by energetic lovemaking in a very unromantic setting (a pickup truck that is stuck in a ditch):

Come on baby, lay me down on my back.
Pretend you don't owe me a thing
and maybe we'll roll out of here,
heaving the past stacked up behind us;
old newspapers that nobody's ever got to read
again.

The desire here is for one moment of intense experience (which happens to be through sex) that annihilates the weight of the couple's long history together. All the accumulated hurts and betrayals (perhaps no more than what most couples rack up during a long relationship) are transcended, and the relationship becomes fresh and whole once more. However, this is only a wish, a thought in the speaker's mind, and it is qualified by the words "pretend" and "maybe," which suggests that she fears it may be out of reach.

These recurring concerns of Ai's—sex, intimacy, transcendence, and violence—are all found in one form or another in "Reunions with a Ghost." Although it can be read on one level as a poem of loss and failure, it also permits a more positive interpretation. It is in fact one of the most tender poems in all of Ai's work, an affirmation of the power of love, even the flawed love of two imperfect people.

This affirmation is present early on, in that the first five lines can be read as a kind of mystic sexual surrender in love on the part of the woman to the man. She gave herself to him completely, but she does not view this as a death ("I didn't die"), because in that act of devotion and self-sacrifice, she has found herself in a new way, with her whole life redirected ("I lived for you"). This is the ultimate experience of love, when the boundaries of self-interest and self-need are at every minute overcome in the desire to serve the beloved one. Disillusionment followed, however, and the woman now complains about the behavior of her lover. And yet as the man reveals to her his pain, as he must have done many times before, she overcomes her frustrations and her anger.

The actions of the man at this point can also be seen as expressions of love and trust. Although he is wallowing in self-pity, he is also open to the woman not trying to hide his wounds. The scar on his thigh that he reveals to her is more than physical; it also stands for every emotional wound he has ever suffered. And he trusts the woman with this, perhaps because she has healed him before through her love.

In touching the scar, the woman indicates that she accepts his pain, his disfigurement, in whatever form it takes; she will not turn away from him sim-

> *The images of tumbling through space suggest a kind of freedom—or loss of the usual boundaries of self—through sexual ecstasy, as if the lovers are borne aloft in defiance of the law of gravity."*

ply because of what he has suffered. He knows this, and he stands in front of her, immobile, as if waiting for the moment when he will be saved from himself, from the torment of his own separateness and guilt, from the shame that he feels about his own life. The origins of this shame are not revealed, but it is clear that his shame runs deep, and he seeks escape from it in alcohol. This is a man who habitually turns inward on himself, away from life, looking back into the pain of the past. The woman with whom he is involved in this turbulent partnership is the one who is capable of dragging him out of his funk and allowing him to face the world, however painful that might be.

Whereas the speaker in "Twenty-Year Marriage" merely hoped for transcendence through sex, this couple come closer to achieving it:

We kiss, we sink to the floor,
but we never touch it,
we just go on and on tumbling through space
like two bits of stardust that shed no light.

The images of tumbling through space suggest a kind of freedom—or loss of the usual boundaries of self—through sexual ecstasy, as if the lovers are borne aloft in defiance of the law of gravity (although the image of stardust that sheds no light somewhat undercuts this sense of spiritual liberation through sexual acts). When the lovers come back to Earth, the speaker's comment, "Nothing's different, nothing," is ambiguous. It could refer to her complaints earlier, in which case she may be saying that the lovemaking has failed to alter anything about this unsatisfactory relationship. On the other hand, she may be saying that after these moments of regained

What Do I Read Next?

- A Japanese novelist much admired by Ai is Yukio Mishima, whose masterpiece, *The Temple of the Golden Pavilion* (translated by Ivan Morris, 1994), first published in Japanese in 1956, is about the burning of a temple in Kyoto by a disturbed Buddhist in 1950.

- Ai has said that her greatest inspiration comes from fiction, especially Latin-American fiction. She is particularly enthusiastic about Gabriel García Márquez's *One Hundred Years of Solitude* (1970), which inspired her poem "Cuba, 1962."

- Ai is an admirer of *Beyond Heart Mountain*, poems by Lee Ann Roripaugh (1999). Roripaugh is part Japanese, and these highly acclaimed poems give voice to the Japanese immigrants of the American West.

- Some readers, including Ai herself, have seen a kinship between her work and that of Norman Dubie. Dubie's *Mercy Seat* (2001) contains many of the poems he has written in a period of over twenty years (to a chorus of critical praise), beginning in the late 1960s, as well as a number of new poems.

- Edited by Gerald Costanzo and Jim Daniels, *American Poetry: The Next Generation* (2000) is an anthology that features the work of many of the best American poets born since 1960.

- *New Selected Poems* by Galway Kinnell (2001) is a collection of poems written over a period of twenty-four years by one of America's foremost contemporary poets, who was also one of Ai's first mentors.

intimacy, she realizes that her feelings for the man are exactly the same as they always were—as they were when she first fell in love with him. Sometimes feelings do not change, whatever strains are placed on them and whatever the rational mind might decide about what it ought to feel. If the latter interpretation is preferred, the woman's state-

ment becomes a powerful affirmation of the bond of love that connects her to this man. It can be tested but not broken.

That is not to say it is easy. There are images of violence in the poem (you "grab me by the hair," for example, which does not sound like the most tender of sexual initiatives), but for the most part they are muted, far more so than in many of the other poems by Ai that deal with sexual love. The potential for violence is instead displaced into the mental rather than the physical realm, in the struggle between them for shared intimacy. The language in which the speaker recalls their sexual encounters suggests combat, war, and struggle. They are pinned down (like wrestlers) until they "give in" (like wrestlers forced into submission). Afterwards they rise "defeated once more" (like a boxer rising after failing to beat the count) and enter a "sanctuary" (like refugees from a war).

Whether the love is in fact defeated depends on how the last line of the poem, "Yes. Yes, I meant goodbye when I said it," is interpreted. It may be that the woman is emphasizing the fact that she is closing the door on this relationship for good, contradicting the man's apparent hope of future meetings. But there is another possibility. Her first "yes" could be a response to his certainty "that we must collide from time to time." She responds in the affirmative: yes, this will indeed happen. Then her thought returns to her goodbye, and she says, "Yes, I meant goodbye when I said it," meaning, although I meant it when I said goodbye, I no longer mean it. The emphasis falls on the second phrase, not the first. In terms of the narrative, this would imply that when the woman looked into the man's eyes for what she thought was the last time and saw in them acceptance and resignation, her heart softened, and she could not maintain her resolve to separate. The pull of love was too great.

Perhaps the different interpretive possibilities presented by the final line is a reminder that poetry, like drama, is a spoken art. Aloud, a reader has a choice in that last line to convey one of two quite opposite meanings, and on that choice may well rest the understanding of the theme of the poem.

Source: Bryan Aubrey, Critical Essay on "Reunions with a Ghost," in *Poetry for Students*, The Gale Group, 2002.

Pamela Steed Hill

Hill is the author of a poetry collection, has published widely in literary journals, and is an editor for a university publications department. In the following essay, Hill looks at the poem twofold—

first, to suggest a possible identity of the man to whom it is dedicated, and, second, to consider why it is a love poem in spite of the unromantic, sordid episode it describes.

Ai is one of those poets that most readers tend to be very opinionated about. One either loves her work or despises it, quite often for the same reason. Her subjects primarily center on sex or violence—sometimes both. Her language is plain-talk and usually crude, and her presentation is at once shockingly explicit and carefully honest. The most common form of poetry she employs is the dramatic monologue, in which she takes on the voice of a famous—or infamous—person, living or dead, and fabricates a story from that individual's perspective. The stories derive from a little bit of fact and a whole lot of fiction. Not all of the speakers in her monologues, however, are real people. Some of these speakers simply give voice to characters she has created, typically murderers, abused women, rapists, child molesters, and so forth. "Reunions with a Ghost" is generally considered one of the latter. But, what if this poem is subtly based on the same people who are more obviously portrayed in the poem that precedes this one in the collection? There is plenty of evidence that points to the possibility. But there is a second aspect here that is perhaps even more worthy of exploration. "Reunions with a Ghost" depicts a sexual act that seems to have little to do with love. As with most Ai poems about men and women, the people within it may be violent, brutish, even disgusting, but they still manage to save a place for love.

The book in which this poem first appeared, *Fate*, is a collection of dramatic monologues, including such speakers as Mary Jo Kopechne (who drowned when a car in which she was riding with Senator Edward Kennedy plunged off a bridge in 1969), Lyndon Johnson, Jimmy Hoffa, General George Custer, and Jim and Tammy Faye Bakker. The poem based on the highly publicized sex scandal that brought about the downfall of evangelist Jim Bakker is called "Eve's Story," but it is more an embellished tale of Tammy Faye and Jessica Hahn, Jim's "other woman," than of the biblical wife of Adam. This lengthy poem alludes to many sordid details of the Bakkers' lives—from Jim at the pulpit to Jim with his pants down, from Tammy's makeup to her mixture of feelings for Hahn—and it makes an interesting lead-in to "Reunions with a Ghost." Perhaps it is just a coincidence, but the dedication line under the title of the "Reunions" poem is "For Jim." The first line, "The

> *Within only a few short lines, the poem has transformed the character of the man from an aggressive, drunken fiend to a helpless, if not humiliated, child forced to show his wounds to the world."*

first night God created was too weak," immediately expresses a religious theme, which quickly blends with the speaker, a woman, describing the beginnings of a sexual encounter. The tension, attraction, and volatility between religion and sex were greatly exploited by the media during the Bakker affair, and it is the kind of controversy that typically inspires an Ai poem. The lines "I was that woman and I didn't die. / I lived for you" are reminiscent of Tammy Faye's tearful, public diatribes on her faithfulness to a man who had betrayed her and her determination to overcome the grief.

Whether evangelist Jim Bakker was ever struck by a train at the age of ten is unknown, but it is not unusual for Ai to introduce seeming "facts" (or exaggerations on reality) to emphasize a theme. What is more poignant about the train, the scar, and the "wonder and self-contempt" is that the "you" in the poem reflects the same remorseful, self-loathing confessions that Bakker did when his sins were discovered. The speaker in "Reunions with a Ghost" says, "you didn't die / and you think you deserved to," echoing her own declaration that death is not an option. It also suggests that the guilt felt by a supposedly God-fearing man who strays from the tenets of his belief is enough to make him think he should be dead. Bakker expressed similar remorse—not going so far as to want to die, perhaps, but certainly sounding very ashamed and self-deprecating. After the sexual encounter, the speaker refers to her and the man's "descent" and "falling." These two words aptly describe the downfall of high-profile celebrities, especially those in religious offices who are expected to be above the temptations of the flesh. "Falling from grace," of course, has been around since the story of Adam and Eve.

If the supposition that the "Jim" and the "you" in this poem refer to evangelist Jim Bakker and that the woman speaker must be Jim's ex-wife, Tammy Faye, still seems dubious, consider a couple more hints that emerge toward the end. Tammy Faye Bakker's signature look was (and perhaps still is) the extremely heavy makeup she wore, especially on her eyes and cheeks. Here, the speaker claims that, after the physical activity, she must "go through the motions of reconstruction— / reddening cheeks, eyeshadowing eyelids" while the man passively looks on. One more religious allusion makes the supposition more tempting: as the man and woman part, she watches him walk away, "arm in arm with [his] demon." With all the media coverage of the Bakker affair, it became common knowledge that Jim's "demon" was a weakness for the flesh, something Tammy Faye acknowledged and, supposedly, something for which she forgave him.

Whether there is any validity in suggesting "Reunions with a Ghost" is a poem whose characters are founded on the Bakkers can be answered only by the poet herself. The only claim here is that the basis for it is certainly plausible, given that the previous poem in the collection is unquestionably about this infamous couple and the other woman, so perhaps the inspiration carried over into a second work. Perhaps not. While the mental musing may be simply an exercise in conjecture, it is also stimulating to take a more serious look at the poem's subject matter—regardless of who the characters are—for it belies something that Ai has claimed is true about the men and women who stock her poems with pain, violence, greed, anger, and less-than-romantic sex: they really do love each other.

In various interviews and articles, Ai has compared her "relationship" poems to those of other poets who, like her, do not shy away from portraying graphically violent and sexual scenes to reflect the most base real-world situations that others may find too disturbing or embarrassing to write about. She has also attempted to distinguish her work from poems that leave only impressions of brutality and hatred and nothing more. In her poems, she claims, there *is* something more, and, while it may be difficult to find what that something is in a great deal of her poetry, at least in "Reunions with a Ghost" the evidence is not too obscure.

The first several lines in this poem depict a very roguish character on the part of the man— the "you" whom the female speaker addresses. Until line 10, all the reader knows of him is that he is a drunk who has dumped his lover only to return to her for a quick, possibly forced, sexual encounter. The language is startlingly brash, reflecting the man's attitude and behavior: "Nobody has trouble like I do, you tell me, / unzipping your pants." The reader's first impression here is that this self-centered ruffian is about to have his way with a woman who "lived for" him, whether she wants it or not. The scene takes a sudden turn when it is revealed that there is another reason he has unzipped his pants. The scar that he displays on his thigh, which apparently the woman is already familiar with, lends an air of vulnerability to an individual who before seemed nothing but ruthless and savage. His weakness is further exposed in the revelation that he speaks of the scar "with wonder and self-contempt" and that he believes he "deserved" to die when the train struck him. The scene becomes pathetic as the woman describes him next: "you just stand there / with your eyes closed, / your pants and underwear bunched at your ankles." Within only a few short lines, the poem has transformed the character of the man from an aggressive, drunken fiend to a helpless, if not humiliated, child forced to show his wounds to the world. Perhaps this is the "something more" that saves the poem. Perhaps without it, the man, the woman, and the entire premise would remain one-dimensional, predictably flat with violence, cynicism, and hate its only themes.

About midway through "Reunions with a Ghost" a hint of love does indeed creep into the otherwise questionable scenario. The line "We kiss, we sink to the floor" is downright romantic, even if it is surrounded by the more aggressive "you shiver / and grab me by the hair" and another allusion to the scar that neither of them will touch. What follows may not be the ideal dream of a beautiful relationship, but there is a sad kind of tenderness in the portrayal of this couple "tumbling through space / like two bits of stardust that shed no light." After sex, all the woman can do is ask, "Is it love, is it friendship" that has drawn them into this intimate encounter, but the question is one that will not be resolved. Nor does it seem that it will ever go away. The cyclical nature of these sexual episodes is evidenced in the confession that the speaker and her lover always "give in, / then rise defeated once more," only to go their separate ways until they meet again, whether for sex or for love.

It seems that the latter is how the speaker would describe it, although she seems almost pained in her admission that what she has just "come through" is the "ordeal of loving once again." *Ordeal* is not exactly the word one normally wants to associate with love.

Those opinionated readers mentioned earlier who find Ai's work too topical, too hateful, too graphic, or too offensive may have a good argument with certain poems, but "Reunions with a Ghost" is not likely one of them. Granted, it may start out that way—the reader is lured into believing that the encounter about to happen is going to be fast, selfish, violent, and, most definitely, loveless. Then, the poem turns, and the reader senses confusion and puzzlement over the strange tenderness of the woman's submission and her analysis of her own position. She claims that she is "sane, whole, wise," while her lover is left with only "acceptance, resignation." Yet, both of them are certain that they "must collide from time to time," and there is no indication that there is an alternative. Surely, this kind of undeniable passion—unwholesome as it may seem—reflects some kind of love, even if it is based more on need than true affection. The last line of the poem only emphasizes the futility of this volatile couple's inescapable attraction to one another. The speaker says she "meant goodbye" when she said it, but she has apparently said it so many times that her conviction is worthless. One can only assume that her ties to this dubious lover are woven in something stronger than the scenario their actions indicates. Something that may actually be called love.

Source: Pamela Steed Hill, Critical Essay on "Reunions with a Ghost," in *Poetry for Students*, The Gale Group, 2002.

Sources

Ai, *Cruelty / Killing Floor*, Thunder's Mouth Press, 1987.

———, *Fate*, Houghton Mifflin Company, 1991, pp. 43–49.

———, *Vice: New and Selected Poems*, Norton, 1997.

Bellamy, Joe David, ed., *American Poetry Observed: Poets on Their Work*, University of Illinois Press, 1984, p. 2.

Kaganoff, Penny, Review of *Fate*, in *Publishers Weekly*, Vol. 237, No. 51, December 21, 1990, p. 48.

Ratner, Rochelle, Review of *Fate*, in *Library Journal*, December 19, 1990, p. 129.

Further Reading

Erb, Lisa, "An Interview with Ai: Dancing with the Madness," in *Manoa: A Pacific Journal of International Writing*, Vol. 2, No. 2, Fall 1990, pp. 22–40.
This is an interview in which Ai speaks of her treatment of eroticism.

Hueving, Jeanne, "Divesting Social Registers: Ai's Sensational Portraiture of the Renowned and the Infamous," in *Critical Survey*, Vol. 9, No. 2, May 1997, pp. 108–20.
Hueving discusses Ai's poetic portraits of famous figures such as John F. Kennedy and Jimmy Hoffa and how these characters are juxtaposed with nameless characters such as dissatisfied wives, priests, and vengeful mothers.

Ingram, Claudia, "Writing the Crises: The Deployment of Abjection in Ai's Dramatic Monologues," in *Literature Interpretation Theory*, Vol. 8, No. 2, October 1997, pp. 173–91.
This is an analysis of how Ai explores the prevalence of violence in modern life by reminding her readers of their cooperation with the violence in language and culture.

Kilcup, Karen L., "Dialogues of the Self: Toward a Theory of (Re)Reading Ai," in *Journal of Gender Studies*, Vol. 7, No. 1, 1998, pp. 5–20.
Kilcup discusses Ai's treatment of sexual violence and female identity in terms of feminist literary theory and criticism.

Mintz, Susannah B., "A 'Descent toward the Unknown' in the Poetry of Ai," in *SAGE: A Scholarly Journal on Black Women*, Vol. 9, No. 2, Summer 1995, pp. 36–46.
This is an analysis of many of the dramatic monologues in Ai's *Fate* as revealing the voicelessness of a multiethnic woman. Her poetry perpetually reveals that the convergence of gender, class, and ethnicity deprives women of color of their voice.

Wilson, Rob, "The Will to Transcendence in the Contemporary American Poet, Ai," in *Canadian Review of American Studies*, Vol. 17, No. 4, Winter 1986, pp. 437–48.
This discusses Ai's books *Cruelty* and *Killing Floor* in terms of Ai's attempt to transcend her ego through assuming a masked identity, while still affirming her own identity over the world of death.

Song of a Citizen

Czeslaw Milosz

1943

"Song of a Citizen" is a poem by the Nobel Prize-winning poet, Czeslaw Milosz. It was written in 1943, during the German occupation of Warsaw and was published in Polish in Milosz's collection *Ocalenie* (English translation, *Rescue*) in 1945. However, the poem was unavailable in English until 1973, when it appeared in Milosz's *Selected Poems* in a translation by the author.

The context of the poem is the enormous social and political upheaval that Milosz has witnessed during his lifetime and the continuing world war in which thousands are dying. And yet even in the midst of all this horror, the poet affirms that it is better to be alive than dead. He seeks a respite from the dark realities that surround him by thinking of the eternal phenomena of nature and the formulae of mathematics. He also recalls times when he seemed to be able to penetrate the mystery of things, and the poem brightens with sensuous imagery and Arcadian visions. But "Song of a Citizen" ends on a strong note of regret, as the poet acknowledges that he may never be able to realize his dreams. He questions God as to why his life has been so full of suffering and who is to blame for it, but he finds no answers.

Author Biography

Czeslaw Milosz was born June 30, 1911, in Szetejnie, Lithuania, the son of Aleksander (a civil en-

Czeslaw Milosz

gineer) and Weronika (Kunat) Milosz. By the time Milosz became a high school student in Wilno (Vilnius), Lithuania had become incorporated into Poland. In 1929, Milosz enrolled in the University of Wilno and studied law. He also became known as a member of a literary group known as the Catastrophic School, and he published his first volume of poetry, *Poem on Time Frozen* (1933). Milosz graduated with a master of law degree in 1934, after which he studied in Paris. Returning to Poland, he published his second book of poems, *Three Winters* (1936), and worked for a radio station in Wilno and later in Warsaw. He was in Warsaw when Poland was invaded by German and Soviet forces in 1939, beginning World War II. Milosz remained in Warsaw throughout the German occupation, writing for the underground resistance. After the war, *Rescue* (1945) was published in communist Poland. This third collection of poetry established his reputation as one of Poland's important writers.

Milosz served as second secretary at the Polish embassy in Washington, D.C., for over four years and was then transferred to Paris, where he defected to the West. He lived in Paris until 1960, publishing frequently. His books included a nonfiction work, *The Captive Mind* (1953); two novels, *The Seizure of Power* (1955), which drew on his experiences in Poland during World War II, and

The Issa Valley (1955); *A Treatise on Poetry* (1957), and an autobiography, *Native Realm* (1958). He received the Prix Littéraire Européen for *The Seizure of Power*.

In 1960, Milosz moved to the United States, and, in 1961, he became professor of Slavic languages and literature at the University of California at Berkeley. Between 1962 and 1974, he published four volumes of poetry in Polish: *King Popiel and Other Poems* (1962), *Bobo's Metamorphosis* (1965), *City Without a Name* (1969), and *From Where the Sun Rises to Where It Sets* (1974). With the appearance of his *Selected Poems* in 1973, many of his poems were made available in English for the first time. Another collection in English, *Bells in Winter*, appeared in 1978.

Milosz also worked to make Polish literature more available to English speakers, publishing translations of Polish poetry and nonfiction works such as *The History of Polish Literature* (1970). He also translated into Polish many writers in English, including Shakespeare, Milton, Eliot, and Whitman.

In 1980, Milosz was awarded the Nobel Prize in literature, and, in that year, his books of poetry were published for the first time in Poland. In 1981, he visited Poland for the first time in thirty years, and the following year he published his tenth book of poetry, *Hymn to a Pearl*. In 1988, *The Collected Poems* was published in English.

In 1990, Milosz received the U.S. National Medal of Arts and was admitted to the American Academy and Institute of Arts and Letters. He was presented with the Order of the White Eagle by the president of Poland in 1994.

Poem Text

A stone from the depths that has witnessed the seas
    drying up
and a million white fish leaping in agony,
I, poor man, see a multitude of white-bellied
    nations
without freedom. I see the crab feeding on their
    flesh.

I have seen the fall of States and the perdition of
    tribes,   5
the flight of kings and emperors, the power of
    tyrants.
I can say now, in this hour,
that I—am, while everything expires,
that it is better to be a live dog than a dead lion,
as the Scripture says.   10

A poor man, sitting on a cold chair, pressing my
    eyelids,
I sigh and think of a starry sky,
of non-Euclidean space, of amoebas and their
    pseudopodia,
of tall mounds of termites.

When walking, I am asleep, when sleeping, I   15
    dream reality,
pursued and covered with sweat, I run.
on city squares lifted up by the glaring dawn,
beneath marble remnants of blasted-down gates,
I deal in vodka and gold.

And yet so often I was near,   20
I reached into the heart of metal, the soul of earth,
    of fire, of water.
And the unknown unveiled its face
as a night reveals itself, serene, mirrored by tide.
Lustrous copper-leaved gardens greeted me
that disappear as soon as you touch them.   25

And so near, just outside the window—the
    greenhouse of the worlds
where a tiny beetle and a spider are equal to
    planets,
where a wandering atom flares up like Saturn,
and, close by, harvesters drink from a cold jug
in scorching summer.   30

This I wanted and nothing more. In my later years
like old Goethe to stand before the face of the
    earth,
and recognize it and reconcile it
with my work built up, a forest citadel
on a river of shifting lights and brief shadows.   35

This I wanted and nothing more. So who
is guilty? Who deprived me
of my youth and my ripe years, who seasoned
my best years with horror? Who,
who ever is to blame, who, O God?   40

And I can think only about the starry sky,
about the tall mounds of termites.

Poem Summary

Lines 1–4

The first three and a half lines of "Song of a Citizen" form one sentence, with the subject ("I, poor man") placed at the beginning of line three. The poet likens himself to a stone in the depths of the sea that has witnessed a cataclysmic disaster. In the disaster, the seas have dried up and a million white fish, deprived of the element that gives them life, leap in agony. Lines three and four continue the metaphor, applying it to the realm of human history. The poet sees many nations deprived of their freedom. The description of them as "white-bellied" links them to the earlier image of

the white fish. Using another image drawn from marine life, the poet sees a crab eating at the flesh of the nations. The image suggests rot and decay in a world in which one living thing feeds on another (crabs eat dead fish).

Lines 5–10

These lines reveal more about the poet, who states that he has witnessed many disasters in human history. He has seen states fall, tribes become lost, and kings and emperors forced to flee. He has also known the power of tyrants. But in spite of this, and even while everything around him is dying, he still believes that it is better to be alive than dead. The allusion is to the verse in Ecclesiastes in the Old Testament: "But he who is joined with all the living has hope, for a living dog is better than a dead lion" (chapter 9, verse 4). This means that it is better to be alive even if one's lot in life is miserable because once a creature is dead, even a noble, powerful creature like a lion, it is as nothing.

Lines 11–14

Repeating that he is a poor man, the poet sits disconsolately in his cold chair and thinks of other things than the horrors of history. He contemplates a starry sky and a space not defined or measured by the principles of Euclidean geometry. (Euclid was a Greek mathematician who wrote a treatise on geometry in the third century B.C.) The poet also thinks of amoebas, microscopic one-celled organisms, and their pseudopodia. *Pseudopodia* is a zoological term, the plural of *pseudopodium*. It refers to a temporary projection of the protoplasm of a unicellular organism (such as an amoeba), by means of which it moves about and takes food, before being withdrawn into the mass of the organism's body. Following this, the poet thinks of tall mounds of termites. Termites are white ants that are found in the temperate zones and the tropics; they eat wood and can destroy wooden structures. Using soil and mineral grains, termites build mounds in which they lay their eggs. Some termite mounds can rise as high as a small tree; in Africa, they can be as high as twenty feet—hence, the reference in the poem to the "tall" mounds.

Lines 15–19

The poet states that his world has become reversed. When he is awake and walking around, it is as if he is asleep. Perhaps this means that he is forced to close his mind to the horror around him, dulling his own reactions. The phrase might also imply that what he has to endure each day is so awful that it puts to sleep his higher aspirations or his sense of purpose or his belief that life should not be so sordid or destructive. The result of having to endure this odd state, in which waking seems like sleeping, is that the poet's dreams become more real to him than his everyday experience. But the dreams are not pleasant. He is pursued by something—he does not say what—and he runs, becoming drenched in sweat. He also dreams of dealing in vodka and gold in the square of a ruined city. The city, with its "marble remnants of blasted-down gates" may have been bombed. Perhaps it is an image of wartime Warsaw. The reference to vodka and gold suggests that the poet dreams that he is selling valuable commodities on the black market during times of privation.

Lines 20–25

This stanza is in contrast to the previous one, which described different kinds of illusions masquerading as reality. Here, the poet recalls that on many occasions he was able to penetrate to the essence of things, the "heart" of metal and the "soul" of earth, water, and fire. He gained momentary insight into the deep truth about life; what was previously unknown revealed itself to him. These were serene experiences, the poet says, but they were fleeting. He compares them to luscious gardens that greeted him but disappeared as soon as he touched them.

Lines 26–30

This stanza appears to continue the thought of the previous one but places it in a more concrete setting, "just outside the window." The images of the beetle and the spider, which are "equal to planets," suggest the infinite significance of tiny things. Even a stray atom can suddenly flare up and seem as mighty as the planet Saturn. The stanza closes with a pastoral image of harvesters drinking from jugs on a hot summer day. The images of nature's tiny creatures are thus linked to human celebrations of the bountifulness of life.

Lines 31–35

The poet speaks personally of his desires in life. The way he places his desires in the past tense ("This I wanted and nothing more") suggests that he has not found what he wanted and does not expect to in the future. He says he had hoped that in his later years he would be like the great eighteenth- and nineteenth-century German poet Goethe, able to understand the natural world, to know it for what it is, and to express that understanding in his work

("reconcile it / with my work built up"). He anticipated that his work would be like a citadel, or fortress, a firm, stable structure, even though it had to be built on the unstable, ever-changing nature of life ("a river of shifting lights and brief shadows").

Lines 36–40

The poet repeats the first line of the previous stanza and then poses a series of questions as he seeks to know why his life has not turned out as he wished and why he has had to endure so many horrors. Who can he blame for this? Who is guilty? Who deprived him of his best years? The final question is addressed to God. However, the questions remain unanswered.

Lines 41–42

In the absence of any answers to the questions that trouble him, the poet returns to the images he used in lines 12–14, of starry skies and mounds of termites. This is all he can think about.

Themes

Destruction and Negation

In the first two stanzas, which establish the context for the whole poem, the poet contemplates destruction on a vast, unnatural scale. In line 1, the apocalyptic, end-of-the-world image of the seas drying up suggests that something is happening that has never happened before. The results are catastrophic, producing mass death and suffering and unprecedented upheavals in human social and political organizations. The catastrophe is clearly man-made, unlike a natural disaster such as an earthquake. It represents a negation of all positive human aspiration, the triumph of everything in the human psyche that leads to violence and evil. In the midst of it all, the poet, by means of metaphor, equates himself with a stone at the depths of the now-disappeared ocean, an image that suggests his helplessness in the face of the destruction he is forced to witness. The remainder of the poem is a valiant attempt by this "stone" to articulate a response to the tragedies that he sees unfolding.

Affirmation

In spite of the distressing position in which he finds himself, the poet still is able to affirm the value and beauty of life. Although deeply troubled, his spirit is not entirely crushed. The affirmations

Topics for Further Study

- Milosz once wrote of the "immorality" of writing poetry when confronted with some great horror in life (such as the German occupation of Warsaw). What do you think he meant by this? Does poetry have an important role to play in society? What might that role be?

- Research what is meant by "survivor guilt," a sentiment that is found in a number of Milosz's wartime poems. What effect does survivor guilt have on people's lives? What might be the best way to deal with it?

- Why did Milosz call his poem "Song of a Citizen?" Explain your answer. In addition, think of alternate titles for the poem and explain why you think these titles would fit the poem.

- Why is the image of the "tall mounds of termites" appropriate to the poem? What might it signify? (Do some research on termites on the Internet to support your view.)

- Why does Milosz mention Goethe in the poem? Who was Goethe, and why is the reference appropriate?

- Is it possible to answer the poet's final question, "Who, / who ever is to blame, who, O God?" Explain your point of view.

take a number of different forms, including a quest for knowledge, a will to survive, and imaginative insight into the true nature of things.

The first affirmation of life comes in the second stanza. The poet states quite simply that even at that very moment, when everything around him is dying, it is still better to be alive than dead. This suggests the power of the instinct to live that is implanted in human beings (as indeed in all living things) that cannot be crushed even by the most dire of circumstances. That the poet has a subconscious desire to survive at almost any cost is suggested in the fourth stanza, in which he dreams of selling vodka and gold in a ruined city. Presumably

this alludes to the role of the black marketeer, who in times of scarcity is willing to put scruples aside and make profit for himself from the sale of valued commodities. Vodka and gold also represent two ways of escape: alcohol alters perceptions of the world and temporarily eases sorrow, and material wealth can ameliorate for a time the pain of the human condition.

The poet also gives voice to deeper, more noble affirmations of life. In the third stanza, for example, he fills his mind with images from the natural world, far removed from the chaos around him. The thought of a starry sky, in its vast and still serenity, creates a calming influence. It suggests lofty thoughts of infinity, which lead the poet to contemplate mathematical concepts ("non-Euclidean space"), which, because of their order and unchanging nature, stand in stark contrast to the turbulence of human affairs. Even the images of the amoeba and the mounds of termites suggest the possibility of a kind of detachment gained through the contemplation of the microscopic and insect worlds that go about their business undisturbed by apocalyptic human disasters.

The fifth stanza contains affirmations of a different kind. The poet recalls moments of imaginative intensity when he was able to penetrate the mystery of being: "I reached into the heart of metal, the soul of earth, of fire, of water." In these serene moments of deep insight, he understood things that were previously unknown. He gives no concrete details of what he learned, resorting instead to images of the gentle coming of night or of a luxurious garden to hint at what such moments of transcendence were like. Perhaps the point is that such moments are ineffable, beyond words, and can only be suggested by images.

These moments of heightened perception are also fleeting, like the gardens "that disappear as soon as you touch them." But the poet is in no doubt of their importance, and in the next stanza he hints at them again. It is clear that his mind is still on these transcendental moments because the first phrase, "And so near," echoes the first line of the previous stanza, "And yet so often I was near." This time, however, instead of the elements of water, fire, and earth, the images are more specific, focusing on tiny creatures in the physical world that contain so much more than appears on the surface: "a tiny beetle and a spider are equal to planets." The significance of the tiny extends into the atomic world, where "a wandering atom flares up like Saturn." The affirmation lies in the poet's insistence that everything in the world, even the tiniest insects and particles of matter, has a significance deeper than can be grasped by mere observation of the surface levels of life.

Desire and Regret

From visionary perception that sees beyond the ordinary, the poet moves to personal expressions of desire and regret. It appears that the moments of deeper insight, the attempt to affirm the integrity and wholeness of life in the midst of chaos, are not enough. The poet reveals that his real desires in life have not and may never be realized. That desire is to know and understand life in all its manifestations and to express that understanding in his own creative work. In the midst of the restless transience of life, the poet had wished to build something that would stand as a permanent embodiment of knowledge. He wanted to reconcile eternity and change, perhaps through understanding the eternal laws that govern the universe (as suggested by his interest in mathematics and biology) and combining the precision of the scientist with the insight of the poet. But now he knows this may not happen, since his youth and early manhood have been so blighted by suffering. But he does not know why this tragedy has happened or who is to blame for it. Since his desire to know is thwarted, all he can do is return to earlier images, of starry sky and tall mounds of termites, which may now acquire a darker connotation than they had when they first appeared. The starry sky is impersonal and does not respond to human desires, and the mounds of termites—intricate structures that display a high level of architecture—are also the breeding grounds of insects that destroy human-built structures.

Style

Style

The poem is written in free verse. The original, in Polish, contained some end rhymes, but Milosz, who translated the poem himself, did not use end rhyme in the English version. However, he does use other stylistic devices: there is alliteration, for example in lines 5 and 6. The "f," "p," and "t" sounds in the "fall of States and the perdition of tribes" are echoed in the same order in the following line by the "flight of kings and emperors and the power of tyrants." Alliteration occurs again in "tall mounds of termites" in line 14 and in lines 17 and 18 with "dawn" and "-down," words that are

close enough in sound to create an imperfect rhyme (also known as near or partial rhyme), in which the consonants are identical but the vowels differ.

The stanzas vary in length from four to six lines, with one two-line stanza at the end. The length of the lines varies also, between dimeter (two feet) and heptameter (eight feet), although most lines fall in between these two. The meter is irregular and creates varying effects. Line 1, for example, is a pentameter that contains three successive anapestic feet (an anapest consists of two light syllables followed by a stressed syllable), and this gives the line what is called a "rising meter," which is entirely appropriate to the meaning, since it reinforces the idea of a stone rising from the depths of the sea (or appearing to rise as the sea dries up). In line two, the spondee (two successive heavy stresses) followed by a trochee (a stressed syllable followed by a light syllable) in "white fish leaping" emphasizes this image. The next line begins with two successive spondees, "I, poor man, see," which brings an emphasis to the speaker of the poem and the subject of the first long sentence, mentioned here for the first time.

In a key passage in the poem, Milosz uses punctuation to create a poetic effect. The theme of the second stanza is that no matter how bad the conditions of life are, it is better to be alive than dead. The poet affirms the value of life and of his own existence with the words "I—am, while everything expires." He does not simply write "I am," which would not have the force that he wants. By separating the subject and verb by a dash, he makes the speaking voice (and the silent reader) pause, and the effect is that both words are emphasized. "I—am" thus becomes the poet's triumphant affirmation of his own existence, almost a moment of revelation. He has prepared the way for this with the repetitions in the preceding line, "I can say now, at this hour," which moves from a generalized "now," which could mean "today" or "this year," to the more specific "at this hour," which sets up the "I—am" that follows, with its affirmation of being in a particular moment.

Historical Context

Warsaw in World War II

Poland has long been a country caught between hostile larger powers. For much of the nineteenth century, Poland was ruled by Russia, but in 1915,

Compare & Contrast

- **1940s:** Up to 1945, virtually the entire world is at war. Germany and Italy battle the United States, Great Britain, Russia, and their allies for control of Europe, while in the Pacific region the United States continues the war against Japan.

- **Today:** Europe is at peace. Former enemies Germany, Italy, Britain, and France are members of the European Community, with economic and political ties that make a future war between them virtually impossible. These countries are also members of the North Atlantic Treaty Organization (NATO) a defensive military alliance. Of other former enemies, the United States and Japan are allies, not adversaries.

- **1940s:** Poland is at first under German control, then after World War II, although nominally an independent nation, it falls under Soviet domination. In 1955, Poland becomes a member of the Warsaw Pact, a military alliance between the Soviet Union and the communist nations of Eastern Europe. The Warsaw Pact is an adversary of NATO.

- **Today:** Poland is no longer dominated by the Soviet Union, which collapsed in 1991. Before that, the Poles, inspired by the labor movement Solidarity, had battled for a decade to overthrow the repressive communist regime. Along with the Czech Republic and Hungary, Poland is also a new member of NATO (joined 1997), marking its transition from communism to a Western-style democracy. Russia opposes this expansion of NATO.

- **1940s:** In wartime Warsaw, copies of Milosz's poems circulate in small numbers in secret. Some of them are copied on typewriters or by hand. Milosz is not known outside his native country.

- **Today:** Milosz is a winner of the Nobel Prize for literature (in 1980), and his poems, translated into English, are known and admired worldwide. He still writes in his native language. Through his efforts, much Polish literature in translation is available in the United States.

during World War I, Germany occupied the capital city of Warsaw, ending a century of Russian dominance. After World War I, Poland enjoyed over twenty years of independence, but this came to an end when Germany invaded the country on September 1, 1939. The Poles resisted, but after a three-week siege, Warsaw, a city of nearly 1,300,000 people, was captured. The Germans began a reign of terror that was to continue until early 1945. There were mass arrests, brutality, public executions, and forced deportations.

The Poles formed an underground resistance movement that carried out acts of sabotage against the Germans, who responded with bloody reprisals.

The city's 400,000 Jews suffered badly under the German occupation. They were herded into a walled ghetto, from which about 300,000 were sent to the concentration camp at Treblinka in 1942. In January 1943, the Germans attempted to deport the sixty thousand remaining Jews but met with resistance from the Jewish Combat organization. In April 1943, German troops attacked the ghetto and were again resisted by the Jews. The Germans responded by setting fire to the ghetto and flooding or smoke bombing the sewers through which many Jews tried to escape. Within a month, the Germans had killed almost all the Jews and completely destroyed the ghetto. Milosz, who as a member of the literary underground was publishing resistance poetry at the time, expressed revulsion at the killings in his poem "Campo dei Fiori," which includes these lines: "Those dying here, the lonely / forgotten by the world."

On August 1, 1944, another rebellion began, known as the Warsaw Uprising. The Polish underground hoped to gain control of the city before it was seized by the Soviets, whose forces had advanced to the banks of the Vistula River, on the other side of which lay Warsaw.

In the early days of the uprising, the fifty thousand Polish fighters gained the initiative. Within three days, they had seized control of most of the city from the surprised Germans. Milosz, who was living with his wife in the outskirts of the city, has described what happened to him on the first day of the fighting. The street in which he lived with his wife and mother-in-law came under fire from German tanks, and he and his wife took shelter with friends who lived on the next street. After the firing died down on the second day, Milosz's wife went back to fetch her mother, who was still in the building, and she also brought back some of Milosz's manuscripts. Not long after this, the building was destroyed by artillery fire.

Their troops under-armed and low on ammunition, the Poles' success did not last. The Germans fought back, bombarding the Poles' defensive positions with air and artillery attacks. Fighting went on for sixty-three days, but the Poles received no help from the Allies. The conflict is vividly described in Sir Winston Churchill's book, *Triumph and Tragedy*, the final volume in the British prime minister's history of World War II. Churchill tried but failed to get help to the Polish insurgents. On August 24, 1944, Churchill wrote to President Roosevelt, quoting eye witness accounts of the battle:

> The Germans are continuing . . . their ruthless terror methods. In many cases they have burnt whole streets of houses and shot all the men belonging to them and turned the women and children out on the street, where battles are taking place, to find their way to safety. . . . In one house, where lived old retired professors of Polish universities, the SS troops forced an entrance and killed many of them.

The Poles were finally forced to surrender on October 2, when their supplies ran out. During the two-month battle, the Poles had 20,000 insurgents dead and 25,000 injured. The toll among civilians was over 150,000. Many of them were killed in massacres that took place in the early days of the uprising. The Germans had 10,000 killed, 7,000 missing, and 9,000 injured.

After the Polish surrender, the Germans took revenge. Adolf Hitler ordered the destruction of Warsaw. Within the next three months, eighty-five percent of the city was reduced to rubble. Thousands of people were deported, and there was famine amongst those who remained.

Milosz, who lived through those terrible times of the German occupation, many years later found it a difficult subject to discuss: "There was the ghetto, for God's sake, and the liquidation of three million Polish Jews, a sin that cries out—on the earth, in all of Poland—to be absolved."

In January 1945, Soviet forces entered the city and established a communist government under Soviet control. The ruined city was rebuilt but remained dominated by the Soviet Union until 1989, when a noncommunist government was elected.

Critical Overview

"Song of a Citizen" was first published in 1944 during the German occupation of Warsaw as one of a cycle of six poems making up the slim volume, *Voices of Poor People*. Like other poetry published in occupied Warsaw, it was produced in secret by printers who were willing to take the risk of being caught and punished by the Germans. Many copies circulated in the city. Milosz tells a story of a Polish boy during the occupation who found a suitcase in the family attic. It had been recovered by his railwayman father from a train, the occupants of which had all been sent to the concentration camp at Auschwitz. When the boy opened the suitcase, he found a copy of *Voices of Poor People* copied on a typewriter. No doubt "Song of a Citizen," as the voice of a Polish poet writing under the German occupation, had inspired many readers long before it became known to the outside world.

The poem did not become known in English-speaking countries until 1973, when it appeared in Milosz's *Selected Poems*, in a translation by the author. At that time, Milosz's work was almost unknown in the United States. *Selected Poems* was enthusiastically received by reviewers. Paul Zweig, in the *New York Times Book Review*, commented that on the evidence of the book, Milosz "seems one of the few genuinely important poets writing today." Zweig also wrote, in a comment that is relevant for "Song of a Citizen," that "Although Milosz is a poet of many subjects, the experience of loss casts shadows across all his work and amounts to an interpretation of life itself." D. J. Enright, in the *New York Review of Books*, referred to the "rational but gentle skepticism" of "Song of a Citizen," quoting the entire second stanza and comparing it to the work of the early-twentieth-century poet, C. P. Cavafy. Enright also commented that Milosz's work was "easy to quote from but difficult to describe, since effect and meaning are so much a matter of tone."

The Warsaw Ghetto during World War II

tant reason Milosz chose this way of expressing himself was as a critique of the nihilism inherent in fascism. Fascism applied the same ruthlessness to the organization of human social life that the laws of nature produced in the evolution of animal life, particularly as shown by Darwinism:

> The universality and unpredictability of death, the struggle for existence determined by strength and the ability to survive . . . and the annihilation without trace of whole groups are all commonly accepted axioms in the biological sciences. But their application to human relations calls the entire humanist tradition into question.

Finally, Leonard Nathan and Arthur Quinn, in *The Poet's Work: An Introduction to Czeslaw Milosz,* interpret the poem, particularly lines 31–40, as Milosz's questioning of his vocation as a poet. They point out that this was more than a personal issue for Milosz, since he and his fellow poets in Warsaw were asking themselves whether poetry was of any use in such extreme times of human suffering.

Although Milosz's output as a poet has been prolific, "Song of a Citizen," a poem written relatively early in his career, still gains the attention of critics. For example, in his essay, "Czeslaw Milosz: Silence . . . Memory . . . Contemplation . . . Praise," in *World Literature Today,* William Riggan quotes the entire poem as being representative of the poems Milosz wrote in the 1930s and 1940s. In the same issue of *World Literature Today,* which is a celebration of Milosz, Krzysztof Dynbciak quotes lines 20–22 of "Song of a Citizen" as an example of one of Milosz's many "enraptured descriptions when being is encountered, where it reveals itself to man."

Aleksander Fiut, in *The Eternal Moment: The Poetry of Czeslaw Milosz,* points out that the first four lines of "Song of a Citizen" illustrate a characteristic way in which Milosz approached the violence of the age and the deaths of so many people: "No Polish poet ever so radically equated the destruction of human beings, races and nations with the death of fish, insects, crabs and reptiles." Fiut argues that there were a number of reasons Milosz did this. First, it was to show that man is part of nature and is subject to its laws, just as lower organisms are. Another effect was to show that during wartime all the trappings of civilization are stripped away, leaving man closer to the animals and "face to face with naked existence." But the most impor-

Criticism

Bryan Aubrey

Aubrey holds a Ph.D. in English and has published many articles on twentieth-century literature. In this essay, Aubrey discusses how Milosz's discovery of the poetry of William Blake influenced his poetic vision in "Song of a Citizen" and other poems.

In his book *The Land of Ulro* (1984), Milosz reveals his high regard for the English romantic poet William Blake (1757–1827). Milosz first discovered Blake's poetry in Warsaw during World War II. Working as a janitor at the university library, which was closed to the public, he taught himself English and read a few of Blake's poems that he found in an anthology. Milosz writes, "In those times and in that landscape so inhospitable to a child's awe before the miraculous, Blake restored to me my earlier raptures, perhaps to my true vocation, that of lover."

Later in his life, Milosz would study Blake's work, including his complex mythology, more deeply. Although he comments that he borrowed little from Blake in terms of literary technique, the influence Blake had on him is clear from the poems he wrote in wartime Warsaw, including "Song of a Citizen." Although Milosz does not say which of Blake's poems he read, it is likely that they were some of the *Songs of Innocence and of Experience* (1794), which were the best known of Blake's poems at the time and were frequently anthologized.

Blake's *Songs of Innocence* are short lyric poems written from the point of view of a child's innocent perceptions. The world is illumined by the light of God, and everything is under the divine protection. The flavor of Blake's *Songs* is echoed by Milosz in his cycle of twenty poems entitled "The World," which he wrote in 1943—the time he was also reading Blake. These are deliberately simple poems that express a serene faith in the order and beauty of the world. Like Blake's *Songs*, their simplicity of tone and diction make some of them resemble nursery rhymes. Milosz subtitled the cycle "A Naïve Poem."

Two of these poems, "Fear" and "Recovery," are clearly modeled on Blake's *Songs*, particularly "The Little Boy Lost" and "The Little Boy Found." In "Fear," a little boy is lost in a frightening dark forest at night. He calls out, "Where are you, Father? The night has no end. / From now on darkness will last for ever." In the companion poem, "Recovery," the father appears and comforts his son as the darkness and fog give way to dawn. Similarly, in Blake's "The Little Boy Lost" a frightened boy loses his father in a dark fen at night; in "The Little Boy Found," God appears like his father in white and rescues him.

If the poems in "The World" are Milosz's "songs of innocence," the cycle of six poems entitled "Voices of Poor People," as well as several other poems Milosz wrote in Warsaw in 1943 and 1944, form his "songs of experience." These are darker poems that face the reality of suffering and the terrible cruelties that exist in the world. Blake subtitled *Songs of Innocence and of Experience*, "Shewing the two contrary states of the human soul," and the epigram is appropriate, too, for Milosz's contrasting perspectives in "The World" and "Voices of Poor People." The latter collection, which includes "Song of a Citizen" provides a series of snapshots of what one man saw, felt, and thought in that dark period of Polish, and European, history.

One such thought concerned the role of poetry and the poet. Some critics argue that in the last stanzas of "Song of a Citizen," for example, the poet questions his vocation, as he realizes that he may never fulfill the poetic dreams and ambitions of his youth. This implicit questioning of what poetry can accomplish becomes the primary theme of "The Poor Poet," one of the poems in "Voices of Poor

> *It is remarkable that Milosz, who at the time had access to only a few of Blake's poems, should so thoroughly have imbibed the spirit of the English poet."*

People." It is a dramatic monologue that traces the evolution of the poet's career. His early poems were joyful, but since then he has seen too much of the world's miseries and now openly states that poetry is unrelated to real life and, therefore, of no use to humanity:

> I poise the pen and it puts forth twigs and leaves, it is covered with blossoms
> And the scent of that tree is impudent, for there, on the real earth,
> Such trees do not grow, and like an insult
> To suffering humanity is the scent of that tree.

The same theme is stated more bluntly in the poem "Dedication," which, although not part of the "Voices" cycle, was written in Warsaw in 1945. It includes the following lines: "What is poetry which does not save / Nations or people?" Later in his career, Milosz wrote of the "immorality of writing when confronted with some horror of the world or of life, the so-called conflict of life and art."

Milosz's tendency at the time to doubt his vocation and the power of poetry to change things was quite different from Blake's, who in *Songs of Experience* exalted the poet as a seer who knows past, present, and future. But Blake's lifelong belief in the power of the poetic imagination to perceive life beyond its surface appearances did have an influence on Milosz, and this is discernible in "Song of a Citizen."

One Blake poem that is often anthologized and which Milosz may have read in Warsaw in the 1940s is "Auguries of Innocence." It begins with some of Blake's most famous lines:

> To see a World in a Grain of Sand
> And a Heaven in a Wild Flower
> Hold Infinity in the palm of your hand
> And Eternity in an hour.

What Do I Read Next?

- Milosz's *Visions from San Francisco Bay* (1988) is a collection of short essays, originally published in Polish in 1969. Milosz moved to California in 1960, so his reflections on American culture figure prominently in these essays—essays that cover a wide range of topics, from literature to religion, philosophy, and history.

- *Postwar Polish Poetry: An Anthology by Czeslaw Milosz* (1983) is a collection by Milosz of 125 poems by twenty-five Polish poets writing since World War II. The emphasis is on poems published after 1956, when the lifting of censorship and the breakdown of official political doctrines produced an explosion of new schools and talents.

- *A Book of Luminous Things: An International Anthology of Poetry* (1996) edited by Milosz includes a wide range of poems selected by Milosz and grouped under thematic headings such as "Epiphany," "The Secret of a Thing," "The Moment," "Woman's Skin," and "Nonattachment." Milosz's introduction and his notes on individual poems give valuable insight into the reasons for his choices.

- *Destroy Warsaw!: Hitler's Punishment, Stalin's Revenge* (2001), by Andrew Borowiec, is a description of the Warsaw Uprising by a man who took part in it and survived. Borowiec gives a lively and sometimes harrowing account of those sixty-three fateful days in 1944 when Polish citizens rose up against the ruthless Nazi occupation forces.

- Polish author Stanislaw Lem's first novel, *Hospital of the Transfiguration*, written in 1948, is the story of a young Polish doctor who begins his career in a mental hospital, hoping to avoid the horrors of the German occupation.

The idea expressed in this quatrain is that somehow the whole of creation (indeed, the whole of being itself) is contained in every part of it, and it is the poet who is able to see this. Surely it is this concept that underlies the otherwise puzzling line in stanza six of "Song of a Citizen": "where a wandering atom flares up like Saturn," since the atom is Blake's "grain of sand" and Saturn is his "world."

Another echo of Blake's quatrain occurs in the second stanza of Milosz's poem "By the Peonies," which is part of the cycle "The World":

> Mother stands by the peony bed,
> Reaches for one bloom, opens its petals,
> And looks for a long time into peony lands,
> Where one short instant equals a whole year.

Other images in stanza six of "Song of a Citizen" have a Blakean flavor. Consider the lines "... the greenhouse of the worlds, / where a tiny beetle and spider are equal to planets." Blake's poetry is full of images of tiny things, including insects, that have a significance well beyond what might be supposed from the evidence of ordinary perception. An example would be the following lines from his long poem "Milton," which Milosz almost certainly did not know at the time he wrote "Song of a Citizen":

> Seest thou the little winged fly, smaller than a grain of sand?
> It has a heart like thee: a brain open to heaven & hell,
> Withinside wondrous & expansive: its gates are not clos'd;
> I hope thine are not: hence it clothes itself in rich array.

Once more, the minute thing contains whole worlds hidden to normal sight (note how in the line from "Song of a Citizen" quoted above, Milosz uses the plural, "worlds," where one would have expected the singular form of the noun).

It is remarkable that Milosz, who at the time had access to only a few of Blake's poems, should so thoroughly have imbibed the spirit of the English poet. Part of the explanation is that Milosz himself had the Blakean gift of seeing, in sudden moments of heightened perception, into the depths of things—a gift which is quite independent of literary influences. It is this aspect of Milosz's work that is apparent in these earlier lines in "Song of a Citizen":

> And yet so often I was near,
> I reached into the heart of metal, the soul of earth,
> of fire, of water.
> And the unknown unveiled its face.

In Milosz's autobiography, *Native Realm: A Search for Self-Definition*, he recalls one such moment from wartime, and it serves as a detailed gloss on the above lines:

> Lying in the field near a highway bombarded by airplanes, I riveted my eyes on a stone and two blades of grass in front of me. Listening to the whistle of a

bomb, I suddenly understood the value of matter: that stone and those two blades of grass formed a whole kingdom, an infinity of forms, shades, textures, lights. They were the universe. . . . I saw into the depths of matter with exceptional intensity.

Milosz would later associate such intense moments with experiencing life in the present, the now, the eternal moment, when consciousness of self is lost and the universe appears to disclose its inner essence and meaning. On some occasions, the poet senses the potential presence of such moments of illumination but they hover just beyond his conscious awareness. In the poem "Mittelbergheim," in *Collected Poems* (written in 1951), for example, he lies half-awake in the early morning and contemplates his many years on earth:

I felt I was attaining the moving frontier
Beyond which color and sound came true
And the things of the earth are united.
. . . .
Let me trust and believe I will attain.

These cryptic lines suggest the elusiveness of such moments, existing as they do in a "moving frontier," and yet they remain central to Milosz's quest for an authentic mode of being. In "This Only," for example, a poem written in 1985 and included in *Collected Poems*, the poet returns to a place of his youth, where he felt great joy in nature's variety and constant movement. Now, on his return, he does not ask for such moments to be repeated:

He wants only one, most precious thing:
To see, purely and simply, without name,
Without expectations, fears, or hopes.
At the edge where there is no I or not-I.

It is in such moments "at the edge," where all distinctions between subject and object vanish in an eternal moment, that poetry—at least a certain kind of poetry—is born. Once again, Blake has the right words, in lines that were well known to the later Milosz:

For in this Period the Poet's Work is Done: and all the Great
Events of Time start forth & are concievd in such a Period—
Within a Moment: a Pulsation of the Artery.

Source: Bryan Aubrey, Critical Essay on "Song of a Citizen," in *Poetry for Students*, The Gale Group, 2002.

Josh Ozersky

Ozersky is a critic and essayist. In this essay, Ozersky considers Milosz's poem as a statement of faith in the power of life.

Czeslaw Milosz, in his acceptance for the 1980 Nobel Prize in Literature, asked what tyranny had

to fear from experimental poetry. His response was that "Only if we assume that a poet constantly strives to liberate himself from borrowed styles in search for reality, is he dangerous. . . . There is no reason why the state should not tolerate an activity." He continued:

that consists of creating 'experimental' poems and prose, if these are conceived as autonomous systems of reference, enclosed within their own boundaries. Only if we assume that a poet constantly strives to liberate himself from borrowed styles in search for reality, is he dangerous. . . . In a room where people unanimously maintain a conspiracy of silence, one word of truth sounds like a pistol shot.

It is telling that Milosz sees the formal aspects of verse as a political decision and compares it to the sound of a shot. Milosz's vision was tested in wartime, and afterwards in the repression of Soviet Poland, from which he defected in 1951. A poet at the center of the century's greatest catastrophe, Milosz is one of the great spirits in contemporary literature, a seer who speaks truth to power through his rich sense of nature and the universal laws that govern it. But can the truth reside in poetry as mystical, abstract, and Olympian as his? For Milosz, as he also said in his Nobel address, is not concerned in his art primarily with the traditionally political. Rather, he believes so strongly in the power of the Truth, that speaking it, on whatever level, serves the ultimate reality, the eternal. This eternal will survive all human catastrophes, Milosz believes, because it exists outside humanity and even outside the natural world:

Complaints of peoples, pacts more treacherous than those we read about in Thucydides, the shape of a maple leaf, sunrises and sunsets over the ocean, the whole fabric of causes and effects, whether we call it Nature or History, points towards, I believe, another hidden reality, impenetrable, though exerting a powerful attraction that is the central driving force of all art and science.

This is heady stuff, mystical and metaphysical. It does not seem the stuff of a poet baptized by fire. Yet it is his very philosophical bent that allows Milosz to see beyond the devastation of his own lifetime. A humane Platonist, Milosz believes in the eternal, in an "impenetrable" reality behind all the forms of the world. Such a cosmic worldview seldom stops to make distinctions between public and private, large or small, or past and present. Life and death, truth and falsehood are its only coordinates. It certainly has no time to pay attention to poetry, a trivial form scarcely fit for attention. For that reason, Milosz' poetry has a weight of meaning that formal experimentation, of the sort

" *Such a cosmic world-view seldom stops to make distinctions between public and private, large or small, or past and present. Life and death, truth and falsehood are its only coordinates.* "

explored by his modernist peers, can never approach. For Milosz, poetry is not just poetry. It is a shot fired in self-defense.

For Milosz, the truth is a weapon, a precious power that alone can defeat despair and death. In "Song of a Citizen" the semi-divine consciousness of the poet conflates and contrasts the horrors of war (it was written in Warsaw in 1943) with the infinite glories of life. And the poet is at the center of it all.

> A stone from the depths that has witnessed the seas drying up
> and a million white fish leaping in agony,
> I, poor man, see a multitude of white-bellied nations without freedom. I see the crab feeding on their flesh.

The poem begins, appropriately, with a horrific image on conquest. Writing in occupied Poland in 1943, Milosz composed this poem at what was probably the nadir of the war. The Nazis had occupied the poet's native land in the first days of the war, in possibly the most one-sided conquest in modern history. Other peaceful countries had followed, as well as other military powers, and now, in his ruined capital, Milosz saw the world as many did: as an ocean of desperate, dying lives, about to be extinguished either by the Nazis or by "the crab" of general devastation. Milosz is rarely explicitly political, in the sense of speaking to the specifics of the time and place, and the "I" of the third line is not necessarily Milosz, any more than the poem is necessarily about Poland.

The next stanza continues on theme of devastation, spoken from an eternal, nameless observer.

> I have seen the fall of States and the perdition of tribes,
> the flight of kings and emperors, the power of tyrants.

I can say now, in this hour,
that I—am, while everything expires,
that it is better to be a live dog than a dead lion,
as the Scripture says.

Notice the weight and formality of the first lines, the slow, stately, iambic cadences—and how they contrast with the rest of the stanza. The general dissolves into the first person "I" and becomes more immediate as the line grows choppier, until it stops dead at the word "am."

Life matters most to the singing "citizen," who is a citizen of life and the world, rather than any particular country. Though "a poor man" caught in the world, his consciousness reaches out to embrace life in all its forms—from the "starry sky" of the heavens to the unimaginable forms of non-Euclidean space to the tiny and shapeless, ever-changing shape of amoebas. And the "I" is not merely the "transparent eyeball" of transcendentalism, but a living, breathing, sweating reality, the perspective of a single human being. For Milosz, reality must be read like a map; seeing is a heroic existential act, in which, as he tells us, "the unknown unveil[s] its face." He tells us, in heroic rhythms, "I reached into the heart of metal, the soul of earth, of fire, of water." The truth is eternal, residing in the elements; in the very stuff of the world. Can such a perspective be enchained by brute force? Throughout "Song of a Citizen," it soars beyond the grasp of warfare and brutality.

> And so near, just outside the window—the greenhouse of the worlds
> where a tiny beetle and a spider are equal to planets,
> where a wandering atom flares up like Saturn,
> and, close by, harvesters drink from a cold jug in scorching summer.

We see developed here the poetic ideas which have been developing throughout the poem begin to blossom. Small and large are equally miraculous; life in and of itself is the one force connecting the separate wonders enumerated by the poet. Even non-poets feel the force of life, "reach into" the elements: the harvesters drinking from the cold jug in hot sun grasp the harmony of extremes.

In this way, Milosz is very "Whitmanesque." Like Whitman, no part of nature is alien to him, nor do contradictions get in his way. "Do I contradict myself? Very well, then, I contradict myself (I am large, I contain multitudes)," wrote Whitman. For Milosz, the power of existence is unconquerable, but unlike Whitman, the poet is himself a flawed and imperfect vessel for that existence. As is his medium.

Milosz regards it ironically. In two stanzas beginning, "this I wanted and nothing more," he regards his own self, daring to take into the context of the world his own puny suffering.

> This I wanted and nothing more. In my later years
> like old Goethe to stand before the face of the earth,
> and recognize it and reconcile it
> with my own work built up, a forest citadel
> on a river of shifting lights and brief shadows.
> This I wanted and nothing more. So who
> is guilty? Who deprived me
> of my youth and my ripe years, who seasoned
> my best years with horror? Who,
> who ever is to blame, who, O God?

The hubris and grandiose self-pity here is a stark contrast to the high-minded exaltation of the narrator up until now. One interpretation is simply that the poet is here being ironic, overdramatizing his own personal problems as a way to put individual pain in perspective. But this would be an oversimplification. Milosz is an intensely emotional poet, one very sparing in his use of ironic artifice. Such an ultra-cool gambit as the one just described would be very unlike him. Nor does it make much sense in the larger context of the poem. Why bother belittling the narrator, when he has already been established as a "poor man" with his eyes fixed in the infinite distance?

Perhaps because, despite his best efforts to the contrary, Milosz in unable to attain the pantheistic rapture he seems on the verge of. Despite his best efforts to the contrary—the poet's imagination, his intellect, his bold grappling with the elements—he is still caught caught inside his own skin. Beyond his philosophizing is a comfortless mystery, the sense every person experiences in times of defeat. The repeated, rhetorical "who?" questions change the tone of the poem from an elevated, eloquent, and philosophical one to one of common exclamation. The penultimate stanza is the most conspicuously "unpoetic" in the poem. It is certainly the most unreflective, the one farthest from the empyrean musings of the poem's first two thirds. It suggests the difficulty of seeing beyond the prison of one's own circumstances. And the final stanza takes a final step away, putting the narrator's outburst back into symbolic context.

> And I can think only about the starry sky,
> about the tall mounds of termites.

These lines reconcile the split in the poem. To whom is a termite mound "tall?" Not the starry skies or the infinite perspective they represent. Is the mound tall to a person? Only given that it is made by creatures so tiny, that its scale is so wildly disproportionate to the beings that produced it. Perhaps, the poet suggests that his own verse is a similar undertaking—as hopeless in the face of the infinite, as ridiculous, and as stark a product of deliberate will.

"Song of a Citizen" is a trivial enough undertaking, after all, given the time and place of its writing. Composing metaphysical verse during wartime can, and was, seen by some as fiddling while Rome burns. But to transcend military defeat, and to defeat war and violence itself, required a great act of the spirit. To some extent, Milosz's entire career has been one long act of liberation.

Source: Josh Ozersky, Critical Essay on "Song of a Citizen," in *Poetry for Students*, The Gale Group, 2002.

Sources

Churchill, Winston S., *Triumph and Tragedy*, Houghton Mifflin, 1953, pp. 128–45.

Czarnecka, Ewa, and Aleksander Fiut, *Conversations with Czeslaw Milosz*, translated by Richard Lourie, Harcourt Brace Jovanovich, 1987.

Dynbciak, Krzysztof, "Holy Is Our Being . . . and Holy the Day," in *World Literature Today*, Vol. 73, No. 4, Autumn 1999, pp. 687–91.

Enright, D. J., "Child of Europe," in *New York Review of Books*, April 4, 1974, p. 29.

Fiut, Alexsander, *The Eternal Moment: The Poetry of Czeslaw Milosz*, translated by Theodosia S. Robertson, University of California Press, 1987, p. 42.

Johnson, Mary Lee, and John E. Grant, *Blake's Poetry and Designs*, Norton, 1979.

Milosz, Czeslaw, *The Collected Poems: 1931–1987*, Ecco Press, 1987.

———, *Native Realm: A Search for Self-Definition*, Doubleday, 1968, p. 204.

Nathan, Leonard, and Arthur Quinn, *The Poet's Work: An Introduction to Czeslaw Milosz*, Harvard University Press, 1991.

Riggan, William, "Czeslaw Milosz: Silence . . . Memory . . . Contemplation . . . Praise," in *World Literature Today*, Vol. 73, No. 4, Autumn 1999, pp. 617–19.

Zweig, Paul, "Selected Poems," in *New York Times Book Review*, July 7, 1974, pp. 6–7.

Further Reading

Carpenter, Bogdana, "The Gift Returned," in *World Literature Today*, Vol. 73, No. 4, Autumn 1999, pp. 631–36.

Carpenter discusses the influence on Milosz of the English and American literature he read in occupied Warsaw during World War II. These poets included Blake, Milton, Whitman, and T. S. Eliot.

Chamberlain, Marisha, "The Voice of the Orphan: Czeslaw Milosz's Warsaw Poems," in *Ironwood*, Vol. 18, 1981, pp. 28–35.

An analysis of the poems Milosz wrote in German-occupied Warsaw. Chamberlain views them as "bitter elegies" arising from the conflict between the poet's energy and his helplessness.

"Czeslaw Milosz: 1980 Nobel Prize in Literature," in *World Literature Today*, Vol. 55, No. 1, Winter 1981, pp. 5–6.

This article contains the entire text of Milosz's Nobel Prize acceptance speech that he made in Stockholm on December 10, 1980.

Mozejko, Edward, *Between Anxiety and Hope: The Poetry and Writing of Czeslaw Milosz*, University of Alberta Press, 1988.

This is a collection of seven scholarly essays that are both a tribute to Milosz and an attempt to give a balanced assessment of his literary output.

Sonnet XXIX

Elizabeth Barrett Browning
1850

Many poems have been written about love: its nature, its causes, its effects, its beginnings, its endings—but Elizabeth Barrett Browning's *Sonnets from the Portuguese* is unique in the history of English literature for the means by which the sonnets were eventually published for all the world to read. According to Margaret Foster's biography *Elizabeth Barrett Browning*, three years after her 1846 marriage to fellow poet Robert Browning, Barrett Browning was listening to her husband rail against "personal" poetry which, presumably, could not handle the greater and more complex themes that he felt poetry should. She then surprised her husband with the question, "Do you know I once wrote some sonnets about *you*?" and then showed him the forty-four sonnets she had composed during their courtship. Astounded by their beauty and power, Browning insisted that they be published, and in 1850, Barrett Browning's *Sonnets from the Portuguese* was read by countless more people than the sonnets' originally intended audience of one.

While the most famous line of all Barrett Browning's poetry is found in "Sonnet XLIII" ("How do I love thee? Let me count the ways"), all of the poems in *Sonnets from the Portuguese* reveal her agile mind that explores the nature of love and its effects on her. "Sonnet XXIX," like several of its companions, offers Browning a glimpse of his beloved when she is not in his presence: beginning with the statement "I think of thee," the poem depicts the workings of Barret Browning's mind as she anticipates her husband's

Elizabeth Barrett Browning

arrival. Although modern readers were not, of course, considered by Barrett Browning as she wrote her poems to Browning, they can still appreciate the skill and force of her verse over 150 years later.

Author Biography

Elizabeth Barrett Browning was born in Durham, England, on March 6, 1806, the oldest of her parents' twelve children. Her father, Edward Boulton Barrett, was a sharp businessman who made a fortune from a number of sugar plantations in Jamaica. Barrett was very stern, and he ruled his home with absolute authority; his household law forbidding any of his children to marry caused a great deal of strife. Barrett Browning grew up in Hope End, her family's country home near the Malvern Hills. As a child, she wrote a number of poems: her earliest known poem was written when she was eight, as a birthday gift for her mother. For her fifteenth birthday, her father had one of her poems (*The Battle of Marathon*) privately printed. Her first brush with sorrow, however, occurred in 1828 when her mother, Mary, suddenly died. After the abolition of

slavery in Jamaica, the Barretts' fortunes declined, and they relocated to London in 1837.

By the time she had moved to London, Barrett Browning's health was poor. As a child, she had suffered a spinal injury and shown signs of a lung condition that was never fully diagnosed; the damp climate of London only exacerbated her illnesses. Many remedies were proposed, and in 1838, she was moved to Torquay, where the sea air would, presumably, soothe her lungs. However, the trip proved a tragic one when her favorite brother, Edward (who had accompanied her at her insistence), drowned in a boating accident on his way back to London from her new residence. Feeling responsible for his death, Barrett Browning became a recluse and practically an invalid. She returned to London in 1841, where she rarely left her room and became dependent on morphine—a dependency that would continue for the rest of her life.

In 1844, her two-volume collection *Poems* was published; while her verses brought her favorable critical attention, her work also brought her the man who would eventually woo, win, and marry her: Robert Browning. Browning (who had yet to make his reputation as a poet) was so impressed by her work that he wrote to her. Over the course of the next few months, he and Barrett Browning wrote to each other almost every day until they finally met on May 20, 1845, and discovered that they were already in love. More letters (over 500 in all) and visits continued until the two were secretly married on September 12, 1846. Fearing the wrath of Barrett Browning's father, the newlyweds fled to Florence. Though the Italian climate greatly improved Barrett Browning's health, her father never forgave her, and she found herself disinherited. She and her father were never reconciled. Apart from a few short visits, Barrett Browning remained in Italy for the rest of her life; in 1849, she gave birth to her only child: her son, Penini.

In 1850, Barrett Browning's *Sonnets from the Portuguese* were published. Although they had been written earlier as a private gift to Browning (who called her his "little Portuguese" due to her olive complexion), her husband was so moved by the forty-four sonnets that he felt they should not be denied to the world. Barrett Browning acquiresed, and this collection stands as her greatest and most well-known achievement. Other significant works include *Casa Guidi Windows* (1856), a political poem in which she expressed her support for the Florentine nationalist movement, and *Aurora*

Leigh (1859), an experimental verse narrative. She died on June 29, 1861, and was buried in Florence. Browning published a collection of his wife's poetry in 1866, just as his own poetic career was at its height.

Poem Summary

Lines 1–4

Barrett Browning's first statement ("I think of thee!") is, in part, the subject of the poem, for the entire sonnet attempts to imitate, through its imagery and sound, the dynamics of her mind dwelling on Browning, her fond yet absent lover. (Though readers customarily use the term "speaker" to note the difference between a poet and the voice behind his or her work, in the case of "Sonnet XXIX" one can speak of Barrett Browning as the speaker, since the poems are deliberate and undisguised addresses to her husband.) Barrett Browning compares her thoughts of Browning to "wild vines" that "twine and bud" about a tree—here, the "tree" is Browning. Like vines, Barrett Browning's thoughts of Browning grow more profuse with the passing of time; eventually, they grow to such length and density (as they "Put out broad leaves") that they cover the tree that gives them a place to flourish. "Soon there's naught to see," she explains, except for the "straggling green" of the vines; in a metaphorical sense, Barrett Browning is suggesting that her thoughts eventually seem to overpower in intensity the thing that allows them to grow in the first place. Her longing for Browning seems to overshadow Browning himself, as eventually the "straggling green" on a tree "hides the wood."

Lines 5–7

Lest her words her be mistaken for an expression of romantic delight with her current situation, Barrett Browning immediately qualifies her previous idea. Calling Browning "my palm tree" as a sign of playful affection, Barrett Browning insists that she could never regard her thoughts (however "wild" and "broad") as a substitute for Browning himself. He is "dearer, better" than any thoughts about him, regardless of how beautifully expressed in verse those thoughts may be.

Lines 7–11

Barrett Browning's thinking about Browning has (naturally) increased her desire to see him, so

Media Adaptations

Barrett Browning's *Sonnets from the Portuguese* is included in the 1997 audio collection *Robert and Elizabeth Browning: How Do I Love Thee?* These cassettes feature a history of the Brownings' courtship, interspersed with performances of both poets' work read by Steven Pacey and Joanna David. The collection is available from the Audio Partners Publishing Corporation.

she asks him to "Renew thy presence" and face her. Extending the metaphor offered in lines 1–4, she commands Browning to act like a "strong tree" and "Rustle" his "boughs." Doing so will "set thy trunk all bare" and cause her thoughts of him (the "bands of greenery") to "Drop heavily down." The image of a tree shaking its own boughs in an effort to free itself of the vines that "insphere" it reflects Barrett Browning's opinion of Browning as a strong, masculine figure who, when "all bare," is beautiful in his simplicity and freedom from her encumbering thoughts. Indeed, Barrett Browning seems to hold little regard for her own thoughts, since she wishes these to be "burst, shattered, everywhere" once Browning appears before her.

Lines 12–14

Barrett Browning concludes the poem expressing the hope that she will soon be in the "deep joy" of Browning's presence and find herself under his "shadow"; as the shade of a tree provides comfort to those who sit under it, so will Browning's overpowering self provide comfort for Barrett Browning, who even describes the "air" under her "palm tree" as "new." Her world is a better place when Browning is in it, and she is willing to remain overshadowed by the force and power of her beloved. Finally, she tells Browning that she is willing to sit in his shadow because doing so will free her from constantly thinking of him; she longs for the time when she will be "too near" him and where thoughts *of* him will be unnecessary.

Topics for Further Study

- Research the critical receptions of Elizabeth Barrett Browning and her husband, Robert. To what extent do biographers and critics use the Brownings' marriage to better understand the poetry produced by this famous couple? To what degree do modern readers think one poet influenced the work of the other?

- "Sonnet XXIX" is one of the forty-four sonnets that comprise the *Sonnets from the Portuguese*. Compose a sonnet sequence of four or five poems in which you trace a speaker's emotional or mental activity as Elizabeth does in her sonnet sequence.

- Research the Victorian era to learn about the book-buying public: Who bought books? Specifically, who bought books of verse? Was reading verse strictly for the upper classes, or did the new middle class discover this pleasure as well? Then, see if you can draw any conclusions about Victorian readers and how they responded to women poets: were such poets received with enthusiasm, skepticism, or both?

- Read Rudolph Besier's 1930 play *The Barretts of Wimpole Street*, which dramatizes the romance between Elizabeth and Robert Browning. What liberties, if any, does Besier take with the known biographical facts? Is the Elizabeth of Besier's play seem like the kind of person who could compose "Sonnet XXIX?"

Themes

The Beloved's Absence

Barrett Browning's artistic challenge in "Sonnet XXIX" is to depict the feelings that come upon her when she is separated from Browning; by extension, the poem applies to anyone who thinks about his or her absent beloved with longing and anticipation of his or her return. Barrett Browning's method is to describe the workings of her mind in organic terms: thoughts are like "wild vines" that wind about the image of Browning, here likened to a tree.

Barrett Browning's comparing her thoughts of Browning to vines that "twine and bud" about him suggests the degree to which his absence (regardless of length) has affected her: "twine" implies that her thoughts continually move in steady ways, while "bud" suggests that they continually grow. One thought of Browning leads to a second, which leads to a third; thoughts engender more thoughts, just as vines keep winding and budding with the progression of time. These vines also "Put out broad leaves," and the size of these leaves suggests the intensity of Barrett Browning's thoughts—an intensity so great that "soon there's naught to see / Except the straggling green which hides the wood." Vines can, of course, kill a tree by wrapping themselves around the branches and effectively cutting off the tree's means of survival, but Barrett Browning does not want to commit "botanical suffocation." Instead, Barrett Browning wishes that she could see Browning in the flesh rather than in her mind's eye. Just as "straggling" vines are no match for the power and beauty of a "strong tree," thoughts of a person are a weak substitute for the person himself. Barrett Browning states, "I will not have my thoughts instead of thee" for this very reason.

Her recognizing that her thoughts of Browning cannot compensate for his absence prompts Barrett Browning to beg him, "Renew thy presence." To continue the botanical metaphor, Browning's return will be like a tree shaking off the vines that cover it: "Rustle thy boughs and set thy trunk all bare," she asks, wishing to see him in all the glory of his strength. ("Set thy trunk all bare" also slyly and playfully suggests Barrett Browning's sexual desire.) As the poem continues, Barrett Browning's wish to see Browning grows more powerful, to the point where she denies the value of her own longing: she hopes that the "bands of greenery which insphere" him will "Drop heavily down" and lie "burst, shattered, everywhere!" The reader gets the sense of Barrett Browning's growing impatience with her own thoughts and their feeble attempts to "insphere" the essence of Browning. Once her "strong tree" has returned to her, she can peacefully dwell in his "shadow" and breathe a "new air," an air made "dearer" and "better" by Browning's presence. Then, she will not *need* to think of him because she will be "too near" him. The physical presence of the beloved precludes any longing thoughts of him because this presence is too overpowering. As Angela Leighton remarks in her 1986 study *Elizabeth Barrett Browning*, "For as long as the speaker thinks her poem, she must miss the presence which supports it." Thus, the poem begins with "I think of thee" and ends with "I am too near thee," to indicate how Barrett Browning moves from wishes of seeing Browning to an imaginary fulfillment of that wish.

Style

The Sonnet Form and Sonnet Sequences

The word "sonnet" comes from the Italian *sonnetto,* a word that means "little sound." The first master sonneteer was Petrarch, who gave his name to the Petrarchan (also called Italian) sonnet: a poem of fourteen lines in which a situation or problem is presented in the opening eight lines (the octave) and then resolved or complicated in the remaining six (the sestet). The rhyme scheme of the octave is *abba, abba*; that of the sestet is *cde, cde* or (in the case of "Sonnet XXIX") *cdc, dcd.* The meter is iambic pentameter (ten syllables per line of alternating unstressed and stressed syllables). Sonnets became popular in England in the sixteenth century, when poets such as Sir Thomas Wyatt, Samuel Daniel, and Edmund Spenser began to employ (and toy with) the form. English interest in the sonnet eventually led to the creation of different sonnet types, the Spenserian and the Shakespearean, both of which still feature fourteen lines but alter the Petrarchan rhyme scheme. The form fell out of favor during the eighteenth century but was resurrected in the nineteenth by William Wordsworth, John Keats, Percy Bysshe Shelly, and, of course, Elizabeth Barrett Browning herself. The sonnet is still widely found in the work of modern poets such as W. H. Auden, Edna St. Vincent Millay, Edwin Arlington Robinson, and Richard Wilbur.

The reasons for the form's broad appeal can be easily understood: it offers readers a compact and intense examination of a specific issue and challenges poets to write about their subjects in a rigidly prescribed form. While the themes explored in sonnets are limited only by their creators' imaginations, the most commonly explored theme in sonnets is love and its effects on the speaker—as is obviously the case with Barrett Browning's "Sonnet XXIX."

"Sonnet XXIX" follows, to an extent, the metrical pattern of the Petrarchan sonnet: the poem's iambic pentameter is mostly regular, except for moments when Barrett Browning toys with the meter to emphasize an idea. For example, when she states

that her "vines" of thought "Put out broad leaves," the words "out," "broad," and "leaves" are all stressed to suggest the weight of her thoughts. Similarly, consider the line describing Browning's shaking her thoughts off his "palm tree" self:

Drop heavily down—burst, shattered, everywhere!

This line begins with a spondee (a foot with two stressed syllables), followed by an iamb, another spondee, an iamb, and then a pyrrhic (two unstressed syllables):

*Drop heav*ily *down—burst, shat*tered, *ev*erywhere!

The sound of this line reflects its sense as the reader's voice reflects the weight of these "heavy" thoughts crashing to the earth.

Rhetorically, the poem also generally follows the Petrarchan pattern, although the poem's "turn" (as the change between the octave and sestet is commonly called) occurs not in the eighth line but in the seventh, when Barrett Browning tells Browning, "Rather, instantly / Renew thy presence."

While "Sonnet XXIX" can be read and enjoyed on its own, it is part of a collection of sonnets titled *Sonnets from the Portuguese.* These forty-four sonnets make up what is commonly called a sonnet sequence, in which each poem serves as one step in a narrative, emotional, or psychological progression. Petrarch's sonnets, for example, explore the poet's feelings for Laura, his beloved, as the poems in Barrett Browning's *Sonnets from the Portuguese* depict her intense love and longing for Browning. Other notable sonnet sequences in English include Sir Philip Sydney's *Astrophel and Stella* (1591), Michael Drayton's *Idea's Mirror* (1594), Shakespeare's *Sonnets* (1609), and John Donne's *Holy Sonnets* (1639).

Historical Context

The Victorian Era

The adjective "Victorian" historically refers to the long reign of Queen Victoria (1837–1901). The first half of her reign was a period of incredible growth and prosperity, the most important example of which was the rise of the middle class as an economic and political power. A specific highlight (and example of English pride) of this half of Victoria's reign was the Great Exhibition (1851), in which hundreds of people from around the world visited London's Crystal Palace to view the fruits of technology and science. The nation enjoyed

Compare & Contrast

- **1800s:** The 1842 Treaty of Nanking ends the Opium War between Great Britain and China and confirms the cession of Hong King to Great Britain.

  Today: In 1997, Hong Kong is relinquished by the British and returned to Chinese rule.

- **1800s:** Karl Marx and Friedrich Engels publish their *Communist Manifesto* in 1848; their work influences a number of world leaders who adopt several of its economic and social ideas.

  Today: With the collapse of the Soviet Union, China remains the world's dominant communist power.

- **1800s:** In 1844, George Williams organizes the Young Men's Christian Association (YMCA) of London, a service organization.

  Today: The YMCA has expanded to include people of both sexes, all ages, and all religions as members. The World Alliance of YMCAs, headquartered in Geneva, Switzerland, has 30 million members in 110 countries.

- **1800s:** In 1849, Elizabeth Blackwell becomes the first woman to earn a medical degree in the United States.

  Today: Women routinely enter the field of medicine, although they are still underrepresented in the upper ranks of many medical schools.

---

perhaps its period of greatest optimism and enthusiasm. As Barrett Browning's husband Browning wrote in *Pippa Passes* (1841):

> The year's at the spring
> And day's at the morn;
> Morning's at seven;
> The hill-side's dew-pearled;
> The lark's on the wing;
> The snail's on the thorn:
> God's in his heaven—
> All's right with the world!

This unbridled enthusiasm, however, was rocked in a number of ways as Victoria's reign continued. In 1859, Charles Darwin published *The Origin of Species* and caused an international uproar from those who viewed his ideas of "natural selection" as heresy. In addition, while the rise of the middle class via the Industrial Revolution marked an achievement of earlier decades, more and more authors and politicians began examining the human cost of so great an economic boom. Writers such as Charles Dickens, John Stuart Mill, and John Ruskin attacked Victorian values in their work while politicians such as Benjamin Disraeli (who twice served as prime minister) attempted to uphold conservative attitudes. Though the term

"Victorian" was first synonymous with English patriotism and a belief that England had a sovereign duty to influence the affairs of the world, the term eventually came to connote an attitude of priggishness, old-fashioned values, out-of-touch conservatism, and a jingoistic nationalism that many English people viewed with scorn, rather than nostalgia. Writers such as Oscar Wilde, George Bernard Shaw, and Joseph Conrad sounded the final death blows of the era in their scathing (and popular) works.

Victorian Verse

While the Victorian age is best known for its explosion in the number of novelists and the refining of that form, the era also saw its share of poets who eventually became giants in the history of English literature. Foremost of these was Alfred Lord Tennyson (1809–1892), whose verse was wildly popular, very refined, and perfectly Victorian in manner and sentiment. (He became poet laureate in 1850.) Though her husband has since eclipsed her in terms of critical reputation, Elizabeth Barrett Browning (1806–1861) was also a well-known poet, despite her reclusiveness; indeed, it was her 1844 collection *Poems* that secured her fame as well as her future husband's heart. Her *Sonnets from the Portuguese* (1850) still stands as one of the finest sonnet sequences in the language. The early work of Robert Browning (1812–1889) received scant attention from critics or readers; it was not until the publication of his *Dramatis Personae* in 1864 that he became a household name; his mammoth series of interconnected monologues, *The Ring and the Book* (1869), cemented his fame.

As the century progressed, two other popular poets reflected the struggle between Victorian values and those of the new (and frightening) twentieth century. Rudyard Kipling (1865–1936) composed several volumes of poems that extolled what he saw as the virtues and inherent rightness of English imperialism; today, many readers view his work as representative of Victorian arrogance. Conversely, Thomas Hardy (1840–1928) wrote a number of verses in which he expressed his pessimism and uncertainty about his seemingly perfect Victorian world. While Kipling saw England as a force for the will of God, Hardy's verse is marked by a skepticism and anxiety that readers have come to recognize as the first sounds in verse of twentieth-century man.

Critical Overview

Since her death in 1861, Elizabeth Barrett Browning's work has received increased critical attention and approbation. As Julia Markus notes in her 1995 study of the Brownings' marriage *Dared and Done*, Barrett Browning's first critical rave came from her future husband, who began his first letter to her with the statement "I love your verses with all my heart, dear Miss Barrett" and who later prompted her to have the *Sonnets from the Portuguese* published because its poems constituted (in his opinion) the greatest sonnet sequence since Shakespeare's. Many critics agree with the assessment of Dorothy Mermin, who (in her 1989 study *Elizabeth Barrett Browning: The Origins of a New Poetry*) calls Barrett Browning "the first woman poet in English literature."

As Margaret Foster points out in her 1988 biography *Elizabeth Barrett Browning*, however, many of the poet's contemporary critics attacked Barrett Browning's poems for their "obscurity, strange images, faulty rhymes and affectation." Some modern critics have concurred with these reviews. In her 1988 work, *Elizabeth Barrett Browning, Woman and Artist*, Helen Cooper quotes Althea Hayter's *Mrs. Browning: A Poet's Work and Its Setting* (1962), in which Hayter argues that the poems in *Sonnets* "are not enough removed from personal relationship to be universal communication." Similarly, Cooper also quotes Lorraine Gray's 1978 essay, "The Texts of Elizabeth Barrett Browning's *Sonnets from the Portuguese*: A Structural Reading," in which Gray faults the poems for failing to "express the universal wisdom expressed in the love sequences of Dante, Petrarch, Sidney, Spenser, Shakespeare and Meredith." Finally, in her 1986 book *Elizabeth Barrett Browning*, Angela Leighton refers to Feit Deihl's 1978 essay, "'Come Slowly—Eden': An Exploration of Women Poets and Their Muse," in which Deihl dismisses the poems as "often sentimental" and "overly self-deprecating."

Such opinions, however, are those of the minority, for *Sonnets from the Portuguese* is widely admired. The aforementioned Dorothy Mermin argues (again in her *Elizabeth Barrett Browning: The Origins of a New Poetry*) that the power of the *Sonnets* lies in Barrett Browning's taking up "the male poet's place": she is both the "object of a poet's courtship" *and* "the sonneteer." Mermin specifically praises "Sonnet XXIX" for its portrayal of how "desire can conceal the object it transforms" and how the sonnet urges Browning to "break free of her entwining imagination." (She also applauds the poem's "joyously erotic" tone.) In her feminist study, *Elizabeth Barrett Browning* (1972), Mary Jane Lupton argues that the poems "capture those insecurities and self-doubts common to many women as they prepare for marriage." In the same vein, the aforementioned Helen Cooper (also in her *Elizabeth Barrett Browning, Woman and Artist*) argues that the fact that Barrett Browning did not write the poems for publication "empowered her voice" and allowed her to use the poems as a "process of discovery." According to Virginia L. Radley (author of the 1972 study *Elizabeth Barrett Browning*), the poems treat the challenge Barrett Browning faced of "how to cope with love" after she had resigned herself to an early death. Ultimately, for both aesthetic and biographical reasons, most critics concur with Julia Markus, who (in her *Dared and Done*) calls *Sonnets* "the deepest and at times the darkest thoughts of a woman of genius, in grave health, who finds in middle life not the death she waits for but the love she never expected."

Criticism

Daniel Moran

Moran is an instructor of English and American literature. In this essay, Moran explores the ways in which "Sonnet XXIX" dramatizes the workings of Elizabeth's mind as she thinks of her absent lover.

In his 1755 *Preface to the English Dictionary*, the lexicographer Samuel Johnson defends his decision not to alter the spellings of the words in his book to suit changes in use or pronunciation. "There is in constancy and stability a general and lasting advantage," he explains, "which will always overbalance the slow improvements of gradual correction." However, Johnson also acknowledges that all debates about spelling and pronunciation are, in a greater sense, almost trivial:

> This recommendation of steadiness and uniformity does not proceed from an opinion, that particular combinations of letters have much influence on human happiness; or that truth may not be successfully taught by modes of spelling fanciful and erroneous: I am not yet so lost in lexicography, as to forget that *words are the daughters of earth, and that things are the sons of heaven*. Language is only the instrument of science, and words are but the signs of ideas: I wish, however, that the instrument might be less apt to decay, and that signs might be permanent, like the things which they denote.

Johnson's admission that words are mere "earthly" tools, used by mortals as "signs" for "heavenly" things may be a defense of his lexicographic methods, but it is also a profound statement about the inadequacies and limitations of language. Only God can give birth to "things"— all mortals can do is invent words that (in many cases feebly) try to capture these things' essences. As Joyce Kilmer famously observed two centuries later, "Only God can make a tree"; all we, as mortals, can do is write about them. Spelling and pronunciation are important, but in the long run, the spelling of a word (whether correct or incorrect, ancient or modern, phonetic or otherwise) does very little service in terms of how well a word captures the essence of the thing it connotes. One can, for example, spell "death" as "death" or "deth," but this will not ease any of our fears about what Hamlet calls "the undiscovered country." For all the time and effort humans put into the use, study, and celebration of language, it remains a tool of limited effectiveness. Language may be the dress of thought, but it is a dressing that is greatly limited in its ability to make human thoughts (and the very process of thinking) understandable to other people. Anyone who has ever tried to compose a resume, love letter, or poem knows this to be the case.

Such is the issue explored in Elizabeth Barrett Browning's "Sonnet XXIX," in which the poet examines the limitations of poetic language (which is presumably richer than other kinds) when faced with a seemingly simple task: how does one put into words the thoughts and emotions that naturally occur when the lover is away from her beloved? Can words ever get close to the complex workings of a lover's mind and then replicate the workings of such a mind on paper? Elizabeth's sonnet ultimately becomes a poem about the inadequacy of poems, a sonnet that becomes obsolete once its subject appears in the flesh, for then a sonnet—and indeed language itself—becomes unnecessary.

The poem begins with Elizabeth stating the occasion for her poetic premise, much as she does in her renowned "Sonnet XLIII," which begins, "How do I love thee? Let me count the ways." "I think of thee!" she exclaims, expressing both her longing for Robert and challenge as an artist: how to make readable and intelligible what actually happens when the action described in these first four words takes place. The rest of the sonnet, therefore, is Elizabeth's attempt to dramatize her thinking of Robert (a "son of heaven") using mere "daughters of earth."

But using the words "I think of thee" to describe the process of thinking does not tackle the task at hand, so Elizabeth turns to figurative language to better replicate her manner of thought, comparing her thoughts to "wild vines" that "do twine and bud" about Robert as vines do "about a tree." As any conscious person knows, one thought leads to another, so her simile makes perfect poetic sense. And as any person who has thought about an absent lover knows, thoughts of the beloved only lead to more intense thoughts of the same. Elizabeth's statement that her "wild vines" of thought "Put out broad leaves" is appropriate in the sense that the vines grow and even flourish as they wind about the image of Robert. Her thoughts, in fact, grow so intense (and the vines, therefore, become so dense) that "soon there's naught to see / Except the straggling green which hides the wood." This image of a tree covered in vines again suggests the intensity of Elizabeth's thoughts, thoughts so numerous that they threaten to smother the tree itself. Calling her thoughts a "straggling green" is Elizabeth's first hint that her thoughts are weak substitutions for the "strong tree" of Robert that prompts them. Still, the only way she can hope to replicate her thoughts is to resort to toying with the "daughters of earth."

Thus, as soon as Elizabeth establishes her simile for depicting her longing thoughts, she undermines it by insisting to Robert that no thoughts (however poetically expressed) can come close to the thing they represent or that she attempts to dramatize in words: "Yet O my palm tree," she explains, "be it understood / I will not have my thoughts instead of thee / Who art dearer, better!" Robert should not take her "wild vines" as ones that Elizabeth pleasantly cultivates; a man is "dearer" (more valuable) and "better" than any thoughts that dwell on him or words that lamely try to describe him. Should Robert knock on her door and appear to her at this instant, the poem would collapse because it would no longer be necessary.

This knocking on the door is what Elizabeth craves, and she presents this craving in the same botanical terms she used earlier to depict her longing: "Rather, instantly, / Renew thy presence," she begs, asking Robert to act "as a strong tree should" by beginning to "Rustle thy boughs and set thy trunk all bare" of the "wild vines" that had encircled it. Though the sexual connotation of these lines is undeniable, the very act of recognizing such a connotation (that is, a toying with words) is what Elizabeth seeks to avoid: she wants Robert, the "son of heaven," perhaps unencumbered by clothes, but definitely unencumbered by her thoughts of him. She wants the man, not the memory—the willful Robert, not these wistful words. Robert's rustling his boughs will make the "bands of greenery" that "ensphere" him "Drop heavily down—burst, shattered, everywhere!" The very sound of "Drop heavily down" suggests the figurative weight of her thoughts and her desire to be freed of their burden. She wants to move to a place beyond thought and beyond the words she must use to describe thought—and the only place where this can happen is at Robert's side. Only then, in the "deep joy" of his presence, where she will be in his "shadow" yet still breathe a "new air," the air of a place in which language is superfluous, since lovers can understand each other's thoughts and moods without their having to write them down. As she explains, "I do not think of thee—I am too near thee" when he is by her side.

The sonnet thus begins with an announcement of Elizabeth thinking and ends with her fantasy of

> **Elizabeth's sonnet ultimately becomes a poem about the inadequacy of poems, a sonnet that falls apart once its subject appears in the flesh, for then a sonnet—and, indeed, language itself—becomes unnecessary."**

not thinking; it begins with her using figurative language to replicate her thoughts and ends with her wish that such language were unnecessary. Whereas William Wordsworth (in his Preface to *Lyrical Ballads*) may have defined poetry as "the spontaneous overflow of powerful feelings recollected in tranquility," Elizabeth would gladly trade those hours in which she tranquilly composes poems for a few moments with these same poems' inspiration. However, as Johnson points out in his preface, definitions are, like the language out of which they are fashioned, inadequate means by which to convey essential truths. The irony of all these ideas about thoughts and language being found in something created from thoughts and language is of course obvious—but what is a poet to do? Almost two centuries after the publication of Johnson's *Dictionary* and one century after Elizabeth composed "Sonnet XXIX," the narrator of Vladimir Nabokov's *Lolita*, Humber Humbert, complained, "Oh my Lolita! I have only words to play with!" Lolita, like Robert, was of heaven, although, unlike Robert, obviously not a son.

Source: Daniel Moran, Critical Essay on "Sonnet XXIX," in *Poetry for Students*, The Gale Group, 2002.

Dorothy Mermin

In the following essay, Mermin examines the critical response to Barrett Browning's works with regard to the content of the work and the sex (and gender) of the author.

"I love your verses with all my heart, dear Miss Barrett"—so began Robert Browning's first letter

What Do I Read Next?

- Barrett Browning's "Sonnet I" from her *Sonnets from the Portuguese* (1850) is notable for its depiction of her surprise at having found love when she thought she would find only death.

- Barrett Browning's sonnet "Grief" (1850) provides an interesting biographical glimpse into the mind of the author; in the poem, Barrett Browning treats the death of her brother.

- Like "Sonnet XXIX," Robert Frost's poem "Bereft" explores the effects of a beloved's absence on a vulnerable speaker.

- A work that contrasts Barrett Browning's "Sonnet XXIX" is Shakespeare's "Sonnet 30," which depicts a speaker who believes that his thoughts of another person provide ample comfort.

- Robert Browning's poem "Meeting at Night" depicts the frantic thoughts of a lover about to meet his beloved; the poem explores the ways in which one's thoughts affect one's perceptions.

---

to the poet he was soon to meet, court, and marry. He went on to praise her poems' "fresh strange music, the affluent language, the exquisite pathos and true new brave thought." Such enthusiasm was not unusual then or later in the nineteenth century, for Elizabeth Barrett was a famous and respected writer whose work was considered learned, innovative, obscure, and difficult as well as expressive and moving. Rossetti, Morris, and Swinburne admired her intensely when they were young and impressionable and much Pre-Raphaelite poetry shows her influence. Her poems offered a vital energy, a new and compelling music, a bold engagement with controversial social issues, and a combination of tough wit with passionate intensity that was more like Donne than anything yet published in the nineteenth century. Coventry Patmore found *Sonnets from the Portuguese* "lofty, simple, and passionate—not at all the less passionate in being highly intellectual, and even metaphysical." Her use of the ballad tradition bore fruit in the work of Morris, Rossetti, and

others, her poems on social themes were popular and influential, and *Aurora Leigh*, her feminist novel in verse, had a huge success (partly *de scandale*) and still charms readers with its wit, psychological acuteness, social comedy, and exuberant energy. But even with the current interest in female writers most of her poetry is neglected, while from *Sonnets from the Portuguese*—her most lastingly popular work and, next to *Aurora Leigh*, her most considerable poetic achievement—critics avert their eyes in embarrassment.

The poem deserves much more attention from literary historians, however, both because of Barrett Browning's influence on later women poets and because it is the first of the semi-autobiographical, amatory, lyrical or partly lyrical sequences in modern settings that comprise one of the major innovations of Victorian literature. The poetry is much more subtle, rich, and varied than one would guess from "How do I love thee"—the only one of the sonnets that most of us know. The poem's enormous popularity with unliterary (presumably female) readers, along with the even more popular legend of the fair poetess, the dashing poet-lover, and the mad tyrant of Wimpole Street partly account for the repugnance—often expressed as ridicule—that *Sonnets from the Portuguese* is apt to inspire. But the real problem is that the female speaker produces painful dislocations in the conventions of amatory poetry and thus in the response of the sophisticated twentieth-century reader, whose first overwhelming though inaccurate impression of the poems is that they are awkward, mawkish, and indecently personal—in short, embarrassing.

The speaker fills roles that earlier love poetry had kept separate and opposite: speaker and listener, subject and object of desire, male and female. While this produces a rich poetic complexity, it also produces embarrassment, which as Erving Goffman says can arise from the clashing of apparently incompatible roles. Traditionally in English love poetry the man loves and speaks, the woman is beloved and silent. In *Sonnets from the Portuguese*, however, the speaker casts herself not only as the poet who loves, speaks, and is traditionally male, but also as the silent, traditionally female beloved. Insofar as we perceive her as the lover, we are made uneasy both by seeing a woman in that role and by the implications about the beloved: the man seems to be put in the woman's place, and—especially if we recall the origins of the female lyric tradition in Sappho—we may seem to hear overtones of sexual inversion. Insofar as the speaker presents herself as

---

the beloved, however, she transfers the verbal self-assertion and many of the attributes which in poems traditionally belong to the subject of desire, to desire's normally silent and mysterious object. The result is a devaluation of the erotic object that casts the whole amorous and poetical enterprise in doubt. For the object is both the speaker and the text, an identity like that which Browning asserted in his first letter to Elizabeth Barrett: "I do, as I say, love these books with all my heart—and I love you too." The identification troubled her, though she could not entirely disavow it: "There is nothing to see in me," she told him; "my poetry ... is the flower of me ... the rest of me is nothing but a root, fit for the ground & the dark." She assumed at first that his love was "a mere poet's fancy ... a confusion between the woman and the poetry." Many of the sonnets say, in effect: *Look at me, and you will cease to desire me.* So solicited, many readers turn away.

They turn from a sight that violates both literary and social decorum: a distinctly nineteenth-century woman in the humble posture of a courtly lover. This blurring of sexual roles is established in the third sonnet, which imagines the beloved as a glorious court musician "looking from the lattice-lights" at the speaker, who is just a "poor, tired, wandering singer, singing through / The dark, and leaning up a cypress tree." Later the speaker compares her bewilderment after seeing her lover to that of a rather Keatsian "acolyte" who "fall[s] flat, with pale insensate brow, / On the altar-stair" (xxx). The traditional poet-wooer, insofar as he describes himself at all, is pale, wan, and weary from unsatisfied desire. Barrett Browning in her essay on English poetry quotes with affection a passage by Hawes that includes these typical lines: "With your swete eyes behold you me, and see / How thought and woe by great extremitíe, / Hath changed my colour into pale and wan." In *Sonnets from the Portuguese*, pallor and weariness belong to the woman both as signs of passion, as in the images of minstrel and acolyte, and—more disturbingly still—as the self-portraiture of an aging woman.

The self-portrait, furthermore, is detailed, unflattering, and accurate. In one of the poem's most vivid scenes from a recognizably nineteenth-century courtship, the speaker gives her lover a lock of hair and reminds him that her hair is no longer dressed with rose or myrtle like a girl's:

it only may
Now shade on two pale cheeks the mark of tears,
Taught drooping from the head that hangs aside
Through sorrow's trick. (xviii)

> *The extraordinary biographical accuracy with which the poem depicts its female speaker violates the decorum of the sonnet sequence almost as much as the sex of the speaker does."*

She has "trembling knees" (xi), "tremulous hands", (xxviii), and "languid ringlets" (xxvii). This is a literally faithful picture of the poet (whereas Shakespeare's description of himself in the *Sonnets* as marked by extreme old age presumably is not). The unfashionable ringlets and the characteristic droop of the head can be seen in her pictures. Elizabeth Barrett was forty years old when she married (Browning was six years younger) and had been an invalid, grieving and blaming herself for the death of her favorite brother, addicted to opium, and mostly shut up in one dark airless room, for years. The extraordinary biographical accuracy with which the poem depicts its female speaker violates the decorum of the sonnet sequence almost as much as the sex of the speaker does.

As is usual in love poetry, there is much less physical description of the man than of the woman. And his appearance, in significant contrast to her own, is always imaginatively transformed when it is described at all. *Her* hair is just "brown" (xviii), but *his* seems fit for verse: "As purply-black, as erst to Pindar's eyes / The dim purpureal tresses gloomed athwart / The nine white Muse-brows" (xix). We can usually accept her exaltation of her beloved—who is characteristically described as royal, whose color is purple, whose merit knows no bounds—because the terms and images are familiarly literary. She gives no sketch of him to match her cruel self-portrait and apologizes for her ineptitude in portraying him:

As if a shipwrecked Pagan, safe in port,
His guardian sea-god to commemorate,
Should set a sculptured porpoise, gills a-snort
And vibrant tail, within the temple-gate. (xxxvii)

No apology is really necessary, however, for this flattering comparison of the lover to a sexy sea-god or for the disarmingly erotic porpoise.

Sometimes she is herself transformed by her own imagination, but into an object unworthy of desire. Her house is desolate and broken (iv), like that of Tennyson's Mariana. She praises him at her own expense: she is "an out-of-tune / Worn viol," but "perfect strains may flat / 'Neath master-hands, from instruments defaced". (xxxii). His imagination, that is, might be able to transform her even if her own cannot. Earlier she had offered herself as the object of his poems (rather than the subject of her own):

How, Dearest, wilt thou have me for most use?
A hope, to sing by gladly? or a fine
Sad memory, with thy songs to interfuse?
A shade, in which to sing of plam or pine?
A grave, on which to rest from singing? Choose.

This extreme self-abnegation is also an incisive commentary on male love poems, however, since the alternatives require not only the woman's passivity and silence but her absence and finally her death. Christina Rossetti makes a similar indirect comment in the lyric that begins "When I am dead, my dearest, / Sing no sad songs for me"—in the dreamy twilight of the grave, she won't hear them. Rossetti's speaker in *Monna Innominata* does define herself within the terms set by male poets, each sonnet in the sequence being preceded by epigraphs from Dante and Petrarch; but her lover goes away and in the last sonnet she is left with "Youth gone, and beauty gone" and "A silent heart," "Silence of love that cannot sing again." Similarly, Barrett Browning's "Catarina to Camoens" presents Catarina on her death-bed musing over Camoens' poetical praise of her eyes, which she recalls at the end of each of the twenty-nine stanzas; Camoens is abroad and she imagines what he might say about her death and how he might come to praise another woman. This poem was one of the Brownings' favorites, and they called her sonnets "from the Portuguese" in a cryptic allusion to the fancy that Catarina might have spoken them. But the speaker in *Sonnets from the Portuguese* initiates and writes her own poems. She does not choose merely to respond to her lover's words, to be silent, to be abandoned, or to die.

And so the sequence works out terms of reciprocity between two lovers who are both poets. His love calls forth her poems, but she writes them. He is the prince whose magic kiss restores her beauty, which in turn increases her peotical power (in love poems as in fairy tales, women draw power from their beauty). He "kissed / The fingers of this hand wherewith I write; / And ever since, it grew more clean and white / … quick … When the angels speak" (xxxviii). He has the "power" and "grace" to see beyond appearances to her true worth; through her outer self—"this mask of me"—he sees her "soul's true face" and "all which makes [her] tired of all, self-viewed," and still "Nothing repels" him (xxxix). His attention encourages her to speak, although in an early sonnet she had briefly adopted the conventional female role: "let the silence of my womanhood / Commend my woman-love to thy belief" (xiii). She says that his poems are better than hers, but we never hear them, and throughout the sequence his role as poet seems to be in abeyance. He let drop his "divinest Art's / Own instrument" to listen to her sad music—"To hearken what I said between my tears"—and although she asks him to show her how to express her gratitude (xLi), we don't see him do so. In the final sonnet she offers him the poems, metaphorical flowers in return for his real ones.

The ultimate source of both her attraction and her power in these poems, however, is simply her own desire. What, after all, does a lyric lover traditionally offer as an inducement to love except his love itself? And if desire confers erotic value, then she herself, being poet-lover, must be an object worthy of desire. Her poem can work if she is humble, but not if she is cold.

Yet love, mere love, is beautiful indeed
And worthy of acceptation. Fire is bright,
Let temple burn, or flax; an equal light
Leaps in the flame from cedar-plank or weed:
And love is fire. And when I say at need
I love thee … mark! … *I love thee*—in thy sight
I stand transfigured, glorified aright,
With conscience of the new rays that proceed
Out of my face toward thine. There's nothing low
In love, when love the lowest: meanest creatures
Who love God, God accepts while loving so.
And what I *feel*, across the inferior features
Of what I am, doth flash itself, and show
How that great work of Love enhances Nature's. (x)

In the quick and subtle reasoning conducted largely through a series of brief analogies, in the flexibility and control with which the verse bends to the argument and to the rhythms of thought and speech, and in the final sonorous generalizations, the poem is more proleptic of Meredith's *Modern Love* than it is reminiscent of Renaissance sonneteers or even of Donne. Like a character in a Victorian novel, she sees herself through another's eyes, but it is the fire of her own love that glorifies her. Later poems in the series develop this realization of the primacy of desire, his and her own. Love me, she says, "for love's sake only" (xiv); and, reciprocally, "Make thy lover larger to enlarge my worth" (xvi).

When the speaker looks at herself in the mirror that traditional love poetry holds up to either men or women, she is apologetic and we are embarrassed. But when she expresses desire, she finds strong new images and a new poetic voice, sensuous, witty, and tender.

> What I do
> And what I dream include thee, as the wine
> Must taste of its own grapes … (vi)

> Let the world's sharpness, like a clasping knife,
> Shut in upon itself and do no harm… (xxiv)

> When our two souls stand up erect and strong,
> Face to face, silent, drawing nigh and nigher,
> Until the lengthening wings break into fire
> At either curved point… (xxii)

She compares her thoughts of her lover to entwined vine-leaves that hide a palm tree, asking him to "renew" his "presence" in terms that suggest a Bacchic rite.

> Rustle thy boughs and set thy trunk all bare,
> And let these bands of greenery which insphere thee
> Drop heavily down,—burst, shattered, everywhere!
> Because, in this deep joy to see and hear thee
> And breathe within thy shadow a new air,
> I do not think of thee—I am too near thee. (xxix)

Readers don't seem to be bothered by erotic passages like these, which use images—knives, grapes, androgynous angels, palm trees, dolphins—that evoke no inappropriate reminders of either courtly love or Victorian manners. What does embarrass us is the feeling aroused by less erotic sonnets that we are eavesdropping on the lovers' private affairs. This feeling has several sources. One is that the disparity between the female role and the traditional poetic lover's, between this speaker and the remembered voices we dimly hear behind her, makes us aware of much that is unconventional, and we assume that what is not conventional is autobiographical, merely personal, mawkishly "sincere." And of course, Barrett Browning herself, like most Victorian readers and writers, valued the appearance of sincerity in poems very highly, and generally achieved it—which is one reason why Victorian readers like the *Sonnets* better than later generations have. Thus Christina Rossetti takes for granted that if "the Great Poetess" had been unhappy in her love she might have written a different set of sonnets, with a "'donna innominata' drawn not from fancy but from feeling" (interestingly enough, Rossetti says

this in a head note implicitly disavowing any autobiographical element in *Monna Innominata*). But women's writing is all too easily read not just as sincere but, more damagingly, as artless and spontaneous. When women's poetry (especially love poetry) is powerful, it is assumed to be autobiographical, and when evidence for this is unavailable, as with Rossetti and Dickinson, critics have deduced it from the poems. And so Barrett Browning's experiments with meter and rhyme were taken as carelessness or ineptitude; even G. K. Chesterton, who found her writing astonishingly "'manly'" and remarked that she is often "witty after the old fashion of the conceit," could not forbear adding that such wit "came quite freshly and spontaneously" to her.

Finally, of course, we know that the story the *Sonnets* tells is true. Elizabeth Barrett was a legendary public figure even before her marriage, by virtue of her poems, her learning, her seclusion, and her sex, and for most readers the personal element has been inseparable from the sonnets since their first publication. We know the story of her courtship, which was largely epistolary and has been available in print since 1899, and the many parallels between the letters and the poems tempt us to assume that the poems were spontaneously produced at the moments they appear to describe.

It is worth noting, however, that the letters themselves don't embarrass us; only the poems do. We are more disturbed by the incongruity we feel between the sentiments and the genre than by the sentiments themselves. Little scenes from Victorian life and characteristically Victorian modes of feeling and turns of phrase give a strange context to the sonnets' erotic intensities and traditional form. They seem to belong in prose fiction instead.

> My letters! all dead paper, mute and white!
> And yet they seem alive and quivering
> Against my tremulous hands which loose the string
> And let them drop down on my knee tonight.
> (xxviii)

The speaker recalls her dead mother's kiss (xviii) and her own childish play among the cowslips (xxxiii). When she addresses her lover as "Dear" or "Dearest" or "Beloved" she sounds more like a Victorian wife than a courtly lover: "I lean upon thee, Dear, without alarm" (xxiv). She likes him to call her by the "pet-name" of her childhood (xxxiii). They exchange locks of hair (xviii, xix). She wonders if she will miss, when she marries, "Home-talk and blessing and the common kiss," the "walls and floors" even, of home (xxxv). Barrett Browning's most sympathetic and discriminating critic, Alethea Hayter, says that *Sonnets from the Portuguese* is too intimate, "emotionally … naked"—and yet all Hayter's well-chosen examples of unduly intimate passages refer to self-descriptions or incidents, not feelings: her pale cheeks, the lock of hair, the pet name, his letters and kisses. The events of courtship as a Victorian woman experienced them don't seem to belong in sonnets—we haven't seen them there before, have we?—so they must be personal, particular, trivial. We are offended by the publication, implicit in the act of writing poems, of what we feel should be kept private.

The legend that has grown up about the *Sonnets* exploits, distorts, and exaggerates the personal element. Barrett Browning herself worried about the question of privacy, particularly no doubt because the poems concerned her husband, whose aversion to literary self-exposure was extremely strong. In 1864 he explained how and why she showed him the *Sonnets* for the first time three years after their marriage:

> all this delay, because I happened early to say something against putting one's loves into verse: then again, I said something else on the other side … and next morning she said hesitatingly "Do you know I once wrote some poems about *you*?"—and then—"There they are, if you care to see them." … How I see the gesture, and hear the tones… Afterward the publishing them was through me … there was a trial at covering it a little by leaving out one sonnet which had plainly a connexion with the former works: but it was put in afterwards when people chose to pull down the mask which, in old days, people used to respect at a masquerade. But I never cared.

This is simple and straightforward enough. But Edmund Gosse's silly, apochryphal version of this episode has followed the *Sonnets* through many printings and still appears in the reprinted Cambridge Edition of 1974. Gosse's tale transfers the reader's embarrassment to the poet herself. She came up behind her husband, Gosse reports, "held him by the shoulder to prevent his turning to look at her, and … pushed a packet of papers into the pocket of his coat. She told him to read that, and to tear it up if he did not like it; and then she fled again to her own room." Afterwards, says Gosse, she "was very loth indeed to consent to the publication of what had been the very notes and chronicle of her betrothal." But Browning makes it clear that his wife's reticence had been mostly the deferential reflex of his own. In 1846 she had answered his question about what she had been writing recently (almost certainly these sonnets) with a wit and self-possession absolutely antithetical to Gosse's emblematic tale of coyness, self-dramatization, and

shame. "You shall see some day at Pisa what I will not show you now. Does not Solomon say that 'there is a time to read what is written.' If he doesn't, he *ought*."

Insofar as the *Sonnets* are autobiographical (and not just spontaneous), however, they inaugurated a new Victorian convention to which almost every significant poet except Robert Browning contributed: the use of autobiographical material in long poems that play specifically "modern" experience against some of the traditions of amatory poetry. Arnold's *Switzerland*, Patmore's *The Angel in the House*, Tennyson's *Maud*, and Clough's *Amours de Voyage* were published in the 1850's, Meredith's *Modern Love* in 1862. Of all of these, only *Sonnets from the Portuguese* does not, so far as we can tell, fictionalize the story or attempt to disguise the personal references. The male poets presented their own experiences and feelings as exemplifying those of modern man, or at any rate the modern sensitive intellectual or poet, but the modern woman's personal experience could not easily be made to carry so heavy a contextual burden. There were no ancestral female voices to validate her own and define by contrast its particular quality. Nor, as Barrett Browning knew, were readers disposed to hear women as speaking for anything more than themselves. Women can't generalize, Romney smugly explains to Aurora Leigh, and therefore can't be poets, and Lady Waldemar repeats the common assumption that "artist women" are "outside … the common sex."

The unusual situation of a female poet in love with a male one was not easy to show as representative, but Barrett Browning worked in many ways to generalize and distance her experience. The use of the sonnet sequence, first of all, seems an obvious choice now, but in fact *Sonnets from the Portuguese* inaugurated the Victorian use of the old genre. Although she noted the absence of female Elizabeth poets—"I look everywhere for grandmothers and see none"—the sonnet sequence offered a way to subsume her own experience into a wider tradition. Within the sonnet form itself she curbed the liberties with rhyme and meter for which she was notorious, although she did not keep to the usual structure of the Petrarchan sonnet, allowed herself great variety of tone, and broke up lines in fresh and surprising ways. She reminds us, too, that she is writing poems, not love letters, when a poem represents what she does not say to the lover (xiii) or suppresses words of his letters that are too private to repeat (xxviii).

She generalizes her situation most clearly and deliberately through literary allusions, particularly in the first two sonnets, which draw on Theocritus, Homer, Milton, and Shakespeare. *Sonnets from the Portuguese* begins: "I though once how Theocritus had sung / Of the sweet years..." This refers to the song in the fifteenth idyll which anticipates Adonis' return from death to the arms of Aphrodite and is proleptic both of the speaker's movement from death to love and of the coming of her lover. The speaker "mused" Theocritus' story "in his antique tongue," she says, thus establishing her credentials as a reader of Greek, a serious, educated person. And as she mused: "a mystic Shape did move / Behind me, and drew me backward by the hair"—a typically female image of passivity, no doubt, but taken from the episode in *The Iliad* when Achilles in his wrath is similarly pulled back by Athena. The allusions are deft and easy, the voice that of one who lives familiarly with Greek texts. The second sonnet draws with the same casual confidence on Milton and Shakespeare. Only she, her lover, and God, she says, heard the word "Love"—and God "laid the curse / So darkly on my eyelids, as to amerce / My sight from seeing thee"—a more "absolute exclusion" than death itself. The word "amerce" recalls Satan's description of himself as by his fault "amerced / Of heaven" (*Paradise Lost* I, 609–10), a highly relevant allusion in the sonnet's context of "all God's universe," "absolute exclusion," and a blinded poet. Then in the background of the sestet we hear "Let us not to be marriage of true minds": if God himself were not opposed, "Men could not part us .../ Nor the seas change us, nor the tempests bend." The rebirth of Adonis, Achilles' injured love and pride, Satan's exclusion from heaven, Shakespeare's celebration of human love—these and not the stuffy room in Wimpole Street are the context in which *Sonnets from the Portuguese* initially establishes itself.

The poem does seem increasingly to take place within a particular domestic interior, but the space it occupies is symbolical and highly schematic. It is sharply constricted on the horizontal plane but open to heaven above and the grave below. At worst, the speaker is like "a bee shut in a crystalline" (xv), in a "close room" (xIiv). In her childhood she ran from one place to another (xxxiii, xxxiv), but the movements she imagines for the future are almost always vertical. Typical repeated words are *down*, *fall*, *deep*, *rise*, *beneath*, and especially *drop*, used eleven times in the forty-four poems, and *up*, used twelve times. Even marriage, leaving one home for another, means that her eyes

would "drop on a new range / Of walls and floors" (xxxv). The reader may feel a bit claustrophobic, but the speaker usually imagines enclosure as protection rather than imprisonment. "Open thine heart wide," she says, "And fold within the wet wings of thy dove" (xxxv). The last sonnet sees "this close room" as the place of fruitful seclusion where the lover's flowers throve and her poems unfolded in her heart's garden (like her "great living poetry" of which Browning said that "not a flower ... but took root and grew" within him.

For the space, which becomes at the end a garden of art, belongs like the story enacted within it as much to Victorian artistic convention as to the setting of Elizabeth Barrett's life. There is a close pictorial equivalent in Dante Gabriel Rossetti's painting *Ecce Ancilla Domini* (1849–50), an Annunciation scene nearly twice as high as it is wide in which the Virgin sits on the bed pressed against the wall, as if cowering away from the tall upright angel who reaches almost from the top to the bottom of the picture and takes up a full third of its horizontal space. In Tennyson's early poems, which often echo through Barrett Browning's, a woman shut up in a house or tower is a recurrent figure for the poet. The speaker of the *Sonnets* is like the Lady of Shalott: people heard her music from outside the "prison-wall," paused, and went on their way (xli). Like the soul in "The Palace of Art," she has "lived with visions... Instead of men and women" (xxvi). She inhabits a figurative dwelling like Mariana's moated grange rather than a solid house in Wimpole Street: "the casement broken in, / The bats and owlets builders in the roof" (iv). (Elizabeth Barrett twice compared herself in letters to Mariana.) In addition, love offers to her as to Tennyson's sensitive, bookish, imaginative, isolated heroes and heroines an escape from self-imprisonment in a world of shadows. "I will bury myself in myself," says the hero of *Maud* (in an early version he plans to bury himself in his books, which is equally relevant), and Maud's love restores him to life. Like the heroes of *Switzerland* or *Amours de Voyages*, the woman in the *Sonnets* finds her lover more passionate and alive than she is herself. He is not imprisoned; her draws her back to life. (In fact, Browning drew Elizabeth Barrett into marriage, motherhood, society, travel, political engagement—the ordinary social, human world that women often represent to their lovers in Victorian poems: but the poem is less proleptically literary than life was and does not anticipate this outcome.) The speaker has the qualities, then, both of the male Victorian poet as introverted self-doubting lover and of the female figures in which Tennyson embodies passive, withdrawn, and isolated aspects of the poetic character.

The unspecified sufferings and griefs that have marked the speaker's face and almost killed her are also signs not only of Petrachan love, feminine weakness, and biographical fact (Barrett Browning's long illness and her brother's death) but of the poetical character too, as many Romantic and Victorian poets conceived it. Matthew Arnold's Empedocles, for instance, renounced poetry because isolation and empathy make poets suffer too much. In the 1844 preface to her poems Barrett Browning discusses the volume's two longest works in terms of the woman poet's vocation and special qualifications. "*A Drama of Exile*," she says, represents the expulsion from the Garden "with a peculiar reference to Eve's allotted grief, which considering that self-sacrifice belonged to her womanhood … appeared to me … more expressible by a woman than a man." And in "*The Vision of Poets*," she says, she has "endeavoured to indicate the necessary relations of genius to suffering and self-sacrifice"; for "if knowledge is power, suffering should be acceptable as a part of knowledge." Thus by an implicit syllogism, suffering is power: women can be poets precisely by virtue of their womanhood.

Another major point of intersection between conventional and personal, male and female, poet and beloved, occurs in the general area in which *Sonnets from the Portuguese* anticipates the Pre-Raphaelites. Here as elsewhere, Barrett Browning is the precursor, though we are likely to read her through expectations formed by those who followed. Sometimes her accents have a Meredithian wit, quickness, cleverness, and variety, as in the tenth sonnet, "Yet love, mere love." Sometimes the poems resemble Dante Rossetti's *House of Life* in their personifications, marmoreal cadences, archaisms, and heated slow simplicities ("Very whitely still, / The lilies of our lives," xxiv or "What time I sat alone here in the snow," xx), and, more pleasingly, in their striking use of Latinate words ("lips renunciative," ix; "Antidotes / Of medicated music," xvii). The speaker is like the tortured husband of *Modern Love* in her subtlety of psychological analysis, intricate arguments and images, and variations of tone and rhythm that can shift in a flash from formal intensity to broken phrases of the speaking voice. She somewhat resembles the speaker in *The House of Life*, too, with her dark allusions to untellable sins and sorrows. But if she speaks like a Pre-Raphaelite poet, she also resem-

bles such poets' favorite subject, the fatal woman: enclosed, passive, pale, deathly. Like Morris' Guenevere or Rossetti's Lilith, she often seems to be looking at herself in a mirror (x, xviii, xxxii). Like the wife in *Modern Love*, she breathes poison (ix). From the lover's point of view, she is silent and unresponsive in the earlier sonnets, hiding her feelings from him and speaking to be heard only by the reader. But she lacks the fatal woman's guile, mystery, and beauty. As speaker she must let the reader hear her, while her bent for self-analysis and formal commitment to lyric self-expression preclude duplicity.

Such persistent doubling of roles accounts for most of the disconcerting strangeness of *Sonnets from the Portuguese*. The speaker is cast as both halves of a balanced but asymmetrical pair, speaking with two voices in a dialogue where we are accustomed to hearing only one. Obviously there are rich possibilities for irony here, but Barrett Browning does not take them—does not appear even to notice them. Nor does she call our attention to the persistent anomalies and contradictions even without irony. This above all distinguishes her from her male contemporaries. The juxtaposition of traditional amatory poetry and the Victorian idea that love should be fulfilled in marriage, combined with the desire of almost every important Victorian poet to write within the context of contemporary social life, inevitably opened up the disjunction between the passionate certainties of literature, and the flawed complexities of life, between the amatory intensity of poetic lovers and the confusion and distractedness of modern ones. Sometimes modern settings produce unintended comedy, as in much of Patmore or the description of Maud's dresses ("the habit, hat, and feather" and "the frock and gipsy bonnet"—"nothing can be sweeter / Than maiden Maud in either") more often, though, Tennyson, Clough, and Meredith exploit the disjunction between literature and contemporary life through self-denigrating irony. *Sonnets from the Portuguese* might well have become the same sort of poem; at any rate, the love letters, kisses, pet-names, childishness, and ringlets rest uneasily with Maud's dresses on the dangerous edge of bathos. Elizabeth Barrett had planned as early as 1844 to write a long poem about "this real everyday life of our age," which she thought as interesting and potentially poetical as past times had been. While her plan was for a novel-poem and in due course issued in *Aurora Leigh*, *Sonnets from the Portuguese* appears to be an earlier fruit of her growing desire to cast off fictional trappings and write from her own time, place, and social class. But neither *Aurora Leigh* nor the *Sonnets* works ironically.

For Barrett Browning does not want to show up disparities: she wants to find a place within the tradition for modern poems, and especially for female poets—not to mark how far outside it she is. Nor can she mock the sonnet tradition from within as Shakespeare and Sidney could, since she wants to assert her right to use it at all. *Sonnets from the Portuguese* is organized around the double discovery that love's seeming illusions are realities, still accessible, and that one can be both subject and object of love, both poet and poet's beloved. Because she does not use irony to mark the points at which the old and the new come together—she wants to create fusion, not show disjunction—she runs the risk of leaving us disoriented and uneasy instead of releasing us, as Clough and Meredith do, into the ironical recognition of a familiar failure. And since success for the poet in this poem involves a happy ending for the lovers, or at least not an unhappy one, there is no release such as Tennyson and Arnold would give us into the lyrical pain of loss.

Barrett Browning knew that embarrassment always threatens to engulf the woman poet, particularly in an amatory context. In a remarkable emblematic incident, Aurora Leigh celebrates her twentieth birthday by crowning herself with ivy leaves, a playful anticipation of the posthumous glory she covets. Recognizing the potentially ambiguous symbolism that a wreath could bear, she had chosen neither the poet's bay nor the lover's myrtle; but when her cousin Romney comes suddenly upon her he sees the wreath simply as a sign of female vanity, flattering to his sense of male superiority, his contempt for mere artists, his love, and his hopes of marrying her. She is memorably embarrassed:

> I stood there fixed,—
> My arms up, like the caryatid, sole
> Of some abolished temple, helplessly
> Persistent in a gesture which derides
> A former purpose. Yet my blush was flame ...

Romney thinks that women cannot be poets. Seen through his eyes, Aurora becomes a work of art instead of an artist, and an archaic, useless one at that. Her aspirations to poetic fame dwindle under his amused, admiring gaze into girlish narcissism. The absolute conflict between her intention and his interpretation immobilizes her: she does indeed become object rather than subject, self-assertive only in the blush that is inherent in her name and the mark of internalized conflict. She marries Romney, years and books later, but by then

he has not only changed his mind about women poets; he is blind and cannot see her.

The extreme paucity of good lyric poetry by Victorian women, which is in such striking contrast to their success in narrative, is largely due to the felt pressure of forms, convention, and above all readers' responses that could not accommodate female utterance without distorting it. This is a problem of the female speaker, not just of the woman writer, as we see in *Bleak House*. Dickens wants to give Esther Summerson narrative authority as well as attractiveness and self-effacing modesty, and the incongruity that results suggests to some readers either intentional irony or authorial failure. Women novelists appear more alert to the problem and usually get round it by avoiding first-person female narrators; only Charlotte Bronte faces it squarely, as part of her battle against conventional notions about female attractiveness, passion, and will. (It is significant that Aurora Leigh's rejected lover's character and fate strikingly recall *Jane Eyre*.) One reason that *Aurora Leigh* seems to many readers fresher and more alive than *Sonnets from the Portuguese* is that the novelistic form of the later poem enabled the poet to speak freely, and without arousing significant conflict in the reader, in her own distinctive, distinctively female voice.

Source: Dorothy Mermin, "Female Poet and the Embarrsassed Reader: E. B. B.'s *Sonnets from the Portuguese*," in *ELH*, Vol. 48, No. 2, Summer 1981, pp. 351–66.

Sources

Browning, Robert, *Pippa Passes*, in *Robert Browning's Poetry*, edited by James F. Loucks, W. W. Norton, 1979, p. 28.

Cooper, Helen, "Poems of 1850," in *Elizabeth Barrett Browning, Woman and Artist*, University of North Carolina Press, 1988, p. 101.

Foster, Margaret, "1846–1861," in *Elizabeth Barrett Browning: A Biography*, Doubleday, 1988, pp. 237–45.

Johnson, Samuel, "Preface to *A Dictionary of the English Language*," in *Johnson's Dictionary: A Modern Selection*, Pantheon Books, 1963, p. 7.

Leighton, Angela, "'How Do I Love Thee?': The Woman's Right To Say," in *Elizabeth Barrett Browning*, Indiana University Press, 1986, pp. 98–111.

Lupton, Mary Jane, "Sonnets and Séances," in *Elizabeth Barrett Browning*, Feminist Press, 1972, p. 38.

Markus, Julia, "Death or Love," in *Dared and Done: The Marriage of Elizabeth Barrett and Robert Browning*, Alfred A. Knopf, 1995, pp. 1, 25.

Mermin, Dorothy, "Courtship, Letters, Sonnets," in *Elizabeth Barrett Browning: The Origins of a New Poetry*, University of Chicago Press, 1989, pp. 130–34.

———, "Introduction," in *Elizabeth Barrett Browning: The Origins of a New Poetry*, University of Chicago Press, 1989, p. 1.

Nabokov, Vladimir, *Lolita*, G. P. Putnam's Sons, 1955, p. 34.

Radley, Virginia L., "Parnassus Attained: *Sonnets from the Portuguese*," in *Elizabeth Barrett Browning*, Twayne Publishers, 1972, p. 93.

Wordsworth, William, "Preface to *Lyrical Ballads*," in *Lyrical Ballads*, Routledge, 1988, p. 266.

Further Reading

Bender, Robert M., and Charles L. Squier, eds., *The Sonnet: A Comprehensive Anthology of British and American Sonnets from the Renaissance to the Present*, Washington Square Press, 1965.

This extensive anthology features headnotes describing the lives and careers of the poets as well as an essay about the history of the sonnet form.

Fuller, John, *The Oxford Book of Sonnets*, Oxford University Press, 2001.

This collection features the work of over one hundred poets, arranged in chronological order so a reader can trace the development of the sonnet form. The collection begins with Sir Thomas Wyatt and ends with Alice Oswald.

Leighton, Angela, and Margaret Reynolds, *Victorian Women Poets: An Anthology*, Blackwell Publishers, 1995.

This collection arranges the work of fifty poets in chronological order, beginning with Felicia Hemans and ending with Charlotte Mew. The work of well-known poets is featured along with work by their lesser-known colleagues; in addition, the collection contains long biographical headnotes and bibliographical information for each poet.

Stone, Marjorie, *Elizabeth Barrett Browning*, St. Martin's Press, 1995.

This critical study examines Barrett Browning's poetic career in light of its Victorian context and contemporary critical opinion.

Southbound on the Freeway

May Swenson

1963

May Swenson is known as much for the content of her poems as she is for the form and sound of many of her writings. Her style is often compared to the styles of e. e. cummings, Elizabeth Bishop, and Marianne Moore. Swenson experimented with poetic language, using such devices as metaphor, alliteration, assonance, and dissonance. By using these devices, many of Swenson's poems are not only intriguing to listen to, but also to read, through her visual inventiveness. May Swenson's poetry is filled with imagery in how it is heard and how it is laid out on the page, with her flowing personal and imaginative observations. As a testimony to her wide range of interests, Swenson wrote books of poetry for children, *Poems to Solve*, and *More Poems to Solve*, along with a book of very personal, very erotic poetry, *Love Poems*. After reading "Southbound on the Freeway," a person will take a second look at what a passing car may truly represent.

Author Biography

Swenson was born May 28, 1919, in Logan, Utah. Following her graduation from Utah State University, she worked as a reporter in Salt Lake City. In 1949, Swenson moved to New York City, where she held various jobs before becoming an editor for New Directions Press in 1959. She resigned the position seven years later to devote her time to

May Swenson

writing. In subsequent years, Swenson was featured as poet-in-residence at several colleges, including Purdue University, the University of North Carolina at Greensboro, Lothbridge University in Alberta, Canada, and the University of California at Riverside.

Best known for the complex wordplay of her poems, which often include riddles and unusual arrangements of type on the printed page, Swenson is generally praised for her technical abilities and explorations of the challenges and possibilities of language. She lectured and gave readings at more than fifty colleges and universities, as well as at the New York YM-YWHA Poetry Center and the San Francisco Poetry Center. In addition, Swenson conducted workshops at the University of Indiana Writers' Conference and at Breadloaf, Vermont, and participated in the Yaddo and Mac-Dowell colonies for writers. Swenson also received numerous awards and grants for her writing over the course of more than three decades, including Guggenheim, Rockefeller, and MacArthur fellowships, and a translation medal from the International Poetry Forum in 1972. In 1970, Swenson was elected to membership in the National Institute of Arts and Letters, and in 1981, she was awarded the

Bollingen Prize in Poetry from Yale University. She died December 4, 1989.

Poem Text

A tourist came in from Orbitville,
parked in the air, and said:

The creatures of this star
are made of metal and glass.

Through the transparent parts   5
you can see their guts.

Their feet are round and roll
on diagrams or long

measuring tapes, dark
with white lines.   10

They have four eyes.
The two in the back are red.

Sometimes you can see a five-eyed
one, with a red eye turning

on the top of his head.   15
He must be special—

the others respect him,
and go slow

when he passes, winding
among them from behind.   20

They all hiss as they glide,
like inches, down the marked

tapes. Those soft shapes,
shadowy inside

the hard bodies—are they   25
their guts or their brains?

Poem Summary

Lines 1–2

This poem starts with the literary conceit, or premise, that an alien life form has come from another planet and observed life on earth. The poem is clear about not taking itself too seriously. First, the alien is referred to with the friendly word "tourist," softening any notion of it being a hostile invader and implying a guest/host relationship. The name "Orbitville" is light, somewhat humorous: it implies small-town America, where names like Kentville, Greenville and Roseville are common. The first half of the name is pointedly un-exotic, using a word that shows an almost childish grasp of the reaches of outer space. When this poem was published, in 1963, the United States and Soviet

Union space programs had put humans into earth's orbit, and the word would have been in the news daily. The use of the name "Orbitville" sets a light, anti-intellectual, child-like tone. Similarly, the action of parking "in the air" implies that this poem is being told by someone with a weak imagination, who borrows from popular science fiction rather than establishing an internal reality within the poem. For young readers this speaker is friendly and non-challenging; more sophisticated readers are amused by the poem's sense of whimsy.

Line 3

Line 3 refers to the earth as a "star." A space traveller would, if it knew anything, know the difference between a star and a planet. In having the visitor describe it this way, the author accomplishes several things. The visitor's naivete is established, making the confusion it is to feel in the coming stanzas more plausible. Also, the word "star" reminds most readers of wonder, of mystery. The emotional associations a reader has with a word constitute the word's "connotation."

Line 4

In Line 4, the theme of technology is introduced. It is not clear at this point in the poem what the visitor is seeing, or if it is actually Earth that is being visited. From the description given here, the reader can only tell that the visitor mistakenly uses the word "creature," which indicates a life form, to talk about something that has been manufactured.

Lines 5–6

"Guts" is a surprisingly informal word for the visitor to use in describing the "creature's" internal organs, but Swenson's purpose becomes clear in the last line of the poem, where the common association of "guts" with "courage" is brought into play. In Line 6, the visitor states the obvious: anything seen within could be considered guts.

Lines 7–10

It is in this part of the poem that it first becomes clear that the visitor is talking about an automobile: only wheels are round and roll where feet would be, and the description previously given, added to the wheels, implies a car. The speaker uses two interesting descriptions for freeways. "Diagrams" implies precise drawings, and to some extent this is exactly what roads are to travellers, although they do not appear to be so from a surface-level perspective. The idea of "measuring tape" stems from the regularly-paced dashes that

Media Adaptations

- The *Music of Claudio Spies*, recorded by CRI in 1996, is a collection of musical compositions based on the words of poets through the ages, including Shakespeare, Dylan Thomas, May Swenson, and others. Specific titles are not mentioned, but three of the songs are based on Swenson's work.

- Swenson's "Symmetrical Companion" is a part of a poems-set-to-music collection, composed by Roger Bourland. Recorded in 1993 by Yelton Rhodes Music, the collection also includes lyrics by James Merrill, Thom Gunn, Allen Ginsberg, Adrienne Rich, and other poets.

divide highways up the middle. In making this comparison, the visitor reverses the human concept of road travel: we think of the road as hardly significant, a detail, but if it were a measuring tape it would be the point of travelling.

Lines 11–12

Lights have often been associated with eyes, probably because the opaque clarity of an eyeball resembles an electric light's glass casing and shines like no other part of the body. The placement of two headlights on a car in relatively the same place as eyes are located on the front of the face makes the visitor's assumption in Line 11 reasonable enough. Seeing tail lights as eyes is a little more conspicuous: since we know nothing about the visitor, it would not be hard to believe that eyes in the back of the head are common to him. But it is not enough to say that this detail is here only because the author wanted to show that the visitor has a different set of assumptions than our own: if that were the only reason, she could have included countless examples, but she chose this particular one. The color red implies fire and passion, and red eyes therefore conjure an image of heated emotion. Paired with the head-lights, that navigate roads with the clarity of light, the creature of earth is shown to be a mix of reason and emotion.

Lines 13–16

The five-eyed creature is a police car, which, in the 1960s, would have had a single red globe on the roof with a bright light rotating when in the process of making an arrest. With a deadpan tone that again indicates naivete, the visitor refers to the frightening figure of authority as "special," a term more cheerful than most people would use. Three red lights to two clear ones on this car tip the balance toward flaring emotions and away from rationality.

Lines 17–20

Here the poem's central question of man's intelligence is implied most clearly. From above, the behavior of automobiles in the presence of police cars seems like primitive reverence, as if they are honoring the police car, possibly because of the mutation on its roof. From the ground, slowing in the presence of a police car is an intelligent thing to do, to avoid a traffic ticket. Contrasting these two perspectives gives a fresh look at what we consider intelligence.

The detail of the police car "winding among them from behind" implies, to a driver, a cat-and-mouse contest of wits and strategy between the motorist and the police car. From a visitor's simplistic perspective, it would appear that wits are not involved, that all parties are participating in a primitive ritual.

Lines 21–22

The hiss in Line 21 implies a snake, a very low order of life, slithering along the ground: to a visitor who can float in the air, this would seem especially underdeveloped. Measuring "inches" (bringing back the measuring tape analogy from Line 9) is another way of implying the car's smallness, fragility, or insignificance.

Lines 23–26

Referring to humans as "soft shapes" points out the vulnerability of the flesh, but in Line 24 the word "shadowy" at least admits that there is a mystery to human beings that the visitor does not understand. The question at the end uses common metaphors to examine man's role in the age of automation: are we the intelligence that controls the machines, or are we just part of the system that makes them run? "Brains" implies intelligence; "guts" implies courage. As indicated by the example of slowing for police cars, this poem asks whether human caution is a question of courage or intelligence. The freeway is an ideal setting for making this dichotomy obvious, since cars and the road system eliminate most opportunity or need for intelligent reasoning, leaving the importance of humans only slightly higher than that of pistons and sprockets.

Themes

Technology Versus Human Intelligence

May Swenson's "Southbound on the Freeway" is a poem that is frivolous on the outside and serious on the inside. Its whimsical premise of a naïve alien from "Orbitville" parking his spacecraft in the air above an American freeway is deceptively simple. But the humorous aspect should not obscure the underlying theme of human intelligence and human control pitted against the machines mankind has created. This is not, of course, a new or unusual theme, but Swenson's treatment of it in this poem is a bit curious. Here, she scrutinizes humanity through the eyes of an inhuman being. This allows for a more objective—albeit, funny and skewed—look at one of the most poignant questions to arise from the age of technology: are humans still in control or are we just trying to hang on for the ride?

Ultimately, the poem leaves that question unanswered, but the lack of resolve only adds to the disturbing assertion put forth by it. To the tourist from outer space who has never before seen an Earthling, all those things racing by below must be the inhabitants of this world or the "creatures of this star." His mistake, of course, is recognized soon enough by the reader who knows that what he is actually describing are vehicles, not people. Cars and trucks, however, are the dominant objects in the alien's sight, so his confusion is not difficult to understand.

The fact that there are so many of these objects reinforces the notion that technology appears to be running amuck. Americans love their automobiles, and, to the unknowing tourist, they are their automobiles. In addition, Swenson cleverly blurs the distinction between man and machine even more by assigning roles and a hierarchy among the cars, much like that of human society. The police car, or other kind of emergency vehicle, "with a red eye turning / on the top of his head" is shown respect by the other cars who slow down or move aside to let him pass. This creature, the tourist assumes, is someone special.

The most significant address of the technology versus human intelligence theme in "Southbound on the Freeway" comes at the end of the poem when the purpose of actual human beings—"Those soft shapes, shadowy inside"—is questioned. Are they the guts or the brains of the "hard bodies" in which they ride? Before one hastily responds that of course they are the brains, perhaps a little pondering is in order. While it is true that cars and trucks and microwave ovens and computers would not exist without the creativity and know-how of the humans that brought them into existence, it is also true that many, if not most, humans have now become dependent on those inventions, among others.

Americans in particular equate driving with freedom, whether it is to travel across country on vacation or across town to go to work. Ask high school or college students today to complete all assignments without the use of a computer and the dropout rate would soar. Swenson's poem was written before much of contemporary technology was as widespread as it is now, but the automobile—perhaps the most sacred of twentieth-century inventions—was already an object of adoration and necessity in 1960s America. One must wonder, then, just how much power has been relinquished from the inventor to the invented. For the tourist from Orbitville, it is a moot point. After all, he cannot distinguish between the two.

Perception and Reality

Swenson makes a clever point in "Southbound on the Freeway" regarding the blurry line between what is real and what is only individual perception. The speaker in the poem may be from another planet, but often human beings on Earth vary widely in their "take" on what they see or hear. While one may be quick to judge the tourist from Orbitville as naïve or even foolish, he is actually calling it as he sees it. Note how sure of himself he seems in describing the "creatures'" body parts: they are made "of metal and glass," the "feet are round," they have "four eyes," and they "all hiss as they glide." These are straightforward, matter-of-fact details that any real human being would say have nothing to do with facts. But from the alien's perspective, they make perfect sense.

Swenson drives home the idea of miscued perception by having the speaker of the poem elaborate on what he thinks are the eyes of the strange inhabitants of this new world. He surmises that the red light on top of the emergency vehicle is a fifth eye and that the behavior of the regular four-eyed creatures indicates that the five-eyed one must be an au-

Topics for Further Study

- What if the tourist from Orbitville had parked his spaceship in the air above a football stadium where a game was being played? How would he have described the "creatures of this star" then, and what provocative question may he have ended his report with? Write your answer as either an essay or a poem.

- Make your case in answering the "guts or brains" question in Swenson's poem. Defend your answer with examples of actual human behavior and tell how and why you arrived at your decision.

- Do some research on the "Roswell incident" and write an essay describing the events that took place in New Mexico in 1947 and the subsequent actions by the U.S. government and military. Why do people still flock to Roswell? Why would there have been a cover-up? What do you believe really happened?

- Other than the automobile, what do you think is the greatest technological achievement in transportation? If you awoke tomorrow and all the cars had disappeared, how would your selected mode of transportation play a role in a society without automobiles? What would be the practical and impractical aspects?

thority figure, someone revered. He sees cars slow down or pull over for the police car or ambulance, but the visitor has no idea that they are simply obeying the law of the land and, hopefully, of human conscience. He has no reason to suspect that what he witnesses—and, therefore, what he believes—is anything other than what he has described.

The value in this theme, of course, is not to point out that aliens from outer space would be clueless in understanding what real life on Earth is like or what real Earthlings are made of. The obviousness of that would hardly be worth calling attention to. But its importance comes to light when the tourist's experience is transferred to that of ordinary human beings. Two people watching the same sunset or the same ballgame or the same crime being committed rarely describe what they have seen in the same way. Often, their reports are completely contradictory. Perception, then, appears to carry as much weight, if not more, than reality itself and even causes one to ponder what is real. Swenson's poem cannot answer that question, but it does a good job of tempting the reader to ask it.

Style

"Southbound on the Freeway" consists of thirteen stanzas of two lines each. It is written in free verse, meaning that there is no consistent rhyme scheme or rhythm pattern. The short stanzas give the poem a look of simplicity, suitable for children's poetry because it requires less attention span. After the first stanza, the poem becomes a monologue by the "tourist from Orbitville," giving the tourist's observations of life on earth's freeways. The poem frequently uses the technique of enjambment, placing significant words instead of punctuation at the ends of lines, to draw attention to those words. The monologue is structured in small, simple words, using familiar images and sometimes using slang.

Historical Context

"Southbound on the Freeway" was written during a time in America when the country was reaffirming its love affair with moving machines. From the automobile to spaceships, technology was taking mobility to new heights in the early 1960s. Two of the most significant developments in this era were space exploration with both manned and unmanned crafts and the construction of an interstate highway system linking cities and towns across America in a manner never seen before. While both developments provided tremendous new opportunities for millions of people, not everyone was supportive of the efforts.

NASA's space programs using manned spaceships and unmanned satellites got underway simultaneously in the late 1950s and early 1960s. With the launching of the *Echo 1* satellite in 1960 and the more sophisticated *Telstar 1* and *Relay 1* in 1962, scientists could bounce radio wave messages off the satellites and redirect them to desired locations, as well as pick up signals that were sent back to Earth. *Telstar 1* provided the first satellite television broadcasts in 1962. Antimissile satellites were also launched in the early 1960s, and the military used satellites with high-resolution cameras to fly over nations and take pictures of facilities that were of interest to the American government. Enemy countries, however, were not the only targets of space exploration, for there were brand new worlds to discover as well. In 1960 *Pioneer 5* was launched on a journey to the Sun; *Mariner 1* and *Mariner 2* left for Venus in 1962; and another pair of Mariners headed for Mars in 1964.

While some Americans grumbled about the expense of the unmanned satellite probes, many others questioned the cost, danger, and effectiveness of sending astronauts into space. The first man in space was actually a Soviet cosmonaut, Yuri Gagarin, who orbited Earth in 1961. But the Americans were not far behind, sending John Glenn into orbit to circle the planet three times in his 1962 mission. Glenn was part of the Mercury space program that saw other launches in the early 1960s, followed by the Gemini program in the mid-1960s, during which American astronauts made their first space walks.

In the latter part of the decade, the Apollo program became the biggest scientific project in history, culminating with the moon landing in 1969. But in spite of the marvels of sending human beings to other planets and of all the discoveries that came from it, many Americans did not find the risk and expense worth it. In the decades since the 1960s, that sentiment has not changed much, particularly in light of the *Challenger* disaster in 1986. But the same is *not* true when it comes to Americans and their cars.

As early as the 1920s, the number of automobiles on the road was increasing at such a fast rate that soon there were millions of cars for only several hundred miles of pavement. Lawmakers began to consider the best ways to fund construction of more paved roads, but the Depression of the 1930s followed by World War II put highway projects on the back burner for nearly two decades. After the war, America saw some of its most prosperous times to date, and much of it was due to new technology. Just as the automobile had replaced the horse and carriage, television replaced radio and for many travelers, airlines became the transportation of choice over buses and trains.

By the 1950s many states had developed their own road construction projects to keep up with the increased traffic, but it was obvious that a major

Compare & Contrast

- **1960s:** The first and probably most famous claim of alien abduction is reported by Barney and Betty Hill of New Hampshire. The Hills state that on a return trip from Canada in September, their car was followed by a low-flying space ship, and, upon stopping to get a better look at it, they both blacked out, losing two hours of memory. Later, under hypnosis, they tell stories of being taken aboard the space craft and examined by aliens before being set free two hours later.

  Today: The U.S. Air Force publishes the "Roswell Report: Case Closed" in an attempt to put an end to rumors that the military tried to cover up a UFO crash in Roswell, New Mexico, in 1947. In the report, the Air Force claims that what witnesses actually saw were remnants of military testing, and Pentagon officials back that claim by saying the "alien bodies" found in the New Mexico desert were probably test dummies.

- **1960s:** *Star Trek* begins airing on television, playing off NASA's intensified space exploration programs of the 1960s. The show becomes an instant hit and is now a cult classic in American science fiction.

  Today: Outer space TV shows and movies are still a major attraction for the American public. The treatment of aliens and humans has become more sophisticated since *Star Trek*, and distinctions between the two beings are not so clear-cut as pointed ears, bulbous eyes, or bald heads used to portray them.

- **1960s:** Activist Ralph Nader begins his consumer protection campaign by lambasting the auto industry for unsafe products. Nader's publication of *Unsafe at Any Speed* led not only to the halt in production of General Motors's "Corvair," but eventually to the creation of the Center for Auto Safety and the Consumer Product Safety Commission.

  Today: While safety features are some of the most touted selling-points of car manufacturers in the United States and abroad, unsafe products are still routinely revealed in the auto industry.

---

undertaking was needed to meet the demands of a highly mobile public. Those demands were met with the passing of the National Defense and Interstate Highway Act of 1956, authorized by President Eisenhower and providing for the construction of over forty thousand miles of four-lane highways all across the country. It was a public-works project rivaled only by the construction of the Great Wall in China.

The significance of an interstate highway system for the military was fueled by Cold War anxieties over possible nuclear or other attacks on American soil. Highways would provide faster movement of troops and military vehicles, more efficient evacuation of citizens, and makeshift landing strips for warplanes facing emergency situations.

But these sobering reasons for building thousands of miles of roadways were outweighed by the more frivolous self-interests of a car-crazy public. Americans love freedom, and the ability to hop in a car and end up at a beach or a mountain resort in a matter of hours instead of days is all a part of being free. Faster travel time was important not only in planning vacations, but in creating one of the most significant cultural changes in the nation's history: the birth of the suburbs. Many urban residents were tired of overcrowded conditions and high crime rates, and the opportunity to move to more open rural spaces and still hold jobs in the cities was very appealing to them.

In the late 1950s and early 1960s, new suburbanites bought up prefabricated homes in communities just outside town as quickly as contractors could build them. Driving to work on the highway became trendy, as well as self-satisfying. But while some historians claim that the interstate system provided new employment opportunities and helped to link rural areas and small towns to the rest of the country, others point out that the creation of the suburbs and the "commuter" worker led not only to the decay of inner cities but to the destruction of farmland and personal property as well. Some even say the massive web of highways simply made Americans more dependent on their vehicles. Most drivers would not deny that, nor would they consider it a problem.

Critical Overview

In the *New York Times Book Review*, Karl Shapiro wrote that "[Swenson's] concentration on the verbal equivalent of experience is so true, so often brilliant, that one watches her with hope and pleasure, praying for victory all the way." Dave Smith, in *Poetr* declared that "May Swenson transforms the ordinary little-scrutinized world to a teeming, flying first creation—she is a poet we want in this world for this world is in her as it is in few among us ever." The transformation Smith refers to becomes active in "Southbound on the Freeway," as Swenson lends her scrutinizing eye to what a car really represents.

Criticism

Pamela Steed Hill

Hill is the author of a poetry collection, has published widely in literary journals, and is an editor for a university publications department. In the following essay, Hill addresses Swenson's use of humor to make a very serious point about American culture in the age of technology.

The humor in May Swenson's "Southbound on the Freeway" is unmistakable, but so too should be the seriousness of the poem's central concern regarding modern humans' dependency on technology and machinery—the automobile in particular. Hardly anyone would deny that Americans love their cars, relying on them for pleasure trips and unmapped adventures, as well as for more practical purposes such as getting to work or traveling for business or important personal reasons. But there may be a darker side to this seemingly wholesome, progressive, even natural human appreciation of technological advancements. "Southbound

on the Freeway" addresses the more dubious side without sacrificing the whimsy and fun of its premise. Perhaps the best way to examine this poem is to look at it with the same mixture of humor and seriousness that Swenson applied to the subject.

"Orbitville" is as hokey as it gets when naming a town in outer space, and Swenson was well aware of that. But it paved the way for such a silly scenario as a naïve alien parking his flying saucer in the air and reporting what he thinks is an account of earthling life, making mistakes all along the way. Some of his errors, though, are simply misconceptions. He has never seen a human being before, so it seems plausible that all those things moving around below are this society's inhabitants. But what is his excuse for calling a planet a star? Surely, a being who hails from a world so scientifically advanced that its people can go on trips throughout the universe must know the difference between the two. (And we can assume that the poet did as well, since she was an astronomy buff and enjoyed reading science material for pleasure.)

Perhaps, though, the key is in the first line of the poem. The alien is a "tourist." Nowhere does it say that he is an astronaut or a scientist of any kind. This adds to the poem's whimsy in that we can liken the speaker to the average-Joe tourist standing in his Bermuda shorts with a camera hung around his neck, gawking at some foreign site which he has never before seen. *He* may not be quite so bright either.

The visitor from Orbitville also makes a curious observation in regard to what he believes are the inhabitants' "transparent parts," obviously, the car windows. He readily assumes that "you can see their guts," but is he referring to the people inside the cars or simply the insides of the vehicles—dashboards, steering wheels, and such? Later, when he describes "Those soft shapes / shadowy inside," it is clear that he is talking about the humans, but his confusion at that point is not evident in the earlier part of his report. It is not necessary to clear up this discrepancy in order to understand or enjoy the poem, but it does hint at the tourist's uncertainty about what he is seeing, making him seem not as self-assured as his matter-of-fact tone first implies. In turn, this doubtfulness is a clever bridge between the humor and the seriousness of the poem. The levity of its surface content is suddenly darkened by the unavoidable question of just *who* or *what* is in control.

But Swenson does not bring that question up until the last line of "Southbound on the Freeway." First, she allows the reader to enjoy getting to know a little more about the alien visitor while he gets to know the people of Earth, or so he thinks. Here, the reader has the advantage of *watching him watch us*, which for most of the poem, is more revealing of the unwary tourist than of humans. Apparently, he is as clueless about roads as he is about the people who drive on them. In Orbitville, everyone must fly, for the alien mistakes the highways for "diagrams—or long / measuring tapes—dark / with white lines." This imagery reappears later in the poem when the tourist reports that the inhabitants "glide, / like inches, down the marked / tapes." But not only do the creatures "glide" down the road, they also "hiss" as they go. This word lends a second, more devious, meaning to the tape measure imagery—snakes. Perhaps this implication is a part of the bridge between fun and sobriety. After all, it does appear just before the question of control arises.

Poet, editor, and critic Dave Smith is a fan of Swenson's poetry, and he asserts in an article for *Poetry* magazine that "There are two central obsessions in her work: the search for a proper perspective and the celebration of life's embattled rage to continue. Her poems ask teleological questions, and answer them, insofar as answers are ever possible." "Southbound on the Freeway" certainly presents a lesson about proper perspective, demonstrating in a light-hearted, yet poignant, manner how warped people's (or other beings') beliefs can be, based on the knowledge they have of the scene set before them. But this is not the core message in the poem. To use Smith's term, the poet was more interested in asking a "teleological" question and letting that be the stimulus to get the reader thinking. "Teleology" is defined as the doctrine that final causes exist, particularly in nature, and that there is an ultimate design or purpose in nature. In this poem, the question is whether the purpose of mankind's intellectual ability and technological intelligence are ultimately designed to make us the masters of the machines we create or simply the guts of the things that have taken on a mind of their own. It is a good question and not one that Swenson necessarily answers.

If the tourist from Orbitville were to take a stab at answering his own question, how may he approach it? Consider what he has observed while parked in the air above the freeway: thousands of similarly shaped, hard-bodied beings move quickly

Artist rendering of space aliens

in parallel lines—some going south, some going north, but all sticking to the track, or "long / measuring tapes," they have been placed on. The scene is similar to a human being standing over a rat maze, in which all the walls of the labyrinth have been configured into straight lines and the confused animals run to and fro, to and fro, without apparent purpose.

Given the alien's limited frame of reference, it would not be surprising for him to decide that "Those soft shapes" inside "the hard bodies" are their guts, not their brains. The movement he witnesses does not show evidence of any intellectual endeavor. Instead, it all appears monotonous and mindless. The only hint of conscious decision making that the tourist sees is the show of respect for the creature with the "red eye turning / on the top of his head." This act, however, is minimal compared to the continuing line of beings moving back and forth in rote fashion. From this perspective, it appears that the ultimate purpose of humanity is to become a *part of* the designs we create.

But not all should be left as doom and gloom in Swenson's poem. A case can be made for a more positive teleological theory as well. Aliens aside, the human capacity for intelligence and technological know-how has proven its worth many times over

> *The scene is similar to a human being standing over a rat maze, in which all the walls of the labyrinth have been configured into straight lines and the confused animals run to and fro, to and fro, without apparent purpose."*

throughout history, and, apparently, pre-history. The fear of American culture being taken over by machines—from outer space or from our own factories—is a more recent concern. The onslaught of the industrial age, followed by the technology age, has caused some human beings to feel out of control of their own lives, even their own destinies. But most people, especially those who grew up with televisions, airplanes, freeways, and, certainly now, computers, do not think twice about the products that they not only *use* everyday, but that they *depend* on. It is this dependency that has riled some people over the past several decades, but it is safe to assume that those same folks do not ride horses or walk everywhere they go and that they do own a TV and have perhaps even briefly surfed the Internet.

The truth is modern human beings do rely on the speed, efficiency, and comfort that has derived from technological advancement, and the automobile is one of the most cherished advances. Its increased use necessitated the construction of a major interstate highway system, and, even if it looks like a long, black measuring tape or a long, black snake, it is still a practical, intelligent solution to the problem of rapid growth. In spite of cynical naysayers and warnings of the coming Armageddon between man and machine, American drivers will not give up their vehicles for anything, including threats of pending disaster. Most would actually be amused at the question posed by Swenson's tourist from Orbitville, feeling quite confident that they *know* who is in charge as they make they way south-

bound, northbound, or in any other direction on the freeway.

Source: Pamela Steed Hill, Critical Essay on "Southbound on the Freeway," in *Poetry for Students*, The Gale Group, 2002.

Lisa Fabian

Fabian is a former student of poetry. In this essay, Fabian discusses how the wonderful use of imagery, metaphor, and simile in this work creates a photograph in the mind's eye.

At first glance, Swenson's poem may seem a bit out of the ordinary to the unsuspecting reader. The reader may inquire as to who this mysterious tourist could be and wonder where this so-called Orbitville is located. Yet, he still continues reading, allowing a willing suspension of disbelief to carry him through the twenty-six lines of simple text. By the end of the first stanza, the reader realizes with a certain delight that the story is told from the viewpoint of a traveler from another planet. What is this mysterious creature observing from above? At first, the reader naturally assumes that the poet, May Swenson, is describing humans because she calls them the "creatures of this star."

As the description continues, the reader begins to comprehend that the visitor is mistaken. For as Swenson slowly begins to flesh out her description, the reader sees that she is describing something inherently more mechanical: these aforementioned creatures are actually automobiles! The genius behind this work is that Swenson never uses the word car, yet all readers are aware by the poem's end that she is describing cars as humans know them. To effectuate this objective, Swenson relies heavily on the poetic devices of imagery, simile, metaphor, and personification to describe the familiar scene of cars traveling southbound on a freeway.

The use of the literary device of imagery is unquestionably the most prominent in the poem and jumps out at the reader with deliberate intention. Imagery can best be described as a picture made out of words. It allows the poem to become a puzzle, or an object of interpretation rather than a literal description such that we would find in a novel. Imagery is the vehicle that makes poetry concrete as opposed to abstract. For Swenson, the world is comprised of images because everything is described rather than named. She paints a verbal picture for her readers so accurately that they can make no mistake as to what is being portrayed on a literal level. The literary understanding of imagery has changed over the generations. Imagery once signified all the objects and qualities of sense perception referred to in a poem, whether by literal description, by allusion, or in the vehicles of simile and metaphor. As the face of poetry evolved, imagery became synonymous with figurative language, and one of the most essential components of the contemporary poem.

The paramount concept behind imagery is that imagery does not necessarily imply a visual reproduction of the object because some readers may experience visual images while others do not after some prompts. Further, even among those who conjure up images in their mind's eye, the details of each reader's image will probably vary greatly. As in this case, a poem may itself be a single image composed of a multiplicity of images. Each line completes another piece of the puzzle, so as to fill in an empty canvas with an increasingly complete picture.

For example, the words "creatures" and "star" in the second stanza demonstrate the use of obscure language to force the reader to stretch his imagination. Although there is little confusion that Swenson means "inhabitants" and "planet," her use of less appropriate words allows the reader to compensate with his own imagination. Her word choice also lends authenticity to the inherently unbelievable premise that aliens are authoring this poem. Certainly, an alien might call Earth a star rather than a planet and would not know to call Earth's inhabitants humans. Those are our words. Swenson comments that "through their transparent parts / . . . you can see their guts." These "transparent parts" may reference windows or sunroofs, and the "guts" perhaps the steering wheel, dashboard, or even the person driving. The notion of aliens perceiving cars as insects or lower life forms is both amusing and grotesque. Further, it gives readers an uncannily new view of the world they once took for granted.

The description of the scene from above is resoundingly beautiful in its simplicity. The four eyes, with the two in the back, are obvious references to head and tail lights. The reader has undoubtedly stood many times next to a car without noticing the eye-like qualities of its headlights. The next description in the poem is that of the five-eyed "creature" with one-turning eye. This is a creature that the others respect, by going slowly and allowing him to wind around them as he passes. Although the description of a bird's eye view of a police car is so obvious to the reader, the reader can readily

> *By deconstructing an aspect of human life so familiar that humans take it for granted, Swenson demonstrates that even the most mundane of objects is a potential subject for a poem."*

see that the alien interpretation is equally feasible. Swenson even employs a sound imagery, in the phrase "they all hiss as they glide." One can nearly hear the sound of the cars whizzing past on the freeway. In this sense, this work employs more than visual sense, which is a pleasant surprise, as most poems are content to only conjure images.

The description of the hissing sound and the notion of the cars "respecting" one another are examples of personification. Personification occurs when the author or poet assigns human or animal traits to objects. An example would be to say that the morning "awoke and stretched its weary arms." Some literary critics also call this device the pathetic fallacy when applied to living but inanimate things like plants, under the theory that it is morbid and unnatural to assign life-like qualities to unnatural objects. Yet, in this poem, the use of personification adds to the authenticity of the premise that automobiles are "alive."

Swenson, a naturalist who revels in depicting ordinary objects with imagination, has assumed a third-person point of view in other works. By deconstructing an aspect of human life so familiar that humans take it for granted, Swenson demonstrates that even the most mundane of objects is a potential subject for a poem. Likewise, in many of her other poems, she utilizes the same gift of creative description to clue the reader in to the object of the work without revealing the specifics. In "Little Lion Face," for example, she describes a sunflower thusly: "Little lion face / I stopped to pick / among the mass of thick / succulent blooms, the twice / streaked flanges of your silk." Using the same metaphorical techniques she uses in "Southbound

What Do I Read Next?

- In 1996, editors R. R. Knudson and Suzzanne Bigelow published *May Swenson: A Poet's Life in Photos*. This wonderful book contains photographs of Swenson from her infancy to old age and includes many pictures of her at functions with family members and with fellow poets. It also includes close to thirty poems in a section at the end entitled "A Life in Poems." This is a must-see, must-read photo album for any Swenson student.

- Ray Bradbury is one of the most respected authors in the genre of science fiction, and one of his most popular books is *The Martian Chronicles*, published in 1950. This collection of stories about colonies of human beings setting out to explore Mars in the then-distant year of 1999 is an important reflection on humanity's treatment of "the other" (in this case, the Martians) and on the tendency to conquer new lands without regard for the inhabitants who came first.

- Tom Lewis's *Divided Highways: Building the Interstate Highways, Transforming American Life* (1999) provides a vivid look at what it took to construct the highway system in the United States and what it has meant to the American public. Lewis contends that the open road used to mean freedom and a gateway to unknown places, and now it often means gridlock, smog, and road rage.

- Elizabeth Bishop was one of America's most noted poets and both a contemporary and close friend of May Swenson. Like Swenson, she wrote highly imagistic poems and was a perfectionist with her own work, always concerned with painting accurate "pictures" with her words as opposed to abstracts. Published in 1983, *The Complete Poems, 1927–1979* provides a comprehensive overview of this important poet's body of work.

on the Freeway," Swenson writes an entire poem about the beauty of a sunflower without once using the word sunflower. One can see strains of the same breed of innocence in "Southbound on the Freeway" because Swenson assumes the same pseudo-childlike levels of observation.

This approach to poetry is philosophically comparable to the approach of abstract or cubist painters such as Picasso. In such paintings, the artist distorts a familiar shape so that the viewer must infuse some imagination into dissecting the meaning behind the art. Swenson gives the reader cryptic verbal clues as to the object portrayed but does not disclose it completely. In this sense, the poet has demonstrated an ability to see the world though geometry, through lines and shapes. In Swenson's world, to write a poem is to reach for a multitude of words in order to describe something rather than divulge the mystery outright. The most interesting aspect of this piece is that it represents a subject and a viewpoint that most poets would not think worthy of exploration with a pen and paper. Why, one may ask, would someone choose such an unusual subject matter and viewpoint for a poem? The skyward view of cars traveling on a freeway is not overtly fascinating, pithy, or romantic. Readers frequently assume that a poem is a vehicle for exposing a facet of an author's personality or background. Unquestionably, some poets view their chosen art form as a medium for sharing some of their hard-learned wisdom with the rest of the world.

At first glance, this poem does not seem to teach the reader anything about the world. Readers might walk away musing at Swenson's creativity, but they may not ask themselves why she chose this particular topic. However, after rereading the lines, the reader may get the sense that Swenson is poking fun at human society. By the poem's end, readers gain a refreshing new insight into the bizarreness of the modern world, where human creations are sophisticated enough to resemble life forms to an unsuspecting extraterrestrial. The fact that an automobile resembles a life form to an unsuspecting observer could be a compliment to the unparalleled technological industry of the contemporary world. However, on the other hand, the fact that an observer from Orbitville could reasonably mistake the hard chassis of a car for an intelligent life form is potentially pejorative for human society. Swenson seems to be saying, "What do humans value in society?" Are human inventions the most apparent and noticeable aspects of this culture? Is engineering reflective of the true brains of human society? One may get the sense that Swenson believes advanced technologies are destructive to the natural world.

In her aesthetic portrayal of unassuming objects, Swenson could even have been described as the fringe of the San Francisco Beat Movement of the 1950s. This movement, which evolved out of intellectual meetings between bohemian poets in San Francisco and New York, spawned such famous names as Jack Kerouac, Allen Ginsberg and Lawrence Ferlinghetti. These unconventional writers were reacting to the post World War II fervor and the beginning strains of McCarthyism, and their writing reflected a subtle angst for American popular and contemporary culture. The three recurring themes of the Beat movement are candor in thought and language, spirituality, and environmentalism. Swenson, who was born into a Morman family in Logan, Utah, often wrote poems depicting nature as a recurring theme. This technique allows the reader to rediscover something ubiquitous in his environment all over again.

Furthermore, the fact that Swenson elected to describe the scene of cars traveling rapidly in open spaces may be indicative of her Western American upbringing. She left Utah after finishing her bachelor's at the University of Utah to move to New York City. Although she worked mostly on the East Coast and never returned to Utah to live, much of her poetry reflects a love of the natural world, which was not likely gleaned from living in cosmopolitan areas. We can almost see her writing this poem while perched on a mountain overlook in Logan, Utah, furrowing her brow at the sight of cars whizzing by on the freeway below her. Once domiciled in New York, she became a poet who corresponded frequently with other influential female poets of the twentieth century, most notably Elizabeth Bishop. Although less known in popular culture than Bishop, Swenson is revered in many critical circles, especially among sensual women writers.

As James S. Terry notes in his annotation of *Nature: Poems Old and New*, "Swenson's gift is to observe and catalog accurately while stretching possible meanings to a higher imaginative level. She is therefore both abstract and concrete at once. A vision akin to William Blake's is mixed with a homely vernacular diction like Robert Frost's or perhaps Roethke's, so that even the darker subjects are luminous with Swenson's unusual or new perspectives." Further, critic Robert Hass, in selecting Swenson's Question as the Poet's Choice in his

Washington Post column on September 13, 1998, called Swenson a "wonderful and not very well-known poet . . . in the quirky tradition of Emily Dickinson and Elizabeth Bishop." Perhaps Swenson will someday posthumously receive the recognition she deserves.

Source: Lisa Fabian, Critical Essay on "Southbound on the Freeway," in *Poetry for Students*, The Gale Group, 2002.

Sources

Hass, Robert, "Poet's Corner," in the *Washington Post*, September 13, 1998.

Shapiro, Karl, "A Ball with Language," in the *New York Times Book Review*, May 7, 1967, pp. 8, 34.

Smith, Dave, "Perpetual Worlds Taking Place," in *Poetry*, Vol. CXXXV, No. 5, February 1980, pp. 291–96.

Swenson, May, "Little Lion Face," in *In Other Words: New Poems*, Alfred A. Knopf, 1987.

———, *Nature: Poems Old and New*, annotated by Terry S. James, Houghton Mifflin, 1994.

———, *To Mix with Time: New and Selected Poems*, Charles Scribner's Sons, 1963.

Further Reading

Knudson, R. Rozanne, *The Wonderful Pen of May Swenson*, Macmillan, 1993.
> This is a biography of May Swenson written by her longtime friend R. R. Knudson. It contains excerpts from her poems and photographs from her personal collection. Although written by an obvious supporter of her poetry, the book presents a candid, honest picture of the poet's life.

Swenson, May, *Dear Elizabeth: Five Poems and Three Letters to Elizabeth Bishop*, Utah State University Press, 2000.
> Just as the title suggests, this collection of personal letters and poems dedicated to Swenson's friend, mentor, and fellow poet Elizabeth Bishop was published through the Literary Estate of May Swenson. It contains copies of actual letters in Swenson's own handwriting and exposes some of her deepest thoughts about a woman she cared deeply for.

———, *Iconographs*, Scribner, 1970.
> Swenson used the word "iconograph" to refer to her "shape" poems—works that typographically and visually represent the subject of the poem. For example, a poem about an animal may reflect that animal's shape on the page. This 1970 collection highlights Swenson's appreciation for nature and science and gives the reader a good idea of how wide her scope was in terms of both subject matter and format.

————, *Made with Words*, edited by Gardner McFall, University of Michigan Press, 1998.

This is an extensive collection of Swenson's prose—from excerpts of her fiction writing to essays about her thoughts on poets and poetry—as well as an interview. The book provides an excellent look at how Swenson created her work and what she believed about the entire creative process.

Story from Bear Country

Leslie Marmon Silko

1981

"Story from Bear Country," first published in Silko's collection of poetry and prose *Storyteller* in 1981, retells a Native-American myth in a simple and direct tone. Silko, an award-winning poet and novelist, grew up in New Mexico where she was raised within three strong cultures—Laguna Indian, Mexican, and white European—which influenced her strong writing voice. Borrowing from traditional Laguna "abduction myths," stories of animals seducing humans and transforming them, the poet uses vivid images throughout to guide the reader through a wilderness where bears are waiting to call people into their world. Before people know it, having wandered too far into the woods, they become "locked forever" inside themselves "dark shaggy and thick," with the poet sending "bear priests" to look for them and help them make the journey back. Silko takes on the role of "storyteller" and "trail guide," speaking directly to the reader, mixing description with instruction as they make their way through this beautiful and enticing landscape.

Author Biography

Silko, who is of Laguna Pueblo, Plains Indian, Mexican, and Anglo-American descent, was born on March 5, 1948, in Albuquerque and was raised on the Laguna Pueblo Reservation in northern New Mexico. As a child, Silko attended schools administered by the Bureau of Indian Affairs and also

Leslie Marmon Silko

learned about Laguna legends and traditions from her great-grandmother and other members of her extended family. From the fifth grade on, Silko received her education at Catholic schools and then went on to college at the University of New Mexico. She graduated summa cum laude in 1969, earning a bachelor's degree in English. Silko subsequently attended law school for a short while before deciding to pursue a writing career. While working on her poetry and fiction, Silko taught at several universities and colleges throughout the Southwest, including the University of Arizona and the University of New Mexico. The recipient of several grants and fellowships, Silko received the Pushcart Prize for poetry in 1977. Silko is the single parent of two sons, Robert and Cazimir, and lives near Tucson, Arizona.

Poem Summary

Lines 1–3

In these introductory lines, the poet establishes a direct address tone, speaking directly to readers, instructing them as if they were about to take a journey and the speaker is the guide. Readers are also introduced to the location, "bear country," which

is probably a general term for any area where bears live and roam.

Lines 4–5

Readers will know they are in bear country by an overwhelming silence. In this unique image, the poet makes "silence" tangible by giving it movement, "flowing" around them as they stand under the juniper trees.

Lines 6–7

Continuing a list of ways readers will know they are in bear country, in these lines, Silko describes the distinctive colors of sandstone in the region. "Sundown colors," or colors associated with the sunset, are most likely referring to red, orange, and yellow.

Lines 8–10

In these lines, the poet uses the sensory detail of smell to help describe bear country. "Yucca" is a commonly found evergreen plant found in the American Southwest, and readers can only guess that bears have "scratched away" the damp earth to expose the roots.

Lines 11–14

These lines help locate readers more vividly in the landscape, surrounded by juniper trees, high cliffs nearby with caves where bears may hide. This is also the first time readers hear the bears, growling and snorting, though they still do not see them.

Lines 15–16

After introducing readers to the surroundings, here the speaker suggests that the bears "call" to them, though it's "difficult to explain" exactly how they do it.

Lines 17–21

Here readers are told not only do the bears call to people, but some people actually follow, joining them, giving up their families and "human" lives. Many traditional stories use other people's examples as warnings, suggesting "be careful or this will happen to you."

Lines 22–23

Although this section does not give readers the exact reason why they would "never want to return," these lines suggest that once people go with the bears, they would have no desire to return to the human world.

Lines 24–26

Here, the poet gives readers an image of beauty that would "overcome your memory" of whatever life was left behind, almost as if people would become entranced by the bears. Note, too, how the season has suddenly changed to winter, the time when bears take refuge and hibernate.

Lines 27–30

In these lines, the poet suggests a transformation from human to animal; people would be trapped inside themselves and see their bodies become "dark shaggy and thick" like the bears who called to them.

Lines 31–32

In the event that people do get trapped in bear country, the poet informs readers that "bear priests," or medicine men specifically knowledgeable of bear magic, would be sent out to rescue them. Native Americans maintain a profound relationship with the natural world, believing animal spirits are just as unique and important as human spirits, each with their own powers and wisdom.

Lines 33–38

These lines describe what the bear priests would be wearing during their search. Taking on the appearance of a bear themselves by painting their legs black and wearing "bear claw necklaces," they would also carry a "medicine bag," which probably contains herbs and medicinal roots.

Lines 39–41

These lines describe the path the bear priest would follow to find people, through canyon and "blue-grey mountain sage," which is an aromatic plant found in the Western United States.

Lines 42–45

The bear priest would follow a person's trail to a clearing in the woods. The poet suggests that this is the place where people first realized their transformation, noticing when they look back that their footprints are no longer human.

Lines 46–49

These lines tell readers that when people hear the bear priests calling, the memories of their families and past "human" life will slowly come back to them and "will writhe around your heart." Even though a very short time may have passed, those memories will seem far away and "startle you with their distance."

Media Adaptations

- In 1978, Leslie Marmon Silko was the subject of a documentary video called "Running on the Edge of the Rainbow: Laguna Stories and Poems," one of a series of videotapes of oral literary performance produced by Larry Evers at the University of Arizona and available from Norman Ross Publishing Co. in New York.

Line 50

"The others" are probably other people who wandered too far into bear country as well, and were also turned into bears.

Lines 51–54

These lines suggest that the songs the bear priests sing are so beautiful, "the others" will have to listen. The poet informs readers that this special skill is crucial for the bear priest; otherwise they would not be able to rescue anyone.

Lines 55–59

Once the bear priests find the people who have been taken, they will slowly and carefully bring them back to the very clearing where they first noticed their transformation, where their footprints switched from human to animal.

Line 60

This line indicates a crucial turn in the poem. Up to this point, the poet has been taking on the role of wise storyteller, more knowledgeable about bear country than those readers who might stumble in and be trapped there. In this line, Silko poses the question "whose voice is this?" to both the reader and herself, perhaps implying everything up to this point was not in her own voice. The oral tradition of storytelling is firmly rooted in Native-American culture, and when someone retells a story, they are linking themselves to a long line of past storytellers. Perhaps the poet wonders if, in telling this traditional myth of animal abduction, she is even using her own voice. Perhaps her ancestors are speaking through her. This single line helps open a new level in the poem, moving from simple narrative to questions of heritage, tradition, and the power of myth.

Lines 61–64

After asking readers "Whose voice is this," here the poet implies that maybe everything up to this point has been hypothetical—people have not been transformed; people are really just hiking alone in the woods listening to the speaker's warnings about how the bears might call to them.

Lines 65–67

These lines help engage readers further in the poem by inventing a life, hiking through bear country while their families wait "back at the car," as if they had just stopped for a short while during a drive.

Lines 68–69

Here, Silko forces the reader to notice himself or herself as an active participant in the story, listening patiently. On one level, Silko is speaking as storyteller to listener, on another as poet to reader. By reading this far into the poem, readers have been listening to her "for some time now."

Lines 70–72

After guiding readers through an imagined bear abduction and rescue by a priest, these lines locate readers back where they started, alone in the woods surrounded by silence, where even the birds are silent. Note, too, that silence was one of the first ways people learned they had entered bear country at the beginning of the poem.

Lines 73–74

Similar to lines 6–7, these lines ask readers to notice the sunset and the reddish-orange light on the cliffs. This recurring image helps frame the poem, returning the reader to a familiar place at the middle of the poem after traveling a great imagined distance through the first half of the poem.

Lines 75–78

In a gentle and consoling tone, the poet returns to the role of storyteller, associating herself again with the bear priests. Blurring the line between myth and reality by saying "we've been calling you / all this time," readers have to wonder whether the abduction was hypothetical or real.

Lines 79–83

In these lines, Silko asks people to look behind them to see whether their tracks are human or bear, making them wonder really how far they have traveled into bear country. Was this all just a myth, or did people really become bears before being rescued by Native-American priests? People will only know if they turn around. On a larger scale, perhaps the poet is also commenting on the ability of myth to transform people—often, when a person becomes engaged in a story, he or she will feel as though he or she gets lost in it, hours passing as if only minutes. Maybe this is the power of myth: through the mutual act of storyteller and listener, stories allow readers to become something else for a while, leaving "normal" lives behind and entering a landscape that is magical and mysterious.

Lines 84–89

At this point in the poem, Silko changes tactics. Instead of addressing the reader directly and having the reader question whether there has been an abduction by bears, the poet instead recounts a story of someone else who has been abducted by bears. In the first line of this stanza, she says, "He was a small child." The "was" indicates that the story is from the past, unlike the first half of the poem, which is entirely in present or future tense. The "small child" is "learning to get around / by himself," implying that he is still young and untrained and needs guidance. The fact that "His family went by wagon," as Silko notes in the next line, indicates that this story took place when people traveled by wagon. In this case, the poet most likely intends the poem to take place in the developing American West, where wagon travel was common.

Lines 90–94

The "mountains" mentioned in the previous stanza are most likely the Rocky Mountains, since "piñons"—edible seeds from pine trees—are often found in this region. While the family is harvesting the edible seeds, the poet offers a suggestion for how the child might have gotten away from the protection of his family. The child, still untrained and unaware of potential danger, tries "to follow his brothers and sisters / into the trees" where they are "picking piñons."

Lines 95–96

Nobody thinks to look for him, because each person thinks that the child is being watched by somebody else.

Lines 97–106

As a result, it is not until "the next day" that the family "tracked him." This long gap of time between the child's disappearance and their search for him implies that the food-gathering process was important enough to forget about the care of the child. The use of tracking indicates that this family is most likely Native American, since tracking was one of the many cultural skills that traditional Native Americans used to survive their environment. When the family follows the tracks of the little boy, they find that he has passed into a "canyon," which is "near the place which belonged / to the bears." The use of the word, "belonged," implies that the bears own this place and that the little boy, and now the adult humans, are trespassing.

This idea is reinforced when Silko describes how the search party goes as far as they can, to the very threshold of the bears' domain: "the place / where no human / could go beyond." At this point, the search party's worst fears are confirmed. The boy's "little footprints" are "mixed in with the bear tracks."

Lines 107–109

Now that the family knows for sure that their son is with the bears, they call in reinforcements, asking a "medicine man" to come help them. Like the "bear priests" mentioned earlier in the poem, a medicine man was a Native-American healer, who used his knowledge of the magical powers of various substances and rituals to perform spiritual cleansings. In this case, the family is certain that the medicine man "knew how / to call the child back again."

Lines 110–112

As the poet notes, "There wasn't much time." The transformation from human to bear can happen quickly, especially for a child who has yet to learn the ways of humanity. For such an impressionable youth, the life of a bear can seem just as natural as the life of a human. For this reason, the medicine man is "running," with his "assistants" in close pursuit, moving much faster than the "loping" bear priests that were called upon to help the reader in the first part of the poem.

Lines 113–115

The medicine man and his assistant, like the bear priests from before, wear items to make themselves appear like bears. In this case, the item is "bearweed," which they wear wrapped around their "wrists and ankles" and their "necks." The bearweed also presumably acts like a charm against the hypnotic influence of the bears, so the medicine man and his assistants cannot be transformed them-

selves while they are trespassing in bear country and trying to save the child.

Lines 116–117

In this short stanza, the medicine man begins to act like a bear: "He grunted loudly and scratched on the ground in front of him." The man is trying to lure the bears out of their cave, the entrance of which he "kept watching."

Lines 118–124

Here, the man's efforts pay off, as his "growling sound" attracts little bears to come out, thinking it is a "mother bear sound." However, the medicine man must grunt and growl "a little more," before he is able to get the child to come out. At this point, the child's transformation into a bear is almost complete. In the absence of human instruction from his family, who was busy picking seeds, the impressionable child has found a new family in the bears. Silko notes that the child "was already walking like his sisters" and that "he was already crawling on the ground." The fact that the child is already close to being part of the bear family underscores the idea that the child is impressionable.

Lines 125–128

Because of this, the child has been all but converted into a bear. As a result, "They couldn't just grab the child." If the family were to do this, they would have one very confused child on their hands. The boy would be stuck "in-between" the human and bear worlds, a disconcerting spiritual state that could lead to his death.

Lines 129–131

Although the child has almost completely turned into a bear at this point, the medicine man is still able "to call him," using the same type of method that the bears use to hypnotize people, to try to slowly coax the boy back to civilization, "step by step." The man is successful, and does in fact bring the child back.

Lines 132–136

However, after getting the boy back from the bears, "he wasn't quite the same." The poet once again draws attention to the fact that this event took place in the past, a "long time ago." Silko also notes that in this time of Native-American myths and legends, the boy was not totally transformed back into a human. The boy had spent time in the company of bears, and this experience will always be a part of him. This is especially true since, when the boy discovered the bears, he was largely untrained. As a result, the bears helped to give him an identity that his human family had not provided yet. And although the medicine man was able to "call" the boy back to humanity, the boy always retained some of his bear-like qualities, which separated him from "the other children."

The story of the boy can be taken literally, as a boy who gets abducted by bears and who must be drawn back to humanity. However, it could also be seen as a symbolic tale, highlighting the struggle for Native-American cultures to preserve their myths and ways of life in the face of European American colonization in the developing American West. Silko uses the first part of the poem to instruct her readers—many of whom are probably not of Native-American descent—in one of the myths of her people, drawing the reader directly into the story by making the reader the focus of it. With this increased focus on myth, Silko then relates an actual story from the myths of her people, where a little boy was permanently transformed—at least in part—by bears.

The boy can be viewed as the symbol of a new generation of Native Americans, who are now out of touch with their heritage, and therefore lack an identity, like young children do. However, if this new generation tries to blindly follow the lead of their older "brothers and sisters," or ancestors, they can lose themselves. This situation is not desirable in a society where such changes of identity would cause them to appear different from others. Differences have historically been used as a method of oppression or exclusion in American society, so Silko seems to be saying that if Native Americans insist on surrendering to their ancient ways, they could be singled out in American society. However, the poem is also a message to Silko's American readers, entreating them not to persecute the new generation for being transformed, at least in part, by its heritage.

Themes

The Individual and the Community

"Story from Bear Country" first appears in *Storyteller*, a collection of poems, photographs, traditional tales, letter fragments, and family history vignettes that is autobiographical yet essentially formed from an "oral" (verbal as opposed to written) tradition whose materials are communal. The idea that tribal stories have the power to teach, guide, and correct individuals is implicit throughout, beginning with the first word, "You."

The direct address to the reader or listener puts us on personal, intimate terms with the author, whose role it is to pass down ancient wisdom in old and new forms for the purpose of connecting us to important Native-American values. "You" is juxtaposed with the "We" of community, which serves as the larger family to whom we are related and that has the power to remind us of who we are. Communal relationships are further complicated by the imposition of "they," which refers both to the bear priests and the bears themselves. The call of the bear is irresistible; their beauty will "overcome your memory like winter sun melting ice shadows from snow." The bear priests' song is also powerful and beautiful. It evokes "faint memories" that "writhe around your heart" entreating you to return to the clan.

The struggle for the individual soul is finally mediated by the narrator, the "me" of the poem, who serves as a universal voice of compassion associated with the natural world. While it is unclear what "footprints" the wandering man in the still canyon may find when he turns (bear claws or human prints) there is still time to heed the call of compassion and avoid being "locked forever inside yourself," lost forever to the human community.

Transformation and Identity

This poem combines elements of traditional Laguna Pueblo mythology ("he" who takes on the aspects of bear) with a contemporary reinvention of the tale that hints at the overwhelming desire for self-transformation and the terrible risk of identity loss. Each person walks a road that will lead either to the recovery of a "memory" or "dream" of the true self (a ritualized form of this rebirth initiation is practiced by Native Americans through vision quests) or a loss or confusion of identity that results from over-identification with another being. This choice creates the tension in the story.

While the poem reverberates with the seductive imagery of the landscape and the "beauty" of bears, the tale is a cautionary one. The child who wanders off, takes on bear aspects, and is finally recovered by the medicine man is never "quite the same after that." Ideally, self-transformation is sanctioned by tribal ritual. Individual rebirth must take place within a human community, forging kinship ties with all of nature but preserving the boundaries that allow us to develop our unique individuality.

The Spirit World

In Native-American cosmology, spirit moves around and within each person. It inhabits animals, plants, rocks, weather, and all things residing in the natural world. A balance is required to keep the earth healthy and in spiritual harmony. Because all things are connected and interdependent in this cosmology, every living thing and element is valuable, both in itself and in its relationship to every other thing. In this poem, bear spirit resides in the dazzling beauty and stillness of the canyons and caves.

Because human identity is flexible and intertwined with all of nature, the spirit of bear can call to a human spirit, coaxing it into a kind of introspective womb-cave that is both powerful and final. Once the call is heard and the transformation made, "you will never want to return." In this spirit world, the intervention of the medicine man is pivotal. He alone has the power to bridge the space between worlds where identity may be caught and forever mutated. But in this poem no simple formula serves to answer the question, "Who am I?" A dynamic uncertainty or ambiguity remains. Readers are asked to weigh the yearning for a miraculous crossing of boundaries into another spiritual realm against the world left behind when someone heeds the call of the bear and surrenders his human self.

Style

"Story from Bear Country" is written in free verse, which means its form grows and varies in relation to the changing moods of the subject matter, unlike formal verse, which is constructed using a set rhyme scheme or number of accented beats per line. Matching this poem's simple tone, Silko uses lines that are short, usually only three or six words long. Similarly, each stanza (which literally means "room" in Italian) is constructed using around seven lines each. Silko arranges one or two images in these "rooms," keeping the poem uncluttered and accessible. In this sense, the poet has constructed a simple framework for a simple voice, the short lines and stanzas helping the reader make the journey through this unfamiliar landscape, wary of bears.

Historical Context

Socially and politically, Native Americans still feel the burden of their separate status as outsiders in

Topics for Further Study

- What is the main "story" of this poem, and how is it rooted in our common experience? What spiritual beliefs are made manifest by the story?

- The belief in self-transformation and rebirth is common among Native-American tribes. Tribe members were initiated into adulthood by undertaking "vision quests" in the wilderness to discover their "totem" animal that was thought to guide them through life. What can this transforming rite tell us about the relationship between humans and animals in Native cultures?

- Storytelling is essential to Native-American oral traditions. Imagine that this poem plays a significant role in educating Laguna Pueblo children. What do you think the poem is trying to teach? Is there a lesson or even many lessons embedded in the poem?

- Poems are meant to be read aloud just as drama is meant to be performed on the stage. Read the poem aloud. What emotion or feeling does the imagery of the poem conjure up for you? How is nature presented; is it filled with terror or beauty or both? Does the author evoke a mood of fear or desire toward wild nature? What specific images create this mood?

- In Native-American traditions, it is important to "walk in balance" with nature. Is something out of balance in this poem? What is the source of conflict or tension in this poem? What can the ambiguous ending tell us about Laguna Pueblo culture?

- Research the significance of the bear as a totem animal in Native-American traditions. What singular, valuable qualities does the bear possess? Relate what you find to the poem.

their own land. Once heir to an entire continent, their communities are mostly confined to reservations on land that is unaccommodating to the way of life that sustained them for thousands of years before European colonization. Joseph Bruchac

Compare & Contrast

- **1400s:** Before contact with Europeans, indigenous peoples of North America lived in long-established tribal homelands and developed cultures that reflected their economic and spiritual relationship with the natural world.

  Today: Many of America's indigenous peoples experience a dual identity, as natives who lost their way of life as a direct result of U.S. policies of aggression and containment and also as patriotic Americans who feel an innate sense of belonging to the continent.

- **1400s:** In Native-American folk legends and narratives of creation, animals were co-creators of the earth. Animals and humans could "talk" to each other, and the natural world was balanced by a sacred respect for all living things.

  Today: New awareness and respect for Native-American traditions has led to a greater sensitivity to the ecological problems facing the planet and our responsibility for preserving and protecting all life forms.

- **1400s:** Since writing was non-existent in Native-American cultures, tribes relied on storytelling to pass down to its members common values, wisdom, and sacred beliefs. This oral tradition relied on both ancient tales and imaginative new stories that would make the past memorable to each generation of listeners.

  Today: Native-American authors write in English and are widely read and celebrated nationally and abroad. But Native-American literacy has not diminished the importance of stories and legends. On the contrary, writing has enabled a new kind of storytelling technique that allows the text to act as the storyteller.

- **1400s:** Native Americans recognized the power of the feminine in creation myths, tribal laws, ceremonies, and rituals. The animating spirit that pervades life is referred to variously in ancient stories as "Spider Woman," "Corn Woman," or "Thought Woman," she who thinks a thing and brings it into being.

  Today: As a corrective to predominately patriarchal social constructs, the power of the feminine is being restored to Native-American stories by such writers as Silko, Paula Gunn Allen, Linda Hogan, and Wendy Rose.

---

writes in his introduction to *Songs from This Earth on Turtle's Back* that "as many as 50 million American Indian people" may have lived on this continent in the 1400s. In the early 1900s, he continues, population figures indicate less than half a million were left.

However, between 1960 and 1980, census figures show that the American Indian population grew from 750,000 to 1,500,000. Simultaneously, the rituals, traditions, and stories of Native Americans underwent a renaissance beginning in the 1960s when N. Scott Momaday won a Pulitzer Prize (in 1969) for his book *House Made of Dawn*. The keen interest in Native-American culture, history, and spirituality is reflected in the new respect accorded Native-American writers and artists and a spiritual awakening in regard to our relationship with the environment and the natural world of which we are a part.

Leslie Marmon Silko was one of the first Native-American writers to be included in the canon of contemporary American literature, and she is well recognized as one of the most gifted fiction writers of our time. Indeed, her home state of New Mexico designated her a living cultural treasure and in her early thirties she was the recipient of a MacArthur "genius" award.

On the back cover of *Storyteller*, the volume in which "Story from Bear Country" appears, it is noted that storytelling in Native-American culture had "a magical quality; [stories] were both real and wondrous, and they had the power to bring the people together as nothing else did." Silko's poem invokes aspects of this "magic" and creates its own mood of wonder by using the ancient tale of the boy being transformed to a bear to discuss the real and problematic nature of identity formation of Native Americans. Because Native-American cultures were destroyed, suppressed or undermined by forced education and absorption into European customs, developing a firm sense of self based on sacred and enduring values has been difficult. Thus, in her capacity as author, Silko is more than a writer. She is both a caretaker of her people's stories and co-creator of new mythologies that serve to continue the tradition of storytelling by which people in the community are sustained and uplifted.

Silko's work, as with many other contemporary Native-American writers such as Paula Gunn Allen, Joseph Bruchac, Linda Hogan, Joy Harjo, Scott Momaday, Simon Ortiz, and Gerald Vizenor (to name a few), invites readers to explore the complex interrelations between individual and community and among human, animal, and vegetable natures. It does so by juxtaposing the language of legends and the anima of the spirit world with the material reality of the everyday physical world. For example, the real problems of despair and alcoholism among Indians and the disturbance of the natural balance by uranium mining in the Southwest regions of the Laguna Pueblo people are important motifs in Silko's popular novel, *Ceremony*. As the hero, Tayo, a Vietnam vet, searches for an authentic self, he must complete his own life-affirming ceremony by remembering the roots of his past and confronting the instruments of death and destruction that threaten the continuity of values embedded in the old stories.

In her poems, essays, novels, and other works of fiction and non-fiction, Silko confronts social and political problems of Native-American life on the reservations, including poverty, alcoholism, social alienation, racism, and suicide. However, Silko places powerful faith in ceremonies that can reverse self-defeating attitudes and outside aggression. That faith is reflected in "Story from Bear Country." Implicit is old Indian wisdom for creating balance and harmony: rely on the strength of community, remember who you are and where you come from, and maintain a respectful kinship with other living things.

Critical Overview

Perhaps best known as a novelist, Silko won the *Chicago Review* poetry prize, soon followed by a national *Pushcart* prize for the best poem published in a small magazine. Although not much has been written specifically about "Story From Bear Country," many critics praise the collection, *Storyteller*, in which it appeared, pointing out the strong Native-American tradition from which Silko writes. Bernard A. Hirsch, writing for the *American Indian Quarterly*, notes how the book "lovingly maps the fertile storytelling ground from which [Silko's] art evolves." Similarly, Linda Danielson, in the *Journal of the Southwest*, concludes that "through the book [Silko] reclaims both personal and tribal traditions about men and women, animals and holy people, community and creativity." According to Hirsch, it is these tribal myths and stories from Native-American culture "that Silko expresses with grace and power through her melding of oral tradition and the written word."

Criticism

Kathy Smith

Smith is an independent scholar and freelance writer. In this essay, Smith explores the significance of Native-American legend and oral traditions to Leslie Marmon Silko's poetics.

"Story from Bear Country" is characteristic of Leslie Marmon Silko's work in that it combines a new tale or "telling" that emerges from old tribal wisdom. The new story is appropriate to be told or read since in Native-American tradition, the story is embedded in the everyday communal life of the people. The poem combines Silko's re-telling of a Laguna Pueblo folktale with an original poem that could easily stand on its own. However, Silko uses the tale of a boy who almost turns into a bear as a kind of "coda" or independent narrative that is powerfully connected to the sacred teachings of Native-American traditions.

The folktale and Silko's contemporary "version" of it work in concert to emphasize the point that the stories must continually be told and retold, adding new words and new meanings so that they remain relevant over time. Silko implies that there is danger in forgetting the stories or in not passing them on to future generations. Since one of the powerful themes of this poem concerns the nature of self, the fragility and fluidity of identity in the interconnectedness of all things, then stories and rituals are imbued with an almost magical power to remind us of who we are and from where we come.

> *There is something wild in us, Silko seems to be saying, that needs the company of other wild things.*"

The poem first appears in *Storyteller*, an auto-biographical collection of poems, photographs, folktales, and family stories that form an oral culture vital to communal life. The storytelling function takes on a sacred quality because stories are used to guide individuals in the ways and beliefs of Native-American thought and being. That the story is meant to be told, that it is meant to include and guide every listener, is implicit from the very first word, "You." This direct address puts us on personal, intimate terms with the ancient wisdom being recycled.

What is it that this "you" is supposed to know? First and foremost, the inner self. But this inner self does not exist outside or apart from either the natural world or the social world of human interaction. So, the first verse orients us to the place in which we find ourselves. It is a particular world of the bear, a country we "will know" by using our senses: to hear and feel "the silence flowing swiftly," to smell the "juniper trees," to see the "sundown colors of sandrock." The images tell us clearly that "you" are in a Southwest landscape; they remind us that "you" are at home in the natural world. The "you" has been here before. As the ominous last line of the first verse indicates, "you" are walking alone, surrounded by the natural world "all around you."

The second verse augments the setting with more images and amplifies them with actions that might be taking place in bear country. The experiences of "you" are less certain. In contrast to the first verse, where the you "will know," the you of the second verse merely "may" smell and hear traces and echoes of bear. The hypothetical language fits the mood. As the "you" walks further into bear country, the poem gives us a sense of disquiet, of meaning that is more ambiguous. This ambiguity is heightened in the third verse when Silko alludes to the mystery of how the bears "call you" and lure you into their realm. The yearning to heed this call of the wild is irresistible, though. Of those who "went," most "left behind families . . . a good life."

There is something wild in us, Silko seems to be saying, that needs the company of other wild things. There is something not quite firm in us, some need to transform ourselves, to transcend ourselves, some desire to lose oneself in the identity of another. The fascination for other life forms, the poem implies, is old and always with us. It has not disappeared, nor will it disappear. It emerges from the very essence of being itself, the nature of connection among all living things.

"The problem is / you will never want to return." These two lines stand by themselves and gain dramatic emphasis thereby. Once you walk too far into bear country, once you identify too strongly with another, you lose track of those that are left behind, including your original self. While the beauty of the bears is seductive, and "will overcome your memory / like winter sun / melting ice shadows from snow," if you stay there you will suffer some consequences. You will be "locked forever inside yourself / your eyes will see you / dark shaggy and thick."

The poem changes focus here with the use of "we" and the introduction of the larger human family to whom we are related and which is endowed with the capacity to "call you back." Communal kinship is further complicated by the use of "they," which refers both to the bear priests and the bears themselves. While the call of the bear is hauntingly persuasive, the "song" of the bear priests is also "beautiful." It evokes "faint memories" that "will writhe around your heart" entreating you to return to the clan. However, these memories already "startle you with their distance." The bear priests dress in their "bear claw necklaces." They paint their legs black to take on aspects of bear. They are "loping after you / with their medicine bags." Their job is to retrieve you, to recall you to yourself "step by step," but you have already seen "only bear prints in the sand / where your feet had been." The listener should now be wondering, is it too late to return?

The struggle for the individual soul is finally mediated by the "me" of the poem, who also has a call or song that emanates from the infinite, from the time of creation, and subsumes all others. It is the voice of compassion calling to the "you" whose wife and sons wait "back at the car." The noncorporeal "me" voice of love reminds the wandering man "hiking in these canyons and hills" that he may

What Do I Read Next?

- *Storyteller* is the autobiographical collection of writings published in 1981 in which "Story from Bear Country" first appears. It is particularly helpful to read the poem in the context of photographs, letters, legends, and family histories, the accumulated experiences of Silko's life that give deeper meanings to Laguna Pueblo culture and her poetic sensibilities. She invites readers to transform themselves by entering a world where memory and imagination recreate the spirit of place, where that place in turn molds the community and the personal interior landscape.

- *Ceremony* (1977), Silko's first novel, reinforces the Native-American wisdom that storytelling occupies a central place in maintaining the health, balance, and strength of community. Implicit in the novel is the notion that without stories to live by, we lose our place in the natural world. Ritual and tribal legends are essential ingredients in healing the spirit and correcting destructive forces. The alienated hero must learn this lesson to complete his journey toward authentic selfhood.

- *Almanac of the Dead* (1991) is Silko's second novel. In it, she attempts to find justice and resolution for the pain, loss, and disenfranchisement of her people. Ironically, it was written during the 1980s, a time dominated by the conservative politics that made life more difficult for the economically disadvantaged and ethnically marginalized.

- In 1969, N. Scott Momaday, a Kiowa poet, novelist, and essayist, won a Pulitzer Prize for his novel *House Made of Dawn*. By doing so, he helped open the doors for other Native-American writers who became established in the American literary canon. In the novel, the protagonist is transformed from an alienated alcoholic war vet to a man whose psyche is finally healed through participation in tribal ritual and reintegration into the fragile web of the cosmos.

- *Songs from This Earth on Turtle's Back* (1983), edited by Joseph Bruchac, is a collection of contemporary American Indian poetry by 52 poets from more than 35 Native-American nations. Each section includes a photograph and brief biography of the poet.

- *The Sacred Hoop* (1986), by Paula Gunn Allen, is a collection of essays whose purpose lies in "recovering the feminine in American Indian traditions." The sacred hoop represents the circle of life, in which every living thing plays a part. The book includes essays on Native-American history and culture as well as reviews of Native-American writers and their art. Allen writes from the perspective of a mixed blood (Laguna and Lebanese) lesbian who is a respected scholar as well as a well-known poet and novelist.

- Joseph Bruchac calls Karl Kroeber's *Traditional American Indian Literatures* "one of the better contemporary books" to explore the heritage of American Indian oral traditions still alive today. Published by the University of Nebraska Press in 1981, Kroeber's book is a wonderful resource for tracing the lineage, range, meaning and relevance of these traditions.

---

safely turn and see his "footprints," that there is still time to heed the call of Native-American spiritual wisdom and avoid being lost forever. The spirit voice is fluid. It easily changes back to the "we" of community. "Don't be afraid," the voice calls. "we love you / we've been calling you / all this time."

Each person walks a road that should lead to the discovery of the true self. The potential confusion of identity is what creates the tension in this poem and in much of Silko's other work. In the folktale that ends this poem, the child recovered from bears by the medicine man is never "quite the same / after that / not like the other children." He has been caught "in between," and his forging of kinship with bears has been gained at the terrible cost of alienation from both groups.

Individual rebirth ideally preserves boundaries that allow us to develop our unique individuality. It is true that in Native-American cosmology, the spirit moves around and within each person. But balance is required to keep spiritual harmony. Because all things are connected and interdependent in this cosmology, every living thing and element is valuable, both in itself and in its relationship to every other thing. In this poem, bear spirit resides in the dazzling beauty and stillness of the canyons and caves where "you" can easily lose yourself. And while no simple formula serves to answer the question, "Who am I?" Silko demonstrates that boundaries are essential to relationships, and relationships are essential to meaning.

Source: Kathy Smith, Critical Essay on "Story from Bear Country," in *Poetry for Students*, The Gale Group, 2002.

Laura Kryhoski

Kryhoski is currently working as a freelance writer. She has also taught English Literature in addition to English as a Second Language overseas. In this essay, Kryhoski considers Erdrich's work in relation to the author's heritage.

"Story from Bear Country" offers a small sampling of Leslie Marmon Silko's ability to weave elements of her ethnicity into the fabric of her work. The poem moves with the rhythms and cadence or beat that is as haunting as it is mystical. The author's Laguna Pueblo (Native American) heritage drives the piece, providing both a traditional framework and a common natural theme, infusing "Story from Bear Country" with a unique sense of spirit and vision.

Silko spins the mystical story of Bear Country in the storytelling tradition characteristic of her Native American roots. The work first maintains an oral quality in its delivery, utilizing such repetitive phrases with slight variations, "You will know," or "You may smell." These phrases and others, scattered throughout the poem, are very inclusive, suggesting that the tale is not only a cautionary one, but one that has been passed along or repeatedly told, from generation to generation. The assumption that the audience "will know" or experience common elements of the tale supports the notion that many have investigated the events of the poem with the same results, thus giving the work a mythic quality. This quality is the hallmark of a myth or

traditional story, defined as one originating in a preliterate society, one dealing with supernatural beings, ancestors, or heroes serving as primordial types in a primitive view of the world. Silko's own natural storytelling ability is an outgrowth of her Laguna Pueblo ancestry.

In *Women Who Run With the Wolves*, Dr. Clarissa Pinkola Estes devotes the afterword of her book to the art and origins of storytelling. She claims that in any of the stories that have been related to her as "authentic" works, "the relating of the story begins with the bringing up, hauling up of psychic contents, both collective and personal." In "Story from Bear Country," these extrasensory impressions are expressed in the first section of the work, in preparation for or anticipation of the story that follows within the body of the same work. The smell of "damp earth / scratched away," or "snorts and growls" echoing in the cliffs and caves beyond, or the "sundown colors of sandrock" compel the reader to respond by playing on the reader's senses. Storytelling is a process by which Silko is affecting the reader, first drawing him into another level of consciousness in preparation for the "actual" story that follows such preparation. Again Estes points to this practice as identifiably one adapted by the storyteller. On one level, a work can involve not just an actual tale but serve as a vehicle for conveying the ancestry of the story, replete or filled with details of the story's origin, "not [just] a long, boring preamble, but spiced with small stories in and of itself."

Structurally, the "Story from Bear Country" falls in two closely related parts. The first part of the work does hint at the geneology driving the story's history. In the third stanza "All but a few who went" to Bear Country "left behind families / grandparents' / and sons / a good life." The quotation hints at generations of Native-American families who have firsthand knowledge of the secrets of Bear Country. But the main thrust or intent of the first section of the poem is to convey the mystical history of human experience in Bear Country. The poet, who expresses her experiences in a series of statements, consequently shares a sense of this history with the reader. Some of her psychic preparation involves the relation of important details in the form of statements akin to "You may wonder," or "You will remain." Other related details come in the form of warnings, such as "They will try to bring you," or "You will never want to return." Such statements, though seemingly ominous or dark in meaning, also lend a supernatural quality to the work itself. In one instance, when a "bear priest" is sent, "loping after you," his beautiful song may not be enough to entice the reader, to draw him from the beautiful songs of the bears. In another, the reader is warned that he may soon discover he is the victim of a mystical transformation. In several places in the poem, the narrator warns of an instance in a "clearing / where you stopped to look back / and saw only bear tracks / behind you."

From a Native-American past also comes an oral tradition based on the retelling of stories that on a psychic level strongly connect both Silko as well as her people to the natural world. In her essay, "Landscape, History, and the Pueblo Imagination," the author explains the intensely intimate connection of her people to the environment. This connection dictates a certain harmony among all things, living and dead in the context of the natural world. This harmony, in turn, is possible because of the belief by Native-American cultures that everything in the natural world is equal, that nature does not solely exist for man's benefit. She explains, rather, that man is co-equal with everything in nature, be it plant, animal, or the rocks that make up the landscape. Nature needs no improvement—the focus of Native-American culture is instead on the reciprocity among all of the elements of creation. Out of this sense of equality also comes a deep spiritual connection for the Native American amongst the various aspects of the natural world, a connection which forms the basis for the group's religious convictions. Silko's work mirrors this spirit. It is recognized for its perpetuation of both an oral tradition and the supernatural energy of the natural world that inspires it.

"Story from Bear Country" is infused or filled with the spirit of the natural world defining Native-American life. It is related in the powerful relationship that entwines both man and bear on a deeper, more religious level of experience. In the beginning of the work, the various sounds of the bears are not only audible but "they call you." In the same instance in the poem, the narrator claims that the power of the bear's beauty "will overcome your memory." These statements foreshadow a potential transformation, from man to bear, as it is slowly recounted in the first half of the poem. At a certain point in the work, both man and bear become synonymous with one another, man developing eyes that will see himself as the bear, "dark shaggy and thick." The transformation is recounted again and again in the poem's insistence of the reader to "Go ahead / turn around / see the shape / of your footprints / in the sand." As the poem con-

> *In one instance, when a 'bear priest' is sent, 'loping after you,' his beautiful song may not be enough to entice the reader, to draw him from the beautiful songs of the bears."*

tinues, backward glances reveal the symbolic melding or mixing of both human and animal tracks, until, at the end of the poem, only bear tracks are clearly visible. Man is not only embraced by the bear, but psychically connected to the bear, hence becoming "one" with the furry creature. Other lines in the poem reinforce this almost familial bond, particularly at the end of the first section of the poem. The narrator warns of a situation in which isolated, alone, the reader may hear the sound of the bear's "voice" calling "we love you / we've been calling you / all this time." The second half of the poem also illuminates the mystical exchange that connects both man and bear in the story of a Laguna Pueblo child who, after having strayed from his parents, must be gently coaxed out of his bear-like trance.

The power of Silko's "Story from Bear Country" is found in the influences of the Laguna Pueblo tradition. The work is a celebration of nature. The splendor and mystery of the celebration is powerful, so much so, that the reader cannot help but be drawn in to the realm of Bear Country, even at the risk of a glance backward to find "only bear prints in the sand."

Source: Laura Kryhoski, Critical Essay on "Story from Bear Country," in *Poetry for Students*, The Gale Group, 2002.

Kate Covintree

Covintree is a graduate of Randolph-Macon Women's College with a degree in English. In this essay, Covintree divides the poem into two sections to examine how Silko develops the idea of transformation, first individually, then as a whole.

Leslie Marmon Silko has divided her poem "Story from Bear Country" into two sections, both different in form and voice. Though the poem is not numbered into sections, a division becomes clear first visually, then stylistically. The first section is aligned to the left side of the page, with occasional lines indented. It is told in second person with the speaker (or storyteller) directly addressing the reader as "you." The second section, written in the center of the page, is a third person narrative. Though both sections are different in form, Silko uses the same strategies with each. Lines are broken according to how they would be spoken, ending a line to create a break, space or emphasis in the narrative. Linda Krumholz, in her essay "To Understand This World Differently," notes that this is an important aspect of Silko's writing. Krumholz states that Silko "uses the ends of lines to indicate verbal pauses, she indents to indicate visually the structural importance of repetition." What is interesting in "Story from Bear Country" is the drastic visual difference between these two sections. Form used in one section (left alignment and indentation) is not used in the other (centering). Krumholz believes "[t]hese textual indicators control the pacing and reception of the stories, increasing the accessibility and emphasizing the poetic and narrative effects for readers." If this is true, then the reader must approach both of these sections differently based on their structural indicators. Though separate, Silko makes it clear, by placing them together as one poem that the greatest understanding of the poem comes when taking the two pieces together. By dividing the poem, Silko allows the reader the opportunity to see how both the poetic (the first section) and narrative (the second section) perspectives of this poem affect her retelling of this Native-American tale and then forces her audience to draw the final understanding.

The first section of this poem is more traditionally poetic. Written in second person, the reader takes an active role and is immediately drawn in to the "juniper trees" and "sundown colors of sandrock" described in the first stanza. Through the detailed description of bear country, the reader can visualize this special place. When the lines are spoken aloud, the reader can see Silko's intentional use of various poetic elements like alliteration in the phrase "because bear priests sing / beautiful songs" and cacophony in the lines "black / bear claw necklaces / rattling against their capes." These elements enhance this section's rhythmic back and forth meter that soothes the reader, almost seducing the reader directly into the section.

The reader is called into the poem like the section's "you" is drawn into bear country. The reader's attraction to the poem and its poetics parallels what the speaker is saying. "It is difficult to explain / how they call you . . . [t]heir beauty will overcome your memory." The journey and the calling become personal. It is the reader's transformation that occurs during the course of this section; the reader's body is now "dark shaggy and thick." The "bear prints in the sand" are from "where [the reader's] feet had been." In this way, what is written alters the readers understanding of self and life. This is a very Native-American concept, and as Krumholz asserts in her article "To Understand This World Differently," published in *Ariel*, "[i]n Native American oral traditions . . . language has the power to create and transform reality."

The speaker makes it clear this is a man being changed, because the reader's "wife and sons are waiting." Even so, Silko makes the bear transformation possible for both genders. Placing this fact near the end of the section gives a female reader plenty of time to relate personally to the poem. Perhaps for a man, the transformation is from man to bear, and for a woman it is from woman to man to bear. In addition, by beginning the next stanza with "[b]ut you have been listening to me / for some time now / from the very beginning in fact" Silko validates the importance of the personal experience and change garnered through the whole section over this one simple fact.

These simple facts ground the reader. They finally allow the reader the opportunity within the poem to return to his or her personal reality and think about his "wife and sons" or his or her lack of these. Also, this same stanza informs the reader about present-day nature of this tale. Until this point in the poem, there is no time frame given. Now, the reader knows that not only are his "wife and sons" waiting, but they are "back at the car." This contemporary word pulls the poem away from ancient or stagnant myth and blurs the lines between past and present, real and imagined.

At times, the speaker's voice also becomes blurred. As the poem itself states, "[w]hose voice is this?" It is unclear exactly who the speaker is. Is this a bear calling the man further in to the wilderness or a bear priest calling the man back out to his family? In this section, the calling bears pull the reader into "caves / in cliffs high above you." Then, with the help of the bear priest, the reader is told to "turn around" and leave "this canyon of stillness." It is as if two voices are playing tug of war for the reader. This contest concurs with a Native-American ritual that David Rockwell discusses in his book, *Giving Voice to Bear: North American Indian*

Myths, Rituals, and Images of the Bear, "[s]hamans often dueled with song." The bear and bear priests can both be seen as shamans. In Silko's poem, the bear priest is shown to be a superior power, "because bear priests sing / beautiful songs . . . they will try to bring you / step by step / back." This is the voice that prevails by the end of the section.

In addition, neither the section's "you" nor the reader can rejoin the bear priest and family until notice of "the shape / of your footprints / in the sand." Silko intentionally breaks these three lines in a manner that places stress on three words, "shape," "footprints," and "sand." Observing footprints, or bear tracks, in the sand is mentioned three times in this section, and it is obviously an important image for Silko. In fact, Silko manipulates these trail markings to reinforce the idea of transformation for the reader. In the first instance, Silko mentions "bear tracks / behind you" that the "you" observes. Then these tracks evolve into "bear prints in the sand/ where your feet had been." Again, Silko has blurred the line, and the reader is forced to contemplate the idea that he or she might have made those bear prints. Finally, Silko tells the reader to return to his or her own "footprints." Though they are called footprints, Silko has already entertained the idea that these could be bear prints or at least a combination of bear/foot print. In doing this, the reader leaves this section with a distinct understanding that the "you" has changed. The "you" is returning, but the "you" is different.

This is the same viewpoint the reader is left with at the end of the second section. In this section's last stanza Silko writes, "So long time ago/ they got him back again/ but he wasn't quite the same / after that / not like the other children." Here, Silko does not use the metaphor of footprints to indicate change but directly speaks of the young boy's transition. Still, the two last sectional stanzas compliment each other so well that, when read in tandem, the reader is left with a more comprehensive understanding of the transformation. Obviously, the "you" from the first section will never be the same, and the young boy may forever carry a memory of his own footprints as bear prints. With the addition of the second section, the reader's awareness deepens.

The second section, in contrast to the first, is distance and straightforward. Told as a narrative, it is clear who the characters are: the small boy, his family, the bears, and the medicine man. The reader is never confused as to who the characters are or what roles they play in the story. The reader be-

> *Obviously, the 'you' from the first section will never be the same, and the young boy may forever carry a memory of his own footprints as bear prints."*

lieves in the story and the speaker is sharing it. Written in simple English, breaks in line now seem especially important for emphasis. Some lines are very short like, "by himself," while others are very long like, "He grunted loudly and scratched on the ground in front of him." Line breaks follow the flow of the story being told, and lead the reader into a better understanding of how the story should sound. Hearing the story, even on the page, is especially important in this section. This is a distinctly external speaker, sharing a story, and using the line breaks to help bring the story to life.

In this way, the second section directly follows the path of traditional Native-American storytelling. By telling the more classic tale, Silko demonstrates that the first section is an adaptation of an old story. There are many tales of bears told by many Native-American tribes. In the title chapter of his book *Giving Voice to Bear: North American Indian Myths, Rituals, and Images of the Bear*, David Rockwell states that one type of tale tells about "a powerful but benevolent spiritual animal [that] help[s] . . . humans." Silko's poem would be a variation of the story type. Certainly, her storyteller introduces the bears as compassionate. These bears take care of the boy when his own family has forgotten him. The storyteller shows that the bears welcome the boy into their family by saying he was "walking like his sisters." In this version, it is carelessness of the family that alters the child. What stops the medicine man from "just grab[bing] the child" is not the violent nature of the bears, but the impact the forced separation will have on the boy.

With this new section also comes a new title for the person who transforms visually into a bear to draw the child or the "you" out from the bears. In the first section, it is a bear priest, complete with "medicine bags / . . . Naked legs painted black/ bear claw necklaces / . . . [and] capes of blue spruce. In the second section, the medicine man comes with assistants and all are dressed with "bearweed / tied at their wrists and ankles and around their necks." They have different techniques and yet each knows the brevity of the situation and is able to accomplish the task set before him.

Unlike the first section, the narrative portion takes the reader right to the caves, not as the child, but as an omniscient observer. Now the reader can not only see what the medicine man wears, but how he behaves in order to move the child out of the den. "He grunted and made a low growling sound… He grunted and growled a little more/ and then the child came out." The reader can notice how the child has already been transformed in his time with the bears. The reader can also witness the child and the bears' reactions to the medicine man's actions. Then, the storyteller explains the reasons behind the medicine man's behavior. The storyteller makes the reader aware of a danger involved for the boy, "he would be in-between forever / and probably he would die." This dark side of the journey into bear country is never apparent in the first section.

With the addition of the second section, Silko widens the reader's understanding of the story. Now the reader is alerted to the danger and separation involved in personal transformation. Silko also reiterates that as caring as the bears (a metaphor for whatever creates change) are, the original home, family, tribe, life, is stronger and more important. This is where everyone returns, and the reader, the "you," and the child are left with an experience that will forever alter their view of the world.

Source: Kate Covintree, Critical Essay on "Story from Bear Country," in *Poetry for Students*, The Gale Group, 2002.

Sources

Allen, Paula Gunn, *The Sacred Hoop*, Beacon Press, 1986, pp. 1–17, 138–46.

Barnes, Kim, and Leslie Marmon Silko, "Interview," in *Journal of Ethnic Studies*, Vol. 13, No. 4, Winter 1986, pp. 33–105.

Bruchac, Joseph, Foreword, in *Native American Stories*, by N. Scott Momaday, edited by Michael Caduto and Joseph Bruchac, Fulcrum Publishing, 1991.

———, Introduction, in *Native American Stories*, by N. Scott Momaday, edited by Michael Caduto and Joseph Bruchac, Fulcrum Publishing, 1991.

———, ed., *Songs from This Earth on Turtle's Back: Contemporary American Indian Poetry*, Greenfield Review Press, 1983, pp. ix–xvi.

Danielson, Linda, "Storyteller: 'Grandmother Spider's Web,'" in *Journal of the Southwest*, Vol. 30, No. 3, Autumn 1988, pp. 325–55.

Estes, Clarissa Pinkola, *Women Who Run with the Wolves*, Ballantine Books, 1995.

Grobman, Laurie, "(Re)Interpreting *Storyteller* in the Classroom: Teaching at the Crossroads," in *College Literature*, Vol. 27, Issue 3, Fall 2000, pp. 88–111.

Hirsch, Bernard A., "The Telling Which Continues: Oral Tradition and the Written Word in Leslie Marmon Silko's *Storyteller*," in *American Indian Quarterly*, Vol. 12, No. 1, Winter 1998, pp. 1–28.

Jaskoski, Helen, *Leslie Marmon Silko: A Study of the Short Fiction*, Twayne Publishers, 1998, pp. xi–12.

Krumholz, Linda J., "'To Understand This World Differently': Reading and Subversion in Leslie Marmon Silko's *Storyteller*," in *Ariel*, Vol. 25, No. 1, January 1994, pp. 89–113.

Rockwell, David, "Giving Voice to Bear," in *Giving Voice to Bear: North American Indian Myths, Rituals, and Images of the Bear*, Roberts Rinehart, 1991, pp. 113–45.

Salyer, Gregory, *Leslie Marmon Silko*, Twayne Publishers, 1997, pp. 1–70.

Sams, Jamie, and David Carson, "Landscape, History, and the Pueblo Imagination," in *Antaeus*, Vol. 57, Autumn 1986.

———, *Medicine Cards: The Discovery of Power through the Ways of Animals*, Bear & Company, 1988, pp. 57–58.

Silko, Leslie Marmon, "Story from Bear Country" in *Songs from This Earth on Turtle's Back: Contemporary American Indian Poetry*, edited by Joseph Bruchac, Greenfield Review Press, 1983, pp. 225–27.

———, *Storyteller*, Arcade Publishing, 1981.

Further Reading

Allen, Paula Gunn, *The Woman Who Owned the Shadows*, Spinsters Ink, 1983.

    As with Momaday's *House Made of Dawn* and Silko's *Ceremony*, this novel propels us into a "ceremonial motion" of Indian chronology that disrupts the linear time of most non-Indian writing. The lessons and experiences of the book's protagonist are understood through stories that take place in dreamtime, the time of mythic tales and history, and dynamic present time.

Deloria, Vine, Jr., *God Is Red: A Native View of Religion*, Fulcrum, 1994.

    A prominent Native-American lawyer, educator, and philosopher, Deloria contrasts Christian traditions and principles to Native-American spiritual beliefs and practices.

Kingston, Maxine Hong, *The Woman Warrior: Memoirs of a Girlhood among Ghosts*, Knopf, 1976.

    The book's heroine discovers that growing up healthy and whole as a Chinese girl in America requires a deep understanding of Chinese values and traditions that her mother passes down to her through powerful and imaginative teaching stories.

Lincoln, Kenneth, *Native American Renaissance*, University of California Press, 1983.
An important guide to Native-American literature, this book includes a smart reading of Silko's novel *Ceremony* as well as reflections on Laguna life and landscape.

Seyersted, Per, "Two Interviews with Leslie Marmon Silko," in *American Studies in Scandinavia*, Vol. 13, 1981, pp. 17–33.
Silko discusses politics, literature, and Native-American life as well as her own experiences growing up as a mixed blood Laguna Pueblo woman.

Sunday Morning

Wallace Stevens

1923

"Sunday Morning," one of the collected pieces in Wallace Stevens's *Harmonium* (1923), has been singled out as one of his most eloquent and thematically resonant poems. Stevens wrote the first version of the poem in 1914, which was published by *Poetry* the next year. Harriet Monroe, the editor of the journal, omitted three stanzas of the poem for its publication and significantly rearranged the remaining five stanzas. Stevens made considerable changes, especially to the ending, by the time he collected it in *Harmonium*.

J. Hillis Miller in "William Carlos Williams and Wallace Stevens," writes that Stevens's poetry is "a prolonged exploration, both in theoretical speculation within the poetry itself and in poetic practice, of the power of language not so much to name reality as to uncover it." This uncovering of reality becomes the focus of "Sunday Morning" as it chronicles one woman's search for spiritual fulfillment in a philosophical dialogue between her and Stevens's poetic persona. Throughout the poem, the two examine two contrasting ideologies: that of Christianity and of paganism. The woman must decide which will help her find the spiritual satisfaction she is seeking.

The poet presents compelling arguments through a series of eloquent images centering on the beauty of the natural world. When the woman notes that this beauty is transitory, the poet counters, "death is the mother of beauty," insisting that the fact of death enhances beauty. After careful consideration of the poet's line of reasoning, by the

end of the poem, the woman determines that a devotion to earthly pleasures and not the dead religion of the past will provide her with divine bliss.

Author Biography

Wallace Stevens was born on October 2, 1879, in Reading, Pennsylvania, to Garrett (a lawyer) and Margaretha (a schoolteacher) Stevens. Stevens's father had a great impact on his education and career choices. He established an extensive library in their home, which he encouraged his son to take advantage of, and promoted the value of education. Stevens prospered in school, and by the time he finished high school, he had been recognized for his fine writing and oratory skills.

In 1897, Stevens entered Harvard, where he studied for three years. During this period, he had articles and poems pubalished in the *Harvard Advocate*. After his third year, Stevens left Harvard due to depleted funds. He soon landed a position as a reporter at the *New York Tribune*, which afforded him the time and the opportunity to record his observations of the city as subject matter for his poetry.

After Stevens grew bored with reporting, his father convinced him to pursue a degree in law rather than devote himself to writing. In 1903, he graduated from the New York School of Law, and in 1904, he was admitted to the New York Bar. After working in various law firms, he accepted a position with American Bonding Company, an insurance firm in 1908.

At the beginning of his long career as an insurance lawyer, which extended until the end of his life, Stevens began a fruitful association with several prominent writers and painters in New York's Greenwich Village, including Marianne Moore, William Carlos Williams, Alfred Kreymborg, and e. e. cummings. By 1913, he resumed writing poetry, and in 1914, he began to publish his work in literary magazines. In 1915, he wrote his first major poems, "Peter Quince at the Clavier" and "Sunday Morning." The next year, he tried his hand at play writing, which resulted in his prize-winning play, *Three Travelers Watch a Sunrise*.

Harmonium, his first collection of poetry, which included "Sunday Morning," was published in 1923. After the publication of his next collection, *Ideas of Order*, Stevens cemented his reputation among a small but influential group of writers

Wallace Stevens

and critics as one of America's most important poets. His work would eventually earn him overwhelming critical acclaim and several awards including the Bollingen Prize for Poetry in 1950, the National Book Award for best poetry in 1951 for *The Auroras of Autumn*, and the Pulitzer Prize for poetry and another National Book Award in 1955 for *The Collected Poems of Wallace Stevens*, which includes "Sunday Morning."

During the early 1950s, Stevens suffered from cancer and was repeatedly hospitalized. He died of the disease on August 2, 1955, in Hartford, Connecticut.

Poem Text

Complacencies of the peignoir, and late
Coffee and oranges in a sunny chair,
And the green freedom of a cockatoo
Upon a rug mingle to dissipate
The holy hush of ancient sacrifice.   5
She dreams a little, and she feels the dark
Encroachment of that old catastrophe,
As a calm darkness among water-lights.
The pungent oranges and bright, green wings
Seem things in some procession of the dead,   10
Winding across wide water, without sound.
The day is like wide water, without sound,

Stilled for the passing of her dreaming feet
Over the seas, to silent Palestine,
Dominion of the blood and sepulchre.   15

II

Why should she give her bounty to the dead?
What is divinity if it can come
Only in silent shadows and in dreams?
Shall she not find in comforts of the sun,
In pungent fruit and bright, green wings, or else   20
In any balm or beauty of the earth,
Things to be cherished like the thought of heaven?
Divinity must live within herself:
Passions of rain, or moods in falling snow;
Grievings in loneliness, or unsubdued   25
Elations when the forest blooms; gusty
Emotions on wet roads on autumn nights;
All pleasures and all pains, remembering
The bough of summer and the winter branch.
These are the measures destined for her soul.   30

III

Jove in the clouds had his inhuman birth.
No mother suckled him, no sweet land gave
Large-mannered motions to his mythy mind.
He moved among us, as a muttering king,
Magnificent, would move among his hinds,   35
Until our blood, commingling, virginal,
With heaven, brought such requital to desire
The very hinds discerned it, in a star.
Shall our blood fail? Or shall it come to be
The blood of paradise? And shall the earth   40
Seem all of paradise that we shall know?
The sky will be much friendlier then than now,
A part of labor and a part of pain,
And next in glory to enduring love,
Not this dividing and indifferent blue.   45

IV

She says, "I am content when wakened birds,
Before they fly, test the reality
Of misty fields, by their sweet questionings;
But when the birds are gone, and their warm fields
Return no more, where, then, is paradise?"   50
There is not any haunt of prophecy,
Nor any old chimera of the grave,
Neither the golden underground, nor isle
Melodious, where spirits gat them home,
Nor visionary south, nor cloudy palm   55
Remote on heaven's hill, that has endured
As April's green endures; or will endure
Like her remembrance of awakened birds,
Or her desire for June and evenings, tipped
By the consummation of the swallow's wings.   60

V

She says, "But in contentment I still feel
The need of some imperishable bliss."
Death is the mother of beauty; hence from her,
Alone, shall come fulfillment to our dreams
And our desires. Although she strews the leaves   65

Of sure obliteration on our paths,
The path sick sorrow took, the many paths
Where triumph rang its brassy phrase, or love
Whispered a little out of tenderness,
She makes the willow shiver in the sun   70
For maidens who were wont to sit and gaze
Upon the grass, relinquished to their feet.
She causes boys to pile new plums and pears
On disregarded plate. The maidens taste
And stray impassioned in the littering leaves.   75

VI

Is there no change of death in paradise?
Does ripe fruit never fall? Or do the boughs
Hang always heavy in that perfect sky,
Unchanging, yet so like our perishing earth,
With rivers like our own that seek for seas   80
They never find, the same receding shores
That never touch with inarticulate pang?
Why set the pear upon those river-banks
Or spice the shores with odors of the plum?
Alas, that they should wear our colors there,   85
The silken weavings of our afternoons,
And pick the strings of our insipid lutes!
Death is the mother of beauty, mystical,
Within whose burning bosom we devise
Our earthly mothers waiting, sleeplessly.   90

VII

Supple and turbulent, a ring of men
Shall chant in orgy on a summer morn
Their boisterous devotion to the sun,
Not as a god, but as a god might be,
Naked among them, like a savage source.   95
Their chant shall be a chant of paradise,
Out of their blood, returning to the sky;
And in their chant shall enter, voice by voice,
The windy lake wherein their lord delights,
The trees, like serafin, and echoing hills,   100
That choir among themselves long afterward.
They shall know well the heavenly fellowship
Of men that perish and of summer morn.
And whence they came and whither they shall go
The dew upon their feet shall manifest.   105

VIII

She hears, upon that water without sound,
A voice that cries, "The tomb in Palestine
Is not the porch of spirits lingering.
It is the grave of Jesus, where he lay,"
We live in an old chaos of the sun,   110
Or an old dependency of day and night,
Or island solitude, unsponsored, free,
Of that wide water, inescapable.
Deer walk upon our mountains, and quail
Whistle about us their spontaneous cries;   115
Sweet berries ripen in the wilderness;
And, in the isolation of the sky,
At evening, casual flocks of pigeons make
Ambiguous undulations as they sink,
Downward to darkness, on extended wings.   120

Poem Summary

In the first stanza, a complacent woman lounges in her dressing gown late into a Sunday morning, eating a leisurely breakfast and enjoying the vivid, vibrant beauty of the natural world around her. She takes great pleasure in her coffee and oranges, her mood reflected by the "sunny" chair and the cockatoo that has been released onto the rug. She is spending a morning at home instead of going to church. The reference to the "holy hush of ancient sacrifice" suggests that the day is Easter Sunday. Initially, the pull of the natural world dissipates the traditional power this day has over the woman, as she has chosen not to take part in Christian rituals. However, as she dreams, the pleasure she experiences this morning is soon extinguished by "the dark encroachment of that old catastrophe," a reference to the crucifixion of Christ. She recognizes that the secular beauty she appreciates is not eternal, and so the colorful oranges and parrot, earlier appearing so full of life, now "seem things in some procession of the dead."

She becomes caught up in Christian dogma as "her dreaming feet" transport her to the "dominion of the blood and sepulchre," symbolic of the ritualistic ceremony in celebration of the Last Supper and Christ's interment. The blood refers to the wine and the sepulchre to the Church of the Holy Sepulchre that contained the tomb where Christ's body was laid on Good Friday. Thus, the sensual pleasure of the late morning coffee and oranges has been replaced by the spiritual satisfaction of the bread and wine communion.

The voice of the poet questions the woman's decision to turn her back on the beauty of the natural world and devote herself to her religion. He insists that she could find divinity through a connection to the splendor of the earth. Her earthly pleasures, which he enumerates in this stanza through images of the seasons, should be as cherished as "the thought of heaven." The poet exhorts her to appreciate the very transience of her world since it encompasses the pleasures and pains of living. These passions, not the superstitions that live in "silent shadows and in dreams," are "the measures destined for her soul."

In the third stanza, the speaker expands his focus on religion to the Greek god Jove who had no traditional family to nurture him and no natural connections to the "sweet land." The speaker links this ancient myth to the birth of Christ through the reference to the star that guided the shepherds and

Media Adaptations

- *Wallace Stevens: Voice of a Poet*, released by Random House in March 2002, features poetry read by Stevens himself.

wise men to Bethlehem. Both myths, he suggests, are disconnected from human reality. As humanity finds the divine in the natural world, the sky will appear "friendlier," no longer marking the division between heaven and earth.

The woman's voice returns at the beginning of the next two stanzas as she questions the poet's argument that earthly pleasures will provide spiritual fulfillment. While nature fills her with contentment, she wonders whether she can find paradise there. Here, the poet reasserts and clarifies his position. In his response, he acknowledges the impermanence of the world but argues that the bliss she experiences observing the beauty of nature is everlasting through immediate observance of the spring and through the vividness of her memory. Christian theology, with its "chimera of the grave" (its dark dreams of the crucifixion of Christ) or even its "melodious isles" will not endure as will the magnificence of nature for her.

She complains that even while experiencing contentment in her relationship to the natural world, she feels "the need of some imperishable bliss," which Christianity insists can be found only in complete devotion to the church. The poet counters, "death is the mother of beauty," asserting that she can only experience true satisfaction through the appreciation of that which is impermanent. To prove his point, he describes the passions of youth, symbolized by the ripening of plums and pears. When death "strews the leaves of sure obliteration on our paths," lovers' desires will be heightened as they realize the importance of the moment.

In stanza six, the poet continues his argument that death is the mother of beauty, juxtaposing it with a counter vision of the stasis of heaven, with its ripe fruit that never falls, hanging heavy in "that perfect sky." The rivers there never pour out into the seas or touch the shores. In contrast, "our perishing earth" of beginnings and endings is colored with "inarticulate" pangs and delicious tastes and odors of pear and plum, where she lounges during "silken weavings" of afternoons.

The next stanza suggests an alternative to traditional worship. The poet describes a pagan, almost savage, celebration of the earth, as a ring of men chant sensuous songs praising the beauty of a summer morning. They do not worship a specific god, but the earth for them has the same intense power that had previously been associated with the Christian God, and thus they are devoted to it. As they strip naked in an act of merging their energies with those of nature, they experience paradise. Their chant encompasses all the elements of nature, "the windy lake" and angelic trees as their songs echo off the hills long after they leave. The poet symbolizes this "heavenly fellowship" between nature and the men by noting the "dew upon their feet" as they dance and chant.

The voice of the poet and that of the woman come together in acceptance of an alternate form of worship in the final stanza of the poem. The single voice here notes the inevitability of decay and death and understands that an appreciation of that mutability enriches present experience. The woman acknowledges that Jesus' tomb was not endowed with mystical spirits, that it only contained his grave. She now turns to the natural world, with its "old chaos of the sun" and its understanding of days and nights, beginning and ends.

This realignment with the pagan world of earthly pleasures releases her from the bonds of her religion so that she is now "unsponsored" and free. The natural world is full of the "spontaneous cries" of its creatures in their beautiful surroundings. The final line reinforces the statement that death is the mother of beauty, as the free flying pigeons, "on extended wings" rise and fall following no prescribed course but eventually descend into darkness at the close of day.

Themes

Belief and Doubt

The woman in the poem moves back and forth between belief and doubt as she enters into a dialogue with the poet about spiritual fulfillment. At the beginning of the poem, she appears to be content in her newfound appreciation of the earthly

pleasures of the natural world. This world with its vivid colors and leisurely breakfasts offers her a sense of freedom in the time she allows herself to appreciate the bounty of nature. Soon, however, doubt over the choice she has made this Sunday morning ruins her serenity. As she appreciates the sensuality of nature, she experiences a growing awareness and dread of its transitory nature. As a result, she becomes filled with spiritual anxiety to the point that she begins to believe that a reversion to Christian rituals and dogma will lead to salvation.

As the speaker tries to convince her to return to her world of earthly delights, she struggles to maintain her belief in traditional theology through a series of questions on the nature of that theology. She wonders whether earth will "seem all of paradise that we shall know" especially given its impermanence. Nature fills her with contentment, yet she asks, "when the birds are gone, and their warm fields return no more, where, then, is paradise?" She continually resists the poet's promotion of a spiritual connection to nature, insisting, "I still feel the need of some imperishable bliss," which she had found in a Christian vision of eternity.

The speaker's voice, however, never wavers from his assertion that she must find divinity within herself, and that this can only be accomplished through a communion with nature. By meeting each question with an imaginative yet logical response, the speaker slowly convinces her to doubt her old beliefs in the divinity of traditional religion. By the end of the poem, she has returned to the position she held at the beginning, again aligning herself with the freedom of birds, "unsponsored" in her attachment to her natural world.

Death and Life

The speaker's strongest argument for the woman to devote herself to an intense relationship with nature comes in the form of an examination of death and life. He continually associates Christianity and the religions of the past with death. In the first stanza, he notes the darkness of "that old catastrophe," the crucifixion of Christ, and of the "dominion of the blood and sepulchre," the important Christian ritual of communion where believers drink the blood and eat the body of Christ. He also finds death in the static nature of heaven where ripe fruit never falls and the "boughs hang always heavy in that perfect sky." In this immutable world, with its "dividing and indifferent blue," she will never, he insists, be able to make an emotional connection.

The speaker points out that a celebration of nature, by contrast, is a celebration of life, even as he acknowledges its cyclical patterns of death and rebirth. He argues that the very fact of inevitable change fills the present with a stronger sense of vibrancy and poignancy. Thus, this form of "death is the mother of beauty" and so should be accepted as a crucial part of an appreciation of the moment.

Imagination

In his "Adagia," a set of musings on poetry and the imagination collected in *Opus Posthumous* (1957), Stevens wrote about the importance of the relation of art to life, since with our modern age's lack of faith in God, "the mind turns to its own creations and examines them, for what they validate and invalidate, for what they reveal, for the support they give." This search for an imaginative connection to the real world becomes another dominant theme in the poem.

The speaker continually engages his imagination to convince the woman that fulfillment lies in her connection with nature. The vivid colors of the oranges and the parrot, the "pungent fruit," reflect the "passions of rain, or moods in falling snow." Birds "test[ing] the reality of misty fields, by their sweet questionings" and the "trees, like serafin" illustrate as no philosophizing could manage the limitless, transcendent beauty and bounty of the natural world and call the woman to a communion with it. Faith in the possibilities of spiritual contentment is thus sustained through the power of the imagination.

Style

Conversation

The poem takes the form of a conversation or philosophical dialogue between the central character, a woman who is on a quest to find spiritual fulfillment, and the voice of the poet, who attempts to aid her during her journey. The poem could also be regarded as a conversation between self and soul, between the social self that feels pressured to conform to traditional religious doctrines and the internal self that desires a more natural connection with the world.

Its fifteen-line stanzas of blank-verse begins with the woman's precarious situation: initially she feels contentment spending Sunday morning at home, surrounded by the comfort and beauty of her

Topics for Further Study

Draw an illustration of the opening scene of the poem, as the woman is contentedly lounging at home.

- T. S. Eliot's famous poem *The Waste Land* also deals with the subject of Christianity. Compare and contrast Eliot's view on this subject with that of Stevens in "Sunday Morning."

- Construct an argument that a Christian would use that would counter that offered in the poem. You could begin by insisting that the imperishable bliss the woman is seeking could only come from a devotion to Christian dogma and ceremonies.

- Define and research the practices of ancient Greek religions. How are these ancient religions used in the poem?

physical environment. But soon, guilt over her dismissal of traditional Christian rituals on Easter Sunday undermines her pleasure, and she becomes filled with spiritual anxiety, conflicted about which path she should take to spiritual fulfillment. After this first stanza, the poem becomes a dialogue between her voice and that of the poet, between the woman's philosophical questionings and his assertion that she can find satisfaction only through a personal, intense communion with the natural world.

Most stanzas begin with a question posed by the woman that is answered by the authoritative voice of the poet, reaffirming his position that sensual pleasures supersede any contentment gained from the dead religions of the past. He presents his argument through association and juxtaposition, continually finding alternate ways to present the same point of view. The cumulative effect of the repeated images results in a convincing argument against a devotion to the tenets of Christianity and for a dedication to an appreciation of and communion with the beauty of nature.

Imagery

Stevens employs two dominant image clusters, which he continually juxtaposes against each other to illustrate his thematic points. He associates the natural world with the warmth of the sun, which the woman enjoys at the beginning of the poem during her leisurely morning at home on this particular Sunday morning. The sun returns in stanza seven, as the speaker personifies his pagan vision in his description of a ring of men chanting "in orgy on a summer morn." The life-giving properties of the sun are echoed in the vibrant colors associated with the natural world. Initially, the woman lounges complacently on this Sunday morning surrounded by the vivid colors of the oranges she is eating and the "green freedom" of her parrot that has been released onto her rug. Stevens evokes the pleasures of other senses in this setting through the odors of plum and pear. Sound ultimately unifies humans with nature when the men's boisterous chant echoes off the hills long after they have stopped.

Stevens links an absence of sound to Christianity, suggesting that those mythological voices do not carry into present realities. He reinforces this sense of absence when the woman hears a voice that tells her that no spirits linger in Jesus' tomb. The vibrant colors of nature are juxtaposed with dark ancient sacrifices, ceremonies of blood. This cluster of images reinforces the speaker's premise that Christianity is a dead religion that can no longer offer contentment and salvation.

Historical Context

Modernism

This term, associated with an important artistic movement during the first few decades of the twentieth century, was reflected in Western literature, painting, music, and architecture. The modernist period in America reached its height in the mid 1910s and extended until the early 1930s. Modernist American literature reflected the growing sense of disillusionment with traditional social, political, and religious doctrines felt by Americans at the beginning of the twentieth century but especially after World War I. Gertrude Stein, an important writer and patron during this period, dubbed the group of writers that expressed the zeitgeist of this age the "lost generation," an epithet Ernest Hemingway immortalized in *For Whom the Bell Tolls*, which like F. Scott Fitzgerald's *The Great Gatsby*, has become a penetrating portrait of this lost generation.

This age of confusion, redefinition, and experimentation produced one of the most fruitful periods in American letters. These writers helped create a new form of literature that repudiated traditional literary conventions. Prior to the twentieth century, writers structured their works to reflect their belief in the stability of character and the intelligibility of experience. Traditionally, novels, stories, and poetry ended with a clear sense of closure as conflicts were resolved and characters gained knowledge about themselves and their world. The authors of the Lost Generation challenged these assumptions as they expanded the genre's traditional form to accommodate their characters' questions about the individual's place in the world.

Modernist Poetry

Modernist poetry contained the same thematic import as its counterparts in fiction. One of the most important poems of this period, or it can be argued of the entire century, is T. S. Eliot's *The Waste Land*, which echoed the disillusionment and anxiety expressed by the lost generation writers.

Poetry in this movement, as with other works of modernism, experimented with new ideas in psychology, anthropology, and philosophy that had become popular in the early part of the century. Freudianism, for example, began to be studied by these writers as they explored the psyche of their characters and recorded their often subjective points of view of themselves and their world.

Imagists

Modernist poetry experiments with new forms and styles in its concern with the verisimilitude of language. A group of poets that were prominent in the second decade of the twentieth century, the imagists had an important effect on modernist poetry in this sense. This group of writers rejected traditional cliched poetic diction and regulated meter in favor of more natural expressions of language written in free verse. One of the leading proponents of this movement, Ezra Pound published his anthology *Des Imagistes* in 1913, with examples of what he considered to be imagist verse by James Joyce, H. D. (Hilda Doolittle), William Carlos Williams, F. S. Flint, Ford Madox Ford, and Amy Lowell among others. Pound included in the work his imagist Doctrine, which insisted on a "direct treatment of the thing"—the essence of what the poet is expressing, the discarding of any language that did not "contribute to the presentation" of this essence, and the emphasis on a sequence of musical phrases rather than of a metronome. In his article on Stevens for *Dictionary of Literary Biography*, Joseph Miller argues that this movement

Compare *&* Contrast

- **1920s:** The modernist writers during this period reflect Americans' growing sense of disillusionment with the tenets of Christianity. Many begin to question whether humanity is being protected by the presence and power of a benevolent God.

  Today: After decades of focus on more secular activities, many Americans are returning to the Church, due to the devastating terrorist attacks in September 2001, which inspire a return to traditional values. A number of conservative Christian groups, usually referred to as the "religious right," are lobbying for a return of Christian ethics in schools, including a return to prayers in the classroom and the promotion of sexual abstinence in sex education classes.

- **1920s:** The flapper, who presents a new, freer female image, becomes the model for young American women as they begin to express themselves more freely in terms of dress and behavior.

  Today: Women make major gains in their fight for equality. Most American women feel free to express their individuality within and outside of the domestic sphere without bowing to the pressure of social strictures.

- **1920s:** American poetry during this period often presents an austerely pessimistic view of contemporary society as a reaction to industrialization, urbanization, and technological innovations. T. S. Eliot's *The Waste Land*, published in 1922, becomes one of the most important poetic expressions of this theme.

  Today: While often less obscure and allusive than the modernists, contemporary poets often continue what has come to be considered the pessimistic zeitgeist of the twentieth century. Their poetry frequently presents this theme in a stripped down form, reflecting the rhythms and diction of contemporary language.

---

had a profound influence on Stevens's work, but "it did not take long for him to recognize the banality of mere images and to see the possibilities of such images as symbols of larger things."

Critical Overview

Harriet Monroe, in her review of *Harmonium* for *Poetry* (the journal she founded), proclaims that readers breathe "delight . . . like a perfume" in response to the "natural effluence of [Stevens's] own clear and untroubled and humorously philosophical delight in the beauty of things as they are." All critics, however, were not as impressed by this volume. Joseph Miller, in his article on Stevens for *Dictionary of Literary Biography*, notes that the few critics who paid attention to the collection dismissed it "as a product of mere dilettantism."

After the publication of succeeding volumes of poetry, Stevens established a reputation as one of America's finest poets that has been maintained to this day. The growing regard for his poetry was due in large part to major critical works written by Helen Vendler and Harold Bloom. Bloom wrote in *Wallace Stevens: The Poems of Our Climate* that the poet is "a vital part of the American mythology" and "the best and most representative American poet of our time."

Today, *Harmonium* is considered to be one of his finest collections. Miller comments that the poems in this volume "reveal Stevens as a poet of delicate, but determined, sensibility, one whose perspective is precise without being precious, and whose wit is subtle but not subdued." He writes that Stevens reveals an "extraordinary vocabulary, a flair for memorable phrasing, an accomplished sense of imagery, and the ability to both lampoon and philosophize."

Special praise has been reserved for "Sunday Morning," considered to be one of Stevens' finest poems. Critics note that its importance lies in its thematic import and its expression. George and Barbara Perkins in their overview of the poem for *The American Tradition in Literature* applaud Stevens' portrayal of "the perturbation and consequent seeking of 'everyman' who "feels the dark / Encroachment of that old catastrophe"—the traditions of Christianity. They note that Stevens appropriately leaves the questions he raises in the poem "beyond the reach of reason."

Criticism

Wendy Perkins

Perkins teaches American literature and film and has published several essays on American and British authors. In the following essay, Perkins examines Stevens's unique employment of the literary motif carpe diem *in this poem.*

Carpe diem, a Latin phrase from Horace's *Odes*, translates into "seize the day." The phrase became a common literary motif, especially in lyric poetry and in sixteenth- and seventeenth-century English love poetry. The most famous poems that incorporate this motif include Edmund Spenser's *Faerie Queen*, Andrew Marvell's "To his Coy Mistress," Edward Fitzgerald's "The Rubaiyat of Omar Khayyam," and Robert Herrick's "To the Virgins, to Make Much of Time." Modern writers have also employed the motif, most notably Henry James in *The Ambassadors* and "the Beast in the Jungle," and obviously Saul Bellow in *Seize the Day*.

Typically the speaker in a poem that uses *carpe diem* as its theme proposes that since death is inevitable and time is fleeting, the listener, often a reluctant virgin, should take advantage of the sensual pleasures the speaker reveals to her.

Wallace Stevens puts a modern spin on this traditional *carpe diem* theme in his celebrated poem, "Sunday Morning." Like his poetic predecessors, he directs his speaker to advise a woman to experience sensual pleasures but not as a prerequisite to losing her virginity. Stevens's speaker urges the woman in the poem to turn from a devotion to Christian doctrines to a spiritual connection with the natural world. Stevens combines the traditional and modern in poem's presentation of the *carpe diem* theme to suggest that a celebration of

earthly pleasures can result in freedom from the strict confines of Christianity.

Most poems present a classical point of view in their expression of the *carpe diem* theme, reflecting the pagan spirit in nature as the speakers try to convince their listeners to give themselves up to sensual experience. For example, in Marvell's "To his Coy Mistress," the speaker's goal is to convince a young woman to join him and become like "amorous birds of prey" and "tear our pleasures with rough strife / Through the iron gates of life."

"Sunday Morning" reverses the order of this classical tradition. The woman begins the poem effectively "seizing the day" by not going to church on Easter Sunday, as is traditionally expected of practicing Christians. She instead spends a leisurely morning lounging in her peignoir, contentedly indulging in the sensual pleasures of breakfast in a "sunny chair." Stevens introduces his main theme in this first stanza through his depiction of the "green" freedom of a cockatoo that she has released from its cage. Throughout the poem, Stevens will assert his point that one should seize the day through a celebration of the natural world, not of traditional Christian theology, to experience true freedom and fulfillment.

The title becomes an apt thematic pun. On this Sunday, a traditional Christian day set aside to worship the son of God, a woman is enjoying a day of nature's sun. Yet, when she recognizes the mutability of the natural world, she experiences a spiritual dread, compounded by her turning away from the rituals of Christianity. As a result, she allows the "encroachment of that old catastrophe" and finds herself passing "over the seas, to silent Palestine," with its promise of eternal life. By the end of the stanza, the woman has exchanged an earthly ritual for a religious one. She turns from her breakfast of oranges and coffee to thoughts of the bread and wine communion.

For the rest of the poem, Stevens turns to the traditional *carpe diem* structure, with the speaker trying to convince the young woman to seize the day; the methods he suggests to accomplish this, however, reflect a modern loss of faith in traditional religion and an impetus toward individual freedom.

Throughout the poem, Stevens presents images of a fearful, death-obsessed Christianity. He juxtaposes the natural world associated with light with the Christian world of darkness, another ironic reversal of Christian symbolism. Thoughts of the death of Christ on this Easter Sunday come in only in darkness (stanza 1) and in shadows (stanza 2), silent like the grave. Christianity's focus on death is illustrated by its "ancient sacrifice" and "dominion of the blood and sepulchre." In stark contrast, the natural world, filled with sunlight is composed of "pungent oranges and bright, green wings."

After introducing these symbolic contrasts between the natural and Christian worlds in the first stanza, Stevens introduces his speaker in the second. Throughout the rest of the poem, the poet's persona engages in a dialogue with the woman, trying to imbue her with a vision of nature that can satisfy her deepest impulses for spiritual and emotional fulfillment.

He first questions her devotion to Christianity by pointing out its association with "silent shadows" in contrast to the natural "comforts of the sun" and the vivid sights and smells that reveal the beauty of the earth, "things to be cherished like the thought of heaven." She can find a more fulfilling divinity within herself, he insists, through a consummation with nature.

He addresses her focus on the impermanence of the natural world, again providing an ironic reversal of Christian doctrine, which promotes eternal life. A large part of his argument is that Christianity is a dead religion, offering its followers nothing but darkness and silence. In contrast, a celebration of the natural world, through an acceptance of its cyclical nature, provides her with spiritual as well as physical satisfaction. Thus, the woman should spend her day not in church, but in contact with nature. He directs her to welcome the very transience of her world since it evokes sadness as well as joy, the pleasures and pains reflecting the wide spectrum of life. These passions, not the superstitions that live in "silent shadows and in dreams," are "the measures destined for her soul."

In the third stanza, the speaker compresses time into a narrative of the evolution of religion to suggest that no natural connections exist between religious myths and the world. The pre-Christian gods had "inhuman" births and did not travel on sweet lands that gave "[l]arge-mannered motions to [their] mythy mind[s]." The speaker links Jove's inhuman birth to Christ's virgin birth, symbolized by the star. He then reinforces the sense of separation between the gods and nature when he points out that religions set up a hierarchical system of heaven and earth, as reflected in the image of a king moving among his hinds, or workers, and a "dividing and indifferent blue." Humans can never

> *The poet links the woman's experience to that of the men through the warmth of the sun that all of them experience, suggesting that she too can feel such imperishable bliss."*

hope to establish a true harmony with the object of their devotion given the strict hierarchical nature of traditional religious practices.

The remainder of this stanza illustrates Stevens's statement in his "Adagia" that "The death of one god is the death of all." The speaker tells the woman that after discarding the dead religions of the past, she can experience a communion between her natural self and the world. As a result of this shattering of hierarchies, the earth will become a paradise. By accepting that life contains "a part of labor and a part of pain," the "sky will be much friendlier" than it was when it divided her from her spiritual fathers.

As Stevens explains in his essay "Two or Three Ideas," in a time when we have lost faith in the old gods, when they have become "the aesthetic projections of a time that has passed, men turn to a fundamental glory of their own and from that create a style of bearing themselves in reality." J. Hillis Miller in his critical work, *From Poets of Reality: Six Twentieth-Century Writers*, suggests that the poem is Stevens's "most eloquent description of the moment when the gods dissolve." Miller argues that the poem suggests that "bereft of the supernatural, man does not lie down paralyzed in despair. He sings the creative hymns of a new culture, the culture of those who are 'wholly human' and know themselves."

The woman responds in the next two stanzas that she is still troubled by the impermanence of nature, when "the birds are gone, and their warm fields return no more." As the poet answers her questions in each, he reasserts and clarifies his position. She notes that observing living nature fills her with contentment. However, when the inevitable

What Do I Read Next?

- T. S. Eliot's *The Waste Land* (1925) offers another poetic examination of loss of faith in Christianity. The poem is considered to be one of the finest examples of poetic modernism.

- Stevens's "The Idea of Order at Key West" (1936) presents a different view of reality through the consciousness of a woman.

- *The Sun Also Rises* (1926), by Ernest Hemingway, one of the "lost generation" writers, focuses on a group of disillusioned Americans living in Paris after World War I. Critics consider this novel to be the voice of its generation.

- *Discontented America: The United States in the 1920s (The American Moment)* (1989), by David J. Goldberg, presents an overview of this fascinating decade and focuses specifically on how World War I affected American society.

cycle of nature turns to winter and encroaching death, she wonders "where, then, is paradise?" The speaker answers by reasserting that the old myths with their "chimera of the grave" or even their "melodious isles" cannot endure "as April's green endures, or will endure." When she desires warm June evenings in the cold of winter, he insists that her memories of "the consummation of the swallow's wings" in the spring will offer her the spiritual satisfaction she is seeking. The reality and the memory of the beauty of the earth create substance not myth. He assures her of the cyclical nature of the world, which will continually replenish itself.

When the woman claims "the need of some imperishable bliss," as in the Christian vision of eternal life, the poet counters, "death is the mother of beauty," asserting that she can only experience true satisfaction through the appreciation of that which is impermanent. The transitory nature of her world infuses it with poignancy and thus divinity. Death enhances beauty as it heightens the experience of the present, acknowledging the inevitable changes that will occur.

The poet illustrates his point in his descriptions of the maidens sitting and gazing at the grass and tasting new plums and pears, as aware of their surroundings as the woman had been at the beginning of the poem, before thoughts of her old religion encroached upon her sunny freedom. The inevitability of death appears in the wind that "makes the willow shiver in the sun." Yet even as the leaves swirl about them, suggesting the impending decay of winter, the maidens stray through them impassioned, fully alive in the moment made more poignant by the knowledge that it will soon fade.

The poet reinforces his vision in his presentation of the stagnancy of heaven, with its ripe fruit that never falls hanging heavy in "that perfect sky" and its rivers that never pour out into the seas or touch the shores. Alternately, "our perishing earth" with its inevitable cycle of change and renewal comes alive with delicious tastes and odors of pear and plum and "silken weavings."

He envisions his new, natural religion in the seventh stanza as a ring of "supple and turbulent" men sing "their boisterous devotion to the sun, not as a god, but as a god might be." Nature does not establish hierarchies that separate her from humanity. The god of nature appears naked among the men "like a savage source" commingling with their blood until the men experience a complete communion with their world, as their chants become a choir, echoing from the hills "long afterward." They know full well of the inevitability of death and rebirth and so celebrate the present beauty and bounty of nature. The poet links the woman's experience to that of the men through the warmth of the sun that all of them experience, suggesting that she too can feel such imperishable bliss.

The voice of the poet and that of the woman merge in the acceptance of a call to live in the moment at the end of the poem. The single voice here no longer turns to the grave of Jesus for spiritual fulfillment, since it understands that there are no "spirits lingering" around His tomb. Christianity has lost its power over the woman who now has become "unsponsored" and free to celebrate a new faith in the sensual beauty that surrounds her. Her more profound contact with nature has become a substitute for the restrictive sacraments of her religion. Through the acknowledgement of the mutability of the natural world, she becomes like the free flying pigeons, "on extended wings" rising and falling in "ambiguous undulations as they sink."

Source: Wendy Perkins, Critical Essay on "Sunday Morning," in *Poetry for Students*, The Gale Group, 2002.

Paul Witcover

Witcover is an editor and writer whose fiction, book reviews, and critical essays appear regularly in magazines and online. In the following essay, Witcover discusses history and technique in this poem.

Wallace Stevens gives hope to late-bloomers everywhere. His first collection of poetry, *Harmonium*, was published in 1923, when he was forty-four years old. His second collection, *Ideas of Order*, did not appear until eleven years later, in 1934. Yet by the time of his death in 1955, Stevens had received virtually every major award and honor the literary community could bestow and was widely acknowledged not only as one of the great poets of the century, but, in the words of critic Harold Bloom in *Wallace Stevens: The Poems of Our Climate*, "a vital part of American mythology."

Not bad for a man who spent his entire adult life laboring as a lawyer for insurance companies! It seems paradoxical that the same man could devote himself with equal diligence if not ardor to poetry and the law, let alone insurance, as if some inevitable clash between imagination and reality, like matter and anti-matter, should render such a harmony impossible. Yet Stevens saw no necessary conflict between imagination and reality; indeed, despite the admitted difficulty of his poetry, its concern with philosophical and metaphysical questions that at times become frustratingly abstract, Stevens wrote in the belief, or in the desire to believe, that imagination and reality should be complementary. By awakening the imagination to its participation in the concrete specificity of the real world, Stevens could achieve for himself and his readers, through a "supreme fiction" of poetry, a kind of transcendent, timeless awareness of creative human involvement in an all-encompassing natural order that would replace the traditional faith in God and divine providence which, at least to certain classes of people in Western civilization, no longer seemed sustainable. For Stevens, the poet's role was not to provide answers but rather to question deeply and persistently in order that readers might construct their own continually evolving answers. Those answers, like the questions that spawned them, would necessarily be grounded in the real or, as Stevens sometimes called it, the "normal." In his essay "Imagination as Value," collected in *The Necessary Angel: Essays on Reality and the Imagination*, Stevens wrote: "The chief problems of any artist, as of any man, are the problems of the normal and

> *For Stevens, the poet's role was not to provide answers but rather to question deeply and persistently in order that readers might construct their own continually evolving answers."*

… he needs, in order to solve them, everything that the imagination has to give."

Just how much Stevens's imagination had to give in this cause was apparent from the start of his career. *Harmonium* is an extraordinarily accomplished debut, a dazzling display of high ambition wedded to prodigious talent. Poet and critic Randall Jarrell, in his essay "Reflections on Wallace Stevens," reprinted in the collection *No Other Book*, wrote that "there are in *Harmonium* six or eight of the most beautiful poems an American has written." "Sunday Morning," first published in a somewhat different form in *Poetry* magazine in 1915, must be ranked among that select number; in the estimation of critic Robert Rehder, writing in *The Poetry of Wallace Stevens*, it is "the first great poem that Stevens wrote. … Here, all at once, the poet is in full possession of his powers."

In the essay "Imagination as Value," Stevens states that "the great poems of heaven and hell have been written and the great poem of the earth remains to be written." "Sunday Morning" is Stevens's first mature attempt to write this "great poem of the earth," a project that would occupy him for the rest of his life; that Stevens originally planned to title his collected poems "The Whole of Harmonium" shows the extent to which he viewed his life's work as a coherent enterprise, a single long poem.

"Sunday Morning" consists of eight fifteen-line stanzas composed in beautiful, seemingly effortless blank verse—blank verse being a kind of poetry that is unrhymed but, in contrast to free verse, written in lines of regular length and meter, generally, as here, iambic pentameter. In tone and style, "Sunday Morning" harkens back to romantic poets like Wordsworth, Keats, and Coleridge. Stevens alludes to the poetry of these and other predecessors throughout his poem; the final stanza, for example, is closely patterned on the last stanza of Keats' "On Autumn." Stevens evokes the romantics to establish a connection of subject and sensibility, yet the consolations that were available to nineteenth-century romantic poets are not, or should not be, available to a twentieth-century American poet. History, if nothing else, demonstrates that the way back is not the way forward.

What marks the poem as modern despite its purposeful romantic echoes is that it takes as a given the loss or futility of religious faith that has come to be recognized as a central theme of modernism. Stevens's focus is on Christianity, but he more than implies that the crisis of belief has extended beyond any one religious system to encompass all religions past and present. The phrase "crisis of belief" is no exaggeration in describing the Western world of 1915, with the carnage of World War I fast eroding traditional notions of faith and patriotism. In 1914, with German troops advancing on Paris, Stevens had contributed four poems to a special "war" issue of *Poetry* magazine, and "Sunday Morning" itself was composed in a year that saw the beginnings of trench warfare and the senseless slaughter it would entail. As critic James Longenbach points out in his essay on Stevens in *American Writers*, "Stevens was not much of a topical poet, but his poetry always emerged in dialogue with the events of his time." This is certainly true of "Sunday Morning," where events on distant battlefields, while not determinative, contribute to the "dark encroachment" that drifts in to disturb the poem's initially peaceful and civilized setting of an upper class woman's boudoir on a lazy Sunday morning. The pun implicit in the title is more than justified by the deeply elegiac mood that will come to dominate the poem.

"Sunday Morning" takes the form of a dramatic dialogue between this nameless young woman and an equally nameless narrator who is probably older, and certainly more experienced. Critic Helen Vendler, in *On Extended Wings: Wallace Stevens' Longer Poems*, advances the intriguing notion that the narrator "is a voice from the sepulcher"; that is, a dead man, a ghost, for whom "all sorrow, triumph, and love are infinitely distanced in some remote and remembered pathos of the past." Both voices, that of the young woman and the older narrator can be thought of as aspects of the poet, of Stevens himself. The poem is a meditation, the record of a mind in dialogue with itself. This is a quality shared by many of Stevens's poems, as Rehder notes: "The poems do not merely represent the mind's mulling and churning; they are doing what they are describing—like all art, they *are* thinking." In terms of physical action and setting, the poem is static, unchanging from the first stanza to the last, although immense distances are traversed in time and space through the evolving thoughts and fantasies of the poet and his personas. The poem does not advance in the machine-like manner of logical argument, marching step by step toward an inevitable conclusion, but unfolds according to the same mysteriously organic patterning of unconscious thought and emotion that produce fantasies and dreams. Which is not to say that the poem is purely imagistic, with nothing to communicate beyond the artifact of itself; "Sunday Morning" eloquently and suggestively addresses a condition of human existence that readers are presumed—and, to judge by the poem's continuing popularity, presumed correctly—to share.

Stanza 1 opens with an obviously well-to-do young woman savoring a late, lazy breakfast of oranges and coffee on a Sunday morning. Instead of attending church, she is still dressed in her peignoir, or nightgown, drowsing "in a sunny chair" while her pet cockatoo, released from its cage, enjoys its "green freedom." The first sentence employs a number of words that are bursting with life, color, and vitality, words associated with nature: "oranges," "green," "freedom," "sunny," "cockatoo." The same sentence also features words and phrases, some explicitly linked to religion, that conjure opposing thoughts of stasis and death: "complacencies," "dissipate," "holy hush," "ancient sacrifice." Here, in simple and stark outline, Stevens sets out the argument about to unfold in the mind of the poet, an argument between life, associated with nature, and death, associated with religion.

The woman may not be in church, but thoughts of church, or at any rate religion, are not far from her mind. The phrases "holy hush" and "ancient sacrifice" in line 5 herald what Stevens beautifully calls, in lines 6–7, "the dark / Encroachment of that old catastrophe." By "old catastrophe," he means both the crucifixion of Jesus and the establishment of the Catholic church. Influenced by these pious and guilty thoughts, in lines 9–11, the woman's dreamy reverie darkens: "The pungent oranges and bright, green wings / Seem things in some procession of the dead / Winding across wide water, without sound." In these lines, one can see the allusion to World War I, "the dark / Encroachment of that old catastrophe" suggesting oppressive thoughts of the war in Europe—that this war was being fought between self-avowedly Christian powers only underscores Stevens's point of the deadening effect of traditional religion. But in the poem itself, Stevens has another destination than Europe in mind; in a striking allusion to one of Jesus' miracles, he sends the woman on "dreaming feet" all the way back to the source: "silent Palestine, / Dominion of the blood and sepulcher." Here "blood" refers to the blood of Christ; far from being associated with the triumph of life over death, as in Christian theology, it is reversed, now serving as a symbol of death's dominion over life. Stevens's poetry can be densely layered with symbol and allusion; a single word or phrase or line often contains multiple embedded meanings. It is a measure of his genius that these constellations of tightly compacted symbols and allusions do not weigh down his poems or turn them into beautiful but lifeless artifacts (like sepulchers) but instead, by unpacking themselves in the minds of readers, actually achieve the opposite, bringing the poems to life.

In stanza 2, lines 16–22, the poem's narrator departs from his passive description of physical and psychological setting to actively enter the poem for the first time by asking and then answering a series of rhetorical questions:

> Why should she give her bounty to the dead?
> What is divinity if it can come
> Only in silent shadows and in dreams?
> Shall she not find in comforts of the sun,
> In pungent fruit and bright, green wings, or else
> In any balm or beauty of the earth,
> Things to be cherished like the thought of heaven?

Note the reappearance of key words from the first stanza; this is a structural technique Stevens uses throughout the poem, repeating words either verbatim or in a slightly altered fashion to get at the words and the associations behind them, from new angles. The word "sunny" in line 2, for example, reappears as "sun" in line 19 and in various guises thereafter. Other important words that echo throughout the poem are "blood," "wings," and "sky." It should also be noted how frequently the appearance of one word calls forth the appearance of an answering word that contains opposing qualities, as again, "sunny" in line 2 is followed in line 6 by "dark." Thus, as Longenbach notes, "the poem moves by association and juxtaposition." Readers experience the poem as the drifting of thoughts al-

most at random, one image calling up a related or opposite image, yet Stevens is in control, carefully building a network of intricately linked associations that will pull tight and then unravel to astonishing effect in the poem's final stanza.

But to return to stanza 2, a divinity that comes in shadows and dreams is a ghost. Rather than look to a ghost, or to the dead son of God, for comfort in her awareness of death and mortality, the narrator advises the woman in lines 19 and 21 to look to the sun and to the "balm and beauty of the earth." She herself must be the residence of divinity; in place of a lifeless tomb or bodiless spirit, a living body of flesh and blood. And not only that; she must recognize that this divinity is present in the rest of the natural world, of which she is a part: "The bough of summer and the winter branch. / These are the measures destined for her soul." Here Stevens expresses the idea of a kind of natural immortality opposed to the unnatural immortality of Christianity. This natural immortality is one of change and cyclical recurrence, and Stevens evokes it beautifully in the image of a branch changing with the seasons. While the span from the leafy green branch of summer to the bare branch of winter is one "measure" of mortality, it is also, and more accurately, seen as a "measure" in a musical sense, part of an orchestrated order in which themes recur just as the seasons pass and recur, the branch that is bare in winter sprouting fresh leaves in the spring.

Stanza 3 traces the history of religion from Jove to Jesus; from pagan beliefs to Christianity. Both systems are found wanting. The former because it had so little of humanity and the earth in it; the latter because it has alienated humanity from the earth and from nature. Instead of an aloof, inhuman god who walks among humans "as a muttering king, / Magnificent, would move among his hinds" (lines 34–35; "hinds" means "servants"), or a god who mingles with humanity only so that humanity might rise above itself, joining him in heaven, the narrator speaks (in lines 42–45) of a future time when the earth itself will be the only paradise humanity knows or can know:

> The sky will be much friendlier then than now,
> A part of labor and a part of pain,
> And next in glory to enduring love,
> Not this dividing and indifferent blue.

The woman speaks for the first time in stanza 4, protesting that while nature in its plenty might confer a measure of contentment, "'when the birds are gone, and their warm fields / Return no more, where, then, is paradise?'" (lines 49–50.) The narrator answers her question as he did his own: paradise lies in the recurrence of the seasons, in the cycle of birth and death. But he goes a step further, stressing that it is the woman's mind, her imagination, that imbues nature's round with human significance. No heavenly paradise, he asserts in lines 56–57, "has endured / As April's green endures; or will endure / Like her remembrance of awakened birds."

The woman is not so easily convinced. In stanza V, line 62, she asserts "The need of some imperishable bliss." The narrator answers in line 63 (in an allusion to the final stanza of Keats' "Ode on Melancholy") that "Death is the mother of beauty." Stevens insists that it is the human consciousness of time and the inevitability of death within time that makes things beautiful; what's more, that is the only beauty humans may know. The transitory yet recurring nature of life is then contrasted, in stanza VI, with a paradise of petrified beauty in which ripe fruit never falls and nothing ever changes. That heaven, the narrator suggests in lines 88–90, is an infantile projection against an equally infantile fear of death:

> Death is the mother of beauty, mystical,
> Within whose burning bosom we devise
> Our earthly mothers waiting, sleeplessly.

What, then, does the narrator offer the woman in place of the solace of Christianity? Stanza 7, lines 91–95, presents a glimpse of a future in which

> a ring of men
> Shall chant in orgy on a summer morn
> Their boisterous devotion to the sun,
> Not as a god, but as a god might be,
> Naked among them, like a savage source.

As the narrator goes on to paint a picture of this future paradise, two things become evident. First, there are no women allowed; it is an earthly paradise made by men, for men, and, one fears, very much at the expense of women. Second, this vision of a future for manly men seems like a bizarre vision of an idealized primitive past. The contrast between the tone and content of this stanza (which, despite its placement, thematically follows immediately after stanza 3) is so striking that one wonders if this is not perhaps the woman's ironic fantasy of what a future paradise will look like rather than the stolid narrator's. There is something either ironic or almost obscene in the elevated language used in lines 102–103, for example, to speak of "the heavenly fellowship / Of men that perish and of summer morn" as though an all-too-earthly "fellowship of men that perish" was not adding to

its ranks each day in the trenches and on the battlefields of Europe. But in fact, the jarring impact of this stanza on a contemporary reader—critic Janet McCann, in *Wallace Stevens Revisited: The Celestial Possible*, calls it "artificial and contrived"—is simply an illustration of the way in which history can intrude to alter forever the interpretation of a poet's lines. Readers cannot blind themselves to the facts or ironies of history; to ignore them when reading a poem or looking at any piece of art is to relegate that art to the realm of the unliving. In view of Stevens's preference as expressed in this poem and others for the living over the sepulchral dead, one can only conclude that he himself would disapprove of such an approach. Yet by the same token, it would be wrong to judge this or any poem solely on the basis of such knowledge, unavailable to the poet. Whatever Stevens's intent in this obscure stanza, it is clear that the vision of a future paradise it puts forward is provisional, a possibility only. If this were not the case, the poem would end, unsatisfyingly, here. Instead, it concludes with the majestic ambiguities of stanza 8, which more than redeem the faults of stanza 7.

In stanza 8, lines 106–108, the woman hears a voice crying out that

> "The tomb in Palestine
> Is not the porch of spirits lingering.
> It is the grave of Jesus, where he lay."

With these lines, which begin in lofty poetic diction yet close in a phrase of simple human dignity, the poem comes full circle, returning to the setting of its first stanza; like the natural paradise of which it speaks, "Sunday Morning" is cyclical. Yet, within the fixed parameters of that cycle, there has been change; Jesus has become fully human, god made in man's image rather than the other way around, subject to death and whatever natural paradise all humans participate in by virtue of living and dying. Jesus died; so did Wallace Stevens; so will all human beings; yet life will go on, the same yet different, and this is all of paradise that humans know or, by a continuing effort of sympathetic and creative imagination, can know. The lines in which Stevens sets forth the final, elegiac statement of his poem are profoundly moving, beginning with line 110, "We live in an old chaos of the sun," and ending, in lines 117–120, with:

> And, in the isolation of the sky,
> At evening, casual flocks of pigeons make
> Ambiguous undulations as they sink,
> Downward to darkness, on extended wings.

The magnificence of these lines is due not only to the stirring poetry with which Stevens imbues them but also to the way in which images and symbols from the poem, which have been carefully repeated and varied throughout, expanding in meaning and gathering substance with each iteration, are here brought together in a masterful culmination that leads not to a resolution but instead to the somehow cathartic uncertainty of that unforgettable final image, which seems to express so well and with such nobility of spirit the paradoxical heart of human existence. One can do no better than to quote Randall Jarrell:

> Here—in the last purity and refinement of the grand style, as perfect, in its calm transparency, as the best of Wordsworth—is the last wilderness, come upon so late in the history of mankind that it is no longer seen as the creation of God, but as the Nature out of which we evolve; man without myth, without God, without anything but the universe which has produced him, is given an extraordinarily pure and touching grandeur in these lines—lines as beautiful, perhaps, as any in American poetry.

Source: Paul Witcover, Critical Essay on "Sunday Morning" in *Poetry for Students*, The Gale Group, 2002.

Laura Kryhoski

Kryhoski is currently working as a freelance writer. She has also taught English Literature in addition to English as a Second Language overseas. In this essay, Kryhoski considers how Stevens urges the reader to find peace in nature.

Wallace Stevens begins his poem "Sunday Morning" in a relaxed, exotic atmosphere, evoking sensual, colorful images of a female protagonist, casually lounging in the warmth of the sun. The vibrancy of the moment is immediately subdued by the mention of a dark "encroachment of that old catastrophe," and the work shifts. In Stevens's careful consideration of language, he has established a new "religion," infused or filled with symbols of an old one. The poet urges the reader to find peace in the spirit of nature, of the present moment, by personifying nature as a nurturing presence. Stevens creates an interesting dichotomy within the work, employing a series of similar contrasts in an effort to come to terms with what many have described as a loss of Christian faith.

The poet relies on vivid images, images heavy with meaning, to establish a dark, serious tone. Towards the end of the first stanza, for example, the reader is transported "over the seas to silent Palestine / Dominion of blood and sepulchre." The sepulchre, or burial vault, of Christ is located in Palestine. The mention of blood and of the grave, coupled with earlier clues, that is, "the holy hush of ancient sacrifice," reinforce images of Christ's crucifixion. Christ is a symbol of ultimate sacrifice in Christianity, a sacrifice of life to purge or wipe clean man's behavioral slate in the world. Christ also surfaces again in stanza four when the poem's female protagonist, in her discomfort, questions the permanence of a paradise on earth. Such imagery inspires assurances by the poet that neither is there a "haunt of prophecy" nor "chimera [imaginary monster] of the grave" that can rival or compete with "April's green." The line again recalls the death of Christ as it was prophesied, and his return as proven by his supernatural appearance.

Curious too is the choice of words the poet uses to describe these images related to Christ. They are not tangible or concrete concepts but are described rather as dreamy, haunting visions of ghosts and monsters. Stevens ponders the relevance of exercising the power of fancy or imagination to invoke the divine in stanza two, asking "What is divinity if it can come / Only in silent shadows and in dreams?" The query solidifies the poet's objective—to present specific images in nature, exposing them as being more practical symbols as well as sources of spiritual comfort than those born of religious ideals. While Heaven is identified as being unrealistic, intangible or out of reach, a glimpse of divinity is easily manifested in nature, "In any balm or beauty of the earth" and made bountiful. In the same stanza, passions and moods described as natural acts reinforce the idea of nature as being a vital part of a total divine experience. The poet insists to his protagonist that "divinity must live within herself; passions of rain, or moods in falling snow." Her passions and moods are described as events in nature, as natural acts. The primacy of her connection to the natural world reverberates or resounds in stanza seven. Its pagan imagery—men supple and turbulent chanting in orgy on a summer morning, dancing in the sun, devoted to it—constitutes a visual feast. Life is real; it is pulsing; Life is warm, loud, rhythmic, alive, and strong in the image of these men who dance in the warmth of the sun.

The historical backdrop for Stevens's work certainly dictated his interest in finding a spiritual connection amidst poetic scribblings. At the turn of the century, Stevens believed that the failings of religion could be overcome by the art of poetry. His published letters, as recounted in Richard Ellman and Robert O'Clair's *Norton Anthology of Modern*

> *Its pagan imagery—men supple and turbulent chanting in orgy on a summer morning, dancing in the sun, devoted to it—constitutes a visual feast."*

Poetry, shed light on such sentiments. Stevens felt that "the great poems of heaven and hell have been written and the great poem of earth remains to be written." He also expressed great concerns that we had "terribly forsaken the earth," ignoring the wonder of its enormity, of its vastness and diversity in favor of creating cityscapes. But ultimately, it was the power of the written word, the limitless potential for self-expression in poetry, that compelled Stevens to embrace it as "the supreme fiction" and "a freshening of life." He pondered a life devoid or without Christian conviction, insisting on finding a suitable replacement. Stevens came to the ultimate conclusion that "I ought to believe in imagination," and that the "imagination is the liberty of the mind."

The true power of the work is indeed found in its ability to embrace death amidst a godless universe. In stanza five, death is described as "the mother of beauty; hence from her, / Alone, shall come fulfillment to our dreams / and our desires." There is no other way to explain what happens after death, states the poet, until you experience it for yourself. Death is the ultimate answer to the most perplexing of human questions inspiring the greatest of fears, namely, the existence of life after death. Death, according to Stevens, is not a fate inspiring terror, but should be seen as an act of intense liberation from fear and doubt. It is not only a point of discovery for the poet, but part of a great continuum.

An embrace of this ominous concept also serves as a springboard for Stevens. Death is not only a means to an end, but it is a part of an ongoing story reflected in nature. The same path of "sure obliteration" is also, reminds the poet, "where triumph rang its brassy phrase." In a similar fashion, "sick sorrow" is paired with "love's tender whisper." These contradictory terms offset one another, the bad with the good, betraying a balance. One term is interdependent on the other to amplify

its meaning—you cannot know one without the other, if you are to truly live. Such systematic pairings or wordplay serve to build a case for enjoying life on earth. Although life has its heartaches, it is also an occasion for great celebration. Throughout the poem, this concept of renewal, of infusing new life into old objects or ideas, is a repeated sentiment, literally as well as figuratively in the text. In one scene, boys pile "new plums and pears / on disregarded plate." Said Stevens, as quoted by Ellman and O'Clair,

Plate is used in the sense of so-called family plate (that is, household silver.) Disregarded refers to the disuse into which things fall that have been possessed for a long time. I mean, therefore, that death releases and renews. What the old have come to disregard, the young inherit and make use of.

Life for the elderly is a worn path, it is withered, dead. In direct contrast, life for the young is a fresh experience, making even the old plate look new. As the "maidens taste / and stray impassioned in the littering leaves," their participation in an innocent seduction is reminiscent of the Fall. Equally powerful are the images of pears and plums, symbols of a woman's reproductive power. Couple these images and the maidens become part of the reproductive process, of the circle of life. Compare again the young of the maidens and the dead, "littering leaves," or the newly-ripened fruit on "disregarded plate," so old, used up—all participate in the life cycle, in the continuous process of death and of renewal.

Wallace Stevens's *Sunday Morning* is no somber affair. During a time of great innovation and change, questions abound about the existence of God and religion. Whereas many found the attempt to embrace scientific progress while maintaining their Christian convictions wearing, Stevens had moved forward, found a solace in his poetry of the every day, inspired by his natural surroundings. He encourages the reader to celebrate a vision of heaven on earth, to look toward "our earthly mothers waiting, sleeplessly," for our comfort and care.

Source: Laura Kryhoski, Critical Essay on "Sunday Morning," in *Poetry for Students*, The Gale Group, 2002.

Herbert J. Stern

In the following essay excerpt, Stern examines the "two conceptions of life" present in "Sunday Morning."

We have already observed that for Stevens the poetic pursuit of pleasure was among the most urgent tasks in which a twentieth-century poet could engage. The poetic enactment of pleasure is, after all, equivalent to what Irving Howe has properly argued to be the main concern of Stevens' poetry: "discovering and . . . enacting the possibilities for human self-renewal in an impersonal and recalcitrant age." This enactment, as we have seen in our examination of "Peter Quince at the Clavier," requires that we maintain our capacity for imaginative, even amatory, response to physical beauty, and from it learn modes of subjective experience worthy of mirroring the external world that feeds the spirit. Stevens' boldest and most famous attempt to embody this process is "Sunday Morning," a poem in which the natural beauty earlier symbolized by Susanna is confronted nakedly as explicit subject. And the poem may properly be called "romantic," not only in the special sense I have discussed, but also because it celebrates, in blank verse that rivals and in some particulars may have been influenced by Wordsworth's own, a physical world sufficient to satisfy those instincts for order, certainty, and comfort which in former times were satisfied by the idea of God.

In his essay on "The Irrational Element in Poetry," Stevens was later to remark:

> while it can lie in the temperament of very few of us to write poetry in order to find God, it is probably the purpose of each of us to find the good which, in the Platonic sense, is synonymous with God. One writes poetry, then, in order to approach the good in what is harmonious and orderly.

The statement, like nearly all of Stevens' prose meditations, is an attempt to make explicit the theory that governed his poetry from the start; and together with his remark that "the great poems of heaven and hell have been written and the great poem of the earth remains to be written," it provides a frame for Stevens' own great poem of the earth. It may be that Stevens nowhere comes closer than in "Sunday Morning" to "enacting the possibilities for human self-renewal." It is certain that here, in a poem that was composed so early in his poetic career, Stevens has already created one of those major works that were to recur throughout his canon: a poem shaped in the image of the Supreme Fiction, looming over the lesser lyrics that surround it like that magical tree of reality in "Le Monocle de Mon Oncle," which

> *... stands gigantic, with a certain tip*
> *To which all birds come sometime in their time*
> *But when they go that tip still tips the tree.*

As usual with Stevens' work, the title provides a complex gloss on the poem that follows it; and

> *It was Stevens'*
> *conviction that although*
> *we can, if only because we*
> *must, learn to live without*
> *God, we cannot, if we are*
> *to remain human, live*
> *without the satisfactions*
> *that belief in God could*
> *formerly provide."*

those who have considered Stevens' titles either merely frivolous or somehow irrelevant to his texts have missed one of the widest portals into his rich world. Sunday, of course, is a day of meditation particularly important to Stevens, who could play his harmonium only during such spare moments as his quotidian responsibilities might allow. The day is also God's day, and the poem is concerned with prescribing the manner of celebrating God—or rather, what "a God might be"—in the modern world. The importance of this point can hardly be exaggerated, since for Stevens, no less than for Matthew Arnold, the salient function of art was one we may legitimately call a religious function. As Stevens put it in the "Adagia,"

> The relation of art to life is of the first importance especially in a skeptical age since, in the absence of a belief in God, the mind turns to its own creations and examines them, not alone from the aesthetic point of view, but for what they reveal, for what they validate and invalidate, for the support that they give.

It was Stevens' conviction that although we can, if only because we must, learn to live without God, we cannot, if we are to remain human, live without the satisfactions that belief in God could formerly provide. Whatever else religion of more devout ages than our own may have done, it did at least supply substance for visions grander than the empiricism of the present age has been able to achieve; and although Stevens seems never to have suffered anguish over the loss of God, he did consider it the burden and the privilege of the poet to rescue from that loss values which man requires and may attain even without God.

On another, less obvious but equally important level, the title reminds us that Sunday is the day of the sun, and that the sun has quite logically been considered in most primitive societies to be the life-giver, the emblem of fertility and procreation. If "Sunday Morning" is a celebration of life, a hymn to things as they are, it is also a poem of potential and renewal, a sermon on things as they might be, an instance of that "world of poetry indistinguishable from the world in which we live, or ... from the world in which we shall come to live." And finally, as Stevens was later to write, "poetry is like prayer in that it is most effective in solitude and in times of solitude, as, for example, in the earliest morning."

"Sunday Morning," then, is a visionary poem; indeed, we might call it the ultimate projection of the romantic vision into the twentieth century. The importance of "Sunday Morning" to Stevens' subsequent poetry is that, although he would never again find it possible to pay, without irony and without qualification, such exultant homage to the sun, "symbol of the good which ... is synonymous with God," the remainder of his work would nevertheless be devoted to the attempt, at times comic, at times ironic, at times heroically triumphant, to create a poetry of exaltation, yet a poetry which is, as he came to think the work of the *Harmonium* period was not, attuned to modern reality. It is Stevens' faith in the possibility of making poetry out of the world as seen in the clear light of reality, out of the Platonic sun that is the source of all knowledge and all truth—the possibility of metamorphosing, somehow without distortion, things as they palpably are into things as the imagination wills them to be—that is the solid core of his most lofty aspiration.

Although the structure of "Sunday Morning" takes the loose shape of meditation and association, not the rigid form of logic, its pattern of thought and feeling, unlike that of many of Stevens' meditative poems, does move toward resolution. The female protagonist suffers at the start the quiet unrest which loss of those consolations attainable through faith in Christ has stirred in her; in the course of the subsequent dialogue between her longings for "some imperishable bliss" and the poet's assurances that transience is all and is enough, she is drawn from religious yearnings to an acceptance of a world without God. Thus, when with the closing image of "casual flocks of pigeons" which, at evening, make

Ambiguous undulations as they sink,
Downward to darkness, on extended wings,

the fact of death is again brought into the foreground, it is no longer a source of terror or unrest, nor does it inspire religious intimations of immortality; now "Death is the mother of beauty," and, as in Keats, through acceptance of earthly transience we are wedded most passionately to the beauty we are certain we must lose.

How many we refine from earth itself sufficient compensation for that "imperishable bliss" promised by heaven? The process begins subtly before the argument of the poem is engaged. Here is one of the few poems by Stevens in which there is no obvious reference, either direct or metaphoric, to poetry itself; yet the opening stanza serves brilliantly to illustrate what in "Three Academic Pieces" Stevens argues to be the singular quality that elevates poetry above other pleasurable things: poetry, he argues there, by revealing "a partial similarity between dissimilar things," intensifies and makes more brilliant the particular element of their similarity. "When the similarity is between things of adequate dignity," he goes on,

> the resemblance may be said to transfigure or sublimate them. Take, for example, the resemblance between reality and any projection of it in belief or in metaphor. What is it that these two have in common? Is not the glory of the idea of any future state a relation between a present and a future glory? The brilliance of the earth is the brilliance of every paradise.

Just as the two closing sentences of this passage constitute a prose summary of one of the central themes of "Sunday Morning," so the argument that precedes them serves to explain the method of the opening stanza. The lady is neither a person nor even a *persona;* she is simply the projection of a mood which, were it to take on a palpable being of its own, would resemble the feminine image Stevens here projects. It should not surprise us, then, if beneath the lady's peignoir we find no flesh. Similarly, her rich ambience is designed not so much to provide "real toads in imaginary gardens" as to foreshadow the imaginative aggrandizement of the material world through which we may come to see that "The brilliance of the earth is the brilliance of every paradise."

The associative richness of the opening stanza is nearly inexhaustible, and within it reality and its metaphoric projection become nearly inseparable. The coffee, oranges, and cockatoo, which at first, as sensual comforts and tokens of a luxuriant mood,

... mingle to dissipate
The holy hush of ancient sacrifice,

become, as the lady's imagination weaves them into dream, into poetry, "things in some procession of the dead," a procession in which the dreamer herself, as if enchanged by her own images, finds herself taking part:

> *The day is like wide water, without sound,*
> *Stilled for the passing of her dreaming feet*
> *Over the seas, to silent Palestine,*
> *Dominion of the blood and sepulchre.*

All roads in the first stanza lead to Palestine, to the lady's meditations on Christ; she, like the earthly riches that surround her, is in reality a thing "in some procession of the dead," for she is mortal; "the pungent oranges and bright green wings" of the cockatoo become, through their tropical associations, fit imaginative companions for her southern journey; and finally, the similarity between the gentle violation of her somnolent mood by thoughts of the Crucifixion ("the dark/ Encroachment of that old catastrophe") and the almost imperceptible manner in which "a calm darkens among water lights," leads her thoughts to Palestine as silently and as surely as Christ himself walked upon the water.

What has occurred in the first stanza is that, in constructing her metaphysical poem, the lady has given "her bounty to the dead." Indeed, her creative act is precisely the kind later rejected by Crispin, "that poetic hero without palms/ Or jugglery," whose

> *... violence was for aggrandizement*
> *And not for stupor, such as music makes*
> *For sleepers halfway waking.*

The lady's imagination and her heart's need having filled her mind with "the holy hush of ancient sacrifice," the second voice, as gentle as the movement of her mind, yet less passive, less feminine, is introduced. Its argument is untouched by any skepticism against her need, but is rather concerned with establishing an alternate solace to the religious comfort she has sought in Christ. And its opening question provides what is at once a delicately articulated transition and an example of Stevens' most subtle wit:

> *Why should she give her bounty to the dead?*
> *What is divinity if it can come*
> *Only in silent shadows and in dreams?*
> *Shall she not find in comforts of the sun,*
> *In pungent fruit and bright green wings, or else*
> *In any balm or beauty of the earth*
> *Things to be cherished like the thought of heaven?*

The fruit, the wings, initially synecdoches for "the balm or beauty of the earth," transported her from their own reality to another balm, the balm of heaven. Yet that more orthodox comforting, although itself mothered by the imagination, depends, as it has always done, on the denial of the poem of earth. The earth, from whose substance we have woven our visionary paradises, is paradise enough to those with sufficient feeling to be *alive* in it.

In an era whose intense self-consciousness has led to an ever-widening alienation from the objective world, Stevens, who is at times the most solipsistic of modern poets, returned in "Sunday Morning" to Coleridge's concept of the "One Life," a poetic and epistemological state to be entered only when "A poet's heart and intellect [are] combined and unified with the great appearances of nature and not merely held in solution and loose mixture with them, in the shape of formal similes." Our divinity consists in an awareness of the "One Life," in our capacity, as Stevens puts it elsewhere, for "Celebrating the marriage/ Of flesh and air," not a marriage of man and God but one whose rituals are celebrated in the closing lines of the second stanza—a marriage of the human and divine within man, to be consummated through an imaginative capacity to unite ourselves with the earth:

> *Divinity must live within herself:*
> *Passions of rain, or moods in falling snow;*
> *Grieving in lonelines, or unsubdued*
> *Elations when the forest blooms; gusty*
> *Emotions on wet roads on autumn nights;*
> *All pleasures and all pains, remembering*
> *The bough of summer and the winter branch.*
> *These are the measures destined for her soul.*

As the second stanza rejects the shadowy bliss of heaven for the certain pleasures (and the certain pains) of earth, the third elaborates the Blakean motto: "All deities reside in the human breast." Just as our emotions may unite us with the paradise of earth, so may the imaginative power with which we created the gods fit us with the requisite dignity to live in this paradise. The argument of the stanza becomes clear enough when we realize that Stevens is in effect quoting scripture to his purpose. The concept of divinity, here emblemized by Jove, becomes a fruitful concept only *after* men have created myths that wed the human to the divine. These myths, conceived out of our hunger for divine magnificence, for breaching the gap between the real and the ideal, comprise, as Stevens knew with Blake, our earliest poetry; born out of longing for the superhuman, these myths conceived in their turn new symbols of human superhumanity, emblemized by the constellations in which Jove's discarded mistresses achieved immortality. Although Stevens confines his argument to classical mythology, the analogy with Christianity is apparent. Christ, too, Stevens reminds us by implication, was born out of our desire to commingle the human and divine; and in the Christian myth as in the pagan, the success of that commingling was symbolized by a star. In both cases, a god has come down to man, and man has in turn been elevated to the heavens.

Stevens' treatment of these myths, it should be apparent, is unmarked by either hostility or cynicism toward religion. He sees religious myths rather as the products of timeless human needs which must be satisfied in a post-religious era no less than in the earlier ages of faith. In short, we still require the transcendental imagination that went into the making of our gods, as it still goes into the making of our poetry. But in a naturalistic universe, the earth itself is the only paradise and the most proximate immortality we can know. Thus, lest "our blood fail," it is through a wedding of our blood to the earth that we can experience the contentment we once experienced in the hope of heaven:

> *The sky will be much friendlier then than now,*
> *A part of labor and a part of pain,*
> *And next in glory to enduring love,*
> *Not this dividing and indifferent blue.*

Through our recognition that the earth is "all of paradise that we shall know" we may come at last to be at home in it—this is the truth visible in the clear light of the sun; this is the attachment to life which for Stevens, as for Camus, only the acceptance of the finality of death can bring.

The dialogue does not end, however, with this lofty conception. The lady, who is not, after all, "A High-Toned Old Christian Woman" but a facet of Stevens' own mind, still demands some satisfaction for the fundamental theistic craving for permanence:

> *She says, "I am content when wakened bids,*
> *Before they fly, test the reality*
> *Of misty fields, by their sweet questionings;*
> *But when the birds are gone, and their warm fields*
> *Return no more, where, then, is paradise?"*

The answer is direct and its limpid rhetoric is persuasive: there is no visionary heaven

> *... that has endured*
> *As April's green endures; or will endure*
> *Like her remembrance of awakened birds,*
> *Or her desire for June and evening, tipped*
> *By the consummation of the swallow's wings.*

Once more the poetry of earth is pitted against that of heaven, and its superiority. Stevens insists, stems from its permanence *as* reality. We are reminded, although he would hardly rejoice in the context of our reminiscence, of Dr. Johnson's injunction to a bereaved friend:

Let us endeavor to see things as they are, and then enquire whether we ought to complain. Whether to see life as it is will give us much consolation, I know not; but the consolation which is drawn from truth, if any there be, is solid and durable; that which may be derived from errour must be, like its original, falacious and fugitive.

To say that the Keatsian fifth stanza is repetitive would be to miss the key fact of the poem's structure, for "Sunday Morning" is, like most of Stevens' longer poems, a set of variations on a theme. Indeed, the lady's final reiteration of the need expressed in the stanza's opening lines ("But in contentment I still feel/ The need of some imperishable bliss") illustrates a technique with which the reader of Stevens becomes increasingly familiar: it is a flat statement of what, in the opening lines of stanza four, was uttered in metaphor. Similarly, the lines that follow in the stanza offer a metaphor for the vision of earth as paradise that is parallel to the vision earlier embodied in the image of the weakened birds. Poetry, Stevens has said, is an "abstraction blooded," and it is clear enough that the abstraction here blooded is that "Death is the mother of beauty." Not so clear, however, is the idea behind lines 13 and 14, in which death "causes boys to pile new plums and pears/ On disregarded plate." The intended meaning of these lines would indeed be impossible to determine with any confidence were it not for Harriet Monroe's objection to them when Stevens submitted the poem to her in 1915. "The words 'On disregarded plate' in No. 5," Stevens wrote to her in reply,

are, apparently, obscure. Plate is used in the sense of so-called family plate. Disregarded refers to the disuse into which things fall that have been possessed for a long time. I mean, therefore, that death releases and renews. What the old have come to disregard, the young inherit and make use of. Used in these senses, the words have a value in the lines which I find difficult to retain in any change. Does this explanation help? Or can you make any suggestion? I ask this because your criticism is clearly well founded.

The lines might read,

She causes boys to bring sweet-smelling pears, And plums in ponderous piles. The maidens taste And stray etc.

But such a change is somewhat pointless. I should prefer the lines unchanged, although, if you like the variations proposed, for the sake of clearness, I should be satisfied.

Miss Monroe like the variation proposed, and Stevens was satisfied, although in the revised lines he indeed lost the value he originally intended.

When we consider the weight of meaning Stevens himself piled on the "disregarded plate," meaning which no unaided reader could possibly taste, it should neither surprise nor dismay us that certain images and even certain poems throughout his work must remain obscure.

With the sixth stanza the current quickens as it carries the argument toward resolution. The permanence we pine for is the static permanence of death:

Is there no change of death in paradise?
Does ripe fruit never fall? Or do the boughs
Hang always heavy in that perfect sky,
Unchanging, yet so like our perishing earth,
With rivers like our own that seek for seas
They never find, the same receding shores
That never touch with inarticulate pang?

A paradise in which all is consummated is a paradise without consummation; a paradise in which all desire is satisfied is a paradise of ennui:

Why set the pear upon those river banks
Or spice the shores with odors of the plum?

We may break Stevens' argument down into three essential points: (1) The most radiant paradise we can conceive is one in which earth's brilliant beauty is perpetual—that is, a paradise in which neither nature nor man is subject to change and death. Essentially, this is the paradise Milton depicts in the prelapsarian Eden. (2) Precisely because the beauty of such a paradise *is* changeless and immortal, it would provide none of the emotional intensity that earthly beauty provides; for that intensity has its source in our awareness that earth's bounties are not ours forever. (3) By extension were we to enjoy, on earth *or* in heaven, that which we most passionately crave—"imperishable bliss"— we would, paradoxically, be robbed of bliss altogether, and be bound instead to the endless reexperiencing of pleasures that would become steadily more cloying through repetition.

Thus, with a cogency never achieved by Dr. Pangloss, Stevens completes his demonstration that this is indeed, the imminence of death notwithstanding, the best of all possible worlds. Nor is it difficult to imagine Stevens' reply to those dark lines of Yeats: "Man is in love and loves what vanishes,/ What more is there to say?" There remains to say, Stevens might have said, that is man were *not* in love with what vanishes, he would not be capable of loving at all. This, in effect, is the argument with which the stanza closes:

Death is the mother of beauty, mystical
Within those burning bosom we devise
Our earthly mothers waiting, sleeplessly.

Death mothers beauty because without awareness of death we would not learn the nurture of our earthly mother, the physical beauty of the world itself, a beauty that is "sleepless" and divine, unlike the hollow divinity that comes "Only in silent shadows and in dreams."

The seventh stanza of the poem might take for its motto Nietzsche's statement that "We have produced the hardest possible thought; now let us create the creature who will accept it lightheartedly and blissfully." The symbolic ceremony of devotion to the life-source that the stanza so grandly describes is not, as Yvor Winters would maintain, a projection of finicky hedonism, but rather an expression of faith in the possible heavenly fellowship of those Nietzschean creatures, "Of men that perish and of summer morn," of men content with the knowledge that

... whence they come and whither they shall go
The dew upon their feet shall manifest.

Nor would it seem a token of spiritual ennui that this poem in celebration of "an old chaos of the sun" should end with an evocation of death in life and life in death the nobility and scrupulous integrity of whose rhetoric requires no gloss:

Deer walk upon our mountains, and the quail
Whistle about us their spontaneous cries;
Sweet berries ripen in the wilderness;
And, in the isolation of the sky,
At evening, casual flocks of pigeons make
Ambiguous undulations as they sink,
Downward to darkness on extended wings.

The cockatoo of the first stanza, the "green wings" of the second, the "wakened birds" of the fourth, achieve synthesis in the "casual flocks of pigeons" whose sinking undulations bring the poem to a close. The lady *does*, in the end, give her bounty to the dead after all; not, however, as she had done initially, by sacrificing sensual experience to the falsifying hope of immortality, but by accepting transience as the necessary condition of our humanity and of our sense of beauty.

Skeptical, yet inspired by a passionate faith, contemporary, yet rooted in a primitive conception of the three-fold tie that binds nature, man, and divinity into an exultant harmony anomalous in an age that conceives "nature" as that which one beholds on picnics, and an age in which the idea of human potential for divinity has become repugnant to humanist and theist alike, "Sunday Morning" stands in the garden of contemporary poetry like some great exotic flowering tree transported into a municipal park by an eccentric millionaire.

Yet the fact remains that "Sunday Morning" *is* an exotic, whose beauty and whose power, as Stevens himself would shortly come to believe, had their nurture in a climate and an age remote from our own. Randall Jarrell came close to recognizing this point when he remarked of the poem that in it "is the last purity and refinement of the grand style, as perfect, in its calm transparency, as the best of Wordsworth…" But for the achievement of that purity and refinement, Stevens was forced to pay a price. In "Sunday Morning" he does not, as he was later to say that the poet must, "move constantly in the direction of the credible." That "ring of men" chanting in orgy "Their boisterous devotion to the sun" may stir us, but will not for long, even as metaphor, win from us a "willing suspension of disbelief." Moreover, Jarrell's reference to "the last purity and refinement of the grand style" is in itself, however unintentionally, but ambiguous praise: Stevens' richly articulated blank verse marks the *end* of a technical tradition, just as his insistence on our source in nature marks the end of a spiritual one. Stevens, like Picasso, began his mature artistic career with mastery of the received tradition; insofar as the vital artist is a pioneer, however, such mastery can bring stasis as leaden as that of a changeless paradise itself. To a degree, then, "Sunday Morning" is at once masterpiece and dead end; and our final response to the poem will be tempered by our recollection of Stevens' own subsequent remarks on Verrocchio's statue of Bartolommeo Colleoni:

> One feels the passion of rhetoric begin to stir and even to grow furious; and one thinks that, after all, the noble style, in whatever it creates, merely perpetuates the noble style. In this statue, the apposition between the imagination and reality is too favorable to the imagination.

"Sunday Morning" is the point of embarkation for the aesthetic voyaging of Crispin, the poet-clown who was to be Stevens' most ambitious vehicle for self-satire. Toward the close of his voyage, shortly before he abandons poetic theory and practice for domestic tranquility, Crispin turns against his own visions, visions of which "Sunday Morning" was the consummate embodiment:

> *These bland excursions into time to come,*
> *Related in romance to backward flights,*
> *However prodigal, however proud,*
> *Contained in their afflatus the reproach*
> *That first drove Crispin to his wandering.*
> *He could not be content with counterfeit,*
> *With masquerade of thought, with shapeless words*
> *That must belie the racking masquerade,*
> *With fictive flourishes that preordained*
> *His passion's permit, hang of coat, degree*

> *Of buttons, measure of his salt. Such trash*
> *Might help the blind, not him, serenely sly.*
> *It irked his patience.*

One wonders whether any obsession can more unsettle the writer of poetry than the indispensable obsession with truth, whether any curiosity can make his task of creation more difficult than curiosity about the ultimate nature of reality. Were Stevens the aesthetic fop that so many contemporaneous readers of *Harmonium* believed him to be, he would have found no grounds for distrusting the romantic incantations of "Sunday Morning"—although it is probable that he would have found no inspiration to write it. His difficulty was that the only poetry he could find ultimately satisfying was poetry of a kind that neither his own skepticism nor the hard contours of the modern world would countenance. For all its impassioned dignity, "Sunday Morning" is, in its primitivism, "Related in romance to backward flights"; for all the beauty of its evocation, it is, as poetry must be, as tenuous in its sanctions as those birdsongs of which the lady says:

> … *"I am content when wakened birds*
> *Before they fly, test the reality*
> *Of misty fields, by their sweet questionings;*
> *But when the birds are gone, and their warm fields*
> *Return no more, where, then, is paradise?"*

And for all the artistry of its rhetoric, it is "counterfeit"; it offers a verbal and philosophical masquerade that may have been workaday costume in the past and could conceivably become so again in the future, but which cannot but distort the present reality, and cannot help but preordain, for him who chooses to wear it, "passion's permit, hang of coat, degree/ Of buttons, measure of his salt"—for to adopt the style of a former tradition is perforce to adopt its vision. Excursions such as "Sunday Morning" must come to seem bland to those inclined to mistrust the comforts of an outworn romantic tradition. The grand style revived was not, for Stevens, what the modern poem had to be: "The poem of the mind in the act of finding/ What will suffice"; it is rather the reiteration of a satisfaction already found, a repetition of "what/ Was already in the script."

Source: Herbert J. Stern, "Adam's Dream," in *Wallace Stevens: Art of Uncertainty*, University of Michigan Press, 1966, pp. 87–104.

Sources

Bloom, Harold, "*The Rock* and Final Lyrics," in *Wallace Stevens: The Poems of Our Climate*, Cornell University Press, 1977, p. 374.

Ellman, Richard, and Robert O'Clair, eds., *The Norton Anthology of Modern Poetry*, 2d ed., Norton, 1995.

Jarrell, Randall, "Reflections on Wallace Stevens," in *No Other Book: Selected Essays*, edited by Brad Leithauser, HarperCollins, 1999, p. 116.

Jeffrey, David Lyle, ed., *A Dictionary of Biblical Tradition in English Literature*, William B. Eerdmans, 1992.

Longenbach, James, *American Writers*, Charles Scribner's Sons, 1998, pp. 295–315.

McCann, Janet, "'The Marvelous Sophomore': The Poems of *Harmonium*," in *Wallace Stevens Revisited: The Celestial Possible*, Twayne Publishers, 1995, p. 10.

Miller, J. Hillis, *Poets of Reality: Six Twentieth-Century Writers*, Harvard University Press, 1966, pp. 254–87.

———, "William Carlos Williams and Wallace Stevens," in *Columbia Literary History of the United States*, Columbia University Press, 1988, pp. 973–92.

Miller, Joseph, "Wallace Stevens," in *Dictionary of Literary Biography,* Volume 54: *American Poets, 1880–1945*, Third Series, Gale, 1987.

Monroe, Harriet, Review of *Harmonium*, in *Poetry*, Vol. 7, November 1915.

Perkins, George, and Barbara Perkins, "Wallace Stevens," in *The American Tradition in Literature*, Vol. 2, McGraw-Hill, 1999, p. 1058.

Rehder, Robert, "The Grand Poem: Preliminary Minutae," in *The Poetry of Wallace Stevens*, St. Martin's Press, 1988, pp. 65, 68.

Stevens, Wallace, "Adagia," in *Opus Posthumous*, 1957.

———, "Imagination as Value," in *The Necessary Angel: Essays on Reality and the Imagination*, Vintage Books, 1951, pp. 142, 156.

———, "Sunday Morning," in *The Palm at the End of the Mind*, edited by Holly Stevens, Vintage Books, 1990, pp. 5–8.

Vendler, Helen, "Fugal Requiems," in *On Extended Wings: Wallace Stevens' Longer Poems*, Harvard University Press, 1969, pp. 56–57.

Further Reading

Burney, William, "Wallace Stevens," in *Twayne's United States Authors Series Online*, G. K. Hall & Co., 1999.
> Burney compares the voice of the central female character in "Sunday Morning" to that of other works by Stevens.

Doggett, Frank, and Robert Buttel, eds., *Wallace Stevens: A Celebration*, Princeton University Press, 1980.
> This collection of articles focuses on the poetic talents of Stevens. In the preface, the editors comment that Stevens's themes and the "inescapable rhythms of his poems . . . are what give his work the important place it holds today and assure that it will be read long after the occasion of his centenary."

Litz, A. Walton, *Introspective Voyager: The Poetic Development of Wallace Stevens*, Oxford University Press, 1972.
> In his analysis of the poem, Litz argues that "by remaining skeptical and open [it] connects with the widest range of our personal and cultural experience."

Maeder, Beverly, *Wallace Stevens' Experimental Language: The Lion in the Lute*, St. Martin's Press, 1999.
> This critique focuses on how the poem's "several subject positions all confront the divine and spiritual with the earthly and bodily."

Newcomb, John Timberman, *Wallace Stevens and Literary Canons*, University Press of Mississippi, 1992.
> In his assessment of the poem, Newcomb asserts that its "subject matter, formal precision, and glorious blank-verse line all fostered the expectation of a strong affirmation of man's existence and artistry."

Three Times My Life Has Opened

Jane Hirshfield

1997

Jane Hirshfield opted to place "Three Times My Life Has Opened" as the last poem in her 1997 collection called *The Lives of the Heart*, and it makes for an appropriate and intriguing closing thought. This poem is rich in metaphor and mystery, and one line probably epitomizes the latter better than any other: "You will recognize what I am saying or you will not." This is the essence of a poem that is presented with an elegant tone, a simple style, and a caring voice that seems to assure the reader that one does not necessarily need to grasp every meaning within it to be moved by it. Instead, the overall gist of this work is most easily comprehended by getting a *feel* for its content without worrying about deciphering a certain message.

The word "Zen" is not mentioned in "Three Times My Life Has Opened," nor is "koan" (an unsolvable, thought-provoking riddle), "zazen," (the act of serious meditating), or "satori" (the attainment of spiritual enlightenment and true peace of mind). Yet the *presence* of these things can be felt within the poem, even though the words themselves are absent. To explain, then, what this poem is about is first to recognize the mystery to which few may be privy and to view it more as a whole than as the sum of its parts. The parts, after all, tend to elude specific definition or reference, but the work in its entirety reflects a philosophy in which ultimate achievement is more about connecting the inner-self to the natural world than to espousing intellectual rhetoric or theory. In short, this poem addresses a spiritual awakening, metaphorically compared to the movement of autumn through winter and into spring.

Author Biography

Jane Hirshfield was born in New York City in 1953. Her father was a clothing manufacturer and her mother was a secretary. Even as a young child, she knew she wanted to be a writer and poet when she grew up and recalls writing a sentence to that effect when prompted by a grade school teacher asking the children about future careers. The first book she bought for herself at age nine was a collection of haiku poetry, evidence of not only her early interest in that genre but also in Japanese writing and culture. Hirshfield graduated from a girls' school in New York and then went on to Princeton from which she graduated magna cum laude in 1973. Also in 1973, she published her first poem, but, in an unlikely move, she put aside her writing for the next eight years to study at the San Francisco Zen Center.

Hirshfield has said that the years she dedicated exclusively to learning and practicing Zen Buddhism have had the most significant influence on everything she has done since—from writing and teaching to her quiet, loving enjoyment of gardening and horses. But the religion of Zen rarely manifests itself in any direct way in Hirshfield's poetry. She does not use Zen language or make overt Zen references, and yet her writing is unmistakably radiant of the introspective, peaceful, and attentive thought that makes up Zen philosophy. After leaving the center in San Francisco in the early 1980s, Hirshfield began to write and teach, and her work began earning awards. Over the past two decades, she has received poetry prizes from several journal competitions, as well as a Pushcart Prize. She was awarded a Guggenheim fellowship in 1985, an Achievement Grant from the Marin Arts Council in 1990, and the Bay Area Book Reviewers Award in 1995. Most of her teaching positions have been at universities and workshops in California, and she has made that state her permanent residence.

The Lives of the Heart, which includes the poem "Three Times My Life Has Opened," was Hirshfield's fourth book of poems, published in 1997. A prolific essayist and translator, as well as poet, Hirshfield simultaneously published a collec-

Jane Hirshfield

tion of essays titled *Nine Gates: Entering the Mind of Poetry* in 1997. She has translated the poems of various Japanese poets, most notably the love poems of Ono no Komachi and Izumi Shikubu. Her most recent poetry collection, *Given Sugar, Given Salt*, was published in 2001.

Poem Text

Three times my life has opened.
Once, into darkness and rain.
Once, into what the body carries at all times within
    it and starts
    to remember each time it enters the act of love.
Once, to the fire that holds all.   5
These three were not different.
You will recognize what I am saying or you will
    not.
But outside my window all day a maple has
    stepped from her leaves
    like a woman in love with winter, dropping the
    colored silks.
Neither are we different in what we know.   10
There is a door. It opens. Then it is closed. But a
    slip of light
    stays, like a scrap of unreadable paper left on
    the floor,
    or the one red leaf the snow releases in March.

Media Adaptations

- In 1999, Bill Moyers recorded interviews and readings with eleven poets who had attended the 1998 Geraldine R. Dodge Poetry Festival in Waterloo Village, New Jersey. The series, comprising nine videocassettes, each running twenty-seven minutes, is called *Sounds of Poetry* and is a production of Public Affairs Televisions, Inc. Poets included are Hirshfield, Lucille Clifton, Stanley Kunitz, and Robert Pinsky, among others.

- Hirshfield recorded more than twenty-five poems from three of her collections on a forty-eight-minute tape catalogued simply as *Reader: Jane Hirshfield*. Recorded in 1995, it is available through the Poetry Center and American Poetry Archives at San Francisco State University. Detailed information can be found online at http://www.sfsu.edu/~poetry/ (last accessed June 13, 2002).

Poem Summary

Line 1

The first line of "Three Times My Life Has Opened" is, obviously, a repetition of the title. But a reader should never be too quick to judge which came first. Perhaps after the poem was written, Hirshfield decided just to call it by its first line. The order makes no difference in interpreting the poem, for this line begs two questions, regardless of how the work got its name: what does the poet mean when she says her life has "opened," and what or when are the "three times" that it happened?

Line 2

The second line of the poem sets the precedent for the poet's description of the times she claims her life has opened. She does not reveal *when* the events occur, but rather what the circumstances are that surround each one—more like *where* it happens than when. Line 2 implies a sad or desolate time, one in which the poet's life experiences "darkness and rain." Keep in mind that the word

"opened" indicates a willingness to receive something. The connotation would have been much different if Hirshfield had said her life fell into, or was forced into, certain situations. Therefore, even though darkness and rain do not seem like anything she would want to welcome into her life, one must wait to see how this episode plays out with the next two openings before reaching that conclusion.

Lines 3–4

These lines describe the second time the poet's life opened, and it seems to reveal a better time than the first. A specific meaning may not be any clearer here, but mentioning "the act of love" implies a moment of contentment, if not blissfulness. The allusion in these lines is to something physical, or natural, for "what the body carries within it" may be water or blood or any other liquid or solid that makes up the human body. But these items do not sound very poetic or like something the body "starts to remember" because the physical makeup of it is not likely to be forgotten. So what the body contains and recalls is open to speculation. Perhaps this second event is a bridge between the dreary darkness of the previous one and the warm brightness of the one to come. Regardless of the specifics, the poet effectively creates a tie-in for the physical being to the physicality of nature described at the end of the work.

Line 5

The third and final opening is "to the fire that holds all," and, again, this image could have either positive or negative connotations. The first inclination may be to imagine something horrific, as opening one's life to flames and burning sounds terribly painful, if not deadly. But fire is also a metaphor for passion and warmth, as well as for mental alertness and enlightenment. Since this fire "holds all," the positive connotation appears to be the most likely intended.

Lines 6–7

These lines are two of the most concrete in the poem, and yet they reveal the core of the poet's message. Although the three events surrounding her life's opening seem to be strikingly different in content—from darkness and rain to lovemaking to fire—Hirshfield claims, "These three were not different." If the reader finds this puzzling, not to worry, for the poet admits, "You will recognize what I am saying or you will not." That may take the reader off the hook, but it does something more as well. In her article "Poetry and the Mind of Indirection," from her book *Nine Gates*, Hirshfield asks, "Why do circuitousness and indirection play so great a role in poetic thought?" The answer she provides is that "only when looked at from a place of asideness and exile does the life of the world step fully forward." So looking at something head-on or trying to analyze something in a straightforward manner usually proves futile. If the reader does not "recognize" what the poet is saying, it is only because he or she wants to bring direction to what is unashamedly indirect.

Lines 8–9

Whereas the previous two lines may be the most lacking in visual imagery, these two virtually bask in it. The setting is late autumn when the bright, colorful leaves of a maple tree are dropping rapidly, foreshadowing the onset of winter. The tree seems to be eager for the new season, for it acts "like a woman in love with winter," who readily disrobes in anticipation of the pleasure it will bring. The sensuousness of these lines draws the reader back to lines 3 and 4, in which the human body and the "act of love" are also the prevalent images. Lines 8 and 9 juxtaposed against lines 6 and 7 make for a stunning contrast between the abstract and the concrete. They seem to imply that no matter what intellectual musings one may entertain, everything always comes back to the visible and the tangible.

Line 10

The "we" in this line refers to the poet and the reader, just as the "You" in line 7 is a direct address to the reader. Line 10 reflects a sentiment similar to that in line 6, but now there is no difference "in what we know." The word "Neither" is a direct reference back to line 6, for the two could easily be put together to read: "These three were not different, neither are we different in what we know." Hirshfield is adamant in assuring the reader of an overall human *sameness*, even though some people appear to have a greater understanding and a knack for unraveling the mysteries of the human mind.

Lines 11–12

These lines present a bit of their own mystery with the somewhat cryptic, somber description of a door simply existing, then opening, and then closing. Perhaps the door is like life, sometimes opening to various experiences and other times closed up, not showing what is going on inside. But, here, a "slip of light / stays" even after the door closes, implying a defiance of total darkness and unenlightenment. The bit of light shining on

the floor is "like a scrap of unreadable paper" lying there, the key word being "unreadable." The one who sees it may not be able to understand what it says, but its *presence* signifies the triumph of light over darkness, comprehension over obscurity.

Line 13

The final line of the poem continues the idea presented in lines 11 and 12, and it also returns to the rich imagery of lines 8 and 9. The slip of light that is compared to a scrap of paper is now compared to "one red leaf" from the maple tree mentioned earlier, which manages to survive winter with its color intact. Come spring, the snow melts and "releases" the leaf, and its presence, like the light that remains, implies the same triumph.

Themes

Awareness and Compassion

Awareness and compassion are themes likely derived from Hirshfield's study of Zen Buddhism, although the connection is invisible in her work. She has noted several times over the years that she does not wish to be labeled a "Zen poet," but readily acknowledges that the components of the religion have become organic to her poetry, her philosophy, and her lifestyle. In "Three Times My Life Has Opened," Hirshfield is keenly aware of her own being and of her relationship to the natural world as a human and, more specifically, as a woman. This self-awareness also makes her attentive to and compassionate toward other beings—in this case, the reader.

Being aware of what goes on in one's life may seem like a given. But most people who can report the facts of life experiences neglect to take the obvious a step further—a step into deeper understanding of not only what has happened but what it all means. Hirshfield's examination of the times her life "opened," as she calls it, includes a metaphorical analysis of where each event falls within the big picture of existence in general. She accepts the periods of "darkness and rain" that each human being inevitably goes through, and she makes no difference between these more dismal episodes and the better times of letting the body have its own pleasures and of the passion and enlightenment of "the fire that holds all." Her acute sense of *knowing* these experiences is as important as the experiences themselves. Her decision to put them into perspective with imagery that encompasses both the natural world (a maple leaf and the

Topics for Further Study

- Write a poem called "Three Times My Life Has Closed" and try to use a mixture of abstract and concrete imagery as Hirshfield does in her poem. Are you able to convey your meaning without revealing too much? Why or why not?

- Choose a religion or philosophy other than your own and write an essay describing its major tenets and where it is most popular in the world. Explain how this religion or philosophy has influenced contemporary followers and whether any significant changes have taken place in its teachings as a result.

- Why have thousands, possibly millions, of Americans turned to the practice of Zen Buddhism? How does Zen differ from mainstream Buddhism and why do the differences make it even more appealing to some people?

- If Hirshfield had decided to write a poem called "*Four* Times My Life Has Opened," what would that fourth event entail? Where would she have placed it within the body of the poem and why would that placement be significant in relation to the three times already mentioned? Try to make your answer "fit" the poem by writing from Hirshfield's philosophical perspective.

- Read the poem "Anasazi," written by Zen poet Gary Snyder, and explain how it compares or contrasts to Hirshfield's poem in its theme, style, and tone. Which poem do you find easier to understand or relate to? Why?

winter season) and philosophical intrigue (an anonymous door opening and closing) speaks of the vitality of each in creating a *wholeness*. The poet is not selfish with her awareness, for she brings readers directly into her thoughts and offers assurance, compassion, and understanding for each.

Despite the ambiguity and mystery of the first half of the poem, there are two lines in the second half that make the confusion take a back seat to a higher purpose. Hirshfield shows both respect for and understanding of a reader's naiveté in lines 7 and 10. She acknowledges that not all people can have the exact same knowledge, but she does not claim that any individual is the better or worse for it. Instead, her declaration that "You will recognize what I am saying or you will not" infers an acceptance of each person's own experiences and says, essentially, *It is ok if you do not get any of the specifics of my message because we are still the same in our efforts and our abilities.*

Transition

"Three Times My Life Has Opened" is a poem of movement, both figuratively and literally. The openings Hirshfield describes are actually periods of transition, and they are natural and healthy even when the moments seem less than desirable. The poet's point is that personal growth comes about through change—change that is sometimes pleasurable, sometimes challenging, but always more beneficial than stagnation. She represents her life's transitions figuratively with the natural elements of darkness, rain, and fire, as well as with a relationship between the body and mind, the physical taking on the mental act of remembering. In the second half of the poem, she likens the changes to the literal movements of maple leaves falling from a tree, silks falling from a woman's body, and the opening and closing of a door. In the final line, in which "one red leaf" is released by the snow in March, the implication is that sometimes transition is circular, just like the seasons of the year revolving one after the other in a continuous cycle. Hirshfield addresses the cyclical motion of transition in her essay "The Myriad Leaves of Words," from *Nine Gates*, in relating a koan, or riddle, to analyze a haiku by seventeenth-century Japanese poet Basho: "'All things return to the One,' a Zen koan states, then asks, 'What does the One return to?' The answer is not to be found in the conceptual mind, yet it swims through this poem like a speckled trout through a stream." The same may be said for Hirshfield's own poem, for, while the forward motion and the circular motion are clearly exposed in "Three Times My Life Has Opened," the destination, or the answer, is unclear, at best, and, perhaps, not to be found.

Style

Free Verse

Hirshfield writes in contemporary free verse, creating poems out of lines that may be easily read as prose sentences as well as verse. Although the style of "Three Times My Life Has Opened" does not involve any traditional pattern of meter or rhyme, it does include striking imagery and carefully placed pauses that give it an effective poetic *feel*. Some of the images are cloaked in enigmatic references that may defy complete understanding but still conjure mental pictures and intrigue the imagination. Ten readers may see ten different images when they consider a life opening "into darkness and rain" or into "the fire that holds all," but, undoubtedly, all ten experience vivid images. Hirshfield also uses very concrete descriptions of a maple tree toward the end of autumn when most of the leaves have fallen or are falling rapidly as winter approaches. This time ten different readers would likely have similar mental images, since the scene is one most people have witnessed. The same may be said for a woman letting her silk lingerie drop to the floor and the one leaf, still red, reappearing in springtime after surviving the winter. All these images are very graphic and make a good contrast to the more mysterious ones.

Sometimes free verse poems rely on *enjambment* for stylistic effect, meaning the running on of a thought from one line or stanza to the next without a syntactical break. In this poem, Hirshfield stops nearly half the lines with periods, forcing short sentences and frequent pauses throughout. Read the poem aloud, making full stops at each period, and listen to the slow, methodical, almost meditative rhythm that the pauses create. Although a specific metrical system is not identifiable, the poet is still able to mimic the strategy of such and to provide clear signals on how to read the work for its greatest effect.

Historical Context

The idea of personal enlightenment theology is not new to America, for various Oriental religious sects began showing up in the United States as early as the nineteenth century. Buddhism was introduced by two priests in San Francisco in 1898 and is still centered on the West Coast, although its popularity has spread across the country. Hinduism came to America via the Swami Vivekananada who introduced the religion at the World's Parliament of Religions in Chicago in 1893. The Self-Realization Fellowship, considered a more practical form of Hinduism, has developed since 1920, stressing greater personal powers through peace of mind and good health. In the 1960s, interest in Hinduism was renewed, especially among the younger generation of the counterculture, when the teachings of Maharishi Mahesh Yogi reached thousands of interested ears through his position as leader of the International Meditation Society. A lesser-known Oriental theology, Bahaism, also arose in the nineteenth century with its major philosophy touting the institution of a worldwide religion. Leaders of Bahaism stress the main themes of the world's three prominent religions and gain inspiration from the great teachers of Christianity, Judaism, and Islam. Although varying sects of these theologies and philosophies find a home with Americans of both Eastern and non-Eastern descent today, perhaps none is as popular among the greatest variety of people as Zen Buddhism.

The Zen form of Buddhism originated in Japan after the arrival in that nation of Buddhism itself, spreading from India into China and then throughout Asia more than two thousand years ago. For centuries, the religion seemed confined to the Far East, but recent times have seen a proliferation throughout the entire world. What attracted young people, including Hirshfield, in 1960s and 1970s America to California to study the ideology of Buddhism and to put its teaching into practice most likely lies in the Zen sect's notion of transforming the *self* to find a oneness with the world and ultimate enlightenment for the individual. Above all, Zen stresses deep meditation by its students, preferably performed alone, although Zen centers attract thousands of people who meditate together in groups. Many followers who come to the Zen religion—or philosophy, as some prefer to call it— belong to centers and attend regular meditation sessions for the rest of their lives. Still others, like Hirshfield, dedicate a sizable chunk of their lives, such as eight years for the poet, and then take what they have learned back into the real world of their everyday lives. There, Zen teaching manifests itself in the things its students say and do—from the most miniscule task to major life decisions—without an intrusion of philosophical language or doctrine. Actually, it is the lack of doctrine and typical religious dogma that is the main attraction to Zen Buddhism for many Americans living in the late twentieth and early twenty-first century. This does not necessarily mean a turning away from traditional theology or worship of a supreme being, as is inherent in more common religions, but it does imply a hunger for greater personal understanding and realization in a time of political, economical, and, perhaps most importantly, emotional instabilities.

Because the U.S. Census Bureau no longer records religious affiliation, estimates of the number of Buddhists in America in the late 1990s cannot be technically determined. However, the trend toward Zen has been unmistakable, and, today, most analysts put the figure at between two and three million. In the midst of presidential scandal, ongoing battles in the Middle East, a roller coaster ride on the stock market, and sensationalized murder stories on the nightly news involving everyone from a football hero to a six-year-old beauty queen, the last decade of the twentieth century had people clamoring for some kind of spiritual comfort and intellectual understanding. Sometimes this need took the form of stronger family bonds and a return to more traditional church-going, and sometimes it meant individuals taking time to pause their lives long enough to observe and appreciate what was most important to them. Some turned to the country's most dominant religions of Christianity and Judaism, and some turned to Zen Buddhism, Islam, and any number of less established sects, as well as to self-created methods of understanding and coping with the world they live in. Although Hirshfield wrote "Three Times My Life Has Opened" and the rest of the poems for *The Lives of the Heart* before the tragedy of September 11, 2001, the same desire for peace of mind and personal enlightenment is just as vital for Americans today—and likely much more so.

Critical Overview

Hirshfield's poetry has been well received by scholarly critics and general readers since she published her first work in the 1980s. Most often, she is praised for her ability to present everyday life experiences in light of their deeper, spiritual meaning, but without becoming erudite or lapsing into philosophical rhetoric. Her use of simple language and soft tone belie the true force of her poetry's messages, and many critics have cited such in their reviews. In a book review of *The Lives of the Heart* for *Booklist*, critic Donna Seaman writes that Hirshfield's "imagery is simple in form but iridescent in implication; her meditative focus on stillness is curiously provocative and illuminating, and the veracity of all that Hirshfield has to say about forbearance and loss makes itself felt first and then is clearly understood." Seaman goes on to say that the poet "celebrates the epic strength of the heart, the sweetness of life, and the value of leaving things as they are"

Red leaves emerging from the snow

and that readers of her work experience "long moments of peace" while engaged with the poems. Very seldom is a writer credited with providing a reader such a gift.

Hirshfield has also been praised for her essays—which often go hand in hand with her poems—and for the readings of her work that draw large crowds. As poet, teacher, and critic Peter Harris states in an article for *Ploughshares*, "Because her poetry is pellucid [transparently clear] and speaks directly to the heart, it is not surprising that readings, from Maine to California, have given her a second means of sustenance." Any occasional reader of poetry understands the significance of Harris's statement and what it means about the acceptance of Hirshfield's work: one who actually makes money by reading her poetry in contemporary America must have something special going on indeed.

Criticism

Pamela Steed Hill

Hill is the author of a poetry collection, has published widely in literary journals, and is an editor for a university publications department. In the

What Do I Read Next?

- *Buddhist Women on the Edge: Contemporary Perspective from the Western Frontier* (1996), edited by Marianne Dresser, consists largely of non-Oriental women discussing the importance of Buddhist thought in their own lives. Hirshfield's "What Is the Emotional Life of a Buddha?" is included.

- Gary Snyder is one of the more prominent Zen poets writing in America today. One of his most popular collections, *Turtle Island* (1974), is also the most revealing of Zen influence in America. The title comes from a Native American term for the continent of North America, and Snyder's poems speak to a desire to reclaim the environmental harmony that once existed here. This book won the Pulitzer Prize in 1975.

- In 2000, *Newsweek* magazine's religion editor, Kenneth Woodward, published *The Book of Miracles: The Meaning of the Miracle Stories in Christianity, Judaism, Buddhism, Hinduism, and Islam*. Here, Woodward uses his easily understood, conversational style to relate the details of how many well-known miracle stories came about. The book is very accessible to the general reader and avoids didacticism in favor of telling a good story.

- Hirshfield is not only a poet but a translator of poetry as well, primarily Japanese. Her 1988 publication of *The Ink Dark Moon: Love Poems by Ono No Komachi and Izumi Shikibu* is evidence of her notable skill in translating the sensual, intriguing poetry of these two Japanese women who lived between the ninth and eleventh centuries A.D. These love poems address the poets' longing for intimacy as well as their fulfillment or disillusionment.

- Though published over twenty years ago in 1980, George Lakoff and Mark Johnson's *Metaphors We Live By* is still one of the best discussions on how the human mind uses metaphorical references to learn and to develop. The book is very readable even though its subject is philosophical, and it is especially appealing to anyone who enjoys writing prose or poetry. The book is full of examples that back up the authors' viewpoints, and it brings some tired old metaphors into new and interesting light.

---

following essay, Hill addresses Hirshfield's claim that poetry is "a path toward new understanding and transformation" and suggests that this belief is the basis for Hirshfield's poem.

It is not difficult to be cynical about the world. It is not hard to let pessimism and doubt thwart any glimmers of serenity that show themselves among dark thoughts and dark days. And it is not unusual for the human mind to surrender to despair when confronted with the more challenging task of going forward in spite of it all, of accepting what comes and moving on. Transition is tough. It means one must face something new, something possibly threatening, possibly life-changing. But then there are those who say: *that's what it's all about—change.* Hirshfield is one of those, and her poetry

speaks eloquently to that effect. The words, like the poet herself, defy negativity even while acknowledging its presence, even when it seems like the dark days are here to stay. "Three Times My Life Has Opened" is a poem of defiance, but it does not stop there. Out of the resolve comes transformation, and out of the transformation comes understanding—that elusive goal so often cast off as unattainable.

Sometimes a poem and the poet are so intimately connected that the reader becomes an intruder—although a *welcomed* one—peering into private thoughts and personal moments. In this poem, the connection is definitely intimate, but the reader is not excluded from it. Instead, Hirshfield twice directly addresses the reader, drawing him or

> *'Three Times My Life Has Opened' not only acknowledges the transience of life experiences, but it also welcomes and even celebrates it."*

her in to share the times the poet's life has "opened," even though "you will recognize" what she is saying "or you will not." Here, *feeling* and *acceptance* are of greater importance than recognition, for they precede whatever enlightenment is eventually to come. To avoid getting bogged down in esoteric philosophizing or abstract assumptions, it is best to let the poet herself explain. Hirshfield has given several interviews over the years, but one of the most interesting and revealing occurred in 1997 just as her collection of poems *The Lives of the Heart* and her collection of essays *Nine Gates: Entering the Mind of Poetry* were hitting the shelves. A writer for the *Atlantic Monthly*, Katie Bolick, spoke at length with the poet and published the interview as "Some Place Not Yet Known" with the magazine's online counterpart, *Atlantic Unbound*. In it, Hirshfield states, "I see poetry as a path toward new understanding and transformation, and so I've looked at . . . poetry's gestures in the broadest sense, in an effort to feel and learn what they offer from the inside." It is safe to assume that feeling and learning were a large part of the creation of "Three Times My Life Has Opened," and even if the reader's mind is left unsure of the poem's *specifics*, its "gestures" speak plainly to the heart.

One of those gestures is the nod Hirshfield gives to life's unhappy moments, the "darkness and rain" that inevitably descend into personal, social, or professional endeavors and that are seen here as opportunities for growth. There is no evidence of the nature of the unhappiness in this poem because that is not what is important. As a matter of fact, the moment is quickly swept aside to move on to the next time life "opened" and the one following that. The descriptions of these times come in rapid succession, as though to hurry up and get to the

main point, which is wrapped up in one line: "These three were not different." While readers may initially think the events are indeed different, another of the poem's gestures helps us understand that the poet knows what she is talking about when she says that they are not. Hirshfield turns to concrete description to draw everyone in to the same picture. Most people can relate to seeing the bright colors of autumn leaves, and most can envision a windy, late fall day when those leaves begin blowing from the trees in large swoops, eventually leaving the limbs bare like a woman who has disrobed, "dropping the colored silks." Suddenly, the abstract gestures have been brought into a real light. No matter how remote from true understanding life's openings may seem, they all come down to "a slip of light" that "stays" or "the one red leaf" in March that symbolizes an intact survival of inevitable transformation.

"Three Times My Life Has Opened" not only acknowledges the transience of life experiences, but it also welcomes and even celebrates it. In Bolick's interview with Hirshfield, the poet states that "It's easy to say yes to being happy, but it is harder to agree to grief and loss and transience and to the fact that desire is fathomless and ultimately unfillable. At some point I realized that you don't get a full human life if you try to cut off one end of it." This explains why the darkness and rain are no different from what the body remembers during lovemaking and the fire that encompasses everything. If the poet wrote only of the good things—of passion and love and pleasant memories—she would not be living a "full human life," which she believes one must do to be enlightened. As if to show the reward in accepting life's transitions, good or bad, Hirshfield takes the poem in a positive direction, making sure it ends on an optimistic note. Even though the door that opens closes immediately, there is a light left visible, a sign of hope for the human spirit. The final metaphor is even more encouraging, as a single red leaf endures the transformation of seasons, outlasting the harshest one to show itself again in spring.

Given all the evidence in this poem that it speaks to transformation as a positive notion, that it is essentially a tool for allowing the poet to achieve deeper understanding, the reader may still ask, "So why not just come out and say it? Why not just tell us what those three times life opened really were?" These are fair questions, especially since this poem is so *likeable*, so appealing to readers that we really want to grasp everything about it. But the focus here is on how the human mind really works, how most people achieve understanding and actually learn something about themselves or about events in their lives. Often, it is done through metaphoric expressions or thoughts, those indirect glances that may provide better insight than intellectual stare downs. Think of how frequently and casually human beings describe the way they feel by using metaphors: a man asks his wife how she feels after a hard day at work and she replies, "Like I was run over by a bus." A couple of teenagers who keep breaking up and getting back together probably think love is "like a roller coaster." An angry man may be told not to "blow his top,"and a cowboy at a disco is "a fish out of water." Songwriters would be out of business if they could not use metaphors, as would most speech writers and, of course, poets. In "Three Times My Life Has Opened," the messages *depend* on metaphoric imagery. Instead of bluntly stating that once life opened into bad times, depression, sadness, or anger, Hirshfield covers all those possibilities with one description: "darkness and rain." Rather than explaining how positive outcomes can emerge from dubious beginnings, the poet *shows* the reader a beautiful autumn leaf still sporting its bright color in spite of being buried under snow for a few months. Ironically, the messages are made stronger by their indirection. As Hirshfield puts it: "instead of simply saying 'I'm sad,' a poem describes rainfall or the droop of a branch." Fortunately for the reader, Hirshfield puts this tactic to wonderful use in her work.

If it is true, then, that this poem is based on a desire to understand and to transform the self, there is one further, similar *use* for poetry that is also at work here. Toward the end of the *Atlantic* interview, Hirshfield states, "And so I see poetry not as an attempt to accurately depict an experience already known but as the making of a new experience that presses into some place not yet known." In this poem, the three times life opened are certainly not "accurately" depicted for the reader, but it seems that they may not be all that much clearer to the poet herself. And that is okay. The darkness and rain, the fire, whatever the body carries within it—all serve as paths to something beyond what they actually are. The door that opens and closes may be a real door, but it is also a mechanism of new experience. It provides the means by which the "slip of light" is able to remain on the floor "like a scrap of unreadable paper." This latter phrase carries even more significance when considered along with the desire to move into "some place not yet known." One may be tempted to con-

note "unreadable" with frustration or inability, but that is not the implication here. Although specific words are not discernible, there is a *feeling* of comfort in the presence of the paper, or in the presence of the light. Compared to the concrete definition of something, a feeling leaves more room for "the making of a new experience," for it is more pliable, more open, and more receptive. Consider, also, the statement, "Neither are we different in what we know." At first, this notion seems to come out of nowhere and even to be out of place in the poem. But it is actually a connection between the poet and the reader that implies both shared *known* and shared *unknown* experiences. Essentially anyone can describe something that has happened, telling who, what, when, and where, but anyone can do something else as well. As Hirshfield puts it, "My job as a human being as well as a writer is to feel as thoroughly as possible the experience that I am part of, and then press it a little further." This may be a bit cumbersome or pose too much expectation on people who find it easier just to let things occur as they will and then either simply forget them or, if necessary, react as nonconfrontationally as possible. Most of us are not keen on the idea of feeling something thoroughly and then pressing it still further, and yet this poet and this poem insist that all of us are capable of it. One must *want* to achieve enlightenment before it can be accomplished, but the desire is not always a given.

Without Hirshfield's own input on her thoughts about poetry in general and on the making of *The Lives of the Heart* in particular, the final poem in that collection would still be engaging and insightful, though perhaps not as much so. Still, it is a good lesson to learn about both writing and reading poetry: sometimes feelings are more important than factual accounts; sometimes sideways glances allow more space to muse and ponder; and sometimes letting the words flow as they may leads to a new understanding that would have otherwise gone unnoticed.

Source: Pamela Steed Hill, Critical Essay on "Three Times My Life Has Opened," in *Poetry for Students*, The Gale Group, 2002.

Michelle Prebilic

Prebilic is an independent author who writes and analyses children's literature. She holds degrees in psychology and business. In this essay, Prebilic discusses how Jane Hirshfield's poem invites readers to experience the wholeness of love, including its dark side.

> *Vulnerability allows the clothing to be stripped away, the leaves to fall, so that the unabashed presentation of love can be enjoyed."*

The poem "Three Times My Life Has Opened," in *Lives of the Heart* by Jane Hirshfield, shares three significant events that caused the speaker's life to be changed in a memorable way. Hirshfield's introductory line proclaims that her life has opened three times. Opened to what, the readers do not know, and this intrigue draws readers to examine the poem repeatedly. This attentiveness will enable the reader to grasp a deeper meaning that can ultimately enlighten or transcend the reader's life. This action is precisely Hirshfield's attempt. She hopes to lure readers into attentiveness, to give them things to think about that will have them eventually walk away from the poem with a greater awareness of themselves, of life. This exercise helps readers live life more fully.

An interpretation of this poem requires a brief insight into Hirshfield's background and influences. Hirshfield's proclivity for writing emerged at an early age; at the age of nine, she purchased her first book, a collection of haiku. As a young adult at Princeton, she created an independent major in creative writing and literature in translation. This shows her willingness to transcend structure and create a framework for herself. Next, according to Peter Harris in the *Ploughshares* article "About Jane Hirshfield," "[w]hat began as a month's commitment turned into eight years of study with the San Francisco Zen Center, including three years . . . living in deep wilderness." Through these experiences, Hirshfield developed her "tripod" of vocations: teacher, reader, and editor, to support herself as a poet.

Her openness to all forms of poetry shows in Hirshfield's depth of writing style. Her influences include both Eastern and Western traditions. According to Hirshfield, in her biography in *Contemporary Women Poets*, "Greek and Roman lyrics, the English sonnet . . . Whitman and Dickinson . . .

Eliot to Akhmatova to Cavafy to Neruda—all have added something" to her perspective and style. Hirshfield's willingness to be open to life, to create her world, and to stay attentive to the moment have promoted a wholeness in herself that she began to express early in her career. This foundation led to her philosophy (as quoted by Harris) that "poetry's job is to discover wholeness and create wholeness, including the wholeness of the fragmentary and the broken."

In considering Hirshfield's influences, a reader cannot help but acknowledge the art of haiku, a precise Japanese verse form. Haiku presents the aspects of nature and contains a reference to a season of the year. Hirshfield uses this literary technique in reference to the maple tree. As the maple tree symbolically steps from her leaves, she leaves herself bare and vulnerable. Hirshfield presents this analogy expertly. Her presentation symbolizes the vulnerability of love. Vulnerability seldom arises in our society as something to cherish or about which to boast. Instead, people consider vulnerability a weakness, a despicable quality to overcome, to make stronger, and to get beyond. Yet, without vulnerability, love would not be complete. Vulnerability allows the clothing to be stripped away, the leaves to fall, so that the unabashed presentation of love can be enjoyed. One cannot truly love without vulnerability. It is this point that Hirshfield strives to make; only through attentiveness to love and acceptance of all of its facets, including the broken ones, can one truly find wholeness and lead a rich life. Her use of haiku to present this analogy works well.

Readers experience Hirshfield's tie to Zen Buddhism as she describes these experiences of the opening of the heart. Zen aims to achieve a state of spiritual enlightenment through meditation called *satori*. As Harris notes,

> the emphases on *compassion*, on the preexistent *unity of subject and object*, on *nature*, on the self-sufficient suchness of *being*, on the daunting challenge of accepting *transitoriness*—all are central to Buddhism.

Hirshfield's attentiveness typifies the thoughtfulness pursued in the practice of Zen Buddhism. She uses simple, short sentences with meaningful words to draw readers into the experience of wholeness.

If readers quietly reflect on "Three Times My Life Has Opened," these innermost ideas of Buddhism emerge. Hirshfield shows compassion when she says that "neither are we different in what we know." She implies unity of spirit. Her use of nature—darkness, rain, fire, a maple tree—develops a unity of subject and object. By using these Earth elements, she suggests the preexistent unity between human experience and natural occurrence. Hirshfield uses both positive and negative symbolic images, such as an act of love and darkness. This approach encourages readers to recognize the full experience of love, not just the elements of pleasure most commonly associated with it.

Readers will note the Buddhist theme of *being* when Hirshfield acknowledges in her verse that they may or may not identify with what she is saying. These lines display Hirshfield's compassion and understanding to readers; it confirms the complexity of her ideas. Nevertheless, Hirshfield gently prods readers on a journey of self-discovery much like the "one red leaf the snow releases in March." Hirshfield hopes that her creativity and attentiveness to things will be contagious and help others to learn and from there, lead a more meaningful life.

Hirshfield starts readers on this journey by beginning her poem with the analogy of darkness and rain. In five simple words "Once, into darkness and rain," Hirshfield immediately gives readers the sense of the completeness of her poem. It brings readers to the awareness that opening to life does not mean experiencing only joy and contentment; darkness and pain are an integral and unavoidable part of life and love.

To examine the deeper meanings of this poem, readers must take some time to focus on each element. At a glance, rain symbolizes the unhappiness or grief caused by an event; writers regularly use it in literature to represent sadness. Darkness in an emotional sense also means sadness, loss, and emptiness. Yet, if one focuses on each element individually, as Hirshfield suggests, additional ideas come to mind.

For example, rain no longer is just water falling from the sky. Readers find that it varies in size of drop, speed of fall, and intensity of the storm. Raindrops can be small and round. Larger drops flatten due to the force of air flowing around them. The largest raindrops alternate between a flattened shape and a stretched out shape. Likewise, many factors affect how rain forms and falls. Storms can be light or heavy, with many variations in between. Only undistracted attention to the raindrops and their journey brings about a full understanding of what rain actually is. Hirshfield's intention is to use nature and elements of unity to bring a deeper perspective of things into readers' awareness.

Hirshfield continues, stating that the speaker's life opened when entering the act of love. This experience invoked a memory of "what the body carries at all time within it." This phrase requires mindfulness in interpretation; it shows extraordinary depth since Hirshfield does not explicitly state what she means. Hirshfield suggests that the "something" that stays with humans becomes more profound with the experience of entering into an act of love. Perhaps entering the act of love may make readers more aware of their hearts, their intentions, their love for another, and their passions.

The third opening occurs "Once to the fire that holds all." Since the times of ancient Greece, people considered fire to be one of the four basic elements of life. Its mysteries have intrigued and frustrated people for centuries. On the surface, fire is the heat and light that comes from burning substances. Yet, a deeper perspective unveils a new outlook. Three conditions must exist before a fire can be made. There must be a substance that can burn. Substances may burn in different ways. The fuel must be heated to its ignition temperature, and there must be plenty of oxygen, which usually comes from the air. Fire takes different shapes, burns in many colors and intensities.

Likewise, in literature, fire can be tremendously complex. It can be used to represent light and the heavens. It can stand for aggression such as a fire-breathing dragon, or an act of God. Symbolically, fire may be a deep desire for someone or something, or a hatred and revenge that's left smoldering. Hirshfield uses fire as a symbol of a desire "that holds all." One assumes that this fire ignited and opened her up to greater attentiveness in life, a deep meaningful experience.

The poem presents darkness, rain, love, and fire and calls on a unity of spirit. "Neither are we different in what we know." Although readers' experiences may be different, and each element may invoke a unique perspective to the each reader, Hirshfield draws on the commonality of human experience. "There is a door. It opens. Then it is closed." What readers get out of it depends on their level of attentiveness, their openness to transformation. Hirshfield notes that "a slip of light stays" after the door closes. It may be that only a faint memory stays behind, like an "unreadable paper left on the floor." On the other hand, it may leave a far deeper meaning, like the "one red leaf the snow releases in March." Regardless, experiences leave some meaning.

Hirshfield makes the point that the meaning depends on the quality of attentiveness. In "Jane Hirshfield in Conversation with Judith Moore," published in *Poetry Daily*, she says that through attentiveness

we can know the nature and qualities of our . . . existence—the entrance gate [to] . . . know it, taste it, consider it, work with it as a potter works with clay.

Only using attentiveness can readers make meaning of Hirshfield's contrasting images. She presents love, desire, and passion along with sadness, darkness, and loss. Hirshfield does not remark on the link between these images but leaves the blending of them to the reader. As a reader absorbs the poem's effects, meanings about the experiences of love and life emerge and grow.

The wholeness of life depends on the level of attentiveness. Thus, the red leaf hangs powerfully in the silence at the end of the poem. It lands brightly on the landscape, clearly out of place for the season, yet naturally occurring. It is not something planned, something contrived. Yet, it concludes that the quality of the experience depends on attentiveness. Hirshfield hopes to help each reader to be receptive to the light and the dark. Both elements add to life's richness, its wholeness.

Source: Michelle Prebilic, Critical Essay on "Three Times My Life Has Opened," in *Poetry for Students*, The Gale Group, 2002.

Kate Covintree

Covintree is a graduate of Randolph-Macon Women's College with a degree in English. In this essay, Covintree explores the structure of Hirshfield's poem and the poem's direct attempt to connect with the reader.

Jane Hirshfield's poem "Three Times My Life Has Opened," the very last poem in her collection entitled *Lives of the Heart*, speaks to the idea of personal revelation and discovery. Almost expressly in the middle of the poem, Hirshfield directly addresses the reader, saying "You will recognize what I am saying or you will not." With this statement, she challenges readers to a more careful examination of both the poem and the self.

Hirshfield's poem is thirteen lines total and comprised of nine short sentences and three long sentences. Hirshfield carefully uses both line and sentence. A line is the grouping of words that comprises one row of writing. Many sentences take up more than one line, and some lines do not hold a complete sentence. Many poets are keenly aware of the difference, and for Hirshfield, she has broken her long sentences into the poetic space of three or four lines each. In doing this, Hirshfield created intentional breaks in her sentences and indents the poem at these line breaks. What is produced is a form to the poem of alternating long and short lines, visually enhanced by the indentations. This self-invented style determines how the poem is read.

The first seven lines of the poem catalog, or list, the times life has opened for the speaker. The first line, a repeat of the title, introduces the list that is to follow. The seventh line, briefly explains what is cataloged. Each of the three instances in the middle of these bookends, begins with the word, "Once," as if each holds equal weight and transience. Though the second example is longer than the others, it is no more detailed or descriptive.

All three are filled with images that are both distinct and unspecific. Hirshfield does not specify the particulars of the "darkness and rain" the speaker has encountered. Nor does she define what type of "act of love" has been entered into or give details as to what the "fire that holds all" is. All three examples could have literal definitions, (it gets dark at night, it rains, someone is having sex, fire consumes) but they can also be open to interpretation (depression, joy, loss). This personal interpretation is part of the poem's goal. As Hirshfield herself stated in a 1997 interview with Katie Bolick in *Atlantic Unbound*, "part of poetry's core activity, both within an individual and within a culture, is to attend to and make visible what Jung called the shadow life."

In each of these three sentences, it is clear the speaker is not describing the same situation. However, it is also clear that her experience to all three is similar. It could be interpreted that these three instances describe stages of life. "Darkness and rain" could be birth. Life could be represented in "what the body carries at all times within it / and starts to remember each time it enters into / the act of love." "The fire that holds all" could be the inevitability of death. Hirshfield has described three stages that are all related and all powerful. However, more importantly, what makes them similar is the revelation stated in the first line. Through these three moments, the speaker's life "has opened."

Then, as alluded to earlier, the poem turns in its focus with the speaker directly addressing the audience and saying, "[y]ou will recognize what I am saying or you will not." Now, the reader is no longer observing someone else but is suddenly challenged to reexamine the earlier catalog for personal life-opening experiences that equal the descriptions Hirshfield lists. As the poet shares in *Atlantic Unbound*, Hirshfield uses poetry as "a place where the thinking of the heart, mind, and body come together." The general statements in this poem allow the reader to inquire within him or herself, generating a personal examination for each reader. If the reader cannot relate to these, the reader is drawn to remember or create his or her own possible list. Has my life opened? When? How? What was my experience?

If self-reflection could still prove difficult, Hirshfield brings the speaker and the reader a new experience, the observation of a maple in fall. The speaker personifies this tree as a woman undressing for her lover, winter. This active example parallels the second experience in the earlier list. Both are two of the longest sentences in the poem. Both reflect on love. In that second listing, the speaker states that her life opened "into what the body carries at all times within it / and starts to remember each time it enters into / the act of love." By shedding a tree of leaves, something a tree carries at all times, because of the tree's love for the next season, Hirshfield brings a more specific understanding to the earlier line.

What is then exposed for the tree is nakedness. Yet, this is a nakedness that is filled with clarity and choice. It is the opportunity to recognize an aspect of the self that is often otherwise hidden. Human bodies do not carry leaves, of course, but when one "enters into / the act of love" what humans do carry is both released and exposed like the leaves—"dropping the colored silks." With this release, the speaker is enlightened and the poet's intentions are seen. "My job as a human being as well as a writer," Hirshfield told *Atlantic Unbound*, "is to feel as thoroughly as possible the experience that I am a part of, and then press it a little further."

This is the hope, but this same metaphor also explores a converse idea to enlightenment. A tree shedding its leaves for winter is a common, simple experience. Whether the poet observes this, the leaves will fall to the ground. The fact the poet sees the experience and can then personalize it is of major importance. The poet is witness to a moment of clarity for this personified tree and her surrender to winter love. But this is the poet's recognition; someone else (even the tree itself) could miss this moment. In this way, the body from earlier often misses the experience of clarity, though the potential, "what the body carries at all times," is ever present. The opportunity for clarity is continuously

> *The poet is witness to a moment of clarity for this personified tree and her surrender to winter love."*

made available, but for the poet, and the reader, the actual ability for recognition is limited.

In this way, the final four lines of the poem reinforce the ease and difficulty of discovering clarity. It is accessible, "[t]here is a door." It is made present, [i]t opens." It is hidden from us, "[t]hen it is closed. Then, each of us is simply left with the memory. By breaking the first line in the middle of a thought with the word "slip" and enjambing the statement "[b]ut a slip / of light stays" Hirshfield uses form to help her in two ways. First, the slip reinforces the door image written earlier in the line, as you can visualize the door opened just slightly or the cracks in the door letting the light through. Secondly, putting slip at the end of the line allows the reader to stop on the word for a moment and recognize the accidental nature of the clarity that has been shown.

This is what the speaker has been left with, not the immediate instance of clarity, but the knowledge that it has been available. The poet is keenly aware of what was present but is forced to let it go. The speaker is also aware that the memory is not equal to full understanding nor as useful. However, the memory, "the one red leaf the snow releases / in March," is sustainable and sufficient.

Source: Kate Covintree, Critical Essay on "Three Times My Life Has Opened," in *Poetry for Students*, The Gale Group, 2002.

Sources

Bolick, Katie, "Some Place Not Yet Known: An Interview with Jane Hirshfield," in *Atlantic Unbound*, http://www.theatlantic.com/unbound/bookauth/jhirsh.htm (September 18, 1997; last accessed: March 19, 2002).

Harris, Peter, "About Jane Hirshfield," in *Ploughshares*, Vol. 24, No. 1, Spring 1998, pp. 199–205.

Hoey, Adam, "Hirshfield, Jane (B.)," in *Contemporary Women Poets*, St. James Press, 1998, pp. 166–68.

Hirshfield, Jane, *The Lives of the Heart*, HarperCollins, 1997.

———, "The Myriad Leaves of Words," in *Nine Gates: Entering the Mind of Poetry*, HarperCollins, 1997, pp. 82–106.

———, "Poetry and the Mind of Indirection," in *Nine Gates: Entering the Mind of Poetry*, HarperCollins, 1997, pp. 107–26.

Kaufman, Ellen, Review of *The Lives of the Heart*, in *Library Journal*, Vol. 122, No. 16, October 1, 1997, p. 86.

Moore, Judith, "Jane Hirshfield in Conversation with Judith Moore," in *Poetry Daily*, Poetry Daily Association, 2002.

Seaman, Donna, Review of *The Lives of the Heart*, in *Booklist*, Vol. 94, No. 1, 1997, p. 53.

Whipple, Elizabeth, "Writers Talk about the Literary Life," in *Library Journal*, Vol. 122, No. 10, June 1, 1997, p. S18.

Further Reading

Brown, Kurt, ed., *Facing the Lion: Writers on Life and Craft*, Beacon Press, 1996.

This is a collection of recorded lectures given by poets and fiction writers at various writing conferences across the country, including one by Hirshfield. The editor saw fit to title the entire collection after Hirshfield's "Facing the Lion: The Way of Shadow and Light in Some Twentieth-Century Poems," as it metaphorically addresses the "lions" that many writers face in trying to make language as effective and important as possible.

Hirshfield, Jane, *Given Sugar, Given Salt*, HarperCollins, 2001.

This is Hirshfield's latest poetry collection, and, like those before it, the work has been praised for its accessibility to all readers as well as its richness in imagery and creative insights. It reads almost as a continuation to *The Lives of the Heart*.

———, *Nine Gates: Entering the Mind of Poetry*, HarperCollins, 1997.

Published at the same time as *The Lives of the Heart*, this collection of essays by Hirshfield makes a useful "companion piece" to the poetry book. The essays provide detailed insight into her "ideas about the art of poetry and its workings," as she describes in the preface.

———, ed., *Women in Praise of the Sacred: 43 Centuries of Spiritual Poetry by Women*, HarperCollins, 1994.

This collection includes poems, prayers, and songs by women throughout history from a wide variety of religious backgrounds. Hirshfield provides biographies and insightful commentary to accompany the poems, and her selection of poets serves to illuminate the values she incorporates in her own work.

Ways to Live

William Stafford

1998

"Ways to Live" was written from July 19 through 21 of 1993, just over a month before William Stafford's death in August of that year. Stafford was well known as a hard worker and diligent poet, often producing a poem a day. This poem comes from his book *The Way It Is: New & Selected Poems,* in a section containing poems that Stafford wrote in his final days that is titled "There's a Thread You Follow." It is a mark of Stafford's dedication to poetry that this collection contains a poem written on the morning of his death at age seventy-nine.

Stafford's method of producing "Ways to Live" is evident in the final product. On the one hand, it is clearly more spontaneous and loosely knit than poems that have been worked over and revised constantly. The four sections could almost stand as separate poems themselves and have only a thin, abstract relationship to each other. On the other hand, Stafford shows the poetic sensibilities that developed over years of daily practice so that even a poem that he had no time to revise shows more clarity and coherence than another poet might get from working and reworking a piece. This is a poem about growing old and giving up life gracefully, and it has the authority of having been written by an expert on the subject, a revered wordsmith at the very end of his life.

William Stafford

Author Biography

William Stafford was born in 1914 in Hutchinson, Kansas. His parents instilled in him moral values and a decidedly nonconformist, independent view of the world. During the Great Depression of the 1930s, the family moved frequently within Kansas. Stafford worked constantly, delivering papers, harvesting beets, or apprenticing as an electrician's assistant. He attended junior college and then the University of Kansas, where he received a bachelor's degree in 1937. When America entered World War II in 1941, Stafford registered as a conscientious objector. In place of military service, he worked in government camps in a program of "alternative service under civilian direction." Throughout the war, he was sent to California, Illinois, and Arkansas, where he was involved in soil conservation projects and battling forest fires. The experience of standing up for his pacifist beliefs during a war that was widely supported made Stafford comfortable with following his own ideas. It also honed him as a writer; because the labor assigned to conscientious objectors was so grueling, he was too tired to write at night, so Stafford and some of the other men in the camps would rise before the sun to write, a practice he continued throughout his life.

During the war, Stafford met and married Dorothy Frantz, a school teacher whose father was a minister. He returned to the University of Kansas after the war and earned a master's degree before moving to San Francisco to work for Church World Services, a relief agency. His memoir about life in the conscientious objector camps, *Down in My Heart*, was published in 1947. He wrote constantly and had several poems published, and then in 1948, he accepted a teaching position at Lewis and Clark college in Portland, Oregon, with which he was affiliated off and on for the rest of his life.

During the first years of the 1950s, he attended the writing program at the University of Iowa, receiving a Ph.D. in 1954. It was not until 1960, when he was forty-six, that Stafford published his first book of poetry with a small press in southern California, selling a few hundred copies. It was his second book, *Traveling Through the Dark*, that made Stafford a major figure on the poetry scene. That book won the National Book Award for 1963. The following year, Stafford won the Shelley Memorial Award from the Poetry Society of America, and two years later, he received a Guggenheim fellowship. Stafford continually wrote and published and kept on teaching in Portland. Throughout the 1960s and 1970s, the generation that opposed the war in Vietnam embraced Stafford's meditative, pacifist beliefs, and he was frequently invited to be a guest speaker at college campuses around the country. Stafford also toured on behalf of the U.S. Information Agency to Egypt, Iran, Pakistan, India, Nepal, and Bangladesh in 1972. Stafford retired from teaching in 1980 but continued to write throughout the rest of his life. "Ways to Live" was written within months of his death in 1993.

Poem Text

1. India

In India in their lives they happen
again and again, being people or
animals. And if you live well
your next time could be even better.

That's why they often look into your eyes   5
and you know some far-off story
with them and you in it, and some
animal waiting over at the side.

Who would want to happen just once?
It's too abrupt that way, and   10
when you're wrong, it's too late
to go back—you've done it forever.

And you can't have that soft look when you
pass, the way they do it in India.

2. Having It Be Tomorrow

Day, holding its lantern before it,   15
moves over the whole earth slowly
to brighten that edge and push it westward.
Shepherds on upland pastures begin fires
for breakfast, beads of light that extend
miles of horizon. Then it's noon and   20
coasting toward a new tomorrow.

If you're in on that secret, a new land
will come every time the sun goes
climbing over it, and the welcome of children
will remain every day new in your heart.   25
Those around you don't have it new,
and they shake their heads turning gray every
morning when the sun comes up. And you laugh.

3. Being Nice and Old

After their jobs are done old people
cackle together. They look back and shiver,   30
all of that was so dizzying when it happened;
and now if there is any light at all it
knows how to rest on the faces of friends.
And any people you don't like, you just turn
the page a little more and wait while they   35
find out what time is and begin to bend
lower; or you can just turn away and
let them drop off the edge of the world.

4. Good Ways to Live

At night outside it all moves or
almost moves—trees, grass,   40
touches of wind. The room you have
in the world is ready to change.
Clouds parade by, and stars in their
configurations. Birds from far
touch the fabric around them—you can   45
feel their wings move. Somewhere under
the earth it waits, that emanation
of all things. It breathes. It pulls you
slowly out through doors or windows
and you spread in the thin halo of night mist.   50

Poem Summary

Lines 1–4

The first section of "Ways to Live" is subtitled "India." The most common religion in India,
Hinduism, holds firm to the belief that all souls are
returned to Earth in new bodies after their deaths—
the doctrine of "transmigration" or "reincarnation."
The first line of this poem mirrors the circular motion of reincarnation with repetition, using "in"
twice (actually, three times, since the sound is part
of "India") and putting "they" and "their" close together. This same effect occurs in the second line

Media Adaptations

- Magnolia Films of San Anselmo, California, released a video entitled *William Stafford and
  Robert Bly* (1994), which documents the friendship between the two poets.

- An audiocassette of *Willliam Stafford's Last
  Reading* is available from Bancroft Poetry
  Archive Sound Recordings. It was taped at the
  Portland Poetry Festival in Oregon on August
  13, 1993, just weeks before the poet's death.

- William Stafford is among several poets who
  participated in making *What Good Is Poetry?*, a
  16 mm film released by Mill Mountain Films of
  Spokane, Washington, in 1979.

with "again and again." This stanza ends with an
optimistic note, of life going from "well" to "better," with no mention at all of a poorly lived life.
This optimism is offered to the reader, since the
poem uses the words "you" and "your" to describe
this better life.

Lines 5–8

In the second stanza, the distinction between
those who believe in reincarnation and those who
do not, between "them" and "you," is made clearer.
"They," the people from India, are the ones who
remember past lives, while Western thinkers, even
the ones who were part of those past lives, do not
remember them. This leads to the odd situation described in the second stanza: an Indian, looking into
the eyes of a Westerner who does not understand
reincarnation, can see a scene from another life,
"some far-off story." The Western person will not
remember it. Oddly, the scene might involve previous incarnations of both participants. Even
though they might be from different parts of the
world in this life, the poem is indicating that they
were both acquainted in a past life.

Line 8 adds an unusual twist to the image of
two people meeting and only one knowing that they
have met in a previous life: Stafford adds "some /

animal waiting over at the side." There is no explanation for this detail, but the fact that animals are beyond philosophical systems makes this one an appropriate way of bridging the differences between Eastern and Western philosophies.

Lines 9–12

In the third stanza, Stafford extols the benefits of reincarnation, phrasing it in terms of opportunity to make up for past mistakes. When life happens "just once," he says, one finds out too late how to avoid things that go wrong. There is a permanence to action that the poem presents as being almost too frightening to think about, making reincarnation seem a much more comforting, preferred system of belief. The rhetorical question at the start of this stanza, in line 9, serves to make readers agree with the narrative point of view, making it seem ridiculous to believe in anything except reincarnation.

Lines 13–14

In the short couplet that ends this section, there are two words emphasized. The first is the word "soft," which is used to sum up the poem's depiction of the way reincarnationists view the world, capturing its gentle and forgiving nature. The second most important word is the last word in this section, "India." Stafford uses this word to refer to the religious theory of reincarnation because it gives the theory a human presence, not a familiar one, but an exotic one, adding an element of mystery and respect that would be missing if he only talked about the abstract concept.

Lines 15–21

The second section of the poem, called "Having It Be Tomorrow," discusses the movement of the sun across the face of the earth. It starts with sunlight represented as the light of a lantern that precedes day. The poem views the earth from far above, tracking the movement of sunlight as it creeps across the face of the globe, but in lines 18 and 19 it focuses closely enough on worldly matters not only to identify shepherds but to identify their purpose for lighting fires before sunrise, for making their breakfast. Line 20 has an abrupt time shift: whereas this stanza tracks the slowly rising sun for five lines, there is a sudden jolt when the poem announces, "then it's noon." After noon, the height of the sun's climb, Stafford does not view the sun in terms of setting but as starting the process that will lead to the sunrise the next day. This mirrors the optimism of the first stanza, which only

presented good and better lives and did not raise any potentially negative aspects.

Lines 22–28

Stafford presents the motion of the sun as a "secret," because most people fail to think of it in the way that he presents it, as a "new land" that arrives over and over again every time a new day begins. For those who look at it this way, the poem promises a continuously new perspective, described here with the "welcome of children" that can be felt constantly in the heart. In the last half of this stanza, he contrasts those who have this ever-renewing perspective with those who lack it. Those people are burdened with negativity—they shake their heads—and age takes its toll on them, turning their hair gray. Although there is opposition between the two ways of viewing things, Stafford does not present it as a bitter contest. The side that he advocates as being the correct view, the one that is always renewed, sees the bitterness of the other side and laughs.

Lines 29–38

The third section of the poem is called "Being Nice and Old." It begins by mentioning a time when old people can look back over their lives. The phrase "after their jobs are done" generally means retirement, in a culture that looks at a person in terms of employment, but the poem implies that it means something more general, referring not just to paying jobs but to responsibilities and personal duties. The previous two stanzas focused, first of all, on making clear distinctions between Westerners and Easterners, and then on the distinction between optimists about the future and those who see no reason for optimism. This stanza has a central distinction between friends and "people you don't like." The friends, lines 32–33 explain, will be lit by memories of "all that was so dizzying when it happened." The poem does not advise bitterness toward enemies, explaining that they will suffer by becoming older and that one can eventually just ignore them until they fall away from notice ("drop off the edge of the world").

Lines 39–50

"Good Ways to Live" is the fourth and final section of the poem. It is a twelve-line stanza that shows the author's awareness and acceptance of his impending death. Nature is presented as a continuum of life. The trees and grass and clouds are moved by the wind. Birds touch the sky, which is seen as a continuous fabric that reaches down to the ground, so that humans on the ground can feel the effect of their flapping. For a short while, in lines 46–48, the poem hints that the life force that runs through all of these things might be dark and sinister: it exists under ground and reaches out to pull people to their deaths. The last line, though, brings the focus of the poem back to the discussion of reincarnation at the beginning. Death is presented as a release that puts the human spirit back into the same atmosphere that "Good Ways to Live" presents as being alive, implying that the spirit will live again in the things of nature. The use of the word "halo" in line 50 hints at a beautification of the spirit as it becomes angelic in death.

Themes

Reincarnation

In this poem, Stafford talks about reincarnation as a second chance to correct the things that were done wrong in this life. His version of this religious belief might be a little oversimplified, in that he presents this doctrine as if it means that one will lead the same life, over and over, with added understanding of what was done right and wrong each time before. If it were that simple, then reincarnation really would be a matter of steering around troubles that one can anticipate coming. True Indian beliefs about reincarnation are, of course, much more complicated, with the spirit ending up in worse circumstances or better circumstances, depending on the *karma* gained in subsequent lives. In Eastern religions, one's chances with reincarnation are more uncertain than Stafford presents them here, but the idea of reincarnation does help this poem make a point about the abruptness of life, as it is understood by Western thinkers.

By personifying the idea of reincarnation, Stafford is able to present a small drama between a stereotypical Indian character, called "them" in the first section of the poem, and a stereotypical Westerner, referred to as "you." "They" have the power to look into "your" eye and see a scene from the past involving both participants. This concept of reincarnation has more poetic than religious significance, but, as a poetic situation, it does provide a powerful image. Stafford seems to understand that the mystical powers that he attributes to Indians are exaggerated, given the way that he says, at the end of the first section, "the way they do it in India." The tone of this line suggests a winking self-mockery, to suggest that he is fully aware that the Indian belief in reincarnation does not operate in the way he has presented.

Topics for Further Study

- Suppose William Stafford were limited to having only three sections to this poem. Decide which section he could most easily give up and explain why.

- Interview several people who are over the age of seventy and ask what they think of the people whom they did not like in their youth. Discuss your findings with others in your class.

- Stafford refers to the Hindu belief in reincarnation. Explore the Internet and find at least three sites by people who claim to have been reincarnated and then explain whether you think their stories are true or not.

- Find another poem that is written in numbered sections like this one is and write an essay explaining why you think poets sometimes choose this technique.

- To symbolize the lights created by people, Stafford refers to shepherds preparing their breakfasts. Make a list of other professions that require people to be at work before dawn and chart what times their lights would come on.

In the last section of the poem, Stafford presents a more spiritual view of reincarnation, as opposed to the exaggeration in the first section. The poem's last line has a dying person "spread into the thin halo of night mist": the person is joined with nature, which the earlier lines in section 4 show to be alive, but is not concerned with past lives and previous episodes that were lived between strangers hundreds of years earlier.

Hope

The metaphor of the sun circling the earth in the second section of the poem is one that radiates a sense of hopefulness. As is often the case, sunlight is used to represent security and knowledge, as a result of the way it overcomes the uncertain shadows of night. Stafford refers to the moments before sunlight arrives, providing readers with a striking visual image of darkened hills lit sporadically with campfires, anticipating the light and heat that will soon blanket the land. As the sun rises over the earth, it is personified, compared to a person lighting a dark place with a lantern, implying that the rising sun is on a mission to bring light.

Most of the first stanza of "Having It Be Tomorrow" focuses on the rising sun, which is almost a universal symbol of hope. When the focus shifts, late in that stanza, to the afternoon sun, there is more than an abrupt time change: the symbolic meaning of the afternoon sun is different. If the sun is charging toward light in the morning, in the afternoon it is charging toward the darkness of night. That is not the way this poem presents it, however; instead, Stafford willfully ignores the symbolic implications of the coming night and views that sun after its zenith as "coasting toward a new tomorrow."

The second stanza of section 2 presents hope as a "secret," one that most people are not aware of. Stafford makes this hope attractive by presenting the benefits that it offers: the land is always new, and "the welcome of children / will remain every day in your heart." Those without hope still have the sun come up upon them every morning, but they do not embrace it, instead facing it with a negative shake of the head. The person with hope faces each new day with a laugh.

Maturity

This poem is about spiritual maturity, but it approaches such maturity through the most familiar sense of the word, that of human aging. The third section of the poem, "Being Nice and Old," uses the word "nice" ironically, to play off expectations that people have about elderly people. There is, in fact, nothing particularly "nice" in the traditional sense about the vision of old age presented here. Instead, Stafford defines what he thinks is nice about growing old. Whereas traditional concepts of maturity tend to discourage looking back at one's life as a kind of weakness, "living in the past," this poem shows a light from the past events that shines on the faces of one's friends. Also, maturity often is taken to include a sort of benign acceptance of those whom one has had trouble with in the past. Stafford's version does include a peace with one's former enemies, but this peace is not reached through a spirit of charity. Characters in this poem reach maturity when they are able to turn away from those whom they do not like. The enemies, he assures readers, will feel the effects of old age, and because they will suffer in this way, there is no reason for the individual to wish ill upon them. Even if they are not punished by old age, the poem

still advises readers to ignore those whom they do not like, and as the reader ages, the others will "drop off the face of the earth." Although the poem does not equate maturity with being charitable, the end result is the same: anger and hatred are ignored, and peace is gained.

Harmony

The end of this poem describes a mystical harmony of nature, with the actions of all things affecting others. The phrase "it all moves or / almost moves" implies an interconnectedness that most people do not see when they look at the world. Stafford gives examples of trees and grass moved by the wind, and, high above, clouds moved by a wind that cannot be felt on the ground. The reference to stars indicates a heightened sense of awareness, since the naked eye cannot generally observe such motion. All of these motions, from the obvious to the sublime, are catalogued under the heading of "Good Ways to Live."

In the middle of the final section, Stafford shifts his focus from things that can be observed visually to things that are connected by touch. The sky is not seen as something far away but as a "fabric" that responds to the motion of birds flying by, so that a person on the ground can feel the ripples made by their wings. By pointing out the harmony between the sky and the ground, Stafford brings together all of nature.

In the end, the poem also brings the supernatural into the equation. Although it had previously denied that Western thinkers—"you"—would have the sensitivity to understand the afterlife, the final lines describe the experience of death as being joined with the other aspects of nature that have already been joined together. Death, "that emanation of all things," rises up from under ground and pulls the essence of the person into the air, turning life into a night mist. The reincarnation explored in the first section is achieved in a more meaningful way than just repetition of past scenes; the rising sun presents the hope of bringing warmth and light to the night mist; and the truest sign of maturity in this poem is a willingness to let go of the good and bad things of life.

Style

Structure

It is not very unusual for a poem to be broken down into numbered sections the way that "Ways to Live" is. The most frequent observation about such poems is that each of the four segments, each of which has its own individual title, could stand by itself as an independent poem. This may be true, but once that is established, it helps to consider why Stafford decided to present them as one entire unit. There are similar themes that run through all of the sections of this poem, drawing relationships between them even when the subject matter of each might seem unrelated to the rest.

The first section, "India," for instance, is narrowly concerned with Hindu religious beliefs, a subject that is not discussed in the rest of the poem. In a more general sense, though, it is about what happens after death, a subject that is implied in the second section in the sun heading toward a new tomorrow and in the fourth by the "emanation" spreading one's life into the halo of night mist that makes all things move. In the third section, the Hindu seeing a "far-off story" in one's eyes is repeated by the way old people see the light of the past on their current friends. This third section, "Being Nice and Old," is the part of the poem that fits least securely with the rest because it is the only one that focuses entirely on worldly events. It comes in the right place for such an unusual stanza: the theme of continuing life is shown in the first section and then anchored by the second section, and, after the third section diverts slightly, the fourth section brings that theme back again.

Audience

This poem is addressed to a fairly specific audience, as is indicated by the frequent use of the second person, "you." In "India," Stafford is quite specific about what he thinks his audience believes, defining his readers by how they differ from "them," who would be the people of India. He is not specifically addressing all of the world's population outside of India, but rather the people who do not hold the particular beliefs that he ascribes to Indians here. Later, in the second stanza of "Having It Be Tomorrow," his reference to "you" allows that his reader might have the sort of insight that was only allowed "them" in the first section. The "you" in the third section is someone that the speaker of the poem is giving advice to, explaining how to deal with friends and family alike. In the fourth section, the reference to "you" is descriptive, showing what happens to any person upon death.

Of course, a poem written in the second person is not limited only to the people described. The effect of addressing readers as "you" is to establish whom the author is thinking of, but that does not mean that other people cannot understand and appreciate the concepts being discussed. For instance, people of India are clearly "them" in the first section, but the sentiments Stafford examines here are accessible to Indian readers. Addressing readers as "you" does not exclude readers who are not described by a poem's use of that pronoun; it just gives readers a fair understanding of whom the author has in mind while writing. Readers can then adjust their expectations and their judgments to help get a clearer sense of the points the author is trying to make.

Tone

The "tone" of a written work is determined by the author's attitude that the author shows toward his audience. In "Ways to Live," Stafford's tone is the one that runs throughout most of his poetry: calm, assured, and insightful. It is not too abstract or intellectual, even though the subject matter of the poem itself has more intellectual depth than many readers are accustomed to. One reason this poem can be viewed as welcoming the reader is its use of "you," which serves to bring readers into the material being discussed. Readers might not feel that Stafford actually knows them, but the use of "you" does establish a conversational tone that tends to make people feel comfortable and to establish them as part of the discussion.

The strongest impression of this poem's tone is one of good-natured forgiving. Emphasis is given to things like light, laughter, and "the welcome of children" that is felt in your heart. The word "halo" in the last line is instrumental in establishing how readers feel about the overall piece. It is a word usually used in a religious context, but it also describes an indistinct, vague light. It is a word that evokes feelings of warmth and spirituality, and this mood fits perfectly with the subject matter being discussed.

Personification

In order to make a greater impact on the reader's imagination, Stafford uses personification in several places in this poem. In several places, he talks about inanimate objects or abstract concepts as if they have human behavior and motivations. In "Having It Be Tomorrow," for instance, "day" is said to be holding a lantern and consciously using that lantern to brighten the earth as it eases across the land. In "Being Nice and Old," the light "knows how to rest on the faces of friends." The most striking examples of personification occur in the last section, "Good Ways to Live." This section starts by hinting that all of the things of the earth move because that is what they want to do. It then goes on to describe the motion of clouds and stars across the sky as "parading," to give a sense of the self-assurance to their motion. The vague concept that is referred to as "that emanation of all things" is treated like a person: it breathes, it waits, and then it moves to abduct a person as if it knows that this is its purpose in this world.

Historical Context

Hinduism

Written in the 1990s, when "multiculturalism" had become a common idea among academics and intellectuals, this poem shows enough awareness about world culture to recognize that reincarnation is one of the central tenets of the Hindu religion, which is the dominant religion of India. Still, it shows little understanding of the details of the Hindu belief in rebirth, other than the broad idea that humans may come back as other forms of life after they have died. William Stafford was a poet well known for his skill in capturing the feeling of the American West, with its open plains representing both desolation and possibility, and for understanding the American moral beliefs that his countrymen so seldom saw represented in print. To some degree, his superficial rendering of Asian religious belief can be considered another facet of his regional identity, since Americans are notorious throughout the world for understanding little about cultures outside of their own.

There are over 790 million Hindus in the world. Of these, nearly 750 million reside in India, making up 80 percent of that country's population. The roots of the Hindu religion can be traced to the year 1500 B.C., when it was brought into India by the Aryans, an Indo-European race of warriors that then merged with Indian intellectualism. As such, Hinduism is one of the world's oldest religions, and its ideas about the existence of an individual soul that continues after death have probably had an influence on all major religions that have followed. It is safe to assume that, when Stafford refers to Indian religious belief in "Ways to Live," he is referring to the religion called Hindu by outsiders, although it is important to note that this religion's practitioners have no such word for their system of beliefs.

The Hindu religion centers on the belief that each individual has a soul, which is a part of Brahma, the Supreme Soul. At death, this soul is separated from the body that it occupied, but it does not leave Earth. Instead, it comes back to life as another living thing. What it comes back as is determined by the *karma* that it has accumulated in the most recent existence. Karma comes from the degree to which one has avoided causing injury. Those who are truly malicious are burdened with bad karma and will return the next time around as a lower form of life, such as an animal or a member of one of the lower classes. Good karma assures one a higher form of existence. Through eliminating passions and gaining knowledge, one can, over the course of several lifetimes, be freed of reincarnation. For followers of the Hindu faiths, the goal is, in the end, to be liberated from suffering and from having to be reborn, and to have one's soul joined to the Supreme Soul.

Critical Overview

William Stafford was recognized as a unique poet, one who focused his attention on common life and moral decisions at a time when most poetry was moving away from a general moral judgment and toward an expression of individual perspective. Critics seldom failed to note Stafford's kind, gentle, fatherly poetic voice, which was perhaps a result of the fact that he was older than many of his contemporaries when he started to gain critical attention—Stafford was forty-six years old when his first book of poetry was published. For example, Louis Simpson, himself a respected poet, noted while reviewing Stafford's first collection in 1961 the way that he was able to maintain a personal voice while writing about significant matters that affect all readers. "Contrary to what many poets believe nowadays," Simpson wrote, "it is not necessary to spill your guts on the table in order to be 'personal,' nor to relate the details of your aunt's insanity. What is necessary is originality of imagination and at least a few ideas of your own." These are the graces that he found in Stafford's work, and this assessment of Stafford stayed fairly consistent over the next thirty years.

Perhaps Stafford's most lasting impression on critics was his independence from the poetic trends of his time. In the 1960s, he became recognized by a small group of writers and intellectuals with his second collection *Traveling Through the Dark*. His audience was impressed with his moral strength in a time of shifting moral values. The public, divided over the increasingly unpopular war in Vietnam, also respected Stafford for his personal history as a conscientious objector during World War II. At a time when he was riding high in public esteem, though, when he could have rested on his popularity, he wrote poems that broke from the style expected of him and took the chance of alienating fans. Gerald Burns noted, while reviewing a 1970 collection, that "Stafford is three very hard things to find in America: an adult, a poet, and an adult poet—and he does a very hard thing in *Allegiances*. He drops out. He can afford to; in his case, it's being a good citizen." Burns explains that the poems are dense and deliberate: "Reading them slowly is almost frightening because you see how thoroughly they are *meant*."

By the 1990s, Stafford was just as respected as he ever was, and just as prolific, still writing a poem a day and publishing dozens each year in little magazines. Ben Howard started a review in *Poetry*, one of the most influential poetry periodicals published in America, by telling his audience directly, "Schools and movements come and go, but over the past three decades the steady, demotic voice of William Stafford has deepened rather than changed." Howard recognizes the fact that Stafford's "casual tone" is frequently incongruous with the subject matter he explored in his old age, such as death and loss of old friends. In his review, Howard points out places in Stafford's poetry where lines that seem intended to spread comfort and cheer to the reader fall flat, making the intelligent optimism he was known for seem forced and unconvincing. Still, he is unwilling to go along with other critics who do not think Stafford has the emotional depth to recognize the negative side of life. As Howard puts it, "Stafford's controversial 'way of writing' has produced its share of ephemera, here as in his previous collections; but it has also allowed access to the 'rich darkness' of the unknown and has strengthened a capacity, rare in contemporary poetry, for intuiting the miraculous." He could have been writing about "Ways to Live," which was written the following year and not published until years later, when he observed that "in the best of his new poems, a poet's sad wisdom fuses with a child's sense of wonder and a grown man's reverence for nature."

The book in which "Ways to Live" was published, called *The Way It Is*, was published five years after the poet's death. In general, it is rare to find a reviewer willing to speak ill of the dead, especially about an author as universally revered as Stafford. The worst that can be said about him, so soon after his death, is that his poetry is still considered outside the mainstream, still frequently overlooked when anthologies are assembled, and too seldom discussed along with the important poets of the twentieth century. By every indication, this is not a reflection of the quality of his work so much as it is a sign that he made poetry look natural and easy.

Criticism

David Kelly

Kelly is an instructor of creative writing and literature at Oakton Community College. In this essay, Kelly explores what aspects of "Ways to Live" make this poem about death believable.

William Stafford's poem "Ways to Live" offers readers advice about life, taking the grandest overall view of it by looking squarely at life's biggest challenge: how to deal with death. It does this with sober sincerity. This is a topic open to many different opinions, but this poem leaves its readers feeling confident that it comes from a poet who knows what he is talking about and secure in the belief that the truth the poem gives corresponds with the way the world really is.

Part of that confidence comes from the poet's biographical situation. Stafford wrote "Ways to Live" over the course of three days, July 19–21 of 1993, just five weeks before his death. It is difficult to ignore the timing: whether he was preoccupied with his approaching finale, as other poems written around the same time seem to suggest, or whether he just knew death was lurking around the corner with the same intuition that shows the Indians in the poem scenes from their past lives, it would be hard for any reader not to believe that Stafford had a considerable amount of insight into what it is like to be near the end. The fact that he was seventy-nine years old alone gives him a perspective that most of his readers will lack.

Another factor that gives readers cause to trust this poem's insights is that it was, after all, produced by William Stafford, whose poetic voice had been clear and honest from the start and then polished daily for almost half a century. It is a voice that rings true to most readers, free of the bends that

What Do I Read Next?

- "Ways to Live" is included along with other poems that Stafford produced in the last months of his life in *The Way It Is: New and Selected Poems*, published posthumously by Graywolf Press in 1998.

- Stafford was well known in poetry circles by the time his first book was published, but it was his second book *Traveling through the Dark* (1962) that attracted attention and established him as an important American author. Most of the poems from this volume have been reprinted in other collections, but it does help to experience them the way the original readers did.

- Judith Kitchen is a preeminent Stafford scholar, who has published several books about the poet. Her most recent study of Stafford's poetry is *Writing the Word: Understanding William Stafford*, published in 1999 by Oregon State University Press.

- In addition to being a poet, Stafford wrote some of the most bright and readable books about the art of writing poetry that are available. His *You Must Revise Your Life*, a tutorial on writing and teaching, is a staple of creative writing classes; it was published by University of Michigan Press in 1986.

- Stafford's book *Writing the Australian Crawl: Views on the Writer's Vocation* is another book of essays that is instructive about the writing business and about the poet's views. It was edited by Donald Hall, himself a major American poet, and published by University of Michigan Press in 1976.

- In 1983, Godine Press published *Segues: A Correspondence in Poetry*. It is the record of a series of letters sent back and forth between Stafford and another poet, Marvin Bell, providing readers with a lively look at the creative process as poems are practically developed as quickly as they can be read.

most people can sense when authors condescend to literary trends. Rhetoric is the art of making things sound true whether they are true or not. The kind of honesty that radiated from Stafford's work, especially his later work, is almost impossible to fake. In Stafford's meek language, his wry wit, and his ease in discussing things of nature, readers recognize that this is not a poet who needs to claim truths that he does not actually feel.

But these are things about the author, not the poem. If sincerity and old age alone were enough to make an effective work of art, then anything he said would be effective. In studying Stafford's latest works, it would be easy to fall prey to admiration and believe that he actually could sit down with a pen at any given time and churn out truth—he was one of the few writers who never coasted along or used the same tried-and-true verbal tricks that served him so well over the course of decades. But there is no need simply to trust that the poem of an honest author is true; there are aspects about "Ways to Live" that in themselves give the poem the authority to advise readers about how to face death.

There is good reason to be suspicious of poems that are too loud about accepting the inevitable, that find beauty in nature and comfort in old age. Too often, writers are able to achieve these positive outlooks only by paying no attention to all of the unpleasant things that become associated with them. Sentimental verse shows mighty eagles soaring and innocent bunnies hopping but has nothing to say when the eagle swoops down for the kill. As the saying goes, "Ignorance is bliss." The great and undervalued thing about "Ways to Live" is that it is a blissful poem that does not need to hide any portion of the truth in order to maintain a convincing balance. In a few short sections, and using an even tone, it presents a range of emotions that conflict with each other but end up offering a well-rounded picture of the world.

For instance, the poem starts out with a section called "India," which touches upon the subject of reincarnation. It touches the subject, but in no way does Stafford claim any sort of expert knowledge about it. One clue of this is the section's title: naming it "India" is the poet's admission that the religious belief he describes is foreign to him, which puts him in the position of being a curious spectator, not a teacher. This idea is made even more forcefully at the end of the section, which is emphatic about the fact that reincarnation is a belief understood by "them," in India, not by the poem's speaker or his probable audience. Americans "can't have that soft look" that comes into the eyes of those who truly understand reincarnation. For Stafford, another culture's religious belief only leads to the commonsense observation that it would be better to have more than one chance to live life right and to redo past wrongs. This is the extent to which he is willing to claim any understanding of Indian religious beliefs.

Separating the parts of the poem with section numbers, subtitles, and different structural styles, Stafford is able to change moods quickly. The second section leaves behind the sad regret of the first. In "Having It Be Tomorrow," one small metaphor is built up to proportions that it could not command if it were not in this particular place in this particular poem. Basically, all this part of the poem does is take the light of the sun, which shines indiscriminately in all directions, and explain it in terms of a lantern beam that is aimed with conscious effort. Sunrise crawls progressively across the face of the earth, and the poem relates that progression to the sense of improvement that is often associated with "tomorrow." Again, Stafford is not so narrow-minded as to claim that things will always be better tomorrow, only that those who fail to see life getting better will feel old, whereas those who do feel the improvement laugh. This is logic that is hard to argue against. If this section were a poem unto itself, and this were all that it had to tell readers, this simple observation would be too lightweight to be worth mentioning. In the middle of a complex piece with changing attitudes, it adds depth and dimension.

"Being Nice and Old" is neither sad, like the first section, nor optimistic like the second. It is sarcastic, although, strangely, in a life-affirming way. A clue to this comes from the use of the word "nice" in the section's title. Readers have to ask themselves what use an author of Stafford's verbal precision would have for a word so vague and weak, so incapable of inspiring anything more than a shrug from readers. What Stafford does here with this unpoetic word makes readers reconsider it. Rather than serving up the tired cliches that usually arise around the concept of niceness, he ends up describing a nice old age as one in which those who disagree have fallen off the edge of the world. It is a calm and carefully phrased idea, not violent nor sweet nor angry nor sad. Ultimately, it is hard-nosed reality: what is peace in old age, or at any age, except for being with friends and being freed of those who disagree? Stafford does not sugarcoat the truth but phrases it coldly, and he highlights his cold phrasing with the use of the word "nice." Added to the

> *The poem goes into optimism and mysticism in places, but it counterbalances these with simplicity and the nerve to tell readers what the author does not know."*

first section's sadness and the second's optimism is this section's unsentimental realism.

The last part of the poem, "Good Ways to Live," uses the sober word "good" whereas the previous section used the candy-coated "nice." It leaves behind relationships between people and, like the second section, focuses on nature. But, unlike section 2, which looked to one natural phenomenon, the progression of the sun, for hope, this section looks at nature in full. "Room," as in "The room you have / in the world is ready to change," is a well-chosen word, denoting both the social space within a house and also the portion of the whole universe that is allotted to one individual. One other word that is worth noting is "ways" in the title of this section. Since the poem only talks about one type of human experience—being drawn out by "the emanation of all things"—"ways" clearly refers to the actions of the birds, clouds, stars, and so forth. They *live* in this poem. Stafford affirms all things, just as he, in this last section, writes off all of the other ways of living covered in the rest of the poem. The Indian way discussed in the first section is incomplete because of that unspecified "animal" that stands on the side, watching the one person remember a past life and the other wish he could. The animal, like the birds in section 4, has a good way to live, too. The anticipation of each new day is good, but it ends with death. The enjoyment of friends, too, is temporal. Stafford has set each part of the poem up to give a truth, but they all fall short when faced with the eternal truth.

A poem that takes life and death as its subject matter has little chance of success. No writers have had the firsthand experience of death, and most bring to the subject all of the preconceptions and prejudices that they have learned throughout their lives. The fact that "Ways to Live" is able to make a meaningful statement comes mostly from the fact that William Stafford, in his old age, was still humble enough to stay away from areas that he did not know about. The poem goes into optimism and mysticism in places, but it counterbalances these with simplicity and the nerve to tell readers what the author does not know. The final image of death as a union with the natural world is the one luxury Stafford allows, the one place where he pretends to know the unknowable. Given who William Stafford was and how he presented himself in his poetry, most readers are willing to allow him that luxury.

Source: David Kelly, Critical Essay on "Ways to Live," in *Poetry for Students*, The Gale Group, 2002.

Adrian Blevins

Blevins teaches writing courses at Roanoke College. In this essay, Blevins suggests that in Stafford's poem, the poet uses extended metaphors to give advice on how people might live with the knowledge of impending death.

In "Education by Poetry," Robert Frost argues that "the height of all thinking . . . [is] the attempt to say matter in terms of spirit and spirit in terms of matter." What he means is that the ability to "say one thing in terms of another" *is what thinking is.* Frost is not the only poet to have made this observation. Pound's advice to go in fear of abstractions, William Carlos Williams's insistence that ideas can only be found in things, and T. S. Eliot's objective correlative are all metaphors for the idea that metaphors are indispensable to poetry (and all serious uses of language). Yet the modernists' interest in metaphor manifested itself primarily as an interest in imagery, and that interest—still strong relatively late in the twentieth century in the deep-image work of poets like Robert Bly and James Wright—may have undermined our willingness to value certain more general—more *rhetorical*—uses of comparison.

"Ways to Live" is one of William Stafford's later poems, and like much of Stafford's later work, the poem is infused with the speaker's consciousness of his own impending death. The poem's title is ironic because although it suggests that the poem is going to be about "ways to live," the poem really concerns the way people might live with the knowledge of imminent death. Although the poem contains a good many images, its effectiveness relies on the way it uses the extended metaphor to express advice about how people might live well

with that knowledge. While an image can be seen as a small "visual" moment in a poem that makes an abstract idea more discernible by making it physical—and while images are typically constructed out of metaphors and similes—extended metaphors are more like analogies in that they extend a comparison further out than most images can, linking large bodies of language with other large bodies of language to say something about being human that could not otherwise be said.

"Ways to Live" is constructed of four titled sections of varying stanza systems and line lengths. Each section presents an alternative way to view the weight of death-consciousness. Because many thinkers have suggested that humankind's foreknowledge of death is the most significant difference between people and animals, Stafford's argument in this poem is especially interesting. The poem's first section, entitled "India," explores the idea of reincarnation in India, celebrating, in deeply metaphorical lines, the notion that individuals might "happen" more than "once." Yet section one does not so much test or explore the idea of reincarnation as imply that people who believe in it give anyone who looks into their eyes "some far-off story / with them and you in it." In other words, Stafford implies in the first section of "Ways to Live" that believing in reincarnation is a "way to live" with the idea of death, since it eliminates the fear of death with a "soft look." This look suggests that, in Stafford's view, people who believe they will return to the earth after death as another human or animal have found a wholesome "way to live" with the idea of ending by dying. In so doing, it suggests that belief systems—the ideas people construct for themselves in order to live in the world—are central factors in living and dying. What is interesting about this observation is that it implies that metaphor itself—certainly Stafford is using reincarnation is a metaphor for the after life in "Ways to Live"—is as central to living as it is to poetry.

The poem's second section, entitled "Having It Be Tomorrow," contains the poem's most beautiful metaphor, suggesting that an additional way to live with the idea of impending death is to be "in on [the] secret" of the notion that each new day is a certain blessing which "[holds] its lantern before it, / [and] moves over the whole earth slowly / to brighten that edge and push it westward." In this section of the poem, Stafford compares people who recognize the "beads of light" that each new day is made of to people who "shake their heads turning gray every / morning when the sun comes up." In other words, Stafford compares people who live without the fear of death with people who do. In so doing, he implies that the wisdom that is the "secret" in this section of the poem is the ability to recognize that "the welcome of children / will remain every day new" in the hearts of people who not only understand, but fully celebrate, the cycle of birth and death. Like the idea in the poem's first section that states that believing in reincarnation will help people live well by preventing the fear of only "[happening] once," this section of the poem, which states that seeing each new day as new, is also a metaphor, signifying that a certain optimistic attitude will help readers see "a new land / [coming] every time the sun goes climbing over it."

The poem's third section, entitled "Being Nice and Old," celebrates old age itself by suggesting that it is possible to be "nice and old" by remembering how "dizzying" the past was and recognizing "the light . . . on the faces of friends." This section of the poem is also ironic, since Stafford suggests that it is "nice and old" to "turn away" from "any people you don't like" and "let them drop off the edge of the world." Our culture famously celebrates youth, but in this section of "Ways to Live," Stafford implies that old age is not as bad as what might be thought. After all, old people can take pleasure in being beyond the "dizzying" past and "turn away" from people they "don't like." In this section of the poem, Stafford suggests that an additional alternative way to live with death is to be at peace in old age. It is interesting to note, too, that in "Being Nice and Old," Stafford links light, which is everywhere in the poem, with love. At the end of the poem, the speaker himself will "spread in the thin halo of night mist," while people he says he does not "like" will "fall off the edge of the world." Although Stafford does not use the terms "heaven" and "hell" anywhere in "Ways to Live," it is clear he is using these mythological terms to address himself, if subtly, to two alternative ways to live and die.

The poem's final section, because it is titled "Good Ways to Live," implies that of all the ways to live with the knowledge of impending death so far explored, a recognition of the way "the emanation of all things" "moves or / almost moves" is probably the best. In this section of the poem, "the emanation of all things" is probably death itself, and what is remarkable about the stanza is the way in which death is being celebrated as a kind of life force. Death here is actually breathing—it "moves or / almost moves" and is related to the natural world in the "clouds [that parade by, and [the] stars

> *. . . what is remarkable about the stanza is the way in which death is being celebrated as a kind of life force."*

in their / configurations." In the poem's final image, death is so vital and so ironically full of life that it "pulls [the speaker] slowly out through doors or windows" until he "[spreads] in the thin halo of night mist." Although the image of a dead man "[spreading] in the thin halo of night mist" is an image—certainly, readers can see the old idea of a spirit rising in this line—the whole notion of death as a kind of life force in this section of the poem is more of an extended metaphor, suggesting that death is not the might that kills life so much as a force that helps to make life *life*.

In the poem's final section, Stafford is borrowing from Carl Jung's idea of the collective unconscious, which puts forward the idea that people do not die but join all others who have died before in an ethereal community of spirit. Yet because Stafford is a poet and not a psychologist-philosopher, he is able to make that idea, which is abstract, concrete with nouns. Here, the collective unconscious becomes a "thin halo of night mist." In other sections of the poem, Stafford uses metaphor and image in much the same way, suggesting that the peacefulness that comes with a belief in reincarnation might produce "a soft look," or that people who understand "the secret" of the blessing of each new day will be able to see the "day" itself "holding its lantern before it."

"Ways to Live" uses both image and extended metaphor to express alternative methods for living with the idea of impending death because metaphor is the only way, as Frost says, that humans *can think*. When Frost states that the "height of all thinking" is the ability "to say matter in terms of spirit and spirit in terms of matter," he is saying that all language is metaphorical. When it is said that a child's hair is like the sunshine, it is a simile being used to make a visual picture so that readers can approximate what the child's hair looks like. But when William Stafford says that living with the idea that people are going to die ought to be conducted "the way they do it in India," *or by* being "in on [the secret] . . . of the "day" with "its lantern," *or by* rejecting the "dizzying" past and seeing "light" "on the faces of friends," *or by* letting death "pull [us] / slowly out through doors or windows," something even more magnificent is happening. In "Ways to Live," Stafford is advising people on how they might approach the most profound and universal of human mysteries from the position of his advanced old age and wisdom. If this is not "the height of all thinking" that leads to what might be called the height of all feeling, nothing is.

Source: Adrian Blevins, Critical Essay on "Ways to Live," in *Poetry for Students*, The Gale Group, 2002.

Frank Pool

Pool is a published poet and a high school English teacher. In this essay, Pool approaches Stafford's poem in relation to the poet's meditations on life in the face of his impending death.

William Stafford wrote "Ways to Live" from July 19 to July 21, 1993, just over a month before his death at the end of August. An exponent of plain speech in poetry, Stafford avoids verbal gymnastics, cultivating his perception and his stance toward his subject and audience instead of polishing his lines with meter and rhyme and all the paraphernalia of formal structure. John Kennedy, writing in *The Antioch Review*, says that, "Stafford's is not a poetry of gimmicks or confessional sensationalism. He minimized the importance of technique and spoke of his poetry as a result of receptivity, not design." Some poets and critics dismissed Stafford because he wrote too much and published too much. Others admire him for his unadorned simplicity of expression. "Ways to Live" is a very plain-spoken poem about four different approaches to life, and, given Stafford's age and health at the time of its composition, about methods to deal with death by reminding oneself of the powers and gifts that life brings.

This poem takes on its own organic design, a four-fold path to practical wisdom. His poem is divided into four parts, each of which is a calm meditation on life and death. Faced with the end of his own life, Stafford writes about the things that are good in life, not in a grandiose, self-gratifying way, not claiming that he has grasped all of life's mysteries, nor is he in any sense regretful or tearful about his impending death. This poem tries to grip the truths of life by pulling forth simple images that

suggest rather than lecture. The poet seeks the moral truth in a world of things; he does not attempt to dazzle, nor to preach loudly. Rather, he gives his readers multiple perspectives, with no pretense of comprehensiveness or intellectual rigor, but he offers them for what one may make of them. His poem is characteristically restrained, understated, and plain. He quietly celebrates lessons he has learned in his life, and he shows them to his reader, all without anxiety.

The first section of his poem is subtitled "India." He ponders the Hindu acceptance of reincarnation and introduces a bit of deliberate awkwardness in the first lines: "In India in their lives they happen / again and again." The expression "in their lives" seems redundant, but as the poem develops, readers see that "in their lives" is a guiding motif throughout all of the four parts. Everything that happens in this poem happens in somebody's life. Their lives are what encompasses all experiences; "they happen" only within that wholeness of being that is a human life. Stafford liberally uses second person, giving the poem an immediacy as well as a universality, "when you're wrong, it's too late / to go back— you've done it forever." This "you" is neither him, nor is it a specific address to a reader; instead, it is a colloquial way of making a general statement about the human condition while maintaining an intimacy of expression. Naomi Shihab Nye has said, in the preface to Stafford's posthumous collection *The Way It Is: New & Selected Poems*, "Rarely has a voice felt so intimate and so collective at once." There is an informality about "you," that is very appropriate to this poem. Stafford relates the traditional Indian view toward death without explicit comment, but he suggests that the Indians have developed an understanding of death that allows them to "have that soft look when you / pass, the way they do it in India." Here, readers see Stafford's unsentimental gentleness. In asserting the eternal recurrence of life, the people of India seem to have found one of the "Ways to Live" the poet contemplates in his last month. To "pass" is merely to move on, to go with the roll of the eternal wheel or to participate in the passing of time. The word "pass" is also, of course, a euphemism for "die," an expression chosen for its mild effect. The tone of the whole poem continues this placid mood.

"Having It Be Tomorrow" is the subtitle of the second section. The poet personifies the day, which "holds its lantern before it," bringing light and life to the entire planet. Stafford evokes the timeless pastoral imagery of shepherds lighting fires, "beads of light that extend miles of horizon." Although the stanza is independent, the connections with the previous one linger, and these shepherds seem to inhabit the uplands of the Himalayas and other exotic peaks. Here, Stafford expresses the long panoramic vista, the immemorial play of light upon the land, painted with unornamented, plain language, and he moves from the largeness of his timeless vision to the intimate particular secret that brings laughter to anyone who shares it. Stafford says that there is a "secret" that allows the world to be seen as new each and every day, keeping "you," presumably the poet, young at heart. Others get gray, but those who know the secret of the sunrise, the possibilities of creation that occur with absolute regularity, every day of one's life, maintain a childlike understanding of the world. Stafford spent a long career developing his distinctive method of composition, writing early in the morning, every morning, letting himself respond to whatever ideas or images moved him that morning, seizing on the newness and freshness each day brings, keeping his imagery and his vision fresh. The morning is the time of his greatest creativity, when the world is young and all is possible. Stafford does not proclaim this secret loudly; he quietly acclaims it as yet another way to live, but readers glimpse his pattern. These ways to live are all good ways, are all approaches to life that enrich human existence.

In the third section of the poem, "Being Nice and Old," the poet describes old people looking back on their lives, "all of that which was so dizzying when it happened" as he constructs a tableau of oldsters who are reminiscing and evaluating their lives, looking at their friends as though they are the light itself. Then in the last five lines of the short stanza, Stafford introduces a metaphorical comparison of lives with a book. It is possible to handle people "you" do not like by developing the ability to "turn / the page a little more and wait," or indeed, to let go of unwanted people by letting them "drop off the edge of the world." The old, Stafford is saying, may at the end of their lives gain a clarity and judgment on their own lives, turning to friendship or, conversely, having the wisdom to ignore persons who do not deserve the attention and vexation that might afflict the young. There is a nice ambiguity in this subtitle, as though the poet wants to be both "nice" in the sense of being kind and honest, and "nice and old" as in having attained, and gained, an important perspective through age and time and reflection. At seventy-nine, William Stafford, honored and elderly poet,

> *He quietly celebrates lessons he has learned in his life, and he shows them to his reader, all without anxiety.*

commends this judicious conservation of friendship and its corollary, the abandonment of troublesome people, as one of his several ways to live.

Finally, in the last section, "Good Ways to Live," Stafford reaches out to the mysterious life force that animates the living and gently transforms the dead. With splendid, calm, confident understatement, the poet says that, "The room you have / in the world is ready to change." In all the parts of this poem, Stafford avoids despair, lament, or any sense of loss, despite clearly mulling over his own, and "your" own mortality. Elemental images, trees, grass, winds, clouds, and birds are all in changes. There is a soul, in ancient Greek a *pneuma* or breath of life, within all things. Here, Stafford invokes a pantheistic universe, in which at the center of the earth, as opposed to some celestial realm, is the living, breathing, inspiring "emanation of all things." Pantheism holds that God, or the consciousness of the world, is not separate or transcendent from the world, but is intimately bound up, immanent, in all the things that make up the world. In this view, God is made up of the things and beings of the world. Consistent images of breath, mist, and clouds create a sense of the respiration of all things, the constant condensation and evaporation of life itself, all in a cyclic process that alludes to the cycles of the first and second parts of the poem, the Hindu cycle of *samsara*, of birth and death and rebirth, and of the diurnal cycle of daylight and the constant newness of the world. When "you spread in the thin halo of night mist" life has shuffled off the mortal coil and reformed itself as an attenuated plume of something—Stafford cannot be precise—that is part of life and beyond life. All these four observations he has chosen to link into one poem because all of them are life-affirming, quietly revealed ways that human beings can come to terms, without sentimentality, cynicism, or sorrow, with their own limited, finite, and yet sacred sense of self.

Source: Frank Pool, Critical Essay on "Ways to Live," in *Poetry for Students*, The Gale Group, 2002.

Sources

Burns, Gerald, "A Book to Build On," in *Southwest Review*, Summer 1970, pp. 309–10.

Frost, Robert, "Education by Poetry," in *Discovering Language*, edited by William Vesterman, Allyn and Bacon, 1992.

Howard, Ben, "Together and Apart," in *Poetry*, April 1992, pp. 34–44.

Kennedy, John, "On William Stafford: The Worth of Local Things," in *The Antioch Review*, Vol. 53, No. 4, Fall 1995, p. 496.

Nye, Naomi Shihab, Preface, in *The Way It Is: New and Selected Poems*, William Stafford, Graywolf Press, 1998.

Simpson, Louis, Review of *West of Your City*, in *Hudson Review*, Autumn 1961, pp. 461–70.

Further Reading

Andrews, Tom, ed., *On William Stafford: The Worth of Local Things*, University of Michigan Press, 1993.
    Several contemporary poets, including Margaret Atwood, Richard Hugo, Linda Pastan, and Charles Simic, contributed essays to this generally positive collection about Stafford's career.

Capps, Donald, *The Poet's Gift: Toward the Renewal of Pastoral Care*, Westminster/John Knox Press, 1993.
    This analysis from a theological perspective looks at poetry from Stafford and Denise Levertov to make the case for spirituality in modern literature.

Carpenter, David A., *William Stafford*, Boise State University Press, 1986.
    At just over fifty pages, this brief survey of the poet's life up to that time was part of the university's "Western Writers" series.

Marshall, Gary Thomas, *William Stafford: A Writer Writing*, Southern Illinois University at Carbondale, 1990.
    Marshall's Ph.D. dissertation analyzing Stafford's career is available on the Internet and also on microfilm from Southern Illinois University.

Pinsker, Sanford, *Three Pacific Northwest Poets: William Stafford, Richard Hugo, and David Wagoner*, Twayne, 1987.
    Pinsker examines Stafford as a regional poet, with other poets from his area of the country providing critical contrast.

Stafford, William, "The End of a Golden String," in *Written in Water, Written in Stone: Twenty Years of "Poets on Poetry,"* University of Michigan Press, 1996, pp. 235–42.
    Stafford's essay, just one of dozens in this book written by contemporary poets, traces the seeds of inspiration, finding them in real life rather than in poetic sources.

What My Child Learns of the Sea

Audre Lorde
1963

When Audre Lorde wrote "What My Child Learns of the Sea" in her daughter Elizabeth's first year of life, she was struggling to come to terms with her identity. The year of the poem's creation, 1963, found Lorde in her first and only marriage, a young mother, writing poetry while also working as a librarian. The United States at the time was in the throes of an energetic and contested civil rights reform movement during the final year of President John F. Kennedy's administration, just before its violent end. Set within the context of the times, "What My Child Learns of the Sea" reflects the anxiety and upheaval in Lorde's personal life. In this poem, Lorde explores the responsibility, legacy, and limitations she felt as a mother and daughter. Avoiding specific allusions to historical events, Lorde focused her imagery on the primal cycles of nature. The language of seasons, including manifestations of growth and decay, give the poem a resilience that transcends the time and place of its creation and ensures its continued relevance and thoughtfulness as an exploration of mother-daughter and parent-child relationships.

"What My Child Learns of the Sea" was published in 1968 as part of *The First Cities*, Lorde's first book. By that year, her daughter Elizabeth was five and Lorde herself turned thirty-four. With its publication in book form, "What My Child Learns of the Sea" reached a wider audience and became part of the turbulent and vibrant cultural and political scene. Between 1963 and 1968, the civil rights movement expanded from a mostly race-oriented effort into a broader societal upheaval that included an outcry for feminist and gay and lesbian rights and for dramatic changes in the status quo, aiming particularly for wider acceptance of diversity in American society. "What My Child Learns of the Sea" can be found in Audre Lorde's 1992 collection *Undersong: Chosen Poems Old and New (Revised)* and anthologized in *The Garden Thrives: Twentieth-Century African-American Poetry* (1996).

Author Biography

Audre Lorde was born on February 18, 1934, in Harlem, New York, the daughter of West Indian-born parents, Frederic Byron and Linda Gertrude (Belmar) Lorde, small-scale real estate managers. Lorde's parents named her Audrey Geraldine, but she dropped the *y* and her middle name by the time she became known to a reading audience. An early romantic poem by Lorde was published in *Seventeen* magazine when she was still a teenager. In 1954, Lorde attended the University of Mexico in Mexico City.

After her return from Mexico, Lorde enrolled at Hunter College, which was then a teacher-training school for women but since 1964 has been a co-educational institution and part of the City University of New York system. She graduated from Hunter in 1959 and proceeded to earn a master of science degree in library science in 1961 from Columbia University's prestigious School of Library Science. Soon thereafter, Lorde became a librarian at the West Chester County, New York, Mount Vernon Public Library, and in 1962, she married Edward Rollins, an attorney. Together, the couple had two children: Elizabeth Lorde-Rollins, born in 1963, and Jonathan Rollins. Lorde wrote "What My Child Learns of the Sea" during Elizabeth's first year. From 1966 until 1968, she became head librarian at the Town School, a small pre-kindergarten through eighth grade institution in New York City.

Lorde's life took a dramatic turn when *The First Cities*, her first book of poetry, was published in 1968. Awarded a grant from the National Endowment for the Arts, Lorde left her library position to become writer-in-residence for six weeks at the predominantly African-American Tougaloo College near Jackson, Mississippi. While there, Lorde met Frances Clayton, who became her long-time partner, continued writing poetry, and dis-

Audre Lorde

covered that she enjoyed teaching. Back in New York City, Lorde taught writing and courses on racism as an adjunct at three colleges and published *Cable to Rage*, a second book of poetry in 1970. In that same year, she finalized a divorce from Edward Rollins. In 1972, she publicly proclaimed her lesbian identity. For the next twenty years, Lorde wrote and published poetry, essays, a novel, and a memoir, gave public readings, became politically active, and taught college English courses for part of that time.

In 1978, Lorde developed breast cancer and underwent a radical mastectomy that she wrote about in a manuscript subsequently published as *The Cancer Journals* (1980). In 1985, she moved to St. Croix in the Virgin Islands and became known locally by her African name, Gamba Adisa. She died in St. Croix on November 17, 1992, from recurrent cancer.

Lorde's awards and achievements include a nomination for a National Book Award in 1974 for *From a Land Where Other People Live*; cofounding The Kitchen Table: Women of Color Press; two National Endowment for the Arts grants (1968 and 1981); the naming of a poetry institute in her honor at Hunter College; and the Walt Whitman Citation of Merit. She was named Poet Laureate of the State of New York in 1991, a title she held until her death. Anthologies of her poetry include *Undersong: Chosen Poems Old and New* and *The Collected Poems of Audre Lorde*. Other works include her novel *Zami: A New Spelling of My Name* and *Sister Outsider: Essays and Speeches*.

Poem Summary

In "What My Child Learns of the Sea," Lorde's speaker muses upon her daughter's future development and growing awareness as a person. One discovers that the speaker is the mother and that "my child" is her daughter. The poem, comprised of four stanzas, turns around the cycles of nature, but not in the typically accepted seasonal order of spring, summer, autumn (or fall), and winter. Rather, three seasons are introduced in the first stanza in this order: summer, spring, and autumn. The poem's title, reinforced by its repetition in the first line of the first stanza, introduces the key phrase "learns of the sea." The speaker's daughter will learn something about the sea and about life. She will learn about mystery, of the existence of "summer thunder" and "of riddles / that hide in the vortex of spring." Given that a riddle is something mysterious and difficult to understand, the speaker's daughter will move from a position of lesser understanding to one of greater comprehension, as if on a voyage of discovery and learning. Because a vortex, by definition, is a dangerous whirlpool, there is an element of danger that will be better understood. The speaker expects that her daughter will better understand these natural mysteries of sea and season "in my twilight." Though the concept of twilight embraces the half-light periods just before sunrise and just after sunset, used here, twilight represents the speaker when she approaches old age. Thus, she projects that her daughter will come to understanding when the speaker is aged. The final two lines of the first stanza introduce the idea of revision, an important part of learning. Because of the incorporation of new sense data, ideas, and reflection, one's initial ideas about the world are periodically revised. In this case, the speaker predicts that her daughter will "childlike / revise every autumn." As a metaphor, autumn can represent a person at or past middle age, but in this instance, it is modified by the word "every," indicating that actual yearly cycles are meant. What happens every autumn that would inspire revision to one's learning? In the United States, the school year begins anew every autumn, and students learn

Media Adaptations

- *A Litany for Survival: The Life and Work of Audre Lorde*, a documentary directed by Ada Gray Griffin and Michelle Parkerson, was first broadcast by PBS as part of its POV series on June 18, 1996. It is available from ThirdWorld Newsreel (www.twn.org).

- *Reading Their Work: Audre Lorde & Adrienne Rich*, a double cassette tape, is available from the National Women's Studies Association as item #AA16 (www.nwsa.org).

new things while revising what they have already learned from previous years.

The second stanza repeats the first line of the first stanza except for the phrase "of the sea." The speaker's daughter will learn as she grows older ("as her winters grow into time") mysterious things that the mature speaker has come to know. Specifically, the speaker refers to her daughter learning about something that "has ripened in my own body." The term "ripened" suggests maturity, full development. One refers to fruit as being unripe or green and not ready for eating, ripeness being the optimal time for eating, and over-ripeness too late. Ripening in one's own body refers to physical as well as mental development. Because "What My Child Learns of the Sea" deals directly with motherhood, the term suggests the development of a girl's body from childhood through adolescence to full maturity. In other words, growing from premenstrual girlhood to the years when most women are capable of childbearing, generally from the teen years into the early or mid-forties. The speaker's daughter will, as she grows older, understand that her mother bore her in her body and gave birth to her and that she herself might become a mother in the future. The stanza ends by saying that the speaker's daughter will see and understand, will learn what the speaker has learned. She will learn things about her mother and herself. This learning will "enter her eyes / with first light"—though she already can see her mother from the time of first consciousness, clearer seeing will only come with physical and mental maturity.

In stanza three, the idea of menstruation and motherhood are reinforced through the words "blood" and "milk." The stanza builds on the second, suggesting that the speaker's daughter will grow beyond thinking of her mother as child bearer and nurturer to become, to the speaker, "a strange girl" who will "step to the back / of a mirror" and will soon be "cutting my ropes / of sea thunder sun." A mirror requires light to reflect images, and the second stanza ended with the notion of the speaker's daughter learning things the speaker knows by seeing "with first light." Stepping behind a figurative mirror, the daughter steps out of and away from her mother's image and cuts the metaphorical umbilical cord, distancing herself from some of her mother's mysteries. The speaker thus speculates that she will seem less magical and mysterious to her daughter as they both grow older. To the speaker, her daughter will become "a strange girl," no longer just a dependent child to be nurtured with milk.

The fourth and last stanza repeats previous seasonal references, autumn from the first stanza and winter from the second. The contrast between the daughter's learning and awareness with the speaker's distance is emphasized by the last line: "I stand already condemned." The speaker projects into the future the fact that her daughter will come into her own but that she (the speaker) will have had a profound impact. Even though her daughter will have come into her own, her mother will have been "condemned" by having left a lasting and unshakable impression. Specifically, the speaker's modeling of how to "taste her autumns" as well as "the words / she will use for winter" will remain with the daughter, despite her growing independence. The introduction of food and taste imagery beyond infant milk is suggested with the descriptive compound "toast-brittle," but this is counterbalanced by the following "warmer than sleep," a phrase that suggests a calm, warm sea and the protective womb before birth. If there is a moral to the poem, it is that once a mother, always a mother, and once a daughter—despite growing autonomy—always a daughter. More generally, the same can be said about any parent-child relationship.

Themes

Growth and Development

"What My Child Learns of the Sea" deals in large part with the growth and development of both a mother and daughter through time. The speaker, as mother, mentions her own "ripening" as a way of comparing and contrasting the things that her daughter will learn both mentally and physically. Both the speaker and her daughter will continue to grow and develop as they grow older. The speaker has already developed into adulthood, so her daughter will only fully come to learn the kinds of things she knows when the speaker has reached her "autumn," or late-middle-aged years. Presumably, there comes a time in one's life (the "winter") when the learning process slows and one comes to terms with death. Early on, especially in infancy, the learning process is rapid and chaotic. Only during the "summer" and "autumn" years can one learn and reflect on a relatively even keel, incorporating new data.

Consciousness

Changes in consciousness over time are suggested throughout the poem. The speaker's daughter will move from a state of dependency on the mother to one of greater awareness. The speaker reflects her own self-consciousness by projecting changes in her daughter's way of seeing things as she grows older while at the same time recognizing her own perceptions. Her daughter will become more conscious as she ages, learning much from her mother but eventually coming to greater consciousness on her own. Consciousness and the articulation of self-reflective thoughts are presumably furthered along by reading and writing. Much of the daughter's basic vocabulary is instilled by the speaker. Therefore the speaker is "condemned" for "the ways" her daughter will comprehend life via her example, or model, and for "the words / she will use for winter."

Introspection

The entire poem shows introspection via the speaker as mother. Like an inner mirror, introspection helps a person reflect upon her or his life. In this case, the speaker (and presumably Lorde) examines her role in life as a mother and, by implication, as a daughter, too. When the speaker imagines her daughter standing behind a mirror and "cutting my ropes," she imagines her daughter as "a strange girl" who has found the ability to reflect about herself on her own. The speaker thereby implies that this is a necessary, if painful, stage for any daughter or child as the child reaches a certain level of maturity.

Instruction and Learning

The theme of learning runs strong through the poem. The speaker's daughter will learn much about the world from observing her mother. She will "re-vise every autumn" what she learns, implying a connection to the conventional American school year from kindergarten though college or university. She learns or will learn about her own body and of her place in the world. She learns much from her mother, but she will eventually learn things not taught her by her mother as well. Certain types of learning, such as learning a foreign language, can best be achieved at an early age, while general wisdom about life may deepen with age.

Nature and Its Meaning

The meaning and mysteries of nature permeate throughout each of the four stanzas of "What My Child Learns of the Sea." The sea, the human body, the seasons, ripening, regeneration, and mortality are all touched upon. The sea, thunder, autumn, winter, and forms of light are all mentioned twice. Nature represents cycles that are part of and beyond the individual person. The sea can represent both the womb and spirituality; it also represents the unconscious aspects of the human mind, such as dreaming. Nature embraces a wide range of phenomena that can be peaceful or dangerous. Terms such as "vortex" and "thunder" tend to evoke images of danger. Nature is full of "riddles" and reflects the mysteriousness of life.

Style

Subject

Two people, the speaker and her daughter, provide the comparison and contrast that propels "What My Child Learns of the Sea" along. The themes of motherhood and the cycles of nature interrelate strongly with these two people. What at least partly separates human beings from other animals on Earth is their advanced learning functions and ability to self-reflect. The speaker and her daughter live, nonetheless, in nature and are subject to its mysterious forces from infancy to death. Though the speaker and her daughter are the subjects, the entire poem is restricted to the speaker's point of view, her reflections on the world, and her imagination about the future.

Symbol

Specific aspects of nature, such as weather and seasonal time, represent both themselves and changes in human consciousness. Symbols such as "blood" and "milk" represent specific functions of

Topics for Further Study

- The sea (particularly the Atlantic Ocean) and its power had a profound impact on Lorde's sensibilities. Her parents were from Grenada in the West Indies, and she resided in the Virgin Islands for the last seven years of her life. In 1991, Hurricane Hugo devastated her small house. Research and analyze the good and bad effects of weather and the sea on the inhabitants of one of these islands.

- The mother-daughter relationship is a crucial element of "What My Child Learns of the Sea." Analyze ways that parents affect their children's lives. Interview a friend and her or his parents or find an autobiography or memoir that examines the author's family. Report on your findings.

- Lorde became a strong feminist as an adult, and she also combated racism. Examine ways that issues of race and gender have interrelated during the civil rights movements of a particular time period.

- Until relatively recently, little was written about breast cancer. Locate a copy of Lorde's *The Cancer Journals* and compare what she wrote with current medical treatment, ideas about prevention and early detection, alternative therapies, and ways that people respond to the disease. What common threads do you find?

- Time spent teaching at Tougaloo College changed the course of Lorde's life by helping her find her calling as poet and teacher. Using the Internet or other resources, research Tougaloo and other predominantly African-American colleges. Is the mission of such schools socially beneficial? Likewise, are single sex schools beneficial? Weigh the pros and cons for each.

female human biology, but they also represent maturation and motherhood. The symbol of the mirror, combined with allusions to light, emphasize the idea of self-reflection and changing awareness of self-image and identity. The symbols of "twilight" and "winter" are used to emphasize middle and old age, respectively. The "sea" often symbolizes the womb, spirituality, and the dream state, but it can also represent any actual large body of water such as the Atlantic Ocean or the Caribbean Sea.

Historical Context

In 1963, when she wrote "What My Child Learns of the Sea," Lorde lived and worked in New York City. The times were rife with protest and change. American participation in the Vietnam War was just beginning to escalate, so most mass protests in the United States at the time aimed for civil rights reforms. John F. Kennedy responded positively to the civil rights movement and used the powers of the federal government to support the reform movement organized by such powerful and persuasive leaders as Martin Luther King, Jr., and Malcolm X. Many of the civil rights reform pressures in 1963 sought to overturn discriminatory policies used primarily against African Americans, but these pressures subsequently broadened and flowered to embrace a wide range of similar issues. In the midst of this movement that would bring significant change in American society, Lorde gave birth to her daughter Elizabeth, the first of two children, and took a short break from her salaried job as a librarian. "What My Child Learns of the Sea" reflects her anxiety as she looked into the future. With all that was happening in the country, what would be her role? By the time of the publication of "What My Child Learns of the Sea" as part of Lorde's first book of poetry in 1968, socio-political changes in the country gave her an opportunity to become a publicly acknowledged poet, supporter of cultural diversity, and proponent of a wide variety of civil rights.

Because "What My Child Learns of the Sea" is not set in any obvious time or place (there are no specific historical references), it can be viewed both within its historical and cultural context and on its own, giving it usefulness as a barometer of Lorde's feelings in 1963 and a transcendent quality not requiring historical anchoring. However, it becomes of added interest when one learns more about Lorde's transformation from a librarian who writes poetry into a public speaker, teacher, and published poet, from a married woman to an outspoken lesbian and feminist. The poem helped her on her way through these dramatic life changes. Its publication in 1968 as part of *The First Cities* prac-

tically coincided with Lorde's residency in Tougaloo College near Jackson, Mississippi, a primarily African-American institution then in the thick of the often violent battle for civil rights. With the launch of her book and her stint outside of New York City, Lorde gained enough confidence and experience to divorce her husband and wholeheartedly join the reform movements of the early 1970s. In a sense, "What My Child Learns of the Sea" is a self-reflective precursor to the massive changes that would happen in her life, partly as a result of its publication in book form.

Critical Overview

Audre Lorde is generally presented as displaying a poetic voice that blends feminism, lesbianism, and Caribbean and African-American concerns in a passionate way. Clarence Major, in *The Garden Thrives: Twentieth-Century African-American Poetry*, places Lorde in a pantheon of African-American writers such as Etheridge Knight, Sonia Sanchez, and Amiri Baraka, who developed in the 1960s and who "tried to give lyrical expression to the complex personal, social, and political issues" of the time. Lorde was personally and professionally befriended and supported by fellow poet Adrienne Rich. According to critic Beverly Threatt Kullii, as quoted in Andrews, et al., Lorde's *The First Cities*, her first published book of poetry (including "What My Child Learns of the Sea"), "was cited as an innovative and refreshing rhetorical departure from the confrontational tone prevalent in African American poetry at the time." Publication of the first edition of Lorde's *Chosen Poems: Old and New* in 1982 (which also includes "What My Child Learns of the Sea") "cemented her reputation." As of the mid-1990s, only a few years after her death, Lorde was considered "an influential and serious talent." Lorde can be found on the world wide web, where she is celebrated in web sites devoted to a wide variety of topics and causes ranging from poetry, feminism, lesbianism, and African-American cultural heritage.

Criticism

Erik France

France is a librarian and college counselor, who teaches history at University Liggett School

Compare & Contrast

- **1960s:** The Civil Rights movement in the United States is bitterly contested. Reforms are made but many people are slain during the process, including major public figures John F. Kennedy, Malcolm X, Martin Luther King, and Robert F. Kennedy.

  Today: The Civil Rights movement is largely confined to consolidating and protecting gains already made, combined with legal challenges and organized protests attempting further reforms, particularly in the area of gay/lesbian rights.

- **1960s:** The first major open gay/lesbian movement is sparked by the Stonewall Riots in New York City, and *Midnight Cowboy*, the first ma-jor movie to depict gay lead characters, is released.

  Today: Gay and lesbian characters on cable television shows such as *Queer as Folk* and *Sex and the City* reflect wider acceptance of gay/lesbian citizens and a more open discussion of sexuality and gender expectations among an interested public.

- **1960s:** Feminism's "Second Wave" advocates massive reforms in academia and the general work place as well as a reshaping of cultural values and a redefinition of gender roles.

  Today: As with civil rights in general, feminists focus on consolidating gains and also electing more women to public office.

---

and English at Macomb College near Detroit, Michigan. In the following essay, France analyzes the prophetic nature of the poem from both a biographical and a textual perspective.

In "What My Child Learns of the Sea," Lorde employs both cyclical and linear imagery to explore the mysteries of human identity from a female perspective. Seasons and weather come in recurrent cycles, while daughters, like sons, typically proceed along a trajectory that takes them from the ignorance and innocence of infancy—via a path of learned experience—toward an awareness of mortality and, finally, to death. All girls and women are daughters, but not all daughters become mothers. In this poem, the speaker is evidently a mother contemplating the changes that will occur in her daughter's awareness and perspective as she grows up.

If one considers "What My Child Learns of the Sea" from the perspective of Lorde's actual life, it works in a number of ways as a sort of prophecy or prediction of the future, especially if one focuses on what "ripened in" Lorde's "own body." First, Lorde gave birth to her daughter Elizabeth around the time she wrote the poem, making her a mother to her daughter, as well as a daughter to her own mother. At the same time, she was struggling with her sexual identity, for though married, she would eventually divorce her husband and redefine herself as a lesbian who identified and oriented herself sexually—exclusively—with women. What also came to ripen in her body was what eventually killed her: breast cancer, a disease that destroyed her via that which had also produced "the milk . . . given" to her daughter. The poem probably also reflects Lorde's self-identity as the child of her own mother, who had been born on Grenada, an island surrounded by the sea and subject to seasonal hurricanes and storms. Lorde herself lived out the last years of her life on St. Croix, another island in the Caribbean, and had her own house visited and damaged by the powerful natural energies of Hurricane Hugo less than two years before she died of recurrent cancer.

But what if one considers "What My Child Learns of the Sea" from the interior vantage point of the text only? Setting aside external biographical facts and focusing on the text, one may still feel the prophetic qualities of the speaker, who in the

> *The speaker's child will learn, and grow, and develop into an adult, and a relative power shift will occur. The child, until this time dependent on her mother for lifeblood and 'milk,' will be able to emerge as an independent person."*

last line says, regarding her daughter's future outlook, "I stand already condemned." This speaker assumes that her daughter will grow up to be independent of her, to move eventually from "riddles / that hide in the vortex of spring" in her early years to become "a strange girl" who metaphorically cuts the emotional umbilical cord of dependency to become her own person and separate self. Spring traditionally represents the childhood and adolescence of a human life. The speaker's child, after surviving the wild mysteries and riddles of her springtime, will, as she crosses into summer, or early adulthood, be able to demythologize her mother and see the world through the reflection of her own mirror. It is important in her development that she see for herself rather than see everything reflected through the eyes of her mother. In other words, the speaker's child will learn, and grow, and develop into an adult, and a relative power shift will occur. The child, until this time dependent on her mother for lifeblood and "milk," will be able to emerge as an independent person. This is essential if she is to reach what psychologists call self-actualization, reaching toward fullest potential as an adult. She will no longer think of her mother as all-powerful. The speaker realizes and laments this. She is also saddened by the fact that with growing awareness, her daughter will come to recognize her own mortality, that she, like her mother, will eventually reach her "winter" and die, for this reinforces the speaker's own sense of mortality. To the speaker, autumn represents the season when one can reflect, can become "childlike," can "taste . . . warmer than sleep." Ideally, a woman in the autumn of life is

allowed to productively pursue her dreams and still remain healthy enough to be able to distract herself from the inevitable approach of the final season. In the poem, despite the speaker's sadness, the daughter's learning process is essentially healthy.

To fully develop as a person, a daughter must ultimately forge her own identity, one that is distinctly separate and not merely an extension of her mother's; this Lorde did. She eventually proclaimed a new adult identity to the listening world, years after the publication of "What My Child Learns of the Sea," an identity that embraced many elements. Calling herself "a black, lesbian, mother, warrior, poet," and feminist, she evidently came to recognize and develop those elements most important to her core personality. Knowing this, one can return to the poem and consider Lorde's developing identity. Her mother had sent mixed messages about being black and of being at least partly of African lineage via the West Indies; her mother had apparently favored her lighter-skinned sisters. Seeing oneself in the mirror according to society's mores reinforces one's self-identity. If one places Lorde's mother into the role of speaker in "What My Child Learns of the Sea," Lorde herself becomes the "strange girl" who metaphorically steps to the back of her mother's—and white-dominated American society—symbolic reflecting mirror, cuts its ropes, and lets it fall crashing to the floor. This cutting is the willful act of a warrior, one who has grown to refuse the socially accepted ways of seeing things. The cutting of the ropes is the first action taken by one ready to challenge and fight against them.

Lorde, by becoming a mother, performed the one role widely accepted by many elements of any society. But in all other ways, she challenged the status quo. She discerned the "riddles / that hide in the vortex of spring" and found the "words" to "use" that would condemn the received social norms transmitted through her mother. Being black meant she was treated as a minority in American society; being feminist put her in the vanguard of her time; being a lesbian and warrior threatened widely accepted ideals of male roles. Lorde is quoted by Margaret Homans in the 1991 publication *African American Writers* as saying: "I learned to speak the truth by accepting many parts of myself and making them serve one another." As a poet, she was able to tap all of these identities. In "What My Child Learns of the Sea," Lorde is just beginning to formulate her answers to the riddles she found in the spring of life. She has entered autumn and can reflect and see forward.

Because of its origin at the time in Lorde's life when she had arrived at a unique forward-looking and backward-looking nexus, "What My Child Learns of the Sea" can be interpreted as a riddle or prophecy that cuts both ways. It reflects upon her position in the world, one that is both cyclical, like the seasons, and linear. Coming from a lineage that ties her through blood to her mother and all the mothers before her, she has helped continue the cycle of human life by giving birth to a daughter; yet her awareness of the linear progression of her life and that of the life of her daughter projected into the future, gives her a sadness derived from the knowledge of mortality. With so much yet to do, mortality seems all the sadder. Still, through "What My Child Learns of the Sea" and other poems and writings, Lorde's vision will carry on. As Lorde explained to Claudia Tate in an interview for *Black Women Writers at Work*: "I write not only for my peers but for those who will come after me, to say, I was there, and I passed on, and you will pass on, too." Like the speaker's child, Lorde passed through life, learning, revising, ripening, condemning the past, and cutting the ropes of old ways of seeing.

Source: Erik France, Critical Essay on "What My Child Learns of the Sea," in *Poetry for Students*, The Gale Group, 2002.

Pamela Steed Hill

Hill is the author of a poetry collection, has published widely in literary journals, and is an editor for a university publications department. In the following essay, Hill suggests that the mother's feelings toward the daughter in this poem are a positive reaction to the poet's negative and hurtful relationship with her own mother.

Critics and readers in general widely accept that Audre Lorde's poetry provides a strong voice for black women everywhere and for all women with feminist views and/or a lesbian lifestyle. Arguably, her work is both staunchly political and direly personal as she addresses the issues of women's and gay rights, as well as the battle with cancer that would take her life decades after she began to write. But these subjects, vital as they are, do not define the real heart of Lorde's creative inspirations as a poet. Her work often explores relationships between people—men and women, female lovers, and mothers and daughters, in particular. The latter is especially poignant in her work, as she frequently writes about her own daughter and the unconditional love, encouragement, fear, and anxiety that all come with raising

What Do I Read Next?

- Simone de Beauvoir's *The Second Sex* (1949) foreshadowed the "second wave" of feminism that arrived in the United States in the 1960s with an analysis of Western gender roles.

- Nancy Friday's *My Mother/My Self* (1977) explores the psychological inter-relationships between mothers and daughters in a provocative but accessible way.

- Betty Friedan's *The Feminine Mystique*, first published in 1963, helped usher in the "second wave" of feminism. Friedan explores the conflicting pressures on adult women at the time.

- Audre Lorde's poetry volume *The Black Unicorn* (1978) embraces African deities and myths and reinforces her lesbian identity.

- In *The Cancer Journals* (1980), Lorde describes in detailed nonfiction form part of her harrowing battle with breast cancer.

a child. Lorde was always forthcoming in the prose she wrote and in interviews when she addressed her own childhood and relationship with her mother. Apparently, her mother was less than encouraging to the young Audre, even resenting her and attempting to repress her inquisitive nature and creative tendencies. But once she became a mother herself, Lorde was determined not to do the same to her own children. "What My Child Learns of the Sea" is evidence of that conviction.

In a interview with critic and editor Claudia Tate, published in *Black Women Writers at Work* in 1983, Lorde had this to say in response to Tate's question, "For whom do you write?":

> I write not only for my peers but for those who will come after me, to say I was there, and I passed on, and you will pass on, too. But you're here now, so do it. I believe very strongly in survival and teaching. I feel that is my work.

This sentiment is echoed beautifully in "What My Child Learns of the Sea," in which the

Life is not a pat movement from one pre-set stage to another but, rather, is interspersed with moments and events that may make a young person feel very old or an elderly individual glow with the freshness of youth."

metaphors reflect a mother's coming to terms with her own mortality and with the aging of her daughter into a woman who will face the same someday. The "survival and teaching" in this poem are actually accomplished through letting go—through the speaker's willingness to accept that the child she has given life to will one day grow into "a strange girl [who] will step / to the back of a mirror / cutting my ropes," and become her own unique, independent person. It is not an easy task for a mother to acknowledge that her daughter's individuality is more vital "than blood / or the milk" she has provided to sustain and nourish the child's life. But, Lorde knows from her own experience that anything less is repressive and detrimental to both physical and emotional well-being. She finds it better to make the ultimate motherly sacrifice of setting the child free, not as a way of abandoning her daughter, but to give her the leeway to learn on her own and make her own choices. This may also be seen as the ultimate act of unconditional motherly love.

The nature metaphors that pervade "What My Child Learns of the Sea" imply the bond between a mother and daughter that should be natural, but which, of course, does not always seem to be. In spite of her own childhood experiences, though—or perhaps *because* of them—Lorde sees her role as a mother as providing a connection between "sea and thunder and spring," while at the same time understanding her child will learn the connection, but then "revise [it] every autumn." This method of teaching is like handing a child a book with much useful information in it, but also with many blank pages on which she can write her own thoughts and

responses to that information. Education, as well as love, it seems, is enhanced by the freedom to discover it on one's own.

Even though the strongest message in this poem is the importance of teaching a child about life with as few ropes and boundaries as possible, it does not mean that powerful ties between a parent and child are less important. On the contrary, the entire premise of "What My Child Learns of the Sea" stems from a very close bonding between mother and daughter, one so close that the knowledge passed from the speaker to the child has already "ripened" in her own body. Like the blood and milk she has given so that her daughter may live, her *teachings* also take on a physical characteristic. In this sense, what the child "learns" is as real and tangible as a ripened piece of fruit that the mother may give her daughter for nourishment. The bond is so strong that the threat of separation is no threat at all. Instead, the mother understands the natural course of life's passing, that she has secured her daughter enough with love that the child will grow to carry on her own life safe in that knowledge even though her mother is no longer there. Whether the last line of the poem is a reference to the poet's acknowledgement of her diagnosis of cancer or simply a metaphorical allusion to an older human being making way for the young, it is probably not intended as harshly as it sounds. Yes, "condemned" is a severe word, but most likely the speaker refers only to death as a natural part of life. There is sadness here, but not bitterness.

It is not unusual for poets to use the seasons of the year to represent time passing or to lament the aging process, and most run the risk of becoming trite with such a common metaphor. In this poem, however, Lorde manages to employ the seasons in a subtle, yet telling manner, avoiding banality and presenting an effective touch. Part of the accomplishment lies simply in the order—or lack of order—in which the seasons are listed. Instead of the typical spring-through-winter narrative, this poem runs summer, spring, autumn, spring, autumn, winter. There seems to be no cohesive pattern and yet the discordant presentation gives the message more credence. Life is not a pat movement from one pre-set stage to another but, rather, is interspersed with moments and events that may make a young person feel very old or an elderly individual glow with the freshness of youth. In "What My Child Learns of the Sea," the speaker, or the poet herself, knows all too well that life's "winter" can arrive early and that someday her daughter will face that season herself, hopefully at a much older age than the mother. She also playfully asserts that whatever the daughter makes of her "summer thunders" or the "riddles / that hide in the curve of spring" she will take the time to "revise" when she reaches the autumn of life, or at least when she *feels like* autumn. Notice that when this third season of the year is mentioned again toward the end of the poem, it is described as either "toast-brittle or warmer than sleep," all depending on how her child, then grown, will "taste" it. Autumn, it seems, can be just the harbinger of winter or it can still bask in the warmth of the summer just gone by.

When a poem is as heartfelt and personal to the poet as this one is to Lorde, it is difficult to separate biography from creativity, but in "What My Child Learns of the Sea" she incorporates the two so well that a reader does not know where one ends and the other begins. Perhaps there are no stopping or starting points, just a continuous mixture of real feelings and intriguing verse. Lorde's claim that she wrote for "those who will come after" her ring thoughtfully true in this poem, as the words she passed on to her daughter reflect that dedication and conviction to the fullest. Clearly, the poet not only overcame a strained, less-than-nourishing relationship with her mother, but succeeded in turning it about-face into a steadfast, loving connection with her own child.

Source: Pamela Steed Hill, Critical Essay on "What My Child Learns of the Sea," in *Poetry for Students*, The Gale Group, 2002.

Deneka Candace MacDonald

MacDonald is an instructor of English Literature and media studies. In this essay, MacDonald considers Lorde's poetry in light of her feminist political ambitions and strong belief in both the "Black mother in us all" and the need to understand the difference.

"What My Child Learns of the Sea," is, like most Lorde poems, a controlled emotional frenzy full of carefully constructed metaphors and cleverly placed images. Moreover, the politics that Lorde advocated in the 1990s are already clearly evident in her poetry in the 1960s.

Audre Lorde's poetry is filled with both a controlled rage and an optimistic voice. As Maggie Humm notes in *A Reader's Guide to Contemporary Feminist Literary Criticism*, Lorde certified that she was a "Black lesbian feminist socialist mother of two." Indeed, this self proclamation is deliberately without punctuation in order to ensure that racism and homophobia are not given the

> *While there is both an angry and discontented tone here, there is also the faint glimmer of hope."*

chance to privilege one term over the other. Consequently, as one might imagine, Lorde spent her life fighting racism and homophobia through her work. Poetry was but one weapon with which Lorde chose to fight this battle.

"What My Child Learns of the Sea" was written in 1963 and published originally in 1968. The images of earth, Mother Nature, and motherhood within the poem are significant to both Lorde personally and to Black feminism as a discourse. Crucially, Lorde has a history of invoking motherhood as an image in her work and consequently makes reference to "the Black mother in us all," a concept similar to the poet Adrienne Rich's "Lesbian continuum"; both concepts invoke the spirit of community among women while still highlighting the difference of experience, thus they have become well used terms within contemporary feminist discourse.

Indeed, the literal mother and the mystical mother (of nature, of spiritualism, etc.) is one of enormous power and significance among Afra-American and African and Aboriginal cultures that venerate the image of mother. Lorde herself argued against the perception that Black matriarchy was a "social disease" in the 1960s and saw this issue as one that took away from Black women's strength and energy. Acknowledging Lorde's issues with mothering, Maggie Humm notes: "this source of energy Lorde locates in the semiotic—in mother-bonding. . . . Many of her poems explore divisions and hatred between mothers and daughters." Thus, it is on the topic of racist oppression that Lorde spent her life working against and helping to bring to the forefront of feminist discourse and criticism.

The 1960s was a time when feminist discourse, theory, and literature were challenging the notion of origin—of specifically male and female authorship and of authority. Feminist criticism itself began to play a large role in the women's movement for the first time during the 1960s and 1970s, leading to the now popular slogan coined by Lorde's contemporary Adrienne Rich, "the personal is political." This concept certainly fed into major feminist literature of the period and Audre Lorde's work is no exception.

"What My Child Learns of the Sea" is divided into three stanzas and has several meanings among its lines. However, at all levels, the poem addresses the challenges that all women face as well as their experiences—both past, present, and future. The first stanza highlights this struggle through the use of natural images: the sea, the seasons, the weather, and time. Contrasting the warmth and safety of summer with the dangerous anger of thunder, Lorde illustrates the concept of unpredictability and goes on to highlight questions and uncertainty that "hide" throughout the many corners of life: "What my child learns of the sea / of the summer thunders / of the riddles / that hide in the curve of spring." While there is both an angry and discontented tone here, there is also the faint glimmer of hope. While she acknowledges that her child will learn of these struggles through naivete, she will also challenge them herself on her own terms: "she will learn in my twilights / and childlike / revise every autumn." Moreover, the child of whom the poem speaks can be seen as a metaphor for all women who are the children of the Great Mother. It is all women who must learn their own experience, follow their own path, and discover in retrospect that the riddles of life must be faced.

While the voice of the poem is ambiguous—real mother/Great Mother, real woman/all women—it is in the second stanza of the poem that Lorde's politics can be seen most clearly: "What my child learns / as her winters grow into time / has ripened in my own body / to enter her eyes with first light." Here, the child/woman has learned and grown wise with her years. She has felt the changes through her body and her knowledge has ripened to "enter her eyes with first light." Light is the provoking term here, as it is a symbolic metaphor which Lorde continually used throughout her life in her personal politics and fight against racism. She saw racism as an invisible enemy, but one that, for Black women, permeated their existence from the day they were born (from "first light"). Light, for Audre Lorde, is a metaphor that illustrates the lack of Black awareness and the marginalization of invisible women who are unseen within dominant white culture—even within feminist white culture. Humm notes that "Lorde's use of the imagery of light, her attention to the very different experiences of Afra-American and Australian Aboriginal women suggest that a Black feminist critique can have global implications." This globalization of recognition for Black women's experience in white (feminist) culture was

an agenda Lorde kept throughout her life and one which is certainly seen among her poetry.

The final stanza of the poem can be seen to have several levels of meaning. On the one hand, the final stanza is a tribute to the initial cutting of the umbilical cord which all mothers face, as well as the growing sense of loss as a child grows older: "cutting my ropes." The mother of the poem has given both milk for nourishment and shed blood for protection. Despite all, the child will emerge, a separate being, to taste her own autumns, walk her own paths, and choose her own words with which to describe her experience. The mother of the poem stands "already condemned" because she cannot assume her child's experience. Because, when all is said and done, one can never understand another's oppression.

On a deeper level, the final stanza of the poem is a message to all women and a political statement about difference. "[M]ore than blood / or the milk I have given" are powerful lines which speak to the historical struggles and tragedy of Afra-American and Aboriginal peoples with Lorde is all too familiar. The image of shedding blood for a child is both literal (as in the birth process) and more profound (as in for protection against danger, for the right for freedom and individuality, for knowledge). The struggle against oppression and the recognition of difference are issues that permeate not only the poem, but all of Lorde's work. In *Feminism, Theory and the Politics of Difference*, Chris Weedon gives an in-depth analysis of the politics of difference and spends a considerable amount of time on the politics of Lorde herself. Weedon highlights the concern of Black lesbian feminist writing within the white middle class academy and notes that "one of the strengths of early second-wave feminism in the west was its emphasis on consciousness raising and the politics of the personal." She goes on to recognize Lorde as one of the key figures in raising this awareness for Black lesbian women. Lorde maintained that difference was key in the understanding of personal struggle and that oppression could not be understood at only one level (that is, the level of experience for white middle class American women). Thus, in "What My Child Learns of the Sea," the voice / child/mother will either taste her autumns "toast-brittle or warmer than sleep"—to each their own, but be aware.

The epiphany of the poem exists in the lines "one day a strange girl will step / to the back of a mirror." Perhaps it is the child who steps forth, the mother herself looking back at the child she once was, or all women who one day look into the mirror and see a strange girl before them. All three are possible and the ambiguousness of the poem's subject is purposeful. It is all three images that the mirror reproduces in its profoundly stagnant reflection.

The mirror is highly significant here as it has become an image throughout literature which is a profound patriarchal symbol and oppressor of women. Issues surrounding mirror myths (beauty myths), metaphors for myths (ponds, water, sea, etc.), and the literal physical mirror itself have become the subject of much critical debate and the source of much feminist criticism since the 1960s. Sandra Gilbert and Susan Gubar (among others) consider the image of the literary woman in *Mad Women in the Attic: The Woman Writer and the Nineteenth Century Literary Imagination.* Importantly, they pivot their analysis of the nineteenth-century woman writer on the image of the mirror. Similar to Lorde's poem, Gilbert and Gubar use the image of the mirror as a metaphor for self analysis, and further, like Lorde herself, they see a woman writer's self contemplation as beginning with a searching glance in the mirror of a male inscribed literary text. Where those "eternal lineaments [are] fixed on her like a mask." In other words, she begins her self analysis with preconceived notions—notions created, maintained and solidified in male dominated literary texts.

Specifically Gilbert and Gubar make reference to Mary Elizabeth Coleridge's nineteenth-century poem "The Other Side of the Mirror" and Walt Disney's *Snow White and the Seven Dwarves* in which women discover that they are prisoners of the mirror. Like Lorde's speaker in "What My Child Learns of the Sea" the woman represented in Coleridge's poem is one who sits in horror as she cannot recognize the image before her in the mirror. Try as she might to escape the image reflected in her looking glass—an image constructed by her social surroundings and estranged from herself—she realizes that she is but a vision, a shadow who cannot escape her domination. Similarly, in the Snow White story, intriguingly the mirror is the essential metaphorical and literal image: on the one hand, the metaphorical mirror which women are trapped and on the other, the literal mirror in which one's imperfect (for it cannot ever be perfect) image is both ensnared and reflected. Thus, Gilbert and Gubar argue that "to be caught and trapped in a mirror . . . is to be driven inward, obsessively studying self-images as if seeking a viable self."

This frightening concept is one that appears often in feminist literature as the image of woman, her relationship with her person and the representation of her body and self becomes more prominent in feminist discourse. Not unlike the mother/daughter relationship in Lorde's poem, Snow White is, of course, a potential replacement for the Queen—a younger version of "woman," a freshly and newly beautiful woman to replace the older and now (sexually) used "mother." However, while Lorde invokes this powerful mirror image for her feminist purposes in "What My Child Learns of the Sea," the woman in Lorde's poem does not simply gaze into the mirror in hopelessness. Rather, significantly, she steps to the back of it, defying it, "cutting [the] ropes" or the chains that have tied her there and shattering the frozen image with her movement.

Audre Lorde worked through her poetry to define herself and capture her own experience as a Black gay woman in America who grew up with the knowledge of race always at the forefront of her life. In the film documentary *A Litany for Survival: The Life and Work of Audre Lorde,* Lorde's acceptance speech for the New York State poet 1991–1993 goes a long way to understanding her poetry:

> I've been asking myself . . . what does it mean that a black, lesbian, feminist, warrior, poet, mother is named as the state poet of New York? It means that we live in a world full of the most intense contradictions, and we must find ways to use the best we have—ourselves, our work—to bridge those contradictions.

Source: Deneka Candace MacDonald, Critical Essay on "What My Child Learns of the Sea," in *Poetry for Students,* The Gale Group, 2002.

Sources

Andrews, William L., Frances Smith Foster, and Trudier Harris, eds., *The Oxford Companion to African American Literature,* Oxford University Press, 1997, pp. 461–63.

Gilbert, Sandra, and Susan Gubar, *The Madwoman in the Attic: The Woman Writer and the Nineteenth-Century Literary Imagination,* Yale University Press, 1979, pp. 15, 37.

Homans, Margaret, "Audre Lorde," in *African American Writers,* Charles Scribner's Sons, 1991, p. 273.

Humm, Maggie, *A Reader's Guide to Contemporary Feminist Literary Criticism,* Harvester Wheatsheaf, 1994, pp. 179, 180–81.

A Litany for Survival: The Life and Work of Audre Lorde, directed by Ada Gay Griffin and Michelle Parkerson, 90 min., Third World Newsreel, 1996, videocassette.

Lorde, Audre, *Coal,* W. W. Norton and Company, 1976, p. 22.

———, *Undersong: Chosen Poems Old and New*, revised ed., W. W. Norton & Company, 1992.

Major, Clarence, ed., *The Garden Thrives: Twentieth-Century African-American Poetry*, HarperPerennial, 1996, pp. xxxix, 122–23.

Tate, Claudia, *Black Women Writers at Work*, Continuum, 1983, pp. 100–16.

Weedon, Chris, *Feminism, Theory and the Politics of Difference*, Blackwell Publishers, 1999, p. 179.

Further Reading

Clark, Darlene, and Kathleen Thompson, *A Shining Thread of Hope: The History of Black Women in America*, Broadway Books, 1998.

Clark and Thompson provide an historical overview of the changing roles of African-American women from colonial times to the mid-1990s.

Lorde, Audre, *Sister Outsider: Essays and Speeches*, Crossing Press, 1984.

This collection of nonfiction writings explore Lorde's engagement in public life, following themes of alienation, diversity, conflict, and the need to find common ground, especially among the historically oppressed.

———, *Zami: A New Spelling of My Name*, Crossing Press, 1982.

This fictionalized treatment of Lorde's childhood gives considerable insight into her upbringing and developing sense of identity.

Glossary of Literary Terms

A

Abstract: Used as a noun, the term refers to a short summary or outline of a longer work. As an adjective applied to writing or literary works, abstract refers to words or phrases that name things not knowable through the five senses.

Accent: The emphasis or stress placed on a syllable in poetry. Traditional poetry commonly uses patterns of accented and unaccented syllables (known as feet) that create distinct rhythms. Much modern poetry uses less formal arrangements that create a sense of freedom and spontaneity.

Aestheticism: A literary and artistic movement of the nineteenth century. Followers of the movement believed that art should not be mixed with social, political, or moral teaching. The statement "art for art's sake" is a good summary of aestheticism. The movement had its roots in France, but it gained widespread importance in England in the last half of the nineteenth century, where it helped change the Victorian practice of including moral lessons in literature.

Affective Fallacy: An error in judging the merits or faults of a work of literature. The "error" results from stressing the importance of the work's effect upon the reader—that is, how it makes a reader "feel" emotionally, what it does as a literary work—instead of stressing its inner qualities as a created object, or what it "is."

Age of Johnson: The period in English literature between 1750 and 1798, named after the most prominent literary figure of the age, Samuel Johnson. Works written during this time are noted for their emphasis on "sensibility," or emotional quality. These works formed a transition between the rational works of the Age of Reason, or Neoclassical period, and the emphasis on individual feelings and responses of the Romantic period.

Age of Reason: See *Neoclassicism*

Age of Sensibility: See *Age of Johnson*

Agrarians: A group of Southern American writers of the 1930s and 1940s who fostered an economic and cultural program for the South based on agriculture, in opposition to the industrial society of the North. The term can refer to any group that promotes the value of farm life and agricultural society.

Alexandrine Meter: See *Meter*

Allegory: A narrative technique in which characters representing things or abstract ideas are used to convey a message or teach a lesson. Allegory is typically used to teach moral, ethical, or religious lessons but is sometimes used for satiric or political purposes.

Alliteration: A poetic device where the first consonant sounds or any vowel sounds in words or syllables are repeated.

Allusion: A reference to a familiar literary or historical person or event, used to make an idea more easily understood.

Amerind Literature: The writing and oral traditions of Native Americans. Native American literature was originally passed on by word of mouth, so it consisted largely of stories and events that were easily memorized. Amerind prose is often rhythmic like poetry because it was recited to the beat of a ceremonial drum.

Analogy: A comparison of two things made to explain something unfamiliar through its similarities to something familiar, or to prove one point based on the acceptedness of another. Similes and metaphors are types of analogies.

Anapest: See *Foot*

Angry Young Men: A group of British writers of the 1950s whose work expressed bitterness and disillusionment with society. Common to their work is an antihero who rebels against a corrupt social order and strives for personal integrity.

Anthropomorphism: The presentation of animals or objects in human shape or with human characteristics. The term is derived from the Greek word for "human form."

Antimasque: See *Masque*

Antithesis: The antithesis of something is its direct opposite. In literature, the use of antithesis as a figure of speech results in two statements that show a contrast through the balancing of two opposite ideas. Technically, it is the second portion of the statement that is defined as the "antithesis"; the first portion is the "thesis."

Apocrypha: Writings tentatively attributed to an author but not proven or universally accepted to be their works. The term was originally applied to certain books of the Bible that were not considered inspired and so were not included in the "sacred canon."

Apollonian and Dionysian: The two impulses believed to guide authors of dramatic tragedy. The Apollonian impulse is named after Apollo, the Greek god of light and beauty and the symbol of intellectual order. The Dionysian impulse is named after Dionysus, the Greek god of wine and the symbol of the unrestrained forces of nature. The Apollonian impulse is to create a rational, harmonious world, while the Dionysian is to express the irrational forces of personality.

Apostrophe: A statement, question, or request addressed to an inanimate object or concept or to a nonexistent or absent person.

Archetype: The word archetype is commonly used to describe an original pattern or model from which all other things of the same kind are made. This term was introduced to literary criticism from the psychology of Carl Jung. It expresses Jung's theory that behind every person's "unconscious," or repressed memories of the past, lies the "collective unconscious" of the human race: memories of the countless typical experiences of our ancestors. These memories are said to prompt illogical associations that trigger powerful emotions in the reader. Often, the emotional process is primitive, even primordial. Archetypes are the literary images that grow out of the "collective unconscious." They appear in literature as incidents and plots that repeat basic patterns of life. They may also appear as stereotyped characters.

Argument: The argument of a work is the author's subject matter or principal idea.

Art for Art's Sake: See *Aestheticism*

Assonance: The repetition of similar vowel sounds in poetry.

Audience: The people for whom a piece of literature is written. Authors usually write with a certain audience in mind, for example, children, members of a religious or ethnic group, or colleagues in a professional field. The term "audience" also applies to the people who gather to see or hear any performance, including plays, poetry readings, speeches, and concerts.

Automatic Writing: Writing carried out without a preconceived plan in an effort to capture every random thought. Authors who engage in automatic writing typically do not revise their work, preferring instead to preserve the revealed truth and beauty of spontaneous expression.

Avant-garde: A French term meaning "vanguard." It is used in literary criticism to describe new writing that rejects traditional approaches to literature in favor of innovations in style or content.

B

Ballad: A short poem that tells a simple story and has a repeated refrain. Ballads were originally intended to be sung. Early ballads, known as folk ballads, were passed down through generations, so their authors are often unknown. Later ballads composed by known authors are called literary ballads.

Baroque: A term used in literary criticism to describe literature that is complex or ornate in style or diction. Baroque works typically express tension, anxiety, and violent emotion. The term "Baroque Age" designates a period in Western European literature beginning in the late sixteenth century and ending about one hundred years later.

Works of this period often mirror the qualities of works more generally associated with the label "baroque" and sometimes feature elaborate conceits.

Baroque Age: See *Baroque*

Baroque Period: See *Baroque*

Beat Generation: See *Beat Movement*

Beat Movement: A period featuring a group of American poets and novelists of the 1950s and 1960s—including Jack Kerouac, Allen Ginsberg, Gregory Corso, William S. Burroughs, and Lawrence Ferlinghetti—who rejected established social and literary values. Using such techniques as stream-of-consciousness writing and jazz-influenced free verse and focusing on unusual or abnormal states of mind—generated by religious ecstasy or the use of drugs—the Beat writers aimed to create works that were unconventional in both form and subject matter.

Beat Poets: See *Beat Movement*

Beats, The: See *Beat Movement*

Belles-lettres: A French term meaning "fine letters" or "beautiful writing." It is often used as a synonym for literature, typically referring to imaginative and artistic rather than scientific or expository writing. Current usage sometimes restricts the meaning to light or humorous writing and appreciative essays about literature.

Black Aesthetic Movement: A period of artistic and literary development among African Americans in the 1960s and early 1970s. This was the first major African American artistic movement since the Harlem Renaissance and was closely paralleled by the civil rights and black power movements. The black aesthetic writers attempted to produce works of art that would be meaningful to the black masses. Key figures in black aesthetics included one of its founders, poet and playwright Amiri Baraka, formerly known as LeRoi Jones; poet and essayist Haki R. Madhubuti, formerly Don L. Lee; poet and playwright Sonia Sanchez; and dramatist Ed Bullins.

Black Arts Movement: See *Black Aesthetic Movement*

Black Comedy: See *Black Humor*

Black Humor: Writing that places grotesque elements side by side with humorous ones in an attempt to shock the reader, forcing him or her to laugh at the horrifying reality of a disordered world.

Black Mountain School: Black Mountain College and three of its instructors—Robert Creeley, Robert Duncan, and Charles Olson—were all influential in projective verse. Today poets working in projective verse are referred to as members of the Black Mountain school.

Blank Verse: Loosely, any unrhymed poetry, but more generally, unrhymed iambic pentameter verse (composed of lines of five two-syllable feet with the first syllable accented, the second unaccented). Blank verse has been used by poets since the Renaissance for its flexibility and its graceful, dignified tone.

Bloomsbury Group: A group of English writers, artists, and intellectuals who held informal artistic and philosophical discussions in Bloomsbury, a district of London, from around 1907 to the early 1930s. The Bloomsbury Group held no uniform philosophical beliefs but did commonly express an aversion to moral prudery and a desire for greater social tolerance.

Bon Mot: A French term meaning "good word." A *bon mot* is a witty remark or clever observation.

Breath Verse: See *Projective Verse*

Burlesque: Any literary work that uses exaggeration to make its subject appear ridiculous, either by treating a trivial subject with profound seriousness or by treating a dignified subject frivolously. The word "burlesque" may also be used as an adjective, as in "burlesque show," to mean "striptease act."

C

Cadence: The natural rhythm of language caused by the alternation of accented and unaccented syllables. Much modern poetry—notably free verse—deliberately manipulates cadence to create complex rhythmic effects.

Caesura: A pause in a line of poetry, usually occurring near the middle. It typically corresponds to a break in the natural rhythm or sense of the line but is sometimes shifted to create special meanings or rhythmic effects.

Canzone: A short Italian or Provencal lyric poem, commonly about love and often set to music. The *canzone* has no set form but typically contains five or six stanzas made up of seven to twenty lines of eleven syllables each. A shorter, five- to ten-line "envoy," or concluding stanza, completes the poem.

Carpe Diem: A Latin term meaning "seize the day." This is a traditional theme of poetry, especially lyrics. A *carpe diem* poem advises the reader or the person it addresses to live for today and enjoy the pleasures of the moment.

Catharsis: The release or purging of unwanted emotions—specifically fear and pity—brought about by exposure to art. The term was first used by the Greek philosopher Aristotle in his *Poetics* to refer to the desired effect of tragedy on spectators.

Celtic Renaissance: A period of Irish literary and cultural history at the end of the nineteenth century. Followers of the movement aimed to create a romantic vision of Celtic myth and legend. The most significant works of the Celtic Renaissance typically present a dreamy, unreal world, usually in reaction against the reality of contemporary problems.

Celtic Twilight: See *Celtic Renaissance*

Character: Broadly speaking, a person in a literary work. The actions of characters are what constitute the plot of a story, novel, or poem. There are numerous types of characters, ranging from simple, stereotypical figures to intricate, multifaceted ones. In the techniques of anthropomorphism and personification, animals—and even places or things—can assume aspects of character. "Characterization" is the process by which an author creates vivid, believable characters in a work of art. This may be done in a variety of ways, including (1) direct description of the character by the narrator; (2) the direct presentation of the speech, thoughts, or actions of the character; and (3) the responses of other characters to the character. The term "character" also refers to a form originated by the ancient Greek writer Theophrastus that later became popular in the seventeenth and eighteenth centuries. It is a short essay or sketch of a person who prominently displays a specific attribute or quality, such as miserliness or ambition.

Characterization: See *Character*

Classical: In its strictest definition in literary criticism, classicism refers to works of ancient Greek or Roman literature. The term may also be used to describe a literary work of recognized importance (a "classic") from any time period or literature that exhibits the traits of classicism.

Classicism: A term used in literary criticism to describe critical doctrines that have their roots in ancient Greek and Roman literature, philosophy, and art. Works associated with classicism typically exhibit restraint on the part of the author, unity of design and purpose, clarity, simplicity, logical organization, and respect for tradition.

Colloquialism: A word, phrase, or form of pronunciation that is acceptable in casual conversation but not in formal, written communication. It is considered more acceptable than slang.

Complaint: A lyric poem, popular in the Renaissance, in which the speaker expresses sorrow about his or her condition. Typically, the speaker's sadness is caused by an unresponsive lover, but some complaints cite other sources of unhappiness, such as poverty or fate.

Conceit: A clever and fanciful metaphor, usually expressed through elaborate and extended comparison, that presents a striking parallel between two seemingly dissimilar things—for example, elaborately comparing a beautiful woman to an object like a garden or the sun. The conceit was a popular device throughout the Elizabethan Age and Baroque Age and was the principal technique of the seventeenth-century English metaphysical poets. This usage of the word conceit is unrelated to the best-known definition of conceit as an arrogant attitude or behavior.

Concrete: Concrete is the opposite of abstract, and refers to a thing that actually exists or a description that allows the reader to experience an object or concept with the senses.

Concrete Poetry: Poetry in which visual elements play a large part in the poetic effect. Punctuation marks, letters, or words are arranged on a page to form a visual design: a cross, for example, or a bumblebee.

Confessional Poetry: A form of poetry in which the poet reveals very personal, intimate, sometimes shocking information about himself or herself.

Connotation: The impression that a word gives beyond its defined meaning. Connotations may be universally understood or may be significant only to a certain group.

Consonance: Consonance occurs in poetry when words appearing at the ends of two or more verses have similar final consonant sounds but have final vowel sounds that differ, as with "stuff" and "off."

Convention: Any widely accepted literary device, style, or form.

Corrido: A Mexican ballad.

Couplet: Two lines of poetry with the same rhyme and meter, often expressing a complete and self-contained thought.

Criticism: The systematic study and evaluation of literary works, usually based on a specific method or set of principles. An important part of literary studies since ancient times, the practice of criticism has given rise to numerous theories, methods, and "schools," sometimes producing conflicting, even contradictory, interpretations of literature in general as well as of individual works. Even such basic issues as what constitutes a poem or a novel have been the subject of much criticism over the centuries.

D

Dactyl: See *Foot*

Dadaism: A protest movement in art and literature founded by Tristan Tzara in 1916. Followers of the movement expressed their outrage at the destruction brought about by World War I by revolting against numerous forms of social convention. The Dadaists presented works marked by calculated madness and flamboyant nonsense. They stressed total freedom of expression, commonly through primitive displays of emotion and illogical, often senseless, poetry. The movement ended shortly after the war, when it was replaced by surrealism.

Decadent: See *Decadents*

Decadents: The followers of a nineteenth-century literary movement that had its beginnings in French aestheticism. Decadent literature displays a fascination with perverse and morbid states; a search for novelty and sensation—the "new thrill"; a preoccupation with mysticism; and a belief in the senselessness of human existence. The movement is closely associated with the doctrine Art for Art's Sake. The term "decadence" is sometimes used to denote a decline in the quality of art or literature following a period of greatness.

Deconstruction: A method of literary criticism developed by Jacques Derrida and characterized by multiple conflicting interpretations of a given work. Deconstructionists consider the impact of the language of a work and suggest that the true meaning of the work is not necessarily the meaning that the author intended.

Deduction: The process of reaching a conclusion through reasoning from general premises to a specific premise.

Denotation: The definition of a word, apart from the impressions or feelings it creates in the reader.

Diction: The selection and arrangement of words in a literary work. Either or both may vary depending on the desired effect. There are four general types of diction: "formal," used in scholarly or lofty writing; "informal," used in relaxed but educated conversation; "colloquial," used in everyday speech; and "slang," containing newly coined words and other terms not accepted in formal usage.

Didactic: A term used to describe works of literature that aim to teach some moral, religious, political, or practical lesson. Although didactic elements are often found in artistically pleasing works, the term "didactic" usually refers to literature in which the message is more important than the form. The term may also be used to criticize a work that the critic finds "overly didactic," that is, heavy-handed in its delivery of a lesson.

Dimeter: See *Meter*

Dionysian: See *Apollonian and Dionysian*

Discordia concours: A Latin phrase meaning "discord in harmony." The term was coined by the eighteenth-century English writer Samuel Johnson to describe "a combination of dissimilar images or discovery of occult resemblances in things apparently unlike." Johnson created the expression by reversing a phrase by the Latin poet Horace.

Dissonance: A combination of harsh or jarring sounds, especially in poetry. Although such combinations may be accidental, poets sometimes intentionally make them to achieve particular effects. Dissonance is also sometimes used to refer to close but not identical rhymes. When this is the case, the word functions as a synonym for consonance.

Double Entendre: A corruption of a French phrase meaning "double meaning." The term is used to indicate a word or phrase that is deliberately ambiguous, especially when one of the meanings is risque or improper.

Draft: Any preliminary version of a written work. An author may write dozens of drafts which are revised to form the final work, or he or she may write only one, with few or no revisions.

Dramatic Monologue: See *Monologue*

Dramatic Poetry: Any lyric work that employs elements of drama such as dialogue, conflict, or characterization, but excluding works that are intended for stage presentation.

Dream Allegory: See *Dream Vision*

Dream Vision: A literary convention, chiefly of the Middle Ages. In a dream vision a story is presented as a literal dream of the narrator. This device was commonly used to teach moral and religious lessons.

E

Eclogue: In classical literature, a poem featuring rural themes and structured as a dialogue among shepherds. Eclogues often took specific poetic forms, such as elegies or love poems. Some were written as the soliloquy of a shepherd. In later centuries, "eclogue" came to refer to any poem that was in the pastoral tradition or that had a dialogue or monologue structure.

Edwardian: Describes cultural conventions identified with the period of the reign of Edward VII of England (1901–1910). Writers of the Edwardian Age typically displayed a strong reaction against the propriety and conservatism of the Victorian Age. Their work often exhibits distrust of authority in religion, politics, and art and expresses strong doubts about the soundness of conventional values.

Edwardian Age: See *Edwardian*

Electra Complex: A daughter's amorous obsession with her father.

Elegy: A lyric poem that laments the death of a person or the eventual death of all people. In a conventional elegy, set in a classical world, the poet and subject are spoken of as shepherds. In modern criticism, the word elegy is often used to refer to a poem that is melancholy or mournfully contemplative.

Elizabethan Age: A period of great economic growth, religious controversy, and nationalism closely associated with the reign of Elizabeth I of England (1558–1603). The Elizabethan Age is considered a part of the general renaissance—that is, the flowering of arts and literature—that took place in Europe during the fourteenth through sixteenth centuries. The era is considered the golden age of English literature. The most important dramas in English and a great deal of lyric poetry were produced during this period, and modern English criticism began around this time.

Empathy: A sense of shared experience, including emotional and physical feelings, with someone or something other than oneself. Empathy is often used to describe the response of a reader to a literary character.

English Sonnet: See *Sonnet*

Enjambment: The running over of the sense and structure of a line of verse or a couplet into the following verse or couplet.

Enlightenment, The: An eighteenth-century philosophical movement. It began in France but had a wide impact throughout Europe and America. Thinkers of the Enlightenment valued reason and believed that both the individual and society could achieve a state of perfection. Corresponding to this essentially humanist vision was a resistance to religious authority.

Epic: A long narrative poem about the adventures of a hero of great historic or legendary importance. The setting is vast and the action is often given cosmic significance through the intervention of supernatural forces such as gods, angels, or demons. Epics are typically written in a classical style of grand simplicity with elaborate metaphors and allusions that enhance the symbolic importance of a hero's adventures.

Epic Simile: See *Homeric Simile*

Epigram: A saying that makes the speaker's point quickly and concisely.

Epilogue: A concluding statement or section of a literary work. In dramas, particularly those of the seventeenth and eighteenth centuries, the epilogue is a closing speech, often in verse, delivered by an actor at the end of a play and spoken directly to the audience.

Epiphany: A sudden revelation of truth inspired by a seemingly trivial incident.

Epitaph: An inscription on a tomb or tombstone, or a verse written on the occasion of a person's death. Epitaphs may be serious or humorous.

Epithalamion: A song or poem written to honor and commemorate a marriage ceremony.

Epithalamium: See *Epithalamion*

Epithet: A word or phrase, often disparaging or abusive, that expresses a character trait of someone or something.

Erziehungsroman: See *Bildungsroman*

Essay: A prose composition with a focused subject of discussion. The term was coined by Michel de Montaigne to describe his 1580 collection of brief, informal reflections on himself and on various topics relating to human nature. An essay can also be a long, systematic discourse.

Existentialism: A predominantly twentieth-century philosophy concerned with the nature and perception of human existence. There are two major strains of existentialist thought: atheistic and Christian. Followers of atheistic existentialism believe that the individual is alone in a godless universe and that the basic human condition is one of suffering and loneliness. Nevertheless, because there are no fixed values, individuals can create their own characters—indeed, they can shape themselves—through the exercise of free will. The atheistic strain culminates in and is popularly associated with the works of Jean-Paul Sartre. The Christian existentialists, on the other hand, believe that only in God may people find freedom from life's anguish. The two strains hold certain beliefs in common: that existence cannot be fully understood or described through empirical effort; that anguish is a universal element of life; that individuals must bear responsibility for their actions; and that there is no common standard of behavior or perception for religious and ethical matters.

Expatriates: See *Expatriatism*

Expatriatism: The practice of leaving one's country to live for an extended period in another country.

Exposition: Writing intended to explain the nature of an idea, thing, or theme. Expository writing is often combined with description, narration, or argument. In dramatic writing, the exposition is the introductory material which presents the characters, setting, and tone of the play.

Expressionism: An indistinct literary term, originally used to describe an early twentieth-century school of German painting. The term applies to almost any mode of unconventional, highly subjective writing that distorts reality in some way.

Extended Monologue: See *Monologue*

F

Feet: See *Foot*

Feminine Rhyme: See *Rhyme*

Fiction: Any story that is the product of imagination rather than a documentation of fact. Characters and events in such narratives may be based in real life but their ultimate form and configuration is a creation of the author.

Figurative Language: A technique in writing in which the author temporarily interrupts the order, construction, or meaning of the writing for a particular effect. This interruption takes the form of one or more figures of speech such as hyperbole, irony, or simile. Figurative language is the opposite of literal language, in which every word is truthful, accurate, and free of exaggeration or embellishment.

Figures of Speech: Writing that differs from customary conventions for construction, meaning, order, or significance for the purpose of a special meaning or effect. There are two major types of figures of speech: rhetorical figures, which do not make changes in the meaning of the words; and tropes, which do.

Fin de siecle: A French term meaning "end of the century." The term is used to denote the last decade of the nineteenth century, a transition period when

writers and other artists abandoned old conventions and looked for new techniques and objectives.

First Person: See *Point of View*

Folk Ballad: See *Ballad*

Folklore: Traditions and myths preserved in a culture or group of people. Typically, these are passed on by word of mouth in various forms—such as legends, songs, and proverbs—or preserved in customs and ceremonies. This term was first used by W. J. Thoms in 1846.

Folktale: A story originating in oral tradition. Folktales fall into a variety of categories, including legends, ghost stories, fairy tales, fables, and anecdotes based on historical figures and events.

Foot: The smallest unit of rhythm in a line of poetry. In English-language poetry, a foot is typically one accented syllable combined with one or two unaccented syllables.

Form: The pattern or construction of a work which identifies its genre and distinguishes it from other genres.

Formalism: In literary criticism, the belief that literature should follow prescribed rules of construction, such as those that govern the sonnet form.

Fourteener Meter: See *Meter*

Free Verse: Poetry that lacks regular metrical and rhyme patterns but that tries to capture the cadences of everyday speech. The form allows a poet to exploit a variety of rhythmical effects within a single poem.

Futurism: A flamboyant literary and artistic movement that developed in France, Italy, and Russia from 1908 through the 1920s. Futurist theater and poetry abandoned traditional literary forms. In their place, followers of the movement attempted to achieve total freedom of expression through bizarre imagery and deformed or newly invented words. The Futurists were self-consciously modern artists who attempted to incorporate the appearances and sounds of modern life into their work.

G

Genre: A category of literary work. In critical theory, genre may refer to both the content of a given work—tragedy, comedy, pastoral—and to its form, such as poetry, novel, or drama.

Genteel Tradition: A term coined by critic George Santayana to describe the literary practice of certain late nineteenth-century American writers, especially New Englanders. Followers of the Genteel

Tradition emphasized conventionality in social, religious, moral, and literary standards.

Georgian Age: See *Georgian Poets*

Georgian Period: See *Georgian Poets*

Georgian Poets: A loose grouping of English poets during the years 1912–1922. The Georgians reacted against certain literary schools and practices, especially Victorian wordiness, turn-of-the-century aestheticism, and contemporary urban realism. In their place, the Georgians embraced the nineteenth-century poetic practices of William Wordsworth and the other Lake Poets.

Georgic: A poem about farming and the farmer's way of life, named from Virgil's *Georgics*.

Gilded Age: A period in American history during the 1870s characterized by political corruption and materialism. A number of important novels of social and political criticism were written during this time.

Gothic: See *Gothicism*

Gothicism: In literary criticism, works characterized by a taste for the medieval or morbidly attractive. A gothic novel prominently features elements of horror, the supernatural, gloom, and violence: clanking chains, terror, charnel houses, ghosts, medieval castles, and mysteriously slamming doors. The term "gothic novel" is also applied to novels that lack elements of the traditional Gothic setting but that create a similar atmosphere of terror or dread.

Graveyard School: A group of eighteenth-century English poets who wrote long, picturesque meditations on death. Their works were designed to cause the reader to ponder immortality.

Great Chain of Being: The belief that all things and creatures in nature are organized in a hierarchy from inanimate objects at the bottom to God at the top. This system of belief was popular in the seventeenth and eighteenth centuries.

Grotesque: In literary criticism, the subject matter of a work or a style of expression characterized by exaggeration, deformity, freakishness, and disorder. The grotesque often includes an element of comic absurdity.

H

Haiku: The shortest form of Japanese poetry, constructed in three lines of five, seven, and five syllables respectively. The message of a *haiku* poem usually centers on some aspect of spirituality and provokes an emotional response in the reader.

Half Rhyme: See *Consonance*

Harlem Renaissance: The Harlem Renaissance of the 1920s is generally considered the first significant movement of black writers and artists in the United States. During this period, new and established black writers published more fiction and poetry than ever before, the first influential black literary journals were established, and black authors and artists received their first widespread recognition and serious critical appraisal. Among the major writers associated with this period are Claude McKay, Jean Toomer, Countee Cullen, Langston Hughes, Arna Bontemps, Nella Larsen, and Zora Neale Hurston.

Hellenism: Imitation of ancient Greek thought or styles. Also, an approach to life that focuses on the growth and development of the intellect. "Hellenism" is sometimes used to refer to the belief that reason can be applied to examine all human experience.

Heptameter: See *Meter*

Hero/Heroine: The principal sympathetic character (male or female) in a literary work. Heroes and heroines typically exhibit admirable traits: idealism, courage, and integrity, for example.

Heroic Couplet: A rhyming couplet written in iambic pentameter (a verse with five iambic feet).

Heroic Line: The meter and length of a line of verse in epic or heroic poetry. This varies by language and time period.

Heroine: See *Hero/Heroine*

Hexameter: See *Meter*

Historical Criticism: The study of a work based on its impact on the world of the time period in which it was written.

Hokku: See *Haiku*

Holocaust: See *Holocaust Literature*

Holocaust Literature: Literature influenced by or written about the Holocaust of World War II. Such literature includes true stories of survival in concentration camps, escape, and life after the war, as well as fictional works and poetry.

Homeric Simile: An elaborate, detailed comparison written as a simile many lines in length.

Horatian Satire: See *Satire*

Humanism: A philosophy that places faith in the dignity of humankind and rejects the medieval perception of the individual as a weak, fallen creature. "Humanists" typically believe in the perfectibility of human nature and view reason and education as the means to that end.

Humors: Mentions of the humors refer to the ancient Greek theory that a person's health and personality were determined by the balance of four basic fluids in the body: blood, phlegm, yellow bile, and black bile. A dominance of any fluid would cause extremes in behavior. An excess of blood created a sanguine person who was joyful, aggressive, and passionate; a phlegmatic person was shy, fearful, and sluggish; too much yellow bile led to a choleric temperament characterized by impatience, anger, bitterness, and stubbornness; and excessive black bile created melancholy, a state of laziness, gluttony, and lack of motivation.

Humours: See *Humors*

Hyperbole: In literary criticism, deliberate exaggeration used to achieve an effect.

I

Iamb: See *Foot*

Idiom: A word construction or verbal expression closely associated with a given language.

Image: A concrete representation of an object or sensory experience. Typically, such a representation helps evoke the feelings associated with the object or experience itself. Images are either "literal" or "figurative." Literal images are especially concrete and involve little or no extension of the obvious meaning of the words used to express them. Figurative images do not follow the literal meaning of the words exactly. Images in literature are usually visual, but the term "image" can also refer to the representation of any sensory experience.

Imagery: The array of images in a literary work. Also, figurative language.

Imagism: An English and American poetry movement that flourished between 1908 and 1917. The Imagists used precise, clearly presented images in their works. They also used common, everyday speech and aimed for conciseness, concrete imagery, and the creation of new rhythms.

In medias res: A Latin term meaning "in the middle of things." It refers to the technique of beginning a story at its midpoint and then using various flashback devices to reveal previous action.

Induction: The process of reaching a conclusion by reasoning from specific premises to form a general premise. Also, an introductory portion of a work of literature, especially a play.

Intentional Fallacy: The belief that judgments of a literary work based solely on an author's stated or implied intentions are false and misleading. Critics who believe in the concept of the intentional fallacy typically argue that the work itself is sufficient matter for interpretation, even though they may concede that an author's statement of purpose can be useful.

Interior Monologue: A narrative technique in which characters' thoughts are revealed in a way that appears to be uncontrolled by the author. The interior monologue typically aims to reveal the inner self of a character. It portrays emotional experiences as they occur at both a conscious and unconscious level. Images are often used to represent sensations or emotions.

Internal Rhyme: Rhyme that occurs within a single line of verse.

Irish Literary Renaissance: A late nineteenth- and early twentieth-century movement in Irish literature. Members of the movement aimed to reduce the influence of British culture in Ireland and create an Irish national literature.

Irony: In literary criticism, the effect of language in which the intended meaning is the opposite of what is stated.

Italian Sonnet: See *Sonnet*

J

Jacobean Age: The period of the reign of James I of England (1603–1625). The early literature of this period reflected the worldview of the Elizabethan Age, but a darker, more cynical attitude steadily grew in the art and literature of the Jacobean Age. This was an important time for English drama and poetry.

Jargon: Language that is used or understood only by a select group of people. Jargon may refer to terminology used in a certain profession, such as computer jargon, or it may refer to any nonsensical language that is not understood by most people.

Journalism: Writing intended for publication in a newspaper or magazine, or for broadcast on a radio or television program featuring news, sports, entertainment, or other timely material.

K

Knickerbocker Group: A somewhat indistinct group of New York writers of the first half of the nineteenth century. Members of the group were linked only by location and a common theme: New York life.

Kunstlerroman: See *Bildungsroman*

L

Lais: See *Lay*

Lake Poets: See *Lake School*

Lake School: These poets all lived in the Lake District of England at the turn of the nineteenth century. As a group, they followed no single "school" of thought or literary practice, although their works were uniformly disparaged by the *Edinburgh Review*.

Lay: A song or simple narrative poem. The form originated in medieval France. Early French *lais* were often based on the Celtic legends and other tales sung by Breton minstrels—thus the name of the "Breton lay." In fourteenth-century England, the term "lay" was used to describe short narratives written in imitation of the Breton lays.

Leitmotiv: See *Motif*

Literal Language: An author uses literal language when he or she writes without exaggerating or embellishing the subject matter and without any tools of figurative language.

Literary Ballad: See *Ballad*

Literature: Literature is broadly defined as any written or spoken material, but the term most often refers to creative works.

Lost Generation: A term first used by Gertrude Stein to describe the post-World War I generation of American writers: men and women haunted by a sense of betrayal and emptiness brought about by the destructiveness of the war.

Lyric Poetry: A poem expressing the subjective feelings and personal emotions of the poet. Such poetry is melodic, since it was originally accompanied by a lyre in recitals. Most Western poetry in the twentieth century may be classified as lyrical.

M

Mannerism: Exaggerated, artificial adherence to a literary manner or style. Also, a popular style of the visual arts of late sixteenth-century Europe that was marked by elongation of the human form and by intentional spatial distortion. Literary works that are self-consciously high-toned and artistic are often said to be "mannered."

Masculine Rhyme: See *Rhyme*

Measure: The foot, verse, or time sequence used in a literary work, especially a poem. Measure is often used somewhat incorrectly as a synonym for meter.

Metaphor: A figure of speech that expresses an idea through the image of another object. Metaphors suggest the essence of the first object by identifying it with certain qualities of the second object.

Metaphysical Conceit: See *Conceit*

Metaphysical Poetry: The body of poetry produced by a group of seventeenth-century English writers called the "Metaphysical Poets." The group includes John Donne and Andrew Marvell. The Metaphysical Poets made use of everyday speech, intellectual analysis, and unique imagery. They aimed to portray the ordinary conflicts and contradictions of life. Their poems often took the form of an argument, and many of them emphasize physical and religious love as well as the fleeting nature of life. Elaborate conceits are typical in metaphysical poetry.

Metaphysical Poets: See *Metaphysical Poetry*

Meter: In literary criticism, the repetition of sound patterns that creates a rhythm in poetry. The patterns are based on the number of syllables and the presence and absence of accents. The unit of rhythm in a line is called a foot. Types of meter are classified according to the number of feet in a line. These are the standard English lines: Monometer, one foot; Dimeter, two feet; Trimeter, three feet; Tetrameter, four feet; Pentameter, five feet; Hexameter, six feet (also called the Alexandrine); Heptameter, seven feet (also called the "Fourteener" when the feet are iambic).

Modernism: Modern literary practices. Also, the principles of a literary school that lasted from roughly the beginning of the twentieth century until the end of World War II. Modernism is defined by its rejection of the literary conventions of the nineteenth century and by its opposition to conventional morality, taste, traditions, and economic values.

Monologue: A composition, written or oral, by a single individual. More specifically, a speech given by a single individual in a drama or other public entertainment. It has no set length, although it is usually several or more lines long.

Monometer: See *Meter*

Mood: The prevailing emotions of a work or of the author in his or her creation of the work. The mood of a work is not always what might be expected based on its subject matter.

Motif: A theme, character type, image, metaphor, or other verbal element that recurs throughout a single work of literature or occurs in a number of different works over a period of time.

Motiv: See *Motif*

Muckrakers: An early twentieth-century group of American writers. Typically, their works exposed the wrongdoings of big business and government in the United States.

Muses: Nine Greek mythological goddesses, the daughters of Zeus and Mnemosyne (Memory). Each muse patronized a specific area of the liberal arts and sciences. Calliope presided over epic poetry, Clio over history, Erato over love poetry, Euterpe over music or lyric poetry, Melpomene over tragedy, Polyhymnia over hymns to the gods, Terpsichore over dance, Thalia over comedy, and Urania over astronomy. Poets and writers traditionally made appeals to the Muses for inspiration in their work.

Myth: An anonymous tale emerging from the traditional beliefs of a culture or social unit. Myths use supernatural explanations for natural phenomena. They may also explain cosmic issues like creation and death. Collections of myths, known as mythologies, are common to all cultures and nations, but the best-known myths belong to the Norse, Roman, and Greek mythologies.

N

Narration: The telling of a series of events, real or invented. A narration may be either a simple narrative, in which the events are recounted chronologically, or a narrative with a plot, in which the account is given in a style reflecting the author's artistic concept of the story. Narration is sometimes used as a synonym for "storyline."

Narrative: A verse or prose accounting of an event or sequence of events, real or invented. The term is also used as an adjective in the sense "method of narration." For example, in literary criticism, the expression "narrative technique" usually refers to the way the author structures and presents his or her story.

Narrative Poetry: A nondramatic poem in which the author tells a story. Such poems may be of any length or level of complexity.

Narrator: The teller of a story. The narrator may be the author or a character in the story through whom the author speaks.

Naturalism: A literary movement of the late nineteenth and early twentieth centuries. The movement's major theorist, French novelist Emile Zola, envisioned a type of fiction that would examine human life with the objectivity of scientific inquiry. The Naturalists typically viewed human beings as either the products of "biological determinism," ruled by hereditary instincts and engaged in an endless struggle for survival, or as the products of "socioeconomic determinism," ruled by social and economic forces beyond their control. In their works, the Naturalists generally ignored the highest levels of society and focused on degradation: poverty, alcoholism, prostitution, insanity, and disease.

Negritude: A literary movement based on the concept of a shared cultural bond on the part of black Africans, wherever they may be in the world. It traces its origins to the former French colonies of Africa and the Caribbean. Negritude poets, novelists, and essayists generally stress four points in their writings: One, black alienation from traditional African culture can lead to feelings of inferiority. Two, European colonialism and Western education should be resisted. Three, black Africans should seek to affirm and define their own identity. Four, African culture can and should be reclaimed. Many Negritude writers also claim that blacks can make unique contributions to the world, based on a heightened appreciation of nature, rhythm, and human emotions—aspects of life they say are not so highly valued in the materialistic and rationalistic West.

Negro Renaissance: See *Harlem Renaissance*

Neoclassical Period: See *Neoclassicism*

Neoclassicism: In literary criticism, this term refers to the revival of the attitudes and styles of expression of classical literature. It is generally used to describe a period in European history beginning in the late seventeenth century and lasting until about 1800. In its purest form, Neoclassicism marked a return to order, proportion, restraint, logic, accuracy, and decorum. In England, where Neoclassicism perhaps was most popular, it reflected the influence of seventeenth-century French writers, especially dramatists. Neoclassical writers typically reacted against the intensity and enthusiasm of the Renaissance period. They wrote works that appealed to the intellect, using elevated language and classical literary forms such as satire and the ode. Neoclassical works were often governed by the classical goal of instruction.

Neoclassicists: See *Neoclassicism*

New Criticism: A movement in literary criticism, dating from the late 1920s, that stressed close textual analysis in the interpretation of works of literature. The New Critics saw little merit in historical and biographical analysis. Rather, they aimed to examine the text alone, free from the question of how external events—biographical or otherwise—may have helped shape it.

New Journalism: A type of writing in which the journalist presents factual information in a form usually used in fiction. New journalism emphasizes description, narration, and character development to bring readers closer to the human element of the story, and is often used in personality profiles and in-depth feature articles. It is not compatible with "straight" or "hard" newswriting, which is generally composed in a brief, fact-based style.

New Journalists: See *New Journalism*

New Negro Movement: See *Harlem Renaissance*

Noble Savage: The idea that primitive man is noble and good but becomes evil and corrupted as he becomes civilized. The concept of the noble savage originated in the Renaissance period but is more closely identified with such later writers as Jean-Jacques Rousseau and Aphra Behn.

O

Objective Correlative: An outward set of objects, a situation, or a chain of events corresponding to an inward experience and evoking this experience in the reader. The term frequently appears in modern criticism in discussions of authors' intended effects on the emotional responses of readers.

Objectivity: A quality in writing characterized by the absence of the author's opinion or feeling about the subject matter. Objectivity is an important factor in criticism.

Occasional Verse: Poetry written on the occasion of a significant historical or personal event. *Vers de societe* is sometimes called occasional verse although it is of a less serious nature.

Octave: A poem or stanza composed of eight lines. The term octave most often represents the first eight lines of a Petrarchan sonnet.

Ode: Name given to an extended lyric poem characterized by exalted emotion and dignified style. An ode usually concerns a single, serious theme. Most odes, but not all, are addressed to an object or individual. Odes are distinguished from other lyric poetic forms by their complex rhythmic and stanzaic patterns.

Oedipus Complex: A son's amorous obsession with his mother. The phrase is derived from the story of the ancient Theban hero Oedipus, who

unknowingly killed his father and married his mother.

Omniscience: See *Point of View*

Onomatopoeia: The use of words whose sounds express or suggest their meaning. In its simplest sense, onomatopoeia may be represented by words that mimic the sounds they denote such as "hiss" or "meow." At a more subtle level, the pattern and rhythm of sounds and rhymes of a line or poem may be onomatopoeic.

Oral Tradition: See *Oral Transmission*

Oral Transmission: A process by which songs, ballads, folklore, and other material are transmitted by word of mouth. The tradition of oral transmission predates the written record systems of literate society. Oral transmission preserves material sometimes over generations, although often with variations. Memory plays a large part in the recitation and preservation of orally transmitted material.

Ottava Rima: An eight-line stanza of poetry composed in iambic pentameter (a five-foot line in which each foot consists of an unaccented syllable followed by an accented syllable), following the *ababababcc* rhyme scheme.

Oxymoron: A phrase combining two contradictory terms. Oxymorons may be intentional or unintentional.

P

Pantheism: The idea that all things are both a manifestation or revelation of God and a part of God at the same time. Pantheism was a common attitude in the early societies of Egypt, India, and Greece—the term derives from the Greek *pan* meaning "all" and *theos* meaning "deity." It later became a significant part of the Christian faith.

Parable: A story intended to teach a moral lesson or answer an ethical question.

Paradox: A statement that appears illogical or contradictory at first, but may actually point to an underlying truth.

Parallelism: A method of comparison of two ideas in which each is developed in the same grammatical structure.

Parnassianism: A mid nineteenth-century movement in French literature. Followers of the movement stressed adherence to well-defined artistic forms as a reaction against the often chaotic expression of the artist's ego that dominated the work of the Romantics. The Parnassians also rejected the moral, ethical, and social themes exhibited in the works of French Romantics such as Victor Hugo. The aesthetic doctrines of the Parnassians strongly influenced the later symbolist and decadent movements.

Parody: In literary criticism, this term refers to an imitation of a serious literary work or the signature style of a particular author in a ridiculous manner. A typical parody adopts the style of the original and applies it to an inappropriate subject for humorous effect. Parody is a form of satire and could be considered the literary equivalent of a caricature or cartoon.

Pastoral: A term derived from the Latin word "pastor," meaning shepherd. A pastoral is a literary composition on a rural theme. The conventions of the pastoral were originated by the third-century Greek poet Theocritus, who wrote about the experiences, love affairs, and pastimes of Sicilian shepherds. In a pastoral, characters and language of a courtly nature are often placed in a simple setting. The term pastoral is also used to classify dramas, elegies, and lyrics that exhibit the use of country settings and shepherd characters.

Pathetic Fallacy: A term coined by English critic John Ruskin to identify writing that falsely endows nonhuman things with human intentions and feelings, such as "angry clouds" and "sad trees."

Pen Name: See *Pseudonym*

Pentameter: See *Meter*

Persona: A Latin term meaning "mask." *Personae* are the characters in a fictional work of literature. The *persona* generally functions as a mask through which the author tells a story in a voice other than his or her own. A *persona* is usually either a character in a story who acts as a narrator or an "implied author," a voice created by the author to act as the narrator for himself or herself.

Personae: See *Persona*

Personal Point of View: See *Point of View*

Personification: A figure of speech that gives human qualities to abstract ideas, animals, and inanimate objects.

Petrarchan Sonnet: See *Sonnet*

Phenomenology: A method of literary criticism based on the belief that things have no existence outside of human consciousness or awareness. Proponents of this theory believe that art is a process that takes place in the mind of the observer as he or she contemplates an object rather than a quality of the object itself.

Plagiarism: Claiming another person's written material as one's own. Plagiarism can take the form of direct, word-for-word copying or the theft of the substance or idea of the work.

Platonic Criticism: A form of criticism that stresses an artistic work's usefulness as an agent of social engineering rather than any quality or value of the work itself.

Platonism: The embracing of the doctrines of the philosopher Plato, popular among the poets of the Renaissance and the Romantic period. Platonism is more flexible than Aristotelian Criticism and places more emphasis on the supernatural and unknown aspects of life.

Plot: In literary criticism, this term refers to the pattern of events in a narrative or drama. In its simplest sense, the plot guides the author in composing the work and helps the reader follow the work. Typically, plots exhibit causality and unity and have a beginning, a middle, and an end. Sometimes, however, a plot may consist of a series of disconnected events, in which case it is known as an "episodic plot."

Poem: In its broadest sense, a composition utilizing rhyme, meter, concrete detail, and expressive language to create a literary experience with emotional and aesthetic appeal.

Poet: An author who writes poetry or verse. The term is also used to refer to an artist or writer who has an exceptional gift for expression, imagination, and energy in the making of art in any form.

Poete maudit: A term derived from Paul Verlaine's *Les poetes maudits* (*The Accursed Poets*), a collection of essays on the French symbolist writers Stephane Mallarme, Arthur Rimbaud, and Tristan Corbiere. In the sense intended by Verlaine, the poet is "accursed" for choosing to explore extremes of human experience outside of middle-class society.

Poetic Fallacy: See *Pathetic Fallacy*

Poetic Justice: An outcome in a literary work, not necessarily a poem, in which the good are rewarded and the evil are punished, especially in ways that particularly fit their virtues or crimes.

Poetic License: Distortions of fact and literary convention made by a writer—not always a poet—for the sake of the effect gained. Poetic license is closely related to the concept of "artistic freedom."

Poetics: This term has two closely related meanings. It denotes (1) an aesthetic theory in literary criticism about the essence of poetry or (2) rules prescribing the proper methods, content, style, or diction of poetry. The term poetics may also refer to theories about literature in general, not just poetry.

Poetry: In its broadest sense, writing that aims to present ideas and evoke an emotional experience in the reader through the use of meter, imagery, connotative and concrete words, and a carefully constructed structure based on rhythmic patterns. Poetry typically relies on words and expressions that have several layers of meaning. It also makes use of the effects of regular rhythm on the ear and may make a strong appeal to the senses through the use of imagery.

Point of View: The narrative perspective from which a literary work is presented to the reader. There are four traditional points of view. The "third person omniscient" gives the reader a "godlike" perspective, unrestricted by time or place, from which to see actions and look into the minds of characters. This allows the author to comment openly on characters and events in the work. The "third-person" point of view presents the events of the story from outside of any single character's perception, much like the omniscient point of view, but the reader must understand the action as it takes place and without any special insight into characters' minds or motivations. The "first person" or "personal" point of view relates events as they are perceived by a single character. The main character "tells" the story and may offer opinions about the action and characters which differ from those of the author. Much less common than omniscient, third person, and first person is the "second-person" point of view, wherein the author tells the story as if it is happening to the reader.

Polemic: A work in which the author takes a stand on a controversial subject, such as abortion or religion. Such works are often extremely argumentative or provocative.

Pornography: Writing intended to provoke feelings of lust in the reader. Such works are often condemned by critics and teachers, but those which can be shown to have literary value are viewed less harshly.

Post-Aesthetic Movement: An artistic response made by African Americans to the black aesthetic movement of the 1960s and early 1970s. Writers since that time have adopted a somewhat different tone in their work, with less emphasis placed on the disparity between black and white in the United States. In the words of post-aesthetic authors such as Toni Morrison, John Edgar Wideman, and Kristin Hunter, African Americans are portrayed as looking inward for answers to their own questions, rather than always looking to the outside world.

Postmodernism: Writing from the 1960s forward characterized by experimentation and continuing to apply some of the fundamentals of modernism, which included existentialism and alienation. Postmodernists have gone a step further in the rejection of tradition begun with the modernists by also rejecting traditional forms, preferring the antinovel over the novel and the antihero over the hero.

Pre-Raphaelites: A circle of writers and artists in mid nineteenth-century England. Valuing the pre-Renaissance artistic qualities of religious symbolism, lavish pictorialism, and natural sensuousness, the Pre-Raphaelites cultivated a sense of mystery and melancholy that influenced later writers associated with the Symbolist and Decadent movements.

Primitivism: The belief that primitive peoples were nobler and less flawed than civilized peoples because they had not been subjected to the corrupt influence of society.

Projective Verse: A form of free verse in which the poet's breathing pattern determines the lines of the poem. Poets who advocate projective verse are against all formal structures in writing, including meter and form.

Prologue: An introductory section of a literary work. It often contains information establishing the situation of the characters or presents information about the setting, time period, or action. In drama, the prologue is spoken by a chorus or by one of the principal characters.

Prose: A literary medium that attempts to mirror the language of everyday speech. It is distinguished from poetry by its use of unmetered, unrhymed language consisting of logically related sentences. Prose is usually grouped into paragraphs that form a cohesive whole such as an essay or a novel.

Prosopopoeia: See *Personification*

Protagonist: The central character of a story who serves as a focus for its themes and incidents and as the principal rationale for its development. The protagonist is sometimes referred to in discussions of modern literature as the hero or antihero.

Proverb: A brief, sage saying that expresses a truth about life in a striking manner.

Pseudonym: A name assumed by a writer, most often intended to prevent his or her identification as the author of a work. Two or more authors may work together under one pseudonym, or an author may use a different name for each genre he or she publishes in. Some publishing companies maintain "house pseudonyms," under which any number of authors may write installations in a series. Some authors also choose a pseudonym over their real names the way an actor may use a stage name.

Pun: A play on words that have similar sounds but different meanings.

Pure Poetry: poetry written without instructional intent or moral purpose that aims only to please a reader by its imagery or musical flow. The term pure poetry is used as the antonym of the term "didacticism."

Q

Quatrain: A four-line stanza of a poem or an entire poem consisting of four lines.

R

Realism: A nineteenth-century European literary movement that sought to portray familiar characters, situations, and settings in a realistic manner. This was done primarily by using an objective narrative point of view and through the buildup of accurate detail. The standard for success of any realistic work depends on how faithfully it transfers common experience into fictional forms. The realistic method may be altered or extended, as in stream of consciousness writing, to record highly subjective experience.

Refrain: A phrase repeated at intervals throughout a poem. A refrain may appear at the end of each stanza or at less regular intervals. It may be altered slightly at each appearance.

Renaissance: The period in European history that marked the end of the Middle Ages. It began in Italy in the late fourteenth century. In broad terms, it is usually seen as spanning the fourteenth, fifteenth, and sixteenth centuries, although it did not reach Great Britain, for example, until the 1480s or so. The Renaissance saw an awakening in almost every sphere of human activity, especially science, philosophy, and the arts. The period is best defined by the emergence of a general philosophy that emphasized the importance of the intellect, the individual, and world affairs. It contrasts strongly with the medieval worldview, characterized by the dominant concerns of faith, the social collective, and spiritual salvation.

Repartee: Conversation featuring snappy retorts and witticisms.

Restoration: See *Restoration Age*

Restoration Age: A period in English literature beginning with the crowning of Charles II in 1660 and running to about 1700. The era, which was characterized by a reaction against Puritanism, was the first great age of the comedy of manners. The finest literature of the era is typically witty and urbane, and often lewd.

Rhetoric: In literary criticism, this term denotes the art of ethical persuasion. In its strictest sense, rhetoric adheres to various principles developed since classical times for arranging facts and ideas in a clear, persuasive, appealing manner. The term is also used to refer to effective prose in general and theories of or methods for composing effective prose.

Rhetorical Question: A question intended to provoke thought, but not an expressed answer, in the reader. It is most commonly used in oratory and other persuasive genres.

Rhyme: When used as a noun in literary criticism, this term generally refers to a poem in which words sound identical or very similar and appear in parallel positions in two or more lines. Rhymes are classified into different types according to where they fall in a line or stanza or according to the degree of similarity they exhibit in their spellings and sounds. Some major types of rhyme are "masculine" rhyme, "feminine" rhyme, and "triple" rhyme. In a masculine rhyme, the rhyming sound falls in a single accented syllable, as with "heat" and "eat." Feminine rhyme is a rhyme of two syllables, one stressed and one unstressed, as with "merry" and "tarry." Triple rhyme matches the sound of the accented syllable and the two unaccented syllables that follow: "narrative" and "declarative."

Rhyme Royal: A stanza of seven lines composed in iambic pentameter and rhymed *ababbcc*. The name is said to be a tribute to King James I of Scotland, who made much use of the form in his poetry.

Rhyme Scheme: See *Rhyme*

Rhythm: A regular pattern of sound, time intervals, or events occurring in writing, most often and most discernably in poetry. Regular, reliable rhythm is known to be soothing to humans, while interrupted, unpredictable, or rapidly changing rhythm is disturbing. These effects are known to authors, who use them to produce a desired reaction in the reader.

Rococo: A style of European architecture that flourished in the eighteenth century, especially in

France. The most notable features of *rococo* are its extensive use of ornamentation and its themes of lightness, gaiety, and intimacy. In literary criticism, the term is often used disparagingly to refer to a decadent or overly ornamental style.

Romance:

Romantic Age: See *Romanticism*

Romanticism: This term has two widely accepted meanings. In historical criticism, it refers to a European intellectual and artistic movement of the late eighteenth and early nineteenth centuries that sought greater freedom of personal expression than that allowed by the strict rules of literary form and logic of the eighteenth-century Neoclassicists. The Romantics preferred emotional and imaginative expression to rational analysis. They considered the individual to be at the center of all experience and so placed him or her at the center of their art. The Romantics believed that the creative imagination reveals nobler truths—unique feelings and attitudes—than those that could be discovered by logic or by scientific examination. Both the natural world and the state of childhood were important sources for revelations of "eternal truths." "Romanticism" is also used as a general term to refer to a type of sensibility found in all periods of literary history and usually considered to be in opposition to the principles of classicism. In this sense, Romanticism signifies any work or philosophy in which the exotic or dreamlike figure strongly, or that is devoted to individualistic expression, self-analysis, or a pursuit of a higher realm of knowledge than can be discovered by human reason.

Romantics: See *Romanticism*

Russian Symbolism: A Russian poetic movement, derived from French symbolism, that flourished between 1894 and 1910. While some Russian Symbolists continued in the French tradition, stressing aestheticism and the importance of suggestion above didactic intent, others saw their craft as a form of mystical worship, and themselves as mediators between the supernatural and the mundane.

S

Satire: A work that uses ridicule, humor, and wit to criticize and provoke change in human nature and institutions. There are two major types of satire: "formal" or "direct" satire speaks directly to the reader or to a character in the work; "indirect" satire relies upon the ridiculous behavior of its characters to make its point. Formal satire is further divided into two manners: the "Horatian," which

ridicules gently, and the "Juvenalian," which derides its subjects harshly and bitterly.

Scansion: The analysis or "scanning" of a poem to determine its meter and often its rhyme scheme. The most common system of scansion uses accents (slanted lines drawn above syllables) to show stressed syllables, breves (curved lines drawn above syllables) to show unstressed syllables, and vertical lines to separate each foot.

Second Person: See *Point of View*

Semiotics: The study of how literary forms and conventions affect the meaning of language.

Sestet: Any six-line poem or stanza.

Setting: The time, place, and culture in which the action of a narrative takes place. The elements of setting may include geographic location, characters' physical and mental environments, prevailing cultural attitudes, or the historical time in which the action takes place.

Shakespearean Sonnet: See *Sonnet*

Signifying Monkey: A popular trickster figure in black folklore, with hundreds of tales about this character documented since the nineteenth century.

Simile: A comparison, usually using "like" or "as," of two essentially dissimilar things, as in "coffee as cold as ice" or "He sounded like a broken record."

Slang: A type of informal verbal communication that is generally unacceptable for formal writing. Slang words and phrases are often colorful exaggerations used to emphasize the speaker's point; they may also be shortened versions of an oftenused word or phrase.

Slant Rhyme: See *Consonance*

Slave Narrative: Autobiographical accounts of American slave life as told by escaped slaves. These works first appeared during the abolition movement of the 1830s through the 1850s.

Social Realism: See *Socialist Realism*

Socialist Realism: The Socialist Realism school of literary theory was proposed by Maxim Gorky and established as a dogma by the first Soviet Congress of Writers. It demanded adherence to a communist worldview in works of literature. Its doctrines required an objective viewpoint comprehensible to the working classes and themes of social struggle featuring strong proletarian heroes.

Soliloquy: A monologue in a drama used to give the audience information and to develop the speaker's character. It is typically a projection of the speaker's innermost thoughts. Usually delivered while the speaker is alone on stage, a soliloquy is intended to present an illusion of unspoken reflection.

Sonnet: A fourteen-line poem, usually composed in iambic pentameter, employing one of several rhyme schemes. There are three major types of sonnets, upon which all other variations of the form are based: the "Petrarchan" or "Italian" sonnet, the "Shakespearean" or "English" sonnet, and the "Spenserian" sonnet. A Petrarchan sonnet consists of an octave rhymed *abbaabba* and a "sestet" rhymed either *cdecde, cdccdc,* or *cdedce.* The octave poses a question or problem, relates a narrative, or puts forth a proposition; the sestet presents a solution to the problem, comments upon the narrative, or applies the proposition put forth in the octave. The Shakespearean sonnet is divided into three quatrains and a couplet rhymed *abab cdcd efef gg.* The couplet provides an epigrammatic comment on the narrative or problem put forth in the quatrains. The Spenserian sonnet uses three quatrains and a couplet like the Shakespearean, but links their three rhyme schemes in this way: *abab bcbc cdcd ee.* The Spenserian sonnet develops its theme in two parts like the Petrarchan, its final six lines resolving a problem, analyzing a narrative, or applying a proposition put forth in its first eight lines.

Spenserian Sonnet: See *Sonnet*

Spenserian Stanza: A nine-line stanza having eight verses in iambic pentameter, its ninth verse in iambic hexameter, and the rhyme scheme *ababbcbcc.*

Spondee: In poetry meter, a foot consisting of two long or stressed syllables occurring together. This form is quite rare in English verse, and is usually composed of two monosyllabic words.

Sprung Rhythm: Versification using a specific number of accented syllables per line but disregarding the number of unaccented syllables that fall in each line, producing an irregular rhythm in the poem.

Stanza: A subdivision of a poem consisting of lines grouped together, often in recurring patterns of rhyme, line length, and meter. Stanzas may also serve as units of thought in a poem much like paragraphs in prose.

Stereotype: A stereotype was originally the name for a duplication made during the printing process; this led to its modern definition as a person or thing that is (or is assumed to be) the same as all others of its type.

Stream of Consciousness: A narrative technique for rendering the inward experience of a character. This technique is designed to give the impression of an ever-changing series of thoughts, emotions, images, and memories in the spontaneous and seemingly illogical order that they occur in life.

Structuralism: A twentieth-century movement in literary criticism that examines how literary texts arrive at their meanings, rather than the meanings themselves. There are two major types of structuralist analysis: one examines the way patterns of linguistic structures unify a specific text and emphasize certain elements of that text, and the other interprets the way literary forms and conventions affect the meaning of language itself.

Structure: The form taken by a piece of literature. The structure may be made obvious for ease of understanding, as in nonfiction works, or may be obscured for artistic purposes, as in some poetry or seemingly "unstructured" prose.

Sturm und Drang: A German term meaning "storm and stress." It refers to a German literary movement of the 1770s and 1780s that reacted against the order and rationalism of the enlightenment, focusing instead on the intense experience of extraordinary individuals.

Style: A writer's distinctive manner of arranging words to suit his or her ideas and purpose in writing. The unique imprint of the author's personality upon his or her writing, style is the product of an author's way of arranging ideas and his or her use of diction, different sentence structures, rhythm, figures of speech, rhetorical principles, and other elements of composition.

Subject: The person, event, or theme at the center of a work of literature. A work may have one or more subjects of each type, with shorter works tending to have fewer and longer works tending to have more.

Subjectivity: Writing that expresses the author's personal feelings about his subject, and which may or may not include factual information about the subject.

Surrealism: A term introduced to criticism by Guillaume Apollinaire and later adopted by Andre Breton. It refers to a French literary and artistic movement founded in the 1920s. The Surrealists sought to express unconscious thoughts and feelings in their works. The best-known technique used for achieving this aim was automatic writing—transcriptions of spontaneous outpourings from the unconscious. The Surrealists proposed to unify the contrary levels of conscious and unconscious, dream and reality, objectivity and subjectivity into a new level of "super-realism."

Suspense: A literary device in which the author maintains the audience's attention through the buildup of events, the outcome of which will soon be revealed.

Syllogism: A method of presenting a logical argument. In its most basic form, the syllogism consists of a major premise, a minor premise, and a conclusion.

Symbol: Something that suggests or stands for something else without losing its original identity. In literature, symbols combine their literal meaning with the suggestion of an abstract concept. Literary symbols are of two types: those that carry complex associations of meaning no matter what their contexts, and those that derive their suggestive meaning from their functions in specific literary works.

Symbolism: This term has two widely accepted meanings. In historical criticism, it denotes an early modernist literary movement initiated in France during the nineteenth century that reacted against the prevailing standards of realism. Writers in this movement aimed to evoke, indirectly and symbolically, an order of being beyond the material world of the five senses. Poetic expression of personal emotion figured strongly in the movement, typically by means of a private set of symbols uniquely identifiable with the individual poet. The principal aim of the Symbolists was to express in words the highly complex feelings that grew out of everyday contact with the world. In a broader sense, the term "symbolism" refers to the use of one object to represent another.

Symbolist: See *Symbolism*

Symbolist Movement: See *Symbolism*

Sympathetic Fallacy: See *Affective Fallacy*

T

Tanka: A form of Japanese poetry similar to *haiku*. A *tanka* is five lines long, with the lines containing five, seven, five, seven, and seven syllables respectively.

Terza Rima: A three-line stanza form in poetry in which the rhymes are made on the last word of each line in the following manner: the first and third lines of the first stanza, then the second line of the first stanza and the first and third lines of the second stanza, and so on with the middle line of any

stanza rhyming with the first and third lines of the following stanza.

Tetrameter: See *Meter*

Textual Criticism: A branch of literary criticism that seeks to establish the authoritative text of a literary work. Textual critics typically compare all known manuscripts or printings of a single work in order to assess the meanings of differences and revisions. This procedure allows them to arrive at a definitive version that (supposedly) corresponds to the author's original intention.

Theme: The main point of a work of literature. The term is used interchangeably with thesis.

Thesis: A thesis is both an essay and the point argued in the essay. Thesis novels and thesis plays share the quality of containing a thesis which is supported through the action of the story.

Third Person: See *Point of View*

Tone: The author's attitude toward his or her audience may be deduced from the tone of the work. A formal tone may create distance or convey politeness, while an informal tone may encourage a friendly, intimate, or intrusive feeling in the reader. The author's attitude toward his or her subject matter may also be deduced from the tone of the words he or she uses in discussing it.

Tragedy: A drama in prose or poetry about a noble, courageous hero of excellent character who, because of some tragic character flaw or *hamartia*, brings ruin upon him- or herself. Tragedy treats its subjects in a dignified and serious manner, using poetic language to help evoke pity and fear and bring about catharsis, a purging of these emotions. The tragic form was practiced extensively by the ancient Greeks. In the Middle Ages, when classical works were virtually unknown, tragedy came to denote any works about the fall of persons from exalted to low conditions due to any reason: fate, vice, weakness, etc. According to the classical definition of tragedy, such works present the "pathetic"—that which evokes pity—rather than the tragic. The classical form of tragedy was revived in the sixteenth century; it flourished especially on the Elizabethan stage. In modern times, dramatists have attempted to adapt the form to the needs of modern society by drawing their heroes from the ranks of ordinary men and women and defining the nobility of these heroes in terms of spirit rather than exalted social standing.

Tragic Flaw: In a tragedy, the quality within the hero or heroine which leads to his or her downfall.

Transcendentalism: An American philosophical and religious movement, based in New England from around 1835 until the Civil War. Transcendentalism was a form of American romanticism that had its roots abroad in the works of Thomas Carlyle, Samuel Coleridge, and Johann Wolfgang von Goethe. The Transcendentalists stressed the importance of intuition and subjective experience in communication with God. They rejected religious dogma and texts in favor of mysticism and scientific naturalism. They pursued truths that lie beyond the "colorless" realms perceived by reason and the senses and were active social reformers in public education, women's rights, and the abolition of slavery.

Trickster: A character or figure common in Native American and African literature who uses his ingenuity to defeat enemies and escape difficult situations. Tricksters are most often animals, such as the spider, hare, or coyote, although they may take the form of humans as well.

Trimeter: See *Meter*

Triple Rhyme: See *Rhyme*

Trochee: See *Foot*

U

Understatement: See *Irony*

Unities: Strict rules of dramatic structure, formulated by Italian and French critics of the Renaissance and based loosely on the principles of drama discussed by Aristotle in his *Poetics*. Foremost among these rules were the three unities of action, time, and place that compelled a dramatist to: (1) construct a single plot with a beginning, middle, and end that details the causal relationships of action and character; (2) restrict the action to the events of a single day; and (3) limit the scene to a single place or city. The unities were observed faithfully by continental European writers until the Romantic Age, but they were never regularly observed in English drama. Modern dramatists are typically more concerned with a unity of impression or emotional effect than with any of the classical unities.

Urban Realism: A branch of realist writing that attempts to accurately reflect the often harsh facts of modern urban existence.

Utopia: A fictional perfect place, such as "paradise" or "heaven."

Utopian: See *Utopia*

Utopianism: See *Utopia*

V

Verisimilitude: Literally, the appearance of truth. In literary criticism, the term refers to aspects of a work of literature that seem true to the reader.

Vers de societe: See *Occasional Verse*

Vers libre: See *Free Verse*

Verse: A line of metered language, a line of a poem, or any work written in verse.

Versification: The writing of verse. Versification may also refer to the meter, rhyme, and other mechanical components of a poem.

Victorian: Refers broadly to the reign of Queen Victoria of England (1837–1901) and to anything with qualities typical of that era. For example, the qualities of smug narrowmindedness, bourgeois materialism, faith in social progress, and priggish morality are often considered Victorian. This stereotype is contradicted by such dramatic intellectual developments as the theories of Charles Darwin, Karl Marx, and Sigmund Freud (which stirred strong debates in England) and the critical attitudes of serious Victorian writers like Charles Dickens and George Eliot. In literature, the Victorian Period was the great age of the English novel, and the latter part of the era saw the rise of movements such as decadence and symbolism.

Victorian Age: See *Victorian*

Victorian Period: See *Victorian*

W

Weltanschauung: A German term referring to a person's worldview or philosophy.

Weltschmerz: A German term meaning "world pain." It describes a sense of anguish about the nature of existence, usually associated with a melancholy, pessimistic attitude.

Z

Zarzuela: A type of Spanish operetta.

Zeitgeist: A German term meaning "spirit of the time." It refers to the moral and intellectual trends of a given era.

Cumulative Author/Title Index

Cumulative Nationality/Ethnicity Index

Subject/Theme Index

*Boldface denotes dicussion in *Themes* section.

A

Abandonment
    Hugh Selwyn Mauberley: 46, 50, 55

Adulthood
    What My Child Learns of the Sea: 249–250

Aestheticism
    Hugh Selwyn Mauberley: 33–34, 39–41

Affirmation
    Song of a Citizen: 127

Allegory
    Business: 7–8

Alliteration
    Much Madness Is Divinest Sense: 86, 89

Ambiguity
    Much Madness Is Divinest Sense: 86, 88–89

American Northeast
    Business: 1, 5–7

American Southwest
    Southbound on the Freeway: 169

Anger
    What My Child Learns of the Sea: 253–254

Apathy
    Hugh Selwyn Mauberley: 49–50, 54–55

Arthurian Legend
    Merlin Enthralled: 71, 73–82

Atonement

    Hugh Selwyn Mauberley: 47–48, 54–55

Awareness and Compassion
    Three Times My Life Has Opened: 215

B

Beauty
    Hugh Selwyn Mauberley: 30–34, 38, 42–43, 47, 49–50, 52–54
    Sonnet XXIX: 150, 154
    Story from Bear Country: 171, 173, 176–177, 183
    Sunday Morning: 188, 191–193, 195, 197–203, 205–210

Belief and Doubt
    Sunday Morning: 192

The Beloved's Absence
    Sonnet XXIX: 142

Buddhism
    Three Times My Life Has Opened: 215, 217–218, 222–223

C

Christianity
    Sunday Morning: 188, 191–198, 200–202

City Life
    Song of a Citizen: 130–131

Civil Rights
    What My Child Learns of the Sea: 243, 248–249

Classicism
    Hugh Selwyn Mauberley: 30–31, 36

Colonialism
    Colibrí: 16

Competition
    Business: 4

Consciousness
    What My Child Learns of the Sea: 246

Courage
    Sonnet XXIX: 148

Creativity
    I Stop Writing the Poem: 61–62, 64

Crime and Criminals
    Business: 5–6

Cruelty
    Hugh Selwyn Mauberley: 31, 33–34, 36–37
    Reunions with a Ghost: 118–123

Curiosity
    Hugh Selwyn Mauberley: 33, 35

Cynicism
    Sunday Morning: 194–195, 206–210

D

Death
    Hugh Selwyn Mauberley: 30–31, 34–37, 47–55
    I Stop Writing the Poem: 57, 59–67
    Merlin Enthralled: 71, 73–78
    Song of a Citizen: 124, 126–132
    Sonnet XXIX: 149–151, 153–154
    Sunday Morning: 188–189, 191–194, 196–204, 206–210
    Ways to Live: 227, 230–241

Subject/Theme Index

Cumulative Index of
First Lines

A

A brackish reach of shoal off Madaket,— (The Quaker
    Graveyard in Nantucket) V6:158

"A cold coming we had of it (Journey of the Magi) V7:110

A line in long array where they wind betwixt green
    islands, (Cavalry Crossing a Ford) V13:50

A narrow Fellow in the grass (A Narrow Fellow in the
    Grass) V11:127

A pine box for me. I mean it. (Last Request) V14: 231

A poem should be palpable and mute (Ars Poetica) V5:2

A stone from the depths that has witnessed the seas
    drying up (Song of a Citizen) V16:125

A tourist came in from Orbitville, (Southbound on the
    Freeway) V16:158

A wind is ruffling the tawny pelt (A Far Cry from Africa)
    V6:60

a woman precedes me up the long rope, (Climbing) V14:113

About me the night moonless wimples the mountains
    (Vancouver Lights) V8:245

About suffering they were never wrong (Musée des Beaux
    Arts) V1:148

Across Roblin Lake, two shores away, (Wilderness
    Gothic) V12:241

After you finish your work (Ballad of Orange and Grape)
    V10:17

"Ah, are you digging on my grave (Ah, Are You Digging
    on My Grave?) V4:2

All Greece hates (Helen) V6:92

All night long the hockey pictures (To a Sad Daughter)
    V8:230

All winter your brute shoulders strained against collars,
    padding (Names of Horses) V8:141

Also Ulysses once—that other war. (Kilroy) V14:213

Anasazi (Anasazi) V9:2

And God stepped out on space (The Creation) V1:19

Animal bones and some mossy tent rings (Lament for the
    Dorsets) V5:190

As I perceive (The Gold Lily) V5:127

As I walked out one evening (As I Walked Out One
    Evening) V4:15

As virtuous men pass mildly away (A Valediction:
    Forbidding Mourning) V11:201

At noon in the desert a panting lizard (At the Bomb
    Testing Site) V8:2

Ay, tear her tattered ensign down! (Old Ironsides) V9:172

B

Back then, before we came (On Freedom's Ground)
    V12:186

Bananas ripe and green, and ginger-root (The Tropics in
    New York) V4:255

Because I could not stop for Death— (Because I Could
    Not Stop for Death) V2:27

Before the indifferent beak could let her drop? (Leda and
    the Swan) V13:182

Bent double, like old beggars under slacks, (Dulce et
    Decorum Est) V10:109

Between my finger and my thumb (Digging) V5:70

Beware of ruins: they have a treacherous charm (Beware
    of Ruins) V8:43

Bright star! would I were steadfast as thou art— (Bright
    Star! Would I Were Steadfast as Thou Art) V9:44

By the rude bridge that arched the flood (Concord Hymn)
    V4:30

C

Celestial choir! enthron'd in realms of light, (To His
    Excellency General Washington V13:212

Come with me into those things that have felt his despair
    for so long— (Come with Me) V6:31

Complacencies of the peignoir, and late (Sunday Morning)
    V16:189

W

Y

Cumulative Index of First Lines

Cumulative Index of Last Lines

A

A heart whose love is innocent! (She Walks in Beauty) V14:268

a man then suddenly stops running (Island of Three Marias) V11:80

a space in the lives of their friends (Beware: Do Not Read This Poem) V6:3

A sudden blow: the great wings beating still (Leda and the Swan) V13:181

A terrible beauty is born (Easter 1916) V5:91

About my big, new, automatically defrosting refrigerator with the built-in electric eye (Reactionary Essay on Applied Science) V9:199

about the tall mounds of termites. (Song of a Citizen) V16:126

Across the expedient and wicked stones (Auto Wreck) V3:31

Ah, dear father, graybeard, lonely old courage-teacher, what America did you have when Charon quit poling his ferry and you got out on a smoking bank and stood watching the boat disappear on the black waters of Lethe? (A Supermarket in California) V5:261

All losses are restored and sorrows end (Sonnet 30) V4:192

Amen. Amen (The Creation) V1:20

Anasazi (Anasazi) V9:3

and all beyond saving by children (Ethics) V8:88

And all we need of hell (My Life Closed Twice Before Its Close) V8:127

and changed, back to the class ("Trouble with Math in a One-Room Country School") V9:238

And Death shall be no more: Death, thou shalt die (Holy Sonnet 10) V2:103

And drunk the milk of Paradise (Kubla Khan) V5:172

And Finished knowing—then— (I Felt a Funeral in My Brain) V13:137

And gallop terribly against each other's bodies (Autumn Begins in Martins Ferry, Ohio) V8:17

and go back. (For the White poets who would be Indian) V13:112

And handled with a Chain—(Much Madness is Divinest Sense) V16:86

And has not begun to grow a manly smile. (Deep Woods) V14:139

And his own Word (The Phoenix) V10:226

And I am Nicholas. (The Czar's Last Christmas Letter) V12:45

And in the suburbs Can't sat down and cried. (Kilroy) V14:213

And it's been years. (Anniversary) V15:3

And life for me ain't been no crystal stair (Mother to Son) V3:179

And like a thunderbolt he falls (The Eagle) V11:30

And makes me end where I begun (A Valediction: Forbidding Mourning) V11:202

And 'midst the stars inscribe Belinda's name. (The Rape of the Lock) V12:209

And miles to go before I sleep (Stopping by Woods on a Snowy Evening) V1:272

and my father saying things. (My Father's Song) V16:102

And not waving but drowning (Not Waving but Drowning) V3:216

And oh, 'tis true, 'tis true (When I Was One-and-Twenty) V4:268

And reach for your scalping knife. (For Jean Vincent D'abbadie, Baron St.-Castin) V12:78

and retreating, always retreating, behind it (Brazil, January 1, 1502) V6:16

And settled upon his eyes in a black soot ("More Light! More Light!") V6:120

And shuts his eyes. (Darwin in 1881) V13: 84

And so live ever—or else swoon to death (Bright Star! Would I Were Steadfast as Thou Art) V9:44

and strange and loud was the dingoes' cry (Drought Year) V8:78

I

I am black. (The Song of the Smoke) V13:197

I am going to keep things like this (Hawk Roosting) V4:55

I am not brave at all (Strong Men, Riding Horses) V4:209

I could not see to see— (I Heard a Fly Buzz—When I Died—) V5:140

I have just come down from my father (The Hospital Window) V11:58

I cremated Sam McGee (The Cremation of Sam McGee) V10:76

I hear it in the deep heart's core. (The Lake Isle of Innisfree) V15:121

I never writ, nor no man ever loved (Sonnet 116) V3:288

I romp with joy in the bookish dark (Eating Poetry) V9:61

I see Mike's painting, called SARDINES (Why I Am Not a Painter) V8:259

I shall but love thee better after death (Sonnet 43) V2:236

I should be glad of another death (Journey of the Magi) V7:110

I stand up (Miss Rosie) V1:133

I stood there, fifteen (Fifteen) V2:78

I take it you are he? (Incident in a Rose Garden) V14:191

I turned aside and bowed my head and wept (The Tropics in New York) V4:255

I'll dig with it (Digging) V5:71

If Winter comes, can Spring be far behind? (Ode to the West Wind) V2:163

In a convulsive misery (The Milkfish Gatherers) V11:112

In balance with this life, this death (An Irish Airman Foresees His Death) V1:76

In Flanders fields (In Flanders Fields) V5:155

In ghostlier demarcations, keener sounds. (The Idea of Order at Key West) V13:164

In hearts at peace, under an English heaven (The Soldier) V7:218

In her tomb by the side of the sea (Annabel Lee) V9:14

in the family of things. (Wild Geese) V15:208

in the grit gray light of day. (Daylights) V13:102

In the rear-view mirrors of the passing cars (The War Against the Trees) V11:216

iness (l(a) V1:85

Into blossom (A Blessing) V7:24

Is Come, my love is come to me. (A Birthday) V10:34

is still warm (Lament for the Dorsets) V5:191

It asked a crumb—of Me (Hope Is the Thing with Feathers) V3:123

it's always ourselves we find in the sea (maggie & milly & molly & may) V12:150

its youth. The sea grows old in it. (The Fish) V14:172

It was your resting place." (Ah, Are You Digging on My Grave?) V4:2

J

Judge tenderly—of Me (This Is My Letter to the World) V4:233

Just imagine it (Inventors) V7:97

L

Laughing the stormy, husky, brawling laughter of Youth, half-naked, sweating, proud to be Hog Butcher, Tool Maker, Stacker of Wheat, Player with

Railroads and Freight Handler to the Nation (Chicago) V3:61

Learn to labor and to wait (A Psalm of Life) V7:165

Leashed in my throat (Midnight) V2:131

Let my people go (Go Down, Moses) V11:43

life, our life and its forgetting. (For a New Citizen of These United States) V15:55

Like Stone— (The Soul Selects Her Own Society) V1:259

Little Lamb, God bless thee. (The Lamb) V12:135

M

'Make a wish, Tom, make a wish.' (Drifters) V10: 98

make it seem to change (The Moon Glows the Same) V7:152

midnight-oiled in the metric laws? (A Farewell to English) V10:126

Monkey business (Business) V16:2

More dear, both for themselves and for thy sake! (Tintern Abbey) V2:250

My love shall in my verse ever live young (Sonnet 19) V9:211

My soul has grown deep like the rivers. (The Negro Speaks of Rivers) V10:198

N

never to waken in that world again (Starlight) V8:213

Black like me (Dream Variations) V15:42

No, she's brushing a boy's hair (Facing It) V5:110

no—tell them no— (The Hiding Place) V10:153

Noble six hundred! (The Charge of the Light Brigade) V1:3

Not even the blisters. Look. (What Belongs to Us) V15:196

Nothing gold can stay (Nothing Gold Can Stay) V3:203

Nothing, and is nowhere, and is endless (High Windows) V3:108

Now! (Alabama Centennial) V10:2

nursing the tough skin of figs (This Life) V1:293

O

O Death in Life, the days that are no more! (Tears, Idle Tears) V4:220

O Lord our Lord, how excellent is thy name in all the earth! (Psalm 8) V9:182

O Roger, Mackerel, Riley, Ned, Nellie, Chester, Lady Ghost (Names of Horses) V8:142

of gentleness (To a Sad Daughter) V8:231

of love's austere and lonely offices? (Those Winter Sundays) V1:300

of peaches (The Weight of Sweetness) V11:230

Of the camellia (Falling Upon Earth) V2:64

Of the Creator. And he waits for the world to begin (Leviathan) V5:204

Of what is past, or passing, or to come (Sailing to Byzantium) V2:207

Old Ryan, not yours (The Constellation Orion) V8:53

On the dark distant flurry (Angle of Geese) V2:2

On the look of Death— (There's a Certain Slant of Light) V6:212

On your head like a crown (Any Human to Another) V3:2

One could do worse that be a swinger of birches. (Birches) V13:15

Or does it explode? (Harlem) V1:63

U

Until Eternity. (The Bustle in a House) V10:62

unusual conservation (Chocolates) V11:17

Uttering cries that are almost human (American Poetry) V7:2

W

War is kind (War Is Kind) V9:253

watching to see how it's done. (I Stop Writing the Poem) V16:58

Went home and put a bullet through his head (Richard Cory) V4:117

Were not the one dead, turned to their affairs. (Out, Out—) V10:213

Were toward Eternity— (Because I Could Not Stop for Death) V2:27

What will survive of us is love. (An Arundel Tomb) V12:18

When I died they washed me out of the turret with a hose (The Death of the Ball Turret Gunner) V2:41

When you have both (Toads) V4:244

Where deep in the night I hear a voice (Butcher Shop) V7:43

Where ignorant armies clash by night (Dover Beach) V2:52

Which Claus of Innsbruck cast in bronze for me! (My Last Duchess) V1:166

which is not going to go wasted on me which is why I'm telling you about it (Having a Coke with You) V12:106

white ash amid funereal cypresses (Helen) V6:92

Who are you and what is your purpose? (The Mystery) V15:138

Wi' the Scots lords at his feit (Sir Patrick Spens) V4:177

Will hear of as a god." (How we Heard the Name) V10:167

Wind, like the dodo's (Bedtime Story) V8:33

With gold unfading, WASHINGTON! be thine. (To His Excellency General Washington) V13:213

with my eyes closed. (We Live by What We See at Night) V13:240

With the slow smokeless burning of decay (The Wood-Pile) V6:252

With what they had to go on. (The Conquerors) V13:67

Would scarcely know that we were gone. (There Will Come Soft Rains) V14:301

Y

Ye know on earth, and all ye need to know (Ode on a Grecian Urn) V1:180

You live in this, and dwell in lovers' eyes (Sonnet 55) V5:246

You may for ever tarry. (To the Virgins, to Make Much of Time) V13:226

you who raised me? (The Gold Lily) V5:127